THE DAWN OF
EUROPEAN CIVILIZATION

EUROPEAN

TEXTS BY

EDITED BY DAVID TALBOT RICE

New York · Toronto · London

McGRAW-HILL BOOK COMPANY

THE DAWN OF
CIVILIZATION
THE DARK AGES

DAVID OATES

R. H. PINDER-WILSON

SIRARPIE DER NERSESSIAN

CYRIL MANGO

J. M. HUSSEY

TAMARA TALBOT RICE

DONALD BULLOUGH

WILLIAM CULICAN

PETER LASKO

DAVID WILSON

CHARLES THOMAS

PHILIP GRIERSON

DENYS HAY

675 illustrations

200 in color

475 photographs, drawings, maps

and genealogical charts

Designed and produced by THAMES AND HUDSON, London

MANAGING EDITOR: Ian Sutton BA

ART EDITOR: Ian Mackenzie Kerr ARCA

EDITORIAL: Mary Bainbridge BA

RESEARCH: R. Davidson-Houston BA, FRAI;
Miriam Shaked BA; A. G. Ward, PhD

RECONSTRUCTIONS: Alan Sorrell RWS, ARCA;
William Suddaby ARCA

MAPS: John Woodcock ARCA, MSIA

PLANS AND DRAWINGS: Gerard Bakker AA DIP; Ivan Lapper ARCA;
P. P. Pratt; M. E. Weaver AA DIP; Jon D. Wilsher

SPECIAL PHOTOGRAPHY: Roloff Beny, Max Hirmer, Edwin Smith, Roger Wood, John Webb

BLOCKS: Klischeewerkstätten der Industriedienst, Wiesbaden, Germany

PRINTED in Western Germany by DuMont Presse, Cologne

PAPER: Woodfree White Art supplied by
Gerald Judd Ltd., London and Apex Smooth Grey
supplied by Frank Grunfeld Ltd., London

BOUND by Van Rijmenam N. V., The Hague, Holland

Library of Congress Catalog Card Number: 65-22962

52194

CONTENTS

Byzantium

Migration and Settlement

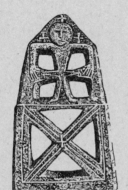

The New Europe

INTRODUCTION

The Myth of the 'Dark Ages'

DAVID TALBOT RICE

UNTIL NOT SO LONG AGO it was sufficient for a student of the age in which we live to concern himself with a study of Europe, but the emergence of Russia, the development of Asia and, more recently, the assumption of independence by a mass of minor states in Africa, have led to a widening of our horizons regarding the present, and a similar change has begun to assail our outlook towards the past. Thus the study of the early medieval phase of the culture of western Europe seemed until recently to be a comparatively simple and limited affair; it was enough for an Englishman to know something of the reigns of kings like Canute and Alfred, with perhaps a grounding in the warlike activities of Queen Boadicea against the Romans; for a Frenchman or a German some information about the wars of Charlemagne and his successors was enough, while an Italian could conveniently forget the whole age between the decline of imperial Roman power and the emergence of Florence in the 14th century. But now we are beginning to realize that a new, more comprehensive approach to our early history is necessary, and that today it is essential to pay very much more attention to certain aspects of man's life that were once wholly disregarded. Events in eastern Europe must thus be studied in addition to those in the west, while some consideration of the age of migrations and wanderings is just as necessary to a true understanding of later ages as an appreciation of the debt left by Rome. And further, it is essential to take into account the interaction of the various regions one upon another and of the influence that was exercised on the West by regions to the East, more especially Syria.

History's New Horizons

In setting out the limits of this book we have been guided by such thoughts as these, and rather than confine our study to the regions that have by convention been thought to play a part in the formation of Europe, we have extended the scope of our enquiry to include a survey, not only of the Byzantine world, but also of Sasanian Persia and early Islam, as well as of south Russia. And in the opposite direction we have included chapters on the situation in Visigothic Spain and the Norse world in addition to those on Merovingian France and Lombardic Italy. More might have been said on Ireland as an independent entity, but space did not permit.

It is in the breadth of its scope that this book can hold out a claim to greatest originality, rather than with regard to detail in respect of the various subjects treated. Previous historians have thus dealt very fully with the more settled cultures of central Europe, like the Carolingian and the Ottonian; the history of the Byzantine world has been familiar since Gibbon wrote his *Decline and Fall*, even if today we cannot always accept the basis of his thesis; the story of the great migrations has been completed in many a detail by the archaeologists; the happenings in Sasanian Persia and the Islamic world have long been familiar to specialists, even if they have received but little attention in more general

works. But it can, we think, be claimed that never before has an attempt been made to draw all of these chapters together with the object of writing an integrated story, or to illustrate their arts so that the influences that the various regions exercised on one another are brought into the limelight; again, some places, like Britain or the Norse world, are far from generally familiar. It is in these directions that our book can claim to cut the newest ground and fill what has hitherto remained something of a vacuum.

The story is taken up in the East, in Persia, when that land was controlled by the great Sasanian dynasty. The Sasanian Empire was both powerful and well organized; it was the only power that had proved itself strong enough to withstand the eastward thrust of the Roman Empire, and that subsequently defied and was at times victorious over Rome's successor, Byzantium. The Roman Emperor Valerian had been defeated by the Sasanian   p 19 (7) Shapur I in the latter part of the 3rd century, and was depicted as suppliant for mercy at Shapur's feet in many a Sasanian rock sculpture. A prosperous and highly developed society had grown up in Persia under Shapur and his successors, and its culture had developed along very individual lines; Persia's kings and nobles were the sponsors of an art of considerable distinction, which was to exercise no small influence both in the Byzantine world and at a later date on Islam; it was also to contribute to western civilization not a few elements of lasting significance. The trading contacts that linked Persia with the lands to the west were of the first importance, and remained virtually continuous even if in the military spheres the powers were at war and the frontiers repeatedly violated. The role played in culture by the 'Silk Road' was indeed more influential throughout most of the period with which we are concerned than were the barriers that were created by Persia's territorial frontiers.

The Fertile Culture of Syria

The zone immediately to the west of that dominated by the Sasanians, the area we know today as Syria-Palestine, together with the adjacent parts of southern Asia Minor, was perhaps even more significant with regard to the influence that it exercised on the development of thought, art and culture as a whole. During the early Christian period it was never the centre of any great imperial power, so that the region boasts no very significant political history of its own prior to the rise of Islam. But it was there that the Christian faith had its origin, together with much of the speculative and philosophical teaching that turned the faith into a world-embracing, universal creed. It was in Syria too that many of the underlying ideas, styles and iconographical systems that went to form Christian art first saw the light, and there, under the Umayyad caliphs, that Islamic art was born. It was thus in Syria that the first aniconic mosque decorations were set up, there that the system of vertical perspective, where things in the distance were placed above those in the foreground, was first developed,

9

and there that a particular type of pictorial presentation came into being wherein the picture, like eastern script, should be read from right to left rather than from left to right. It was there too that the conception of Christ as a bearded, awesome figure first came into prominence, in opposition to that dominant in the classical world, where He took on the attributes of a youthful Apollo. And it was in the same region that the belief that the representation of the saintly or divine form in art was anathema first arose—subsequently to affect the whole of Islam and to dominate in the Byzantine world during the age we know as the Iconoclast (726–843). Many of these ideas spread from Syria to influence the early Christian art of Rome and Italy and the growing art of Byzantium. They even affected the West as far as the Atlantic seaboard, especially in the realm of iconography. Thus the sculptures that decorate many of the stone crosses of Ireland derive from Syrian rather than Byzantine or Italian prototypes, while with regard to style, Geza de Francovich also attributes the strange, transcendental character that dominates Ottonian miniature painting to the influence of Syrian thought. Indeed, without the contribution made by Syria, Islamic art would never have developed in the way that it did, Byzantine art would in many respects have remained a mere decadent version of Roman art, while the Christian arts in Italy, France, Germany, and Britain would have lacked many of the features that were eventually to become characteristic of them.

Syria again exercised a considerable influence on Armenia, both in art and in the realm of dogmatic thought, though there developed in that country at an early date an individual and an independent way of life of considerable distinction. It was the Austrian scholar Strzygowski who first drew the attention of the historians and archaeologists of the West to the area, but epoch-making though many of his discoveries were and stimulating his theories, our knowledge of Armenia has remained somewhat restricted as the result of wars and closed frontiers, so that the land and the many important buildings that survive all over it have remained something of an enigma. Strategically the country occupied an unenviable position, for it stood as a buffer first between the Sasanian and the Byzantine Empires, and then between Byzantium and Islam. But the Armenian people were never aggressive and if their territory was often a battle-ground, it was through none of their own choosing. Politically the influence of Armenia was however very effective, for she gave to Byzantium quite a number of emperors and also a great many

Constantine the Great, whose reign, from 306 to 337, in many ways epitomizes the break between the classical and medieval worlds. He took two critical decisions—to move the capital from Rome to Byzantium and to adopt Christianity as the official religion of the Empire. (3)

ideas and inventions, and the influence exercised by Armenian art in developments in Byzantium and even in the West was considerable. But if we can still hardly explain how constructional systems which were to become characteristic of Romanesque and Gothic architecture were brought to a considerable degree of perfection in Armenia several centuries before they were developed in the West, we can at least make ourselves more familiar with the history, thought and art of this little known but important area. Georgia's role was less significant than that of Armenia during the period with which this book is concerned, but there were some important early buildings there also, though it is only at a date later than the year 1000 that serious consideration must be given to that country's contribution so far as relations with the West are concerned.

The role played by Islam in our story was of a rather different character. Around 640 the conquering Arab armies, spurred on by fanaticism, succeeded in wresting Syria and Egypt from the control of Byzantium; north Africa was conquered, and the Sasanian Empire was eliminated; within a few years an Arab force was threatening the walls of the mighty stronghold of Constantinople itself. Thenceforward skirmishes along the frontiers that separated the Islamic and the Byzantine Empires were more or less continuous, till affairs were brought to a head as a result of the defeat of the Byzantine forces by the Seljuk Turks at the Battle of Mantzikert in 1071. But even if there were hostilities, trade was but temporarily interrupted, and there was a constant give and take, as is attested by the numerous Islamic elements to be found in Byzantine art from the 9th or 10th century onwards. Even the West was affected, for Islamic textiles and other works *f 1, 2* of art found their way into cathedral treasuries at quite an early date, while rather later a fuller realization of Islam was brought clearly before the West as a result of the Crusades and the West's debt to Islam became of the very first consequence. It was thus the Islamic world that gave numerous new techniques as well as the words by which they were known to the West, it was there that certain aspects of classical learning were best conserved, and thence, rather than from Byzantium, that ideas in mathematics and the sciences were transmitted to Europe. Even if the more forceful contacts were established after the year 1000, the foundations were laid earlier, and the role played by Islam in the building of Medieval Europe was fundamental.

One of the most striking features of the period covered by this book is the number of cultural links between peoples divided by race, religion and historical background. The double-headed eagle, for example, originated in Persia, was adopted by Islamic patrons, then by Byzantine, and finally found its way on to the cathedral vestments of western Europe. These two designs are from silk fabrics—Islam (left) and Byzantine (right). (1,2)

Capital of the Civilized World

Vital though the role of Islam was, however, that of Byzantium was of even greater significance, for the capital of the Empire, Constantinople, was not only the centre of the most advanced and sophisticated civilization in the world between the fall of Rome (410) and the year 1000, to which the rest of Europe was repeatedly to turn; it was also the parent stem on which the Slav civilizations were founded and to which they owed the very essence of their being. There is hardly a saint, archbishop or ruler of the West who was not buried in Byzantine grave clothes, numerous embassies were exchanged and marriages effected between Western states and Byzantium, and works of Byzantine art were both acquired in the West and imitated there. But the Western debt to Byzantium, however important, was interrupted and intermittent, whereas that of the Slavs was fundamental, and was indeed so all embracing that Slav history may well be regarded as a later phase of Byzantine history, both with regard to countries like Bulgaria and Yugoslavia, which were for long periods of their history intrinsic parts of the Byzantine empire, as well as with regard to Russia, which was always independent, despite very close religious and political ties. The arts of the eastern Slav lands, moreover, are essentially Byzantine; it was actually in the Slav areas that Byzantine art saw some of its most important later developments, though these were to come after the close of our period.

f 3   In the year 313 the Emperor Constantine had openly accepted Christianity, and seventeen years later he transferred the capital from Rome to a site on the Bosphorus which had till then been occupied by the small city of Byzantium, first a colony established by Megara in Greece, then a typically Hellenistic trading town, and finally an outpost of the great Roman Empire. It was thenceforth to be called Constantinople in honour of its new patron. In the political, economic and artistic spheres the event was of outstanding importance, for it paved the way for the formation of a new culture in place of that proper to classicism, in spite of the many classical elements that were revived from time to time in the course of Byzantium's long history. And the city's role was to prove little less significant in the sphere of religion, for it was really the transference of the capital to the East that threatened the religious supremacy of Rome and brought about, some four hundred years later, a split between the two major branches of the Christian church, the Roman Catholic and the Orthodox. True, the churches were in theory united till 1054, but the city of Con-

stantinople grew in importance while Rome declined; the patriarch in the new capital was in daily association with the all-powerful emperor and was in consequence not very ready to pay attention to a pope far away in Rome who was, through much of the period with which we are concerned, not even a citizen of the Byzantine state; above all, the thought and outlook of the Greek citizens of the eastern capital was basically different from that of the Latin population of Rome, and though Latin was at first the official language of the state, it had, by the 7th century, given place to Greek. Moreover as new powers grew up in the West they became jealous of Byzantium, and the Byzantines tended to resent them, so that religious differences were exploited for political ends, especially by the popes, who were suspicious of the growing independence of the eastern church.

The Great Migrations

It was, however, only after the coronation of Charlemagne at Rome in the year 800 that relationships with the West began to cause serious anxiety in the Byzantine world. Before then it was the northern frontier that was a source of danger. Through much of the 1st millennium peoples were assembling, forces regrouping on the soil that is now south Russia, and the effects of these movements were to prove extremely wide-sweeping. It was from the plains of south Russia that the various peoples who were to pour into eastern Europe around the middle of the 1st millennium began their westward movements, and they took with them the so-called polychrome style in ewellery which had first been developed in the area by the Scyjthians and Sarmatians. The style was one which we would term barbaric, though it nevertheless left a lasting legacy in Lombardic Italy, Merovingian France and Visigothic Spain which was not only important in itself, but also exercised an influence on the development of more sophisticated arts like the Carolingian and the Ottonian, and was to affect the Norse world even more considerably. No great kingdoms or empires were involved, but instead comparatively small groups of peoples, who were to penetrate into Europe in a series of waves, some of them to pass on rapidly, leaving no more than a wake of destruction along their path, while others were to halt and colonize large tracts of the northern and western parts of the continent, so that a new ethnic complex evolved shortly before the end of the 1st millennium which set the stage of the Europe we know today. Thanks to the Roman system of defence, which was taken over by the Byzantines, these peoples were in the east

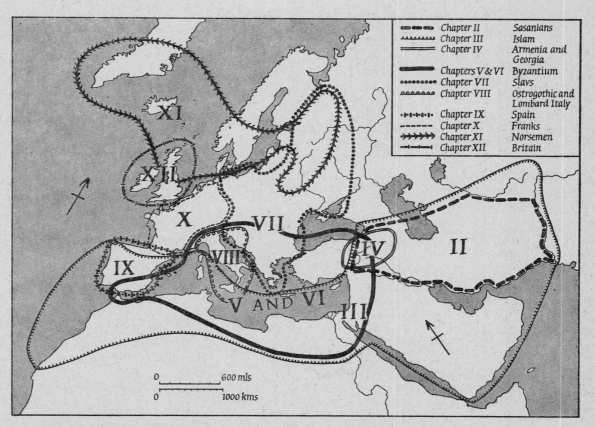

A bird's-eye view of the whole volume, showing in simplified form the areas covered by the various chapters. (4)

▰▰▰▰▰ Chapter II	Sasanians
⋏⋏⋏⋏⋏ Chapter III	Islam
═══════ Chapter IV	Armenia and Georgia
▬▬▬▬ Chapters V & VI	Byzantium
•••••••• Chapter VII	Slavs
⌢⌢⌢⌢ Chapter VIII	Ostrogothic and Lombard Italy
⊷⊷⊷ Chapter IX	Spain
–––––– Chapter X	Franks
»»»»» Chapter XI	Norsemen
⊢⊢⊢⊢ Chapter XII	Britain

0 — 600 mls
0 — 1000 kms

of Europe retained to the north of the river Danube, and to the frontier defences the Byzantines added an elaborate system of payments to keep the barbarians in check. When once their westward advance had penetrated to central Europe, however, the invaders spread out to the north and south. The Goths, Ostrogoths and Lombards, in successive waves, invaded and settled in northern Italy; the Visigoths penetrated into parts of France and into Spain; diverse tribes of the same blood dominated northern France and Germany and established links with the Norse world, while in Britain the development of art and culture was profoundly affected by the penetration of Germanic peoples into what had formerly been a Celtic stronghold.

Last of all came the Slavs, moving southwards from the region of the Pripet marshes, to establish themselves in the Balkans and in the eastern parts of central Europe as well as in the southern parts of Russia. They were converted to Christianity towards the end of the 10th century thanks to the missionary zeal of two brothers, Cyril and Methodius; the name of the former is preserved in that of the script which he devised for rendering the Slav tongue in writing, namely the Cyrillic. Eventually the Slavs of the West, the Czechs, the Slovaks, the Slovenes, the Croats and Poles, became Roman Catholics, while those of the East, the Serbs, the Bulgars and the inhabitants of Russia itself, adopted the Orthodox faith. In the end the latter became so numerous that they constituted the major branch of the entire church. The debt that they owed to Byzantium was immense, and it became more and more significant as time went on, till as a result of the Turkish conquest of Constantinople and the Balkans in the middle of the 15th century the mantle of the chief Orthodox state was assumed by Russia, and if Constantinople was the second Rome, Moscow was the third. The early history of Russia is thus to no small extent Byzantine history, and it is in a study of the Byzantine outlook that an answer to part at least of the enigma that is Russia is to be found.

p 142 (3)

A New Europe takes Shape

These events, the rise of the East, the establishment of Byzantine civilization, and the story of the great migrations, are all dealt with in the first three parts of this book. All of them had their beginnings in the 4th century, and they make of it a clearly marked dividing line in history. Major developments in all these spheres were more or less complete by the year 1000, a date which marks another great divide, for it was then that began the history of medieval Europe in the aspects with which we are most familiar: features like feudalism and chivalry, court and monastery, nobles and serfs. But long before that divide new cultures had begun to spring up in the West and North, like those of Northumbria, Mercia and finally Wessex in Britain and of the Vikings in Scandinavia. The role of Britain was important, for its art was highly developed by the end of the 7th century and was thereafter to exercise an important influence on that of the Carolingian world, while the Celtic church in Britain, though it was but short-lived, constituted a significant chapter in Christian history. The role played by the Vikings in Scandinavia, and subsequently in Britain and along the western sea-board of Europe, was again important. Even if, so far as the arts of those regions were concerned the Vikings were responsible for a good deal of destruction, they also had much to give, and the Norse sagas live with us still. Their art, too, was often of great beauty, even if it was in the main non-representational; it is of great interest if only because we see developed there some of the elements that began their life in Central Asia and Persia many hundreds of years before.

It might be held that the civilizations which are dealt with in the last section of this book, the Carolingian and the Ottonian, also began to develop as early as our dividing line in the 4th century, though in this case the period of gestation was very much more prolonged than with regard to Byzantium. Thus, soon after Constantine moved his capital from Rome to the Bosphorus, an independent emperor set himself up in the West, and from the year 364 onwards one emperor ruled in Italy and another in Constantinople. The Western Empire lasted for rather more than a century, and under the great Justinian (527–565)

there was something of a return to the grandeur that was Rome, though his capital remained in the East. His Empire stretched from Persia to Spain and from North Africa to the Alps, so that, but for Britain and Gaul, it was as considerable as the Roman had been at its widest extent. But when once Justinian's firm rule came to an end the West soon fell a victim to the invading barbarians and centralized control came to an end except for that of the petty papal state in Rome. It maintained continuity, and was able to pass that continuity on to Charlemagne by the ceremony of his crowning in Rome in the year 800. Charlemagne's new Western Empire was thus in a sense the successor of the old Empire of the West, and though the Carolingian line was soon to peter out, the Ottonian emperors again represented a virtually direct succession. But the West was never united in the same way as Byzantium, though culture was perhaps more widespread, for in an attempt to reconstruct a picture of the age we must follow up the story in numerous centres, whereas in the Byzantine world art and thought was very much concentrated in the capital.

The Written Word

Throughout the 1st millennium the art that was produced both in the barbarian and in the civilized worlds was often of very high quality; literature, on the other hand, was at a rather low ebb. In the Byzantine world, so renowned for the luxury of its life and the sumptuousness of its material products, literature was in the main confined to theological writings and to history; in the West there was even little of history. But the works of classical writers were highly valued and were copied in the Carolingian and Ottonian *scriptoria* as well as in Byzantium, and Christian texts were regarded with great reverence; numerous commentaries were written regarding them, and great care was taken and considerable expense was devoted to the production of manuscripts. The importance of this subject is perhaps in danger of being lost by the way this book has been divided, and it may therefore be useful to give it some space here.

As written languages, Greek and Latin used different alphabets and their individual letter-forms were variously modified to produce both a rapid informal script (cursive) for notes and *f 5 (a)* documents and more formal, calligraphic, scripts for literary manuscripts. In the course of the 2nd and 3rd centuries AD writers of Latin adopted a new way of forming and (where appropriate) joining the letters in their various scripts, although changing the shapes of only a few of them: the varieties of writing in use thereafter are the ancestors, directly or indirectly, of all the medieval and later scripts in the West.

A majority of the surviving Latin manuscript books (codices) older than the 8th century are written in a (normally) spacious, firm script ('uncial') in which thick and thin strokes are combined, *f 5 (b)* without sharp angles, to form letters of approximately equal height. Missionary clergy introduced writing to peoples among whom it had hitherto been unknown: and around 700 scribes at Wearmouth-Jarrow made copies of the Bible in a supremely beautiful uncial. By contrast the famous Gospel Book written at Lindisfarne in the same period was in a highly-distinctive heavy script created there or in Ireland from various older models. *f 5 (c)* The type of writing most widely used in the British Isles in the *f 5 (d)* 8th and 9th centuries however, was a compact angular script adapted from the less formal hands in use on the Continent. In the 7th and 8th centuries stylized versions of ordinary cursive *f 5 (e)* were adopted by the Papal chancery and by the writing-offices of the Frankish kings for their most formal documents. Many writing-centres on the Continent were simultaneously trying to create from this type of writing a script that required less writing-space than uncial but was appropriate for literary manuscripts; but not until Monte Cassino and other south Italian churches had developed the so-called Beneventan script could any of *f 5 (f)* these attempts be said to have been successful.

By this time, however, the problem of creating a complete and consistent minuscule alphabet (i.e. with letters of the type p,d instead of P,D) that combined legibility, grace and a flowing line and yet possessed a strength that survived its use by scribes of very different ability had long been triumphantly solved—at

The production and copying of manuscripts was perhaps the most valuable single contribution of the Dark Ages to later civilization. Below are a few examples illustrating the development of script during the period. Others are shown in later chapters. (5)

(a) Roman cursive script of the 4th century, the basis for most subsequent forms of writing in the West.

(b) The heavy 'uncial' hand used from the 4th to the 8th century.

(c) Anglo-Irish semi-uncial of the late 7th century.

(d) Anglo-Saxon minuscule of the 8th-9th century.

(e) Minuscule semi-cursive, 8th century.

(f) The beautiful 'Beneventan' script, evolved at Montecassino. This was the basis of the Carolingian minuscule illustrated on p. 294.

(g) English 'Winchester School' hand, 11th century, a version of Carolingian minuscule.

(h) 'Gothic' script, evolved during the Middle Ages and used in Germany until modern times.

(i, j) Two 'humanist' scripts, created in 15th-century Italy, which form the basis of modern 'Roman' and 'Italic' type-faces.

The most important development of Greek script was the formation of the new 'Cyrillic' alphabet designed to record the Slav languages. Above: the Codex Sinaiticus, 4th century. Below: the Slav translation of Manasses' Chronicle, 14th century. (6)

the court of Charlemagne or in one of the monasteries that was closely linked with it in the last years of the 8th century. With St Martin's at Tours as the main centre of dissemination 'Caroline minuscule' established itself in most writing-centres within the Western Empire in the next two decades. In the later 10th century it was adopted in England and Spain. Naturally, regional and local varieties emerged and quality varied enormously, but a fundamental change of character is not apparent in most places until the later 12th century. The 'Gothic' scripts which then evolved from it were rejected by the Humanists, who attempted to imitate the better Caroline hands in the belief that they were Antique; and when printed books began to take the place of manuscripts in Italy, writing *all'antica* inevitably provided the models for type-faces which in five hundred years have only been modified in points of detail.

p 294
(f 8)
f 5 (g)

f 5 (h)

f 5 (i, j)

Greek manuscripts of the period 200–1000 reveal less experiment and regional variety. At the earlier date the distinction between literary and documentary hands is much less marked than it is in Latin manuscripts. As literacy became less widespread, however, the script used for almost all books was a remarkably regular 'majuscule' script which is seen at its best in the 4th-century *Codex Sinaiticus* of the Bible. The dominant influence of Constantinople and its court may partially explain why the extant Greek manuscripts of the next four centuries show very little evolution in their scripts. Round about the year 800 a new minuscule script was created (we do not know where) from the cursive script that was in use for documents and provoked an outburst of copying in the capital and elsewhere. In the Middle Ages Greek was written in a more restricted area than Latin; but its alphabet was on several occasions exported and freely adapted to the needs of other languages, notably, by the 9th-century missionaries to the Slavs. The respective limits of the Latin and Cyrillic alphabets, the latter so-called after the missionary to the Slav world, Cyril (although not all scholars would agree that it is his creation), are still one of the significant cultural divisions of Europe.

f 6

An Age of Regeneration

Unfortunately there is no very convenient term by which to describe this phase of history. The term 'Dark Ages' is generally familiar. Yet both text and illustrations belie the accusation of darkness. Constantinople indeed was the most glorious of cities and the Byzantine age one of the most sumptuous that the world has ever seen. The period is also sometimes called 'The Age of Migrations', but the migrations only affected the regions north of the Danube and certain, but not all, parts of the West, while large tracts of Europe and the nearer East enjoyed a predominantly stable life. Still less could it be called the 'Age of Barbarism', though there were barbarian elements. The 'Early Christian Era' was already spent before our book begins, the 'Middle Ages', as characterized by such features as chivalry and romance, feudalism and serfdom, had not really developed. The 'Macedonian Renaissance' or 'Second Golden Age' are terms restricted wholly to the Byzantine world, the 'Carolingian Renaissance' to a limited period in the West. In the six hundred years before our story begins one could speak of the 'Hellenistic Age', but it would not be correct to think of calling our period the 'Romanistic' (even if such a term were current), for many other elements than those stemming from Rome were at play. Nor did the 'Byzantesque' element form more than a part of the general complex. It could indeed be called 'The Triumph of Christendom', for that is a theme that binds together the accounts of France and of Armenia, of the Carolingian world and of Byzantium, and even of the wandering peoples like the Goths and Lombards. Yet it is only one theme out of several, and three chapters would fall outside its limits—those dealing with Sasanian Persia, the Islamic world and the Vikings.

The concept which includes and transcends all these is that of 'Europe' and European civilization. Essentially Christian as it was, it was still the product of many forces from before and outside Christianity, and it is from this point of view that the book has been organized; so the title THE DAWN OF EUROPEAN CIVILIZATION has been chosen. How a culminating point was reached in the West

13

around 1000 is told in the last chapter, where progress towards a realization of the consciousness of Western Christendom is studied. This western realization was something very different from that which had developed in the East over several continuous centuries. In Byzantine eyes the church was essentially a part of the everyday world in which people lived, with the emperor at its head as Christ's vicegerent on earth, just as he was in the same way head of the state. Only the emperor could sanction the appointment of a subordinate ruler, only he could choose and nominate the head of the Church. It was not for the patriarch of Constantinople, still less, in Byzantine eyes, for the pope of Rome, to crown a rival sovereign, and any such action could not be recognized by the Byzantine emperor. Never, by the remotest chance, could the patriarch have become a virtually independent ruler making and unmaking kings, as did so many popes in the West. And the conception of the faith was different too; in the Byzantine world it was simultaneously profoundly spiritual and curiously practical, but it was never, as in the West, dualistic or to a considerable degree political.

In dealing with this long and extremely diverse phase of history different techniques have had to be used. In writing of the highly developed cultures like the Byzantine, the Carolingian or the Ottonian, the approach has been more purely historical, for records, though they are often incomplete, are none the less plentiful. But with regard to the Slavs, the Lombards, the Merovingians and the Visigoths, not to mention Britain and the Norse world, our knowledge has often been acquired mainly through excavations, and the relics of material culture are more plentiful than the written records. Their interpretation has demanded an archaeological rather than an historical approach. In general however an attempt has been made to treat all periods as much as possible in the same way, according more or less equal attention to actual events, to the political situation, to the social background and to the arts. Throughout, the illustrations have been chosen not only with the aim of illuminating the text, but also with that of giving as full and accurate a picture as possible of the various ages and civilizations concerned.

Acknowledgements

The Editor would wish to take opportunity of recording his thanks to all those who have helped in the production of this book. He thanks Mr Donald Bullough for information on script incorporated in the Introduction, and all the authors for their willing and expert help in collecting the illustrations and supplying material for the captions, though final responsibility for these remains with the publisher. He would also like to express his warmest appreciation of the work done by the editorial and research staff of Thames and Hudson, and more especially to thank Mr I. R. Sutton, who has followed the book through all its stages from first to last. Finally, both Editor and publisher are deeply indebted to all those throughout the world who have so readily answered queries and provided photographs, especially M. Paul Perdereau, Curé de Germigny-des-Prés; Mr W. Douglas Simpson, CBE, University Librarian, King's College, Aberdeen; Prof. Joachim Werner, Ludwig-Maximilianus-Universität, Munich; Prof. George Zarnecki of the Courtauld Institute of Art in London, and the Directors, Keepers, Librarians and Staff of the following museums, galleries, libraries and institutions:

Forhistorisk Museum, Aarhus; Bibliothèque Municipale, Abbeville; Musées d'Arles; Bibliothèque Municipale, Arras; Bibliothèque d'Autun; Walters Art Gallery, Baltimore; Staatliche Bibliothek, Bamberg; Musée de la Tapisserie, Bayeux; Staatliche Museen, Berlin; Bernisches Historisches Museum; Rheinisches Landesmuseum, Bonn; Musées de Bourges; Moravské Museum, Brno; Institut Royale du Patrimoine Artistique, Brussels; Bibliothèque Municipale, Cambrai; Corpus Christi College and the Fitzwilliam Museum, Cambridge; Nationalmuseet, Copenhagen; Hessische Landes- und Hochschulbibliothek and the Hessisches Landesmuseum, Darmstadt; The Manx Museum, Douglas; Hauptstaatsarchiv, Düsseldorf; Edinburgh University Library; Real Biblioteca de San Lorenzo de El Escorial; Münsterschatzkammer, Essen; Museo Nazionale (Bargello), Florence; Stadt- und Universitäts-Bibliothek, Frankfurt am Main; Musée d'Art et d'Histoire, Fribourg; Bibliotheek der Universiteit, Ghent; Niedersächsische Staats- und Universitätsbibliothek, Göttingen; Landesmuseum für Vorgeschichte, Halle; Tiroler Landesmuseum, Innsbruck; Bibliothèque de la Ville, Laon; Bibliotheek der Rijksuniversiteit, Leyden; City of Liverpool Museums; the British Museum (Departments of British and Medieval Antiquities, of Coins and Medals and of Manuscripts), the Legation of the People's Republic of Bulgaria, the Victoria and Albert Museum and the Warburg Institute, London; Biblioteca Nacional, Deutsches Archäologisches Institut and Museo Arqueológico Nacional, Madrid; Römisch-Germanisches Zentralmuseum, Mainz; Domstiftsbibliothek, Merseburg; Musées de Metz; Bayerisches Nationalmuseum, Bayerische Staatsbibliothek and Schatzkammer der Residenz, Munich; Landesmuseum für Vor- und Frühgeschichte, Münster; Metropolitan Museum of Art, New York; Universitetets Oldsaksamling, Oslo; Ashmolean Museum and Bodleian Library, Oxford; Ecole des Hautes Etudes and Musée des Arts Décoratifs, Paris; Civici Istituti di Arte e Storia, Pavia; Philadelphia Museum of Art; Muzeum Archeologiczne, Poznan; Princeton University Library; Deutsches Archäologisches Institut, Rome; Stiftsbibliothek, St Gallen; Musée des Antiquités Nationales, St-Germain-en-Laye; Stadtbibliothek, Schaffhausen; Schleswig-Holsteinisches Landesmuseum für Vor- und Frühgeschichte, Schleswig; Kungl. Vitterhets Historie och Antikvitets Akademien, Stockholm; Württembergisches Landesmuseum, Stuttgart; Stadtbibliothek, Trier; Museo Civico, Turin; Universitetsbiblioteket, Uppsala; Aartsbisschoppelijke Musea and Bibliotheek der Rijksuniversiteit, Utrecht; Biblioteca Apostolica Vaticana, Vatican City; Biblioteca Nazionale di S. Marco, Venice; Kunsthistorisches Museum and Österreichische Nationalbibliothek, Vienna; Gotlands Fornsal, Visby; Rijksdienst voor de Monumentenzorg, Voorburg; Państwowe Muzeum Archeologiczne, Warsaw; Freer Gallery of Art, Washington DC; Herzog August Bibliothek, Wolfenbüttel, and the Schweizerisches Landesmuseum, Zürich.

II BEYOND THE FRONTIERS OF ROME

The Rise and Fall of Sasanian Iran

DAVID OATES

The Empire of Iran during the Sasanian period, 3rd–7th centuries AD

Between Mesopotamia and India

lies the great tract of land known at various times as Persia, Iran and Parthia. The civilization which grew up there in the 6th century BC (the heir of ancient Sumer, Babylon and Nineveh) was to be the rival—the only permanent rival—of Greece and Rome throughout the entire classical age, and on into the Byzantine. Its history is chequered but culturally continuous, the various periods into which it is divided—Achaemenid, Seleucid, Parthian and Sasanian—denoting dynastic changes (and to some extent changes in the racial character of the ruling class) rather than the conquest of one people by another.

The Parthian Empire (so called because its founder, a Scythian chieftain, first seized power in Parthia, south-east of the Caspian) lasted from the 2nd century BC to the 3rd century AD. In 224 the last Parthian King, Artabanus V, was defeated by Ardashir, the founder of the Sasanian dynasty (named after his grandfather Sasan). Although he and his successors did their best to establish a new order, they still belonged to the Parthian tradition and inevitably inherited the same role towards the West. What the Parthians had been to the Roman Empire—a threat, an unsleeping enemy ready to exploit any sign of weakness—the Sasanians were to prove to the Byzantine.

With Ardashir I and his son Shapur I, Iran achieved a splendour that recalled the great days of Darius and Xerxes. But an even higher peak was reached in the mid-6th century under Khusro I (531–579), who reorganized the administration, initiated large-

scale public works and inflicted crushing defeats on the Huns in the north and the Hephtalite kingdom in the east. As part of the never-ending war against Byzantium he invaded Syria and sacked Antioch. His court at Ctesiphon became one of the most brilliant the world had ever seen.

The gold dish known as the 'Cup of Solomon' (right) dates from this time and has as its centre an engraved rock-crystal with a portrait of the King. He sits enthroned, holding his sword of state and wearing an elaborate head-dress (every Sasanian king had a new crown specially designed for him). His throne is a wide bench supported by winged horses. Beside him is a pile of cushions, which were handed one by one to the most distinguished men who sought audience with him. The stones surrounding the crystal are coloured glass paste—white and red rosettes and green lozenges. According to tradition, this bowl, which is now in Paris, was given to Charlemagne by the Caliph Harun ar-Rashid. The style of ornamentation is one that was carried to Europe by nomads invading from the East and spread even as far as the Atlantic coast.

Khusro's reign was almost the end of Sasanian greatness. His grandson Khusro II revived the brilliance of his court and began to emulate his conquests and even captured Jerusalem, but the effort was too great. He was defeated by the Byzantine Emperor Heraclius in 628. Eight years later the Muslim invasions began. Ctesiphon fell in 637 and soon the whole of Iran had become part of the Arab world. (1)

16

Roman victories in the 2nd century AD helped to seal the fate of the Parthian dynasty, the Arsacids. Between 197 and 199 the Emperor Septimius Severus (above) invaded Mesopotamia and captured Ctesiphon. It was one more stage in a war that had lasted for hundreds of years. For Romans the name of Parthia still meant Carrhae—the dreadful slaughter in which Crassus and all his legions had perished in 53 BC. (2)

The Parthian army—often invincible in sudden attacks but ill-suited to long campaigns or the occupation of territory—relied for its main strength on mounted archers (this small terracotta dates from the 1st–3rd centuries). Organized on a feudal basis, the cavalry were furnished by the land-owners, the infantry consisting of their peasant retainers. (3)

King Ardashir I, founder of the Sasanian monarchy, came from a family already powerful in the province of Fars. His father had successfully rebelled against the Arsacids and seized the throne of Istakhr. Ardashir succeeded him in 208, building a new capital at Firuzabad. In 224 he met and defeated the last Arsacid King. The rock-relief (above) shows his symbolic investiture at the hands of the divine Ahuramazda. The god, on the right, holds out the diadem, which the King grasps in his right hand. Ardashir's crown is surmounted by a *korymbos*—a bundle of hair wrapped in a piece of silk. Under their horses' hooves lie the enemies of Ahuramazda—Ahrim, the Evil Spirit—and of Ardashir—Artabanus V, the defeated Arsacid King, seen (left) in a Parthian relief. (4, 5)

Shapur I, Ardashir's son, succeeded him in 241. This portrait (above) is part of a huge statue over 26 feet high carved in the living rock of a cave which was probably his burial place: the top of the crown and feet are still part of the ceiling and floor of the cave, but the statue itself was broken loose by an earthquake. Hieratic in pose, with large staring eyes and impassive countenance, the great King embodies authority and command. In the carved gem (left) is represented Shapur's greatest military achievement—his defeat and capture of the Roman Emperor Valerian in 260. Valerian, on the left, raises his sword against Shapur who, without troubling to draw his own, seizes him by the wrist. Valerian never returned to Rome, and is believed to have died in captivity in Iran. (6, 7)

The sacred place of the old Achaemenid rulers of Persia had been Naqshi-Rustem, a cliff-face about four miles north of Persepolis. Here Darius the Great, Xerxes, Artaxerxes and Darius II were buried. Ardashir, claiming descent from the pre-Alexandrian house, carefully preserved their temples and rock-cut reliefs, adding new ones of his own, so that they seemed one continuous—legitimate—dynasty. Part of the sanctuary is shown here (right). The two cruciform façades, with their rows of columns, inscriptions and reliefs, are the tombs of Xerxes and Darius the Great, dating from the 5th century BC. Beneath that of Xerxes is a Sasanian carving showing a victory of Hormizd II (302–309), enlarged below: the King, lance in hand and riding at full gallop, charges his adversary who falls headlong. Between the two Achaemenid tombs, near the ground, is a scene showing Shapur triumphing over Rome: the Emperor Philip the Arab (who was forced to pay tribute to the Sasanian King) kneels in front of him, while Shapur holds Valerian by the wrist—as in pl. 7 a conventional sign that he had been captured.

On the extreme right of the photograph, under the tomb of Darius, are two reliefs showing Vahram II (276–293) and Hormizd II in battle against the enemy. Single combat was favoured by the Parthian and Sasanian warriors—there is a tradition that Valerian was actually taken prisoner by Shapur personally in this way.

The man and woman in the foreground give an idea of the immense scale of these reliefs. (8, 9)

20

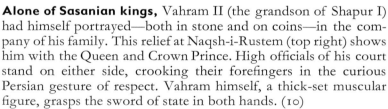

Alone of Sasanian kings, Vahram II (the grandson of Shapur I) had himself portrayed—both in stone and on coins—in the company of his family. This relief at Naqsh-i-Rustem (top right) shows him with the Queen and Crown Prince. High officials of his court stand on either side, crooking their forefingers in the curious Persian gesture of respect. Vahram himself, a thick-set muscular figure, grasps the sword of state in both hands. (10)

Mithras and Ahuramazda, the chief gods of the Iranian pantheon, hand the diadem to Ardashir II, who reigned from 379 to 383 (right centre). The Sun-god Mithras, wearing a rayed headdress and standing on a lotus-flower, holds the sacred *barsom,* or bundle of reeds (similar to that held by Ahuramazda in pl. 4). Ardashir II, about whom little is known, is standing on a prostrate enemy who seems to be a Roman. The technique here is flat and linear, in contrast to the rounded reliefs of a century earlier. (11)

The last rock-carving of the Sasanian kings (bottom right) is set at the back of a deep niche cut into the cliff and shows another royal investiture, though it is uncertain which king is meant— either King Peroz (457–483) or Khusro II. Ahuramazda, as usual, gives him the diadem; the figure on the left is the water-goddess Anahita. In the lower register stands an equestrian statue of the King in chain mail—one of the greatest works of Sasanian art. All the figures here are notable for the detailed rendering of their armour, costumes, jewellery and weapons. (12)

The royal hunt,

the killing of a wild animal at the hands of the king himself, was an age-old symbol of power, possibly stemming from the time when man pitted his strength against the beasts in earnest. The art of later Iran, as well as that of Nineveh and Babylon, is full of displays of kingly prowess. On this page we show three characteristic scenes of Sasanian boar-hunts. Left: Shapur II wielding bow and arrow—a repoussé silver dish, engraved and partially gilt. Right: stucco plaques made from three moulds showing King Peroz attacked by two boars (right), killing them with his lance (left) and the herd fleeing (centre). Each mould has been used twice. Below: an elaborate scene in which the identity of the protagonist is not known. The hunt takes place in an enclosed preserve (note the fence which surrounds it, the posts secured to bushes with ropes). The King is rowed across a lake accompanied by female musicians. In the centre he stands, shoots and slays; the dead animals are taken away on elephants. (13, 14, 15)

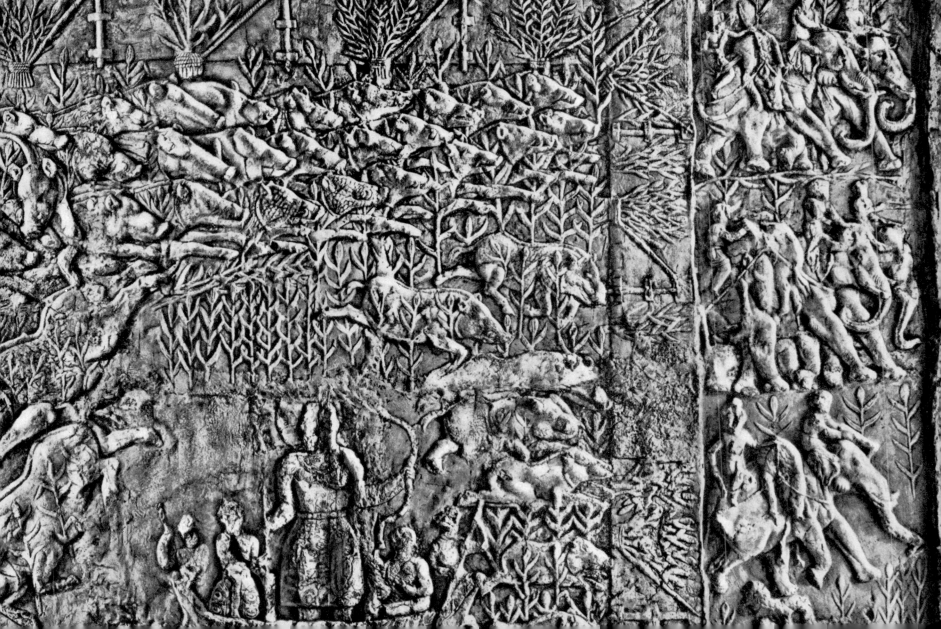

Bishapur, 'beautiful city of Shapur', the new residence built by Shapur shortly after his victory over Valerian in 260, lay in his native province of Fars and was planned not in a circle like other Sasanian cities, but in the Greek chequerboard style. One whole section was reserved for the royal palace and here recent excavation has revealed one of the most splendid buildings of the period—'the Sasanian Versailles', as the excavator, Roman Ghirshman, has called it.

At its centre was the Great Hall (reconstructed right), a huge domed room 37 metres wide and about 25 metres high. Its plan was square with four rectangular bays added on each of the four sides, so that the impression from inside was of a series of projecting angles—a device adopted by the architect in order to solve the problem of the vaulting, since it reduces the central area to 22 metres square. This could easily be covered by a dome, while the four outer bays, at the end of which were the four doors into the hall, could be vaulted with tunnel vaults.

The decoration can be reconstructed with a high degree of certainty. The lower parts of the walls consisted of a series of stucco niches, painted red and surrounded by a Greek-key pattern. Above them ran a line of beautifully moulded foliage, surmounted by a cornice. Of the dome itself only fragments have survived; it was painted in fresco in floral designs, chequer-patterns and triangles. Near the doors stood vividly coloured plaster statues of animals—a yellow and black horse and an elephant with eyes of green glass. In the days of Shapur the total effect must have been one of rich and sombre magnificence. (19)

A mosaic floor in the nearby banqueting hall (left) shows Shapur's court in a mood of gaiety and relaxation. Mosaic was an art foreign to Iran and must have been introduced from the West; the style and imagery have many Roman characteristics, but modified to suit Sasanian tastes—the faces, clothes and manner of sitting, for instance, are typically Persian, as is the custom of having portrait heads 'cut short at the chin' and not showing anything of the shoulders or neck. Top: a woman reclining on a cushion. Centre: a harpist. Bottom: portrait of an old man. The panels are all on a fairly small scale (none larger than 3 feet) and form the border of a stone floor—exactly like a Persian carpet or rug. The other subjects are similar to those shown—portraits of members of the court, aristocratic ladies, and nearly-nude girl dancers and musicians. (16, 17, 18)

Life at the Sasanian court,

rich, luxury-loving and magnificent, is reflected in the sumptuous works of art by which it was surrounded. Silverware has survived especially well. There are scores of plates, bowls, jugs and drinking cups, many with engraved scenes showing the king feasting, hunting or at war.

Dancing girls, whirling their light veils over their heads (below), or the sensuous music of the pipes (above) were among the delights of a royal banquet. On the bowl (right) a king and queen sit together. The king hands his wife a festal garland. The ram's horns on her head symbolize fertility, while the three boars' heads below stand for the king's successful hunt. (20, 21, 22)

'Let us pass round the golden cup that Persia has decked with diverse images', wrote a later poet of Muslim Iran. Many drinking vessels portray animals or fantastic hybrid beasts. Below and right: two *rhytons* in the form of horses. The sitting war-horse shows the Sasanian fashion of grooming, with elaborate harness, tuft of hair on the forehead and plaited tail. The bit and bridle are missing. The *simurgh*—a combination of peacock, lion, griffin and dog (top right)—was a creature of good omen. (23, 24, 25)

The supreme god of the ancient Persian religion was Ahuramazda, 'the Wise, the Lord' whom we have already seen in reliefs at Naqsh-i-Rustem and elsewhere. Zoroaster, a great teacher who lived about the 7th century BC, reformed Mazdaism, as it is called, purging it of its crudest features and introducing ethical standards and a doctrine of rewards in an afterlife. It was this faith which was adopted by the Sasanian kings, and they made it into a state religion. Central to its ritual was the maintenance of an 'eternal fire', and two fire-altars at Naqsh-i-Rustem are shown above, about 5 feet high and carved out of the solid rock. The intaglio (top) depicts the fire-god, son of Ahuramazda, rising from such an altar. (26, 27)

The ruin of the Sasanian Empire

was due as much to internal weakness as to invasion from outside. After the heavy defeats inflicted by the Byzantine Emperor Heraclius a more ominous threat appeared—the armies of Islam in their first impetuous burst of conquest. The Sasanian state crumbled. The last King, Yazdgard III (left) had neither the talents nor the resources for resistance. In 637 the Arabs entered Ctesiphon, the city in Iraq chosen by Ardashir as his capital, and were dazzled by its wealth and grandeur.

Part of the façade of the great palace still stands (below). Like other Sasanian palaces, it consisted of a wide tunnel-like recess flanked by ornately decorated wings (the right-hand one collapsed as recently as 1908). At the end of the recess is a doorway leading into the royal apartments. The outstanding achievement of its architect is the huge brick vault, nearly 100 feet in span, and over 100 feet high—a feat comparable with the greatest works of Roman and Byzantine architecture. (28, 29)

The Rise and Fall of Sasanian Iran

DAVID OATES

The great god Ahuramazda, carved above the head of Darius the Great at Behistun. The worship of Ahuramazda was taken over by the Sasanian kings, in its modified Zoroastrian form, and was one of the features by which they sought to show their unity with the Achaemenid line (Darius and Xerxes). Ahuramazda was the principle of Good, in perpetual conflict with the power of Evil. (1)

ON THE STAGE of world history Iran played its most important role during the period from the fall of Assyria in 612 BC to the coming of Islam in the 7th century after Christ. Long before this time the country had reached a high level of material culture and had contributed to the development of Near Eastern civilization, but it had never been politically united. Yet within a century after the sack of Nineveh all the lands from the Nile to the Hindu Kush were provinces of the Iranian Empire under the Achaemenid dynasty.

It was inevitable that, lacking an imperial tradition of their own, the early Achaemenid kings should adapt to their own needs and to the special character of Iranian society the methods, and in part the outwards forms, of the Mesopotamian empires which they had so rapidly supplanted. Their administration was modelled on two thousand years of Mesopotamian experience, but their officials were Iranian nobles. Their palaces were decorated with stone reliefs in the Assyrian manner, arranged and executed in accordance with Iranian taste. Above the head of Darius the Great, on the grandiose relief which he cut on the rock of Behistun, there floats the figure of his divine patron Ahuramazda, in appearance almost identical with Ashur, the great god of Assyria. This infusion of the Iranian spirit into a hybrid of native and foreign traditions created a civilization and a system of government which, for all its obvious weaknesses, endured without fundamental change for more than a thousand years.

Its political continuity was interrupted by the conquests of Alexander and the brief supremacy in the East of his Hellenistic successors. They achieved a lasting effect in wresting from Iran the control of the East Mediterranean lands, and by implanting in Iranian culture a tenuous thread of Hellenism. But they learnt more than they taught, and there is more than a little of the Oriental monarchy in the institutions they developed and in the legacy they eventually transmitted to the Roman Empire.

The Seleucid kings who were Alexander's nominal heirs in Iran did not long maintain their authority beyond the Euphrates, where during the 2nd century BC the Iranian empire was rebuilt by the Arsacid dynasty of Parthia. The full revival of Iranian power, however, came only when the Sasanian dynasty of Fars (Persis), the home of the Achaemenids, supplanted the Arsacids in the early 3rd century AD. The Sasanian monarchy was a conscious restoration of Achaemenid glories, and became both an object of emulation to the contemporary Byzantine Empire and a model for the later Abbasid caliphate. Its influence on Byzantium and even on medieval Europe, though less immediate, was not inconsiderable, particularly in the sumptuary arts for which it was renowned. Its history forms the subject of this chapter. But in order to understand it we must first look at the nature of the country and the important ways in which it influenced the character of Iranian society.

'The Desert and the Sown'

The Iranian plateau is bounded on the west and south-west by the Zagros mountains, on the north by the Elburz chain and on the east by the outlying ranges of the Hindu Kush. These formidable barriers, rising to heights between 10,000 and 20,000 feet, intercept the moisture of the rain-bearing winds. Their valleys are well-watered and fertile, but limited in extent and sometimes difficult of access. Little rain reaches the heart of the plateau. Circumscribed areas of cultivation exist where water for irrigation is supplied by a river rising in the mountains or can be collected in *qanat*, vented tunnels which tap the subterranean drainage from the hill-sides. These *qanat* systems, some of considerable extent, have been the mainstay of agriculture over wide areas of Iran at least since the time of the Achaemenid kings.

The land which supports the greater part of the settled population of the plateau is thus distributed in a broad arc around its mountain fringe, either in the rain-fed valleys of the several ranges or in oasis-like pockets where local conditions permit the development of irrigation systems. It may be said to form another Fertile Crescent, but it differs in two historically significant respects from the plains of Mesopotamia and Syria to which the name is traditionally applied. There the cultivable land forms an almost continuous belt with few natural features to define the boundaries of individual settlements or to hamper communication between them. Moreover, the desert within the horns of the Crescent does not utterly forbid either nomadic occupation or the passage of travellers. Many of the local communities of Iran, on the other hand, have evinced a fierce independence in their dealings with one another and with any central government that has tried to control them. And the effect of their local separatism is increased by the presence, across the middle of the plateau, of great salt deserts which prevent direct and rapid communication between the extremities of the country.

Such conditions encourage the existence of small towns in commercially favourable locations, and of rural communities of limited size whose leading figures, often landlords or their representatives, have been one of the most important elements in Iranian society. The city is not, in much of Iran, the traditional form of local government as it was in Mesopotamia, where early empires could be formed by the subjection of cities and administered by the inflation of their existing bureaucratic systems.

Two other features of the country have tended in its long history to emphasize its lack of political cohesion. Large areas which receive an annual rainfall at or below the minimum required for agriculture, and have no water available for irrigation, can provide seasonal grazing. Tribes of nomad herdsmen, whose migrations often brought them in conflict with the settled peasants and the townsmen, form a disruptive and sometimes politically dangerous element in the population.

Secondly, despite the apparently formidable barrier of its frontier mountains the Iranian plateau is by no means impenetrable from without. The passes of the Zagros afford communication with the west, and the plateau lies open to intrusion from the Eurasian steppe on the north, either through the passes of the Caucasus or across the lowlands of Khorasan immediately to the east of the Caspian. Contacts with Mesopotamia have been primarily commercial and cultural; only Alexander and the Arabs successfully invaded Iran from this direction. In cultural transmission an important role was played in ancient times by the extreme south-westerly province of Khuzistan (Susiana), which forms geographically a salient of the south Mesopotamian plain into the foothills of the Zagros. From the northern steppe have come waves of nomadic invaders, each successful intrusion adding to the Iranian population a heterogeneous element which, though it might accept the sedentary life and be apparently absorbed in the amalgam of Iranian culture, often retained its ethnic identity, its language or dialect and its internal loyalties. Even when the attacks were unsuccessful, the pressure on the northern frontier remained an important military and administrative problem.

The Three Estates

Against this background it is easier to understand some characteristics of Iranian society in the Sasanian period, which define the problems of government and delimit their possible solutions. There were by long-standing tradition three estates, the priests, the warriors, and the peasants and craftsmen. The last-named, which also included those engaged in trade, was by far the most numerous, but its members were of little account. It was almost impossible for them to attain a higher rank, and difficult even to change their hereditary craft or occupation. Individuals, notably merchants, might amass considerable fortunes and even lend money to the king, but this entitled them to no social pretensions. The great majority of this class comprised the peasants who lived in a condition approaching serfdom. The bourgeoisie of Iran was never an effective political force, nor could it provide an alternative to the land-owning classes as a source of administrative manpower.

p 18 (3)

The warriors were the land-owners, great and small, who furnished the heavy cavalry and the mounted archers, the effective strength of the Iranian army. The infantry were a rabble of their peasant retainers. The composition of this army and its character as a feudal levy made it a formidable field force, capable of devastating raids but ill-suited to the permanent occupation of territory. Socially the 'warriors' ranged from the 'free men', probably small proprietors, up to the seven great families who had existed in Iran as early as the Achaemenid period, owned vast estates and held by hereditary right some of the traditional offices of state. Typical of these were the Suren and Karen clans, who figure constantly in both civil and military affairs under the Arsacid and Sasanian dynasties. The small landlords and the heads of single villages also played a significant, though less conspicuous part in politics. Their hereditary loyalties were to the head of a clan or tribe, often a feudal overlord, but the effective strength of these ties would vary with the circumstances of the moment. In times of weak government self-interest and the need for security would lead them to support their local or tribal leaders. On the other hand a ruler strong enough to give them protection could use them as the basic framework of his own administrative system, thereby diminishing the power of the great nobles. The social and political significance of hereditary estates helped to emphasize the importance of marriage alliances, which were arranged with great care. It is doubtless one, though not the only, explanation of the peculiar good fortune which was thought to attach to marriage between father and daughter or brother and sister, a practice common in the great families and the royal house.

The Mazdaean priesthood exercised great influence at all levels of Iranian society. At this period their religion had departed considerably from the monotheism of the prophet Zoroaster, and it is probable that in many parts of the country the original polytheism had never been radically altered. Modern accounts of the Zoroastrian creed suggest a mysticism, complicated by theological exposition, that can hardly have fulfilled the requirements of popular worship. However that may be, the precepts of religion which were at some time during the Sasanian period gathered into the written Avesta ordered every aspect of life. The *magi*, as exponents of these traditions, gained a formidable authority over the individual from the cradle to the grave, and their public prestige was further enhanced by their exercise of judicial functions in the local law courts. They owned considerable estates, particularly in Media, and their wealth was increased by endowments given by the pious for their souls and those of their families. The political importance of the hierarchy was greatly strengthened when the Sasanian dynasty established Mazdaism as the state religion of Iran. Thenceforward we find the *mobadhan mobadh*, or chief *magus*, and the *herbadhan herbadh*, the head of the administration of the fire temples, ranked with the greatest of royal officials.

p 27
(26, 27)

In this system the king had no original place, except as a member of one of the great families. His formal position is summed up in the only substantive royal title that has no earlier Mesopotamian counterpart, 'King of Kings', a paramountcy which might be real or purely nominal according to circumstances and the character of the monarch. The early Sasanian kings set out to reinforce both the theory of kingship and its effective power. The theory is represented by the claim of divine authority for the king as the viceroy of Ahuramazda, even perhaps in the later period the divinity of the royal person, and by his presentation as the invincible conqueror of man and beast, the embodiment of the fortune of his people. It is these aspects of royalty that we see depicted in every form of Sasanian art that we possess; the endless repetition had a propagandist and also a talismanic value. The reality of power depended on the creation of a loyal administration under effective control, and this ran counter to the traditional interests of the nobility. The internal history of the Sasanian Empire is largely the history of the struggle that ensued.

p 18 (4)
f 1

Decline and Fall of Parthia

At the beginning of the 3rd century AD the Parthian Empire was disintegrating. The greater part of its territory had always been divided among petty rulers or hereditary satraps whose loyalty to the King of Kings depended on the hope of reward or the threat of retribution. Its army was composed, in the main, of feudal contingents under the command of great nobles, whose hereditary privileges and vast estates gave them a dangerous preponderance in affairs of state. Although there had been an apparently deliberate revival of Iranian culture and a consequent rejection of Hellenistic traditions early in the 1st century AD, the Arsacids remained tolerant of diversity in religion, language and custom among their nominal subjects and did little to encourage a national feeling that might have redounded to their benefit. The paramount kingship belonged by right to the Arsacid family, but the succession was often determined by the nobility in their own interest. The real power of any Arsacid ruler thus rested to an outstanding degree on his personal qualities of administrative, military and diplomatic ability, and he faced the constant threat of deposition in favour of some other member of his family, when either his incompetence or his excessive zeal displeased his too powerful subjects.

The military security of Parthian territory had long been threatened on two fronts, in the east by the rise of the empire of the Kushans, which reached the peak of its power under Kanishka (AD 144–173), and in the west by the Roman Empire. There is no evidence to suggest that either power seriously aspired to the conquest of Parthia. On the history of the eastern frontier we are ill informed, although it was certainly the scene of considerable fighting in the latter half of the 2nd century. In the west the constant struggle for the control of lesser kingdoms which lay between the two great powers reflects the lack of a satisfactory natural frontier and the concern of either side for the security of the wealthy provinces of Syria and Babylonia. The strategic key to the situation, now and later, lay in the control of northern Mesopotamia and Armenia; a glance at the map will show that troops stationed there could outflank a threatened attack from either side.

f 4

In 197–8 the Roman Emperor Septimius Severus led an expedition into the heart of Parthia, capturing Ctesiphon and Seleucia and taking 100,000 prisoners. The arch erected in the Roman Forum in 203 to celebrate this triumph was carved with reliefs (now badly weathered) illustrating incidents from the campaign. This 19th-century engraving of one of the scenes shows (top left) the siege of a riverside city and, on the right, its submission to the emperor. Below is seen another city besieged by Roman soldiers while the mounted enemy takes to flight—one of them perhaps the Parthian king himself escaping from his capital of Ctesiphon. (2)

p 18 (2)

f 2

There were three major Roman attacks during the 2nd century, the last of which, under the great soldier Emperor Septimius Severus in 197–199, placed Rome in a commanding position. Not only was the capital, Ctesiphon, taken and sacked as it had been on previous occasions, but northern Mesopotamia as far as the Tigris at Nineveh became a Roman province garrisoned by two newly formed legions. The existence of this forward base was a threat to Parthia's richest provinces and a damaging blow to Arsacid prestige, made explicit when Caracalla, son of Septimius, invaded Media and Adiabene and desecrated the Arsacid tombs at Arbela. Although the balance of honour was redressed by a bloody but inconclusive battle near Nisibis, which forced Caracalla's successor Macrinus to buy peace with a large indemnity, Rome retained her Mesopotamian province and her strategic advantage. The struggle must have sapped the resources and the confidence of Parthia, and the existence at this time of two claimants to the throne was a symptom and an aggravation of her weakness. Vologases IV, who had survived a serious revolt in Fars as well as the invasions of Septimius Severus, died in 208/9 and was succeeded by Vologases V, who was evidently in control of the south until 223. As early as 213, however, Media and the north were ruled from Ecbatana by Artabanus V, the opponent of Caracalla and Macrinus. The combination of external pressure and internal dissension proved fatal to the Arsacid house.

The House of Sason

Sasan, from whom the Sasanian dynasty took its name, was a high official of the temple of Anahita in Istakhr, the principal town of Fars (Persis) since the decline of its greater Achaemenid neighbour Persepolis. Sasan must have been of noble origin, for he married a woman of the Bazrangi family, the ruling house of Istakhr. There can be no truth in the story that the Sasanians were the offspring of a common soldier, but there is equally no evidence concerning their own claim to Achaemenid descent. Papak, son and successor of Sasan, was able to secure for his younger son Ardashir the command of the garrison at Darabjerd in south-east Fars. Papak himself later usurped the throne of Istakhr, while Ardashir extended his own power by the conquest of many towns in the province. Following the death of his father and, opportunely, of his elder brother Shapur whose accession he had refused to recognize, Ardashir was installed as King of Istakhr in 208, the year that was later held to mark the founding

of the Sasanian dynasty. The neighbouring province of Kerman was soon overrun, and Ardashir built himself a new capital and palace at Gūr, modern Firuzabad. Its remains survive, as one of the earliest domed buildings that we know. His pretensions could no longer pass unchallenged by the King of Kings. Artabanus V ordered the King of Ahwaz to march against him, but Ardashir, having meanwhile possessed himself of Isfahan, defeated the new adversary and added Khuzistan to his dominions. He now controlled the whole of south-west Iran, and his position was further strengthened by an expedition up the Tigris which brought him alliances with the rulers of Kirkuk and Erbil (Arbela), whose defection was doubtless encouraged by their desire for a more vigorous champion against the Roman threat. Finally in 224 he met and defeated Artabanus V, and in 226 he was crowned King of Kings.

f 3

p 18 (5)

Resistance to the new ruler continued for some years in the north and north-west, where it was fomented by the Arsacid King of Armenia and supported by the power of Rome, and in the east, where members of the former royal family had found refuge with the King of the Kushans. In 232–33 a Roman invasion under the Emperor Severus Alexander was successfully checked, but seems to have led to the acceptance of a Roman garrison by the Arab ruler of Hatra, a desert city just west of the Tigris which had long served as the principal Parthian fortress on the north-west frontier and had withstood many Roman sieges. In 237–38 Ardashir counterattacked, laying unsuccessful siege to Dura Europus, the Roman outpost on the Euphrates, and invading northern Mesopotamia. A fort on the Severan frontier road leading to Nineveh was captured at this time and apparently not reoccupied. Further to the north-west Carrhae and Nisibis fell into Iranian hands, but Hatra still held out. Armenia likewise resisted Ardashir's early attempts to subdue it, and in general his western campaigns seem to have stabilized the area of Iranian control without permanently extending it. His eastern frontier seems to have approximated to that of modern Iran.

f 4

Ardashir's New Order

We know too little about Parthian administration and the dating of individual features of the Sasanian system to determine precisely the degree of innovation that Ardashir introduced in the government of the country. But Iran had long possessed the forms of bureaucracy, descended through Hellenistic institutions from

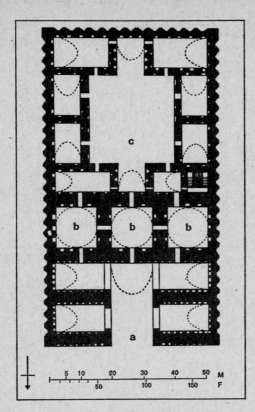

Ardashir's palace at Firuzabad consisted of a large tunnel-like recess (a) flanked by symmetrical walls and leading into a range of three domed halls (b). Behind these was a courtyard (c) from which the residential quarters opened. It was built by Ardashir shortly after his accession in 226, on the outskirts of his new capital. (3)

Achaemenid and eventually from Mesopotamian models. It is likely that the system persisted under the Arsacids in an attenuated form, and that Ardashir's task was to revive and reinforce it. He could not have changed the nature of Iranian society even had he wished to do so. He was obliged to find his chief ministers among the great families and his minor officials among the lesser landowners. But he replaced the hereditary satraps and the countless petty kings of Arsacid Iran with governors who held office during his pleasure, equal in honour to their predecessors but inferior in power. Their responsibilities seem to have been largely military, in the defence of the frontiers and the provision of troops to the royal army, while the civil administration and the all-important collection of the revenues were carried on through a hierarchy of officials, based on the small landlords and the heads of villages, and responsible ultimately to the royal secretariat. The most important provinces were often, as a double safeguard, entrusted to members of the royal family.

Military affairs were likewise set on a new footing. The supreme military office was henceforward confined to the Sasanian house, and the size of the standing army was increased. Governors still led their provincial levies in the field, but their authority now derived from royal appointment rather than hereditary right, and only the contingents of a small number of client kings still owed their primary loyalty to their own leaders rather than the King of Kings. The latter's standing with his army and his generals, however, inevitably depended on his own military prowess, and it is no accident that the greatest of the early Sasanian kings were brilliant soldiers.

It is clear that the efficacy of these reforms depended in many respects on the energy and judgment of the King in appointing and supervizing his subordinates. Ardashir could not guarantee the competence of his successors, but he did all that lay in his power to increase the prestige of royalty, an undertaking which was the more necessary since he occupied the throne only by right of conquest. In this light we may see his claim to be the legitimate successor of the Achaemenids, and the propaganda which represented the Arsacid dynasty as Hellenized interlopers, the Romans as usurpers of the rightful dominions of Iran. He established Mazdaism for the first time as the official state religion. This had the twofold effect of strengthening national feeling and

of focussing the loyalty thus engendered on the person of the King, who was represented as the viceroy of Ahuramazda. The concept of the divine origin of royal authority found dramatic expression in the investiture reliefs, where the King is shown receiving the ring of power from the hand of the god. The conscious reversion to Achaemenid ideas is again obvious, but it is noteworthy that Ahuramazda is no longer an echo of Ashur, but an unmistakeable Iranian aristocrat.

p 18 (4)

Shapur I: Consolidation and Conquest

Shapur I (241–272), son and heir of Ardashir, continued his father's policy of internal reorganization and external aggression. In the year of his accession he was engaged in consolidating his control over the northern and north-eastern provinces, but was soon called westwards by a Roman attack under Gordian III. Shapur later claimed a victory, but the actual course of the campaign is obscure. It ended with the assassination of Gordian, whose throne was usurped by his praetorian prefect, Philip the Arab, in 244. Philip, anxious to establish his claim in Rome, accepted a peace treaty by which Armenia and Mesopotamia were to be surrendered and a large indemnity paid. The terms were probably never carried out, for Philip's brother was later governor of Mesopotamia and a Roman protégé was King of Armenia as late as 250. It is likely, however, that the Roman garrison was withdrawn from Hatra and that the frontier posts in the extreme south-east of the Roman province of Mesopotamia were finally abandoned. Shapur took no further action, probably because affairs in the east demanded his attention; it must have been at this time that he completed the conquest of the Kushan kingdom.

p 19 (6)

In his great inscription on the walls of an Achaemenid shrine, the so-called 'Ka'aba of Zoroaster' at Naqsh-i-Rustem, he claims the Roman failure to observe the treaty as an excuse for his second western campaign, which began in 252. Now at last Armenia was conquered, and Mesopotamia was again invaded. Hatra must have been besieged and taken as a prelude to these operations, if it had not fallen earlier. Its capture, which according to legend required a siege of three years, was followed by the virtual abandonment of the city, and the role of its Arab princes as the lords of the Mesopotamian desert passed to another Arab dynasty, the Lakhmids, who had settled at Hira in southern Mesopotamia during the last years of the Arsacid dynasty. The Lahkmids in turn were to play an important part in the wars between east and west.

f 6

The Roman fortress of Dura Europus on the Euphrates may have passed briefly into Iranian hands in 253, and Shapur claims to have sacked many cities of Syria itself. But the raid cannot have been of long duration, for Dura Europus was soon in Roman hands again and its final destruction came in the first stage of Shapur's third campaign in 256. This was the crowning success of his military career. Syria was overrun and Antioch, the capital of the Roman East, was sacked and burnt. In 260 the Roman Emperor Valerian, attempting to stem the tide of disaster, was defeated in a battle near Edessa and taken into captivity with the greater part of his army, said by Shapur to have numbered 70,000 men. The Iranian forces then spread out to ravage the rich southern parts of Asia Minor, laying waste the province of Cilicia and penetrating as far as Iconium (Konya). In the event their confidence in success led to the piecemeal defeat of some of their scattered detachments, and when Shapur finally withdrew he was harried by the Arab prince of Palmyra, Odeynath, who claimed to have relieved him of much of his booty. But these successive humiliations of the Roman power which had brought down the Arsacid monarchy symbolized the rebirth of Iran under Ardashir and Shapur. It is significant that Shapur, in the Naqsh-i-Rustem inscription and the numerous reliefs which present his achievement to his subjects and to posterity, chose to describe the wars with Rome even to the exclusion of his victories on other frontiers.

p 19 (7)

The Naqsh-i-Rustem inscription provides a convenient index, not only of the growth of the Empire in the number of provinces and of tributary kings that it lists, but of the parallel expansion of the central administration with its nobles and high officers of state in the immediate service of the King. As an important part of his achievement Shapur includes the establishment of shrines and the endowment of offerings for the souls of members of the royal house, the kings, nobles and officials who served under him and his predecessors. We see that of those whose services to the Sasanian dynasty had earned this recognition, eight were the retainers of Papak, King of Istakhr, thirty-one of Ardashir and sixty-six of Shapur himself. By far the greater part of the increase in each reign can be seen to consist of officials with specific responsibility for departments of the royal household or administration.

This pious act and the prominence accorded to it in the official record also reflect the King's concern for the state religion. But Shapur, unlike some of his successors, was not intolerant of other beliefs. He is said to have authorized the translation of Greek and Indian works on science and philosophy, and gave protection and encouragement to the prophet Mani, whose teachings were a compound of Mazdaean, Buddhist and Christian doctrines. We cannot know whether this patronage of a new religion, bitterly opposed by the Mazdaean hierarchy, sprang from personal sympathy or from a calculation of its political advantage. Certainly Shapur's official expressions of piety both in the inscriptions and the reliefs were orthodox. But he may, as the first to adopt the title 'King of Kings of Iran and non-Iran', have anticipated some benefit from the spread of a creed which embodied elements of all the major religions of his Empire and might prove acceptable to his non-Iranian as well as his Iranian subjects. He may, too, have wished to deny a monopoly of spiritual power to the *magi* who might, and later did, translate it into a temporal influence subversive of royal authority.

The practical side of Shapur's administration can best be seen in his efforts for the development of agriculture, the ultimate source of his revenues. Recent survey has confirmed the Sasanian date of large-scale irrigation works in Khuzistan, and Shapur himself tells us that Valerian's captured troops were settled there. There is no reason to doubt the tradition that their labour and engineering skills were used to lay the foundation of this system,

Vahram I (273–276): the king wears the traditional Sasanian head-dress of a cap surmounted by symbolic flames, and the curious ornament known as the 'korymbos'—a bunch of hair drawn to the top of the head and wrapped in a silk cloth. (5)

parts of which are still in use today. Western influence is also to be seen in the new city of Bishapur, laid out on the Hippodamian chess-board pattern rather than the circular plan adopted by Ardashir at Firuzabad. The form of the monumental buildings, both palace and fire-temple, remain uncompromisingly Iranian, but the floor mosaics of the palace and the iron-clamped ashlar masonry of the temple are obviously the work of Western, probably Syrian, craftsmen.

p 24-5 (19)

p 24 (16-18)

The Heirs of Greatness

The reigns of Shapur's immediate successors afford a good illustration of the weakness still inherent in the Iranian monarchy despite the reinforcement of the royal administration which Ardashir had initiated. Ardashir and Shapur had each nominated his heir, but this privilege was afterwards exercised only by the most powerful of their successors. At other times the succession was determined by the nobility and the high officers of state, whose interest rarely dictated the choice of the most forceful candidate. Hormizd I, son of Shapur, who had been designated Crown Prince in his father's lifetime, was succeeded after a reign of only one year by his brother Vahram I (273–276), whose rela- *f 5*

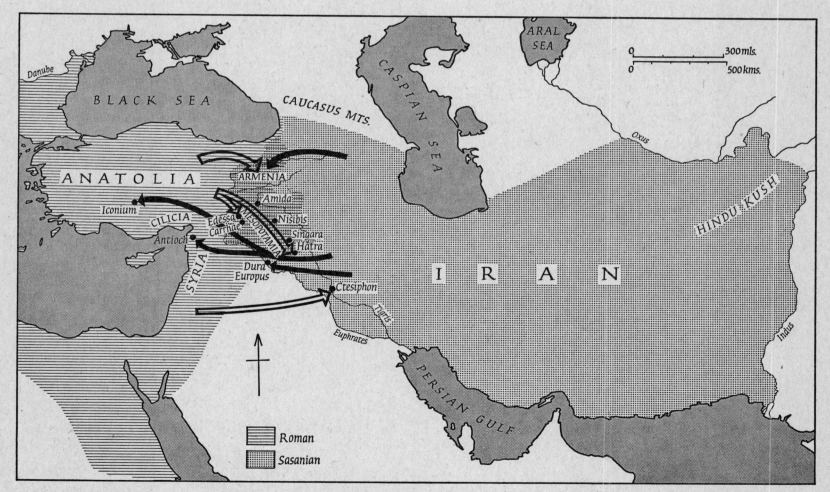

The Roman and Sasanian Empires in the Middle East in the 3rd century. The boundary between them was never constant. Armenia and northern Mesopotamia perpetually changed hands, as did the frontier towns such as Hatra and Dura Europus. More ambitious incursions into enemy territory were occasionally attempted: Shapur I penetrated as far west as Antioch and Iconium, and in turn the Roman Emperor Carus managed to reach Ctesiphon, but in neither case was any permanent conquest achieved. (4)

tive insignificance in the Naqsh-i-Rustem inscription suggests that his father had not regarded him as a candidate for the throne. It is probable that his elevation, and that of his son and grandson of the same name, was brought about by the chief *magus* Kartir. Kartir left a number of inscriptions, of which one was cut on the 'Ka'aba of Zoroaster' immediately below that of Shapur. In it he recounts his service during five reigns, from Ardashir to Vahram II, and the growth of his influence is apparent both in the degree of responsibility he exercised in the religious affairs of the Empire and the titles he was given by successive kings. The prophet Mani was arrested and executed under Vahram I and Kartir records the persecution of his adherents, together with Christians and Buddhists, in a spirit of intolerance which is altogether at variance with the policy of Shapur I.

Vahram II (276–293), son of Vahram I. It was during his reign that the internal family conflicts began which were in the end to weaken the Sasanian Empire. Perhaps as a propaganda measure to promote unity at home, Vahram included portraits of his wife and children on his coins and official monuments. (6)

Of the family of Vahram I only his son, Vahram II (276–293) is worthy of note. During his reign the war with Rome broke out afresh when the Emperor Carus led an army to Ctesiphon, but his sudden death in 283 brought the campaign to an end. Vahram, however, was simultaneously faced with a rebellion in the eastern *f 4* marches of the Empire and was forced to sign an unfavourable treaty with Rome, ceding Mesopotamia and Armenia. The rebel, the King's brother Hormizd, was crushed and the east was placed under the governorship of Vahram's son, later Vahram III. This was the first of the open dynastic conflicts which often threatened the cohesion of the Empire and weakened its external policy.

Perhaps the most interesting feature of the reign is the way in which its major preoccupations are illustrated in the numerous rock reliefs. Two of them, at Naqsh-i-Rustem and Sar Meshed, depict Vahram II in the company of his wife and children. The *p 21* inclusion of the royal family is unparalleled in Sasanian rock *(10)* carving, and on his coins he again departed from convention in *f 6* showing the heads of the Queen and Crown Prince as well as his own. This strongly suggests, not merely family feeling, but a concern with dynastic problems, and the use of reliefs both as propaganda and as talismans to ensure the succession of his own immediate descendants. At Naqsh-i-Rustem a number of dignitaries, perhaps including Kartir, signify their allegiance to the royal family. At Sar Meshed the King defends his family from the onslaught of a lion which, pierced through the belly by his sword, falls dying at his feet, and the theme is clearly victory over the enemies of the royal house. Victory is again depicted in more conventional fashion in a second relief, also at Naqsh-i-Rustem, where Vahram charges and unseats an adversary with his lance. And at Naqsh-i-Bahram he is shown seated on the throne and attended by his officials. The frontal pose here employed apparently served in Parthian and Sasanian art to enhance the talismanic value of the representation. It is next adopted in the great relief of Shapur II at Bishapur, where it clearly denotes the King triumphant.

Looking at these reliefs in conjunction with the inscription of Kartir, we gain the impression that a branch of Shapur's family was attempting to establish an exclusive claim to the succession with the backing of the orthodox priesthood. The unsuccessful revolt of Hormizd may be seen as a reaction to the dynastic plan and perhaps even the religious policy, for it was in the east and in the extreme west that the prophet Mani had achieved his most conspicuous success; the political situation in

the west was an obvious factor in the later reversal of the policy. This took place under Narseh, son of Shapur I, who deposed Vahram III after a reign of a few months in 293. Narseh called a halt to persecution, and even attempted to obliterate the memory of his predecessors by attaching his own name to the investiture relief of Vahram I at Bishapur. In the representation of his own investiture at Naqsh-i-Rustem Narseh is seen on foot, receiving the ring of power from the hand of a goddess, probably Anahita, and not from Ahuramazda. Again there must be some religious or political implication, but in the absence of other evidence it cannot be defined. More obvious in its significance is the presence, between the King and the goddess, of a small figure, clearly Narseh's son Hormizd whose right to the throne is thereby proclaimed and reinforced.

Narseh's efforts to redeem the situation on the western frontier met with failure. After an initial success against Galerius, and despite the propaganda value of his tolerant attitude toward the Manichaeans of whom there were now many in Rome's eastern provinces, he met with defeat in a second encounter with Galerius in 298 when his family was captured. As the price of their ransom Mesopotamia and parts of Armenia east of the Tigris passed once more into Roman hands, but it is noteworthy that even at this favourable moment the Romans made no attempt to restore the old Severan frontier of Mesopotamia, and Singara and Nisibis remained the frontier towns.

Against Rome — and Against Christ

The brief and undistinguished reign of Hormizd II was followed *p 20 (9)* by a contest for the throne, which ended, according to legend, in the coronation of the future Shapur II, one of Hormizd's sons, *p 22* while still in his mother's womb, the babe's sex having been *(13)* guaranteed by the Magi. 'A royal bed on which the queen lay in state was exhibited in the midst of the palace', states Gibbon, 'and the diadem was placed on the spot which might be supposed to conceal the future heir of Artaxerxes.' He proved during a reign of seventy years to be one of the greatest of Sasanian monarchs. His first task when he came of age was to break the power of the Kushans, who had taken advantage of earlier weakness to reclaim their independence. When the east had been reduced to order he was able to turn his attention westwards, and from 339 until 364 he was engaged in almost constant warfare with Rome, interrupted only when an incursion of nomads from the south Russian steppe demanded his presence in the northeast. The outcome of the war was a resounding triumph for Shapur when the Emperor Julian was killed during a campaign directed against Ctesiphon, and his successor Jovian bought a safe retreat with the surrender of the frontier fortresses of Nisibis and Singara and the territories east of the Tigris; the Romans also agreed to subsidize the defense of the Caucasus passes, to be undertaken by Iran in the common interest.

The nature of the fighting is of some interest, in part because it is so vividly described by Ammianus Marcellinus, himself an officer on the Persian front under Julian and one of the few ancient historians who understood military matters. The character of the Roman army had been radically altered, with the legions, diminished in size and status, serving as garrison troops and the field forces, reinforced with mailed cavalry on the Iranian model, as a mobile strategic reserve often under the Emperor's direct command. On the other hand the Sasanians had learnt from their opponents the techniques of siege warfare in which the Romans had hitherto been unrivalled. The war unfolds itself in the pages of Ammianus as, in the main, a series of prolonged sieges of fortress cities, Singara, Nisibis, Amida, Edessa, conducted with extraordinary ferocity on both sides. The changed strategy encouraged the development on the Roman side of a refined military architecture which reached its monumental climax in the walls of Constantinople, built in the first half of the 5th century, and set the pattern for European fortification until the age of gunpowder.

The increased virulence of feeling between the combatants may be ascribed in part to the emergence of Christianity as a factor in international politics. The conversion of Constantine had made Christianity the official religion of the Roman Empire, and its

Most of the decorative details on Sasanian buildings have disappeared, but some idea of their effect can be gained from pictures engraved on metalwork. This fortress appears on a silver dish. It stands on a stepped plinth; the ground floor consists of a line of high blind arcading; then a series of horizontal zones of patterning, leading to an ornate gallery. Another gallery at the top is supported on brackets. The doorway is divided into two by a central shaft, and the arch is pointed. Sasanian decoration was quite unrelated to structure. (7)

almost simultaneous adoption by Terdat, the pro-Roman ruler of Armenia, had brought that vital kingdom more closely into the Roman orbit. Shapur could no longer afford to exercise the tolerance of his immediate predecessors towards his Christian subjects, who were numerous in the disputed areas of Mesopotamia and might be presumed to be sympathetic to the Roman cause. Thus the war was accompanied by the persecution of the Christians within the Sasanian Empire, although this was probably more local and intermittent than the violently partisan accounts of martyrdom would lead us to suppose.

Kings, Priests and Prophets

The death of Shapur marks the end of the first great phase of Sasanian expansion and the beginning of a decline in royal power, subject to dynastic disputes fomented by the ambitions of the nobility, which lasted for a century and a half. It would be tedious to follow in detail the fortunes of Shapur's feeble successors. But the period as a whole is a reminder that the system developed by Ardashir and Shapur I did not guarantee strong government, although it provided the machinery for the comparatively few kings throughout Sasanian history whose talents and personality qualified them to use it. Certain individuals and events, however, demand our attention.

One of the most famous of Sasanian kings, celebrated by poets and artists for centuries after the fall of the Empire, was Vahram V, *f 9* surnamed Gōr. The events of his reign characterize the main preoccupations of rulers of Iran at this time. He came to the throne in 421, apparently as the candidate favoured by Mihr Narseh, his father's chief minister, and supported by the forces of Mundhir, the Arab prince of Hira under whose tutelage he had been educated. His father Yazdgard I in the early part of his reign had shown tolerance towards his Christian subjects as part of a policy of rapprochement with the Byzantine Empire, heir to Roman power in the East. A Council held at Seleucia in 410 defined the organization and the dogmas of the Church in Iran, whose existence was henceforward officially recognized by the government. But the offensive and intolerant attitude of some of the Christians themselves lost them the royal favour, and a new persecution followed at the time of Vahram's accession, perhaps instigated by Mihr Narseh and certainly directed by the chief *magus* Mihr Shapur. This led to frontier troubles and a brief, unsuccessful war with the Byzantines, in which the Iranian army was commanded by Mihr Narseh.

The succeeding treaty provided for religious toleration in both empires, and renewed the agreement on Byzantine subsidies for the defence of the Caucasus passes. That this problem was of real interest to both powers had been demonstrated by a Hunnic invasion in 395, which penetrated through Armenia to Cappadocia, Cilicia and even Syria. Much of Vahram's own military activity was directed against Chionite nomads who threatened Khorasan. He also reaffirmed Iranian control over Armenia by deposing its king and reducing it to the status of a province under an Iranian governor. In internal affairs he seems to have been a figurehead, leaving real power in the hands of Mihr Narseh, three of whose sons held high offices of state during their father's lifetime.

The palace at Sarvistan was built during the 5th century in Fars, the home province of the Sasanian dynasty. The façade was made up of three large arches forming a long porch or loggia. From the central arch a square hall roofed by a dome on squinches was entered; the courtyard and living rooms lay behind. On either side of the hall were attractive narrow rooms roofed by tunnel vaults on short coupled columns. (8)

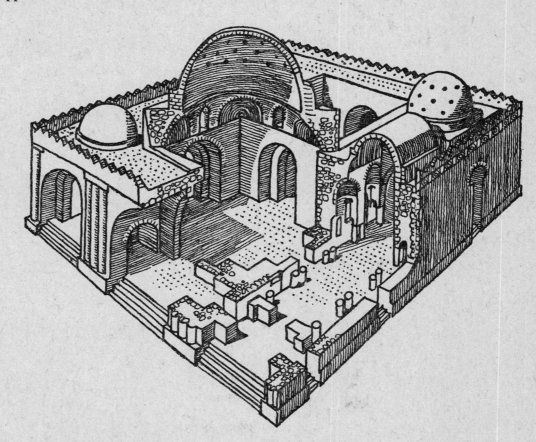

Vahram V (420–438), known as 'Gŏr', 'the wild ass', because of his impulsive temperament. In later ages he was remembered as a great hunter, poet and musician, but he seems to have left the government largely in the hands of ministers. (9)

The decline of the monarchy is symbolized by the nature of the traditions which made Vahram Gŏr the hero of later legend. According to one tale he gained his throne by killing two lions which had been set in an arena to guard the royal insignia. The story must be apocryphal, but it aptly expresses the heroic qualities demanded of the monarch as the personification of his country's virtue and well-being. Vahram's skill as a huntsman no doubt reflects his real attainments in the favourite pastime of the Iranian gentleman, but it is also one of the qualities of the ideal figurehead, an interpretation of kingship which suited the ambitions of a powerful nobility.

p 22-3
(15)

Two major events of the 5th century illustrate the external and internal weakness of Iran at this time. The Hephtalites, a people similar in origin to the Huns though probably of a different stock, had succeeded in establishing a powerful state on the territory of the old Kushan kingdom, threatening the eastern provinces of Iran. A series of unsuccessful attempts to restore the situation culminated in 484 with the complete destruction of the Iranian army and the death of the King, Peroz. The Hephtalites then extended their control over Iranian territory and forced the Sasanians to pay them tribute. The effect of the disaster was further aggravated by the repeated failure of crops through drought, resulting in a prolonged and widespread famine.

p 23
(14)
p 21
(12)

About this time there arose a new preacher, Mazdak, whose religious ideas seem to have been founded on a version of Manichaean doctrine propagated some two centuries before. One of his precepts laid down that a man, in order to learn asceticism, must have the opportunity to experience satiety in the good things of life. In the circumstances of the time and particularly in the rigid social system of Iran, this was all too readily translated into a revolutionary creed of the common ownership of property and even of women, encouraging the poor to distribute among themselves the possessions and the households of the rich.

The Road to Renewal

In this situation the well-meaning but ineffectual Valash, brother of Peroz, was soon found to be inadequate and was deposed in 488 in favour of Kavadh I, son of Peroz, who had spent some time as a hostage at the Hephtalite court and may thus have seemed a politic choice. The new King surprisingly championed the Mazdakite cause. The motive of his policy may have been religious, but its results were political. The first years of his reign were marked by hostilities in Armenia, the incursion of Arab tribes in Mesopotamia, and minor rebellions in Iran. He succeeded in disposing of two powerful ministers by encouraging their mutual jealousy, but this success and his Mazdakite sympathies earned the enmity of the nobility which led to his deposition in 496. He escaped and took refuge with the King of the Hephtalites, whose daughter he married. His successor proved incompetent and after two years Kavadh was restored to the throne, which he occupied until his death in 531.

During this time he gradually rebuilt the prestige of the monarchy and the power of the Empire, laying the foundations, like Ardashir I before him, for the more obvious brilliance of his successor. He restored discipline within the Empire, and during a brief war against the Byzantines Amida fell into Iranian hands for the first time since the reign of Shapur II. In internal affairs it is sometimes difficult to distinguish between the reforms of Kavadh and those of Khusro I, his son and heir. But Kavadh

was probably responsible for two measures which greatly diminished the power of the chief minister, an office which in the hands of men like Mihr Narseh had overshadowed the throne. He created a new post charged with some of the minister's duties in the central government, and appointed four viceroys in the four quarters of the Empire to divide between them the minister's responsibility for the supervision of provincial administration. Although more circumspect in his attitude to the Mazdakite leaders than he had been at the beginning of his reign, he may be suspected of using them to counterbalance the pretensions of the *magi* who were their religious opponents and the nobility who were the targets of their political agitation. He introduced social reforms, and probably planned a fiscal reorganization which would alleviate the lot of the poorer classes, the farmers on whom his revenues ultimately depended. Not until his reign was drawing to a close, in 529, did he permit the final suppression of Mazdak and his followers. Their capital crime was not, it appears, forty years of communist subversion in a rigidly aristocratic society, but a threat of interference with the king's plans for the succession.

The Last Great King: Khusro I

Khusro I (531–579) continued the work of strengthening Iran and the monarchy which his father had begun, although implicitly and perhaps explicitly condemning his revolutionary methods now that the need for them had passed. He redeemed the stability of Iranian society and the ideal of the just king as its protector by a series of measures designed to repair the damage caused by Mazdakite appropriation of the property and the women of the upper classes. By accepting responsibility for the upbringing of children born of forced marriages he created a new class of men, devoid of loyalty to families which would not own them and

p 17 (1

Persian textiles were famous throughout the world and fetched enormous prices at Byzantium. This fragment of silk with the head of a wild boar is from Astana (now in Chinese Turkestan). The technique of spinning and weaving silk originated in China, but by the reign of Shapur II the fabrics made in Iran were completely Persian in style. Birds, horses, lions and boars were among the most popular subjects. (10)

A silver ewer, with repoussé lions. The lion was among the most popular of Sasanian motifs, and it was probably from this source that it passed, by way of Syria and Byzantium, into the art of Romanesque Europe. (11)

dependent entirely on the Crown, who would serve him faithfully in official positions. The device was an ingenious solution of one of the crucial problems of government, but its effect was limited and came too late.

The scars of a generation of insecurity in the countryside were mended by the rebuilding of villages and roads, the repair and extension of canals; the irrigation system of Khuzistan, initiated by Shapur I, probably took on its final form under Khusro. The reform of the fiscal system projected by his father was put into effect, based on a new survey of the resources of the country and a reassessment of taxation. The collection of revenues was thereby rendered more efficient and less burdensome to the peasantry whose earlier sufferings had led to the excesses of the Mazdakites.

In the structure of administration Khusro made further changes in keeping with the policy of his father. The heads of three departments of state under the supervision of the chief minister were henceforward appointed by the King himself and were granted the right of direct access to his person, thus diminishing still further the authority of their nominal superior. The post of commander in chief was abolished and its duties assigned to four commanders, one in each of the four quarters of the Empire. The army itself was rendered more effective by the introduction of a form of compulsory military service, and it was supplemented in the defence of the frontiers by the settlement in crucial areas of warlike tribes from other parts of the Empire, a device much used by the Assyrian Empire and, in later times, by the Ottoman Sultans.

In foreign affairs Khusro was no less successful. In the east he first discontinued the payment of tribute to the Hephtalite kingdom in 542, and twenty years later destroyed it for ever.

The northern frontier was secured against the Huns, and in the south the Yemen was brought under Sasanian rule. In the west he had inherited a war with the Byzantines, born of the squabbles of their respective Arab client princes, the Lakhmids of Hira and the Ghassanids who controlled the Syrian side of the desert. Peace was made in 532, but in 540 Khusro felt strong enough to use another border incident as an excuse for reopening hostilities. He invaded Syria and sacked Antioch. Despite a truce in Mesopotamia in 545, the war dragged on in Armenia for another twelve years and it was not until 651 that a treaty was signed.

An interesting feature of the struggle is the political significance of the theological quarrels which at that time rent the Christian world. The Byzantine Empire under Justinian was officially Orthodox, but the Monophysite heresy had many adherents in Syria, especially among the Arab frontier tribes of the Ghassanid confederacy, and in Constantinople it enjoyed the powerful support of the Empress Theodora. The recognized Christian church in Iran was Nestorian, but many of the Arab subjects of the pagan Lakhmids were Monophysite, and the Monophysite church was strong in Armenia. Justinian was torn between his desire to reconquer Orthodox Italy and to retain the loyalty of his Syrian subjects. We find Harith, the greatest of the Ghassanid princes, on whom Justinian had conferred the highest rank in the Byzantine nobility, visiting the capital in 563 to discuss the affairs of his confederacy with the Emperor and the business of his Church with the Monophysite Patriarch whom Justinian held in prison. Khusro, on the other hand, maintained the Nestorian Patriarch as an honoured member of his entourage, and at the same time encouraged the foundation of Monophysite churches in Mesopotamia to prevent his Bedouin subjects from visiting the great

Bronze bust of a Sasanian king of the 6th or 7th century. Although unidentified, this small figure bears all the symbols of royalty—particularly the fantastic horned head-dress—which appear on the coins and reliefs of the dynasty. (12)

37

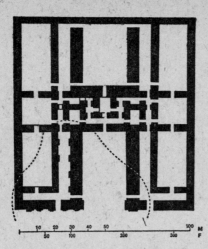

The last monument of Sasanian greatness was the palace at Ctesiphon, built by Khusro I in the mid 6th century (see p. 28, pl. 29). Its plan was essentially the same as that of Firuzabad—a huge arched entrance—recess leading to the state rooms and royal apartments. (13)

Syrian sanctuaries where they might contract undesirable loyalties. One of these churches, St Sergius in Beth Arbaye north-west of Mosul, has recently been identified. It was built on the model of the great basilica of St Sergius at Rusafa, an architectural form quite foreign to the native tradition. We may notice, too, that one of the pretexts for the outbreak of war in 540 was the complaint of Byzantine oppression made by an Armenian embassy to Khusro, and at a council held in 554 the Church of Armenia declared its independence of Constantinople. Thus war was carried on against a background of religious subversion which lends added point to formal pronouncements such as the guarantee of freedom of worship embodied in the treaty of 561.

Portents of the End

War broke out once more in 572, and peace negotiations were still in progress when Khusro died in 579. He was justly remembered in later legend as the greatest ruler of the Sasanian line, and the surviving ruins of his great palace at Ctesiphon, a unique achievement in ancient architecture, are a fitting memorial to his grand concept of the Iranian monarchy. His successor, Hormizd

f 13
p 28
(29)

IV, had the virtues of his father without his political sagacity and force of personality, and lost ground once more in the struggle with the nobility. Vahram Choben, a capable and popular general whom Hormizd attempted to deprive of his command, revolted and the rebellion quickly spread. One faction of the nobility deposed Hormizd in favour of his son, Khusro II, but Vahram Choben claimed the throne for himself and Khusro was forced to take refuge with the Byzantine Emperor Maurice. This was the first occasion on which the right of the Sasanian family to the throne had been challenged, and it was a portent of disaster.

p 21
(12)

Restored to the throne with Byzantine help, for which he paid in the customary fashion by the cession of Armenia, Khusro revived for the last time the military glory of the Iranian Empire and the splendour of its court, and in so doing reduced it to fatal exhaustion. Between 610 and 616 his armies overran Anatolia and reached the Asiatic shores of the Bosphorus, then conquered Syria and Egypt and once more appeared before Constantinople. But the effort was too great, and the Emperor Heraclius was quickly able to reconquer the lost territories, invade Azerbeijan and besiege Ctesiphon. Khusro, refusing to make peace, was deposed and killed.

The character of Khusro II was marred by avarice, suspicion and cruelty. The glittering façade of his court, the fabulous wealth of his treasury and the extent of his conquests were made possible by the ruinous taxation of his country. He used the administrative and military system built up by his grandfather to its utmost potential, and the strain revealed its defects. He was not himself a soldier, and was forced to entrust the new, more powerful armies to the command of nobles whom he suspected, with or without cause. His death may fairly be regarded as the end of Sasanian power. The Empire continued to exist, at first under a bewildering succession of puppets supported by the factions of the aristocracy, then under the last king, Yazdgard III (632–651). In 636 the invading Muslims defeated the Iranian army at the battle of Qadisiya, and they captured Ctesiphon in the following year; their astonishment at the wealth of the great palace is legendary. The last formal resistance ended with the battle of Nihawand in 642, and the Empire disintegrated into a confusion of petty principalities. Yazdgard, a fugitive from province to province with neither troops nor revenues, was assassinated in the region of Merv in 652.

p 28
(28)

III THE EMPIRE OF THE PROPHET

Islam and the Tide of Arab Conquest

R. H. PINDER-WILSON

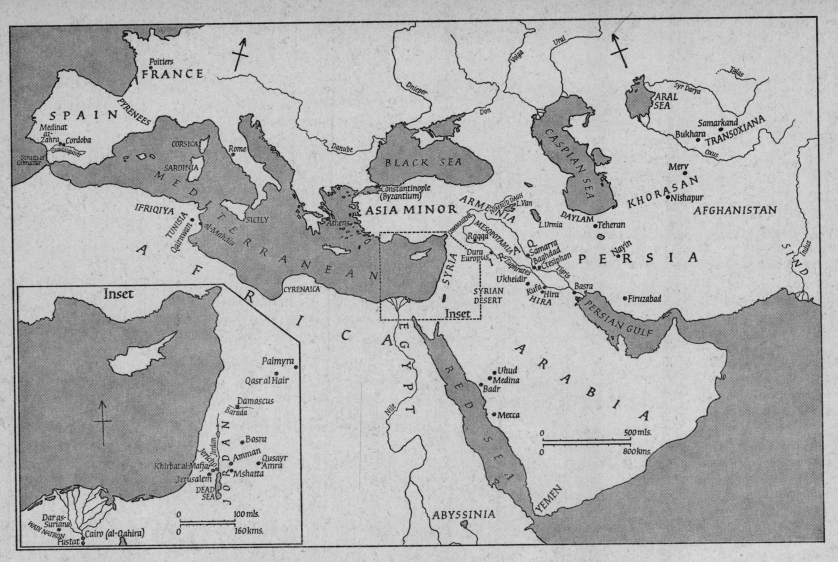

The extent of the Arab Empire

The sudden eruption

of the Arab peoples in the 7th century is something unique in history. In three generations a collection of scattered tribes, some settled, some nomadic, living by trade and subsistence farming had transformed itself into a rich and powerful empire dominating the whole of the southern Mediterranean and the Near East from Afghanistan to Spain. How was it achieved?

In some ways, circumstances made events. The two great powers of Byzantium and Persia had fought each other to a standstill; Arab tributary armies had been employed and exploited by both sides—an experience which embittered them as effectively as it taught them the art of war; even Arab Christianity, which was widespread (there were pictures of the Virgin and Child in the Ka'ba during Mohammed's lifetime), far from bringing them under Christian influence led to hostility and a radical break in the name of monotheism, the rejection of the Trinity.

It was Mohammed, a magnetic personality and statesman of genius, in whom all these forces coalesced. Beginning with a devoted few, the new movement grew into a powerful force, strictly centralized and under Mohammed's absolute authority. Mecca, from which he had fled in 622, year 1 of the Muslim era, was re-entered in triumph; the Ka'ba was purified and rededicated to Allah, the One God. Arab unity was a reality.

The new faith itself, Islam, was not wholly revolutionary—rather it seemed to sum up what had long been implicit in Arab religious thought. Combining features from the old paganism, from Judaism and from Christianity, it claimed to purify and complete all these rather than to reject them utterly. The astonishing rapidity with which it was accepted is proof of this. It did not need to be argued, it had only to be proclaimed.

When he died in 632 Mohammed had transformed the Arab world but had made little impression beyond it. Abu Bakr, his oldest adherent and father-in-law, was elected Caliph (*khalifa*, 'successor') and led the armies of Allah, inspired by a new fervour, into the Sasanian and Byzantine empires (where the population welcomed them as liberators), and in a few years was the ruler of the whole of Syria, Upper Mesopotamia, Armenia, Persia and Cyrenaica.

'Umar, the second Caliph, was murdered. So was the third, 'Uthman. The fourth was 'Ali, Mohammed's cousin and the husband of his daughter Fatima. 'Ali was opposed by Mu'awiya, a cousin of the murdered 'Uthman. It was the beginning of a schism in Islam that has never healed. Mu'awiya eventually triumphed, becoming the first of a line of caliphs, the Umayyads. But 'Ali's party, refusing to admit his authority, was to emerge as a separate sect, the Shi'ites, though their doctrines became increasingly theological and non-political.

The manuscript reproduced opposite is datable to AD 1307, but is probably based on a much earlier version and is clearly sympathetic towards the Shi'ites. Mohammed, on the left, declares 'Ali his successor; 'Ali carries the famous two-pointed sword, the Sword of Islam.

For Islam was not a pacifist religion like Christianity. It aimed at world-dominion, if necessary by force. At the same time it inherited, and had to come to terms with, the rich and ancient cultures of the Near East. The result was the creation of a new social and intellectual pattern—Islamic civilization—with decisive effect upon medieval Europe and upon the subsequent history of mankind. (1)

'But to those who believe, and who do the things that are right, He will pay them recompense. God loveth not the doer of evil.' This fragment of parchment (left) is from the earliest datable manuscript of the Qur'an. It was made, as an inscription on a second leaf tells us, at the expense of Amajur, governor of Damascus from 869 to 877.

The Qur'an consists of Mohammed's oracular utterances delivered on various occasions for the moral or practical guidance of his followers and now arranged arbitrarily in order of length. It is accepted by Muslims as the inspired word of God. The pilgrimage to Mecca, one of its ordinances, which every believer must perform at least once in his lifetime, is in fact far older than Mohammed. It goes back to the remote pagan religion of Arabia, but Mohammed purified its rites, making it a potent source of Muslim unity. (3)

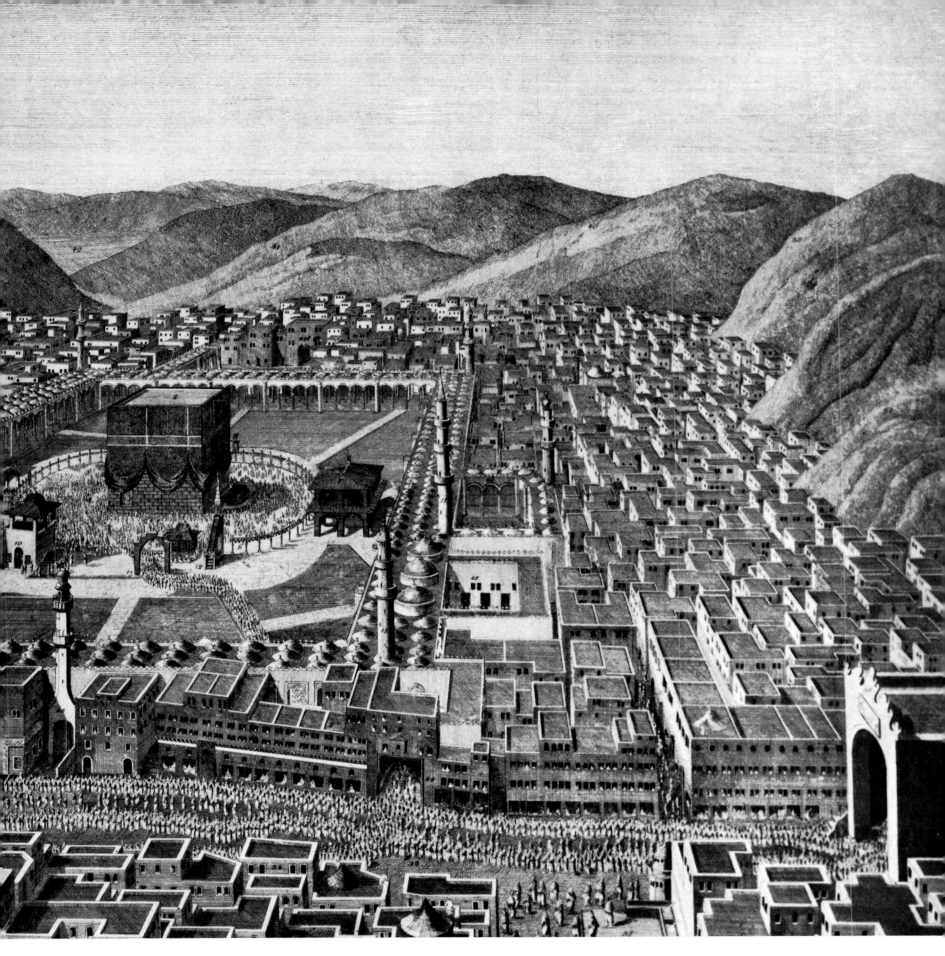

Mecca, the Holy City, as it appeared in about 1800. In the centre stands the Ka'ba, or 'Ancient House' (of Abraham), a windowless stone building in the shape of a cube, with a door seven feet up one side. It has been rebuilt several times since the days of Mohammed. On the external wall near the south-east corner about five feet from the ground is set the 'Black Stone', an ancient cult object, probably a meteorite. The pilgrimage includes a night's devotion on Mt Arafat (top left), pelting the devil with stones; running seven times round the Ka'ba, and kissing the Black Stone. (2)

Every Muslim turns in prayer towards Mecca, whose direction is indicated inside the mosque by an ornamental niche, the *mihrab*. This is often the object of lavish decoration, as in this example (left) at Qairawan. (4)

43

The oldest Islamic building,
the Dome of the Rock, at Jerusalem
(left), was built as a sort of rival Ka'ba,
over the spot where Abraham had
offered his son for sacrifice and from
which, it was believed, Mohammed
had ascended to Heaven. The dome
covers the Rock itself; round it runs
a double ambulatory for pilgrims to
walk round the shrine as they did in
Mecca. The exterior is octagonal and
approached through graceful arcades
of four arches. Built in 691 the Dome
of the Rock is not characteristic of
later Muslim architecture. The mosaic
decoration (above, the impost of one
of the columns) is based on Roman
acanthus and Persian palmette motifs. (5, 6)

In Persia, the old Sasanian traditions
merged into Islamic without a break.
Under Isma'il, the founder of the
Samanid dynasty, the provinces of
Khorasan and Transoxiana saw a
brilliant flowering of ceramics, calligraphy and architecture, and Isma'il's
own mausoleum (above), built between 913 and 943, recalls the design
of a Sasanian fire-temple. (7)

The new worship demanded a new ritual and a new setting—the mosque. Its characteristic features, already present by the end of the 7th century, were a large vaulted hall or sanctuary for prayer, a spacious courtyard surrounded by porticos, and at least one minaret—the high tower from which the call to prayer was given.

Above: three details from the Great Mosque at Damascus (begun 706)—the façade of the sanctuary, a mosaic decoration from the portico and the south-west corner of the courtyard. Below and left: interior and air view of the Great Mosque at Qairawan. The massive minaret is the earliest still standing. (8–12)

'The most unprofitable thing

that eateth up the wealth of a believer is building', Mohammed is reported to have observed, and the great palaces later built by the Umayyad and Abbasid caliphs would doubtless have confirmed him in his opinion. They were often as large as small towns. Three examples of their rich ornament are shown above. Left: the top of one of the towers flanking the main entrance at Qasr al-Hair;

centre, part of the façade of Mshatta, with deeply undercut floral patterns; right, an exquisite stone knot, formerly part of a gable, at Khirbat al-Mafjar. Below: the ruins of Ukheidir, perhaps the grandest palace of them all. Rectangular in plan, with a large 'annexe' to the north (left, in the photograph), its four brick façades with their great plain buttresses dominate the lonely desert. (13–16)

The spiral minaret (right) at Samarra ▶
links Islam with the ziggurats of
Assyria and Babylonia. As each storey
is the same height the slope becomes
steeper as it goes up. It was built in
about AD 850. (19)

◀ **Sasanian manners** and the memory
of the Sasanian courts inspired the
early caliphs. Far left: Qusayr 'Amra,
an Umayyad hunting-lodge in Jordan
with a vaulted audience hall and baths.
Left: the palace of Jausaq al-Khaqani
at Samarra; the central arch, or *iwan*,
as in Sasanian palaces at Firuzabad or
Ctesiphon, led into smaller halls and
then into the main courtyard, the
other two into guardrooms. (17, 18)

From the ends of Asia
traditions, motifs and techniques came
together to form the unified 'Islamic'
style. The beautiful textile (right), silk
on cotton woof, was probably woven
at Nishapur or Merv. Basically it is
still Sasanian, but such details as the
gryphons between the elephants legs
point to the Far East. (20)

Bird-catchers in a garden appear on
textiles, ceramics and ivory. From the
forms of vegetation developed the
characteristic Islamic 'arabesque'. This
fragment of a tunic, 8th century, is
from Syria or Egypt. (21)

In emulation of T'ang China the Muslim potters evolved a technique which combined a *sgraffito*, or scratched decoration, with tin
glaze. This dish from Samarra is obviously copied from similar
mottled ware in China. It is evidence both for the trade links
between China and the Persian Gulf and for the readiness of the
Muslim artists to absorb new ideas. (22)

Human figures do not appear on the pottery of Samarra, but this
jar, painted in lustre with a hieratic figure, must also have been
made in Mesopotamia and dates from the 10th century. The floral
ornament down the sides is comparable to the third style of
Samarra (see pl. 37) while the peacock's 'eyes' at the top possibly
derives from Roman *millefiori* glass. (23)

48

A pagan goddess—Gaea—painted in a clearly Hellenistic style (below) is among the unexpected features of Qasr al-Hair (see pl. 13). She holds a napkin filled with the fruits of the earth. (25)

Kufic script, a stylized form of Arabic widely used as decoration, originated in the town of Kufa in Mesopotamia. The inscription on this slip-painted dish (left) reads 'Blessing on the owner'. (24)

49

In palace, court and castle life achieved a degree of sophisticated elegance which is still legendary. Left: two scenes from the frescoes of Qasr al-Hair—a lute player and flautist under an arcade, and a hunter shooting at a gazelle; the great courtyard of Qasr al-Hair seems to have served as a game preserve. Below: an ivory casket from Cordoba showing two horsemen plucking dates; birds fly above their heads and bear-cubs sit behind them; in the corners are lions attacking another animal, a peacock, antelopes and two wrestlers. (26, 27)

Luxury ware (right) from the tables of the Arab aristocracy. Top: a lustre-painted dish showing a lady at her toilet. Centre: a bronze ewer from Egypt with a spout in the shape of a cock. Bottom: a jug carved out of rock crystal, one of the specialities of Fatimid Egypt. (28, 29, 30)

Abstract patterns in almost endless variety are characteristic of all the arts of Islam. Sometimes they incorporate alien elements, as in this panel from the *mihrab* at Qairawan (above) which is essentially a Greco-Roman niche-hood supported on columns. Below: a carved wooden panel from the *mimbar* (pulpit) at Qairawan. (31, 32)

The sacred text of the Qur'an (above) lies enclosed like a relic in the centre of its exquisitely decorated page. The manuscript was copied in Persia probably in 1036, soon after the fall of the Samanid dynasty. (34)

How a pattern evolves from the natural object to a purely formal arrangement of shapes is seen in these three details from Samarra (right). First: vine-leaves and stems accurately carved in stucco. Second: also carved, but with the buds only and without stems. Third: the stucco moulded instead of carved and reduced to a continuous band of repeated curves. (35, 36, 37)

Light and shade: a fragment of deeply undercut floral ornament (left) from Medinat az-Zahra, near Cordoba. (33)

The Umayyad dynasty fell from power in 750 and its place was taken by the Abbasids, with a new capital at Baghdad. But in Spain the Umayyads held out, independent of and largely separated from the rest of Islam. Muslim culture was here mingled with Visigothic and Jewish and produced, as its most exotic flower, the city of Cordoba. At its heart was the Great Mosque, begun by 'Abd ar-Rahman in 785 and enlarged in the 10th century. Left: the interior of the sanctuary, with its two levels of horseshoe arches. Below left: the mosaic arch above the *mihrab*. Below: part of the façade over a side entrance. (38, 39, 40)

For a caliph's mistress, az-Zahra ('the flower'), the concubine of 'Abd ar-Rahman III, the palace-city of Medinat az-Zahra was built, five miles outside Cordoba, in 936. It was filled with works of the choicest art from Byzantium, Syria and even Ottonian Germany. The courtyard (above) is still typically Umayyad in its decorative forms. (41)

Islam and the tide of Arab conquest

R. H. PINDER-WILSON

THIS CHAPTER is concerned with the disruption of the East Roman Empire and the emergence of a new political and religious force. The mainspring of this movement was the religion of Islam; its progenitors the Arabs. Inspired by the faith propounded by one of their own number they issued from the Arabian peninsula to promulgate their beliefs and to win new lands for Islam. Within a few decades of the Prophet's death they had wrested from the East Roman emperor the provinces of Syria and Egypt and the greater part of the southern shore of the Mediterranean. In the East they defeated the armies of the Sasanian king and won for Islam Mesopotamia and Persia. Within a century or more they had succeeded in welding together peoples of divers beliefs and language into a unified society based on a common religion, a common language and common institutions.

'The First of the Muslims'

Arabia is largely desert imposing on its inhabitants a nomadic existence. Only in the north where it borders the fertile lands of Syria and Mesopotamia did the Arabs come in contact with communities open to Roman and Persian civilization. In the south-west physical conditions were favourable enough for the growth of a civilized community, but by the time of Mohammed the once flourishing kingdom of south Arabia had become little more than a memory and the region had fallen under the influence of Abyssinia. Elsewhere and over a large part of the country the inhabitants had remained Bedouin, that is, nomads. These were organized in tribes: political combinations between the tribes were but rarely achieved.

If the conditions of life in Arabia were harsh, its geographical position allowed its inhabitants to think of wider political horizons; for it lay between Syria, Mesopotamia, Egypt and Abyssinia. It was this circumstance which contributed to the importance of the city of Mecca situated in western Arabia on the highroad running north and south; an advantage fully appreciated by its merchant aristocrats.

Just as there was no political cohesion so there was no single religion. Stone fetishes seem to have played an important role in the religious beliefs of the Arabs; and many tribes boasted their own exclusive idol. The Meccans possessed an ancient sanctuary containing the Ka'ba or black stone which seems to have been the highest sanctuary in central Arabia; for it was much venerated by the Bedouin who during certain sacred months refrained from interfering with the caravan traffic—the source of Meccan wealth. At Mecca were worshipped three goddesses each endowed with her own particular attributes. The Meccans also believed in a supreme deity, Allah (al-'ilah, the God) whom they recognized as the 'Lord of the Ka'ba' and creator of the world. This deity is certainly the Allah of Mohammed, for in one of his revelations he is commanded to worship the Lord of the House (i.e. the Ka'ba). It is possible too that the Jewish and Christian communities settled in Arabia helped to foster this belief in a supreme deity.

Mohammed was born about AD 570. The family of Hashim from which he sprang belonged to the tribe of the Quraysh, the ruling aristocrats of Mecca; and seems to have been respected if not rich. Mohammed's parents died when he was still a child and he was brought up successively by his grandfather and uncle. When he was twenty-five, he married the wealthy forty-year-old widow Khadija in whose service he had been employed as camel driver in the caravan trade, and so acquired a certain measure of economic security. Although tradition has endowed him with a religious piety from his early years, it was not until his fortieth year that he received his decisive religious experience when he was charged by the Archangel Gabriel with Allah's revelations. These were revealed to him in the form of rhymed prose at various intervals until his death. When all were collected they became known as the Qur'an (Koran) and were divided into chapters and verses.

The earliest revelations are concerned with the vision of the Day of Judgment: of the punishment that will be meted out to the damned in Hell and of the joys of the redeemed in Paradise. Faith is belief in Allah and the Last Day. Mohammed's preaching reiterates the omnipotence and oneness of Allah and the need for submitting to His will. So central was this last idea in Mohammed's message that the Arabic word *Islam*, meaning surrender, came to designate his religion. 'I am the first of the Muslims', he declares. His teaching and in particular his conception of judgment, retribution and good works, shows the influence of Christian—possibly Nestorian—ideas; while his introduction of Old Testament figures into the Qur'an presupposes Jewish influence. Mohammed claimed that the Qur'an was Allah's revelation to the Arab peoples in their own tongue; and for this reason he acknowledged as divine the corresponding revelations made to the Christians and the Jews, whom he called Peoples of the Book.

Apart from a handful of devoted adherents, Mohammed made little headway among the Meccans; and in AD 622 he and his followers migrated to Medina, some two hundred and fifty miles to the north of Mecca, at the request of its citizens. At this time the city was split by dissensions between two hostile tribes who were also involved in disputes with the three Jewish tribes settled there. Mohammed was invited to settle their differences.

This date AD 622 is known as the year of the Hijrah, that is, the Flight, and marks the turning point in Mohammed's mission. For this reason it was chosen as the beginning of the Muslim era. Mohammed was now established as the political head of a community which was soon to become the Muslim state. In his efforts to maintain the peace between his followers and the inhabitants of Medina, he emerges as a true statesman, and as the number of his adherents increased he felt able to settle accounts with his native city which had rejected his teaching. A successful military engagement at Badr in 624 was followed by a reversal at Uhud; but alliances with the Bedouin and skilful negotiations with the enemy secured for Mohammed the final victory. In 630 Mecca surrendered and the greater part of its citizens embraced Islam.

In the two remaining years of his life Mohammed laid down the five religious duties required of the Muslim: (1) profession of faith in Allah and in His Prophet Mohammed (2) recitation of the five daily prayers (3) fasting during the month of Ramazan (4) payment of the poor tax (5) the performance of the pilgrimage to Mecca if possible at least once in a lifetime.

Mohammed's Heirs—the Caliphate and Conquest

The testing time of the young Islamic community came with the Prophet's death in 632. Most of the Bedouin tribes had accepted Islam; but would they continue to adhere once deprived of the Prophet's personal authority? This danger was fortunately averted by the election of Abu Bakr, one of his foremost followers, as Mohammed's successor—not of course as prophet but as political and religious head of the community. The holder of this supreme office was henceforward known as the *khalifa* or successor. Abu Bakr re-established the authority of the government and set in motion the first Muslim campaign against the Byzantines which had been planned in the Prophet's closing years. When he died in 634, the choice fell on 'Umar, another companion of the Prophet and an equally remarkable character. Under his leadership the first great wave of Islamic conquests was undertaken: Syria, Egypt, Upper, Mesopotamia, Armenia,

f 7

p 42-3
(2)

p 41 (1)

p 42 (3)
p 51 (34)

f 1

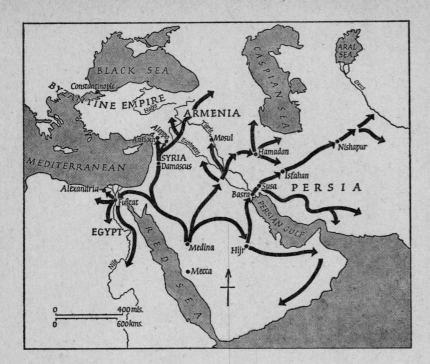

Map showing the Islamic conquests in the time of the first caliphs. No conquests outside Arabia were undertaken in Mohammed's lifetime, but in the reign of his successors the Arabs occupied large parts of the Byzantine and Sasanian Empires, including Egypt and north Africa. (1)

Persia and Cyrenaica. The Muslim forces were composed of the Beduin tribes who were actuated as much by desire for booty as by zeal for spreading the faith. Troops were settled in military camps in the conquered territories. Sometimes these were existing fortresses and sometimes new sites such as Kufa and Basra in southern Mesopotamia or Fustat south of the present city of Cairo. The foundation of Kufa shows more clearly than any other city this process of the creation of new towns. Here the Arab tribes were settled on a tongue of sand penetrating the lands irrigated by the Euphrates. This lay in front of the site of the ancient city of Hira, capital of the one-time Arab kingdom of the Lakhmid dynasty allied to the Sasanian emperors. Kufa shared in the prosperity which the Umayyads brought to Iraq, as a result of bringing the valley and delta of the Euphrates under one rule. Ships from India unloaded their cargoes at Basra so that a poet says of Basra that it is 'already India'.

The third Caliph, 'Uthman, belonged to the ruling aristocracy of Mecca, the house of Umayya. A man of piety, his main preoccupation was with religious affairs. It was on his initiative that the canonical text of the Qur'an was established. The favours which he showed to the members of his own family was one of the reasons for the storm of opposition which he aroused. In 656 he was murdered and the Prophet's son-in-law and only male descendant, 'Ali, was elected Caliph. 'Ali was unable to quell the civil war which ensued. This was concerned with the succession to the caliphate. On the one hand were those who held that the caliphate was vested in the descendants of 'Ali and who came to be called Shi'ites (Arabic *Sh'ia*, ['Ali's] party); and on the other hand were those who refuted this claim adhering to the *Sunna*, or tradition, whence they became known as Sunnites. 'Ali was assassinated in 661 and the succession was seized by Mu'awiya the governor of Damascus. Like his cousin 'Uthman, he belonged to the house of Umayya.

p 41 (1)

Islam Triumphant

Mu'awiya founded the dynasty of the Umayyad caliphs who ruled in hereditary succession until 750. Early in the 8th century the second wave of conquests began. In 711 the Muslim forces crossed from north Africa into Spain and after crossing the Pyrenees were only brought to a halt at the battle of Poitiers in 732. In the East they drove down to the Indus valley and annexed the province of Sind. In 714 they reached Kashgar on the confines of China. The Umayyads aspired to winning the throne of the East Roman Empire and carried the war into Asia Minor.

f 7

But they had little permanent success, although the Empire was hard pressed when the Muslims besieged Constantinople in 717 and 718.

Out of these widespread territories, the Umayyads created what has been called the Arab Empire. Damascus was chosen as the seat of government and Arab governors were appointed by the caliph to rule the provinces. Two administrative measures had far reaching consequences in uniting the Empire. First, Arabic was adopted as the official language. Secondly, the Empire was provided with a standard coinage. Hitherto the caliph had issued coins based on Byzantine or Sasanian prototypes. The new coins set the pattern for almost all future Islamic coinage: portrait heads and other symbols were replaced by the legend proclaiming faith in Allah and his Prophet and the superiority of Islam over all other faiths. There could be no more fitting symbol of the universal pretensions of the Umayyads.

f 2, 3

Tolerance was exercised towards the non-Muslim population of Syria and Egypt—that is Jews and Christians—who were required to pay the poll tax and land tax. Indeed the Christians of these two countries seem to have welcomed their new rulers rather than otherwise. In its efforts to impose orthodoxy the Byzantine administration had alienated the local churches. The Arabs wisely declined to interfere in ecclesiastical disputes; and had moreover to rely on the native bureaucracy for administration.

In Persia the Arabs inherited the state created by the Sasanians, the structure of which was largely feudal. Administration remained in the hands of the nobility. The Zoroastrian religion was tolerated, but Islam spread rapidly among the lesser nobility so that an Islamicized local aristocracy was able to secure positions of authority; and it was thanks to them that Persian traditions and culture were kept alive, to blossom again at a later time.

p 44 (7)
p 27
(27)

A New Art is Born

There is little to suggest that art was taken into the service of religion at Mecca and Medina during the lifetime of the Prophet. The first mosque in Islam was Mohammed's house in Medina which consisted of a square court with huts ranged along its eastern wall. Against the southern wall a shelter of palm leaves supported on palm trunks was erected in order to protect the faithful from the heat of the sun when they assembled for the corporate act of prayer. At first the faithful, when praying, turned towards Jerusalem but when Mohammed quarrelled with the Jews the direction of prayer (Arabic, *qibla*) was changed to Mecca and the venerated Ka'ba. This improvised mosque could hardly claim to be architecture. Indeed Mohammed seems to have had little concern for the building of monuments and his biographer credits him with the saying, 'the most unprofitable thing that eateth up the wealth of a believer is building'. Nor was there much in the way of an architectural or artistic tradition in Arabia. The prevailing atmosphere under the first four caliphs —at least as it appeared to subsequent generations—was one of piety and apostolic simplicity.

p 42-3
(2)

The early development of Islamic coinage. Left: coin of Abdallah (year 56), closely following Sasanian prototypes (see Chapter II) with inscription in Pehlevi. Right: one of the first purely Islamic coins; the portraits and symbols have now been replaced by an inscription proclaiming the oneness of Allah and the universal mission of Islam. (2, 3)

In Syria the situation was very different and it was here that Islamic art was born, under the patronage of the Umayyad caliphs during the first century of the Hijrah. The Arabs brought with them a dynamic religion and a superb language: but they were without an artistic tradition. Universal empire exacted of the rulers all the external manifestations of power, and there was a strong element of rivalry in the growth of Islamic art. The caliph—at once the peer of the emperor of Byzantium and the heir of the last Sasanian king—required palaces worthy of his status. The superiority of Islam would be proclaimed by mosques that would outshine the most splendid of the Christian churches. It was natural therefore that the caliph and his representatives should have recourse to those of the subject peoples with inherited artistic traditions. Two great traditions were at hand: the Greco-Roman art of Syria and Egypt and the Sasanian art of Persia and Mesopotamia.

p 47
(17, 18)

The art of Syria too represents a branch of the Greco-Roman family although, as in Persia, the Hellenic elements had to a great extent been subordinated to the oriental. Thus in its sculpture and painting there is an increasing preoccupation with spiritual expression and a neglect of naturalistic effect. This was no doubt partly due to the fact that the mystery religions and more particularly Christianity had grown up in these regions. The trend can be traced in the stone sculptures set up at Nimrud Dagh by the Arsacid Antiochus of Commagene in the 1st century BC, in the funerary monuments of Palmyra of the 2nd and 3rd century AD, and in the paintings of AD 85 discovered at Dura Europus on the middle Euphrates.

The Dome of the Rock

In architecture far greater prominence was given to the decoration of surfaces than had been the case in the Hellenistic world. The trend away from naturalism can also be observed in the treatment of decorative motifs. The acanthus and vine scroll were rendered with a naturalistic plasticity in Hellenistic art. Here they were reduced to a linear scheme in which the contrast between light and shadow was sought for purely decorative effect. Characteristic are large panels sculptured in more or less flat relief with floral ornament and abstract patterns drawn from textiles and mosaic floors. This preoccupation with surface decoration—the play of light on lace-like patterns and the glitter of mosaics—was the legacy of the East to Islam as well as to Byzantium.

p 44
(6, 8)

Islam's earliest surviving monument—perhaps too its most impressive—is the Dome of the Rock in Jerusalem. It is a unique building inasmuch as it was designed for a particular purpose. It was built in 691 by the Caliph 'Abd al-Malik who according to tradition intended it to be a rival sanctuary to that of the Ka'ba in Mecca which at that time was in the hands of a rival caliph. It is likely too that 'Abd al-Malik who did more than any of the other Umayyad caliphs to build the foundations of the Arab Empire, wished to erect a monument that would outshine those of his non-Muslim subjects. The dome of this building covers the rocky summit of Mount Moriah, believed to be the 'Altar of Burnt Offering'. It is not a mosque but a shrine built over a sacred place; and tradition has it that the faithful circumambulated the rock as they did the Ka'ba at Mecca. This would explain why the particular structural plan of the Dome of the Rock was adopted: an octagonal building with two octagonal ambulatories and a central area enclosing the rock. This central area is covered by a wooden dome set on a high drum. The plan is closely related to the Christian architecture of Syria; and the centrally planned Cathedral of Bosra or the Church of the Ascension at Jerusalem may have served as the model for the architect who was probably a Christian. Originally both the inside and outside of the building were covered with mosaics but only those of the interior have survived. These too are thought to be the work of local Christian mosaicists. They decorate the drum and the faces and soffits of the arches consisting principally of the Roman acanthus scroll and the Persian palmette rendered in green and blue tones on gold ground. On the inner face of the drum and therefore looking on to the rock are depicted jewels and crowns including a Persian diadem. It has been

f 4
p 44 (5)

44 (6)

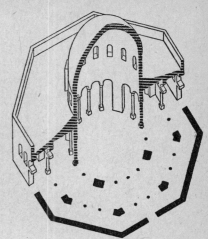

The Dome of the Rock, Jerusalem, the earliest surviving Islamic building, begun by 'Abd al-Malik and completed in 691–2. It covers the summit of Mt Moriah, the traditional place of both the sacrifice of Abraham, whom the Arabs revere, and the journey of Mohammed into heaven. (4)

suggested that these were introduced not only in order to provide a worthy decoration to this sacred place but also to symbolize the surrender of their sovereignty by the defeated enemies of Islam. The Qur'anic inscription which runs round both faces of the intermediate octagon proclaims the unity of God and refutes the Trinity of the Christians. In succeeding centuries Muslims believed that the rock was that from which the Prophet Mohammed made his miraculous ascent to Heaven: but it is more likely that 'Abd al-Malik had in mind the rock's association with Abraham, since this was by tradition the spot where he offered his son as a sacrifice. This too would have emphasized the universality of Islam: Abraham was revered alike by Christians, Jews and Muslims.

The Congregation of the Faithful

The Dome of the Rock however played little or no part in the development of Islamic architecture. For the Umayyad contribution to architecture we have to turn to the congregational mosque. In the early years of Umayyad rule, there was no building of mosques in Syria since the Muslims availed themselves of churches. This they did by using the wall of the southern aisle as the *qibla* or sanctuary wall. In the new garrison towns, however, mosques which had been hastily improvised in the period of the conquests had to be rebuilt. One of the first of these was that at Kufa where the new mosque formed a square with each side 200 cubits in length. On three sides were columned porticos while on the fourth and south side was the five-aisled sanctuary, its roof supported direct on stone columns without the supervention of arches.

Of far greater consequence for the future were the features incorporated in the great mosque of Medina when it was rebuilt by the Caliph al-Walid. In the centre of the *qibla* wall a concave niche was introduced. Before this niche, or *mihrab* as it was called, stood the *imam*, that is the leader of the prayers. The mihrab became an essential feature of a mosque. In order to give prominence to the mihrab a raised central nave was erected down the centre of the sanctuary. As the most sacred mosque in Islam the mosque of Medina was to set the pattern for many of the great mosques of the Umayyad period.

p 43 (4)

The most remarkable of these is the great mosque of Damascus which is still known as the Umayyad Mosque. When they occupied Damascus the Muslims had converted to their own use a part of the Basilica of St John the Baptist built by the Emperor Theodosius at the close of the 4th century. This church had been built in the precincts of the temple of Jupiter. In 706 the Caliph al-Walid decided to provide the capital with a new mosque. The church was demolished and the perimeter walls of the mosque were those of the temenos of the ancient temple. The square towers at the corners became the first minarets of Islam; and three of the ancient entrances and a great monumental propylaeum were incorporated. The vast court of the mosque forms an oblong rectangle with shallow porticos on three sides covered with wooden roofs sloping in towards the court. The sanctuary occupies the whole of the south side of the temenos and consists of three aisles running east to west. These aisles are formed of two-tiered arches supported on columns or piers.

p 45
(9–11)
f 5

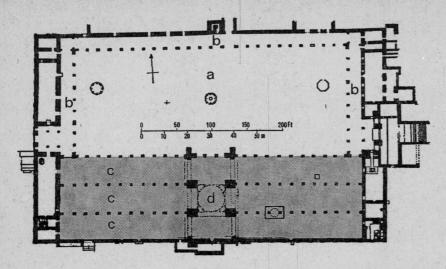

Plan of the Great Mosque at Damascus. It stands on a site previously occupied by a church and before that by a Temple of Jupiter. The former temenos became a courtyard (a), surrounded on three sides by porticos (b). The mosque itself, on the south side, consists of three aisles (c) cut at right angles by a domed 'nave' (d), whose roof rises above that of the rest of the building. (5)

The most striking feature of the sanctuary is the great central nave which cuts across the aisles of the sanctuary and leads to the mihrab. In the central bay of this is a lofty dome. The roof of the nave is raised above the rest of the sanctuary. The somewhat monotonous exterior of the sanctuary looking on to the court is relieved by the majestic pedimented façade of the nave.

In the middle of the side opposite the sanctuary a square minaret was erected, although the existing one is not the original. The practice of placing the principal minaret on the side of the court opposite the sanctuary and on the main axis formed by the central nave and mihrab was an Umayyad innovation. The oldest surviving example is probably the massive minaret of the great mosque of Qairawan and dating from the close of the Umayyad period.

p 44–5
(8–12)
p 51
(31, 32)

Originally the interior was covered with panels of marble and mosaics. Much of this decoration was destroyed by fire in 1893. Among the mosaics which have survived is the famous panorama of the River Barada that flows through Damascus. This depicts an ideal landscape of a tree-lined river bank, fantastic palaces and pavilions, a hippodrome, hills crowned with villages and even a church. The panels are wrought with extraordinary skill: it has been claimed that no less than twenty-nine colours have been employed including gold and silver. In style they are related both to earlier Syrian mosaics and to those of the Great Palace of the Byzantine emperors at Constantinople; Arab historians relate that the emperor of Byzantium sent mosaicists to Damascus at the request of al-Walid. One conspicuous feature is the absence of human figures: for although the official proscription of human representation in art was not formulated until later, such representations were in fact already excluded from religious buildings.

Flowers in the Desert: the Umayyad Palaces

Our knowledge of the religious architecture of the Umayyad period is necessarily limited owing to the destruction or restoration of mosques by successive generations. We know rather more about the secular architecture of the period, for the ruins of some thirty Umayyad castles have been discovered in Syria. It may seem strange that these palaces and castles should have been allowed to decay shortly after their foundation. One reason is that the centre of government moved in 750 to Iraq; another is that in Islam the building of his own palace was the symbol of an individual prince's power, so that the life of a palace was usually coextensive with that of its founder.

Of the town palaces of the Umayyad caliphs or governors no example survives. It is clear, however, from contemporary descriptions that the palace was normally joined to the congregational mosque and situated to the rear of the *qibla* wall.

Umayyad palaces of which ruins do still exist seem to have been country retreats rather than administrative centres. It has been said that the Umayyad caliphs ruled in the manner of patriarchs. Although patricians of Mecca, their ancestors had felt the lure of the desert. The Umayyad prince, too, liked to live the nomadic life. When the spring came he would leave the close confinement of the city to find the freedom of the desert.

He had tasted too much of the delights of the city to find repose in the simple bedouin tent which moreover would not have befitted his imperial dignity. His encampment became a fortified palace with an imposing gateway either of stone or brick and equipped with suites of rooms and galleries, a great audience chamber where he might receive the leading dignitaries of the state and foreign ambassadors, a complex system of baths (the steam-bath seems to have been as popular as it was in the ancient world), an oratory, and guard-rooms. In order to supply the needs of the royal household extensive irrigation systems had to be made and the surrounding land brought under cultivation. In some cases this involved the construction of an aqueduct.

One of the most impressive of these is Qasr al-Hair al-Sharqi, (the Eastern Castle of the Enclosure), situated in the Syrian desert north-east of Palmyra. It was founded by the Caliph Hisham in 728 and consists of two square fortified enclosures of dressed limestone and brick. Each side of the larger enclosure measures about 525 feet. At the corners of each are half round towers with intermediate towers on each side. The entrance of the lesser enclosure is an impressive composition with its two great flanking towers and semicircular relieving arch above the door lintel. Surrounding these two enclosures was yet another perimeter wall enclosing an area of over three square miles. It has been suggested that the purpose of this wall was to prevent the wild animals from getting out, for we know that the hunt was a favourite pastime of the Umayyad princes.

p 46
(13)
p 49
(25)

The art and architecture of the Umayyads is a fusion of artistic traditions of the subject peoples whom the Arabs ruled. This syncretism is well illustrated by the castle of Mshatta (the 'Winter' castle) about 20 miles south of Amman in Jordan. It was founded probably in the closing years of the Umayyad period but was left unfinished. Like the castle of Qasr al-Hair al-Sharqi, it consists of a square fortified wall strengthened by massive half round towers. The square proportion is typical of the Roman fortresses on the Syrian frontier: the towers however belong rather to the Persian tradition of military architecture. The entrance on the south side had an elaborately carved façade which is now preserved in the Berlin Museum. Deep cutting by drill and chisel produce the strong contrast of light and shadow. Between richly carved mouldings an acanthus frieze is arranged in a zigzag to form great juxtaposed triangles each containing a floral medallion. Around the latter is carved floral and vegetal ornament; the most prominent is the curling vine growing from a vase. Elsewhere there are paired creatures—some fantastic—such as the lion and griffin drinking from a chalice, birds perched in the scrolls and even human figures. In some of the triangles the ornament is restricted to vine scrolls arranged in regular volutes; and the tendency to stylization already seems to foreshadow the arabesque. While most of these elements are taken from the Hellenistic

f 6
p 46
(14)

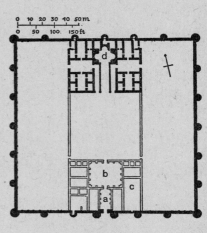

Mshatta, one of the last and most ambitious of Ummayad palaces, was never finished, its construction probably being interrupted by the death of its builder. Much of it, however, (shown here in black lines) was fairly well advanced, and the foundations of other parts already laid (hollow lines). The entrance passage (a) led into a spacious hall (b). A room to the right (c) must have been a mosque since it included a mihrab. Across a wide courtyard was another block of buildings entered by a three-arched entrance, the central one leading to a triple-apsed throne-room (d). (6)

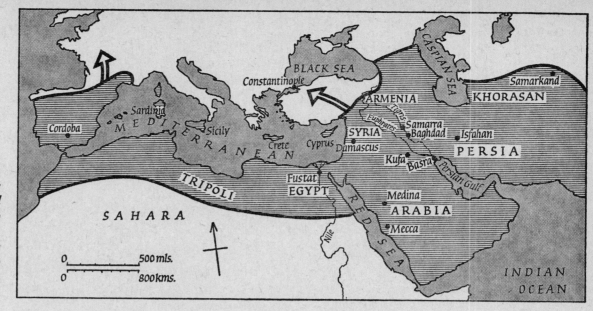

Map showing the extent of Islam in the 9th century. At the time of the Abbasid caliphs the empire of Islam included north Africa, most of Spain, parts of Italy, Crete, Sicily and the Indus valley. The attacks on France and Asia Minor which in the 8th century had seemed to threaten Europe from both sides, had been checked. (7)

repertory, the compositions betray the influence of Persia and the treatment of the vine scroll that of Coptic Egypt.

This monumental entrance gives access to a long passage leading to a spacious room: another square room to the west of the entrance was clearly a mosque, for there is a mihrab niche in the south wall. A vast open court separates this complex from the palace buildings beyond. These lie behind the façade on the north side; three imposing arches give access to three vaulted aisles of which the central one terminates in a square-domed chamber with a semi-circular apsidal niche in each of its three sides. This domed chamber was the throne-room. The triple-apsed hall occurs in Syria as early as the 5th century AD but this combined with a nave preceding it is first found in Egypt. But the domed chamber preceded by an oblong nave was the typical Sasanian throne room.

The Sasanian Legacy

After failing to realize their dream of winning the throne of Constantinople, the Umayyads looked to the East and assumed the external majesty of the Sasanian monarchs, of whom they were the heirs and successors. They adopted the elaborate etiquette of the Sasanian court which was designed to inspire awe for the person of the king. At Qusayr 'Amra, an Umayyad hunting lodge in Jordan, there is a famous wall painting depicting the caliph seated on his throne and wearing the winged crown of the Sasanian kings. It is therefore not surprising to find the Umayyads adopting the plan of the Sasanian audience hall. What is interesting here is the way in which the Arabs also incorporated a number of non-Persian features.

p 46 (17)

It is also possible that the basilical feature of the congregational mosque was an adaptation of the audience chamber of the Umayyad palace to religious usage. The most important part of the Friday service was the reading of the *khutba*—a kind of homily or locution which proclaimed the name and titles of the ruling prince. It also preserved an opportunity for addressing the assembled congregation on political as well as religious matters. On such occasions the caliph or provincial governors sat in the mihrab niche and this would explain how the three elements of the secular audience hall found their way into the mosque sanctuary in the form of a raised central nave, dome and concave mihrab.

Thus new forms in architecture were created by borrowing whatever was appropriate from different traditions and adapting them to the dictates of the Islamic religion. The same process was at work in the decorative arts. Painting, of which a few rare frescoes have survived, oscillated between the Hellenistic and Sasanian tradition. This can be observed in two floor paintings from the Western Qasr al-Hair between Damascus and Palmyra. The dominant feature of the first is the central roundel. This contains a female bust evidently intended as the goddess Gaea, personification of the earth. A snake is entwined about her neck

p 49 (25)

and the napkin which she holds is filled with fruits. Marine monsters with human torsos occupy the upper field and animals and birds the lower. Both the treatment and subject matter of the painting are Hellenistic. The second painting is divided into three registers: in the upper a female lute player and a male flautist stand each within an arcade, in the middle one a horseman shoots an arrow at a gazelle and in the lower one an attendant leads an animal into the enclosure. The spirit of this painting is Sasanian; music making and the chase were familiar themes in Sasanian silverwork, and the motifs of the paintings follow Sasanian prototypes closely.

p 50 (26)

Khirbat al-Mafjar near Jericho was founded during the reign of the Caliph Hisham (724–743). It comprises a gateway of honour, two-storied porticos around an open court, a mosque, underground rooms for use in the hot weather and a sumptuous bath house. Fine stone and stucco carvings, mosaic floors and fragments of wall paintings were recovered during the course of excavations. Many of the floor mosaics are based on highly intricate designs and are related to those of the Syrian churches. Human figures play a part in the stucco decoration.

Of even greater interest are the examples of floral and geometric ornament. While many of the motifs such as interlacings, grape vine and acanthus belong to the classical repertory, the way in which they are treated and combined into a harmonious ensemble is wholly distinctive. Particularly prominent are the designs in which compartments are repeated in a regular series of correspondences. This system was to become an established principle in Islamic art.

p 46 (15)

Umayyad art leaves an impression of amazing richness and vitality but not of a fully integrated style. Nor had it developed a distinctively Islamic character. It was not possible in the dynasty's life of less than a century to produce the perfect alloy from such heterogeneous elements. It was born in Syria and with the fall of the Umayyads that country was eclipsed by the eastern provinces which assumed the cultural and political hegemony of the Islamic world. Yet by some miracle the Umayyad tradition was to survive, for a scion of the house secured for himself the Muslim kingdom of Spain; and it was under Umayyad rule in Spain that Umayyad art was to attain full maturity and in course of time radiate its influence to the Muslim kingdoms of north Africa.

A New Dynasty: Baghdad and the Abbasids

Umayyad rule had been based on Arab supremacy and Arab privilege. The movement which brought about the downfall of the dynasty was largely a protest of the Islamicized population of eastern Persia against Arab domination. In accepting Islam the Persians, although exempted from the poll-tax, were required to pay the land-tax. They now looked to the family of the Prophet in the hope of securing equality of treatment according to the precepts of the Qur'an. Their hopes were centred on the descend-

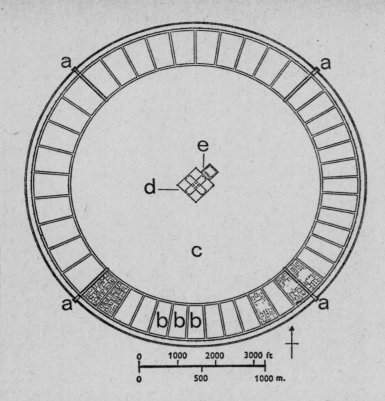

The Abbasid dynasty moved the seat of the caliphate from Damascus to Baghdad and in 763 the second Abbasid Caliph, al-Mansur, laid out a great new city whose plan was a perfect circle. It was surrounded by a double wall pierced by four gateways (a). Round the inside were the residential quarters (b, b), within which the planning was irregular (merely indicated in a few sections of the plan). In the centre of the city, and occupying the greater part of it, was the palace area (c), approached by arcaded streets from the gates but inaccessible from the residential quarters. Al-Mansur's palace (d) was square, with a mosque (e) adjoining it on one side. Nothing of this extraordinary city survives, but it is known from the detailed descriptions of contemporaries. (8)

ants of the Prophet's uncle, 'Abbas. The rebellion broke out in Khorasan where the Arab colonists combined together with the local Persian aristocracy under the leadership of a Persian, Abu Muslim. In 749 the rebels marched into Mesopotamia and in the following year decisively defeated the forces of the last Umayyad Caliph, Marwan II. The first Abbasid Caliph was proclaimed as Abu'l 'Abbas as-Saffah (Shedder of Blood); and the seat of government was fixed in Mesopotamia. The political centre of the Islamic world shifted from Syria to Mesopotamia and in 762 as-Saffah's brother and successor, al-Mansur, laid out a new capital at a Christian village called Baghdad on the Tigris. Because the Abbasids had been brought to power largely through the intervention of the Persian Muslims, Persia became the paramount influence in the new state. The Abbasids completed the process of Persianizing the institution of the caliphate—a process already initiated by the Umayyads. The caliph participated less and less in affairs of state which passed into the hands of the principal administrator known as the *wazir*. Persians, such as the family of the Barmakids which served the caliphs until their overthrow in 803, increasingly filled the high offices of state.

The Abbasid Empire achieved its greatest splendour under the Caliph Harun ar-Rashid (786–809) and his son al-Ma'mun (813–833). The administration was reorganized on Persian lines. An efficient fiscal system was introduced, thus ensuring a stable revenue subject to strict control. A postal service secured rapid communication between the provinces and the central government besides providing the caliph with first hand intelligence service covering the remotest corner of the Empire. Stable government brought economic expansion: the trade routes to India, China and Ceylon as well as to the Mediterranean were opened up and foreign trade stimulated the growth of industries. This prosperity was reflected in the growing refinement of court life and the increasing demand for luxury articles which stimulated the growth of the decorative arts such as pottery, glass, metalwork and textiles.

p 50
(28–30)
p 48–9
(21–25)

The Muslim Enlightenment

United by a single religion and a single language, the Islamic world began to create a unitary culture in which Arab and non-Arab shared. The spirit of the age is one of intellectual adventure and curiosity to which the Abbasid caliphs contributed by their tolerance and enlightened patronage. Literary and artistic activity was focussed on Baghdad. The influence of the subject population of Syria in the development of Umayyad art has already been mentioned. Hellenistic thought now became the principal inspiration of the intellectual movements of the period. The Aramaic speaking peoples of Syria and Mesopotamia had been subjected to Hellenistic influence since the time of Alexander: Greek philosophy, astronomy, medicine and science were studied in the Christian monasteries and in the Sasanian academy of Jundi-Shabur near Ctesiphon. Contact with these ancient centres stimulated Muslim activity in the profane sciences—experimental medicine, astronomy, physics, mathematics and geography. At Baghdad the Caliph al-Ma'mun founded the Bait al-Hikma (House of Wisdom) where Greek philosophical works were translated into Arabic. Greek thought had a far-reaching influence on all branches of Muslim learning: above all, Aristotelean logic brought method and order into their intellectual activity. Philology was studied primarily to elucidate the meaning and language of the Qur'an but these studies were now systematized according to Greek categories. Theology, too, was caught up in the Hellenistic revival. The so-called Mu'tazilite movement which earned the favour and support of al-Ma'mun tried to reconcile revelation with Greek logic and eventually its adherents were condemned by the orthodox: yet even the latter were obliged to have recourse to Greek dialectic when it came to formulating their principles.

The Empire Breaks Up

In their efforts to maintain the religious and political unity of the Empire the Abbasid caliphs were less successful. For one thing the caliph himself was beginning to lose effective control of events. The army of the Umayyads had been composed exclusively of Arab troops: but now the Arabs became less and less inclined for military service. A permanent standing army was more than ever necessary to maintain the security of the central government against the civil disturbances which troubled Mesopotamia in this period. Having failed to recruit either the indigenous population of Mesopotamia or the Persians the caliph called in Turkish mercenaries from central Asia. By the time of al-Ma'mun's death the caliph's forces had become virtually a Turkish army: and in the course of the 9th century acquired the status and function of a 'praetorian guard' exercising an ever tightening control over the caliph's person and even assuming the right of appointing the successor to the highest office in Islam. Because of the constant friction between the Turkish soldiers and the townsfolk, the Caliph al-Mu'tasim decided in 838 to remove the court from Baghdad to Samarra higher up on the Tigris; and Samarra remained the seat of government until 883 when the government was once again established at Baghdad.

The caliph's authority was also being questioned in the provinces. Tahir, Governor of Khorasan proclaimed himself ruler there and founded a short-lived dynasty to be replaced by that of the Saffarids. In Egypt, Turkish generals were invested with the governorship in the second half of the 9th century: certain of these remained in Samarra sending a representative to govern in their name. One such deputy, Ahmad ibn Tulun, ruled Egypt as an independent sovereign from 868 until his death in 883, when his son succeeded him and reigned until 896. Further west, the province of Ifriqiya, corresponding to the modern state of Tunisia, had become independent under the Aghlabids whose founder Ibrahim ibn Aghlab had been invested with the governorship of that province by Harun ar-Rashid. The Aghlabids gave only nominal recognition to the caliph. Their ambitions were directed northwards and by 875 they had secured possession of Sicily which remained in Muslim hands until its capture by the Normans in 1060. In the farthest west and across the Straits of Gibraltar, the Muslims held the greater part of Spain. In 756 the sole survivor of the Umayyad house to escape the avenging hands of the victorious Abbasids had succeeded in establishing an Umayyad kingdom of Spain with the support of those Arab tribes loyal to the dispossessed house. In 929 his descendant 'Abd ar-Rahman III proclaimed himself Caliph, thus reviving its ancient glory. The Umayyad rule in Spain was to endure until 1031.

The separatist movements so far described were political. More disturbing and of greater consequence for the future were those with a religious as well as a political basis. The most important of these were connected with the Shi'a movement which originated as we have seen in a difference of opinion regarding the succession to the caliphate. Although the movement was now split into various groups, all its protagonists were unanimous in believing the succession to pass through the Prophet's daughter Fatima and her husband 'Ali. They were not all agreed, however, on the subsequent succession.

The Shiites differed amongst themselves as to who were the legitimate successors or *imams* of 'Ali. Those who recognized Isma'il ibn Ja'far as the seventh *imam* were known as Isma'ilites. Owing to the eclectic and esoteric nature of their beliefs, they remained a secret sect. One branch of the Isma'ilite movement was that of the Fatimids. Its leader, 'Ubayd Ullah, claimed descent from the Prophet through his daughter Fatima and refusing the Abbasid's title to the caliphate claimed to be the only lawful leader of the Islamic community. His declared intent was the abolition of the caliphate of Baghdad. By means of effective propaganda he won over the Berber tribes of Ifriqiya to his cause and was invested with the title of Caliph. In 909 he overthrew the Aghlabids and established his capital at the town of al-Mahdia on the coast of Tunisia. Sixty years later his successors were powerful enough to turn their attention to the East. In 969 al-Mu'izz, the fourth Fatimid Caliph, conquered Egypt and so brought about the final detachment of that country from Abbasid control. The new ruler built his capital near the old city of Fustat and named it al-Qahira (Cairo) 'the Victorious' because it was founded when the victorious planet Mars was in the ascendant; and so inaugurated the brilliant civilization of Fatimid Egypt which lasted for two centuries. Although the Fatimids secured possession of Syria and for a brief period were recognized in Mesopotamia, they never succeeded in destroying the Abbasid caliphate.

While these two rival caliphates—the one in Spain and the other in north Africa—were being established, the position of the Abbasid Caliph in Baghdad was becoming increasing straitened. Ruler in nothing more than name he was at the mercy of his Turkish 'praetorians' whose chiefs came and went in rapid succession. In the 10th century one after another of the provinces

was lost to the central government—losses which were accompanied by diminishing returns to the central revenue.

In the East the Saffarids had been succeeded by the Samanids, a Persian family whose kingdom comprised Khorasan and Transoxiana. During the century of their rule the Samanids brought about a veritable renaissance of Persian culture which had lain dormant during the period of Arab control. Their principal cities were Bukhara and Samarkand in Transoxiana and Nishapur in Khorasan. Thanks to their patronage, the revival of the Persian language made possible the first and perhaps the finest flowering of Persian poetry.

Culture and Religion—the Forces of Unity

By about AD 1000 Islamic civilization had come into being with as distinctive a character as that of Christendom. This was achieved thanks to a common language and a common religion which engendered a common outlook. The significance of the proliferation of religious sects and of independent states within Islam can be over-stressed: for on the fundamental articles of faith there was unanimity and the same political social institutions were to be found throughout the Islamic world. Within that world no frontiers were closed. Trade and the pilgrimage to Mecca and other sacred shrines encouraged the movement of persons and the exchange and dissemination of ideas. It was above all in the great cities that Islamic culture was born and where the patronage of prince and merchant attracted the talent of the age. When we turn to architecture and the arts we cannot but be struck by the distinctive stamp which dominates diversity of expression.

In the days of its greatest power and prestige, the Abbasid court set the standards for the provinces; and not without justification has the expression 'international Abbasid style' been applied to the art of the period. The city of Baghdad itself was a *f 8* remarkable achievement of town planning, for it was based on a circular plan. There was an outer wall and a concentric town wall flanked by round towers. Four gateways divided this great circle into quadrants, each joined by an inner and outer road between which were residential districts separated by radial streets. The inner side of this residential area was arcaded and looked out on to the great circular court containing the congregational mosque and the palace of al-Mansur. To the Arabs this round city seemed a startling innovation: but it is probable that al-Mansur took as his model certain round cities with concentric walls that are known to have existed in Persia.

No trace of al-Mansur's round city has survived. The walls however must have resembled those of Raqqa, parts of which can still be seen today. Raqqa on the middle Euphrates was founded by al-Mansur in 772. Its walls are laid out in a horseshoe plan. A part of the Baghdad Gate still stands: like the walls it is *f 9* built of baked bricks. Its eastern face consists of a great arch flanked by two niches above which is a row of three-lobed niches supported on engaged columns. The composition of the façade recalls that of the Sasanian palace of Ctesiphon where niches are employed with a similar decorative function. Of particular interest is the way in which bricks are used to produce an ornamental effect in the lower niche. This device was to become a regular device in the architecture of Persia.

The city of Samarra, which was the seat of the Abbasid caliphs *p 51* for close on fifty years, can still be traced from its ruins which *(35–37)* were excavated before the First World War. It stretches for more than twenty miles along the bank of the Tigris, a network of streets, canals, mosques, palaces and houses. The great mosque of Samarra was built by the Caliph al-Mutawakkil between 847 and 852. Although a ruin, it has been possible to reconstruct its plan and structural details. The enormous enclosing wall of baked brick flanked by semicircular towers is longer than it is broad and makes it the largest mosque in the world. The porticos and sanctuary were covered by a flat roof supported on great octagonal piers of brick with marble columns at the four corners. The sanctuary has neither raised central nave nor dome. The minaret which lies outside the wall opposite the sanctuary is a *p 47* helicoidal tower with an external ramp running spirally to the top. *(19)* This unusual minaret has been connected with the Babylonian ziggurat which may have been its prototype.

The Baghdad Gate, at Raqqa. Raqqa was founded by al-Mansur nine years after Baghdad, and parts of its surviving walls give some idea of those of the capital. The use of decorative riches on this gate is a Sasanian feature. (9)

p 46
(18)   The palace known as the Jausaq al-Khaqani was built at Samarra by the Caliph al-Mu'tasim. A part of this still stands on a terrace overlooking the Tigris. It consists of a brick façade in which is an enormous niche or *ivan* flanked by two lesser ones. This central ivan was probably used for the Caliph's receptions and is reminiscent of the great arch of Ctesiphon which had the same function.

p 46
(16)   Grandest of all in conception is the palace of Ukheidir some seventy-five miles south west of Baghdad. It was probably built in the reign of the Caliph al-Mahdi, father of Harun ar-Rashid, and is thus some sixty years earlier than the Jausaq al-Khaqani at Samarra. Its plan has many features in common with that of Mshatta. The palace proper stands inside a fortified wall with round flanking towers and a great gateway which also serves as entrance to the palace. The latter, as at Mshatta, has an entrance hall flanked on the right by a mosque and leading to the court of honour and the audience hall beyond. Ukheidir is built mostly of stone except for brick which was employed for the vaults and arches. The three-aisled throne-room of Mshatta is here replaced by a great vaulted niche opening on to the court of honour of which we have already had occasion to speak in connection with the palaces at Samarra.

An Art of Pattern Making

p 46
(13–15)   Of particular interest is the style of decoration employed in architecture of the Abbasid period. Thanks to the excavations at
p 51   Samarra we know much about how it was employed as well as
(31–33,   the repertory of ornament. Wall surfaces of palaces were richly
35–37)   decorated with carved or moulded stucco, fresco painting, tiles and, though apparently rare, mosaics; wood, carved and painted, was used for ceilings. There is no reminder of the Greco-Roman tradition of Umayyad decoration. The Abbasid style is a survival and development of the Sasanian. In the wall paintings, compositions are restricted to decorative friezes and the handling is heavy. Stucco dadoes of houses are carved with repeat patterns of polygonal framing bands containing vine leaves and grapes, palmettes and the Sasanian wing palmette in varying degrees of stylization and relief. One group is quite distinctive and is executed in what has been described as the 'bevelled style'. Here the composition is reduced to a purely linear design in a single plane, the contours of the decorative elements being indicated by a bevelled edge cut back to the ground. So stylized are these elements that it is often hard to determine their intention. This style has a striking affinity with the Scythian animal style: and it is probable that it was developed by the Mesopotamian artists to accord with the taste of the Turkish element at the court and was based on the decorated weapons, horse trappings and jewellery which these nomads of the Steppe brought with them from their homes in central Asia. Perhaps this gives added significance to the employment of the bevelled style in the
f 10   magnificent mosque which Ahmad ibn Tulun, the Turkish ruler of Egypt, built in Cairo.

The stucco styles of Samarra gained wide currency, for examples have been found in houses excavated at Fustat in Egypt as well as in the Christian monastery of Dar as-Suriani in the Wadi

Carved lintel from the sanctuary door of the Mosque of Ibn Tulun, Cairo. There were nineteen doors to the mosque, but the carving has been preserved on only two of them. It is an example of the bevelled style favoured by the Turkish mercenaries who brought it from Samarra. (10)

60

Natron, also in Egypt. They turn up in the mosque of Nayin in western Persia and in the dwelling places excavated at Nishapur in Khorasan. Traces of the bevelled style occur in the art of Seljuk Persia and even later.

In their employment of carved stucco and in the decorative style they adopted, the architects of Mesopotamia were following the Persian Sasanian tradition of which examples have been recovered at Ctesiphon and other Sasanian sites. The stylization and absence of undercutting in one group may have been dictated by the need for speedy delivery. The bevelled style was a wholly new invention and again may have acquired favour, since, being   p 51
moulded, it dispensed with the more laborious process of carving.   (37)

Ceramic Renaissance

The pottery finds from Samarra are an eloquent tribute to Mesopotamian inventiveness. In fact there was a veritable renaissance of the ceramic art under the early Abbasids. The range of Sasanian pottery was relatively limited: the best was a turquoise glazed ware sometimes with relief decoration. This ware continued to be produced in Mesopotamia and Persia into the Islamic period and, indeed, throughout the Middle Ages. Early in the 9th century the Mesopotamian potters discovered the technique of lustre painting on pottery. The earliest examples   p 48
are dishes decorated with relief patterns of geometric interlacings,   (23)
palmettes and the angular Arabic script known as Kufic on a ground of tiny raised dots. A lustrous golden film was then   p 48
applied over a transparent lead glaze: in some examples touches   (24)
of green glaze are added. No doubt these were inspired by the splendid golden dishes for which the Sasanian goldsmiths were famous.

A powerful stimulus to pottery production was the porcelain and stoneware of T'ang China which was finding its way to the Near East now that ships plied between the Persian Gulf and the Far East. Several of the Islamic wares of this period can be explained as an attempt by the Muslim potters to imitate these Chinese porcelains and stonewares. Because they never succeeded in acquiring the technique of true porcelain, they developed an opaque white tin glaze which when applied to the earthenware body of the vessel gave the appearance of porcelain. Not content with a plain white surface they then learned the secret of painting on the tin glaze in cobalt blue and green. The most spectacular achievement was the technique of painting in lustre on the white tin glaze. In some pieces several tones of lustre were used ranging from a rich ruby to a pale yellow. At Samarra, lustre decoration consisted of floral and geometric motifs; but other examples of Mesopotamian lustre ware include human and animal representations though these may date from the following century.

Another ware represented at Samarra is decorated with splashes of aubergine, yellow and green and was evidently inspired by the mottled wares of T'ang China. The Muslim potters however added for further effect engraved designs of an Islamic character beneath the glaze and having no relation to the polychrome splashes.

Not only glazed vessels but also glazed tiles were produced in Mesopotamia. A beautiful series of polychrome lustre painted   p 51
tiles decorates the mihrab of the Great Mosque at Qairawan and   (31)
we know from contemporary sources that these were ordered   p 43 (4)
from Baghdad about 862 when they arrived accompanied by a Baghdad potter.

Pottery was manufactured at Baghdad as well as Samarra where, according to Arab authors, potters were drawn from Basra and Kufa. That the skill of the Mesopotamian potters was in great demand is shown by the lustre painted pottery that was being produced at Fustat in Egypt during the reign of Ahmad ibn Tulun.

Local Variations: Syria and the Persian Tradition

This international Abbasid style however did not succeed in ousting local styles. More often than not local traditions were mingled with others. This can be seen in the Great Mosque of   p 44–5
Qairawan which in spite of later restorations and changes is still   (8, 12)
largely the work of the Aghlabid rulers of the 9th century; the

scalloped niche-hood supported on columns maintains the Greco-Roman tradition. We have already had occasion to mention its minaret which is probably of the Umayyad period, inspired as it is by the bell towers of the Christian churches of Syria and placed in the middle of the side of the court opposite the sanctuary like the minaret in the Umayyad mosque of Damascus. The sanctuary and court however date from the 9th century; the former consisting of seventeen aisles perpendicular to the *qibla* wall. The central bay is broader than the others and is raised. It terminates in the mihrab and has a dome at either end. The flat roof of the sanctuary and porticos are supported on horseshoe p 44 (8) arches carried on coupled marble columns taken from pagan or Christian buildings. Because the latter are of varying height, wooden imposts have been inserted between columns and arches as well as wooden tie beams connecting the imposts to prevent lateral movement of the supports. Both wooden impost-blocks and tie beams were used in the mosque of Amr at Fustat when it was restored in 827 and must have been in the minds of the Aghlabid builders when they set to work to rebuild their mosque some years later. The beautiful domes with their external ribbings seem to have been inspired by the architecture of Mesopotamia. Besides the lustre painted tiles the mihrab is decorated with delicately carved marble panels with interlacings apparently derived from north African mosaics. Painted wood panels from p 44 (6) the mosque are decorated with floral motifs reminiscent of the mosaics in the Dome of the Rock in Jerusalem.

One of the most striking features of Mesopotamian art of the 9th century is the domination of the Persian tradition. In fact there is no reason to believe that there was ever any break in this tradition. The influence of Sasanian forms and style is seen in a bronze ewer found in a grave in upper Egypt and said to be that of the last Umayyad Caliph Marwan II who made his last stand p 50 there against his pursuers. The cock modelled on the spout and (29) the crenellated mouth, the traced arcades around the body of the vessel give it an unmistakable Sasanian stamp.

This Persian tradition increased with the growth of political separatism in the 9th and 10th centuries. A bronze medal struck f 11 in Baghdad in 975 in the name of the Buwayhid Prince 'Izz ad-Daula Bakhtiar is known only from a cast in the British Museum. It shows the King crowned and with cup in hand seated between two attendants; on the reverse is a seated musician playing the lute. Here the composition is Sasanian though the treatment is Islamic. It has already been mentioned that the Buwayhid princes aspired to revive the Sasanian monarchy.

It is appropriate at this point to allude to the role of Arabic writing in Islamic art. Because Allah chose to make his revelations to the Prophet in the Arabic language, the actual written words of the Qur'an in course of time came almost to be endowed with a sacred character. The copying of the Qur'an was considered an act of merit; and calligraphy was given a position high among the arts. Sacred texts of the Qur'an were introduced into religious buildings. We have already referred to the verses executed in mosaic in the Dome of the Rock. In the Umayyad period there was a cursive script employed for everyday docu-p 49 ments and a more formal script known as Kufic—tradition (24) ascribes its origin to the the town of Kufa—which was used for monumental inscriptions in stone and other materials. In the Kufic, the curvilinear element is less prominent than in those scripts which were developed later and for this reason it strikes a note of majestic severity.

Writing materials in the early Islamic period were papyrus manufactured in Egypt and parchment; the pen was a reed and indeed has remained so ever since. The earliest copies of the Qur'an which we possess are written on parchment in the Kufic script. The most characteristic format is broader than it is long although the codex format of the antique period is not unknown. Many of these early manuscripts must have comprised many volumes since as few as three lines of writing occupy a single p 42 (3) page. One such copy is a Qur'an copied for a certain Amajur, an Abbasid Governor of Syria in the second half of the 9th century. Manuscripts were bound in tooled leather bindings—a technique which was probably learned from the Copts of Egypt. The art of illumination was already practised in some of these early

Bronze medal, struck in 975 for Prince 'Izz ad-Daula Bakhtiar. The Prince, crowned, sits with a cup in his hand, attended by two servants. The whole setting reflects the ambition of the Buwayhid princes to emulate the Sasanian emperors. (11)

Qur'ans: chapter headings were enclosed within frames of p 51 geometric or floral ornament, verse divisions were indicated by (34) rosettes placed in the margins and occasionally single pages were entirely reserved for illumination.

The East under the Samanids

The first truly distinctive style that **we** know of in Persia occurs in the dominions of the Samanid rulers of Khorasan and Transoxiana. The skill and architectural sense of their builders can be seen in the Mausoleum of Isma'il, founder of the dynasty p 44 (7) who died in AD 907. This is the second earliest surviving funerary monument in Islam. It is a simple square building of baked brick surmounted by a dome. There are engaged piers at the corners and pointed arched doorways in each of the four sides. In addition to the central dome there are four lesser domes at the corners. It is probable that the general plan of the building is a reminiscence of the Sasanian fire temple. Its essential features—a p 27 square structure surmounted by a dome and with an entrance (27) door on each of its sides—remained the pattern of the Islamic tomb monument for the following centuries.

The excavations at Nishapur have revealed something of the high civilization of the Samanid court. Besides the wall paintings and carved stucco decoration, both related to those from Samarra, a wholly distinctive type of glazed pottery was recovered. A similar type of pottery has also been found at Samarkand the other important Samanid centre. The potters of eastern Persia and Transoxiana did not at this period know of the opaque tin glaze: instead they painted in coloured clay slips on the surface of the vessel which they then covered with a transparent lead glaze. Although there is no great variety of shapes among these slip painted wares—straight sided bowls are the commonest—the range of decoration is considerable, as much by its rich polychrome palette as by the variety of motifs. Geometric interlacings and stylized rosettes and palmettes were popular; perhaps the most successful designs are those dishes decorated with a circular band of superbly drawn Arabic inscription in a brilliant tomato red on a white ground. Most of the Arabic inscriptions which the Samanid potters employed are of a gnomic character.

Samanid patronage of learning has already been mentioned. Great libraries were amassed: and eastern Persia was an important centre for Arabic calligraphy. Arabic was employed as architectural decoration at Nishapur where there was found a splendid frieze containing a Kufic inscription on a scrolling ground and carved in stucco. The finest of the painted inscriptions on Samanid pottery must have been after the designs of masters of calligraphy.

The secret of paper manufacture had been discovered according to tradition as the result of information given by a Chinese captured during a military engagement between Arabs and Chinese on the Talas river in 751. In the 10th century paper ousted the much more expensive parchment and papyrus and must have had a beneficial effect on book production. In the course of the same century Kufic was gradually yielding to the more curvilinear scripts. Book production was now a securely established art; the Islamic *scriptorium* must have been a complex organization in which scribe, illuminator and binder combined in making the finished manuscript for the delectation of prince or scholar. A Qur'an manuscript now in the British Museum p 51 gives some idea of the quality of the books made in the Samanid (34) period although it was copied in 1036—nearly forty years after the fall of the dynasty. There is a perfect harmony between writing and illumination: there are, too, a number of pages decorated solely with illumination combining intricate interlacings and floral scrolls. The names of both the scribe and illuminator are recorded in the manuscript.

Egypt: the Fatimids

By 1000 the Fatimids were securely established in Egypt: and the foundations of Fatimid art—one of the most fertile influences in the development of Islamic art—were securely laid. Soon after the foundation of Cairo, the Caliph al-M'uizz built the college and mosque of al-Azhar as a centre for the dissemination of Isma'ili beliefs in Egypt and the Near East. It is the first Fatimid religious foundation in Egypt; owing to the important role it has always played in the Muslim world little has remained of its original state. Its plan combined elements from the great mosque of Qairawan on the one hand and from the mosque of Ibn Tulun on the other. Parts of the original façade of the court still remain and give some impression of the style of early Fatimid stucco carving. More important however is the mosque, built by the Caliph al-Hakim and completed in 1003, on account of the decoration of the portico and its two minarets. Here for the first time we are confronted with the arabesque, that most typical of Islamic ornaments. In origin it was a free interpretation of the classical acanthus scroll and in its earlier stages retains a recognizable plant form, but in the Fatimid period naturalism is subordinated to linear effect. Yet however schematized, it retains the organic nature of its origin. The Fatimid artists in evolving the arabesque scroll established the principle of the split leaf and the continuous stem; and their manner of combining arabesque and geometric motives such as star forms united by interlacing bands determined the whole future character of Islamic decoration. They also introduced human and animal figures into their decorative schemes; but generally reduce their function to one of decoration.

The greatest achievements of early Fatimid art are the rock crystal carvings. The art of crystal carving was practised in Egypt from the period of Ahmad ibn Tulun and may have been introduced from Mesopotamia. Some half-a-dozen ewers represent the high water mark of the Egyptian crystal carver's skill. These have pear-shape bodies standing on a foot-ring, slightly projecting spout and handle joining the mouth to the body. An example in the Treasure of St Mark's, Venice bears a dedication to the Caliph al-'Aziz (975–996). The most beautiful is that in the Victoria and Albert Museum which is anonymous and without date but which cannot be far removed in time from the ewer in Venice. There could be no better illustration of the nature of Fatimid art than the refinement of form and decoration manifested in this ewer where the arabesque scrolls and the motif of the bird of prey attacking a gazelle achieve a perfect harmony.

p 50
(30)

Spain: the Brilliant Flowering of Cordoba

In certain respects, the Iberian peninsula in this period stands somewhat apart from the rest of the Islamic world: for here the Muslims were settled on European soil. Communication with the east was often hazardous owing to the presence of hostile forces in the Mediterranean and to the uneasy political situation in north Africa. In Spain, which the Arabs called *al-Andalus* after the Vandal settlers in the south, Arab and Berber Muslims lived alongside the indigenous Christian population. Unlike Syria, Egypt and Persia, the number of Christian converts to Islam was exceedingly small. Both Christian and Muslim contributed to the creation of Umayyad civilization in Spain which thus came to form a real bridge between the West and the East. This was a strange world in which the Arab poet could make play with the vernacular and Christians who spoke Arabic retained the Latin liturgy.

Cordoba became the Umayyad capital six years before the founding of Baghdad and was soon to rival that city. In the 10th century it possessed seven hundred mosques besides the Great Mosque (perhaps the noblest in the Islamic world), three public baths, a palace with four hundred halls and rooms and a city library with four hundred thousand books. Apart from twenty churches there were many monasteries, some even endowed by members of the royal house.

The greatest monument of the Umayyad period in Spain is the Great Mosque of Cordoba. 'Abd ar-Rahman I founded it on the site of a Christian church near the bridge which spans the Guadalquivir. His mosque was a court and sanctuary of eight aisles with a broad central nave. In the following century this was enlarged by the addition of two aisles and the extension of the *qibla* wall by eight bays. The Caliph al-Hakim between 961 and 966 added a further twelve bays and constructed the great mihrab and the dome with its two flanking domes which precede the mihrab. In order to raise the height of the roof the architect of the Great Mosque employed a system of superposed arches of horshoe form, the upper supported on piers placed between the extrados of the lower. This system is thought to have been adopted from the arch system of the Roman aqueduct. The hemispherical dome caps are supported on intersecting ribs which provide the necessary transition to the square space below. This vaulting system probably originated in the East. The domes and the framing bands of the mihrab are faced with mosaics on a gold ground, the work of a Byzantine mosaicist sent to Cordoba by the Emperor of Constantinople at the Caliph's request.

p 52
(38–40)

The mosque was still further enlarged in 987 by al-Mansur the powerful minister of the Caliph al-Hisham who added eight aisles on the east side of al-Hakim's mosque and made corresponding additions to the court. When Cordoba passed into the hands of the Christians in the 13th century the mosque was converted into a church. In the 16th century the canons of the cathedral built a lofty choir in the centre of the mosque, thereby providing an illuminating contrast between the upward thrust of the church and the uniform level of the mosque ceiling—two opposed aesthetics.

'Abd ar-Rahman III founded in 936 a royal city five miles outside Cordoba. The site of Medinat az-Zahra has been investigated by archaeologists since 1910: and the finds have added considerably to our knowledge of the Umayyad art of Spain. Above all the capitals of columns, carved pilasters and wall revetments provide us with a repertory of Umayyad ornament. As has been suggested earlier the feeling and treatment of this decoration is related to that of the Umayyad art of Syria. Like their Syrian forbears, the masons who carved the decoration at Medinat az-Zahra exploited the effects of light and shade by deep drilling. There is great variety of floral forms, and scrolling includes acanthus leaves, vine-leaves and palmettes. Repeat patterns of flowers or palmettes within interlaced polygonal framing bands are reminiscent of the decoration at Khirbat al-Mafjar. Typical of Umayyad decoration are the carved stone capitals of columns: some of these are carved with a lace-like pattern of small leaves arranged in the form of a highly schematized Corinthian capital.

p 52
(41)

p 51
(33)

In the second half of the 10th century there was a flourishing school of ivory carvers in Cordoba. A number of their productions have survived; one of the finest is the cylindrical casket with domed lid now in the Louvre. According to the inscription around the lid it was made in 968 for al-Mughira, a younger brother of the Caliph al-Hakim and son of 'Abd ar-Rahman III.

p 50
(27)

The carving is the work of a great master. Every inch of the surface is worked but there is no impression of a superfluity of ornament. Rather is the decoration so ordered that every element whether figural, geometric, floral or epigraphic, combine to produce a sense of harmony and repose which is the mark of every true work of Islamic art.

IV BETWEEN EAST AND WEST

Armenia and its divided history

SIRARPIE DER NERSESSIAN

Armenia and Georgia; the area is now divided between Russia, Turkey and Iran

Armenia was the shadow

of the great nation that she might have been. Between the 7th and the 11th centuries she was the source of advances whose significance is only now being fully realized—in theology, in liturgy (the Armenian rite is still practised by the Armenian, in communion with the Roman Catholic Church), in scholarship, in the arts, and perhaps most fruitfully of all in architecture. Yet her geographical position, which made her the meeting point of so many influences and ideas, also doomed her to be the thousand-year battlefield of Europe and Asia, to be denied the full flowering of which she was so supremely capable, and to suffer conquest, division, oppression and finally annihilation.

By a treaty of AD 387 Armenia was divided between Byzantium and Persia, the lion's share going to Persia. Three hundred years later, during the Arab invasion, she was fought over by both sides and ended by becoming a province of the Caliphate.

In the 9th century the tide turned. Ashot I, a member of a great princely family, the Bagratunis, proclaimed himself an independent sovereign. It was the beginning of Armenia's brief Golden Age. Her kings ruled in wealth and luxury. On the walls of King Gagik's palace at Aght'amar, we are told by the chronicler Thomas Artsruni, were painted 'gilt thrones, on which were seated, in gracious majesty, the King surrounded by young pages with resplendent faces, groups of musicians and marvellous maidens'.

Aght'amar, the city on an island in Lake Van, is now a deserted ruin, but King Gagik's church still remains. Among the reliefs on the exterior is the Virgin and Child (opposite). It is characteristic of the Aght'amar carvings that all the faces have large piercing eyes gazing out at the spectator. The small figure beside the throne is the Archangel Gabriel. It was said to have been above this island-city that the Virgin appeared in a vision to the great poet and mystic Gregory of Narek.

The rule of the Bagratunis lasted until about AD 1000 and ended when the central authority became too weak to organize its own defence. By the end of the 10th century there were six virtually independent kingdoms in Armenia. The Byzantine Emperor Basil II was claiming large parts of the western frontier, while a new wave of Asiatic invaders, the Seljuk Turks, were carving out an empire in the east. In 1064 they captured the capital, Ani. Seven years later Armenia ceased to exist.

The later history of the Armenian people lies outside the scope of this book. They moved south and founded another kingdom in Cilicia, which lasted until the 14th century. When that too fell to the Mameluke Turks the Armenians were left scattered throughout the Near East, a Christian minority living under alien masters, treasuring their ancient language and culture and the memory of their past greatness. (1)

64

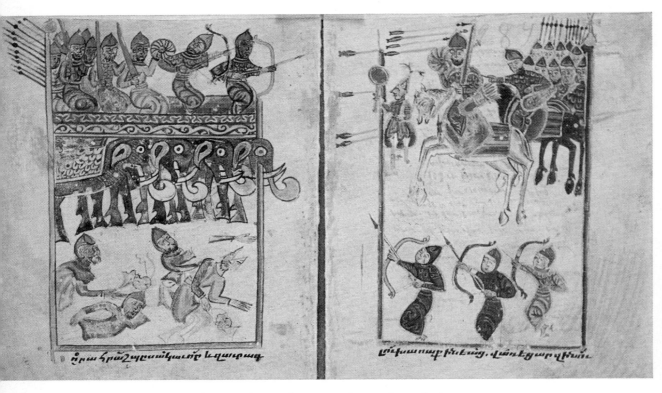

An epic battle, which took its place in Armenian poetry and legend, was fought in AD 451 on the plain of Avaraïr. A small Armenian force, fighting with desperate bravery, was wiped out by the Persians. The Armenian leaders became national saints, and the battle is here depicted in a Hymnal made just over 1000 years later in 1482. The Persians ride elephants, the Armenians are either on horseback or on foot. The man in front of the Armenians, holding a shield on a pole, was supposed to provoke the enemy with insults so that he lost control of the battle. (2)

At Armenia's heart stands the snowy peak of Ararat, rising to a height of 17,000 feet. Since Old Testament times it has been regarded with particular veneration, and it was in the region at its foot that the Bagratunis established their first strongholds. To Armenians of today it is still a living symbol of the land from which they are exiled. (3)

The magnificent churches of the 9th and 10th centuries show that the Armenians were, at the time, among the leading architects of the world. One of them, Trdat, was called in to repair the dome of Hagia Sophia in Constantinople in 989. Ani Cathedral (left) was built by Trdat between 989 and 1001. Its plan is a cross within a rectangle, and a dome (now fallen) surmounted the central crossing. The clustered piers, the pointed arches and vaults anticipate the European Gothic style by a century. The exterior shows the typical Armenian decoration of blind arcades.

Right: the church of the Holy Cross at Aght'amar. The main space, covered by a dome, is flanked on all four sides by niches (polygonal on the exterior), with smaller niches in the corners. Armenian churches display a brilliant series of variations on the centralized plan. (4, 5)

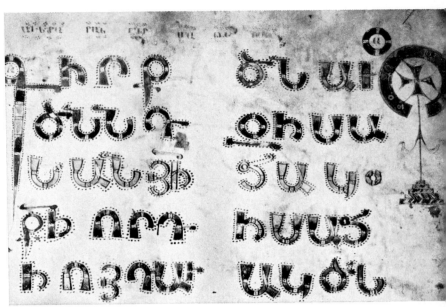

Armenia is the oldest Christian state.
St Gregory 'the Illuminator of the Armenians' (seen, left, in a Georgian miniature added to an Armenian New Testament) converted King Tiridates in 301 and Christianity was adopted as the official religion. As with the Slavs, this led to the language—so far only spoken—being written down for the first time, and a new alphabet being invented for the purpose. It was the work of a learned priest, Mesrop Mashtots', and is shown below in its most elaborate form, a highly ornate manuscript of the 11th century. Armenia soon produced a prolific literature, both translated and original. (6, 7)

Among the oldest of Armenian buildings is the monastic Cathedral of Etchmiadzin (below left), though not much of the original 7th-century fabric now remains. The Cathedral of Kars (below), mid 10th century, is another variant of the quatrefoil plan. (8, 9)

King Gagik (right) crowned and nimbed presents to Christ the church of the Holy Cross he had erected between the years 915 and 921. His robes, richly adorned with foliage and birds, show the type of textiles woven by the Armenians and the Muslims during this period. (11)

Ashot I, of the Iberian branch of the Bagratunis, presiding Prince and Curopalate of Iberia (813–830), presents the church of Opiza (above). (10)

The Church of the Redeemer at Ani (below) was built in 1034 as a chapel for a relic of the True Cross. Services were to be held in it every night until the Second Coming. It is octagonal inside, sixteen-sided outside, with blind arcading at two levels. (12)

'The living and life-giving Christ

we represent in every medium', wrote the Catholicos John Otsnets'i in the early 8th century. Armenian wall-painting is sparse and ill-preserved, but the rich treasure of manuscript illumination that survives bears witness to the outstanding qualities of the artists. Above: the Holy Women at the Sepulchre, from a Gospel book made in 1038. Right: the Baptism, from the Etchmiadzin Gospel; the book dates from 989, but this miniature, painted on a leaf bound in at the end, originally formed part of a manuscript of the 6th or 7th century. Opposite: the Annunciation and Visitation, from the Gospel of Mugni, of the mid-11th century. (13, 14, 17)

Masterpieces in enamel stem largely from Georgia. The 10th-century crucifixion (left) shows Adam's skull, under the cross, with the Virgin, the Church Triumphant (catching Christ's blood), St John and the Synagogue (turning away from Christ). The plaque above is of the same date. (15, 16)

Georgia, lying further to the north, shared much of Armenia's history and culture, though distinct in language and religion (the Georgians belonged to the Greek Orthodox church and were thus closer to Byzantium). Georgia was slower to develop than Armenia, but she was destined to be the longer-lived. As Armenia broke up in the 11th century Georgia seemed to gather strength and was in fact united for the first time under King Bagrat III in 1008. Between then and the 13th century was the most splendid period of Georgian history.

Georgian art and architecture are broadly in the Armenian tradition. Above: sculpture over the west door of the church of the Holy Cross at Djvarî near Mtskheta, typically Georgian in its combination of figures and ornamental work. Right: Samtavisi Cathedral, built about 1030. Below: the church at Oshki, c. 958. Both buildings have the normal dome on squinches. (18, 19, 20)

Armenia and its divided history

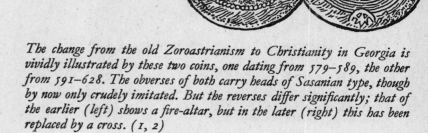

SIRARPIE DER NERSESSIAN

The change from the old Zoroastrianism to Christianity in Georgia is vividly illustrated by these two coins, one dating from 579–589, the other from 591–628. The obverses of both carry heads of Sasanian type, though by now only crudely imitated. But the reverses differ significantly; that of the earlier (left) shows a fire-altar, but in the later (right) this has been replaced by a cross. (1, 2)

THE PERIOD STUDIED in the present chapter extends from the conversion of Armenia and Georgia in the beginning of the 4th century to the Seljuk conquest in the 3rd quarter of the 11th century. The main emphasis will be on Armenia, and events in Georgia will be considered in so far as they form part of the general history of this area, for the two countries were connected with one another by many ties and had, in many respects, a similar fate. Throughout the Middle Ages, and even later, these nations stood as the eastern bastions of Christian thought and civilization against the great empires which developed on their eastern borders and, more than once, slowed down the westward advances.

Armenia is that part of the high plateau of Hither Asia which lies east of the Euphrates. Its boundaries are roughly marked by the Chorokh and Kura rivers on the northwest and north, by the river Araxes and the Lake of Urmia on the east, and by the mountains of Kurdistan and the valley of the Tigris on the south. Mountain ranges, with the majestic peak of Mount Ararat rising to a height of about 17,000 feet, run across the plateau in an east-westerly direction and divide the country into a number of separate basins, through which the mountain torrents cut deep gorges. The geographic conformation of Armenia explains to a large degree the course of her history. Each one of her powerful neighbours sought control or possession of this natural fortress, of great strategic importance for defence or attack. The division of the land into separate basins strengthened the separatist tendencies of the feudal lords, and prevented unity among them; but on the other hand it also prevented the conquering nations from being complete masters of the land.

Georgia lay to the north and north-west of Armenia, beyond the Kura and Chorokh rivers, with a long coastline on the Black Sea. The mountains of the north and the high plateau on the south contrast with the fertile valleys of the Rion and the Kura. Further removed from the routes which from Iran and Mesopotamia passed into Asia Minor, it was less exposed to the march of the great armies. To the east of Georgia and extending to the Caspian Sea, was the smaller country of the Albanians. No literature in their own language is preserved, and our main sources of information are the works of the Armenian historians, in particular of Moses of Kaghankatuyk' who wrote the *History of the Albanians.*

T e political history of this entire period is dominated by the struggles between the Roman and Byzantine Empires on the one side, and the Sasanian and Arab Empires on the other; Armenia, and to a lesser degree Georgia, were frequently the battlefield and almost always one of the targets. Jointly with these wars, runs the long succession of revolts against the occupants, whatever their nationality. No common ground for a durable peace could exist between the conquerors and those who ceaselessly aspired to retain or regain their independence. The situation was further complicated by rivalries between the leading families, their internecine wars, and also by their differences of allegiances, some of them favouring an entente with their western and others with their eastern neighbours.

Roman power was in the ascendancy during the early 4th century. After the victorious campaigns of Galerius and the peace treaty signed with the Persians at Nisibis (298), Roman protectorate extended far into the provinces which lay beyond the Tigris. Tiridates, a scion of the ruling Arsacid family, was restored to the throne of Armenia by the Romans, and in Georgia Mihran received from the latter the royal insignia. Through the conversion of Tiridates by Gregory the Illuminator (301) Armenia was the first country to recognize Christianity as the official state religion. The conversion of Georgia, followed by that of Albania, brought these three countries into closer contact with the West, especially after the proclamation of the Edict of Milan and the transfer of the capital to Byzantium, while, on the other hand, a new source of conflict was thus created with Mazdaist Iran.

p 68 (6)

f 1, 2

p 67 (3)

Under Persian Rule

The Persian invasion of 338 broke the truce signed at Nisibis; the war between Persia and the Byzantine Empire continued intermittently for almost half a century. Georgia was the first to be partitioned into two kingdoms; the western part was submitted to Byzantine suzerainty and the eastern part to that of Persia. The same fate befell Armenia shortly after (387). Persia being stronger at the time received about four fifths of the land, that is the provinces which lay east of a line passing from Theodosiopolis (Erzerum) in the north, to Martyropolis (Meyafarkin) in the south. The Arsacid king retained a nominal power in each section, but after the death of Arsaces III (c. 391) Byzantium appointed a *comes* for the administration of the country. In Persian Armenia there remained an Armenian king until 428; after that date a *marzpan* or margrave was appointed by Iran. In Albania the local kingship was also abolished before the end of the 5th century, while in Georgia the Mihranid dynasty retained its nominal rule until 580.

In speaking of the new organization of Persian Armenia, the historian Eghishe (Elisaeus) states that the kingship of which the king had been deprived passed, in effect, to the Armenian *nakharars*, for although the taxes were sent to the Persian treasury, yet in time of war the entire Armenian cavalry was led by the *nakharars*. Despite some exaggeration in the use of the term kingship, these remarks give an accurate picture of the state of affairs, for the Persians did not succeed in maintaining complete and permanent control of the country.

Armenia had at the time a fully developed feudal organization. At the head of the hierarchy were the four *bdeashkh* (*vitascae*), the hereditary, viceregal lords and defenders of the marches or frontier regions; their role disappeared with the fall of the Arsacid dynasty. Next in importance came the *nakharars*, the heads of the princely houses. Their hereditary, patrimonial domains constituted autonomous principalities; the 'head of the house' exercised absolute military, juridical and administrative powers, and his chief duty, as vassal, was to furnish cavalry troops to the king in time of war. The *nakharars* also held important offices, many of which were hereditary. Such were for instance the office of the Coronant, reserved for the Bagratuni family; that of the Commander in Chief of the armies (*sparapet*), the prerogative of the powerful Mamikonian dynasty; or that of the general administrator of the realm (*hazarapet*), reserved for the Gnunis. In special circumstances the king called the assembly of the *nakharars*

Ա ա a	**Կ կ** k[g]	**Ռ ռ** rh
Բ բ b[p]	**Հ հ** h	**Ս ս** s
Գ գ g[k]	**Ձ ձ** dz[ts]	**Վ վ** v
Դ դ d[t]	**Ղ ղ** gh	**Տ տ** t[d]
Ե ե e [1]	**Ճ ճ** ch[j]	**Ր ր** r
Զ զ z	**Մ մ** m	**Ց ց** ts'
Է է ē	**Յ յ** y [2]	**Ւ ւ** w
Ը ը ĕ	**Ն ն** n	**Փ փ** p'
Թ թ t'	**Շ շ** sh	**Ք ք** k'
Ժ ժ zh	**Ո ո** o	**Օ օ** ō
Ի ի i	**Չ չ** ch'	**Ֆ ֆ** f
Լ լ l	**Պ պ** p[b]	
Խ խ kh	**Ջ ջ** j[ch]	
Ծ ծ ts[dz]		

The Armenian alphabet. Compiled by Mesrop Mashtots' in the early 5th century to meet the needs of the Armenian language, it has special signs for vowels, and all consonants whether simple or compound are expressed by single characters. (3)

and sought their advice. The historical sources speak of senior and junior *nakharars*, a distinction dependent partly on the size and importance of their domains, but even more on the order of their precedence at Court, established by a Throne-list (*Gahnamak*).

The next group in the hierarchic order was formed by the *azats* or the free-men, owners of small fiefs, and vassals of the king or of the *nakharars*. They owed military service to their feudal lords and formed the cavalry troops. They participated in the administration of the feudal domain and just as the king called at times the assembly of the *nakharars* for consultation, the *nakharars* also called the assembly of the *azats*. They were subject to taxation, but were exempt from corporal punishment. It was also from this class of free-men that many of the minor court officials were selected.

The majority of the common people (*ramik*) consisted of peasants (*shinarar*). As in Medieval Europe they were serfs, attached to the soil, which they tilled for the benefit of their masters, retaining only a small part of the products for their own use; they could own their house and a few animals, but most of them lived in great poverty. They were called upon for all the public works, such as the construction of fortresses, roads or bridges, and in war time they were enrolled in the army without receiving any pay or any part of the spoils. The majority formed the infantry; some were horsemen but these companies were distinct from the cavalry of the nobles.

The large cities had their own rules of government and their inhabitants, especially the artisans and traders, enjoyed greater freedom than the peasants.

A document designated as the Military Register (*Zoranamak*) lists the size of the cavalry troops that each *nakharar* could raise. Although this document, like the Throne-list, is only known through a compilation of late date, comparison with information furnished by the ancient historians shows that in its main lines the estimates are fairly accurate, and that during the Arsacid

period the military potential of Armenia varied approximately from 70,000 to 120,000 men. The senior *nakharars* usually contributed 1,000 men, a number which was substantially increased in times of great necessity, even after the fall of the monarchy. In view of the importance of the cavalry troops raised by the *nakharars*, and the well-known valour of these warriors, one can easily understand that both Byzantium and Persia were anxious to gain control of Armenia and use the Armenian contingents in the defence of their borders, as well as in their own wars. But it becomes equally clear why the control of the land could never be complete so long as the *nakharars* retained their feudal powers. Entrenched with their cavalry in their fortified towns and mountain strongholds, they formed important centres of resistance. United they might have been able to save the fatherland, but as in all feudal organizations their patriotism had often a local character. Jealous of their prerogatives, independent to a fault, they rarely subordinated their personal aspirations to the national interests, and fought with the same energy with one another as against the common foe.

In Byzantine Armenia, imperial policy aimed to eliminate these centres of resistance by reducing the power of the *nakharars*. The Emperor Zeno forbade the *nakharars* 'to transmit the office to those connected with them by kinship', and he ordained that on each occasion different men of the Emperor's choosing should succeed to these offices, just as is the rule in all the other offices of the Romans (Procopius, *De aedificiis*, III, i). This measure struck at the roots of the feudal organization, and the hereditary transmission of power within each family. Equally drastic changes were introduced by Justinian. The daughters who, according to Armenian feudal custom, had been excluded from the paternal inheritance, were granted equal rights with the sons and were also entitled to a dowry. This led to a greater division of the feudal domain and consequently diminished the effective power of the head of the house, already reduced by Zeno's law.

The Persians did not try to abolish the feudal organization which was similar to the one prevailing in their own country. Individual measures were taken against the *nakharars* and their privileges were frequently curtailed, but by and large the relations between the Sasanian king and the Armenian *nakharars* were those of suzerain and vassals. The hereditary laws were maintained, the *nakharars* still raised their cavalry troops which they placed at the service of their suzerain in time of war, but as we shall see they had the control of these troops and with them opposed the Persian forces during the national revolts. The process of the Iranization of Armenia was attempted through the channel of religion, by trying to impose Mazdaism and to destroy the Armenian church, one of the principal bulwarks of national life.

'To Teach, Write and Translate'

The national consciousness aroused by the conversion to Christianity had been reinforced in the early 5th century by the invention of the Armenian alphabet, an event of foremost importance for the entire history of the Armenian people. Until then Armenian was a spoken language; the religious services were performed in Syriac in Persian Armenia, or in Greek in Byzantine Armenia, and priests well trained in these languages orally translated the Scriptures and services to the people. The absence of a written language increased the possibilities for the work of assimilation relentlessly pursued by the Empire, and in Persian Armenia it left a free field for the dissemination of Mazdaist writings. The King of Persian Armenia, Vramshapuh, and the Catholicos Sahak, a man of great erudition, were conscious of these dangers and of the urgent need for a national script. The task was entrusted to the learned cleric Mesrop Mashtots'. After a long journey of consultation and study, which took them to Amida, Edessa and Samosata, Mesrop and his companions returned to Armenia bringing with them the alphabet they had devised, an alphabet admirably adapted to the Armenian language, *f 3* consisting of thirty-six letters corresponding to all the subtle p 68 (8 variations of the phones.

A great work lay ahead: 'to teach, write and translate'. Mesrop undertook a journey to neighbouring Georgia and Albania, he sent his disciples to Edessa and Nisibis for further study of the Syriac language, and with special instructions to bring back manuscripts of the Scriptures and works of the famous Syrian writers, such as Ephraim, in order to translate them into Armenian. Monastic schools were established in different parts of Armenia, where students were trained and the foreign works translated. Such schools could easily be founded in Persian Armenia where the Catholicos resided and where there was still an Armenian king, but in Byzantine Armenia imperial authorization was needed. Mesrop therefore proceeded to Melitene (421/2) and, leaving several of his pupils in this city, passed on to Constantinople, where he was received by the Emperor Theodosius and the Patriarch Atticus. Having obtained the necessary permission Mesrop established schools in Byzantine Armenia; he also sent students to Constantinople, and brought back with him a number of precious manuscripts.

The spoken language had reached a high degree of development and the writings of the 5th century constitute the golden age of Armenian literature. The Bible which had first been translated from the Syriac, was retranslated from the Greek by the Catholicos Sahak himself, together with Mesrop and his pupils; they also translated all the books needed for the liturgy, the writings of the Greek and Syrian Church Fathers, as well as secular works such as the Romance of Alexander. The significance of this intensive activity is not confined to Armenia; in several instances works of which the originals are lost are only known through these translations, such as the Chronicle of the 4th-century ecclesiastical historian, Eusebius. Even when Greek or Syriac manuscripts have survived, the early date and accuracy of the Armenian translations have been of great assistance to scholars in establishing the original form of the text. Finally it was the Armenian version of the Gospels, as well as of several writings of the Church Fathers that the Georgians used for their own translations. The creation of original works proceeded side by side in Armenia with the task of translating. The historical writings which go back to the early, legendary history of Armenia and give valuable information on contemporary events in Armenia and the neighbouring countries occupy the first place, while theological treatises, like the *De Deo* by Eznik, one of Mesrop's disciples, throw a vivid light on the philosophical and theological culture of the Armenian clergy during this period.

Rebellion and Revival

The Persian rule had become more oppressive after the abolition of the monarchy; the heavy taxation, the religious persecutions, and the forceful measures to impose Mazdaism undertaken by Yazdgard II immediately after his accession (439) finally led to a general revolt. The church, the nobility and the people rallied around Vardan Mamikonian and determined to resort to war, even though part of the cavalry was still with the Persian army, fighting against the Huns, and Byzantium had refused to send armed assistance. After a series of minor engagements won by the Armenians, the decisive battle was waged in the plain of Avaraïr (451), an epic encounter between a small army of determined men fighting for their faith and independence, and the vastly superior forces of the Persians with their select troop of the 'Immortals' mounted on their elephants. In spite of their valour, the Armenians, whose ranks were depleted at a crucial moment by the defection of Iranophile *nakharars*, were defeated; their leader Vardan Mamikonian and the flower of Armenian chivalry fell on the battlefield.

A state of unrest prevailed in Armenia and Georgia during the second half of the 5th and the entire 6th century. There were numerous revolts and, moreover, the war that broke out again between Byzantium and Iran (502) was fought principally on Georgian and Armenian soil. The Iberian monarchy was abolished in 578–580 and in 591 both Georgia and Armenia were partitioned between Byzantium and Iran. The treaty favoured the Byzantines: the line of demarcation passed from Tiflis in the north, to Martyropolis in the south, thus ceding to the Empire the greater part of Georgia and Armenia.

The city of Dvin, near the river Azat, a tributary of the Araxes, was the centre of economic life during this period. It had been

p 66 (2)

founded by Khosrov II (330–338) as the new capital of Armenia; after the Persian conquest it became the residence of the *marzpan* and the centre of administrative life. The seat of the Catholicos had also been transferred to Dvin early in the 5th century. Its importance is attested by the numerous references of the Armenian historians and by Procopius who wrote: 'Now Doubios (Dvin) is a land excellent in every respect, and especially blessed with a healthy climate and abundance of good water; and from Theodosiopolis it is removed a journey of eight days. In that region there are plains suitable for riding and many populous villages are situated in very close proximity to one another and

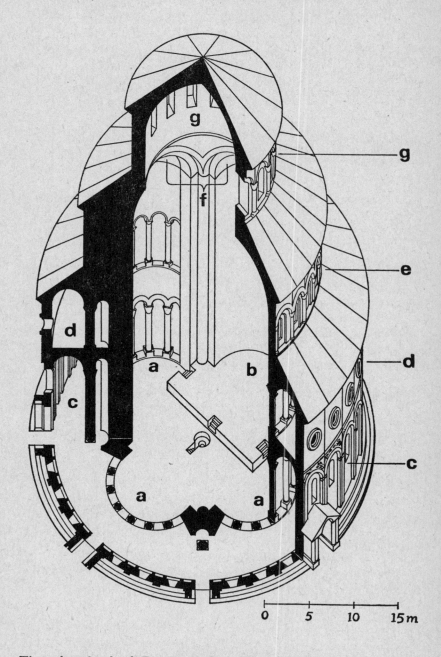

The palace-church of Zvart'nots', built by the Catholicos Nerses III between 641 and 666, was one of the most brilliant of all Armenian buildings. The centre was quatrefoil in plan; three lobes were open exedrae (aaa) and the fourth a solid apse for the altar (b). Each exedra rose through three storeys; the first opened through arcades into the ambulatory (c); the second through another arcade into a gallery (d); while the third contained windows (e)—three to each lobe—which lit the central space. Four arches (f) connected the four main piers of the quatrefoil, and from them, by means of pendentives, rose a dome on a circular drum (g) with another ring of windows. The exterior was circular at all levels. The first level included the ambulatory (c) lit by long windows, and the gallery (d) lit by circular ones. The next level consisted of the ends of the four lobes of the quatrefoil connected up into a circle and given windows (e) equally spaced apart—though only three windows in every quarter of the circle could admit light to the interior. And finally the circular drum of the dome (g). This drawing follows the reconstruction suggested by Toramanian. (4)

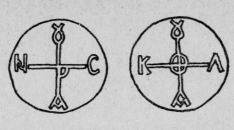

A capital from one of the exedra arcades of Zvart'nots'. Its bold eagle with outspread wings shows the influence of Byzantium. Above: the monogram of Nerses III, 'the Builder', carved on two sides of another capital. The first circle stands for NAPCOY, the second KAΘOΛIKOY, i.e. Narsou Katholicou—'(the work) of Nerses the Catholicos'. 'Catholicos' was the title of the Patriarchs of Armenia. (5, 6, 7)

numerous merchants conduct their business in them. For from India and the neighbouring regions of Iberia and from practically all the nations of Persia and some of those under Roman sway they bring in merchandise and carry on their dealings with each other there.' (*History of Wars* II, xxv).

In addition to this active transit trade Armenians exported manufactured goods and raw products from their mines. The material prosperity of the leading classes can be judged from the numerous and sumptuous buildings erected during the latter part of the 6th century and in the course of the 7th by the Catholicoses and the *nakharars*. Earlier monuments were also restored or transformed during this period. By the originality and variety of their plans, the ornamental and figured reliefs carved on the façades, these churches mark one of the high points of Medieval architecture. The Catholicos Nerses III (641–660), surnamed the Builder because of his numerous foundations, built a palace next to the remarkable church of Zvart'nots', and also houses for the people whom he invited to live there, granting to them the privileges enjoyed by the city dwellers.

This was also a period of intellectual activity. The group of translators designated as the 'Philhellene school', which established close contacts with Byzantium, was greatly attracted by philosophical and scientific studies, and, through their translations, they introduced into Armenia the writings of Aristotle and of his commentators, the works of the Neoplatonists Porphyrius and Olympiodorus, those of Philo Judaeus, and of the grammarian Dionysius Thrax. The schools established in Armenia, in particular those of the provinces of Shirak and Siunik', received a new impetus, and Armenian literature was enriched by original scientific treatises. Let us recall, by way of example, the mathematical, astronomical and chronological studies of the 7th-century author Ananias of Shirak, and the 'Geography' erroneously ascribed to Moses of Khoren. Composed between the year: 591 and 610, as has recently been proved by S. Eremyan, the Geography originally comprised a set of fifteen maps, being thus one of the earliest Medieval attempts at cartography. The text itself with its varied information on the natural resources, the products of the different cities, the routes joining Armenia to the neighbouring countries, is a most valuable document for the economic as well as the political history of the time. In Georgia interest in philosophical and scientific works awakened much later; the literature of this period consists primarily of

f 5, 6

f 4, 7

ecclesiastical writings. But the arts flourished, and many important buildings remain of which the Church of the Holy Cross near Mtskheta is one of the most interesting examples.

f 8
p 72
(18)

In Byzantine Armenia the emperors pursued their policy of de-Armenization. Tiberius and Maurice transplanted large sections of the population and settled them in Cyprus and Thrace, and the religious question became a source of constant conflict. The Armenians had rejected the decisions of the Council of Chalcedon and proclaimed their fidelity to the profession of faith promulgated at the Council of Ephesus; the emperors used therefore every means to bring them into the fold of the Greek Church. During the period of anarchy following the murder of the Emperor Maurice, the Persians had recovered the major part of Byzantine Armenia and they held these provinces until the victorious campaigns of Heraclius brought them once again under Byzantine obedience.

The Coming of the Arabs

The religious policy of Heraclius had widened the rift between the Armenian partisans and opponents of collaboration with Byzantium; moreover the conflict between Byzantium and Iran had weakened both countries and paved the way for the advances of the Arabs. With startling rapidity their armies had occupied Syria, Palestine and Mesopotamia, and overthrown the Sasanian kingdom. While their main forces were engaged in the conquest of North Africa, the Arabs made only destructive raids into Transcaucasia. They invaded Armenia in 640, 642/3 and in 650, meeting with strong resistance on the last two occasions. In 645 the Georgians had been obliged to acknowledge their suzerainty and agree to pay tribute; in 652 the Armenian general Theodore Rshtuni concluded a treaty with the Caliph, also recognizing his suzerainty over Armenia.

The Arabs gave the name Arminiya to the vast area which included Armenia, Georgia and Albania and thus extended to the Caspian Sea. In Georgia the Caliph's representative resided in Tiflis, while in Armenia Dvin was the seat of the Arab governor, as it had been that of the Persian *marzpan*. The principal functions of the governor were the collection of the taxes, and the protection of the country, but his army was stationed in Azerbeijan. The civic administration was in the hands of the *nakharars* who had retained their feudal prerogatives; their suzerain was now the Caliph to whom they were bound to bring armed assistance in time of war.

The occupation of Armenia and Georgia by the Arabs was not readily accepted by the pro-Byzantine elements in both countries nor by the Empire itself. Several expeditions were sent by Byzantium, and under Justinian II Byzantium reclaimed the suzerainty of Armenia, Iberia and Albania, but these successes were not durable and by the end of the 7th century the Arabs were again in full control. The wars and the cruel repressions which followed each conquest, or uprising—as in 705 when the leading *nakharars*, their families and followers, 12,000 persons in all, were assembled by ruse in a church and burnt—had ruined and decimated the country. The Syrian historian Dionysius of Tell Mahre who had passed through Armenia in 716/7 states that the entire area, once remarkable for the number of its inhabitants, the abundance of the vineyards, cereals and magnificent trees, was now devastated and deserted.

The situation became much worse when the Abbasid dynasty replaced the Umayyad (750). Many of the privileges which the *nakharars* had retained were curtailed; they, as well as the clergy, were subjected to heavy taxes, and the oppressive fiscal policy reduced the population to extreme poverty.

In 771 (or 774?) the *nakharars*, headed by the Mamikonians, rose in revolt, but they had been able to muster only a small army of 5,000 men and after initial successes they were defeated in the plain of Bagrevand by the overwhelming forces of the Arabs, numbering 30,000 men. After this disaster, which had deprived Armenia of the leading members of most of the feudal families, the Arabs tightened their hold even more; they plundered the churches and monasteries and persecuted the Christians. Two of the Artsruni princes, Hamazasp and Sahak, were seized by the governor Khuzaima ibn Khazim and put to death because they would not abjure their faith; by order of the same governor the Iberian prince was beheaded.

Those who could flee sought refuge in the western borderlands or in the Byzantine territories; thus in 791 Shapuh Amatuni left with 12,000 men, barely escaping the Arab pursuers. The abandoned estates were seized and partly populated by Muslim immigrants; a number of Arab emirates were thus founded in Armenia, of which that of Mantzikert was one of the most important. Throughout this period war with Byzantium continued intermittently; the Khazar tribes also made repeated raids, capturing Tiflis in 799/800.

Two Centuries of Eclipse

Invasions, persecutions and excessive taxation had devastated and impoverished the country, while the wars between Byzantium and the Arabs had virtually closed the trade routes which passing through Armenia led to Asia Minor and the Black Sea. Cities such as Dvin, Theodosiopolis, Nakhitchevan and Ardjesh had owed their prosperity to this transit trade which no longer existed; they were now primarily military outposts or administrative centres and their inhabitants were deprived of their chief source of livelihood. The general impoverishment, together with the religious intolerance of the Abbasids, can be judged from the fact that for almost two centuries no churches or monasteries were erected, whereas the period which immediately preceded the Arab conquest and continued during the earlier part of Umayyad rule had been one of intense artistic activity. Intellectual life as well suffered an eclipse, but not as much as the artistic life, for the monasteries, though often molested, still offered havens where studies could be pursued.

Internal dissensions, the separatist tendencies of the Arab and Persian emirs, the increasing importance in the affairs acquired by the Turkish elements had greatly affected the power of the caliphate in the course of the 9th century. The fortunes of war also changed, for Byzantium now took the offensive, and although after the great victory under Michael III (863) the imperial armies suffered some reverses, they did not lose their momentum and gradually recaptured large sections of the territories that had once belonged to Byzantium. The Armenians were not long in taking advantage of the altered circumstances. The Mamikonians, who had played a prominent role in the national history, had been dispossessed of the greater part of their domains by the end of the 8th century; many members of this family had gone to Byzantium where they occupied high posts. Two other ancient families were now in the ascendancy, the Bagratunis and the Artsrunis. The latter were established in the province of Vaspura-

kan in the south-eastern part of Armenia and their possessions extended to the province of Ayrarat in the north and to the Lake of Urmia in the east. The domains of the Bagratunis were more scattered. One branch, which had not taken part in the revolts of the 8th century, remained in the province of Taron; the elder branch sought refuge in the mountain strongholds of the northwest, close to the Byzantine territories, while a younger son Vasak passed to Iberia. Vasak's son, Adarnase I founded the principality of the Iberian Bagratunis which enjoyed Byzantine protection; the dignity of Curopalate was conferred upon him, and later his son was recognized by the Arabs as Prince of Iberia.

The rise to power of the elder line of the Bagratunis began in 806. The caliphate needed local support against the Arab emirs of Armenia who were striving to become independent; to entrust this task to the Artsrunis, the most powerful of the feudal families at the time, would have been contrary to the Arab policy and their choice fell on the Bagratunis. Harun ar-Rashid conferred on Ashot the title of Prince of Armenia; by this show of favour he also hoped to prevent Byzantine influence from penetrating into the territories held by Ashot as it had in the princedom of the Iberian Bagratunis. Ashot Bagratuni, an able general and a wise politician, fully exploited the situation. By suppressing the revolts of the emirs and by bringing his support to al-Ma'mun in the war of succession after the death of Harun-al-Rashid he served the interests of the caliphate, but he also saw to the interests of his own house and enlarged his domains, partly by conquest, partly through purchases thanks to the proceeds of his silver mines. This could not please the caliphate. To prevent further aggrandisement and consequently concentration of power in a single hand, his son Smbat was appointed *Sparapet* or General-in-Chief after his father's death in 826, while the title of Prince of Armenia was conferred on Bagarat Bagratuni of Taron. No further measures were taken so long as the Armenian forces were needed against the Byzantines or the rebel emirs, but when al-Mutawakkil ascended the throne (847) he decided to take energetic action against the growing independence of the Armenians. After two expeditions, the first of which was repulsed while the second made prisoner Bagarat of Taron, a large army entered Armenia, led by the Turkish Emir Boga (852). Passing from the southern into the northern provinces the armies laid waste everywhere, massacring the population, sending their leaders as prisoners to Samarra. They next marched into Albania and Georgia where their advance was finally stopped by Bagrat, around whom had rallied all the Bagratuni leaders who had not been seized by Boga, and whose resistance was helped by Byzantine contingents (855).

'Prince of Princes' and 'King of Kings'

No drastic changes seem to have been introduced into the actual organization of the country after the expedition which had been so disastrous; after some years the Caliph conferred on Ashot Bagratuni, the son of the General-in-Chief Smbat, the title of 'Prince of princes of Armenia, Georgia and the lands of the Caucasus', which carried with it the office of general-in-chief and the right to levy taxes. By judicial alliances, through marriages with members of the powerful Artsruni family and the feudal lords of the eastern province of Siunik', Ashot forestalled marked opposition on their part; he had the support of the Catholicos who resided on his domains, and this support was important, for the moral authority of the Church was great. Ashot was moreover ably seconded by his brother in his struggle against the local emirs and the recalcitrant members of the aristocracy. He allied himself with the Iberian Prince Bagrat and together they defeated Bagrat's brother Guaram and divided his estates. The happy result of these efforts, and of his caution in keeping aloof of the struggle between Byzantium and the Caliphate, was his election as King by the Catholicos and the assembly of the *nakharars* (885/6). This election was confirmed by the Caliph, who sent Ashot a crown, but he still considered himself as the suzerain of the Armenians who continued to pay tribute. Shortly afterwards Basil I also recognized Ashot's elevation and sent him a crown. Thus the monarchy was restored after a lapse of more than four centuries and the event was greeted with a joy

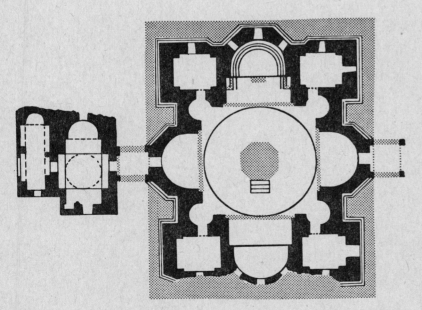

Plan of the church of the Holy Cross, near Mtskheta. Roughly contemporary with Zvart'nots' (it was built between 619 and 639) it shows another variant of the central-plan, an apsed square with miniature apses in the diagonals and then four square chapels at the corners, producing an interior of great spacial complexity. (8)

of which the echo resounds in the works of the contemporary and later historians. Ashot spent the last years of his life in consolidating his rule; he undertook a journey to Constantinople to the court of Leo the Wise and died on his return journey (890).

Smbat (890–914), lacked the wisdom and ability of his father; he was unable to impose his authority on the Armenian nobility or to maintain peace with the Arabs. The major internal crisis of his reign was provoked by Gagik Artsruni who allied himself with Yusuf, the Emir of Azerbeijan, and through his intermediary received a royal crown from the Caliph (908). By withdrawing their support from the Bagratunis and conferring it on their rivals, the Artsrunis, the Muslims were following their usual tactics of weakening the stronger party. But the way had been opened to them, this time, by the ambition of Gagik who, not content with his initial success, took up arms against Smbat and joined Yusuf when the latter invaded the province of Siunik'. After a long resistance Smbat was forced to cede; he was tortured and put to death (914), and Yusuf sent the king's body to Dvin to be nailed on a cross so as to strike terror in the hearts of all the inhabitants. There followed a period of cruel religious persecutions but the resistance also continued. The *nakharars* rallied around Smbat's son, Ashot II, and carried on a guerilla war; they were assisted by their Iberian and Albanian allies and the Iberian King Adarnase placed the crown on the head of Ashot, just as he himself had received it in 898 from the hands of Ashot's father. Ashot undertook a voyage to Constantinople where he was received with great honours by the Emperors, and he returned to Armenia laden with presents and the promise of Byzantine assistance. Faced with this rapprochement and the increasing successes of the national resistance, the Caliph was obliged to accept the *fait accompli* and named Ashot 'King of Kings', sending him a royal crown. Peace was also restored between Ashot and Gagik who, realizing his mistake, had withdrawn from his alliance with Yusuf, and agreed to bear only the title of King of Vaspurakan. Ashot took energetic measures against the feudal lords and the foreign invaders and succeeded in bringing peace to his war-torn country.

In the years that followed, the Abbasid caliphs, threatened by the rapid advances of the Byzantine armies, were no longer in a position to interfere seriously in Armenian affairs; the Arab emirs of Armenia had recognized the King's suzerainty, and the invasions by more powerful dynasties established in neighbouring territories, in particular that of the Hamdanids who for a while imposed tribute, had no lasting effects. Discontent among the population resulted in local uprisings during the early 10th century, particularly in the provinces of Ayrarat and Siunik', and for a long time the country was disturbed by the spread of the dissident sect of the T'ondrakians, severely and often ruthlessly suppressed by the rulers and the clergy. But the 10th and the early 11th centuries were, on the whole, a peaceful era, and as we shall see, one of great prosperity, during which buildings of importance were set up and fine art produced.

Among the various factors which eventually led to the destruction of the Bagratuni rule, one of the most important was the fragmentation of the territory through the creation of minor kingdoms and principalities. Though founded with the reluctant consent of the 'King of Kings' whom they recognized as their suzerain, the very existence of these separate entities weakened the central authority and prevented strong, unified action against the enemy.

The province of Taron, in the south-west, held by the minor branch of the Bagratunis, had remained outside the royal domain; these princes had maintained friendly relations with Byzantium and had received the title of curopalate and later that of patrice. In 968, pressed by circumstances, the two brothers Gregory and Bagrat (Pankratios) ceded their principality to the Empire. This was the first of the series of annexations thanks to which Byzantium was to gain possession of Armenia, a policy which in the end had results equally disastrous to both, for they facilitated the Seljuk conquest of Armenia and thereby opened the path to the advance of the Turkish armies into Asia Minor.

Within the royal domain the first division occurred in 963, when Mushegh, who had been appointed governor of Kars by

Coin of David the Curopalate (literally 'Guardian of the Palace'). David (983–1001) was a Georgian prince who won an independent principality for himself in Iberia with the support of Byzantium. His alliance with Smbat strengthened the Bagratuni dynasty. (9)

King Gagik I (989–1020) from a statue on his church of St Gregory at Ani. Gagik—not to be confused with a previous King Gagik of Vaspurakan—succeeded his brother Smbat II at Ani. During his reign both the Bagratuni dynasty and the kingdom of Armenia reached the peak of their prosperity and influence. (10)

his brother Ashot III, proclaimed himself King. His example was followed in 970 by Smbat of Siunik' who raised his princedom to the rank of a kingdom, and in 982 by the brother of King Smbat II, Prince Gurgen. The small kingdom founded by the latter in the district of Tashir, north of Lake Sevan, with the capital city of Lori, was to last longer than any of the others, surviving until the middle of the 13th century. During the reign of Smbat II, despite some defections, such as that of the King of Kars who, for a while, took up arms against his suzerain, the royal authority was maintained. The alliance with David the Curopalate of Iberia strengthened Smbat's position, and at the *f 9* same time it brought to the former, and to Bagrat III King of Iberia, the military assistance of the Armenians against the King of Abasgia. The long reign of Gagik I (989–1020) marked the *f 10* apogee of the Bagratuni monarchy; his marriage with Katramide, the daughter of the Prince of Siunik', helped to heal the rift between the Catholicos and the metropolitans of Siunik'. Gagik was also in very friendly relations with his northern neighbour, Bagrat III, in whose person the kingdoms of Iberia and Abasgia had been united.

Armenia's Golden Age

The reign of Gagik I also marked the apogee of the material prosperity and cultural revival of Armenia. The transit trade, interrupted during the first century of Abbasid rule, was revived with the accession to power of the Bagratunis. Except for brief periods, Armenia was no longer the principal battlefield of the struggle between the Empire and the caliphate; consequently the caravan routes were not closed to traffic; moreover the Byzantines and Arabs needed a neutral ground where they could exchange their products, even when they were at war with one another, and Armenia was geographically well situated for such transactions. New cities came into existence along these routes, or rather their importance gradually increased. Such was the city of Kars which was in the province of Vanand on the junction of two important routes: one, led to Trebizond (Trapezus), the other, turning northward, passed by the important Georgian city of Ardanuch and reached the eastern shores of the Black Sea. Kars also communicated with Tiflis and other cities of Georgia. King Abas suppressed the robberies which had plagued the countryside so that, writes the historian Asoghik of Taron, one could go around safely by night as if it were daytime, and walk in deserted areas as if one were in a palace. During the reign of Abas and his son Gagik, the capital of the small kingdom was an important centre of learning, the cathedral erected by Abas, and the p 68 (9) sumptuous Gospel illustrated for Gagik testify to the high skill of the artists of Kars.

Another vital centre was Artsn, near Theodosiopolis. It too owed its prosperity entirely to its trade; it was an open city, and when the fortifications of Theodosiopolis were dismantled the population was transferred to Artsn. Aristakes of Laztivert speaks of it in lyrical terms, comparing the city to a young bride who by her beauty and her brilliant adornments arouses the envy of everyone. He praises the honesty and generosity of its merchants, who were great builders of churches and of houses for the clergy, and who were also charitable towards the poor. According to the Byzantine historian Michael Attaliates, all that Persia, India and the rest of Asia produced was brought there.

f 11 Most important of all, however, was the city of Ani, situated on a high plateau some 25 miles east of Kars. During the early Middle Ages it had been the stronghold of the Kamsarakan family; the Bagratunis had acquired it in 826, but it was only during the reign of Ashot III (953–977) that it became the capital of the kingdom. The deep gorge of the Arpa-Tchai which encircles the city on the east and south east, and the valley of the Aladja-Tchai, which borders it on the west, already offered a

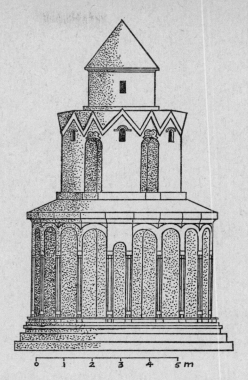

The small Shepherd's Chapel at Ani (c. 1000) is one of the most original of Armenian designs. It is raised on a circular platform, and the lowest storey of the exterior is divided into eighteen niches, triangular in plan—twelve large and six small—with round arches over them. A similar alternation, this time of large and small gables, occurs in the hexagonal upper storey, the smaller ones over niches, the larger over flat wall surfaces each containing a window. The top storey is again circular. Inside, six arches on double columns supported a stone vault from which rose the hexagon, which in its turn supported the drum of the dome. (12)

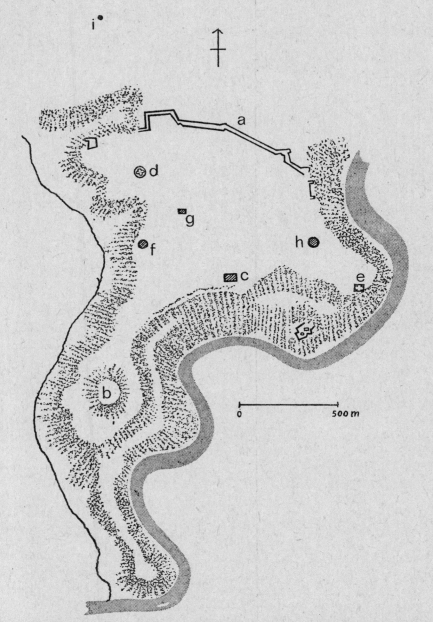

Ani, 'the city of a thousand and one churches', became the capital of Armenia during the reign of Ashot III (953–977). It was a place of great natural strength, defended on two sides by rivers and high cliffs and on the third by a double line of fortifications (a). Today it is deserted, with only the ruins of some of its buildings to recall its past glory. The Citadel (b) occupied the highest point, and there are still substantial remains of the Cathedral (c), and the churches of St Gregory of Gagik (d), St Gregory of Tigran Honents' (e), St Gregory Apughamrents' (f), the Holy Apostles (g) and the Holy Saviour (h). The Shepherd's Chapel (i) lies outside the walls to the north. (11)

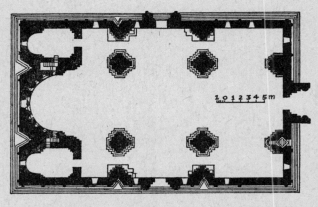

Ani Cathedral, designed by the most famous Armenian architect, Trdat (see p. 66, pl. 4). The plan is simple, but again based on symmetrical spaces—a cross inscribed in a rectangle, with a dome over the crossing. (13)

natural protection, but Ashot also fortified it. The population had rapidly increased, and in 989 Smbat II built further to the north a double line of walls fronted by a moat, which almost trebled the area of the city, and of which the imposing ruins still stand. Bridges across the Arpa-Tchai enabled the caravans coming from Iran to pass directly through Ani. Numerous buildings were erected within the walls and also beyond them; they comprised a royal residence, private houses, baths, caravanserais for the merchants and, especially, so many churches, that with poetic exaggeration the Armenian historians called Ani the city of a thousand and one churches, a term repeated by the Franciscan monk William of Rubruck who visited the city in 1255. Several of these churches are still preserved, though in a ruined condition. They bear witness to the remarkable artistic activity of the period, to the great skill of the architects and also of the sculptors who carved the delicate ornaments around the doors and windows, and on the blind arcades of the façades. In the Cathedral, the work of the famed architect Trdat (who was invited to Constan-

p 69 (12)

f 13

p 66 (4)

tinople to rebuild the fallen dome of Hagia Sophia), and in the
Shepherd's Chapel outside the walls, new modes of construction
presaged in an astonishing manner the forms that were to be
later developed in Gothic architecture in the West.

The splendours of the small kingdom of Vaspurakan were
comparable to those of the court of the Bagratunis. The historian
Thomas Artsruni and his continuator relate and often describe
in some detail the constructions of King Gagik: works of public
utility, like the underground stone conduits which brought the
water from the summit of Mount Varag; the numerous churches;
the palace and pavilion built at Vostan on the south shore of
Lake Van, and they dwell especially on the city he founded on
the island of Aght'amar. The palace with its throne room decorated with secular scenes which glittered, and were probably
executed in mosaics, the houses, the terraced gardens, the harbour
have all disappeared, only the Church of the Holy Cross still
stands, its façades entirely covered with figured representations,
animals and floral ornaments, a unique example of the Christian
art of this period.

Wealth, Industry and Trade

To these and other churches, as well as to the monasteries they
founded, the kings, the Catholicos and nobles donated gold and
silver vessels, reliquaries adorned with precious stones, bronze
and copper lamps, silk and embroidered vestments and hangings.
The excavations of Ani brought to light a large polycandilion,
decorated with animals in open-work technique, and the silk
dress of a child delicately embroidered with gold threads. A few
fragments of silks woven with animal and geometric designs
have also been found in the bindings of old manuscripts. They
serve to indicate that the textile industry was greatly developed
in Armenia; indeed, these manufactured goods constituted one
of the chief exports of the country and also formed part of the
tribute paid to the caliphs. For instance, among the revenues of
the reign of al-Ma'mun, Ibn Khaldun lists twenty large carpets in
relief from Armenia.

The Arab historians and geographers give valuable information
about the different kinds of carpets and textiles made there.
According to Djahiz the best and most expensive draperies were
the crimson Armenian goat-hair cloths with a double woof which
he rates higher than the striped silks and brocades. Among the
articles of merchandise exported 'to every country and province'
Ibn Hawkal mentions the Armenian trouser-bands made at Salmas,
in the province of Vaspurakan, which 'had no equal in the world',
the fabrics made at Dvin, the Armenian cushions and carpets
with a raised pattern, and the brocades. Both he and Istakhri
especially praise the wools and silks dyed a red tint with the
kirmiz, a worm found on a plant growing on the slopes of
Mount Ararat. Artashat, near Dvin, was the principal place
where these dyes were prepared and Baladhuri calls it *karya
al-kirmiz*, the kirmiz-village. The Armenian historians also speak
of the magnificent robes worn by the clergy and the nobility, or
used for presents. Thus the Catholicos historian Hohannes relates
that when he was sent by King Smbat to appease the Emir
Yusuf, he took with him from the royal treasury robes in gold
brocade and cushions embroidered in many colours by the women
of Armenia.

Besides these manufactured goods other exports constituted
important sources of income. Armenian furs were highly valued,
as well as all kinds of leather goods; we learn from Constantine
Porphyrogenitus that the Byzantine emperors used to take with
them on their campaigns leather bathtubs 'prepared in the Armenian fashion'. Thanks to a good system of irrigation, the country
was rich in all kinds of products, especially cereals, and wheat
was exported to Baghdad. In the forests which still covered the
slopes of Mount Ararat and other mountains, grew very large
trees which were sold to the neighbouring countries, while the
rivers and lakes had an abundance of fish which were also
exported. The Armenian horses, mules and donkeys were especially prized for their strength. Finally a variety of minerals was
extracted from the soil for the use of the local industries and for
export: there were silver and gold mines in the valley of the
Chorokh; the region of Lake Van was rich in borax and arsenic;

f 12

p 69
(11)
p 65 (1)
p 67 (5)
f 14

p 67 (3)

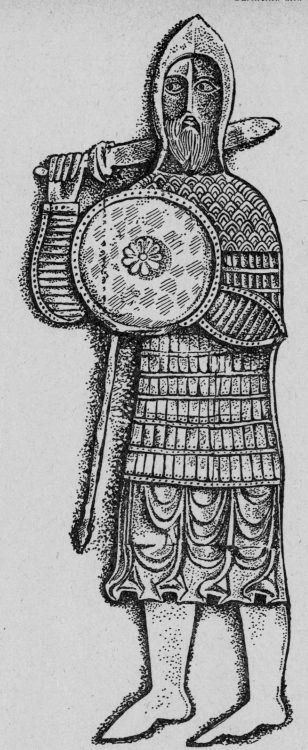

*An Armenian warrior of the early 10th century. This relief, from the
exterior of Gagik's church at Aght'amar, in fact represents Goliath, but
the arms and armour are probably close to contemporary equipment. (14)*

there were salt mines in different parts of the country; the
important copper deposits had been exploited ever since the time
of the Urartian kingdom, and Armenia exported the raw material
as well as arms and other objects made of copper and bronze.

As can be seen from this rapid survey, the proceeds from the
transit trade formed only part of the revenues, the prosperity of
the country was also due to the exploitation of the natural
resources and to the export of manufactured goods. The extensive
building programme undertaken by the rulers of the different
principalities and by the higher clergy, as well as the demands
for luxury goods by the aristocracy and by the new class of
wealthy merchants in the large cities encouraged the development
of the arts and crafts. Separate corporations began to be formed,
but unfortunately we have very little information about their
organization. The artisans of the cities were principally laymen,
some of whom rose to great prominence. The absence of any title
or addition of the word cleric or monk leads one to suppose that
the architect Trdat of Ani, and Manuel, the 'man full of wisdom'
who built the Church of Aght'amar belonged to the laity.

'Skilled Painters and Incomparable Scribes'

In the course of the 9th and 10th centuries the monasteries had acquired great wealth; the records of the donations made by the princes include not only farms and tracts of land, but also large sums of money. Some crafts were only practised in these centres, chief among them being the work of the illuminators, for the scribe himself was sometimes the painter. The illustrated manuscripts of the period, such as the Gospel which Queen Mlk'e offered to the monastery of Varag in the province of Vaspurakan, or the Etchmiadzin Gospel written in the province of Siunik' in 989, or again the Gospel of King Gagik of Kars show the great skill of the painters both in figural representations and the rich ornamental designs.

The schools established in these monasteries contributed greatly to the cultural revival. The schools of Siunik' had a long tradition. In the 5th and 6th centuries their scholars had actively participated in the translation of Greek writings, and had produced original works as well. Cultural contacts with Byzantium were maintained in the 8th century; Stephen, Bishop of Siunik', had visited Constantinople, he had translated the writings of Dionysius the Areopagite, several works of Gregory of Nazianzus, and after his return to Armenia he had continued to correspond with the Patriarch Germanos. In the 9th and 10th centuries the monastery of Tat'ev became an important centre of learning; we are told that close to five hundred priests and monks lived there, scholars and philosophers, 'skilled painters and incomparable scribes'.

Within the limits of the kingdom of Lori were the famed monasteries of Sanahin and Haghbat, both founded in the 10th century, large complexes of buildings comprising several churches. The eastern façade of the Church of the Saviour at Sanahin, erected by King Ashot III and Queen Khosrovanush, is decorated with the portraits, in high relief, of their two sons holding the model of the church: Gurgen, who was later to proclaim himself King of Lori, and Smbat, the successor of Ashot at Ani. In the early 11th century, Dioscoros, the learned Abbot of Sanahin, built a separate library and gathered many scholars around him. At Haghbat, the portraits of the two brothers Gurgen and Smbat again adorn the eastern façade of the principal church. The collection of manuscripts housed in the imposing building of the Library was considered as one of the largest in Armenia. It was at Haghbat that Hovhannes Sarkavag, the reformer of the Armenian calendar, had received his training. He later went to Ani and founded a school in which he emphasized the study of mathematics and philosophy, especially of the commentaries of Aristotle. The monastery of Narek near Lake Van was reputed

Two sons of Ashot III, Gurgen and Smbat, together dedicate a model of their church at Haghbat. After Ashot's death Gurgen ruled the province of Lori and Smbat succeeded his father at Ani. The church, another centrally planned structure, is possibly also the work of Trdat. (16)

for its musicians; the great mystic poet of the 10th century, Gregory of Narek, was one of its shining lights.

The principal exponent of classical studies was Prince Gregory Bahlavuni, surnamed Magistros, one of the few lay authors of this period. Political intrigues had forced him to retire for a while to his domains in the province of Taron and he founded there a school, personally directing the work of a small, select group of men. In 1044 Gregory had gone to Constantinople; Constantine Monomachus conferred on him the title of magistros; later he was entrusted with the government of the provinces of Vaspurakan and Taron, annexed by Byzantium, and given the title of Duke of Mesopotamia. Gregory was a man of vast erudition, a Greek and Syriac scholar, equally familiar with pagan and Christian thought. References to Greek mythology, and to ancient writers abound in his correspondence. Unlike many of his contemporaries whose philosophical studies were centred on Aristotle, Gregory was a great admirer of Plato and had translated two of his dialogues, the *Timaeus* and the *Phaedo*. He had also begun to translate Euclid's geometry. His own writings include a number of versified works and detailed commentaries on grammar.

It was natural that this period of national independence should have inspired the contemporaries to relate the events they had witnessed and the 10th and early 11th centuries produced a number of historians. Several of them have already been mentioned in passing: the most important were Thomas Artsruni who deals primarily with the history of the province of Vaspurakan; Stephen Asoghik of Taron, more concerned with that of the Bagratuni rulers; Aristakes of Laztivert who gives valuable information on the years immediately preceding the Seljuk conquest and on the conquest itself; Moses of Kaghankatuyk', our main source for the history of the Albanians. Most important of all is the history written by the learned Catholicos Hohannes who played an active part in the affairs of the realm.

This was also a period of economic prosperity in Georgia. Tiflis was an Arab enclave, but Ardanuch in Tao-Klardjetia was the active trading centre of Iberia. 'The city of Ardanoutzin', wrote Constantine Porphyrogenitus, 'is very strongly defended, and has moreover a considerable suburban area like a provincial city, and the commerce of Trapezus and of Iberia and of Abasgia and from the whole country of Armenia and Syria comes to it, and it has an enormous customs revenue from this commerce.

A detail from the stele of Usaneti, Georgia, carved between 791 to 802. John the Baptist and an Angel stand on either side of Christ, while above his head the Holy Ghost descends in the form of a dove. (15)

The country of the city of Ardanoutzin, the "Arzyn", is both extensive and fertile, and it is a key to Iberia and Abasgia and the land of the Mischians.' (*De administrando imperio*, chap. 46). The monasteries founded in this area by St Gregory of Khandzt'a, especially his own monastery and those of Shatberd and Tbet', played a vital role in the cultural life of the country. Others were established by the rulers, for instance the Monastery of the Virgin at Khakhuli in Meskhia, by the Curopalate David, and the monastery of Gelati near Kutais by Bagrat III.

While Armenia was weakened by the division of the territory into a number of small kingdoms, Georgia acquired new strength through her national unification. In 978 the King of Abasgia, Theodosius III, was deposed and his nephew Bagrat, the son of the Iberian King Gurgen, was appointed in his place. At the death of Gurgen (1008) Bagrat III fell heir to both thrones and eastern and western Georgia were united for the first time. Thus, despite the passing successes of the Byzantine armies and the destructive raids of Alp Arslan, Georgia was able to maintain her independence and the period which lasted to the 13th century was to be the most brilliant era of her history.

The Seljuk Conquest: an Era Ends

In Armenia Bagratuni rule suffered a rapid decline after the death of Gagik I (1020); the rivalry of his two sons resulted in a further partition of the royal domain. These unfortunate events occurred at a time when the security, and the very existence of the country, were seriously threatened, for on the west Byzantium was actively engaged in extending her borders, while on the east the raids of the Seljuk Turks had increased in intensity. Taron had been annexed in 968, as mentioned above. In the year 1000 Basil II had taken over the principality of David of Taik' whose domains included the province of Apahunik', with the capital city of Mantzikert, so that Byzantine rule now extended to the borders of the province of Vaspurakan. In 1020 Senek'erim of Vaspurakan, hard pressed by the Seljuk forces, also ceded his kingdom to Basil II, receiving in exchange the city of Sebastia in Cappadocia and the neighbouring area as far as the Euphrates. According to the continuator of Thomas Artsruni, 14,000 persons, without counting the women and children, followed the King, and although the number may be exaggerated, it is nevertheless a fact that many of the leaders and a large number of the population left the country. The turn of Ani was to come next. Hohannes-Smbat had supported the King of Iberia in his unsuccessful struggle against Basil II; fearing reprisals, and probably persuaded by the pro-Byzantine elements, he had named Byzantium as heir to his kingdom. But at the death of the King (1041) the Armenians refused to recognize the claims of the Empire; Gagik, the nephew of Hohannes-Smbat, was crowned, a Byzantine expeditionary force was repulsed, and the troubled conditions in Constantinople provided a short period of respite. In 1045 Gagik was invited to Constantinople with false promises; during his absence Ani was taken by the imperial armies and the kingdom annexed to the Empire.

These territories were not destined to remain long in Byzantine hands. 'Just as the subjugation of Bulgaria had removed the buffer state between the Empire and the nomads of the north, so the annexation of Armenia under Constantine IX had facilitated the Seljuk attack. The internal weakness of the Empire and the collapse of its system of defence meant that the way was open into the heart of the vital Byzantine provinces. Led by Alp Arslan, the second Seljuk Sultan, the Turks broke into Armenia and took possession of Ani (1065), laid waste Cilicia, forced their way into Asia Minor and stormed Caesarea (1067). The policy of the Byzantine rulers of the day thus stood condemned.' (G. Ostrogorsky). After the Byzantine disaster at Mantzikert (1071) Seljuk rule was firmly established in Armenia; the kingdom of Kars, annexed shortly before by Byzantium, was conquered and only the two small kingdoms of Siunik' and Tashir-Lori retained a semblance of independence; Siunik' until 1170, Tashir-Lori until the middle of the 13th century.

V THE HEIR OF ROME

Byzantium from Justinian to Theophilus

CYRIL MANGO

Chief cities and provinces of the Eastern Mediterranean during the early Byzantine period

'The City of Constantine',

Constantinople, was to be the New Rome. It was dedicated on 11th May, 330, and the ceremony marked—was intended to mark—a new era, though like all such symbolic 'turning points', its immediate effects were not dramatic. The Roman world continued to be administered as before, on the system inaugurated by Diocletian, but by moving the government to the threshold of Asia Constantine had both altered its character and ensured its survival, although neither could have been easy for men to realize at the time. After Theodosius (379–395) the whole Empire was never ruled by one man. As the West succumbed to the barbarian attacks, the new capital inevitably acquired a quality that made it different from the old, no matter how deeply rooted in precedent its citizens believed themselves to be. Constantinople was Greek and Eastern, and therefore open to a flood of cultural, intellectual and artistic influences which Rome could select and assimilate as she chose; it was Christian and therefore the centre of theological controversy, a wholly 'modern' phenomenon; it was exposed to attack, and therefore aware of itself as the guardian both of Christianity and of classical civilization itself.

The task of defence rested to a dangerous degree on troops who were themselves non-Roman—Goths and Alans from the Balkans, Isaurians from Asia Minor. For a time these alien elements threatened to take over complete control, but the end of the 5th century marked a return to more balanced and responsible government under Anastasius. It was the beginning of Constantinople's first Golden Age.

The spirit of renewed confidence is caught in the ivory relief shown opposite, although the identity of the emperor is still a matter of dispute. Anastasius is the most likely. He is known to have received an embassy from India in 496, an occasion which the two figures on the right of the lower panel seem to commemorate. They bring ivory tusks and wild beasts. The emperor himself rides forward in triumph, Victory hovering beside him and an Asiatic prisoner crouching behind his spear; at his horse's feet sits Earth holding fruit. The two panels at the sides showed warriors presenting statuettes of Victory (one is missing). At the top a youthful Christ gazes out between two more winged Victories. (1)

The Emperor was nominally the apex of the state, as well as being the vicegerent of Christ on Earth, 'the Thirteenth Apostle'. Yet his real power was likely to be as varied and uncertain as the path by which he came to it. Leo I (left) was the puppet of his Alan minister, Aspar. The next Emperor, Zeno, was Leo's son-in-law; the next, Anastasius (pl. 1), the choice of the widowed Empress Ariadne. Justin, who succeeded him, owed his elevation to the army, but he took over a financially sound empire, and under his nephew, Justinian (right), Italy, Spain and North Africa were recovered. But the state's resources were strained, and Justin II (left) found it impossible to maintain the same programme. He died insane, to be followed by Tiberius II and then by Maurice (right), a fine soldier and administrator, but whose reign is a record of failure in the East, on the Danube and in Italy. In 602 his army revolted and put their own leader, the semi-barbarian Phocas (far right) on the throne. Maurice was brutally murdered. (2–6)

Heraclius (left), military governor of Africa, overthrew the hated Phocas and began to win back some of the ground that had been lost. He was menaced by enemies in the north and in the east, but in 622–28 gathered an army, invaded Persia and inflicted a crushing defeat on the Sasanians. His success was ironic, for a few years later the Arab conquests began, and by 641 when he died everything was lost again. The second half of this century is one of the darkest periods in Byzantine history. The dynasty of Heraclius tottered to its fall; its last member was Justinian II (below left) who led the state into anarchy and chaos. The Bulgarians were in the suburbs of Constantinople; the Arabs occupied the opposite shore. The question seemed to be not whether the city would fall, but only to whom. But now a new dominant personality emerged — Leo III (right), a soldier from Syria. He broke the Arab blockade and drove them back beyond the Anatolian plateau. He is remembered as the saviour of Constantinople, and also as the first Iconoclast Emperor. Carried to its extreme by his son Constantine V, Iconoclasm aroused fierce persecution and resistance. But the next Emperor, Leo IV, attempted conciliation and in 787 his widow, Irene (bottom right), re-established for a time the veneration of images. (7–10)

'To keep the pure Christian faith inviolate, and to defend the Catholic and Apostolic Church from any harm' was, said Justinian, the first duty of the sovereign. Yet theological controversy characterizes the history of Byzantium to an extent far surpassing any other nation or people. Patriarchs and emperors were made and unmade; riots, rebellions and wars provoked; men and women martyred, over questions which today excite only the most sedate scholarly disagreement. In part the causes were political; parties or peoples might become identified with a certain doctrine and cling to it as a symbol of their independence—for instance the Arianism of most of the northern peoples, or the Monophysitism of the eastern provinces. In part, however, this was genuine *odium theologicum*. Christian doctrine was still young. Some of its vital issues were still subjects of debate and their settlement was not to be achieved without passion.

That Christ was not equal in dignity and co-eternal with the Father, but only the first of his creatures (in technical terminology, that he was not 'consubstantial' with the Father) was the doctrine maintained by Arius, a presbyter of Alexandria. Hardly had Christianity won official toleration than it was faced with this disastrous threat to its unity. Although condemned as heretical at the Councils of Nicaea (325) and Constantinople (381) Arianism continued to flourish for the next two centuries, especially among the newly converted barbarians. This 9th-century painting (above) represents the patriarchs and priests gathered for the Council of Constantinople. It was here that the Creed in its present form was finally approved. The Gospel book open on the throne symbolizes Christ's presence.

From the same manuscript (the Sermons of St Gregory of Nazianzus) come two more vivid scenes of the strife caused by the Arian controversy (left). In the lower one Arians burn down a church belonging to the Orthodox, and in the upper a group of Orthodox, including a bishop, flee for their lives in a boat. (11, 12)

87

Into Constantinople

flowed the wealth and culture of both West and East, and its dual nature is apparent in almost everything that was made there. Its religion united Jewish Christianity with Hellenistic philosophy; its architecture combined the classical orders (Greek), the arch (Roman) and the dome (from the East), while in painting and mosaic the naturalism of the Roman Empire merged or ran side by side with the stiff, hieratic, spiritual style of Syria.

The Ascension (left) from the Rabbula Gospels, was painted in 586 at Zagba, in northern Mesopotamia. The manuscript, which is in Syriac, has five full-page illustrations, all predominantly eastern in style and iconography. The bright colours, formal poses and stylized gestures of this art were soon to become typically Byzantine. (13)

Fully-formed Byzantine art first emerged in the 6th century. The Rossano Codex is an early example of much of the iconography adopted by the Middle Ages. The scene of Pilate inviting the Jews to choose between Christ and Barabbas (above), for example, with its elimination of depth and expressive faces and gestures, was to be repeated in similar terms up to the 13th or 14th century. (15)

The antique world lives on in both the subject and style of this dedication page (left). The book is a treatise on herbal medicine by Dioscorides (1st century AD), and this copy of it was made on the orders of Princess Juliana Anicia. She is shown between two personified virtues, attended by other allegorical figures in the triangles around. The date is about 512. (14)

Iconoclasm—the ban on the representation of Christ or the Saints—caused a break in religious art of about a century (726–843). No illuminated Bibles or Lives of the Saints were produced during this time; icons and mosaics in churches were destroyed; and even figural painting in non-religious contexts seems to have diminished to a mere trickle. Indeed only one such manuscript has survived from this period—the Vatican copy of Ptolemy's *Astronomy*, made between 813 and 820. It clearly imitates an earlier model. Classical texts continued to be studied and copied throughout this time. Not only Helios in the centre, with his chariot and four white horses, but the other figures and signs of the Zodiac are unmistakably Hellenistic in inspiration. (16)

The ivory carver's art served both state and Church, giving to both the same hieratic dignity. The panel below, one half of a diptych, celebrates the Lampadius family. Though possibly made in Rome, the scene seems to represent the Hippodrome at Constantinople, with the Theodosian obelisk in the middle. (17)

Consuls, a legacy of the Roman republic, continued to be appointed every year, one in Rome and one in Constantinople, until 541. To mark the occasion, the consul would issue ivory diptychs as souvenirs for distribution to high officials. This one commemorates Anastasius, who held the office in Constantinople in 517. He is shown twice, with theatrical scenes below—on the left amazons and tragic actors, on the right a circus with the audience in the corners. (18)

The Archangel Michael stands with orb and staff, the bearer of divine authority. This relief, one of the finest works of the Byzantine carvers, was probably made in the capital during the 6th century. (19)

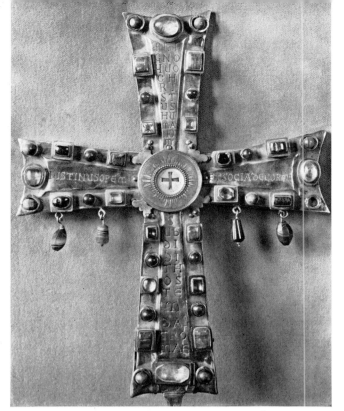

Christendom was as yet undivided, except between Orthodox and heretic. The Councils still spoke, in theory, for the whole Church, though already it had crystallized into two main groups—the Western church, under the Pope, and the Eastern which accepted the Emperor as the final authority. When Justinian reconquered Italy the popes were obliged to accept the same situation, but feelings ran high and there were ominous signs of schism. Justinian's successor, Justin II, seems to have attempted conciliation and presented this cross (right) to the Pope in about 575. It has been much restored. (20)

The ivory throne of Archbishop Maximian (of which five panels are shown below) is a witness to the complex history of the Church in the age of Justinian. Ravenna, reconquered from the Arian Ostrogoths, became the centre of the Eastern church in Italy, with Maximian as its Bishop. The panels of his throne are the work of various artists, probably from Alexandria or Constantinople. John the Baptist, in the centre (below), is flanked by the four Evangelists. On other parts of the throne are scenes from the life of Christ and the story of Joseph, a subject that was more popular in Egypt than elsewhere. (21)

The two streams of Byzantine culture had still not completely merged by the 7th century. The silver plate (far right) with a scene of David killing a bear might easily be mistaken for a Greek work of six centuries before; memories of Hercules and the ancient heroes lie behind it. The silver liturgical fan, on the other hand, looks eastward for its iconography. The edge is lobed, with a peacock's feather design, and on both sides are engraved eight-winged cherubim, with huge hands and staring eyes. The smaller circles are flaming wheels. (22, 23)

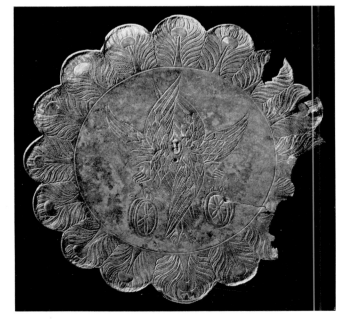

The brilliant art

of glass mosaic, which reached its peak in the 6th and 7th centuries, was the perfect medium for Byzantine Christianity. Walls and the concave ceilings of apses and domes were now covered with thousands of minute tesserae, each pressed into the plaster at slightly different angles so that the surface shimmered with light as the spectator moved. Rich, luminous and unfading, mosaic exactly fulfilled the requirements of the new style: intensity of feeling plus rigidity of composition. Most of the great works of this period were destroyed by the Iconoclasts, but a few have survived by accident or inaccessibility. The large Transfiguration (right) occupies the apse of the monastic church of St Catherine in Sinai. Dating probably from c. 560, it has only recently been cleaned and photographed. Christ Glorified rises in the centre, with Elias and Moses beside him. The Apostles John, Peter and James crouch in fear at his feet. Below left: St Demetrius with Bishop John, from the church of St Demetrius, Thessalonica. Below right: the Virgin and Child, from Kiti, in Cyprus. Both these mosaics are of the 7th century. (24, 25, 26)

In the Great Palace of Constantinople mosaic decoration continued to follow the less ambitious classical precedent. This is a floor-mosaic, with tesserae of coloured stone, though the blues and greens are of glass. It is different in content and in style from the wall mosaics in the churches. Four fragments are shown here: a man leading a camel, a bear attacking an antelope, a farmer milking a goat, and a 'barbarian' head surrounded by scrolls. (27–30)

Buildings of matching beauty

arose to meet the spirit of the new age. Byzantine architecture has been analysed and its elements traced to a variety of sources—the high brick vaults to the great *thermae* of pagan Rome, the colonnades and clerestory lighting to the Early Christian basilicas, the domes on pendentives to Sasanian and Armenian buildings. Yet the result is clear, organic and distinct. On the left are three important churches of Constantinople. Top: St John of Studius (463) looking east. The plan is basilican, but differs from the basilicas of the West by being much wider in proportion to its length. Centre: St Irene (532 and 564), a combination of basilican and central plan; the nave consists of two square domed bays. Bottom: SS. Sergius and Bacchus (527–536). Here the nave is octagonal, covered by a single dome and surrounded by an ambulatory. This church was extremely influential. It was the model for S. Vitale at Ravenna, which in turn was copied by Charlemagne at Aachen. None of these buildings is in its original state: the first is a ruin, the second an empty shell, the third a mosque. (31, 32, 33)

The living ritual of the Church gave meaning and purpose to the buildings. This small ivory relief shows a relic being brought in procession to one of the churches. Doors and windows are crowded; people are even clambering on the tiled roof of the church. (36)

The bleak exterior of a Byzantine church normally gives little hint of the splendour within; it merely reveals the mechanics whereby the interior effect has been achieved. This applies even to Hagia Sophia (left), whose essential structure consists of a shallow dome covering a square central space, supported on the north and south by massive brick buttresses and on the east and west by smaller semi-domes. The minarets and domed chambers in the foreground are Turkish. (34)

The south doors of Hagia Sophia still hang where they were placed in 839. They are of bronze with silver inlay and are made up of earlier panels with Greek-key and acanthus patterns complemented by panels of Byzantine manufacture. These doors are of especial interest because they belong to the Iconoclast period. (35)

'Whoever puts foot within the sacred fane' would live there for ever, and his eyes fill with tears of joy.' So wrote Paul 'the Silentiary' (a court official) in 563, about 30 years after Hagia Sophia had been finished. He goes on to give an exact description, in over 700 flowery hexameters. The reconstruction given here (right, fold-out) represents the church in c. 900 when most of its mosaic decoration had been restored after Iconoclasm. We are looking from the south west corner, diagonally across the central space; on the extreme right the south aisle leads away in the direction of the altar. Opposite is the north wall, with its two ranges of arches, supported on columns of green Thessalian marble. Above them, in the huge lunette of the arch, are mosaics of bishops and church Fathers, surmounted by two rows of windows. Another ring of windows pierces the base of the dome. Vast mosaics of cherubim fill the pendentives. To the east lies the chancel, flanked by two further open exedrae, again with

two levels of columns (purple below and green above). All the columns, according to Paul, had gilded capitals. Across the chancel stood an elaborate screen and projecting from it into the body of the church was a striking and (to modern eyes) unexpected feature—the *ambo*, a sort of pulpit from which prayers and lessons were read and which was used during coronation ceremonies. It was a substantial structure of marble, ascended by flights of steps at the east and west, and lavishly decorated with ivory and silver. A passage of green marble connected it to the chancel-screen, and passage, *ambo* and screen were adorned with images of Christ and the saints in silver, ivory reliefs and candle-sticks. Hundreds of other lamps, including large circular candela-bra suspended a few yards above the floor by chains from the dome, lit the church, so that at night, says Paul, 'verily you might say that you gazed at the bright constellation of the Heavenly Crown'. (38)

Fold out ▶

Justinian presents his church and Constantine the city he found-ed to the Virgin: a mosaic placed over the south door of Hagia Sophia probably towards the end of the 10th century. The model in Justinian's hands may be compared with the view in pl. 34. Note too the fine marble veneer and carved stucco frieze of the 6th century. (37)

For a complete impression of what a Byzantine interior of the ▶ 6th century was like one must go to Ravenna. Right: the chancel of S. Vitale, with all its mosaics well preserved—in the vault Christ with angels and saints, on the wall Justinian and his court, in the lunette Abraham and Sarah entertaining the angels and the sacri-fice of Isaac. (39)

A bare handful of icons

escaped the Iconoclast fury, and few from any major centre of painting. The three illustrated here owe their survival to the fact that they were preserved in relatively remote Egyptian monasteries. In the 6th and 7th centuries, however, such small wooden panels must have been widespread in all Christian communities.

Christ and St Menas (right) is provincial Egyptian (Coptic) work, its bright colours and odd proportions betraying a certain lack of sophistication. Menas was an Egyptian saint, martyred under Diocletian. (40)

St Peter (below) is by contrast executed in an accomplished classical style clearly derived from late Roman portraiture. It is painted in the encaustic technique, by which wax is applied to the wood with a hot spatula, not a brush. (41)

The Virgin and Child with saints and angels (below right) represents a style mid-way between the other two: the two angels, for instance, seen half-face, are more Roman than the frontal and formalized Virgin and Saints. Both these icons are in the monastery of St Catherine, Sinai. (42)

The use of images

in worship aroused one of the bitterest feuds in the history of the Church. Its origins go back to the Jewish roots of Christianity. The representation in art of God, Christ and the Saints savoured of idolatry; after the reign of Justinian this is actually what it seemed in danger of becoming, and the victories of the Arabs were seen as God's punishment. The reformers gained ground and in 730 Leo III issued an edict forbidding the veneration of images.

The images, however, had passionate defenders. For more than a hundred years the Byzantine Empire was divided over the question, but almost all the icons, mosaics and frescoes which had previously adorned the churches were torn down, destroyed or—in more fortunate cases—painted over with whitewash. This post-Iconoclast illumination shows one such operation taking place. (43)

Constantine V (above left), the son of Leo III, urged forward the movement for the destruction of icons and persecuted those who clung to them, the monks. After his death the reforming impulse slackened. Images were allowed again in 787, but for many years their position was precarious. Leo V re-imposed the ban in 815. **Michael II** (centre) confirmed it, though his energies were mainly directed towards defending Constantinople against the Slavs. His son **Theophilus** (above right) was the last Iconoclast emperor; he too was constantly engaged on war, this time against the Arabs. When he died in 842 icon worship was reintroduced. (44–46)

Instead of images the Iconoclasts used abstract patterns or symbols. In many churches the apse mosaic of Christ or the Virgin was replaced by a cross. This one (which can be seen in the background of pl. 32) survives in St Irene. (47)

ГОУБНТЕЛЬМАЖЬНЗЛОУТН ВЪНОТРОВННН ЧЄРОДЬН:-

ПЕРСН РѢБЖТЪ
А ЦРНГРА

ſub iſto coſtantino venit p.

Byzantium was never at peace. She was menaced from Asia first by the Persians and then (after the 7th century) by the Arabs, and from Europe by the Slavs, the Avars and the Bulgarians. This later miniature from a Bulgarian chronicle shows an attack of the Persians during the reign of Heraclius. On the left six towers and two hard-pressed archers stand for Constantinople. Under the hooves of the Sasanian horses lie the mangled remains of the dead.

The city was often under siege, and the massive defences by sea and land that were erected during this period still bear witness to both her danger and her strength. The land-walls (right) were the work of Theodosius II between 413 and 447. They consist of a double rampart with ninety-six towers and a moat or ditch on the outside. (48, 49)

The secret weapon of the Byzantine navy was Greek Fire, a mixture of quick-lime, petroleum and sulphur which burst into flame when the quick-lime came in contact with the water. Brought into use c. 675, it was of crucial importance in the struggle with the Arabs, who did not possess it. This illustration from a 14th-century manuscript shows it in action. (50)

πῶμμκῶρ· Ἡραϊοδὲκαὶ τῶόκλαςῶ πρωολόω τ πυρί·

ϛόλεερωμαψ πυρπολ τὸν τῶν ἐ ηαντιϛόλον·

Byzantium from Justinian to Theophilus

CYRIL MANGO

THE PROLONGED CRISIS which the Roman world underwent in the 3rd century led to the ruination of the western provinces without seriously affecting the prosperity of the eastern ones. As a natural consequence of this, the gravitational centre of the Empire shifted from west to east, a state of affairs that was already quite apparent in the reign of Diocletian (284–305) who maintained his customary residence at Nicomedia (Izmit). The work of this great Emperor is of direct relevance to the Byzantine historian: first, because he elevated the imperial office to a level altogether inaccessible to simple mortals; second, because he carried out a complete overhaul of government machinery which he entrusted to a vast bureaucracy. This new system, perfected by Constantine, was to form the basis of Byzantine administration.

The reign of Constantine (co-Emperor 306–324; sole Emperor 324–337) represents, of course, a radical change in religious policy: no consideration of political, much less military expediency could have persuaded him to adopt the religion of the Christian minority. This we must ascribe to his personal conviction. But in other respects he followed Diocletian's policy: even the foundation of Constantinople cannot be regarded as an entirely new departure. It is difficult for us to say what purpose Constantine was trying to achieve when he transformed the little city of Byzantium into a seat of government. We may note that Constantine himself maintained his court at Nicomedia, and that Constantinople did not become the permanent residence of the Eastern Emperor until 380. The system of the Tetrarchy instituted by Diocletian (i.e. the division of the Empire for administrative purposes between two senior Augusti and two junior Caesars) excluded the notion of a fixed capital: while Rome was deliberately downgraded, the seat of government was wherever the emperor and his suite happened to be at any particular moment, whether this was Nicomedia, or Milan or Aquileia. In other words, the emperor was supposed to be ubiquitous. But in the perspective of later centuries the foundation of Constantinople assumed an entirely different meaning; it came to be believed that Constantine deliberately and, to use the contemporary phrase, *instinctu divinitatis*, set up a Christian capital to supplant the old pagan capital; that this constituted a *translatio imperii* or transference of empire, upon which indeed later Byzantines predicated their claims to universal dominion and their entire conception of history; and that to the accompaniment of heavenly choirs the new city was dedicated to the Virgin Mary. In the realm of historical myth the foundation of Constantinople certainly marks a new era.

A Beleaguered Capital

Half a century had not elapsed since the dedication of Constantinople when the tide of a Germanic invasion swept over the Empire. On 9th August 378, when the Emperor Valens was defeated and slain by the Goths at Adrianople, it might have looked as if the capital on the Bosphorus was doomed. But the Germans were deflected towards the west and the story of the next hundred years is that of the piecemeal collapse of the Western Empire; in the East it is that of an insidious German penetration from within. The irony of the situation was that the imperial army, which had the task of defending the frontiers against the advancing Germans, was itself largely German in composition, especially since the time of Theodosius I (379–395) who sought to neutralize the enemy by admitting large masses of Goths within the Empire and conferring upon their tribal chieftains the highest military commands. As a result of this shortsighted policy, effective power both in the East and in the West passed into the hands of barely Romanized German generals. On several occasions thereafter Constantinople almost fell prey to the ambition of these generals, as for example in 400 when it was momentarily seized by the Goth Gainas, or between 457 and 466 when Aspar, an Alan, ruled through the Emperor Leo I. In the end, however, the manpower reserves of the Eastern Empire proved sufficient to counterbalance the German element in the army. The same Emperor Leo called to his help the warlike Isaurians of southern Asia Minor; and after the Isaurians had enjoyed their period of supremacy in the reign of their chieftain Tarasicodissa, renamed Zeno (474–491), they too were expelled. On Zeno's death, the populace of Constantinople, tired of barbarians and heretics (the Goths were Arians, while Zeno made concessions to the Monophysites), clamoured for an emperor who was orthodox and a Roman. Anastasius I (491–517) was a Roman, even if he was not quite orthodox; better than that, he proved to be a financial genius. The enormous reserves he accumulated in the treasury made possible the partial recovery of the West that was boldly undertaken by Justinian I (527–565).

p 86 (2)

p 85 (1)

p 86 (3)

The West Reconquered

It is customary to censure Justinian for having dissipated the resources of the Empire for the sake of his own colossal ambition; and for having neglected the real interests of the state, which lay in the East, by embarking on the reconquest of the West, a reconquest that was bound to prove ephemeral. There is no denying that Justinian had a very exalted idea of his own mission; but to censure him in this fashion is to require from him a degree of prescience that no political figure has ever possessed. Actually, when we look into the political situation of the West in the early 6th century, we must grant that Justinian judged it rather shrewdly. In the West all was chaos; and Justinian probably saw what modern historians have come to realize, namely that those Vandals who ruled North Africa, those Ostrogoths who ruled Italy, those Visigoths who ruled Spain, even perhaps the Franks who had conquered Gaul, were simply squatting on the ruins of the Roman civilization; that they had introduced nothing of their own, no principle of order or organization. He must have perceived the instability of those barbarian rulers who constantly murdered and sold one another; he judged the time was ripe to throw the intruders out.

f 1, 5

If Justinian over-reached himself, it was because he had to cope with two full-scale wars against Persia; the first (526–532) resulted in a draw, while the second (540–561) proved much more disastrous. These wars were fought between equals and both sides put into the field armies that were quite substantial by the standards of those days (30,000 to 40,000 strong). When, however, we consider the reconquest of the West, we are astonished by the smallness of the forces involved. Even allowing for the incompetence of the Vandal King Gelimer, it is remarkable that the overthrow of his kingdom should have been accomplished in three months by means of 5,000 cavalry (533). The occupation of Sicily required 8,000 men. Continental Italy could have been recovered with almost the same ease had it not been for dissensions within the imperial command and the failure of the central authorities to support the expeditionary force; as a result of which the operation got out of hand and the reconquest, which dragged on for twenty years, had to be consolidated by the despatch of an unusually large force of 22,000. As for the reconquest of southern Spain (which was to remain in Roman hands for about seventy years), it was accomplished by a small armament, headed by an eighty-year old senator without any previous military experience (550). All in all, Justinian cannot be accused of having underestimated the stability of the German kingdoms. The biggest flaw of his military policy is that he did not make sufficient provision for the defence of the Danube frontier. He did, it is true, erect a line of forts along the right bank of the

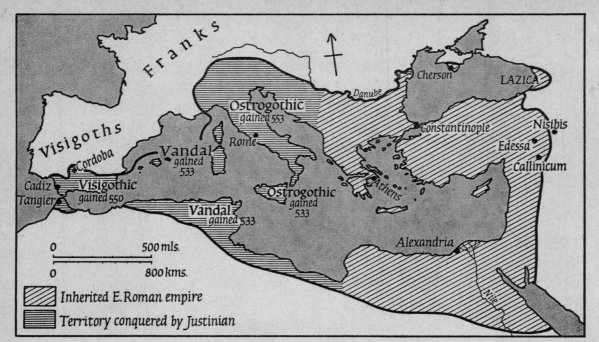

river, but in the absence of a standing garrison force it was always possible for an invader to march right through this line, as was repeatedly done by the Huns and Bulgars who spread their depredations throughout northern Greece and to the very suburbs of Constantinople. Justinian did what he could to cope with the situation by means of diplomacy, but the constant flux of the populations north of the Danube frustrated the efforts of his agents. To the Germans (Gepids and Heruls) and Huns living in these parts were now added the Slavs and a little later the Avars. Under their thrust the Danubian defences began to crack in the latter years of Justinian's reign; they collapsed completely twenty years after his death.

Problems of Co-existence

The restoration of imperial authority along practically the entire coast of the Mediterranean offers a suitable opportunity for reviewing some of the principal features of the Later Roman Empire.

In the first instance, we should examine the position of the Empire on the international scene. Now, the only other civilized state at that time was the Sasanian Empire of Persia. Contact between the two was, however, rather limited in a manner that is strangely reminiscent of the co-existence of the democratic and Communist blocs today. Ambassadors were treated with elaborate decorum, but carefully supervised. Commercial relations were limited to the border, and even so to three points only, Callinicum on the Euphrates, Nisibis near the Tigris, and Artaxata in Armenia. There was indeed some cultural seepage, but most of it went into, rather than out of Persia. The Persians were particularly anxious to profit from the superior technical skill of the Romans and whenever they captured a Roman garrison they took care to transport it to a distant part of Iran. The spread of Christianity into Persia, especially in its Nestorian guise, was a form of Roman penetration, as a result of which Christians were often persecuted there. The corresponding spread of Manichaeanism through the Roman Empire does not appear to have had the same political implications. The great Persian King Khusro I (531–579) is said to have been an assiduous student of the Christian scriptures; we do not hear of any Roman emperor reading Zoroastrian books.

A fact of particular importance is that the relative position of the two empires remained stable in the course of the 4th and 5th centuries. After the wars of 337–363 which, like most other conflicts between the two states, originated in Armenia, there was almost uninterrupted peace until the beginning of the 6th century. It is surely due to the stability of the Persian frontier that the Eastern Empire was able to withstand the Germanic invasions. The equilibrium between Persia and Constantinople depended on the existence and respective allegiance of several buffer states: such were the tribal principalities of Arabia Deserta,

that of the Ghassanids and that of the Lakhmids, the former clients of the Romans, the latter of the Persians; such were also the Caucasian states, Armenia, Lazica, Iberia and Albania. In 522 this equilibrium was upset by the conversion to Christianity of the King of the Lazi, and this led to Justinian's first war against Persia. This war followed the traditional pattern: fighting was limited to the border, neither side penetrated very deep into the territory of the other, frontier fortresses were laboriously attacked, and in the end nothing was changed. But the second war, which flared up in 540 as a result of a dispute between Arab tribesmen, showed that relations between the two great empires were entering a new, a desperate and envenomed stage. For this time the King of Kings marched right into Syria and captured Antioch, the third city of the Empire, which was burnt to the ground and its inhabitants led away into captivity. The final duel between the two giants of the late antique world was beginning.

Treasures of a Great Empire

When we look within the Empire, the first, if rather obvious observation we may make is that it was still, during this period, a vast and immensely rich state. The fact that Anastasius I, even after reducing taxation, was able on his death (518) to leave in the treasury the sum of 23 million gold pieces is sufficient evidence of the financial resources of the Empire. It is, however, through the study of monuments that we obtain the most graphic illustration of the Empire's wealth in the 4th, 5th and 6th centuries. Whether we look at the hundreds of vast basilicas dotting every province of the Christian world, even an area then as underpopulated and economically depressed as Greece, with their colonnades of imported marble and their mosaic pavements; or at the dead cities and villages of northern Syria built for eternity in solid stone; or the Land Walls of Constantinople, nearly four miles of a triple rampart rising to a height of 40 feet; or at the scores of massive fortresses by which Justinian sought to guard reconquered Africa, we cannot help reflecting that these noble monuments stretching from the Atlantic to the Syrian desert could have been produced only by a great empire. It is, above all, in Hagia Sophia (built in 532–537) that we can appreciate the impact of imperial majesty. Even without its altar-screen and ambo of beaten silver, its altar table made of an amalgam of gold and precious stones, its silver doors and purple hangings, it produces an effect of grandeur that is not equalled by any other building. We may doubt that Justinian expended 320,000 lbs of gold on the erection of Hagia Sophia; but, however much he had to oppress his subjects by taxation, he was evidently able to raise the necessary funds. One has to think, by way of comparison, of the minuscule churches of medieval Athens to grasp the difference in scale between the world of Justinian and that of Byzantine times.

Secondly, we may observe that in the 6th century the Empire contained a multitude of urban centres, many of which had a

p 102
(49)

p 95
(34, 35)
p 96 (3
p 97–8
(38)
f 2

lively cultural tradition of their own. Confining ourselves to the Eastern half of the Empire, we naturally think first of Alexandria, with its great library, the city not only of Plotinus and Hypatia, but also of Arius, Athanasius and Cyril. Next we may think of Antioch which still lives for us on the pages of Libanius and John Chrysostom; of Gaza so vividly described by the rhetor Choricius; of Berytus (Beirut) with its great law school; of Caesarea in Palestine, the see of Eusebius and birthplace of the historian Procopius.

By the end of the 4th century Constantinople too was rapidly becoming a great cultural centre. But a point may be made here which has considerable importance for later Byzantine history: namely, that with the exception of stagnating Athens, the last stronghold of the Neoplatonists, most of the culturally alive provincial cities lay in Egypt, Syria and Palestine, i.e. in lands which in the 7th century were lost to the Empire.

The Last Agony of Paganism

Down to the 6th century there existed in each provincial city a leisured and cultivated class which, along with the landed gentry, kept alive the traditions of antique culture. Paganism, which began to be persecuted in the middle of the 4th century, subsisted certainly until the end of the 6th. It was strongest among the aristocracy, the teaching profession and the peasants. Even in Asia Minor, one of the first countries to have been evangelized, mass conversions in rural areas were still being conducted under Justinian. For the medieval historian, however, the most significant aspect of the prolonged agony of paganism is perhaps to be sought in the realm of education. We know that the pattern of liberal education was elaborated during the Hellenistic period and thereafter underwent little change until the end of the ancient world. Its orientation was 'Classical', i.e. it was indissolubly wedded to the reading and imitation of approved ancient authors from Homer downwards; and it normally culminated in the study of rhetoric, since eloquence was thought to be the prime characteristic of the cultivated man. There was a wide gap between the ideal of the *mousikos aner* and the Christian ideal; indeed, the stricter Christians rose in opposition to pagan education. It was in vain. The Church had to accept the existing educational process which, in any case, was required for a 'professional' career: pagans and Christians mingled in the same schools, on the whole with a minimum of friction. Two developments are worth noting: first, that the Church failed to set up a Christian educational system; second, that the monastic school had little diffusion in the East, and this, on the whole, is true even of the Byzantine period (in complete contrast with the West). Why? Because a monastic education (apprenticeship is a better term for it) prepared a young man only to become a monk; it did not prepare him for a career in the world. Which brings us to two further aspects of the Later Roman world: monasticism and what we may call *étatisme*.

It is difficult for us to imagine that the year of Plotinus' death (270) was probably also the year when St Anthony began to practise in the Egyptian desert. The father of monasticism was a Copt who never washed and spent most of his time fighting off a multitude of demons whom he spied in every corner. Anthony enjoyed an immense success and became the prototype of the solitary hermit, while the monastic community or *koinobion* was organized by his younger contemporary Pachomius. From Egypt monasticism quickly spread to Palestine, Syria (where it assumed its most bizarre forms) and Asia Minor. The reform of the Pachomian system by St Basil, Archbishop of Caesarea in Cappadocia (died 379), gave eastern monasticism its definitive form. While the solitary hermit's life was recognized as being fit for a chosen few, the ordinary monk spent his life in a community where he divided his time between prayer, study, manual work, meals and sleep; social work was of far less significance than in the West. By maintaining monasticism in its 4th-century form, the Byzantine Empire showed itself once more as the true heir to the late antique world.

The life 'within the world' from which the monks sought to escape was regimented to an extraordinary degree. Every calling was regulated by the state: the humble *colonus* who tilled the land was tied to his plot in the interests of taxation; skilled workers, be they bakers, weavers or brick-makers, were organized into hereditary corporations, as were even the sea captains; in addition, the state possessed its own manufactures, such as mining, arms, purple cloth, etc. where service was likewise hereditary. The regulation of practically every aspect of life was entrusted to an immense bureaucracy. Service in the bureaux (which likewise tended to become hereditary) was organized along military lines and had its own uniforms. The pyramid of the civil bureaucracy was however, strictly separated from the military pyramid; their apices meeting only in the person of the emperor. Absolute master of his subjects, sole legislator, supreme judge and great pontiff (hence head of the Church), the Late Roman emperor was responsible only to God.

Justinian's age was not only one of territorial expansion: it also produced the last flowering of Graeco-Roman culture. Apart from pagan philosophy which had died with Proclus (485), almost every branch of learning was represented: mathematics by Anthemius, the architect of Hagia Sophia; medicine by his brother, Alexander of Tralles. Juridical science, under the chairmanship of Tribonian, produced the *Code* and the *Digest*. Procopius, the last in the great line of ancient historians, found a worthy subject in the story of Justinian's wars. He shows such complete detachment in matters of religion that modern critics have had trouble in deciding whether he was a Christian at all. For example, he dismisses theological speculation with the dictum that 'it is a foolish absurdity to scrutinize the nature of God'—and this two years before the Fifth Ecumenical Council! The court poet, Paul the Silentiary, not only described Hagia Sophia in Homeric hexameters, but also wrote epigrams to his mistresses. 'If anyone finds fault with us', he exclaims, 'let him remain in the penury of the monogamist!' We catch here our last glimpse of the easy-going antique life before it is engulfed by the gloom of the Middle Ages.

Art in the Service of the New Religion

The survival of antiquity is also a feature, though not the only p 100 feature, of the great artistic activity of Justinian's age. What is (41, 42) usually called Early Christian art is nothing else but Graeco- p 92 Roman art pressed into the service of a new religion; and Graeco- (27–30) Roman art itself, whether pagan or Christian, had begun already p 90 in the 3rd century to shed its classical values. Indifference towards (17, 18) perspective and scale, a rigid two-dimensional frontality, the p 94 decline of sculpture in the round, the proliferation of ornament— (36) these are some of the symptoms that marked the slow transition p 88 from antique to medieval representational art. This development (14) was not uniform; it varied from region to region and from one

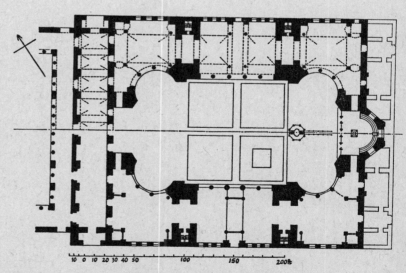

The Emperor Justinian rebuilt the church of Hagia Sophia ('Divine Wisdom') after the first church had been burnt down in 532. The work was begun under the supervision of Anthemius of Tralles and Isidorus of Miletus and completed in 537. In this plan the upper half shows the church at ground level and the lower half the level of the galleries which flank the large central domed area. Although the plan is almost square the internal effect is of an aisled basilica, as can be seen in the reconstruction on pages 97–8. (2)

Byzantine architectural sculpture is seen to its best advantage in the carving of capitals. The favourite motif was an adaptation of the classical Corinthian acanthus capital (above). In the Byzantine version, an extra row of leaves is added instead of the classical egg-and-dart ornament between the volutes, and the rosette in the abacus is frequently replaced by a cross or monogram, or in this case, a head in high relief. In other variants of the Byzantine capital the foliage is more stylized and elaborately interwoven (below). Deep undercutting and drilling have been used to give an effect of light and shade. Monograms and animal forms are also frequently used, standing out boldly from the dark under-surface of the marble. (3, 4)

social class to another: the 3rd-century tombstones of Anatolian peasants are much more 'medieval' than the refined objects made for the Roman aristocracy at the end of the 4th century. Sometimes the whole trend appeared to go into reverse: Constantinian art, for example, is often less antique than Theodosian art.

We may think of Justinian's age as achieving a synthesis, setting the stamp, as it were, on the artistic development of subsequent centuries. In architecture our first impression is one of diversity and inventiveness: next to the traditional basilica, we find buildings of all shapes, square, polygonal, cruciform. Yet it is evident that the prime concern of Justinian's architects was with the dome, i.e. with the creation of a centralized interior space; the formula, once perfected, was to last to the end of the Middle Ages. The 'impost capital', another creation of the 6th century, became the norm for all later Byzantine architecture. We could make similar observations regarding ornamental sculpture, painting, mosaics, iconography. It was from the great pool of Justinianic art that later Byzantine art continually drew its inspiration.

To obtain a vivid impression of 6th-century art, we must naturally go to Ravenna. The noble basilicas of S. Apollinare

p 94
(32, 33)

f 4

p 99
(39)

Nuovo and S. Apollinare in Classe, the octagonal church of S. Vitale, the baptisteries, the archiepiscopal chapel astound us with their wealth of marble and mosaics, the gleaming gold, the hieratic figures of saints and emperors. More remote but more authentic specimens of the same art (because untouched by the restorer's hand) may be seen in Cyprus and Mount Sinai; while the mosaic pavements of Antioch, Apamea, or Constantinople show us how faithfully the antique style could be reproduced until the end of the 6th century. A few illuminated manuscripts, like the Dioscorides in Vienna, the Gospels of Rossano and Florence (the so-called Rabbula Gospels), ivory carvings, like Bishop Maximian's chair at Ravenna, help us to visualize more fully the splendours of this largely vanished art and to understand the irresistible attraction which Justinian's golden age exerted on the centuries that followed.

p 92–
(26–30

p 88
(13–1

p 91
(21)

'An Accursed People called Slavonians'

Justinian's immediate successors were neither fools nor weaklings: Justin II, as long as he kept his sanity (in the end he lost his mind and would 'mew like a cat'), the handsome Tiberius II, and in particular the ill-fated Maurice, an excellent soldier, hardworking, economical—all of them strove energetically to maintain the territorial integrity of the expanded Roman Empire. Alas, the situation was gradually becoming untenable. In 568 Italy was invaded by the Lombards and soon passed almost entirely into their hands. War with Persia broke out once more in 572 and thereafter continued with only short interruptions until the collapse of the Sasanian Empire half a century later. Most serious of all, the Slavs, spearheaded by the Avars, invaded the entire Balkan peninsula and began to form permanent settlements there. 'In the third year after the death of the Emperor Justin [II] . . . an accursed people, called Slavonians overran the whole of Greece, and the country of the Thessalonians, and all Thrace, and captured the cities, . . . and made themselves masters of the whole country, and settled in it by main force, and dwelt in it as though it had been their own without fear.' For ten years the Emperor Maurice fought the barbarian hordes on the Danube frontier; in the end his own army revolted and placed on the throne a rude soldier called Phocas. Maurice and his family were brutally murdered (602).

p 86 (

p 86 (

f 5

p 86 (

At this tragic juncture the chain of Greek historians breaks off. If the reign of Justinian is so well known to us, this is due largely to the detailed and urbane narrative of Procopius. The remainder of the 6th century is also well illumined. But practically the entire period stretching from 602 until the beginning of the 9th century is seen only by the dim light of two chronicles which, to make matters worse, often draw on the same information. The Chronicle of the Patriarch Nicephorus, written at the very end of the 8th century, covers the years 602–769 in 74 printed pages of small format; the rather fuller Chronicle of Theophanes the Confessor devotes 213 pages to the period 602–813. It would be futile to pretend that an adequate history of the Byzantine Empire in the 7th and 8th centuries can ever be written; all we have is a chronological skeleton, a meagre outline of the doings of emperors, of wars and battles, mentions of earthquakes and other portents, and much verbiage on theological disputes. And yet it was precisely these two centuries that witnessed the transformation of the Later Roman Empire into a medieval state.

The reign of Phocas, the brutish centurion (602–610), conveys an impression of unrelieved terror and confusion. While the Emperor was exterminating the aristocracy of the capital, the occupation of the Balkan peninsula by Avars and Slavs continued unchecked; and the Persian King, ostensibly to avenge the murder of Maurice, launched a great offensive, occupying the heart of Asia Minor and even coming within sight of Constantinople. At length the banner of revolt was raised in North Africa and the saviour appeared in the person of Heraclius who overthrew the hated tyrant and was crowned Emperor. Now, in the growing penumbra, we witness the final struggle between the Roman and Persian empires: first the Persian offensive, synchronized with an Avar drive through the Balkans; the fall of Jerusalem (614), the destruction of the Holy Sepulchre and the loss of the most precious of all palladia, the Holy Cross; renewed penetration of

p 86 (

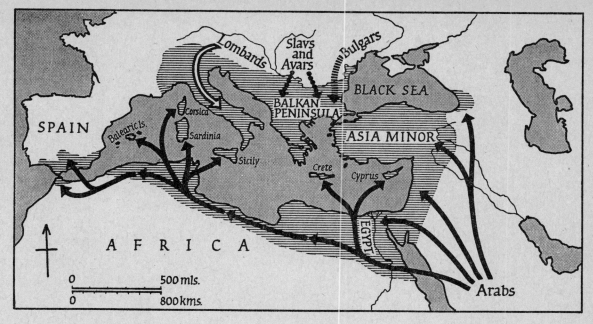

Asia Minor; the conquest of Egypt (619). Then, after careful preparation, Heraclius counterattacked in Armenia; for six years (622–628) he remained in the field, reinforcing his army with Caucasian tribesmen and Khazars from the Volga, attempting again and again to strike into Persia. During his absence Constantinople underwent its first great siege at the hands of both Persians and Avars (626); the attempt was foiled by the supremacy of the imperial fleet, and now Heraclius felt strong enough to invade Persia. The decisive battle was fought before Nineveh (627) and the Persian army was wiped out. The following year the Sasanian Empire capitulated.

It was a great triumph and one which the sentiment of succeeding ages enveloped in a shroud of pious fiction. Heraclius was made to appear as the first Crusader, his war against Persia being inspired by the theft of the True Cross. In 630 the precious relic, implausibly unharmed, was restored to Holy the Sepulchre. What does it matter if, as the evidence indicates, it was a clever *mise en scène*?

The Catastrophe of the Seventh Century: Islam

And now we come to one of the great accidents of history. The year when Heraclius set out on his Persian campaign (622) was also the year of the Hegira. The Cross had barely been returned to Jerusalem when the unleashed Arabs were overrunning Syria, crushing the Byzantine army on the Yarmuk (636), capturing Antioch, forcing the surrender of Jerusalem, invading Egypt, while they simultaneously overturned the Sasanian Empire and reached even distant Armenia (640). To all of which Heraclius put up hardly any resistance. When he died (641) practically his whole life's work had been undone and the entire complexion of the Near East irretrievably changed.

The historian cannot fail to observe that the onslaught of Islam occurred at the precise moment when the two great powers of antiquity had all but knocked each other out. Is this sufficient

explanation for the catastrophe of the 7th century? The questions have often been asked how Heraclius was able to win his epic victory over Persia, and why the same Heraclius showed such singular passivity in the face of the Arab onslaught. An explanation that has won wide acceptance is that Heraclius' success was due to a reform of provincial and military organization; and that he did not have the time to apply the same reform to the areas that he had won back from Persia, viz. Syria, Palestine and Egypt. The previous administrative system, as we have seen, was based on the separation of civil and military authority. The provinces were governed by praetorian prefects stripped of all military power; the sphere of each prefect was further subdivided into dioceses, each governed by a *vicarius*. The military organization, on the other hand, came under the command of *magistri militum* who were responsible directly to the emperor. One can readily see that such a system was bound to be wasteful and inefficient in a period of stress; and already at the time of Justinian individual exceptions began to be made, although the doctrine of the separation of powers was maintained. Going further from the Constantinian system, Maurice instituted the so-called exarchates of Italy (with its seat at Ravenna) and Africa (seat at Carthage), each exarch being in effect a vice-emperor. But it is only in the 7th century that the combination of military and civil powers becomes a coherent system. From this time on the provinces are gradually split up into units called *themata* or 'themes', each governed by a *strategos* or general. It was truly a *régime d'état de siège*: in each province was quartered a corps of soldiers, each soldier receiving a grant of land on condition of hereditary military service. The Empire's army, from being dependent on barbarian recruits (as it had been heretofore), now became a caste of soldier-farmers, largely self-supporting. It was a development of capital importance and a telling symptom of 'medievalization'; but we are hardly justified in regarding it as the cause of Heraclius' success against the Persians. For one thing, our evidence suggests that the 'themes' were developed gradually throughout the course of the 7th century and even later; secondly, the very nature of the reform would have required a long period before it became effective, much longer than the few years that Heraclius had at his disposal.

Monophysitism: The Single Nature of Christ

Another factor that is usually invoked to explain the rapid loss of Egypt, Syria and Palestine is the religious one. The Christian population of these areas was largely of Monophysite allegiance: in other words, they repudiated the Council of Chalcedon and held that Christ's human nature had been swallowed up by his divine nature. The orthodox government of Constantinople was bound by its guiding ideology to impose religious unity. Outright persecution offered a ready tool against small groups of heretics and non-Christians; but the Monophysites were too numerous to be coerced in this fashion. As a result, the govern-

ment vacillated between conciliation and the use of force: neither worked. Justin I had tried persecution without success; Justinian was under the illusion that he could reach a compromise. But a compromise is possible only when both sides are willing to make concessions, a phenomenon of rare occurrence in ecclesiastical history: the harder Justinian worked at reaching an acceptable formula, the deeper he got into trouble not only with the Monophysites, but even with his own party. So in the end he, too, felt obliged to resort to persecution, which his beautiful spouse did her best to counteract. Thus beleaguered, the Monophysites organized themselves more tightly, and it was in Justinian's time that the Jacobite Church was formed in Syria. The problem became acute once more in the reign of Heraclius: for when the eastern provinces were regained from Persia, it was found that the orthodox bishops had been removed from their sees and replaced by Monophysites. Like Justinian before him, Heraclius attempted a doctrinal compromise which may be crudely expressed as follows: why bother about the two natures if they acted in unison? Christ, even if he had a double nature, had a single energy or will *(thelema)*. Alas, it was to no avail. The only result of Heraclius' endeavours was the emergence of a new heresy (Monothelitism) which continued being a source of trouble even after the Monophysite problem had been solved in an unforeseen way—by the Arab conquest.

It is quite clear that the oppression of the Monophysites hastened the loss of the eastern provinces. We must not, of course, imagine that the Copts and Syrians were, under cover of their heterodoxy, animated by nationalism, and that they welcomed the invader in order to be rid of the hated Roman overlord: such notions were foreign to the ancient world. The Romans were hated not as Romans, but as tax collectors and Chalcedonian heretics to boot. As we read the story of the conquest of Egypt told by a contemporary Monophysite, we perceive a mood of resentful resignation: the Arab scourge was a punishment meted out by the Lord in atonement for the sins of the Chalcedonians. Who is to resist God's decrees? But a day would come when the Lord would overthrow the execrable Muslims as He once overthrew the Egyptian Pharaoh.

Aided by such an attitude of the local population, the Arabs continued to advance. Under the Caliph 'Umar (634–644) the *f 5* conquest of Syria was completed, while the general 'Amr, acting on his own initiative, invaded Egypt and won the capitulation of Alexandria (642). A little later the energetic governor of Syria, Mu'awiyah, built a fleet and attacked Cyprus; Rhodes was occupied in 654 and the famous Colossus sold to a Jewish merchant. An attack on Constantinople was now expected. To forestall it, the Emperor Constans took a stand with his fleet on the Lycian coast, but was utterly defeated, barely escaping with his life (655).

Disastrous as the situation was in the East, this was not the sum total of the Empire's troubles. The wholly unnecessary Monothelite affair was producing profound discontent in North Africa and in Rome; provincial governors were revolting; and meanwhile the Lombards were pursuing their conquest of Italy. Profiting from a lull in the Arab offensive, Constans betook himself to the West (663). Already in 619, when the Persian danger stood at its peak, Heraclius had thought of transferring the capital of the Empire to Carthage; now Constans was contemplating moving it back to Rome. He did visit Rome, the last Byzantine emperor to do so until the 14th century; but we may imagine that the melancholy ruins of the Eternal City made him change his mind. Instead, he set up his residence at Syracuse from where he tried to conduct operations against the Lombards; and there, a few years later, he was murdered in his bathtub (668).

Christendom's Darkest Hour

When the caliphate passed into the hands of Mu'awiyah, the Arab offensive resumed once more. The loss of Byzantine North Africa was merely a matter of time, and was completed in 709 when the Arabs reached the Atlantic. But it was in Asia Minor that the decisive struggle was waged. From 673 until 677 an p 102 Arab fleet blockaded Constantinople. It was then that a Syrian (50) architect invented Greek fire—an inflammable mixture presum-

ably containing saltpetre that was to serve as the secret weapon of the Byzantine navy for several centuries to come. With the help of this mysterious fire the Arabs were repulsed; it was the first serious setback they received, and this produced a great impression all over Europe. But the advantage was of short duration; indeed, the close of the 7th century and the beginning of the 8th are among the darkest periods of Byzantine history. The Heraclian dynasty was tottering to its fall; its last member, Justinian II, was violent and unbalanced, cruel to his subjects p 86 (9) and reckless in foreign affairs. In 695 he was deposed; his nose was cut off and he was exiled to the Crimea. For the next twenty years there was complete anarchy as one ephemeral emperor succeeded another. A new enemy had meanwhile appeared in the Balkans—the Bulgarians who, after freeing themselves from the Avars, invaded the territory of modern Bulgaria (c. 680) and *f 5* subjugated the Slavic tribes that had settled there earlier. In 711 the Bulgarian Khan Tervel was ravaging the suburbs of Constantinople at the same time as the Arabs were pushing deeper into Asia Minor along a front that extended from Amasia in Pontus, through Galatia and Phrygia, to Pergamum on the Aegean coast. In 717 the Arabs stood once more before Constantinople.

Was it by design that the second Arab attempt to capture Constantinople nearly coincided with the Arab offensive through the Pyrenees into Gaul and with a similar offensive through the Caucasus into the land of the Khazars? Were the Arabs spurred on to a supreme effort because they expected the end of the world to come in the year 100 of the Hegira (AD 718)? There is no proof that the Caliph of Damascus was masterminding a plan for the subjugation of Europe; but as we view the events of these fateful years we realize that never did Christendom stand in such grave peril.

The Arab tide, was, however, checked. At its darkest hour Byzantium found a new leader in the person of Leo III, a general p 86 (8) of Syrian extraction (though he is commonly known as Leo the Isaurian). The siege of Constantinople (717–718) was broken. It is customary to compare this event with the decisive defeat of the Arabs at the battle of Tours (732); but it is seldom remembered that the year 730 was marked by a no less resounding defeat of the Arabs by the Khazars on the plains of Azerbeijan. The Pyrenees and the Caucasus remained henceforth the extreme limits of Islam vis-à-vis Christian Europe.

Never again did the Arabs lay siege to Constantinople; but the struggle for Asia Minor went on for another two centuries and a half, and it was on this struggle that the chief energies of the Byzantine Empire were bent. Leo III succeeded in clearing the Anatolian plateau. His son, Constantine V (741–775), pushed p 101 the theatre of war back to Syria, Mesopotamia and Armenia. This (44) coincided with the fall of the Umayyad dynasty and the transference of the Arab capital from Damascus to more distant Baghdad. From this time on the relative position of the Byzantine and Arab empires became somewhat stabilized: warfare did not cease, but it was limited, as a rule, to border raids repeated with monotonous regularity summer after summer.

'Thou Shalt Not Make unto Thee any Graven Image'

Leo III is remembered not only as the saviour of Constantinople, but also as the instigator of a religious reform, Iconoclasm, which was first introduced in 730 and continued to agitate the Byzantine world for over a century. No aspect of Byzantine history has been the object of so much study as Iconoclasm; indeed, it would be no exaggeration to say that the interpretation of Iconoclasm has reflected every major trend in European historical thinking since the middle of the last century. All kinds of explanations have been offered, internal and external, theological and philosophical, social and economic. The paucity of the evidence has actually encouraged the multiplication of speculative theories.

The major facts of the Iconoclastic controversy are these. In 730 Leo III published, at the instigation of certain Anatolian p 101 bishops, an edict fobidding the use of images in religious worship. (43, 47) The defenders of images suffered a persecution which was not *f 7* apparently very severe; there was an unsuccessful revolt in Greece; more important, the new 'heresy' accentuated the rift between the Emperor and the Pope with the result that a little later the Papacy allied itself with the Frankish kings. Iconoclasm reached its peak under Constantine V who, unlike his father, took an active part in the theological debate. In 754, a council attended by 338 bishops met in a suburb of Constantinople and ratified the Iconoclast doctrine. Having thus obtained the sanction of the Church, the Emperor proceeded to a systematic destruction of icons and to a persecution of their chief supporters, the monks. There were many martyrs who defied the crowned Antichrist as the early Christians had defied Nero or Diocletian. During the brief reign of the next emperor, Leo IV (775–780), persecution was replaced by conciliation. After his death, the veneration of images was re-established by his widow Irene at the Seventh Ecumenical Council (787). The iconophile interlude continued until 815 when another Oriental, Leo V (813–820) banned once more the use of religious images. The second period of Iconoclasm is generally considered as lacking the vigour of the first; but there was renewed persecution, especially during the reign of Theophilus (829–842). It was only after the latter's death that Iconoclasm was finally suppressed, although it retained a small band of supporters for another twenty or thirty years.

The spectacle of a great Empire deeply divided for more than a hundred years over the question of religious painting is naturally puzzling to the modern mind. Hence the question has persistently been asked: Was not Iconoclasm a mask concealing another, non-theological issue? If this issue has not yet been discovered, it is not for lack of trying. We have been asked to believe that Iconoclasm was really a resurgence of Hellenism or, conversely, of Orientalism; or that it was an anti-monastic movement; or a campaign for the confiscation of ecclesiastical treasure; or an attempt to strengthen imperial absolutism; or an expression of the class struggle. However much we may be tempted by such explanations, we must, I think, reject them: Iconoclasm was surely what it purported to be, namely a religious quarrel; which is not to say that there were no political, social or economic problems in the 8th and 9th centuries.

Iconoclasm had deep roots in the Christian past. Indeed, the early Church, surrounded as it was by idolatry, was uncompromising in its rejection of the representational arts. Had not the Old Testament explicitly condemned such arts? It is true that by the 4th century a Christian art did arise, but it was not without protest. Recent scholarship has justifiably laid emphasis on the objections that were sporadically raised against the use of religious images in different parts of the Christian world from the 4th century until the outbreak of Byzantine Iconoclasm, and has noted that opposition was particularly strong among the Monophysites. Another important consideration is that the veneration of icons experienced a remarkable intensification in the period after Justinian and throughout the 7th century. The worshipper was no longer content to regard the icon as merely a symbol, a pictorial reminder of the saintly person represented; to his credulous eyes the icon and the saint were one. Icons began to speak, to bleed when wounded, to defend themselves when attacked; their veneration manifested itself in the burning of incense, the lighting of tapers, in kissing and genuflection. A new class of icons made its appearance, those 'not made by hand' (*acheiropoietai*), i.e. produced miraculously without human intervention, like the Holy Face of Edessa which purported to be the impression of Christ's features on a napkin. Now, the significant fact is that the emperors of the late 6th and 7th centuries, taking advantage of the new direction that the religiosity of the masses was taking, made deliberate use of icons for political and military ends. Icons were made to be the defenders of cities and were carried into battle by the army. Had they worked the miracles that were expected of them, the chances are that there would have been no Iconoclasm; but they had not worked. And this surely brings us very close to the immediate causes of Iconoclasm.

We must attempt at this point to think ourselves back into the world of the early 8th century. In 726, when Leo III began to express his Iconoclast beliefs, the Arabs had just been repulsed from Constantinople, but they were still overrunning most of Asia Minor. In that same year Caesarea in Cappadocia was cap-

Even when icon worship was officially forbidden it still went on in private, not least among members of the imperial family. In this manuscript illumination the Empress Theodora is surprised kissing an icon by the court jester, peering in from the garden. As soon as Theodora came to power (she acted as regent for her six-year-old son Michael III) she gradually removed Iconoclasts from all positions of authority and was finally able to restore Orthodoxy. (7)

tured; the following year two Arab armies were laying siege to Nicaea, a day's journey from the capital. The situation was desperate enough; and anyone looking back over the previous century could see nothing but disaster following disaster. Now, to a medieval mind this could mean only one thing: that the Byzantines were being punished by the Almighty for some religious infraction. Why had the Christian armies carrying their icons into battle been consistently defeated? Why had city after city, each boasting a palladium in some miraculous icon, fallen to the unbeliever? Clearly, this was because the Christian faith had become tainted, because the emperors themselves had put their trust in painted images which even the Saracens rejected.

The Origins of Iconoclasm

Let us now see what the Greek sources have to say about the origin of Iconoclasm. It all allegedly started with a Palestinian Jew who approached the Caliph Yazid II (720–724) and promised him a long reign if the latter would destroy all representational images in the churches of his Christian subjects as well as in the streets and market places. Yazid, who was a foolish man, complied with this request, but his early death belied the Jew's prophecy. It was from this source that the Emperor Leo drew his heretical beliefs; he was aided and abetted by his companion Beser, a Muslim renegade, and by the Bishop Constantine of Nacoleia.

Some details of this story are admittedly suspect. But is there anything inherently improbable about such a derivation of Iconoclasm? It is an established fact that Yazid II issued an ordinance against the use of images and enforced its execution. It is known that the Jews of the diaspora had admitted human representations into their synagogues, but beginning about the 6th century returned to a stricter interpretation of the Law and henceforth showed implacable opposition to all such images. It has also been shown that the early Umayyad princes had used representational painting and sculpture in their palaces, and, except for the reign of Yazid II, continued to do so into the 8th century, after which time this practice was banned. We also know that Jewish thinking exerted an influence on the Umayyad court. All the evidence is indeed remarkably consistent. I see no reason to doubt (although some modern scholars have done so) that Byzantine Iconoclasm originated in the same milieu as Arab Iconoclasm; that it spread to the Byzantine army of the eastern borders, an army containing a high proportion of Armenians and other Monophysites, and found a sympathetic reception among the clergy of Asia Minor. If this ferment had occurred at a time when the Empire was strong, Iconoclasm would probably have been confined to the eastern marches; but the times were desperate, and Byzantium was waiting for its *homme providentiel* who appeared in the person of Leo III. In a situation of this kind a minority (such as the Iconoclasts were) can usually impose its will on a demoralized majority for as long as it remains successful. But by making the Empire more secure, by removing the stress of defeat and desperation, the Iconoclasts were inevitably preparing their own downfall.

The success of Leo III and Constantine V cannot be denied. We have seen how they cleared the Anatolian plateau, pushing the Arabs back to the Euphrates. The growing menace of Bulgarian expansion was dealt with no less energetically. Constantine V led nine counterattacks into Bulgarian territory, defeating the enemy time and again. He was the idol of his army and even managed to win over the populace of Constantinople by making bread cheap. What did it matter that the Iconoclast emperors neglected their Italian possessions, that Ravenna fell to the Lombards (751), and that the Pope, no longer able to rely on Byzantine protection, placed himself at the service of the Frankish kingdom? Italy was very far away. Even the Fathers of the Seventh Ecumenical Council, who had little love for the two great Iconoclast emperors, acknowledged 'their victories over the foe, the subjection of barbarians ... their solicitude concerning their subjects, their counsels, their trophies, their civil ordinances, the rebuilding of cities'.

p 290

A Woman 'Emperor'

After the brief reign of Leo IV (775–780) the throne passed to a ten-year old boy, Constantine VI, his mother Irene acting as Regent. Beautiful, cruel and ambitious, Irene appears as the ideal heroine of a historical novel. The official restoration of icon-worship which she effected in 787 has earned her the undying gratitude of the Church; in other respects, however, she proved to be a thoroughly frivolous ruler. She selected her advisers from among eunuchs and monks who had no experience of public affairs. In an attempt to win popular support taxes were irresponsibly lowered; worse still, the army, which was as before the stronghold of the iconoclasts, was deliberately undermined—a policy which immediately resulted in serious defeats at the hands of the Arabs and allowed the threatening growth of Bulgarian power. To top it all, a horrible drama was being enacted at court. Irene had little use for her son and was determined to keep him in the background: as soon as he grew up, she cancelled his projected match with Charlemagne's daughter and forced him to marry an obscure wife instead. After undergoing further humiliations, Constantine managed to depose his mother with the support of the army (790); but two years later she was back in the palace, bent on discrediting her son. Her intrigues proved so successful that in 797 she was able to have Constantine arrested and blinded; for the next five years she ruled alone under the title not of Empress but of Emperor. It was the first time that a woman assumed sole rule over the Empire, and it provided Pope Leo III with the excuse of crowning Charlemagne to fill the allegedly vacant throne (800). The uncouth Frank who allow-

p 86
(10)

p 291

During the reign of Michael II, Thomas the Slav, a soldier from Asia Minor, gathered an army of Arabs, Persians, Armenians, Iberians and other Caucasian people, and raised a revolution against the Iconoclast sympathies and the oppressive taxation of the Emperor. Civil war split the empire, and Thomas launched an attack on Constantinople (illustrated here from the 14th-century manuscript of John Skylitzes) which might even have succeeded if the Khan of the Bulgars had not come to Michael's aid. In 823 the movement collapsed and Thomas himself was captured and executed a few months later. (8)

ed himself to violate the most cherished political idea of the Middle Ages, that of the single empire, must have felt rather insecure in his new role; and it is reported that in 802 there arrived at Constantinople ambassadors from Charles and the Pope proposing a marriage between the Emperor of the West and the Empress of the East. Historians cannot help speculating what course European history might have taken if this union had occurred; but a few months after the arrival of the embassy there broke out a palace revolution. Irene was quietly removed and died soon afterwards on Lesbos.

Iconoclasm Restored

The man whom the revolution placed on the throne, Nicephorus I (802–811), was a middle-aged treasury official. Indifferent towards popularity and theological disputes, he made it his task to replenish the exchequer by raising taxes, to strengthen the army, and to re-establish the dignity of the Empire which had fallen so low under the previous administration. Byzantine chroniclers paint an odious portrait of the crowned tax collector; even so, he commands our respect. The most pressing problem that Nicephorus had to face was posed by the Bulgarians who had profited not only from Irene's laxity, but even more from the destruction of the Avar state at the hands of Charlemagne. In 809 the Bulgarian Khan Krum captured Sardica (Sofia), one of the key points in the Byzantine line of defence. Nicephorus, leading his army in person, struck at the Bulgarian capital and with stubborn determination came within an inch of crushing the enemy; but in 811 he was unexpectedly trapped in mountainous country, himself slain and his army destroyed. Nicephorus' brother-in-law and successor, Michael I Rangabe (811–813), was not man enough to save the situation. The Bulgarians advanced capturing important strongholds on the Black Sea and defeating the entire Byzantine army near Adrianople. Michael was thereupon overthrown and a more capable leader placed on the throne in the person of Leo V the Armenian (813–820).

The disasters sustained by the Empire since the accession of Irene were obvious enough, and it was difficult to resist the conclusion that they had been caused by the re-establishment of icon worship. Leo V, a rough soldier, reasoned as follows: 'Why are the Christians suffering thus and are subdued by aliens? In my opinion, this is because the icons are worshipped and for no other reason ... For you see that all the emperors who have acknowledged and worshipped icons met their death either in exile or in war; and only those emperors who did not worship them died a natural death on the throne and received glorious burial in the imperial sepulchres ... So I too intend to imitate the latter and destroy the icons so that both I and my son may live a long time and our dynasty continue to the fourth or fifth generation.' After the immediacy of the Bulgarian threat had been averted by Krum's timely death, Leo V proceeded to re-impose Iconoclasm as the official doctrine of the realm. Alas, his hopes of a long life were not fulfilled, and on Christmas day 820 he was murdered by his former companion in arms, Michael the Amorian.

Michael II (820–829) is presented to us as an abominable heretic tainted by Jewish doctrines; not an overt Iconoclast, he was nevertheless an Iconoclast-sympathizer. The first three years of his reign were taken up in fighting a formidable revolt led by the enigmatic figure of Thomas the Slav. With Arab support, Thomas assembled a miscellaneous host containing every Oriental nationality. He became master of the greater part of Asia Minor and proceeded to lay siege to Constantinople. The strength of the capital's walls and the unexpected intervention of the Bulgarian Khan Omurtag caused the failure of the revolt. Nevertheless, the Empire was greatly weakened and could not resist the occupation of Crete and part of Sicily by the Arabs, thus marking a further stage in the decline of Byzantine sea-power in the Mediterranean.

Michael's son Theophilus (829–842) was the last Iconoclast emperor. Although engaged in constant warfare with the Arabs, sometimes successfully but more often disastrously (as when Ancyra and Amorium were captured by the enemy in 838), he showed real interest in Arab culture. At no other time, it would

p 101
(45)

f 8

f 5

p 101
(46)

seem, were the courts of Constantinople and Baghdad so similar. Even in his personal idiosyncracies Theophilus was very much like an oriental despot: witness his childish love of pomp and gadgetry (he had a golden tree on which mechanical birds warbled) or his proverbial justice which he dispensed rather arbitrarily by inflicting especially on rich or influential wrong-doers punishments quite disproportionate to their misdeeds. For this, of course, he was much loved by the common folk. Alone among the Iconoclasts, Theophilus escaped the condemnation of posterity, and was even represented in a 12th-century Byzantine text as one of the judges of the underworld.

The 8th century had seen very little accomplished in the cause of letters; in the reign of Theophilus, however, we notice a distinct cultural uplift. The key figures of this revival are unfortunately rather shadowy. There was, first of all, Leo the Mathematician who is said to have been invited to Baghdad by the Caliph al-Ma'mun, but was not allowed by the Byzantine government to depart from Constantinople and was instead set up as a public teacher. Leo appears to have cultivated geometry and astronomy and may also have dabbled in the occult. Another noted scholar was John the Grammarian who served as the last Iconoclast Patriarch (837–843) and whose scientific knowledge earned him the reputation of being a powerful magician. It was also in the reign of Theophilus that the future Patriarch Photius must have acquired his prodigious classical learning. This renewed interest in letters and science led to the re-copying of ancient Greek texts in the newly introduced minuscule script; and it is on these manuscripts produced in Constantinople from the early 9th century onwards that our knowledge of the Greek classics is largely based. The scholarly movement which began under Theophilus, although the target of savage attacks on the part of obscurantist monks, came to fruition in the next reign when the University of Constantinople was refounded.

f 7 Theophilus died in 842 leaving a minor son, Michael III, and the regency was assumed by his pious widow, Theodora. For the next year the liquidation of Iconoclast leadership was quietly conducted behind the scenes; and on the first Sunday of Lent, 843, a solemn ceremony marked the re-establishment of icon worship. This occasion is still celebrated by the Eastern Church
f 9 as the Feast of Orthodoxy, and it marks a turning point in Byzantine history. Modern scholars have seen in the events of 843 the victory of Hellenism over the Orientalism of the Iconoclasts; it would be more correct to say that it was not so much Hellenism that triumphed as the concept of the pre-Iconoclast Christian Empire. In the eyes of contemporaries the suppression of Iconoclasm, the last great heresy, meant the attainment of the perfect Christian world; and this entailed the notion of a 'renovation', meaning (as always in the Middle Ages) not the creation of anything new, but the reconstitution of the old, i.e. the empire of Constantine and Justinian. This 'renovation' was reserved for the glorious reigns of Michael III and Basil I.

Cut Off from the West

Having reached the chronological limit of this chapter, we may pause to survey the condition of the Byzantine Empire as it emerged after weathering the storms of the 7th and 8th centuries. The approximate extent of the Empire c. 850 is shown on p. 129. What the map does not show, however, is that some of the areas marked as Byzantine were only under nominal control and that the really 'operative' parts of the Empire were Asia Minor this side of the Taurus and Antitaurus ranges, and Thrace.

We may begin by asking the question: How did the Byzantine of the early 9th century look on the world around him? Of the West, even including Italy, he had only the vaguest notion. The chronicler Theophanes, our principal source for this period, knows less about Charlemagne, who was his contemporary, than does a modern schoolboy. The alienation between East and West has often been blamed on the policy of the Iconoclast emperors; rather, it seems to be attributable to larger developments and in particular to the Slavic occupation of the Balkans. We have seen that in the late 6th century the Slavs poured south of the Danube and gradually made themselves masters of practically all the Balkan possessions of the Empire; only Thrace and a few coastal

On the first Sunday of Lent, 843, icon worship was officially restored, an event still celebrated in the Eastern Church by the annual Feast of Orthodoxy. This miniature, of the mid-11th century, shows a deacon standing on the ambo of Hagia Sophia (see p. 96) and reading the decree which anathematized the Iconoclasts and proclaimed the condemnation of their doctrine. (9)

cities of the Aegean and Adriatic remained in Byzantine hands. The Slavs did not form any organized state (except that part of them were subservient to the Avar and later to the Bulgar khans) and remained as tribal groups which are called 'the Sclavinias' in Byzantine sources. We learn with some surprise that in 688/9 Justinian II had to fight his way from Constantinople to Thessalonica, and he barely managed to return. For two centuries the Byzantine government made little effort to draw the Sclavinias within its cultural orbit. The reconquest of Greece, begun in the late 8th century, was continued in the early 9th, but even c. 820, as we learn from the travels of St Gregory the Decapolite, it was virtually impossible to cross the Balkans by land without falling into the hands of Slavic brigands. Communication between Constantinople and Italy was maintained only by sea; even so, the journey could hardly be accomplished in less than two months.

The Slavs thus drove a wedge between East and West and in so doing they created not only a physical but also a linguistic barrier. As long as the soldiers of the Later Roman Empire were recruited from Illyricum, some knowledge of Latin persisted in the East; but with the loss of Illyricum the use of Latin disappeared. The self-styled Roman Empire was henceforth ignorant of the Roman tongue; and how abysmal this ignorance was may be judged from the story that the Emperor Leo VI (886–912), one of the most learned men of his age, bestowed a reward of 30 lbs of gold on an Italian who was able to read a Latin inscription in Constantinople.

If the average Byzantine knew almost nothing of the West, he was, on the contrary, very much interested in the affairs of his immediate neighbours, the Arabs and the Bulgarians. In spite of the hostility of these two powers, contact with them was intimate and sustained. Incursions from one or the other side were almost a yearly occurrence; prisoners were taken and exchanged. What is more, the Caliph had among his subjects a large Christian population, part of which was of Chalcedonian allegiance and continued to regard the Byzantine emperor as its legitimate head. Was not St John Damascene, the pillar of orthodoxy in the 8th century, an official at the Muslim court? Did not the patriarchs of Antioch, Alexandria and Jerusalem reside in Arab country?

A Medley of Nations

When we enquire into the ethnic composition of the Empire, we readily understand why its population should have had closer links with the East than with the West. The centre of the Empire, as we have said, now lay in Asia Minor, a country that presented the most bewildering medley of half assimilated nationalities. The ancient peoples of this area, such as the Phrygians, Cappadocians,

Isaurians, Lycaonians and others, appear to have retained something of their identity and the use of their respective languages until about the 6th century; thereafter they mostly adopted Greek. To what extent these nationalities were absorbed and Hellenized in the succeeding centuries we are unable to say; but it would be rash to affirm that the process had been completed by the 9th century. Meanwhile, many other elements had been installed in Asia Minor. More important than the arrival of refugees fleeing from Arab occupied Syria, was the deliberate policy of transplantation pursued by the Byzantine government for military ends. Most prominent among the new settlers were the Armenians, the mainstay of the Byzantine army from the late 6th century onwards. They were brought in by thousands, starting in the reign of Maurice and all through the 7th and 8th centuries, and given lands in Asia Minor and Thrace. Similar measures were applied to the Slavs: we are told, for example, that Justinian II settled upward of 30,000 Slavs in Bithynia and Constantine V another 208,000 in the same district. The prevalence of heresies in Asia Minor is also a gauge of the ethnic confusion that reigned in that area: in the 9th century we hear of Athingans, Quartodecimans and especially of the Paulicians whose extermination entailed not only persecution but even military expeditions.

The addition of so many foreign elements to the Byzantine army, coupled with the fact that military organization was based on land-holding, naturally affected the composition of the aristocracy. The old ruling class, decimated under Phocas and Justinian II, and financially ruined by the Persian and Arab invasions, appears to have faded out in the 7th century; in the 8th a new aristocracy emerged which was Anatolian and in large part Armenian. It is roughly at this period that we first encounter such names as Skleros, Musele, Rangabe, etc.—families that were to play a leading role in subsequent Byzantine history.

It is difficult to give a clear account of the agrarian situation into which this new landed gentry inserted itself. Broadly speaking, Byzantine agricultural history is presented to us in the following terms: the economy of the Later Roman Empire up to the 6th century, we are told, rested on the exploitation of large estates by serfs and *coloni*; this gave place in the 7th and 8th centuries to a system of free village communes which gradually, but especially from the 9th century onwards, began to merge once more in the hands of 'feudal' lords. The formulation of this development requires a great deal of qualification: one can point out, for example, that in Syria big estates were already breaking up in the 6th century, as archaeological findings indicate; one can also question the predominance of petty freeholding during the transitional period and quote the case of the 8th-century Paphlagonian magnate who owned 48 domains, 800 horses of pasture, 1,200 sheep, etc. These exceptions probably do not invalidate the over-all curve: after all, the settlement of hundreds of thousands of Armenian and Slav soldier-farmers could have been effected only by the fragmentation of existing estates, whether these were private or crown property. As a result, the proportion of petty freeholding must have increased very considerably.

In discussing agrarian problems we cannot neglect a development of even broader significance, namely general depopulation. Unfortunately, we have few figures to guide us; but the impression one gains from reading the sources is that the population of the Empire declined sharply, starting with the great plague of 541–544 which in Constantinople alone is said to have killed over 300,000 persons. The downward trend must have continued until the situation was somewhat stabilized at the end of the 8th century. The repeated invasions of both the Asiatic and European provinces of the Empire, entailing massacres and the destruction of crops, were surely the most important factor in this development. We hear of entire cities being abandoned as, e.g., Tyana on the Anatolian plateau. In addition, there were repeated epidemics (including a plague of extraordinary virulence in 747) and a succession of destructive earthquakes. The loss seems to have been borne to a greater extent by the cities than the countryside. How low the population of Constantinople had sunk by the middle of the 8th century may be judged by the fact that there was not sufficient manpower to repair the city walls that had

been damaged by the terrible earthquake of 740; and that in 766 Constantine V had to import artisans from the provinces in order to repair an aqueduct.

But what of the provincial cities? That they continued to exist on paper is made clear by episcopal lists, which, however, do not tell us anything about the size of these cities. An adequate answer to this problem can be provided only by the excavation of Byzantine urban centres, preferably in Asia Minor. Until now, most of the excavating that has been done in this area has been concerned with prehistoric or classical antiquities, so that whatever Byzantine material happened to be in the way has been accorded scant attention. Even so, the information that has come to us from sites such as Ephesus, Pergamum, Sardis and Priene points to a dramatic decline in the middle of the 7th century. Not only was construction almost at a standstill from this period until the 9th or 10th century; there was also a corresponding drop in the circulation of coinage. The Arab author Ibn-Khordadhbeh, who visited the Empire in the forties of the 9th century, knows of only five important cities in Asia Minor: Ephesus, Nicaea, Amorium, Ancyra and Coloneia. For Amorium we have some incomplete figures referring to the year 838 and we can still survey on the spot the extent of the medieval town: it could hardly have contained a population of over 20,000. We do not know how the inhabitants of Amorium occupied themselves, but we may imagine that in time of peace many of them would go out of the walled enclosure and till their lands, as, incidentally, was the case in Thessalonica in the early 7th century.

The Survival of Antiquity

When we survey the parallel developments of depopulation, ruralization and fragmentation (as reflected by the *theme*-system), we naturally wonder why the Byzantine Empire did not, like the west of Europe, go to seed and, after lying dormant for a couple of centuries, was not reborn in a new form. I would suggest that the explanation of this problem is to be sought in Constantinople. No matter how low the capital sank in the 8th century, it somehow managed to hold on to the traditions of an antique *polis*. It preserved some semblance of its former civic organization with its *demes* and circus factions even after these entities had lost all political reality. It continued as a centre of industry and maritime trade when most other towns had become walled refuges for country farmers. It also remained the seat of a vast bureaucracy which had to be somehow trained. In the provincial towns one could obtain a secondary education of sorts; the equivalent of a university education was available only in the capital. We know very little of the history of education in Constantinople from the middle of the 7th century until the beginning of the 9th; it could not, however, have been entirely extinguished as our biased sources would have us believe. To take one instance, the Patriarch Nicephorus, who began his career as a civil servant, obtained quite a respectable schooling in the seventies of the 8th century. Now, the remarkable thing is that when the 'University' was re-organized in the middle of the 9th century, it retained the characteristics of the original foundation that had been set up by Theodosius II in 425: in other words, it was a lay body which taught philosophy, geometry, astronomy and rhetoric, but no theology. It would be difficult to find a more graphic illustration of the manner in which Constantinople clung to its ancient heritage.

We must not underestimate the effort that must have been required to salvage the antique values when the Arabs and Bulgarians were beating on the gates of Constantinople. Conservatism proved its worth and, in a world of barbarism, it placed Byzantium in the lead of European civilization. Later on, however, it degenerated into a habit that could not be shaken off. Just as the Byzantine Church closed its books after the Seventh Ecumenical Council of 787 and declared that henceforth nothing could be added to or subtracted from the doctrine of the Fathers, so the Byzantine intellectual was content to rest on the rhetorical and philosophical teaching of the Later Roman Empire. The negative side of this conservatism does not, however, concern us here: the price for it did not have to be paid until the high Middle Ages.

VI THE CHRISTIAN CITADEL

The Byzantine world of the ninth and tenth centuries

J. M. HUSSEY

The eastern Mediterranean, showing the sites important in the 9th and 10th centuries

'King of the New Romans',

reads the inscription on one side of the page (opposite) and 'Basil trusting in Christ' on the other. The manuscript is a Psalter made at Constantinople in about 1017, and the Emperor is Basil II, who reigned between 976 and 1025, gaining the surname of Bulgaroctonos, 'Slayer of the Bulgars'. In this frontispiece eight of the defeated race are shown grovelling at his feet as he gazes sternly over them, armed and implacable. Above him the Archangel Michael hands him his spear, Gabriel places a crown on his head and Christ promises him a heavenly crown; while on either side military saints seem to assist and partake in his triumph.

Basil II was the most outstanding member of an outstanding family—the Macedonian dynasty founded by Basil I (the Macedonian) in 867. For nearly 200 years it was acknowledged as the legitimate imperial line, although the real power was frequently in the hands of co-emperors, thus partially solving one of the thorniest problems of the early Byzantine period—the succession. Continuity was achieved, for successful usurpers had at least to make some pretence of connection with the Macedonian house.

It was in fact a time of prosperity for most of the Empire. Religious turmoil had subsided. The army was well organized and well led, the provinces efficiently governed, the treasury full.

Constantinople was without rival the richest city in the world and, ringed with foes as she was, had never fallen to the enemy.

The threats came from east, west and north. In 913 Symeon, ruler of the Bulgars had reached her gates, but a hundred years later his kingdom was a Byzantine province. In the endless struggle with Islam there was no such decisive defeat, though there were considerable gains. The eastern frontier was advanced; Cyprus and Crete were recovered and Armenia added to the Empire. With the Western Empire under the Ottonians and Popes an uneasy peace was maintained.

These conditions favoured both the Church and the arts. It was the great age of monasticism, the foundations on the Holy Mountain of Athos alone constituting almost a world of their own. The classical tradition, Christianized and transformed by contact with the East, was yet a living reality. Above all the city of Constantinople itself—as yet unpillaged by Crusader or Turk, filled with the treasures of antique Greece and Rome and the tribute of the richest provinces of Europe and Asia—was a place of wonder to all who came to it: Arab, Jew, Ostrogoth, Lombard or Norseman. 'God dwells there among men', wrote an envoy from Kiev in the 980s; 'we cannot forget that beauty.' (1)

War: the Byzantine campaigns of conquest or defence are barely represented in contemporary art, which was more concerned to teach than to illustrate. The primitive drawing of an armed rider (right) is Bulgarian. It was found on the wall of a fortress and dates from the 9th century, a time when Bulgarian expansion seriously menaced the Byzantines. Miniatures of Old Testament scenes—now and throughout the Middle Ages—often provide the best glimpses of contemporary warfare. The capture (below) of the city of Ai (Joshua, VIII, 19–20) seems inspired by the war against the Arabs. More typical of Byzantine official art is the ivory casket-lid (bottom) also showing, in symbolic terms, the capture of a city. The horseman is an emperor and the little figure emerging from the gate carries the city's crown. (2, 3, 4)

Peace: life in rural areas can have differed little from that of the Greek or Turkish countryman of today. These scenes are taken from illustrations to the Psalms, the Gospels and the Sermons of St Gregory Nazianzus. Left: masons at work—a column has been raised by pulley. Below: sheep-shearing, trapping hares and sailing; and (below them) work in the vineyard. The 9th and 10th centuries were relatively prosperous times for the small farmer. After the death of Basil II taxation, high rents and invasions made life increasingly hard. (5–9)

The weaver at his loom, painted to illustrate Exodus XXXVI, 8–19, describing the hangings of the tabernacle. (10)

'Flight from the world, and from all those in the world, for the sake of the Lord' was represented by a 6th-century abbot of Mt Sinai as a symbolic ladder leading to heaven. Each rung represents a virtue attained, a vice conquered. But each step up—even the very topmost—carried with it the risk of falling. (11)

At the foot of Mt Sinai, where Moses received the tablets of the Law, Justinian built a church (its mosaic of the Transfiguration is shown on pp. 92–3). Here the hermits who had been scattered in separate cells among the rocks came to live—one of the earliest of eastern monastic houses (left), later known as St Catherine's, world-famous for its collection of icons and precious manuscripts. The religious way of life spread and flourished, becoming one of the pillars of Byzantine society. Its heart was another Holy Mountain, on a tongue of land jutting from the northern coast of Greece: Mt Athos. The first endowed monastery was founded in 963; soon there were over twenty, of which that of Dionysiou (below) is characteristic—a large fortified rectangle enclosing a church, splendidly sited on cliffs overlooking the Aegean. By a decree of 1045, still enforced, not only women but female animals are entirely excluded from the whole promontory. (12, 13)

The stern spirituality of Byzantine religion reasserted itself in art as soon as Iconoclasm had passed. Above all the figure of Christ the Judge, the Almighty, 'Pantocrator', dominates the monastic churches of the 9th to 11th centuries, wherever in the Byzantine world they may be. Above left; a symbolic representation of the Eucharist, from Ochrida, in Yugoslavia. Above: Christ the Judge, from Hosios Loukas, near Delphi in Greece. Below: the Kiss of Judas, a fresco from one of the strange rock-cut chapels of Cappadocia. (14, 15, 16)

'**These riches and buildings** are equalled nowhere in the world,' wrote the Jewish traveller Benjamin of Tudela, visiting Constantinople in 1161—and he had seen Rome, Damascus, and Baghdad. This reconstruction, based on recent research, shows it between the 9th and 11th centuries. It was laid out on the grand scale, along axial roads leading from the main gateways to the Great Palace. The early defensive system built by Constantine (*1*) was superseded by the more elaborate walls of Theodosius (*2*), which defied the invader for a thousand years and which still stand (see p. 102). They were pierced by five major gates and several smaller ones, and from each gate straight Roman roads converged on a series of spacious arcaded squares. This was the Triumphal Way, by which the Emperors entered their capital. It began in the west at the Golden Gate (*3*), continued with one change of direction, to the first cross-roads and then turned east to the Forum of Arcadius (*4*), the Forum Bovi (*5*), the Forum Tauri (*6*), the Forum of Constantine (*7*) and finally the Augusteon (*8*). Here one had the Hippodrome (*9*) on one side and the Cathedral of Hagia Sophia (*10*) on the other, and beyond, descending in a series of terraces, galleries and courts to the water's edge, the rambling Palace of

the Emperors (*11*). Of the hundreds of other churches, some of the most notable were St Saviour in Chora (*12*), St John of Studius (*13*), St Irene (*14*), the Holy Apostles (*15*), SS. Sergius and Bacchus (*16*) and the monastery of Constantine Lips (*17*).

Constantinople was ideally placed as the capital of a great empire, lying both on the main trade-route between Europe and Asia, and at the narrowest point of the channel that joined the Black Sea with the Mediterranean. In this bird's-eye view the coast of Asia is just out of sight on the right; in the foreground is the Sea of Marmora, and on the other side of the city the Golden

Horn, which enemy shipping could be prevented from entering by a chain stretched across the mouth (*18*). The opposite shore was also fortified, by ramparts and the Tower of Anastasius (*19*). The main harbours were in the Golden Horn, but if wind or current were too strong for ships to round the point they could use those on the south side. Other features of the public works that stand out are Justinian's Bridge (*20*), the aqueduct of Valens (*21*) and the huge cisterns (*22*)—others were underground—which contained the city's water-supply.

The medieval traveller approaching by sea saw a skyline

'**Kings removing their diadems** take up the cross, the symbol of their Saviour's death', wrote St John Chrysostom; 'on the purple, the cross; in their prayers, the cross; on their armour, the cross; on the holy table, the cross; throughout the universe, the cross. The cross shines brighter than the sun.' The True Cross, according to legend, was discovered by St Helena, the mother of Constantine, captured by the Persians, recovered by Heraclius and brought to Constantinople. Medieval Europe was full of fragments of wood claiming to be part of it, enclosed in reliquaries of gold and venerated as the holiest objects in Christendom. The two reliquaries on the right are both covered by inlays of cloisonné enamel, a medium which reduces the figures to simple but highly expressive forms. On the opposite page is the lid of a reliquary made for Constantine Porphyrogenitus. It is adorned with jewels and enamels representing, in the centre, Christ flanked by John the Baptist (with Gabriel) and the Virgin (with Michael) and the Apostles above and below. (20, 21, 24)

Gorgeous silken shrouds for the burial of saints and rich liturgical robes are among the most splendid works of Byzantine art. Above: textile showing two riders spearing lions. Right: the shroud of St Germain l'Auxerrois—each eagle is nearly two feet high. The strong eastern influence in both is not surprising: the production of silk was for long a Persian monopoly, and was only introduced to the West by Justinian. (22, 23)

The rich decoration and lavish colours of Byzantine architecture have mostly succumbed to Turkish repainting or the passage of centuries. This 12th-century Ascension, from the Sermons of James of Kokkinobaphos, however, is thought to be based on a destroyed church at Constantinople: the Holy Apostles. Both exterior and interior are represented. There are five domes, a large one over the central crossing and four more over the arms of a Greek-cross, a plan that was copied at St Mark's, Venice, whose original appearance may be seen in a mosaic above one of the west doors (left), and in Romanesque France. (18, 19)

dominated by the domes of churches. Over them all, on the high ground that forms the backbone of Byzantium, and from which the streets slope so steeply that some of them are simply flights of steps, rose Hagia Sophia, that 'great incomparable work', as the 6th-century writer Evagrius called it, 'which, excelling in beauty, far surpasses power of description'. (17)

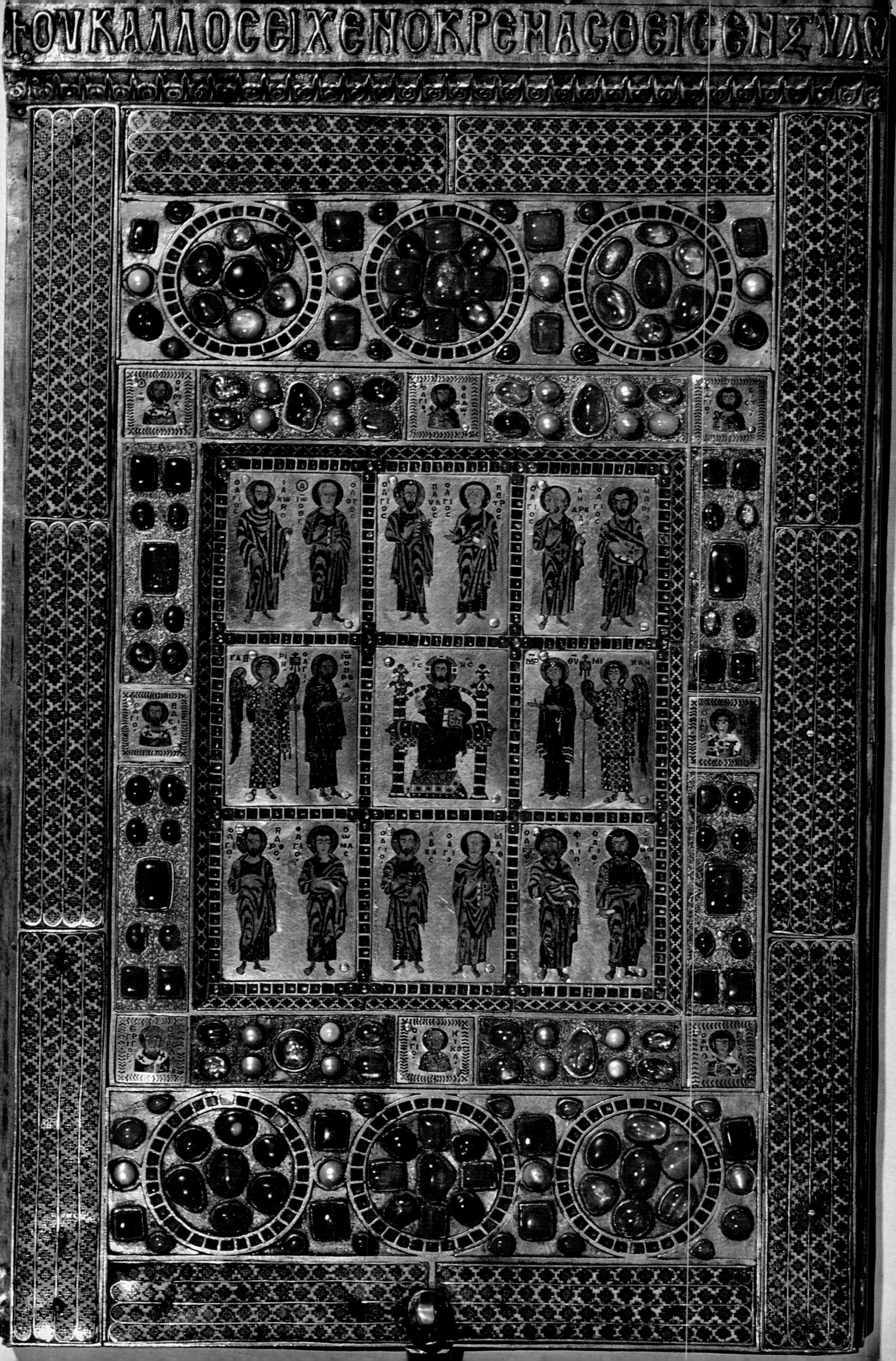
ΟΥΚΑΛΛΟϹΕΙΧΕΝΟΚΡΕΜΑϹΘΕΙϹΕΝΞΥΛΩ

'Through God, Autocrator, King of the Romans':
the ivory relief (right) of Christ crowning Constantine Porphyrogenitus epitomizes the relation of church and society in Byzantium. As Christ ruled the universe, so the emperor ruled the Empire, the governor his province, the father his family—all part of the same hierarchy of delegated authority. Left: a city, perhaps Constantinople, offers a diadem to the conquering Basil II. Below: two more scenes that express the semi-divine nature of the imperial office: Constantine I leads his troops into battle at the Milvian Bridge under the sign of the miraculous cross (a manuscript of the 9th century). And the acclamation of David as King—an Old Testament illustration in which David is seen as a Byzantine prince, raised on a shield by his legionaries and hailed as Emperor. (25, 26, 27, 29)

The old pagan world still lived on, innocently, in much secular art and literature, standing in sharp contrast to the powerful Christian imagery whose origins are ultimately in the East. The Rape of Europa (below) from the exquisite Veroli Casket, dates from the 10th or 11th century, but its spiritual home is the Hellenistic Greece of 1000 years earlier. (28)

The Byzantine Church had its own unique and consecrated role in the hierarchy of the state, and never, as in the West, grew into a separate power capable of independent political action. It was the emperor who had the deciding vote in the election of a patriarch. This 9th-century miniature shows the consecration of a bishop, Gregory of Nazianzus. (30)

The Saints, the Fathers and the Councils had hammered out the basic dogmas of the faith: a union of Eastern religious concepts with Greek rationality. The arts show the same dual inspiration. These saints (James, John the Theologian, Peter, Paul and Andrew) are contemporary with the Veroli Casket, but the repeated frontal poses and static composition stem from Syria. (31)

Leo VI, the Wise (below) kneels at the feet of Christ, a mosaic in the narthex of Hagia Sophia. Leo reigned from 886 to 912; he was unfortunate in his private life, for he married four times before he got a son, the infant Constantine Porphyrogenitus, to whom he left the throne. It was, however, generally a period of prosperity, and Leo earned his surname of 'the Wise' by completing the Digest of Justinian's Laws and composing numbers of poems, orations and epigrams. (33)

The Macedonian dynasty ended in the 11th century amid confusion and discord. Constantine VIII, the weak brother of Basil II, died in 1028 leaving a daughter **Zoe,** one of those characterful women who seem so often to have seized the reins of Byzantine history. She married first Romanus III, but tiring of him had him murdered in order to marry Michael the Paphlagonian, whom she rapidly had crowned. When Michael died she first adopted his handsome nephew Michael V Calaphates who ruled for only a short time, and then she took a third husband, **Constantine IX** Monomachus, with whom she reigned until her death in 1055. The leadership of the state was then at a low ebb, leading to the rise of a powerful new dynasty, the Comnenian house. In the mosaic above, also at Hagia Sophia, Zoe appears on the right. The Emperor on the other side was originally her first husband Romanus, but in about 1042 the head of Constantine IX was apparently substituted; the first word of the inscription above him has clearly been altered and the last is an addition. (32)

The Byzantine World
of the Ninth and Tenth Centuries

J. M. HUSSEY

Symeon the Bulgar burns a church under the walls of Constantinople. In the political upheavals which took place during the minority of Constantine Porphyrogenitus, Symeon was among the dominant figures. In 913 and 924 his armies penetrated to the very walls of the capital. But those massive defences proved once more to be impregnable and the projected marriage of Symeon's daughter to the young Emperor never took place. The old Bulgar foe was successfully kept at bay by the co-Emperor Romanus I. (1)

FROM 820 UNTIL AT LEAST 1025 Byzantine affairs at home and abroad were in the hands of unusually capable statesmen and generals. A practical arrangement was evolved whereby an associate or co-emperor was accepted and duly crowned during a minority or when an emperor of the legitimate house happened to be uninterested in active government. Thus a fiction of legality was cast over what was often in practice an usurpation of the imperial authority of the reigning house. The Byzantines, though there were sporadic periods of quick change, tended to cling more and more tenaciously to an established dynasty even to the length of putting up with two elderly women (one an ex-nun unwillingly dragged from the cloister), the last of the Macedonian dynasty (founded by Basil the Macedonian), which reigned from 867 to 1056. The highlights of occasional revolution should not be allowed to obscure long periods, particularly during the years 842–1025, when continuity of policy prevailed and was marked by spectacular success.

Ninth-century Byzantium could build on the sound administrative foundations of the 7th-century Heraclian and 8th-century Isaurian emperors but it also inherited certain unsolved problems, such as the unwise military and financial policy of the Empress Irene (orthodox though she was in religion), the continued undercurrent of as yet unsolved ecclesiastical controversies, the Bulgar menace in the Balkans, the rise of the Frankish Empire in the west, and the encirclement by hostile Muslim forces to the south-east and in the Mediterranean.

Ringed by Enemies: The Slavs and Bulgars

Byzantium was at all times ringed by hostile neighbours and its continued existence is due to its vigilant diplomacy, effective defences and rich resources. The welcome influx of fresh Slav blood into its multi-racial society was accompanied by the establishment of Slav principalities in the old Roman provinces in the Balkans, and these were near enough to be dangerous enemies. During the years 800–1025 two facts of significance occurred in Byzantino-Slav relations. Firstly, the Slavs were converted to Christianity and after some hesitation chose to accept the missionaries of Greek Constantinople and not of Latin Rome which brought them within the sphere of influence of imperial Byzantium. Secondly, Bulgaria, the first young Slav state to go into action—it was in fact a fusion of Slav and Turkic Bulgar—was defeated in its bid for Constantinople and the prize of imperial authority. In 913 Symeon, the ruler of the First Bulgarian Empire, stood at the gates of the Queen of cities, aspiring to become father-in-law of the Macedonian boy Constantine VII Porphyrogenitus (Born-in-the-purple). He eventually met his match in the Byzantine admiral Romanus who adroitly insinuated himself into the position coveted by Symeon. The Bulgar Tsar was effectively put in his place by both the Patriarch and Romanus. There exists a report of the meeting between Symeon and Romanus in which the Bulgar is told to accept his place in the hierarchy of kings and recognize the superiority of imperial rule and the necessity for the promotion of peace. Symeon shortly afterwards died, probably of cerebral haemorrhage, and his son Peter proved a more pliable vassal of the Empire. But later in the century, recognizing the potential danger of Bulgaria, Byzantium was strong enough itself to adopt

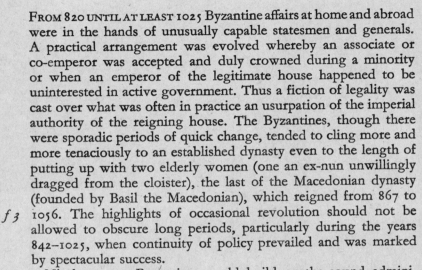

a policy of active conquest. Under John I and Basil II there was an added reason for action, because the powerful Kievan state was taking too close an interest in Bulgaria. John I conquered north-east Bulgaria and incorporated it into the Empire as the provinces of Paristrium and Sirmium. Strong national feeling led however to a revived Bulgarian Empire in the south-west in Macedonia where the Tsar Samuel made Ochrida his capital.

Basil II was a tough and persistent campaigner. Perhaps too he preferred to concentrate on an area whose conquest, unlike the south-east Asian borders, would not increase the authority of the Greek magnates of Asia Minor. By 1014 this western Bulgaria was reduced and Samuel dead, and by 1018 it too had become a Byzantine province. But this was an uneasy conquest. The Bulgarians never willingly accepted Greek rule and much of their resentment found an outlet in the dualist heresy of the Bogomils which arose in the 10th century and never died out during the Middle Ages, even after the re-assertion of Bulgarian independence at the end of the 12th century. Byzantium kept a wary eye on the fluctuating politics of the countryside behind the Dalmatian coastal strip where the Serbs and Croats were growing to maturity. Here it had a rival in Hungary which was to extend its influence south over Croatia, while Byzantium was to some extent successful in exercising a fitful suzerainty over the various groups of small Serb principalities, though it never brought these under its direct control.

The Life and Death Struggle with Islam

On its eastern front and in the East Mediterranean Byzantium had to meet a more implacable foe. The Slavs had been successfully converted to Christianity, but the faith of Mohammed, classed by the Byzantines as a heresy, proved singularly impervious to Christian influence. Wars against Islam took on the form of a crusade and soldiers in campaign were spurred into battle to the accompaniment of the Christian exhortations of priests and cantors. The upsurge of Islam in the 7th and early 8th centuries had driven Byzantium out of Egypt, Palestine and Syria and the infidel was firmly entrenched in the mountain ranges of the Taurus and Anti-Taurus on the eastern boundaries of Asia Minor. As yet Islam had not penetrated into either Asia Minor or the Christian Caucasian kingdoms. But it was a dangerous foe, established first in the Umayyad capital at Damascus and then after 750 centred in Baghdad under the Abbasid caliphate. As long as Byzantium kept Asia Minor it ensured certain vital resources both of men and commodities, and events after 1025 were to show that with the virtual loss of this area to the Seljuk Turks and others the Byzantine lifeline was seriously threatened. But under the Amorians and the Macedonians Byzantium seemed on

f 3

f 2

f 1

126, 7
(29)

p 115
(1)
p 126
(25)

p 116
(2–4)

p 107
(f 5)

f 2

the crest of the wave and during the years 842–1025 moved victoriously forward. For more than a hundred years since the beginning of the 8th century the mountain passes which guarded Cilicia had seen continuous warfare. Each year at certain favourable times the Arabs regularly conducted raids to pillage the Christian frontier lands. From the mid-9th century with the establishment of the Amorians the Christians successfully took the offensive. Under the regency during the minority of Michael III (842–867) the dowager Empress and her minister Theoctistus sought to crown the restoration of orthodoxy in the Church with a victorious drive against the infidel. At the same time this was also to the advantage of the landed magnates in Asia Minor who might reasonably hope to enlarge their own estates by the reconquest of the lands to the east. The revival of both naval and military power showed itself in expeditions which were launched against Crete while Cyprus, for a time at any rate, had been recaptured from the Arabs. Advances were made in Asia Minor and in the Taurus and Anti-Taurus ranges. Byzantine forces moved to the river Euphrates and beyond. Under the co-Emperor Romanus I (919–944) and his successors 10th-century Byzantium achieved still more spectacular victories.

At this time its military and its naval resources were deployed to advantage under a series of brilliant military and naval leaders. The Byzantine general Curcuas penetrated into Mesopotamia. In a series of campaigns, not fought without some reverses, he pressed home his attacks and even captured Edessa and the revered relic of the cloth on which the imprint of Christ's face was marked (the mandylion). After the downfall of Romanus I (he was relegated to a monastery in 944) the life and death struggle between Christian and Muslim for the control of North Syria continued. In the days of the minority of Basil II and Constantine VIII the Asian general (and then co-Emperor) Nicephorus II Phocas reclaimed the Taurus regions and took Antioch, as well as recapturing the islands of Crete (961) and Cyprus (965), while his fellow general and successor, the Armenian co-Emperor John II Tzimisces, was eventually strong enough to move south beyond Antioch into Palestine, successfully reaching Nazareth. It looked as though the Holy Places of the Christians were within Byzantine grasp. But John II died unexpectedly in 972, perhaps poisoned at the instigation of the powerful minister Basil the Grand Chamberlain who feared for his position. John's successor, the Macedonian Basil II, who was now of age, only took control

p 115
(1)

of affairs into his own hands after a fierce struggle with would-be co-Emperors who had cast him for the role of a second Constantine VII. They were mistaken. Basil II did not take after his illustrious and cultured grandfather. Adverse circumstances moulded him into a soured, hardened campaigner who appeared to have none of the traditional Byzantine love of letters, though

he was reputed to have a witty turn of phrase and was something of a patron of art if one may judge from the superb Psalter that bears his name and is now in the Marcian Library at Venice.

Basil II was a realist in his foreign policy as well as at home. He had no use for overpowerful magnates and took stringent measures to curb their authority and their lands. Though he gave equal if not more attention to the Balkans, he also strengthened his eastern front. By diplomacy and campaigning he secured Georgian lands. He subdued Armenian Vaspurakan and made a treaty whereby the remaining portion of the Armenian kingdom would fall to Byzantium on the death of its ruler. Further south around Antioch Basil's swift action and powerful army repulsed the attacks of the Muslim Fatimids of Egypt and the ruler of Aleppo was the Christian Emperor's grateful vassal. The eastern conquests were organized as provinces *(themes)* and the Byzantine position secured in North Syria and in Mesopotamian and Caucasian lands. It may be questioned, in the light of subsequent development, whether his Armenian policy was wise; it might have been more advantageous to retain an independent Armenia, possibly as an ally, but also as a buffer against the eastern enemy. This was all the more so, as Armenians and Greeks did not generally get on. Armenians resented Greek rule, and their church did not hold what the Greeks regarded as orthodox teaching; moreover the Greeks disliked the Armenian propensity for obtaining high office and correspondingly high salaries in imperial service, though grudgingly forced to recognize their ability.

Byzantium and the West

Byzantine successes in the Balkans and on the eastern front were not paralleled in relations with the West. Here Byzantium never fully realized the dangerous nature of rising forces, tending to think of itself as still the only Empire, supreme over all the 'barbarian' principalities. This point of view is illustrated in the 10th-century Italian Bishop Luitprand of Cremona's account of his second embassy to Constantinople in 968. Admittedly Luitprand was deliberately peevish in his alleged report (in reality probably a propaganda pamphlet against the Greeks). But it is in fact clear that the Byzantine Emperor, Nicephorus II, deliberately teased him about the youthfulness of western ecclesiastical tradition and boasted about his naval strength, and though Luitprand evidently had a good place at the imperial dinner party opposite the Emperor (who leant over to speak to him) he was not given formal precedence over the 'unwashed' Bulgarians, as he angrily described them. It was also made clear that his master, Otto I, was regarded by the Byzantines as a mere 'king' and not as an 'Emperor', and in fact considerable Greek resentment was shown both at the German ruler's assumption of the imperial title and at his intrusion into central and south Italian politics.

p 323

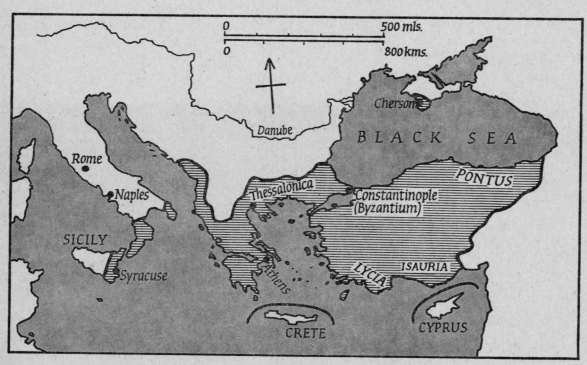

The Byzantine Empire in 850, after it had been shorn of its provinces in the west and south by the invasions described in the last chapter. (2)

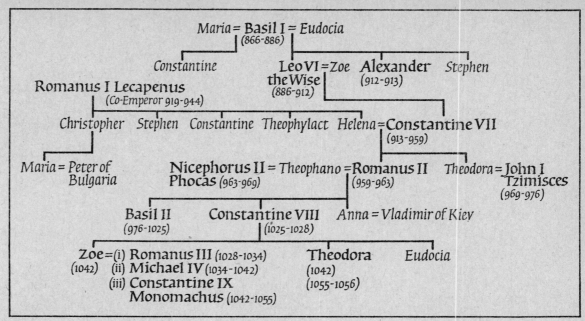

Family-tree of the Macedonian dynasty, which ruled the Byzantine Empire from 867 to 1056. Although the imperial succession was virtually continuous, colleagues, co-emperors and ministers often exercised the real power. (3)

Byzantine relations with the West had in fact been somewhat soured by the Iconoclast controversy, and the Carolingians had made the most of this in order to further their own strong interests in north Italy and the northern Adriatic. But the Franks did not want an open rift with Constantinople; hence Charlemagne's various proposals for marriage alliances. It was only under duress and for a very short time that Byzantium recognized his claim to the title of 'Emperor', at the same time making it clear that their ruler was 'Emperor of the Romans' with all its implications. Byzantium in the 9th century, although it had lost its central and north Italian lands to the Carolingians and the papacy, still kept the southern provinces of Apulia and Calabria and took full diplomatic advantage of the rivalries of the small south Italian cities and principalities, such as Naples, Salerno or Benevento. Rome, too, under the mid-10th century Alberic, the 'Roman senator and ruler' (died 954), was well disposed to Constantinople and hostile to the Saxons. But with the establishment of Saxon control in the northern *regnum italicum* of Lombardy and from 960 onwards to some extent over the papacy, the situation changed. Nicephorus II might laugh at Otto's ambassador Luitprand when he came to ask for a Byzantine princess for Otto I's son, and Otto's military efforts against the Byzantines in Apulia failed. Nicephorus' successor John I was a more subtle diplomat and he thought it advisable to concede something to the West. He compromised in 972 by sending as bride Theophano, a Byzantine noblewoman, not the Macedonian princess for whom Otto had asked (apparently Anna, who was however later married off in 989 to the Russian Vladimir). Her union with Otto and their mutual coronation is commemorated in an ivory now in the Musée de Cluny, an essentially Byzantine work with an inscription in Greek. The marked Byzantine influence in Ottonian art of the time has been explained by the suggestion that Theophano may have taken Byzantine objects and even craftsmen with her to the West. Byzantines may have been forced to give more attention to the Balkans and the eastern front, but they never abandoned their claims to lands in Italy, and indeed stoutly maintained the 8th-century Iconoclast Leo III's transference of the south Italian (and Greek and west Balkan) dioceses from papal to patriarchal ecclesiastical jurisdiction, though this was a perennial source of irritation to Rome and one pope after another pressed for its reversal, at any rate as far as Italian lands were concerned. Ravenna and the central duchies had been lost to the West in the 8th century, the island of Sicily in the early 9th century to the Arabs who indeed also constantly threatened the west coast of Italy. The Byzantine diplomatic service made attempts to establish an alliance with the late 9th-century Frankish 'Emperor' Louis II against Arab inroads into Italian coastal areas, but western and Byzantine military and naval methods differed and each reproached the other for lack of success. In the mid-10th century Otto I was a more powerful adversary; the maritime cities south of Rome, such as Naples, Gaeta or Amalfi, were virtually independent,

though willing to give their allegiance to Constantinople at a price. Alberic of Rome died in 954 and after 960 Otto I laid a heavy hand upon the city, controlling papal elections and to some extent internal politics. Otto even led an expedition against the Byzantine city of Bari in his pique at not being given a Greek bride for his son as quickly as he had hoped. He was defeated and wisely reverted to further diplomatic efforts which eventually succeeded.

Otto II's son Otto III, was therefore half Byzantine, and he tried to build up in the West a Latin counterpart to East Rome's conception of a hierarchy of rulers with the Emperor at the apex, a Christian 'family of kings' under the Roman Emperor. This was primarily a Byzantine idea, no doubt instilled into the young ruler by his Greek mother and his Greek tutors. But in trying to put this into practice in the West he was also influenced by an imperial tradition which went back to Charlemagne. He held his court in Rome and was affianced to a Byzantine Macedonian princess, Zoe, the niece of Basil II. But Otto III died in 1002 and his dream—and the possible union of the two empires—came to nothing. His successors had other views, and Basil II planned a systematic reorganization of the Byzantine south Italian provinces which he intended to use as a base for reconquering Sicily. It is highly doubtful that he ever intended the marriage of Zoe and Otto III to bring about the union of the two empires and had Zoe married into the German house, a different successor would surely have been found to her father Constantine VIII, Basil II's indolent brother, possibly his daughter Theodora, who never had much chance in straight competition with Zoe.

One factor which the Byzantines underestimated in the West was the Latin church. The swift succession of popes and antipopes after the Ottonian intervention gave a false impression of weakness and masked the stamina of reforming ecclesiastics and the vital upsurge of popular religious feeling which came to a head in the reformed papacy of the mid-11th century and the crusading movement. In the north the Byzantines had to admit the growing power of Venice, a city which they had always regarded as being under their suzerainty. Basil II granted commercial privileges to the republic, the forerunner of more to come as the Venetian navy grew indispensable to a weakened Byzantium whose own fleet fell into disrepair after the mid-11th century.

New Troubles

Thus when in 1025 the mighty Basil II the Slayer of the Bulgars died, Byzantine successes in foreign policy, could only be maintained at the cost of constant naval and military vigilance. Between 1025 and 1081 there were however twelve different short reigned rulers, only three of whom had any pretensions to statesmanship and military ability. Further there was a deadly feud between the military party and the aristocracy of the court and the higher civil service, and for the greater part of this period the navy and army were deliberately starved by the latter who were usually in

f 2

p 323

p 325–6

f 9

p 128 (32)

the ascendancy. Added to this, Norman adventurers appeared and established themselves in southern Italy, and the Turks who had overrun the caliphate broke down the eastern defences of Asia Minor and established the sultanate of Rum in the heart of the Empire. And from 1096 onwards the western crusading movement brought bands of marauding Latin soldiers across the highways of the Empire and added to Byzantine troubles by setting up Latin states in Syria and Palestine. It is therefore not surprising that the first signs of the downfall of the Byzantine Empire can be found in the mid-11th century. This decline was not due entirely to external attacks nor, it should be noted, was there any fall off in the cultural activities of Byzantium which continued to flourish however much the frontiers contracted.

The Imperial Office

The pivot of the central departments, and indeed of every sphere of Byzantine government, was the Emperor. The Byzantine constitution, if it can be so called, was an autocracy tempered by respect for law. Imperial election and acclamation came to be normally something of a formality save in time of revolution, when a usurper in search of the throne naturally relied on military and popular support as symbolized by their 'acclamation'. Often the throne passed from father to son or to the nearest suitable kinsman. To safeguard the dynasty a son would often be crowned in infancy as joint emperor. But much of the success of Byzantium under the Macedonians was due to the practice of having a second or co-Emperor during a minority, or when a ruler of established dynasty was pre-disposed to other than governmental activities, as for instance the scholarly Constantine VII. The acceptance of the statesmanlike admiral Romanus or the distinguished general Nicephorus Phocas as co-Emperor ensured firm control and military success.

The senior, or 'great', Basileus, as he was known, had supreme control in every sphere; administration, legislation, the judiciary, defence and foreign policy, all ultimately depended on his will, as in most other contemporary royal circles. He was advised by a small informal body of councillors whom he could dismiss or summon as he wished. The senate no longer had any real authority as such, for its membership had become merely honorary. But lack of constitutional organs in the western European sense did not however imply irresponsibility. Limits on imperial authority were imposed by respect for law as well as by a keen sense of expediency. The Emperor inherited a deeply ingrained acceptance of certain imperial responsibilities which included not only the maintenance of good order and the effective defence of the Empire but the preservation of Christian orthodoxy and the Christian Church.

Christianity was a formative influence in shaping both the Late Roman and the Byzantine Empire and this is reflected in the Byzantine conception of the imperial office. The medieval Christian Emperor, like his predecessor Constantine the Great 'the thirteenth apostle', was regarded as the representative or vicegerent of Christ on earth and the Empire over which he ruled was thought of as the terrestrial reflection of the celestial realm. The Emperor was then actuated not only by the desire to do justice, but by the Christian virtue of compassion towards mankind, by the divine attribute of *philanthropia*.

p 126
(25–27,
29)

The 'Poor' and the 'Powerful'

Two particular problems of internal government exercised 9th- and 10th-century Byzantine rulers. These were the maintenance of justice for all and security of tenure for the small farmer. In different ways both these exemplify the imperial concern for their subjects, and, it may be added, also for their own finance and safety.

Basil I, the peasant founder of the Macedonian house, began by setting up a commission to recodify and revise the laws. This work was continued by his son Leo VI the Wise, who is depicted in mosaic prostrate at Christ's feet above the western door of Hagia Sophia at Constantinople. The resulting corpus, which was in Greek and was known as the *Basilics*, became the basis of medieval Byzantine law, but only very gradually, for it was many years before it superseded Justinian's corpus. This was

however a great task and the legal activity of the time is also reflected in several smaller handbooks, some of which were unofficial publications but which nevertheless throw light on existing practice and opinion.

Contrary to the impression often held, the Byzantine administrative system possessed considerable flexibility and was modified as circumstances demanded. By the 9th century the extensive central organs of the early period under a powerful minister had been split up and the head of each differentiated department was now directly responsible to the Emperor. The pressing problem of Byzantine internal government in the 9th and 10th centuries was not so much the building up of administrative organs, as the provision of secure tenure for the small farmer. This was closely related to a basic problem which exercised most medieval governments, i.e. the central authority's control over the provincial magnate.

The problem of the small-holder's security of tenure was by no means exclusive to the Amorian and Macedonian period. It involved imperial finance and imperial defence as well as the danger of the over powerful provincial magnate. Whatever its origins it is clear that by the late 9th and early 10th centuries there was a fairly widespread system of granting small farms in return for military, or in coastal regions, naval, service. The grants went from father to eldest son who had to turn out and do so much military service. At the other end of the provincial scale was the powerful landowner with widespread and rich estates, with local influence and resources to enable him to weather droughts or pestilences and to hold his own *vis-à-vis* the tax collector. It was all too usual for the small farmer faced with bankruptcy to be forced to sell, perhaps becoming the tenant farmer of a local lord, or even to abandon his holding in flight, going to swell the beggar population of some town. Romanus I, and later Basil II, made special efforts to help smallholders and to give villagers the right of pre-emption. In certain cases lands bought up by wealthy families or by ecclesiastical landlords had to be restored. Basil was particularly ferocious in his attack on the powerful provincial landowner whose armed retainers in their thousands might so easily threaten the safety of the throne. Finance was also involved and imperial efforts were made to safeguard dues owed to the exchequer and to control any movement of tenantry which might alienate the rights of the central fisc. Meagre surviving records, mostly from a later period when Basil II's firm hand was withdrawn, show how powerless even imperial legislation was to control the rich landlord. And monastic or episcopal stewards were as predatory as the layman's bailiff, persistently mopping up an olive orchard here or a vineyard there in their relentless efforts to extend their estates at the expense of men too poor to sustain unending actions in local courts where they might in any case have little chance of success.

But under Basil II the poorer farmer was deliberately protected. Basil transferred to the 'powerful' the responsibility for the taxes of defaulters which had previously fallen on the village community as the taxable unit. Thus he further crippled the resources of a class already laid low by his ruthless confiscations. But after his death in 1025 conditions worsened for the small farmer, particularly in Asia Minor where marauding attacks from the Turcomen were added to the relentless squeeze of both tax collector and local magnate. The best chance of survival was to become a tenant on a big estate preferably in the European provinces.

Church and State: Patriarch and Emperor

There was inevitably an essential connection between the Byzantine state and the Greek Orthodox Church. To conceive of the possibility of a clear cut separation between the two is to misunderstand the framework of the Byzantine world. The Emperor was the guardian of the Church, the convenor of its General Councils and its protector. It could not be otherwise with the vicegerent of Christ. This was not to deny the vital role of the consecrated episcopate and the ordained priesthood. Headed by its patriarch, the patriarchate of Constantinople had its own place in Christendom along with the other four historic patriarchates. By the

p 127
(30, 31)

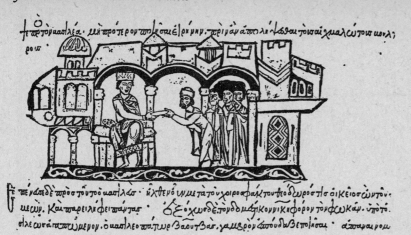

A Byzantino-Bulgarian peace is negotiated. Symeon's original quarrel with Byzantium had been over trade rights. His attacks on the Empire in the end forced Leo VI to concede the disputed points and to pay an annual tribute to the Bulgarian kingdom. (4)

9th century three of these, Jerusalem, Antioch and Alexandria, were in Muslim territory, leaving Latin Rome and Greek Constantinople as the two forces in a Christian world, now no longer bilingual as in the days when both Greek and Latin were understood. Relations between the two fluctuated but there was as yet no prolonged schism.

The patriarch of Constantinople was the head of the Byzantine Church and it was he who crowned the emperor and received his profession of orthodoxy. Although the emperor had a deciding voice in the patriarchal election, patriarchs were by no means entirely subservient. When in the mid-10th century the general John Tzimisces murdered Nicephorus II Phocas and proposed to marry his widow, the unsavoury and already twice-wed Empress Theophano, the Patriarch decisively intervened and refused the Emperor entry to the cathedral of Hagia Sophia until he had promised to abandon this project. But such extremes were rarely necessary, and normally the patriarch and emperor worked together reasonably well. They were both cogs in the same wheel and the smooth running of the close-knit affairs of Church and state depended on their co-operation. The court ceremonies at Epiphany or Easter needed both Emperor and churchman; the extension of the imperial frontiers and imperial influence likewise needed the cooperation of both, and as in the western world friction was as far as possible avoided.

In the late 9th and 10th centuries there were no great ecumenical councils to pronounce on trinitarian and christological issues as in the days of the early Byzantine Empire. The raging controversy over the icons had found its solution in the Seventh General Council of 787, confirmed in 843. But this did not mean that theological development ceased or that ecclesiastical problems vanished. Iconoclasm left its aftermath in the antagonism between the passionately orthodox extremists and the less fanatical moderate churchmen. This tension was reflected in the prolonged disputes which surrounded the enigmatic figure of one of the most learned laymen of the Amorian and early Macedonian renaissance, the famous Photius, who became twice Patriarch of Constantinople and protagonist in the disputes between the sees of Rome and Constantinople. Such disputes had far-reaching implications—jurisdictional, doctrinal and political. The affair of Photius' appointment to the patriarchate and the appeals to Rome by his rival's party were bound up with dynastic imperial policy in Constantinople and ecclesiastical (and political) clashes in the missionary field, particularly in Moravia and in the Balkans. Later generations up to the present day have been misled by the deeply ingrained western view that Photius himself was to some extent responsible for the rift between the two churches and by the mistaken idea that he died in schism. In actual fact, as the brilliant researches of Catholic scholars have now shown, Photius, though he supported the older version of the Creed without the *filioque* clause and had stormy clashes with Rome, died in communion with the Holy See. It was left for unfortunate developments in the 11th and subsequent centuries to bring out and intensify

certain underlying differences between eastern and western Christians which were to result in an ecclesiastical rift which is not yet healed.

An Expanding Faith: Russia and the Balkans

It is sometimes implied that the epoch of the Church Fathers was succeeded by a period in which all really worthwhile development ended. This is not so. The achievement was of a different nature. The concentrated intellectual activity of the patristic age was now bearing fruit at home and abroad. The work of the Fathers had articulated a body of teaching which could be developed within the Church and handed on to its converts. It is of course true that Byzantine missionaries were not always successful. Islam, considered to be a Christian heresy, remained impervious to the claims of Christianity and did indeed prove its own expertise in the mission field. The insidious dualist heresy of the Bogomils (so-called after their leader Bogomil) arose in the 10th century and gained a firm hold on certain districts in the Balkans and persisted there throughout the Middle Ages.

But the Greek Church could claim credit for some pioneer work among the Hunnic peoples migrating westwards from central Asia across the southern steppes of Russia as well as in Moravia, Bohemia and Hungary. Their achievement was still more obvious in the Balkans and in the Russian principality of Kiev. Bulgaria was the first Balkan settlement to crystallize into a state and after a brief period of playing off Rome against Constantinople, its ruler Boris (852–889) realized where his interests lay and threw in his lot with the Greek Church. Except along parts of the Dalmatian coast, the other Balkan peoples did likewise. Byzantium fortunately had men well equipped to introduce Christianity to the Slavs. The *Lives* of the missionary-scholars, Constantine, better known as Cyril, and Methodius, give a vivid picture of their activities among the Khazars in the Caspian regions, as well as in Moravia and elsewhere. Photius, himself a learned and able churchman, knew the advantage of sending out men who were highly trained philologists as well as dedicated Christians. It was thus possible to help the Slavs to produce a written language, and more important still, to give them the Christian church services in their own language and to set up centres where the rich doctrinal and liturgical heritage of the Church could be studied and translated into Slavonic. *p 142 (2)*

Thus from the 9th century onwards the Balkans were brought into close contact with their Byzantine neighbours who had much to offer besides Christianity. They learnt their statecraft from the Byzantine court, they often received their education in the imperial capital, they imported Greek administration into their own princely circles and grafted it on to their native customs and traditions, and from the 10th century onwards they increasingly married into Byzantine families. As they grew to political stature these Balkan principalities became an integral part of the network of international diplomacy, though in the mid-10th century, as we have seen, it was still difficult for an Italian bishop to stomach the presence of the Bulgarian ambassadors at the *f 4* Byzantine court and the honour which was diplomatically accorded them. But Bulgaria (as Constantinople had good cause to know) was a much nearer neighbour and a greater potential danger to Byzantium than the Saxon king whom the Italian Luitprand represented, even though Otto I did have ambitions in Italy.

North of the Black Sea another principality was brought within the sphere of the Orthodox Church during the Macedonian regime. In 957 the Princess Olga of Kiev visited Constantinople to be received with customary splendour. She herself was a convert to Christianity. It was not however until the end of the 10th century that the Kievan state formally recognized this faith when Olga's grandson Vladimir (972–1015) accepted it for himself and his people and married the Byzantine Princess Anna of the Macedonian house. The entry about this event in the *Russian Primary Chronicle* conveys something of the appeal which the Greek Church made. The Russian envoys telling Vladimir of their visit to Hagia Sophia were at a loss to describe their experience, 'We only know that God dwells there among men and their service is fairer than the ceremonies of other nations; for

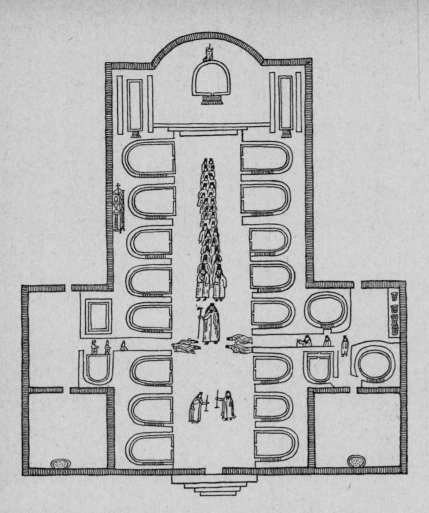

The refectory of the Great Lavra Monastery, Mt Athos. Refectories were usually kept separate from the rest of the monastery buildings. Here the abbot is shown leaving in procession after a meal. At the top, on a dais, is the high table, and down both sides D-shaped tables for the monks. The two rooms right and left of the entrance are concerned with water and wine-supplies; the baskets in the corner of the right-hand transept are for bread. Against the wall on the left stands the pulpit from which the Gospels or the works of the Fathers were read during the meal. (5)

we cannot forget that beauty'. Thus another young church came under the Patriarch of Constantinople and in its early days owed much to Greek advice and to Greek spirituality.

The Christian World
In the East Mediterranean and in the Slav worlds Christian grace was mediated through a double channel, through the sacraments and through the spiritual gifts *(charismata)* of holy men and women. In a Slav or Byzantine diocese the usual hierarchy of secular clergy functioned, ranging from the bishop to the parish priest. The cathedral church might even have such hordes of clerics that their numbers had to be limited. If it had a miracle-working shrine it would attract large crowds especially on its patron saint's anniversary, when a fair would also be held, perhaps on an almost international scale, as that of St Demetrius of Thessalonica in October. Often the spiritual needs of the countryside would have been poorly served but for some nearby monastery. A large house with rich, perhaps imperial, endowments would have alms to administer on a lavish scale and the chapels in the monastic grounds could be used by the villagers. The small and humble monastic house, as saints' lives show, also served the neighbourhood no less faithfully.

p 117–8 Monasticism had become an integral part of the life of Byzan-
(11, 12) tium. To regard monks as escapists is to misunderstand the aims of this Christian way of life. From its inception in Egypt and Palestine in the 4th century monasticism had continually inspired Christians to dedicate themselves to the worship of God in liturgical services day and night and in contemplation accompanied by the perpetual struggle for self-mastery. Whatever form their life might take, contemplation leading to knowledge of God was the

aim of these eastern monks. Some were isolated hermits, some lived grouped round a spiritual leader in what was called a *lavra*, and others followed a common life in a monastery under an abbot. These different ways were not mutually exclusive but, under authority, might be interchangeable. Service to mankind was something which, if need arose, was inevitable though subordinate. The holy saint, whether a hermit recluse or the abbot of a cenobitic house, bore with the needs and problems of the ordinary man and was never indifferent to the drought threatening the villagers' livelihood or the beggar shivering at night in the dark alleyway.

Symeon the New Theologian belongs to the late 10th and early 11th centuries and he is one of the outstanding Byzantine saints. He admirably demonstrates much that Byzantine monasticism stood for. He developed from an undisciplined novice who was expelled from the Studite monastery in Constantinople for insubordination into an experienced abbot of another house nearby and the chosen confessor of the laity in the capital. Driven out of the city at the instigation of a jealous ecclesiastic he built up yet another house in the neighbourhood. His life was written by his disciple, Nicetas Stethatus, who shows Symeon's place in public affection as well as his qualities as a spiritual guide. But it is especially Symeon's own writings, sermons and accounts of his experiences in the contemplative life, which were used from his own times to the present day, serving later generations in modern Greek or Slav translation. In these works the highest aims of the monk lie revealed and it is clear why Orthodox spirituality did not wither.

It is sometimes implied that there was a fundamental antagonism between monks and humanists. Up to a point this is true. But however emphatic monastic repudiation of 'secular learning' might be, it was almost impossible for an ascetic to cut himself off completely from his Greek heritage. Simply reading the church fathers and the commentaries on their works might bring him into contact with pagan gods and myths and perhaps illustrations of these. Classical sources exercised a potent influence over Christian iconography, not only in manuscripts for devout reading but in the decoration of the church walls. Though many a pious monk might not be aware of it, the prototype of the Anastasis or of the infant Christ having his bath in the Nativity scene which caught his eye when at service in chapel, might be some figure of classical mythology. Within monastic scriptoria the books copied were not exclusively religious, and during the lifetime of Symeon the New Theologian a certain monastic scriptorium in Constantinople produced *inter alia* Thucydides, Lucian, Aristotle, Demosthenes and a military handbook, the *Tactica*.

Symeon the New Theologian was himself a product of a world whose classical and Christian traditions were inextricably interwoven. No one who reads his works is likely to take at its face value his repudiation of all secular learning. His style, vocabulary, range of reading, all contradict such a claim. His mainspring was the grace of God, his theme was the spiritual life, yet his tools were provided by a long tradition of Greek learning which he shared albeit unconsciously with Byzantine humanists.

Mt Athos: The Holy Mountain
It fell to Symeon's lot to live and work for most of his life in a great city or its environs. During his lifetime monasticism was taking root in one of its most famous medieval strongholds, Mount Athos, a magnificent steeply wooded tongue of land to the east of Thessalonica. Here in 963 the Emperor Nicephorus Phocas, who himself had certain leanings towards the ascetic life, founded and endowed the monastery known as the Great *f 5* Lavra under the guidance of his old confessor St Athanasius, and presented to the monastery a reliquary and a book-cover which still survive there. Though there had previously been some intermittent monastic activity on the peninsula, it was only from now onwards that the splendid series of foundations began. *f 6* Mount Athos' renown as a monastic centre spread far beyond p 118, 9 its own shores and beyond the imperial frontiers. It was visited (13) by monks from distant parts of the Christian world, from Kiev or from Rome, while countries such as Georgia, Serbia or Russia

were to set up their own houses on the Holy Mountain which in the late Middle Ages and beyond was one of the spiritual power houses of the Orthodox Church. Greek monks also travelled and not only north or eastwards. Rome had its apostolic shrines to be visited and there are instances of eastern monks who even settled in western communities. In the 10th century a monastery for Greek and Irish monks was founded by the Bishop of Toul, and there were of course Greek houses in Rome and elsewhere in Italy at this time. It was from another 'Holy Mountain' in south Italy that St Nilus went to found his Greek house of Grottaferrata in 1004.

Monasticism was one of the pillars of Byzantine society whether in its heyday as in the 10th century, or later in the time of its distress, and it has left in its still living tradition a more tangible witness than the less articulate everyday religious life of the laity could do. But though the holy man might pass beyond the ordinary sacramental channels, the spiritual life of most, whether laity or monks, was normally nourished through the Divine Liturgy, the sacrament of communion. The memorial of countless unknown men and women lies in the churches which have survived in town or countryside, some with their interior decoration of mosaic, or more often fresco. Here the reality of the Byzantine intermingling of time and eternity can be seen; here the Liturgy took place, perhaps against the frescoed background of the heavenly celebration of Christ offering communion to the angelic host as in Ochrida, or the congregation would worship surrounded by mosaics of the saints of earlier generations together with those of the holy men of the neighbourhood, as the 10th-century St Luke of Stiris in the monastery of Hosios Loukas still standing in the mountains of Phocis.

p 119
(14)

p 119
(15)

A Cosmopolitan Empire: Underlying Rifts

Like the Roman Empire of classical times, Byzantium contained many different races, from Armenian highlanders or nomad Vlach shepherds to Greek fishermen or Slav farmers. These were united by the bonds of their common citizenship and Christian faith and at a more sophisticated level by Greek intellectual traditions. However diverse their racial origin and their background it was remarkable how those Byzantines who rose to key positions adapted themselves to the hierarchical system which bound together the society and political life of Byzantium. But in spite of the emphasis constantly placed on the Hellenic heritage it should however be remembered that Byzantium was at all times open to other influences, particularly from the Muslim world. On the frontiers there was a kind of marcher culture drawing on both Muslim and Christian traditions and even in the very heart of the Empire there was a two way traffic. Muslim

scholars visited Constantinople and Byzantines went to work in Muslim circles. Even emperors did not hesitate to adopt certain customs of the caliph's magnificent court. Many lands within or near the Empire preserved their own distinctive traditions, as among the Caucasian or Slav peoples. They kept their own language too, though a knowledge of Greek was essential for all who hoped for advancement. Greek remained the language of political life and of cultured Byzantine circles. Though there were long enduring hostilities—for instance the Greeks and Armenians hated each other—there was no racial discrimination as such, nor was low birth a bar to promotion. Basil I came of humble stock; so did the admiral, and later co-Emperor, Romanus I Lecapenus. Great estates and aristocratic forebears might even be an embarrassment, as in the days of Basil II, who distrusted men with powerful relatives and strong economic backing.

In contrast to the military provincial aristocracy there was an intellectual *élite* closely associated with the capital and the court. This underlying dichotomy in Byzantine society was to become a dominating and disastrous feature of the years between Basil II's death in 1025 and the accession of Alexius Comnenus in 1081 during which period it developed into a prolonged and fatal struggle. The germs of this bitter antagonism can already be discerned during the late 9th and 10th centuries, though any head-on clash was usually quashed by rulers strong enough to assert effective central control. But differences of policy and underlying tension showed up clearly when the 10th-century Nicephorus II Phocas of landed Asia stock went back on some of Romanus I's legislation in protection of the small farmer and boldly stated that this had been unfair to the larger landowner. Basil II, who reversed this, had no illusions about the ability of the 'powerful' to look after themselves. In the event he was proved right. No amount of imperial edicts could check the growth of the strong, and often disruptive, local units which were to characterize the economy of surviving Byzantine lands in the later Middle Ages.

Secular Learning: Christian Values

The intellectual aristocracy bound together by their devotion to Hellenic culture found their natural centre in the capital and at court. Education was never the monopoly of the Church and it had a strong secular flavour. At the lowest level there is some evidence for village schools; better-off families had tutors for their children, both boys and girls. In middle-class households sometimes the early teaching came from the mother of the family. In a well-off household books would be available. Symeon the New Theologian mentions that as a boy he had read John Climacus before he went to Constantinople to his uncle to

p 120–2
(17)

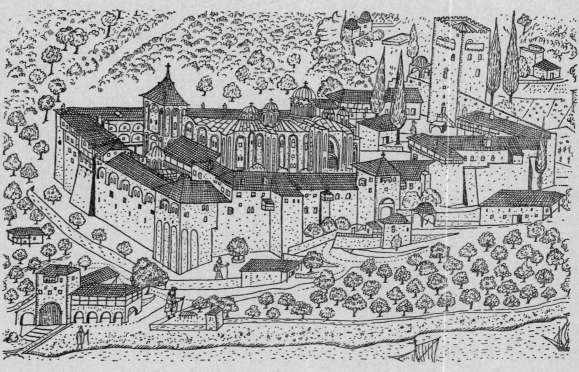

A typical monastery on Mt Athos in the 18th century. In the second half of the 10th century the promontory began to be occupied by these monastic foundations. The actual fabric of the buildings has been constantly renewed up to modern times—the church is nearly always the only ancient part—but the basic plan has not varied. The monastery formed a rectangle with the church inside it and at some point a fortified tower. (6)

A scene showing students and teachers. Constantinople was well-known for its university, and scholarship was encouraged by many Byzantine rulers. Constantine Porphyrogenitus, for instance, was a generous patron of the arts and of learning, and under his rule the Empire reached new heights of achievement. (7)

complete his education; various books are listed in the will of the later 11th-century country landowner Eustathius. Sometimes education (with opportunity for sport as well as letters) might also be obtained in monasteries and girls might be educated in a nunnery. Often monks or nuns would have had their education in the secular world before entering the house, though there were establishments run by churchmen, such as the patriarchal school in Constantinople. There were at most times private coaches who catered for pupils in the bigger towns, and often the household of a rich patron attracted and provided for young would-be scholars. At the highest level Constantinople had superseded earlier centres such as Gaza or Athens famed for philosophical, or Rome and Beirut for legal, studies. A university had been founded in the capital as early as 425 (then with Latin as well as Greek chairs, while theology was noticeably absent). This centre usually depended on imperial patronage and had its ups and downs. Bardas Caesar, the uncle of Michael III and a contemporary of the learned Photius, appears to have taken an active part in stimulating higher studies, and subsequent members of the imperial circle, including the Emperor Leo VI and his son Constantine VII were possessed by the Byzantine passion for letters. There was too a practical side to imperial support of the university, since its legal school turned out trained civil servants, at all times a necessity for a highly developed state such as Byzantium.

The emphasis of Byzantine studies was on elegant presentation and for this reason the rhetorical aids of the classical world were specially valued. There was almost an over-emphasis on tradition which made an artificial Attic style the language of polite circles. In the early Byzantine period the Greek Fathers had taken the lead in adapting the intellectual equipment of the classical world to the service of Christianity, as their theological works witness. Now in the 10th century the emphasis was to some extent on preservation, imitation and reproduction. In the scriptoria copies were made of the plays of Euripides, or of Hellenistic handbooks on practical subjects such as veterinary surgery. The charge is sometimes made that Byzantines in the middle and later medieval periods were so busy turning out stylized rhetorical occasional pieces and letters, or compiling handy anthologies to provide a store of apt quotations from classical or patristic writers, or writing commentaries on the Bible and classical authors, that they had no time for thought or indeed for creative work of any kind. That is not so. To take only the 10th and 11th centuries, there was excellent historical writing, like that of the 10th-century Leo the Deacon or the 11th-century Psellos; there were the admirable handbooks on foreign policy or on court ceremonial which we owe to Constantine VII; there was poetry, whether secular verse in the classical metre as that of John Geometres, or liturgical, as the canons of John Mauropous, or the rousing epic *Digenis Akrites* in a syllabic metre; there was the development of church music closely related to liturgical poetry; and above all there were some of the finest masterpieces of the spiritual life in Symeon the New Theologian's sermons and mystical works called *Hymns of the Divine Loves* (not written in any artificial or archaic style). And this is apart from achievements in the fields

of art and architecture, whether in surviving illustrated manuscript or in monastery and church, or in the mosaic-decorated palaces which are now known to us only through literary evidence.

Economics of an Age of Brilliance

Byzantium was a wealthy society, judged by contemporary standards, as well as an educated one, though it was only the minority who enjoyed the material luxuries and intellectual heritage for which it was renowned. Social and political life were focussed in the capital, in the complex of buildings known as the Great Palace. Here, next door to the magnificent cathedral of Hagia Sophia, the daily life of the court throughout the Christian year was lived according to protocol set out in detail in the 10th-century *Book of Ceremonies*. Even a cursory glance at this shows how important was the role of the Christian religion and the buildings and works of art associated with it. In the palace itself the living quarters, halls of audience, barracks and open courts alternated with churches, and the number of churches and religious foundations in the town itself was legion. In most of them relics, of great religious significance, were preserved, most of them housed in caskets of ivory of mounts of gold, silver, enamel or precious stones, while an elaborate decoration of the walls in paint and mosaic above and marble below was virtually as much an essential part of the building as the roof itself. Vessels of gold and silver were similarly associated with the ritual, and it was their profusion which served to acquire for this age the appellation of sumptuous.

But though more is known about the religious art than the secular, it would be wrong to think that no secular art existed. The ivory caskets, adorned with classical scenes, that survive in many western museums and treasuries represent one aspect of this, and existing texts tell of the multitude of gold and silver vessels on the tables in the banqueting halls of the Great Palace. There too the walls were coated with marble, or with rich hangings, and there were precious carpets on the floors, while the courtiers were clothed in the finest silks. There was a special factory in the palace, called the Zeuxippos, which was employed in their manufacture. Visitors to the Byzantine court, perhaps from Kiev or Baghdad or Cremona, have left eye-witness accounts of magnificent processions, banquets and receptions, of Byzantine nobles in their official robes of office and of the silence before the sacred majesty. But even emperors had their moments off, and there were polo grounds and imperial yachts and barges and frequent hunting parties. Emperors found time to write: Constantine VII was absorbed by his scholarly interests and his well-educated daughters helped him in his work. The tough soldier Basil II characteristically did not bother to look at anything but military handbooks.

Among the most useful and valued of Byzantine civil servants were the 'curiosi', or informers, whose business it was to observe and report on the loyalty of both officials and general public. This 13th–14th-century illustration shows two such 'curiosi' taking down the conversation of two conspirators in a private house. (8)

The imperial palace, a vast complex of buildings of all dates from the 4th century onwards, adjoined the Cathedral of Hagia Sophia. Here Theodora, the last of the Macedonian dynasty, is seen passing from the cathedral to the palace when, just before the blinding and deposition of Michael V Calaphates, she was raised to power in 1042 to rule with her sister Zoe, who is addressing the crowd while the senate is assembled in the palace. (9)

p 120–2
(17)
f 11

Within the splendid fortifications of the capital there were the mansions of the wealthy, as well as those scattered along the slopes of the wooded hills on either side of the Bosphorus. In the city markets and bazaars, merchants and shopkeepers, beggars and visitors of every race crowded and jostled. Visiting traders, such as the Rhos (Rus), had their own quarters and their activities and privileges were carefully controlled by treaty. Coming down the waterways of Russia, they bought ermine and sable and other furs, as well as slaves, honey and wax. From eastern trade, especially with the Arabs, came perfumes, spices, ivory and more slaves. The local traders and manufacturers of the capital, such as bakers or raw-silk merchants or fishmongers or perfumiers, were organized into guilds. The early 10th-century *Book of the Prefect* sets out regulations for trade and industry in Constantinople in some detail, giving glimpses of the economic life of the most important city of the Empire. Raw-silk merchants were strictly forbidden from spinning silk or from selling raw silk in their homes privately. Penalties varied from a substantial fine to being flogged and shaved, or even banished. Slaves might be used in business transactions but their masters had to take full responsibility for their actions. The conditions of journeymen's employment were controlled; raw-silk merchants could only make a contract with them for a month at a time.

p 117
(10)

Import and export trade was controlled by imperial officials throughout the Empire. Customs duties formed an important source of imperial revenue. The government also controlled many manufactured articles, whether the materials of war or goods for its own household or luxury gifts for use in foreign diplomacy. The full social and economic history of Byzantium has yet to be written. In considering it, perhaps attention is sometimes too exclusively focussed on Constantinople. The machinery of state involved a highly complicated and far-ranging organization only some of which is hinted at in 10th-century documents. The horses and mules for the army and for imperial use which came from the royal studs or from various other sources even including monasteries, the obtaining of materials for the manufacture of purple and paper, the working of the gold, silver, lead and iron

mines in the Balkans and in Asia Minor—it was these and countless other activities in all parts of the Empire which made possible the day to day maintenance of the administration and the civilization of 10th-century Byzantium.

Life in Town and Country

Outside urban centres, such as Constantinople or Thessalonica, land was the important factor. Government restrictions on trade and industry may have been one reason why many preferred to put their wealth into land; another factor in the 10th century was the opportunity for acquisition created by the victorious advance on the eastern frontiers. Small farmers and free villagers existed but often succumbed before the extortions of tax collectors or

Excavations in recent years have gone some way towards establishing the plan of the Imperial Palace, though so much has disappeared for ever that attempts at a reconstruction are bound to be largely conjectural. Contemporary writings, however, often provide clues to the various buildings, their functions and relations with one another, and in this drawing the literary evidence has been used to supplement the archaeological. Some of the most important structures are the following: the Hippodrome (A); the Covered Hippodrome (B); the Chrysotriclinos, or Golden Hall (C); the House of Justinian (D); the Lighthouse (E); the Cathisma or Imperial Box (F); the Triconch (G); the Church of St Stephen (H); The Consistorium (J); the Baths of Zeuxippus (K); the quarters of the palace guards (L); the Milion Arch (M); Justinian's Column (N); the Bronze Gate, the entry into the Palace from Hagia Sophia (O); the Magnaura (P); the Cathedral of Hagia Sophia (Q); the Senate House (R); the Polo Ground (S) and the 'New Church' (T). (10)

the ravages of hostile elements. The powerful landowner was a menacing feature of the Macedonian period. His large estates were worked partly by tenant farmers, partly by agricultural labourers and slaves. In spite of half-hearted prohibitions, slavery was found in every walk of life, in trade, on estates, in imperial service. Those in debt might sell themselves into slavery, and then there were prisoners of war as well as a flourishing import trade. Eunuch slaves were a valued gift at court and Luitprand of Cremona brought four as a present for Constantine VII when he came on an embassy in 948. The marcher lord Digenis Akrites had 'ten handsome long-haired eunuchs' given him as a wedding present by his eldest brother-in-law's wife. In the late 9th century Danielis, a rich widow, numbered slaves on her estates in the Peloponnese by their thousands. She brought 500 as a present to Basil I and when she died 3,000 were given their freedom.

It was only the minority who enjoyed life in the wealthy household of a Danielis with its works of art in gold, silver and bronze, its owner's extensive wardrobe, and its Arabian perfumes and spiced delicacies, or who rejoiced in the princely life of a border warrior, such as Digenis Akrites with his gold-belted grooms and immense 'gold-embroidered' tent with silver poles (not to mention his twelve well-trained hunting leopards and other animals). For most in the countryside it was a struggle for subsistence, and villagers lived on the bare essentials which they themselves produced, barley bread, vegetables, cheese and olives and wine, with fish if they were near coast or river. But they too had their entertainments, perhaps from travelling acrobats or jugglers. Or if they lived near a popular shrine they would then, as now, troop up the mountainside on the saint's day to visit the oratory or monastery at the place where the holy man was buried. Many homely details of country life are revealed in the lives of its saints and hermits, the holy men who in spite of their detachment often had close links with the villagers. The affairs of humbler country people were less spectacular than those of statesmen and generals, or even of merchants and guildsmen, but they were no less important an element in the life of East Rome.

p 117
(6–10)

One of the earliest extant plans of Constantinople, by the Florentine traveller Buondelmonte. Though greatly simplified it is interesting because it represents the city as it was in 1422, some 30 years before her fall to the Turks. On the right is the great domed Hagia Sophia, which the artist has mistakenly placed in the precincts of the Hippodrome (see pp. 120-2). Left of it, close by the river, is the Church of the Holy Apostles (see p. 123 pl. 18), later destroyed by the Turks; and in the extreme left corner, behind the Golden Gate, stands St John of Studius. (11)

VII THE CRUCIBLE OF PEOPLES

Eastern Europe and the rise of the Slavs

TAMARA TALBOT RICE

Map showing the area covered by the Slav races

Christianity came to Russia

early in the 10th century and was officially adopted in 988/9. It was a sign that Russia was now to be considered a part of Christendom, but it was by no means the beginning of Russia as a European state. Already by the 9th century the cities of Novgorod and Kiev were the centres of organized national groups, and Kiev at least constituted a serious threat to Byzantine interests in the Black Sea area. At first the ruling class was of Norse descent, but the native Slav population was soon to predominate.

It was to the Slavs, in fact, that the new pattern of Eastern Europe was largely due, after nearly a thousand years of confused tribal movement. They had left their early homes in the south-east of Central Europe at the end of the Bronze Age, and had split up into three main branches. The Eastern Slavs (ancestors of the Ukrainians and Russians) established themselves along the Dnieper; the Western Slavs (later the Czechs and Poles) round the Vistula and Oder; and the Southern Slavs (Serbs, Croats, Macedonians) in the Balkans. During the years between AD 600 and 900, apart from Russia, independent Slav kingdoms had arisen in Poland, Croatia, Moravia and Bulgaria. In the face of Byzantine pressure only Russia and Poland preserved their autonomy without interruption, but the others established their identity and, throughout, they managed to retain their language and essential traditions.

Christian missionaries went to work among them in the 9th century. Bulgaria became Christian in 865 and soon afterwards a Byzantine bishop (later made an archbishop) was appointed to southern Russia to minister to the converts. Olga, Queen-Regent and mother of Svyatoslav I, was baptized in Constantinople in 957, and the country became officially Christian under her grandson Vladimir (978–1015), the founder of medieval Russia. The 12th-century chronicler known to early historians as Nestor tells how Vladimir sent envoys to the Catholics in Germany, the Muslims in the kingdom of the Eastern Bulgars and the Greek Orthodox in Byzantium, in order to choose the best religion. In Ottonian Germany they saw 'no beauty'. From the Eastern Bulgars they reported 'there is no gladness, only sorrow and a great stench; their religion is not a good one'. But at Constantinople, where spectacular ceremonies were organized for their benefit, they were overwhelmed and hardly knew whether they were in heaven or on earth. So it was, according to popular belief, that Russia became attached to the Greek Orthodox Church.

The illustration opposite is from one of the earliest Russian manuscripts, a Gospel book transcribed and illuminated in 1056/7 for a Novgorodian courtier at Kiev, Ostromirov, by the deacon Gregory. It shows St Luke at the moment of inspiration, in a setting reminiscent of cloisonnée enamels. The Byzantine source of both style and iconography is clear, but already a characteristically Russian manner has begun to show itself. The reigns of Vladimir, his son Yaroslav and grandson Svyatoslav II was the great formative period of Russian Christianity, the age of the earliest icons, the first books and the beginnings of church architecture. (1)

Bulgaria's history is illustrated on these two pages from a unique manuscript now in the Vatican. It is a Slavonic translation, made for the Bulgarian King John Alexander in 1345, of the 12th-century Byzantine historian Manasses.

The conversion of the Western Bulgars was achieved by two brothers from Thessalonica, Cyril and Methodius. For many years they worked among the southern and western Slavs, being finally appointed bishops by Pope Adrian II. Cyril died in Rome in 869 and was buried in the church of S. Clemente. An 11th-century fresco (above) in the crypt portrays them both kneeling before Christ in the presence of angels and St Andrew and St Clement. As part of their missionary activities they succeeded in creating a script thereby enabling the liturgy to be recorded in the Slavonic language: the Cyrillic alphabet, a few lines of which can be seen in the manuscript below. It shows the baptism (by immersion) of the Bulgarians in 865 with their King, Boris, and his Queen standing beside the font. (2, 3)

War against Byzantium: in 811 the Emperor Nicephorus (top) led an army against Krum (802–814), greatest of the Bulgarian kings, but was trapped in the mountains and forced to surrender. In the lower scene Krum, with members of his bodyguard, taunts Nicephorus who stands with his hands bound, about to be beheaded. (4)

The Russians invaded Bulgaria twice between 946 and 971. In this scene (right) Svyatoslav is the central figure, dressed in red and brandishing his sword. The Bulgarians flee, leaving their dismembered dead on the battlefield. (5)

The 'Slayer of the Bulgars', the Emperor Basil II (see p. 115) inflicted a crushing defeat on King Samuel in 1014 (right, above), taking 15,000 prisoners. They were all blinded, only one in every hundred being left as guides for the others, and sent back to the Bulgarian King (lower picture), who died of sorrow. (6)

The kingdoms that failed,

Bulgaria, Croatia and Moravia laid the foundations of their national cultures during this opening phase of their history. Under King Samuel Bulgaria, in addition to her present-day territory, included most of what is now Albania and Yugoslavia, but his empire collapsed after his death. Much later, in the 13th century, it became the centre of the heretical Bogomil sect (or Cathars), in revolt against the rest of Christendom. Moravia was even more short-lived, under constant attack from Avars, Franks and Magyars, though one of its component peoples, the Croats revived in the 10th and 11th centuries.

King Samuel's capital was at Ochrida in Macedonia, where many relics of his time still survive. Left: the apse of the church of Hagia Sophia. Centre: the walls of his citadel, with their original round towers. Right: one of the 14th-century Bogomil tombstones from Bosnia. (7, 8, 9)

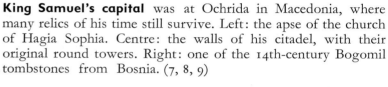

Vladimir succeeded to the throne of Kiev in about 978. He is the first Russian prince to mint his own coins, stamping them with his portrait and crest. His long reign of thirty-five years made Russia a European power and a part of Christendom. Right: Vladimir's envoys visit Constantine IX at Constantinople and return (far right) to Kiev. (10, 11)

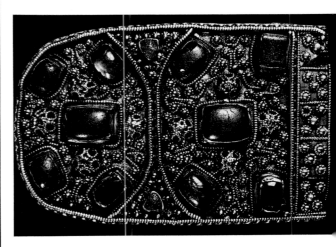

The brief flowering of Moravia can be glimpsed only in a few accidental relics like this silver plaque (left), showing a young man out riding with his hawk. (14)

In their art the Slavs looked back to their nomadic ancestors and contact with Asia. Above: a silver-gilt belt-end, 9th century, from Moravia, reflecting the fondness felt by the Sarmatian nomads and the Goths for polychrome decorations. (15)

Vladimir left twelve sons to quarrel over his throne. The one who emerged victorious was Yaroslav, 'the Wise'. He was a cultured man, fond of Greek literature; even his sarcophagus (far left) is strongly Byzantine in character. Left: four of Yaroslav's daughters, a fresco in Hagia Sophia at Kiev. The eldest (not seen here) married King Harald Hardrada of Norway, the second Henry I of France and the third Andrew I of Hungary. (12, 13)

Under Svyatoslav II, Yaroslav's son, a collection of writings from the Church Fathers was finished (1073). One of the four illustrations (right) shows the authors gathered in an ornate church. (16)

'In this great city, which is the capital of the realm, there are more than forty churches, eight market-places and countless multitudes of inhabitants.' That is the earliest description of Kiev, dating from a time (early 11th century) when Yaroslav himself was laying the foundation stone of the greatest of all Kiev's churches, the Cathedral of Hagia Sophia. Reconstructed here from the north-east, this basically Byzantine structure already embodies some essentially Russian features; its large dome and twelve smaller ones introduced a new skyline to Russia. Open arcades surrounded it on the north, south and west. The upper sections of the walls are of brick, the lower of *opus mixtum*, rough blocks of red quartzite set in pink mortar with a cord to simulate a straight edge round each stone. Inside stood the archbishop's throne with inlaid mosaic panels similar to some that have survived at Novgorod (above). Below: a cloisonné enamel pendant made in Kiev at about the same time; its ace-of-spades motif points to Central Asian influence. (17, 18, 19)

William Suddaby

Closest to the West

of the new Slav communities was Poland, which grew up around Gniezno in the 9th century. In 996 Poland became Christian, but she joined the Roman church, not the Byzantine. This was to be of the utmost importance for the future, for it made Poland look west rather than east – a difference which marked her off from her neighbour, Russia, almost until modern times. Right: Boleslav I (992–1025), one of the founders of Polish greatness, portrayed—over a century later—on the bronze doors of Gniezno Cathedral. (20)

Poland's long struggle first for survival, then for security and civilization, is characteristic of all the Slav nations. Below left: an earth-work fortification with wooden ramparts of the type built in the 8th–9th century. Right: a grave-hoard containing various silver ornaments buried in the first half of the 11th century. Bottom: a silver bowl of the 11th century showing warriors in contemporary armour. By this date Poland's western affiliations are well defined, and the Romanesque style is clear in her art. (21, 22, 23)

Eastern Europe
and the rise of the Slavs

TAMARA TALBOT RICE

ANYONE CONTEMPLATING the long and chequered history of the Slavonic people may well wonder why the various tribes belonging to that ethnic group became animated by a vigorous, almost aggressive spirit towards the end of the 6th century AD rather than at any other moment in the course of the three and a half thousand years of their previous existence. It was this sudden surge of activity that led to a series of developments which culminated in the establishment of the communities we know as Europe's Slavonic nations.

In the 3rd millennium BC the Slavs lived in the East Carpathians or the south-east of Central Europe, but by the end of the Bronze Age they had spread east and west in two main groups—the Eastern Slavs to the Dnieper area (forerunners of the Russian, Ukrainian and White Russian peoples) and the Western Slavs around the Vistula and the Oder (who developed into the Poles and the Czechs). In the 5th century AD a third group, the Southern Slavs, made up mostly of Western Slavs but with a few Eastern, settled in the Balkans and became the ancestors of the Serbs, Croats, Slovenes and Macedonians.

A Subject Race—the Slavs under the Scythians and Goths

The Eastern Slavs were doomed to be conquered again and again by bellicose invaders coming from the East, among whom the Scythians, in about 800 BC, were the most important for the future. Their domination of the native Slav population in the south Russian plain is shown not only in such features as burials (the Scythian being elaborate and rich, the Slav simple and poor) but also in the imprint which it left on Russian art, certain facets of which can trace their origins back to Scythian prototypes.

The work of these nomads was essentially decorative; basically it was a carvers's art, and so for a time was that of the Eastern Slavs. The latter adopted certain nomadic designs to their own needs, and transmitted them to their descendants. It was in this way that these designs were not only incorporated in the folk art of south Russia, but also eventually played a part, if only a small one, in moulding the decorative traditions of western Europe.

The Slavs seem to have shown an innate aptitude for work in metal. The motifs which they took over from the Scythians were either animal (cock and horse) or geometric patterns (e.g. the wheel, rosette and cross, often associated with the sun-cult), and both types survived into Russian folk art.

Between the 2nd century BC and the 4th century AD south Russia was the scene of large-scale national movements. First the Scythians were replaced by the Sarmatians, another people of Asiatic origin. The Romans took over the Greek colonies around the Crimea, and in 342 the Goths, a Germanic tribe from the Baltic region, reached the Black Sea and began to overrun eastern Europe. All these waves of invaders, particularly the last, left their mark on Slav culture.

The earliest examples of the art of the Eastern Slavs that survive date from this period, and they consist entirely of metal articles, the majority of which were intended for personal adornment. Most of them are cast, and many reflect the Goths' fondness for bird-motifs and geometric decoration in coloured inlays and enamels. Even when these surface decorations are lacking, the influence of the Goths is often reflected in the geometric shapes of the open-work sections of the designs.

The only known bronze plaque of East Slavic origin to bear a human figure disappeared during the Second World War. It was dated to between the 3rd and 4th centuries AD and came from Novgorod-Seversk, where it was preserved. Though decorated with enamel inlay with Gothic associations, it displayed a stylized rendering of the Great Goddess whose cult had been transmitted to the Slavs by the Scythians. In this instance the goddess was shown with upraised arms, in the position in which she appears in many 19th-century Russian peasant embroideries. Indeed, to gain some idea of the art of the Eastern Slavs during the opening centuries of our era, it is often relevant to study the decorations on the wood-carvings, toys and textiles which were produced throughout the centuries by the peasants of Eastern Europe.

The Scythian element in Russian art goes back to the time when the Eastern Slavs were subject to Scythian domination between the 8th and 4th centuries BC. This silver amulet in the shape of a horse (6th century AD) found at Martynovka near Kiev reflects Scythian conventions in the treatment of its mane and hooves. (1)

The First Bulgarian Empire

The last and most violent incursion of Asiatic tribes into Europe was that of the Huns. Nomadic, brutal and ruthless, they moved faster and caused more desolation than any previous invaders, crossing the Don in 360, reaching Hungary by 430 and penetrating as far as Gaul by the 450s. Here they were halted; their King Attila died, and they fell back towards Asia even more swiftly than they had left it.

When the holocaust had burnt itself out the racial map of Europe had assumed a new shape. The Sarmatians, apart from a small pocket called the Antae, had been virtually wiped out. The Slavs had for the most part escaped death to survive as an agricultural population, but some abandoned their homes in the south to settle in the northerly park lands between the Volga and the Don.

Here, however, they were subject to pressure from two kindred groups of Asiatics, both offshoots of the Turco-Tartar Empire—the Khazars and the Bulgars. The Khazars had settled in the lower reaches of the Volga in the 4th century AD, and by 651 had established themselves as a powerful kaganate which, with its capital of Itil, close to the Volga's mouth, was to exercise its power throughout the 8th and 9th centuries as far westward as Sambat, the Kiev of the future, and as far south as Kherson.

The Bulgars created an even more long lived, though less belligerent, kaganate north of the Khazars, on the central and upper reaches of the Volga. (With its capital, Bulgar, on the bend of the river, it was to endure as a Muslim state till the 13th

The only East Slavic representation of the human figure was on a bronze plaque from Novgorod-Seversk, which unfortunately disappeared during the Second World War, leaving only this drawing. It shows the Great Goddess in an attitude with raised arms—an ancient image inherited by the Slavs from the Scythians and extremely persistent in later Russian folk art. It even appears in 19th-century peasant embroidery. (2)

century, when it was destroyed by the Mongols.) Some of them seem to have participated in the Hunnic invasion of Italy. From there a number must have moved to the Danube since in 448 we find a group of them opposing the Gothic invasion. Indeed their leader Buzan met his death fighting the Goths on the banks of the Save. These Bulgars were fierce and determined soldiers. By pushing westward they reached Illyria by 502. Within two years they were again at war with the Goths, and although on this occasion they failed to win any victories of importance they nevertheless succeeded by 512 in gaining a firm foothold in the Balkans, where they soon became a real danger to the Byzantines. To ward against them and to safeguard Constantinople the Byzantine Emperor Anastasius I (491–518) built a wall sixty-five kilometres from Constantinople, stretching from the Sea of Marmora to the Black Sea. Yet, regardless of Byzantine opposition, they succeeded in the 6th century, in the time of Justinian, in establishing a Danubian kaganate, soon to develop into Slavonic Bulgaria. This group is known as the Western or White Bulgars, to distinguish it from the Eastern or Black Bulgars who remained in the Volga region.

Once established in the Balkans the White Bulgars fused very rapidly with the Southern Slavs, yet it may have been this admixture of Asiatic blood that led many Slavs living in that area to come together in the 6th century and to form a block conducting a series of military campaigns which were to prove of the greatest political importance. Their attacks were directed against Byzantium and were carried out by Bulgars aided mainly by Western and Southern Slavs, relatively few Eastern Slavs participating. They raided the Empire in 527, 530, 540, 547, 549, 550/51 and 556. These operations herald the dawn of an age during which Slavic nationalism was to develop till it culminated in the establishment of the various Slavonic kingdoms of later times.

In 557 the Slavs crossed the Danube and entered Thrace, where they were joined by further contingents of Western Slavs. They then pushed into Macedonia and Thessaly. By 589 they had reached the Peloponnese and, by the end of the century they were also advancing westward and northward. The former group penetrated into Dalmatia and Istria to reach the Adriatic, where its members became assimilated with the native Dalmatian population. The latter turned towards the Alpine valleys, moving into what was long known as Bohemia and Austria, to become the Slovenes, Croats and Czechs of later times. The Slavs who remained in what is now Bulgaria had, as we have seen, intermingled with the White Bulgars and had begun to exercise so great a threat to Byzantium that, in 592, the Emperor Maurice (582–602) thought it essential to lead an army against them. Fighting did not end with the murder of Maurice in 602 by his own soldiery, for the war dragged on throughout the first quarter of the 7th century. In spite of this and of Avar interference the Slavization of the Bulgars progressed, and by soon after 650 the Slavs constituted a definite majority in the Balkans.

The Avars were actually off-shoots of the Huns, in whose wake they had entered western Europe. By about 550 they had established themselves in Dacia and had reached the Elbe. Within another fifty years they had founded a large kaganate which, in addition to its western territories, also comprised much of southern Russia. Their depredations in what is now southern Russia were encouraged by Justinian and dislodged a number of Eastern Slavs from their homes. These dispossessed agriculturalists turned north-westward in search of security, and eventually penetrated into the forests to the south of the Gulf of Finland. Though Finnish and Esthonian hunters had come to regard the area as their own these Slavs were able to form a wedge between these two ethnic groups.

Christianity and the Alphabet

Meanwhile, in the west, the Slavicized Bulgars, perhaps inspired by the achievements of the Slavic King Samo of Moravia, had grown into a major political force in the Balkans. By 681, perhaps even as early as 674, they had forced the Byzantine Emperor to agree to pay them an annual tribute in order to keep them at bay; in 716 they had obliged him to recognize Bulgaria's independence,

to accept a definite frontier between their kingdoms, and to give valuable trading concessions to their merchants. The Bulgarians were in consequence able to forestall the other Slavs in establishing themselves as a fairly enduring sovereign state. Their first kingdom, with its capital at Pliska, was founded in 681 and survived till 1018. It reached its zenith in the 9th century under the rule of King Krum (802–814) who, in 811, trapped and killed p 142 the Byzantine Emperor Nicephorus in battle, advanced to the (4) Black Sea and defeated the Greeks on the outskirts of Adrianople. As a result Bulgaria's territory stretched from the left bank of the Danube to the Theiss and from the Carpathians to the Dniester, whilst extending southward to include the region of modern Sofia (Sardica) and part of Macedonia. It was Krum's successor, Omurtag, who founded the town of Preslav which *f 3* replaced Pliska as the country's capital.

Bulgaria was the first of the Slavonic countries to accept Christianity. It took this momentous step in 865, under King Boris (825–888), following upon the missionary activities carried out there in 863 by the saintly Macedonian brothers Cyril and Methodius. As all the other Slavs excepting the Poles were to do when accepting Christianity, the Bulgarians chose to join the Greek Orthodox Church of Byzantium in preference to the Roman Catholic. Even though the Byzantines refused for a long time to recognize the autonomy of the Bulgarian church, just as they were later to refuse to grant full independence to the churches of Kievan Russia and of Serbia, the converted Slavic states remained staunch members of the Greek Orthodox church, only the Slavs living in Bohemia eventually ceceding from it to join the Church of Rome.

Cyril and Methodius were born in Thessalonica. Their zeal as p 142 missionaries spurred them to evolve a Slavonic alphabet for the (2) use of the Bulgarians. This alphabet was to prove a very important factor in the creation of Bulgarias' native culture since it enabled the Bulgarians to conduct their church services in their own tongue instead of in Greek. This use of the national language contributed very significantly to the preservation and development of Bulgaria's Slavonic traditions. It was used, for example, for the new legal code which was introduced at an early date in the young kingdom; this drew on Byzantine sources for many of its clauses but it also included a considerable number of important laws of basically Slavic origin. Again it played an important role when, following upon Moravia's collapse early in the 10th century, the best among the pupils of Cyril and Methodius came to Bulgaria and founded a number of schools. Foremost among them were Clement, a second Methodius, and Naum. To meet the teaching needs of these foundations certain Greek works had been translated into Slavonic without loss of time. Under their stimulus learning and the arts began to flourish, though unfortunately, the period of greatest progress coincided with the outbreak of a series of wars directed against the Byzantines and the Magyars.

Omurtag, Prince of the Bulgarians, receiving Byzantine ambassadors in his tent. When Omurtag succeeded to the throne of Bulgaria, his predecessor Krum had reduced the Byzantine Empire to a state of considerable weakness. Omurtag, however, took little advantage of this situation. His ambitions were chiefly directed to the internal consolidation of his kingdom and to its expansion towards the north-west. To achieve this he needed security from reprisals by the Emperor, and therefore concluded a thirty years' peace treaty with Byzantium. (3)

These sapped the country's financial resources and led to an acute economic crisis. Reduced to dire poverty, the people became restive and the general dissatisfaction encouraged the growth of various heresies. One of the most virulent of these, the Bogomil, succeeded not only in taking firm root in Bulgaria, but later spread to Bosnia and Herzegovina, where its followers were responsible for the setting up of a number of interesting though enigmatic stone monuments.

In 963 Svyatoslav, Prince of Kiev, having become involved in the war as an ally of Byzantium, managed to annex the eastern section of Bulgaria. He was, however, forced to cede it to the Byzantines in 971, but already by 969 conditions in Bulgaria verged on the chaotic. Led by the Chichmanides, in an attempt at self-preservation, the western section of the country managed to break away and to form an independent kingdom comprising Macedonia, Albania, the district of the Morava and the regions of Vidin and Sofia. Under the great King Samuel (977–1014) Macedonia became the country's cultural centre, with Ochrida serving to some extent as its capital, for the Tsar established his court in the town's citadel, building the round towers which survive as ruins today. However, within four years of Samuel's death the Byzantines had annexed his realm and the first Bulgarian Empire had come to an end.

p 144 (9)

p 143 (5)

p 143 (6)

p 144 (7, 8)

Moravia's Short-lived Empire

In central Europe another Slav kingdom, Moravia (originally the area roughly occupied by present day Czechoslovakia), promised early to become a great empire, but as such it was unable to survive more than a few centuries. It gained prominence in the 7th century under Samo's leadership by its revolt against the Avars, when it was joined by a large number of other central European Slavs and Czechs. With the aid of the Franks, these Slavs managed to stem the Avar advance by deflecting it eastward and the victorious territories subsequently adopted Samo as their sovereign. Their independence was sealed when they managed to withstand the attack of the Frankish King Dagobert who claimed supremacy over them for the support he had given. Samo's empire, which included Bohemia, Moravia, Lower Austria and, from 631, White Serbia, had only a short existence however. When Samo died in 658 his kingdom fell apart, the various groups it comprised resuming their independence, and it was not revived until the 9th century, when a new Moravian state was established, with its capital of Velegrad on the March (the Morava in Czechoslovakia). This was founded by Mojmir I, and so greatly expanded under his successors, Ratislav and Svyatopluk that it earned the title 'Great Moravia' of the Byzantine Emperor Constantine Porphyrogenitus. It was never secure, however, from Frankish invasion and in 906 its old enemies formed an alliance with the Magyars and, less than a century from its birth, destroyed it. Later in the 10th century, however, the Slovenes succumbed to the Magyars, and that which survived of Samo's old Moravian kingdom reformed under the Czechs, with its capital at Prague. Its significance increased in the following century when the Polabian Slavs, whose territory had contained such important towns as Schwerin, Rostock and Lübeck, were in their turn wiped out by the Germans.

p 145 (14)

The old Moravian kingdom had included the Slovene and Croatian Slavs. It was in the 6th century that the Slovenes had captured the land of the Illyrians and had turned towards the Alps, where they were obliged to contend against the *Langobardi* (Lombards) and the Bavarians in order to join forces with King Samo. At the latter's death they were conquered by the Franks, and although they rallied in the 9th century they did not succeed in regaining their independence. The Croats were more successful in their efforts to retain their autonomy. They managed to withstand both the Avars and the Franks, and to found a kingdom which, between 815 and 822, embraced a small part of Dalmatia. By 925, when Christianity had made great strides among them and when their Prince Tomislav had proclaimed himself their first King, their country had become so important that it aroused the jealousy both of the Byzantines and the Venetians. The Croats did not hesitate to resist both these powers and by 1058, when their King Peter Kreshinin ascended the throne, they were in control of most of Dalmatia.

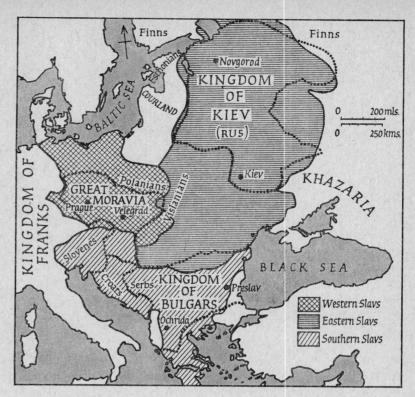

Slav states in the 9th century. The Slavs had spread in three main groups (indicated by shading) over most of Eastern Europe, establishing separate states that included Croatia, Great Moravia and Bulgaria, a fusion of Southern Slavs and Bulgars who had migrated from their kaganate on the Volga. In the 9th century the Eastern Slavs and Scandinavian settlers formed the kingdoms of Novgorod and Kiev, which in 881 were combined by Oleg into one large state, Kievan Russia. (4)

Their neighbours, the Serbs, were forced to contend the longest for their independence for although they had firmly established themselves in the Danube's basin in the course of the 6th and 7th centuries, they had devoted themselves from the 8th to the 10th centuries to endeavouring to break loose from Bulgarian control. From 819 the struggle entered a particularly acute stage because the Serbs, even though the activities of Roman Catholic missionaries were undermining their unity, found it necessary also to fight the Franks. As a result, it was not until early in the 13th century that the Serbs officially adopted Christianity, joining the Greek Orthodox church. The delay in doing so may well have retarded their political development, for it was not until 1018, when the Byzantines were able to reconquer Bulgaria, that the Serbs began ardently to desire independence, and not until late in the 12th century under the leadership of their great King Stephen Nemanja, that they were able to achieve it.

The Beginning of Russia

The 6th and 7th centuries marked a significant advance not only in the political consciousness of the Western Slavs but also in that of the Eastern Slavs, for it was during that period that the latter started out on the first stage of that gradual process of organization which eventually led to their unification and to the establishment of the first Russian state. The latter is generally referred to today as Kievan Rus. In the 8th century historians divided the Slavonic forebears of the early Russians into twelve major tribes. These included the Polinians living on the middle Dnieper, on what was soon to become Kievan soil. This group should not be confused with the very similar Polanians, who were the founders of Poland and who, like the Polinians, derived their name from the word 'pole', meaning field.

In Eastern Europe certain of these tribes were by then beginning to evolve into self-governing, slave-owning communities whose members lived in settlements of considerable size. These were laid out either on a square or a round plan and were often enclosed by a vallum, but most of the dwellings still took the form of partially sunken mud huts. In the 6th century Byzantine writers referred to these huts and to the primitive habits of their inhabitants with scorn, but Grekov and other Soviet scholars suggest that, at any rate in the Kievan area, such huts were inhabited only during the summer months in the manner of the *yaylas* in present day Turkey, and that the winters were spent in villages which were largely made up of wooden dwellings. Grekov asserts that by the 8th century an average sized village occupied some 5,000 square metres of land whilst some of the larger ones were as much as seven times as big. In the more populated areas these settlements often lay only some five to eight kilometres apart. In all of them married men appear to have lived with their families in separate huts, but since the settlers continued to adhere to the patriarchal way of life, the huts were often connected by covered ways which led to the chieftain's house situated at the centre of the settlement.

This state of affairs points to the establishment of the family as a definite unit, for even those settlers who still accepted the authority of a head man had begun to form themselves into a democratic society based to some extent on the communal ownership of property. The more advanced communities were by then already governed by elders in place of a chieftain, and it was they who decided on such matters as political alliances or participation in war. Many of these men were rich and owned slaves, but it is not known whether they were elected to office or whether they inherited their position. They formed the upper class of the Slavic community and, to judge from the contents of the hoards dating from that period that have been discovered, they owned a good many valuable objects fashioned in precious materials. Some of those objects were of Byzantine workmanship and may well have fallen into their hands as war booty, but some must have been acquired by barter. The latter indicate that the Eastern Slavs had by then begun to regard trade as an alternative occupation to husbandry.

Nevertheless, the majority of the Eastern Slavs continued to rely on agriculture for their livelihood, and since, at any rate in the northern districts, they were still cultivating the land on the cut and burn principle, which depended upon triennial moves to virgin soil, they had by then spread over a considerable area of southern and central Russia. Many of those who had penetrated to the north-eastern regions had begun to advance into the forest belt, settling in small groups and at convenient points along the rivers which intersect the country.

The Dulebian and the Volynian Slavs were among the first to unite, doing so soon after the Avars had succumbed to Charlemagne. They thereby laid the foundations of the Novgorodian state but it was the Polinians of the middle Dnieper who, though subjected to the Khazars, were responsible for transforming the Khazar fortress of Sambat into either the actual site of Kiev or into that of Vyshgorod, which was to become one of Kiev's outer defences. It was in this way that they planted the seed from which the Russia of the future was to grow. Legend, however, attributes the foundation of Kiev to three brothers who were so devoted to each other that although they settled on three adjoining hills they surrounded their households by a single wall; the elder brother Kiya, who was to give Kiev his name, lived on the highest hillock. By the 8th century the Tmutarakan group of Slavs were also growing into a strong community, whilst to the north the Krivichian Slavs were founding the settlements which were to develop into the towns of Smolensk, Pskov and Lubech, and the Severian Slavs were in the process of laying the foundations of Chernigov.

Fortune-Seekers from the North

These developments did not attract the attention of foreign historians. Byzantine writers in the 9th century continued to dismiss the Eastern Slavs as rough and primitive, though they mentioned their love of music, their honesty, hospitality and fierceness in battle, noting with surprise their fondness for hot baths. In the 8th century the interest of foreign observers was not so much directed to the Eastern Slavs as to the Khazar capital of Itil. The Muslim conquests in Transcaucasia and central Asia had led to so great an expansion of trade in the Caspian area that Itil had suddenly developed into a centre of considerable commercial importance. Merchants of divers nationalities were flocking to its markets. As a result, by the 8th century many Scandinavian

adventurers, the majority of them Swedes, had begun to seek their fortunes in eastern Europe in preference to joining their Norwegian and Danish kinsmen in raiding the coasts of Britain and Gaul. These Scandinavians were to become known in ancient Russia as Varangians.

It is significant that the earliest traces left by them on what is now Russian soil are to be found along the routes which once carried goods eastward to the Orient and southward to the Caspian, and not along the Dnieper waterway, which was later to connect Scandinavia to Byzantium and to go down in history as 'the road leading from the Varangians to the Greeks'. Braun has shown that the Russian sites which have produced hoards containing mostly Arabian coins have also provided the greatest number of Scandinavian objects. Braun infers from this that the Norsemen acted as middlemen in the trade which developed between the eastern world and the richer trading centres of north-eastern Europe.

At the turn of the 7th century three routes at least existed connecting the Scandinavian area to the Caspian. Travellers went by boat, hoisting their vessels onto wheels at specific points of the journey to drag them overland to the next waterway. The routes started respectively from the Gulf of Finland, the Baltic and Lake Chudskoye, to converge on the Volga and lead the travellers to Itil. Most of the Varangians ended their journeys at the Khazar capital, but eastern writers mention some who went as far as Baghdad, doing the last stages by camel caravan. The earliest that are known to have travelled as far had done so by 846, when the writer Hordad Bey mentioned their arrival in Baghdad.

Whilst some Varangians were penetrating to Mesopotamia others had begun making their way across the Black Sea to Byzantium, embarking for the purpose at a port situated somewhere on the Volga–Don–Dnieper route—Tsarytsin renamed, Stalingrad (and now renamed Volgograd), has been suggested as a possible location for this as has a port in the neighbourhood of the Khazar fortress of Sarkel (Belaya Vezha), where the remains of Varangian fortifications and a settlement have been discovered. Meanwhile, in the north, other Varangians, aided this time by Danes, had entered the Baltic area in an attempt to conquer Courland. They had little difficulty in reaching a point situated somewhere between the Dvina and the Niemen, and within a short time they were exacting tributes from the Novgorodian Slavs, the Krivichians and outlying groups of Finns.

The Kingdoms of Novgorod and Kiev

Scandinavian sagas contain many references to *Rus* (called 'Rhos' by many contemporary writers); the country is described in them as rich in towns remarkable for the size of their buildings as well as for the wealth of their inhabitants and the luxuries with which they surrounded themselves. According to Russian legends it was in answer to an appeal by the Novgorodian Slavs that Ryurik and his brothers, Sivers and Travor, came to Eastern Europe in 862 to establish themselves there respectively as Varangian Princes of Novgorod, Pskov and Izborsk. It is, however, far more probable that some Norsemen had risen to positions of eminence in parts of what are known today as Russia several decades earlier. Indeed, some historians think that Ryurik's mother was a Slav; if so, Ryurik must have been born on Russian soil. Even if this was not the case it seems clear that another Varangian, Askold, became ruler of Kiev several years before the accepted date of Ryurik's rise to power in Novgorod.

The Varangians did not take their women with them into eastern Europe. This attitude helps to account for the speed with which the newcomers became Slavicized. The process appears to have been accomplished within a century and a half, even in the case of the princely families. Thus, the examination which was recently carried out on the remains of the body of Yaroslav the Wise (1019–1054) showed that his skull was not of Nordic type. Furthermore, although the Varangians, constituting as they did the ruling class and the military hierarchy throughout the initial period of Norse penetration, were at first alone eligible for service in the bodyguards of the ruling princes, it was not long before Slavs were being enrolled to serve with them as their equals.

The Scandinavian conquest of Courland (854) led to the establishment of the Niemen-Pripet route connecting the Baltic to the south-western section of the Eurasian plain. It may have been as a result of this development that Askold decided to set out for Kiev. He must in any case have been firmly established as ruler of Kiev by 860, when the Eastern Slavs launched a major offensive against Byzantium, for it is now considered probable that it was Askold who concluded the peace treaty of 867 which marked the end of the campaign. If so, there is every reason to suppose that it was he who was also responsible for the venture. To have undertaken it at all proves that his army must have been both large and loyal for although his cavalry must have consisted of Norsemen, since in the formative period of Russia's growth only members of the princely bodyguards were entitled to fight mounted, yet the bulk of his infantry must undoubtedly have been made up of Slavs.

Though Ryurik had been ruling Novgorod during the last five years of the war, yet, on coming to terms with the Greeks, Askold lost no time in challenging Ryurik's strength by attacking Polotsk, a town of major importance and a dependence of Ryurik. The incident did not however lead to a full scale war, perhaps because both princes were anxious to consolidate their positions and to increase their lands by absorbing neighbouring groups of Slavs which were still independent. The subjection of these tribes was necessary as much for economic as for political and territorial reasons, for the ruling princes depended upon the tributes they were able to levy from their vassals both for their national revenue and their private incomes, since they retained for their personal use a third of every tribute they imposed.

Askold must have acquired considerable prestige both by his attack and by the peace negotiations with Byzantium, for his Kievan territory soon started to acquire the outlines of a state. The new status of southern Rus was tacitly recognized by Photius, Patriarch of Constantinople, when he dispatched Bishop Michael to eastern Europe as his envoy. Photius' successor, Ignatius, raised Michael's rank to that of Archbishop. It is not known precisely where in eastern Europe Michael resided; some scholars think that his appointment assigned him to the Slavs of Tmutarakan; if so, this would imply that Askold had been assisted in the war against the Greeks by this powerful, autonomous group. However, it seems more likely that Michael's headquarters were situated somewhere within Byzantium's Crimean territories, whence it would have been safer for him to conduct his missionary activities than would have been the case had he been living among the ardently pagan Slavs. Though certain scholars now believe that Askold became converted to Christianity at about this time there is no conclusive proof of this, and the church which was standing in Kiev by 882 was probably intended to meet the needs of foreign merchants rather than of native converts.

The Highway of the Dnieper

Askold was not the only Rhos prince to attract the attention of his neighbours; Ryurik was also arousing interest by his effort to open up the Dnieper waterway in order to link Scandinavia to Byzantium. Once established, this waterway was found to possess several important advantages over the older, more easterly, routes for it not only provided a direct road to Constantinople, but it also ensured greater safety to travellers since it lay to the west of Khazaria's boundaries and also beyond the reach of the predatory Asiatic nomads who had penetrated into the European section of the plain. Though the Khazars still retained a nominal hold over the plain almost as far west as the walls of Kiev they were unable to control these nomads, perhaps because they had themselves largely forsaken the nomadic way of life to establish towns which were developing into important commercial centres, frequented alike by Jewish and Arabian merchants. Under the influence of the former the ruling house had become converted to Judaism but the bulk of the Khazars had either remained pagan or had adopted Shamanism.

The stimulus of commerce, much of it connected with the slave trade, had brought such prosperity to these towns that, in the 9th century, they had drawn upon themselves the covetous eyes of another group of Asiatic nomads, the Pechenegs or Patzinaks. On entering Europe these peoples moved steadily westward, advancing by means of a series of predatory raids.

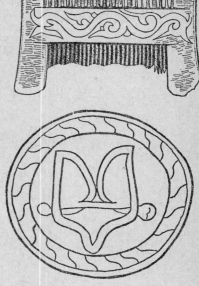

Sarkel (Belaya Vezha) was founded as a fortress by the Byzantine Emperor Theophilus. It was strategically situated at a point where the Volga and the Don flow close together, and became a place of some importance in the Kievan state. This bone plaque with a prince's crest and ornamental comb were found there. (5, 6)

Sensing the danger underlying these thrusts the Khazars had appealed to the Byzantine Emperor Theophilus (829–842) for technicians capable of constructing strong defensive outposts. Accordingly, in the year 835, the Emperor despatched the spatharocandidate Petronius Camatirus to Khazaria, to build the fortress of Sarkel (Belaya Vezha) on the left bank of the Don, at a point where the Volga and Don rivers flow fairly close to each other and where, even at this early date, they may well already have been linked by a canal. Finding no stone in the district Camatirus was obliged to construct a kiln in which to bake the bricks he needed for building the fortress. When completed Sarkel was manned by three hundred men. Unfortunately, neither this unit nor the fortifications themselves succeeded in deterring the Pechenegs, who continued to raid the Dnieper Slavs to the west of Sarkel at will, whilst obliging the Khazars to remain concentrated on the banks of the Volga. *f 5, 6*

The incursions of the Pechenegs did not extend as far northward as Novgorod which served as the capital of an area inhabited by Slavs who were free and not, as in Kiev's case, vassals. In the Kievan area the eastern Polinians were still at this date subjected to the Khazars and the western to the Magyars—a Mongolian people who had penetrated into the Pannonian plain at the turn of the 8th century, separating the northern Slavs from the southern. The Khazars had proved no more capable of arresting these invaders than they were of protecting their Polinian vassals from the depredations of the nomads. In 840, only five years after the fortress of Sarkel had been completed, a large caravan of merchants suffered grievously at the hands of the Pechenegs, and in 867 the latter launched their first attack on Kiev. For the next hundred and fifty years they were to raid the town on many occasions. Askold was so much angered by the Khazars' inability to restrain the Pechenegs whilst at the same time continuing to levy a tribute from the Polinians that he went to war with the Khazars and succeeded in freeing the Polinians from this imposition.

Oleg at the Gates of Byzantium

Askold reigned over Kiev for some twenty-seven years, during part of the time with Dire as co-ruler. However, at Ryurik's death around 881 Oleg, as Regent and guardian of Ryurik's infant son, Igor, determined to annex Kiev. By resorting to a ruse he managed within a year to kill both Askold and Dire, and to capture their capital. Soon after he transferred his own court from Novgorod to Kiev, so that the latter town became the capital of a principality rather than of a small fief. Its geographical situation endowed Kiev with commercial and political advantages which made it a key point from which to implement Oleg's policy of East Slavic unification. By about 890 Oleg had as a result succeeded in winning over four of the most important tribes and was thus in a position to go to war against the Magyars. However his enemies broke away after some indecisive fighting to turn, at Byzantium's request, on the Bulgars, who, in the teeth of intense opposition, were striving to form an independent kingdom. Faced with war on two fronts the Bulgarians invoked the aid of the Pechenegs, and these intrepid nomads contrived to traverse southern Russia and to attack the Magyars, inflicting such a trouncing upon them that in 897 the latter abandoned southern Russia for ever.

His hands freed by the Magyar collapse, Oleg was able in the course of the next ten years to win the allegiance of the two Slavonic tribes living on the banks of the Dnieper. He thereby gained full control of virtually the whole of that river—an advantage which led him to develop two major islands on its lower reaches, Khortitza, which was to be renamed St Gregory in Christian times, and Berezan, the future St Aetherius, into naval bases as well as assembly ports for the use of merchants travelling along the Dnieper waterway. The advantages afforded by the naval bases, and the increase in the size of the army, made possible by the assimilation of subjected tribes, convinced Oleg that he was in a position to go to war against Byzantium.

Oleg planned his campaign as a combined land and sea operation. In 907, having despatched his cavalry westward to strike the Byzantines from the Balkans, he embarked his infantry into some two thousand vessels and sailed with them across the Black Sea. Disembarking on the western bank of the Bosphorus his men managed to drag their boats ashore, hoist them onto wheels and haul them overland to the Golden Horn. Having in this way avoided the chain barring its entrance Oleg was able to re-embark his men on its placid waters to assault Constantinople's northern sea defences. After some bitter fighting the Greeks had to admit defeat and Oleg was able to pin his shield to the walls of the greatest capital in Christendom. The peace treaty of 911 which followed forced the Byzantines to agree to terms which were very much to the invaders' advantage. The text of the treaty was drawn up in both Greek and ancient Russian, and Oleg, as he stood at the walls of the mighty capital, swore in the name of the pagan gods Volos and Perun to abide by its terms.

Each of the Russian principalities which had participated in the campaign, and these included Kiev, Chernigov, Perejaslavl, Polotsk, Rostov and Lubech, together with the names of the princesses in their own right who had contributed to the war, were specifically mentioned in the treaty; merchants from these territories alone were to benefit from the commercial concessions which had been exacted from the Byzantines. The latter agreed to raise a large indemnity which was to be set aside to meet the costs of their upkeep and travel but insisted on specific safeguards, stipulating that no Rhos merchants were to visit Constantinople during the winter months or ever to reside within the capital's walls; that none were ever to enter the city carrying arms, or to remain within its walls after nightfall, or to enter the town unless accompanied by a Greek, or to do so in groups numbering more than fifty. In return the Byzantines undertook to provide special quarters for the Rhos in the Monastery of St Mamas situated just outside the walls, where the Rhos could spend six weeks a year, food and lodging being provided free of cost and of similar standard to that reserved for foreign envoys. In addition to transit goods from northern Europe these Rhos merchants were to bring furs, slaves, wax, honey, flax and linen to Byzantium.

However, Oleg did not regard this victory as a reason for laying down arms. Instead he looked eastward, in 913 leading a large force to the Volga in an attempt to engage the Khazars in battle, but the latter withdrew into country where Oleg was unwilling to follow them. Oleg therefore turned towards the Caspian, raiding Tabaristan. At the approach of winter he decided to lead his booty-laden men home, but as they travelled up the Volga the Khazars, who had been lying in wait for them, were able to attack them in the rear and to kill many of them. The defeat was all the more bitter to accept since, notwithstanding Oleg's truly remarkable achievements, it meant that at his death—which occurred either in 921 or 922—Kiev's lands still extended only some fifty to a hundred miles eastward. Beyond stretched the 'pole'—the no man's land in which Russia's legendary heroes

performed their gallent deeds—and still further to the east lay the territory of the crumbling, but still irritating Khazar khanate.

Oleg was succeeded by Ryurik's son, Igor. In 941, perhaps in retaliation for some provocative act, Igor raided Byzantium, penetrating as far as Nicomedia before withdrawing. Three years later he again led his men against the Greeks, but this time he suffered so sharp a defeat that, in 945, he was forced to agree to peace terms which deprived him of some of the valuable economic advantages which Oleg had obtained in 911. It also obliged the Kievan principality to furnish military aid to the Byzantines if called upon to do so. The wording of this treaty is of particular interest to historians both because it is the first document in which the term Rhos was used officially to describe the Kievan principality and also because it refers to both Igor's pagan and his Christian subjects. Igor was killed by Slavic tribesmen soon after he had signed the treaty on the grounds that he had attempted to exact from them two payments of a tribute where they considered that only one was due. His son Svyatoslav, the first Kievan prince to bear a Slavonic name, was too young to rule and control of the state's affairs was therefore entrusted to Igor's widow, Olga.

The Kievan Kingdom under Olga

Olga was a woman of outstanding intelligence. There is reason to think that she was born in Pskov of a Slav mother. In Kievan Russia women enjoyed many of the same rights as men, and Olga is known to have owned a good deal of property before her marriage. This had taken place when she was no longer altogether young, and on coming to power she made use of the experience she had gained in managing her estates to introduce a number of changes in the existing constitution. Her first and most significant reform was designed to abolish the custom which obliged a prince to set out on an annual tour of visits to his vassals in order to collect the tribute he had imposed on them. It was this method of levying funds which had cost Olga's husband his life. She replaced it by a centralized financial administration, employing regional officers to collect the tribute and to forward it to the main assembly point. This new method of collection made it necessary to substitute for the old assessment of the tribe as a corporate body a tax based on the family unit. Accordingly townsmen were henceforth to be rated by the number of hearths they possessed and agriculturalists on their ploughed land. The change struck a final blow at the old tribal system. It was in any case in the process of breaking up for in country districts chieftains were being replaced by local communes with elected elders, while in the towns the *veche*—a form of general assembly or parliament—was coming into being. All adult males other than slaves were entitled to take part in the public meetings of the *veche;* these were soon being held regularly in the main market square of every town.

Though the country's social structure had undergone a basic change, the old two-class grouping of society had survived. The upper class was now made up of the prince of Kiev, who was still often referred to by the Khazar title of *kakhan*, together with his family, bodyguard, courtiers and relatives, as well as the regional princes. The working class included freemen and slaves. Soon, however, society started to produce intermediary categories. These included the traders and artisans, both of whom were equally essential to a rising commercial nation. The wealthier merchants were therefore quickly accepted into the upper class, whilst the smaller tradesmen and artisans came to form a middle class. The artisans soon became both numerous and highly skilled in various trades, and by the 11th century Theophilus was to rank their metal workers as the best of their time. Although the latter were both the most numerous and the most important of the artisans, there were many others who followed a variety of occupations, becoming potters, textile workers or makers of a wide range of implements, tools, arms and utensils. Excavations at Tsarskoe Gorodishche, the 7th- and 8th-century site of Rostov, have revealed a rich variety of objects, the workshops found there including studios which were well equipped with artists' materials.

The country's highly developed trade was one of the factors which was responsible in the 10th century for a sharp decrease in illiteracy. Though the first Slavonic alphabet is thought to date back to the 3rd or 4th centuries AD and to have been evolved in the Black Sea area, it was a difficult one to master for it consisted of a blend of Runic, Greek and Hebrew signs. It was, however, the only one in existence till 863 when the alphabet evolved by Cyril and Methodius was introduced. The latter quickly superseded the native alphabet in so far as commercial and diplomatic affairs were concerned, though many writers continued for several centuries more to use the older form for literary purposes.

The social and economic advances which were being achieved in Kievan Russia did not escape the notice of missionaries and, in Olga's day, men preaching diverse faiths came to Kiev hoping to convert the inhabitants to their own particular beliefs. However, the reigning house and the bulk of the population remained pagan, worshipping, in addition to their ancestors and the Great Goddess of antiquity, a number of deities associated with the elements. Yet both the largely Jewish and still powerful Khazars, and also the fervent and militant Muslims had begun to make an impact on the people. Shaman preachers were also meeting with a measure of success and so too were Christian missionaries. It is impossible to judge of the impression made on the Kievans by the missions which Cyril and Methodius carried out in Khazaria in 861 and in Bulgaria in 863, but the Rhos princes do not appear to have shown the slightest desire to change their religion; if Askold did in fact do so, he must have kept his conversion a closely guarded secret. Even Olga's son, Svyatoslav, remained wholeheartedly pagan. Olga, however, decided to take the momentous step of adopting a new faith. It is now thought probable that she was secretly baptized in 955, but her official conversion took place in 957, whilst she was on a state visit to Byzantium. The ceremony was conducted with great pomp and magnificence in the great cathedral of Hagia Sophia at Constantinople, the Patriarch of Constantinople and the Emperor of Byzantium officiating.

Olga's state visit to the Emperor of Byzantium, still the foremost ruler of Christendom, and her conversion established her position as sovereign of an autonomous state, but before her country could start to play a part in international affairs certain tasks had to be done. It was thus essential for the nation as a whole to accept Christianity and to aim at establishing an autonomous church, and it was also necessary for it to enter into diplomatic relations with the great powers of the day. Olga may have thought the last task of prime importance for, in 959, she despatched an envoy to the Emperor Otto. However, that monarch attached little value to her overture and it was not until 961 that he sent to Kiev the monk Adalbert of the Monastery of St Maximin at Trier to return the courtesy. By that time it was too late for either the Kievans or for the Roman Catholic envoy to establish friendly relations for Olga had by then been succeeded on the throne by her son Svyatoslav and the latter was so militant a pagan that Adalbert found it necessary to depart from Kiev hurriedly.

War on Two Fronts

Though Svyatoslav disapproved of his mother's religious views he shared her desire to extend Kiev's territory. He was anxious to do so at the expense of the Khazars and he was so clever a commander that, within a few years, he was able to put an end to their existence. His victory brought him great territorial gains, yet it left his eastern frontiers exposed to invasion from Asia, with the result that thereafter it fell to Russia to act as an effective bulwark between the two continents.

It was in the same year that the Byzantines, taking advantage of the political dissensions which were undermining Bulgaria, determined to invade her. To ensure the success of their enterprise the Emperor Nicephorus Phocas instructed the chief magistrate of Cherson to invoke Russian aid in accordance with the terms of the treaty agreed to by Igor in 945. Svyatoslav was always punctilious in military and diplomatic matters and he unhesitatingly assented to the Greek demand. Withdrawing from the East he entered Bulgaria and within the year conquered the whole eastern section of the country. However, he was then obliged to interrupt his campaign in order to hasten to the relief

The leader of a mission from Kiev inquires about the Christian faith from a Byzantine bishop. In the background is part of the Palace at Constantinople. When the Russians officially adopted Christianity under Vladimir it was to Byzantium that they looked for instruction. Their first bishops were appointed by the Patriarch of Constantinople, and Byzantine influence was supreme in theology, religious music and art. (7)

of Kiev which, at the instigation of the Bulgarians, had been besieged by the Pechenegs. It was not until 971 that Svyatoslav was able to return to the Balkans to resume the offensive, but by then the Byzantines had succeeded in conquering the whole of western Bulgaria, and Svyatoslav was now confronted by a large combined Byzantine and Bulgarian force. Even so, he managed to capture Preslav, the Bulgarian capital. But the situation reached a stalemate. On realizing that he could no longer hope for an outright victory Svyatoslav agreed to peace terms which obliged him to restore his conquered territories to their Bulgarian and Byzantine masters. Yet as he marched homewards, the Pechenegs, who had once again been treacherously alerted by the Bulgarians, contrived to ambush and kill him.

The Age of Vladimir

In Russia six years of fratricidal war followed till the late ruler's youngest son, Vladimir, succeeded to the Kievan throne in c. 978. Within another eleven years Vladimir had become converted to Christianity, joining the Greek Orthodox church of Byzantium in preference to the Roman Catholic; he had married Anne, the sister of the Emperor of Byzantium, and had had his people baptized. By the time of his death in 1015, Vladimir had destroyed the pagan idols and temples all over his kingdom, and had replaced them by churches adorned with mural decorations and icons in the Byzantine style; he had introduced economic and legal changes along Byzantine rather than Western lines; he had founded schools and some essential charitable institutions; he had built himself a palace at Kiev, the splendours of which are recorded in legends, for it is believed to have housed at least seven hundred people and is known to have included among its many dependencies workshops in which sumptuous pieces of metal work were produced. Vladimir also erected modern fortifications to defend his kingdom which now stretched from lake Ladoga in the north and the Klyazma in the east to the upper Bug. The lower Oka and the eastern Bug had not yet been won, whilst Galicia for many years to come continued to change hands with Poland.

Vladimir established in Russia the artistic and architectural styles which were current in Byzantium. His people had always been musical, but Vladimir added the Gregorian canon to their repertory. When Vladimir's son, Yaroslav, succeeded his father— once again after contending for the throne for four years—it was as a result of Vladimir's efforts, that Kievan Russia possessed artists, builders, jewellers, craftsmen, and entertainers of various kinds who, though working in the Byzantine style, were creating masterpieces containing many specifically Russian characteristics. It was, however, largely due to Yaroslav that Kievan Russia came to rank as a European power and that his house was respected by the rulers of Christendom. Yaroslav had himself married Ingigerd, a daughter of the King of Norway. Later he widened his family circle and foreign connections by uniting his children to the foremost ruling houses of his day. Thus one of his daughters became the wife of Harold Hardrada, the future king of Norway;

p 144
(10, 11)
f 7

p 144
(12)

p 146, 7
(17–19)
p 141 (1)

p 144
(13)

another married Henry I of France and yet another was wedded to Andrew I, the future king of Hungary. Of his sons, three married German princesses and at least two princesses of Byzantium. And it was at Yaroslav's court that the dispossessed children of Edmund of England sought security from Canute. Kievan Russia had indeed at last become part of the European scene.

A New Slav State: Poland

p 148
(20–23)
The 9th and 10th centuries also witnessed the birth of another Slavic nation. To the north-west of Kiev the Vislanian tribe, with its centre on the site of present day Cracow, and the Polanians, with their capital at Gniezno, had started to lay the foundations of Poland. In the 9th century the Vislanians had been considered so dangerous by their Moravian neighbours that the latter determined to destroy them. In 880 they succeeded in doing so, capturing the Vislanian prince and annexing his territory. The Polanians were more fortunate for, towards the end of that century, they managed to gain possession of the region which is now the heart of Poland. It comprised Poznan, Kruszwica and Kalisz. The founding of their capital at Gniezno is to be assigned to the end of the 8th century; by the 10th it had become the residence of Poland's first princes. The founder of the dynasty, Siemowit, had had to fight fiercely for his power, but he was able to hand his throne on to his son Leszak, who in his turn contrived to leave it to his own son, Siemomysl. These three rulers saved their people from being wiped out by the Germanic knights who had destroyed the Polabian Slavs on the Elbe. Siemomysl's son, Mieszko I, was thus able in his turn to rule over his people as their uncrowned king and to control an area which embraced the whole of what is today central Poland, that is to say, the districts of Leczyca and Sieradz, Mazovia, Chelmno and possibly even parts of Pomerania. However, western Pomerania remained autonomous, whilst Silesia and Malopolska were incorporated in Bohemia. Like those of Kievan Russia, so too Poland's rulers consolidated their hold gradually, slowly yet steadily extending their boundaries. By the second half of the 10th century their territory was fully integrated, and when, in 966, the Poles became converted to the Roman Catholic faith, their country qualified for recognition as an autonomous state. Yet Mieszko was anxious to add western Pomerania to his possessions. After securing the safety of his south-western border by entering into an alliance with Bohemia he therefore led his army into the coveted area. By 967 he had reached the mouth of the Oder. Two years later he successfully resisted the Emperor Otto II's efforts to reconquer the ground and was able to establish his frontier along the line of the Oder and the Baltic. He was as a result in a position to enter into direct contact with Scandinavia and to marry his daughter, Swietoslawa, to Eric Segersäl, King of Sweden. Later she was to marry Svein, King of the Danes, and to become the mother of Canute. These contacts and Poland's entry into the Roman Catholic church led the country to form close ties with Western Europe with the result that Romanesque art reached the area and became firmly established there.

Miezsko died in 992 and was succeeded by his son Boleslav the Brave. Boleslav set out to establish cordial relations with Otto III, and the Western Emperor consented to visit Gniezno in 1000, though he did so primarily in order to pay homage at the tomb of his friend, St Adalbert, who had met a martyr's death when serving, at Boleslav's wish, as a missionary in Prussia. It was during that visit that Otto III officially recognized the sovereignty of the Polish ruler. This act displeased Otto's successor, Henry II, who distrusted Boleslav's imperialistic aims. Thinking it wiser to forestall a future attack, he decided to declare war on Boleslav in 1004, before the latter had recovered from his unsuccessful attempt to annex Bohemia. Fighting dragged on till 1018, to end with a peace which entitled the Poles to retain the disputed territory. Boleslav was now free to turn to the support of his son-in-law Svyatopolk who, as the eldest son of Vladimir and brother of Yaroslav, the future ruler of Rus, was contending against his brothers for the Russian throne. Advancing swiftly eastward Boleslav surprised Yaroslav in Kiev and forced him hurriedly to retreat to his own principality of Novgorod. Yet when Svyatopolk was reinstated on the Kievan throne he foolishly quarrelled with his father-in-law. Greatly angered, Boleslav decided to abandon Svyatopolk to his fate and to return to Poland, but as he marched homeward he took many Russian prisoners back with him, and he also seized the group of Ukranian towns known as the Cherven cities. Though the latter were recaptured in 1031 by Yaroslav and his brother Mstislav, and although the surviving prisoners were then freed, the episode left an indelible mark on the memory of the Russians.

Throughout the remainder of his life Boleslav continued to stand out against the German Empire and, in 1025, at a time when the Emperor of the West was deeply concerned with internal affairs, he had himself crowned King of Poland. At his death his son Mieszko II also had himself crowned, both in order to establish a precedent and also to emphasize Poland's sovereignty and independence. By that time the Balkan Slavs were entering on a dark period in their history for Bulgaria had succumbed to the Byzantines in 1018. But although the Byzantine Emperor Basil II (976–1025) spent thirty years demolishing the Bulgarian kingdom and slaughtering its people, thus earning for himself the appellation of Bulgar Slayer, he nevertheless failed to break the spirit of the people. As a result Asen I was able to establish a second Bulgarian kingdom in 1186; it endured till the Turkish conquest. Serbia was in her turn able to break free from Byzantine control in 1168, when Stephen Nemanja founded a dynasty which survived till the Turkish victory at Kossovo in 1389. Thus, although by the year 1000 the Slavs had, as we have seen, assimilated the alien races they had encountered in the territories in which they had settled, in the 11th century only Kievan Russia and Poland had become permanently established as enduring kingdoms. Their importance, though already considerable, was to grow with the passing years and from then onwards to play an increasingly significant part in the political and cultural life of western Europe.

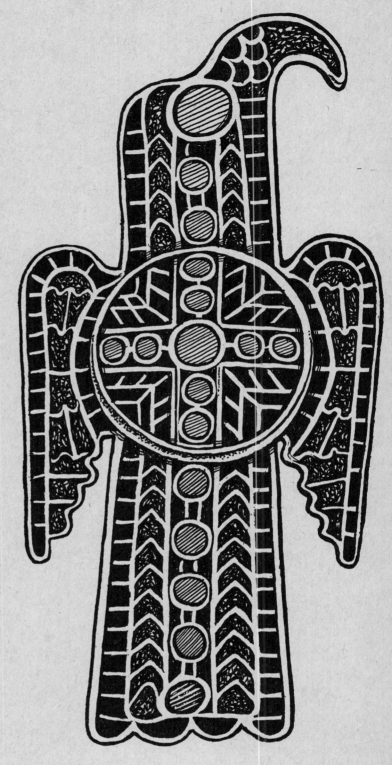

VIII GERMANIC ITALY

The Ostrogothic and Lombard kingdoms

DONALD BULLOUGH

Italy at the time of the Ostrogothic and Lombard invasions

Italy's fate

was in many ways more bitter than the rest of the Western Empire, since she had more to lose and was less reconciled to losing it. Rome was the prize that tempted wave upon wave of barbarian enemies across the Alps—the Visigoths, in 403 and 410, the Huns in 452, the Vandals in 455, the mixed army of Odovacer in 476 and the Ostrogoths in 493. During this period, in the intervals of devastation, there were two centres of power: Rome, where the Papacy was emerging as a strong political force, and Ravenna, where the Emperor and Senate had fled in 402. By paying barbarians to fight barbarians the imperial administration managed to survive, but it was crippled by chaotic conditions and lack of leadership. Finally in 476 the army deposed the last Western Emperor, a boy of twelve, and proclaimed their own leader, Odovacer, ruler of Italy.

The invasion of the Ostrogoths thirteen years later was mainly due to the Eastern Emperor Zeno's desire to rid himself of their presence in the Balkans. Theodoric was commissioned to regain Italy on behalf of the Empire. He did so. Once more the wealth of the country had to be shared out among new masters, but although Theodoric's rule was in fact no less autocratic than Odovacer's, he remained constitutionally a subject-king of Byzantium. 'Our royalty,' he wrote to the Emperor Anastasius, 'is an imitation of yours, a copy of the only Empire on earth.'

His portrait on the gold solidus (opposite, top) reflects this estimate of his position. Its inscription reads *Rex Theodoricus*

Pius Princis, but he wears neither diadem nor robe—only the Emperor could do that. Unusually for a coin portrait, both hands can be seen, the left holding a globe on which stands a victory.

Theodoric saw himself as the successor of Augustus. When in AD 500 he visited the old capital of Rome he was welcomed by the Pope, the Senate and the people; he sponsored commemorative games in the circus and distributed free grain to the poor; his coins bore the figures of Romulus and Remus and the motto *Invicta Roma*.

He died in 526 and was buried in a magnificent tomb outside Ravenna (opposite), which looks back primarily to Roman and Early Christian mausolea, but also perhaps, distantly, to the rock-tumuli of his Germanic ancestors. It is of stone (all the other buildings at Ravenna were brick) and in two stories, the lower —containing the porphyry sarcophagus—decagonal, the upper circular. Round the upper level ran a gallery, of which only the cavities in the outside wall remain. The roof, with its frieze of barbaric ornament, is one enormous slab weighing 470 tons, and the twelve strange 'loops' round its edge bear the names of the Apostles; possibly statues were intended to stand there.

Theodoric is the one great figure of the Ostrogothic Kingdom in Italy. When he died the end was already in sight and the Eastern Emperor was preparing to reclaim the whole country. The Ostrogothic domination lasted only sixty years (493–553). Theodoric had reigned for over half of them. (1,2)

The new capital

was Ravenna, on the Adriatic coast, where Honorius had taken refuge from the Visigoths in 402. It had been a Roman naval base (*Classis*) and still had an important harbour, but the sea was receding, leaving acres of marsh fed by the sluggish waters of the Po. It was almost impregnable. Odovacer held out here for three years and then only surrendered to a trick.

One of the churches built there by Theodoric was S. Apollinare Nuovo. Its walls were covered with mosaic decoration extolling Arian Christianity and the glories of the Ostrogothic state, most of which were destroyed by Justinian when he captured the city in 540. But two relatively innocent panels were allowed to remain—one showing the port of Classis and three ships, one with sails set (right), the other the royal palace with the city of Ravenna beyond (far right). Even in the latter, however, Justinian's artists cut out the portraits of Ostrogothic nobles who formerly stood between the columns and replaced them by curtains. Their faint 'ghosts' can still just be made out. The palace itself, PALATIUM, is shown schematically: the arcades at the sides are the two wings of the inner courtyard, projecting at right angles to the portico. (3,5)

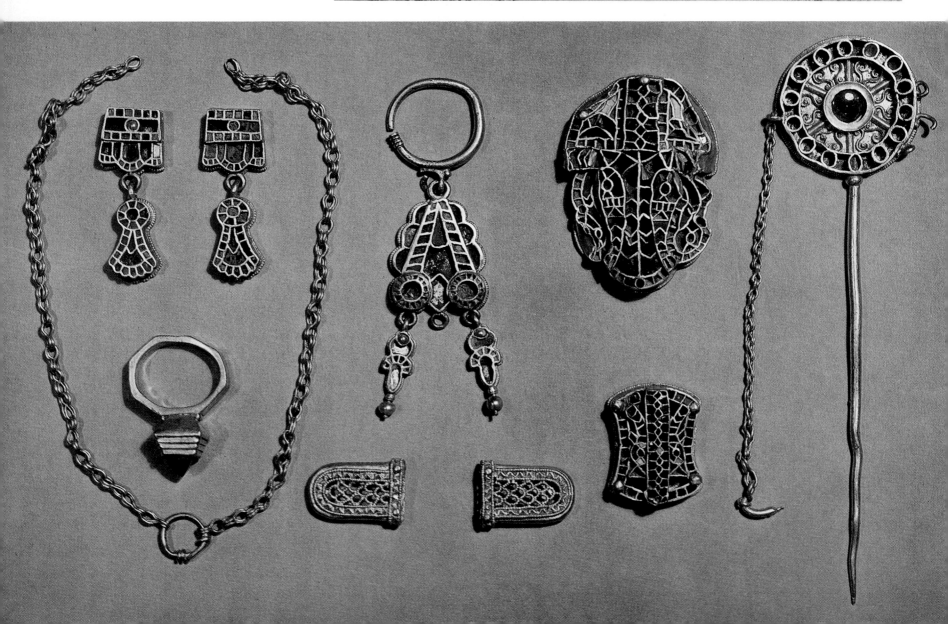

Red and gold characterize Ostrogothic jewellery. Most of the pieces from the Cesena treasure (left), dating from the lifetime of Theodoric and found twenty miles south of Ravenna, are of gold set with garnets. From left to right: a gold chain with, inside it, two pendants from a necklace and a heavy gold finger-ring; a large earring with garnets and pearls; a pair of casings, possibly parts of knife-sheaths; two jewelled crosses flanked by fish, an Early Christian symbol; a large hairpin; and a jewelled eagle-brooch, a design that was widespread among all the Gothic peoples. (4,6)

A woman's make-up jar (right) was among the objects found at Desana as recently as 1941. The collection seems to have been a jewel-chest. It also included several silver spoons like the one shown here, and some inlaid fibulae. The little rouge-jar was studded with forty-two amethysts (four remain) and had an ingenious lid secured by a pin. (7)

The heirs of Theodoric

could do little but preside over the decline of the Ostrogothic Kingdom. When he died his daughter Amalsuntha ruled on behalf of her young son Athalaric (below left). A suggestion has been put forward that the Byzantine ivory on the left represents the Queen; this identification is very difficult to accept though her appearance may have been similar. Athalaric died at the age of eighteen and Amalsuntha married Theodoric's nephew Theodohat (below centre)—an ambitious and ruthless man who soon seized complete power and had his wife put to death. In 536 the Goths deposed Theodohat and put Witigis on the throne. But the Byzantine army was now in Italy; Rome was captured; Ravenna fell; Witigis became a prisoner. Under Totila (below right), the last outstanding figure among the Ostrogoths, they fought on for another twelve years. But in 553, with Totila dead, the whole of Italy again became part of the Byzantine state. (8–11)

Under Byzantine rule Ravenna was governed by a prefect and later by 'exarchs', officials appointed by the emperor. The brick and marble palace façade (below) probably belongs to the last decades of this period, though it incorporates an earlier structure. Charlemagne took marble columns from this palace for his chapel at Aachen. (12)

Ostrogothic art was the exotic offspring of Roman and barbarian taste. A Roman coin, for instance, might be given a bizarre setting of spirals and heads (far left). The fibula from Desana (left centre) marks the zenith of the style—gold inlaid with emerald and garnet. The second fibula is the product of decadence. Made after the defeats of 552–3, it is poor in quality, the ornament crudely scratched on the surface. (13,14,15)

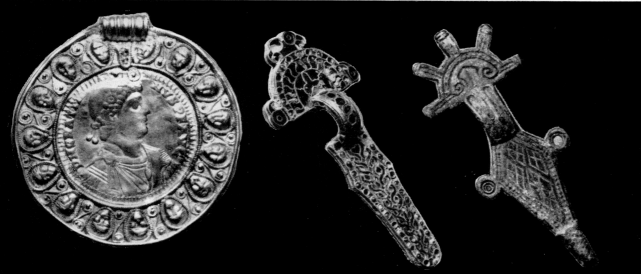

The interval of peace was short.

Sixteen years after the final dissolution of the Ostrogoths a new barbarian people appeared from across the Alps—the Lombards. They had come from northern Europe by way of the Danube and the Hungarian plain, entering Italy in 568. Although more loosely organized than the Ostrogoths under Theodoric, by 572 they had taken Pavia and occupied all the land north of the Po. Under King Agilulf (590–615) their kingdom was strengthened and expanded. All of northern Italy except Ravenna and a strip of the Adriatic coast was lost to the Eastern Empire; Rome remained under papal control. The Lombards reached their peak in the 8th century under their greatest King, Liutprand (712–744), but this very power now aroused anxiety among their neighbours. The Pope called upon the Franks for help, and not in vain. When Charlemagne answered another appeal in 773 and besieged and captured Pavia, the Kingdom came to an end.

Artistic contact with both Franks and Goths, going back to the period before the invasions, is evident in much Lombard metalwork. This silver-gilt brooch (originally it ended in two birds' beaks with garnets for eyes) is of early 6th-century manufacture. (16)

The gold brooch with central turquoise (bottom) and the saddlebow (top) show the style of the following century. In the saddlebow animal shapes—lions, bird-heads and twisted dragons—combine with knots and interlacing cords to form the face of an ox. (17,18)

King Agilulf holds court, guarded by Lombard warriors in armour. On each side winged victories (they carry signs saying VICTURIA) usher in other figures bringing tribute to the King. This unique relief of gilded copper was made as part of a helmet decoration. The classical tradition is still clear, as is the relative crudity of the Lombard artist's attempt to interpret it. (19)

A Lombard nobleman lay buried with his weapons, shield and jewellery in this ornate coffin (right). The wood has been renewed, but all the metal fittings are original. (20)

An enamel portrait, perhaps of a royal lady, forms the centre of the Castellani brooch (below). Possibly made in the Byzantine part of Italy, it is set in four concentric zones, two of pearls and gold loops, one a series of circular patterns and the fourth a simple frame for the portrait. The three loops at the bottom were for pendants, now lost. (22)

'They had their hair parted on either side of their forehead, hanging down their face as far as the mouth.' It is interesting to compare this description of Lombard fashions by Paul the Deacon with the eight faces of Christ which decorate the Cross of Gisulf (below). It was found in a sarcophagus thought to be that of Duke Gisulf, a nephew of Alboin, the King who led the Lombard invasion of Italy in 568. The cross was sewn on to the dress of the dead man. (23)

Agilulf's succession, as told by the chronicler Paul the Deacon, has the flavour of romance. King Authari died in 590, leaving his Queen, Theudelinda, a widow: 'Then all the Lombards, since Theudelinda pleased them well, decided that she should remain Queen, and whosoever she should choose as her husband should wear the royal crown. She therefore chose Agilulf, Duke of Turin, for this double honour . . . And when they had met, after some words spoken, she ordered wine to be brought. And he, receiving the cup from the Queen, reverently kissed her hand; but she, with a blush and a smile, said: He ought not to kiss my hand who has the right to kiss my lips.'

Agilulf died in 615, Theudelinda in 628. They were buried in their favourite city of Monza, where some fascinating relics of them still survive. Above: the jewelled cross from the funerary crown of Agilulf. The crown itself, on which his name was inscribed, was stolen in Paris in 1804, the gold melted and the jewels sold. The small cross, however, remains; it hung down from the edge in the manner of the Visigothic crowns illustrated on pp. 180-1. (21)

Queen Theudelinda is one of the few figures of this age who can still live as a personality—in the pages of Paul the Deacon and in the letters which Pope Gregory the Great wrote to her. Right: diadem from the Queen's crown, probably of Gothic workmanship. Above: a hen and seven chicks, in silver-gilt. This may be one of the gifts which Pope Gregory is known to have sent her, but its exact origin and meaning remain mysterious. Was it simply decorative, or did it symbolize the Lombard state? (24, 25)

The little town of Cividale, in Friuli, northern Italy, is the only spot where the memory of the Lombards can still be recaptured. The seat of a duke and a patriarch, it was enriched during the 8th century with the finest Lombard art. Above: the interior entrance-wall of the church of S. Maria-in-Valle—six female figures, in a style strongly influenced by Byzantium. (26)

Lombard and Eastern motifs come together in two more works at Cividale—the Pemmo Altar (above) and the baptismal font of Patriarch Callistus (right). Both contain a wealth of abstract and animal carving: doves, peacocks, lions and fantastic hybrid beasts. The altar, erected by King Ratchis (744–749) in memory of his father Duke Pemmo of Friuli, shows Christ in glory flanked by seraphs whose wings, following Ezekiel's description, are 'full of eyes round about'. (27,28)

The Ostrogothic and Lombard kingdoms

DONALD BULLOUGH

f 1 When Theodoric the Amal entered Italy in 489 with his Ostrogothic followers, the peninsula was long familiar with invasion and Germanic settlement. The Empire had barely been saved from complete destruction in the later 3rd century; and in the 4th it was still an arduous task to keep the barbarians at bay and letters ('without which we are put on a level with the barbarians') alive. The newly-powerful Christian church made a great contribution to the latter but could give little help with the former; and the estates of the again powerful senatorial class, although farmed predominantly by rigorously-controlled tenants, proved an unsatisfactory source of military recruits. Hence, the seemingly insatiable need of the Empire for soldiers was met by bringing in barbarians to fight barbarians; and before the end of the 4th century Italy and the western provinces were already partly Germanized. The most dramatic of the invasions o Italy, those of the Visigoths in 401/3 and 408/10, led to no permanent settlement, only to widespread destruction. The later one also gave inspiration to Augustine and through him assurance to those who believed that paganism, not Christianity, was to blame; the earlier caused the Emperor in the West to move his court from Rome to Ravenna—then a city very different from now, set amid marshes and the various branches of the Po, with canals between the houses, and hitherto famous otherwise for its asparagus. For nearly three-quarters of a century those who ruled from it or, from mid-century, intermittently from Rome had to cope with a succession of barbarian soldiers-of-fortune who crossed the Alps in search of portable wealth and land.

'Tyrannical Sway of the Intruders'

In 476 the 'army' stationed in the northern part of Italy revolted against the nominal Emperor in Rome and the Patrician at Ravenna who was the real ruler: it demanded 'one-third of the land of Italy', i.e. the third shares *(tertiae)* of estates of existing landowners, that had come to be considered the appropriate rewards of confederate soldiers. As the Byzantine historian Procopius wrote later: 'Under the specious name of alliance the state fell under the tyrannical sway of the intruders'. The demand was rejected. The predominantly Germanic *foederati* acclaimed one of their leaders, Odovacer, as King; Patrician and Western Emperor were disposed of; the imperial insignia were returned to Constantinople with the request that the Emperor should appoint Odovacer 'patrician' in Italy. What degree of recognition the rebel leader actually received is debated. Two documents written by 'Romans' refer to him as *rex* and attribute to him several formerly imperial prerogatives. Coins of silver and bronze struck at Ravenna show him with a thick moustache—a barbarian characteristic already noted by the biographer of St Severinus when Odovacer passed through Noricum in the 460s—but without insignia and without title; his gold coins imitate those of Byzantium, as was the normal practice in the barbarian kingdoms. The administration remained as it had been before 476, with the leading offices held by men drawn from a limited number of native landowning families. Scholars have generally assumed (probably rightly) that the 'thirds' which Odovacer's ten thousand or so followers acquired after their successful revolt were located in the plainland of the Po from

Pavia to Ravenna or in the critical north-east, and that the change of rule was little noticed in the south. Odovacer remained a usurper none the less: his successive support (however qualified) of a Pope unacceptable to Constantinople and of an imperial pretender, followed by his decisive defeat of the Rugians on his northern frontier whom the Emperor had hoped to use as a counter-threat, were fatal to him. The instrument of imperial vengeance was found in the Ostrogoths.

The Ostrogoths Move West

Unlike the Huns, the Ostrogoths cannot boast a characteristic ethnology or physical anthropology: but they have an archaeology; and, thanks in particular to two writers of the 6th century —one Roman, one Gothic—they have a history, with an appropriate element of myth. And their last seventy years of existence display a triumph and a tragedy of truly classic quality.

The undifferentiated Goths were the largest of several groups of Germanic peoples who about the beginning of the Christian era moved southwards from the Baltic. By the later 3rd century, when the name Ostrogoth is first recorded, they were established in the plains and low hills north of the Black Sea. Here, they received Christianity in its Arian form and came into touch with the artistic techniques and styles both of the Asiatic Steppe peoples and of the Mediterranean world. The art that resulted before the end of the 4th century is perhaps best represented by the Szilágy-somlyó hoards which show, often combined in a single piece, the use of filigree, *cloisonné* settings for precious stones and enamel and debased figural ornament: but other Germanic peoples early took up the new style and it is impossible to be confident about the ethnic connections of most of the early examples.

For many decades the Ostrogoths were under the control of the Huns. After the break-up of Attila's empire they moved westwards across the Danube into Pannonia, where according to a near-contemporary they grew wheat and the poorer cereals such as millet without rotating their crops. Their resources were supplemented by *strenae* (annual bounties) from the imperial treasury and by raids on their neighbours: but 'as the spoil diminished, the Goths began to lack food and clothing and peace became distasteful to men to whom war had long furnished the necessities of life'. In the 470s and 480s the Ostrogoths, under their Kings Thiudimer and Thiudariks (Theodoric) who was acclaimed in 474, rampaged through the Balkans and even threatened Constantinople. It was as much to remove this threat as to recover a province of the Empire that seemed to be passing out of his control that in 488 the Emperor commissioned Theodoric—to whom he had already shown innumerable favours and even put up an equestrian statue of him before the Great Palace in Constantinople—to 'secure Italy' at the expense of Odovacer. p 159 (1)

Some groups of Ostrogoths chose to remain where they were, presumably as imperial *foederati*: the fortified settlements of one such group were identified some years ago in northern Bulgaria and others have been claimed in Roumania. The bulk of them loaded their families and possessions on to wagons and, driving their flocks and herds before them, followed Theodoric westwards, to enter Italy by the now traditional route of invasion across the Julian Alps. Odovacer and his forces were defeated in three successive battles; and his erstwhile followers and supporters transferred their allegiance piecemeal to the newcomer, until almost the whole of Italy acknowledged his authority. Odovacer himself was able to take refuge in Ravenna and hold out for three years while the price of corn rose to fabulous levels. At the end of February 493 he sought peace. Theodoric was acclaimed King by the clergy of Ravenna and by his army and entered the city that was henceforth to be his capital. Shortly afterwards Odovacer was treacherously killed—as was early believed, by Theodoric's own hand.

King Theodoric

Theodoric ruled Italy—and subsequently Dalmatia also—as King of both Goths and Romans, although not at first acknowledged as such at Constantinople: in 497, however, he was sent the *ornamenta palatii*, i.e. the insignia dispatched to Constantinople in 476. Clearly Theodoric's position was not strictly comparable f 2

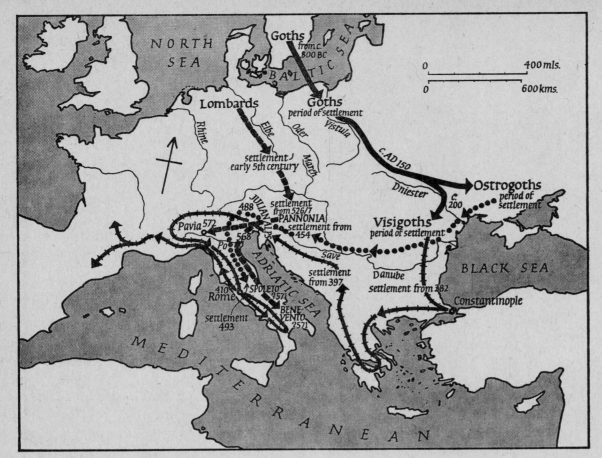

The three most important waves of invaders of Italy are shown on this map: the Visigoths, who sacked Rome in 410, but who then moved on to southern France and Spain; the Ostrogoths, who migrated from the East Roman (Byzantine) Empire with the active help of the Emperor; and the Lombards, a less Romanized people who came more directly from their home on the shores of the Baltic. (1)

with that of other barbarian kings; and the difficulty of expressing it adequately was evidently felt by the composer of the inscription who added to the title of *gloriosissimus adque inclytus rex* the (imperial) epithets of *victor ac triumfator semper Augustus!* Theodoric's own view of his relationship with the Roman Empire was no less ambiguous, as may be gathered from the words of a letter sent in his name to the Emperor Anastasius in 508 or 509: 'you', he says, 'are the health and salvation of the whole world, whom all other nations rightly regard with reverence, because they know that in you there is something unique.... Our royalty is an imitation of yours, a copy of the only Empire on earth; and in so far as we follow you do we excel all other nations'.

Theodoric's constitutional position may be uncertain. The effective basis of his authority is not. This depended, firstly, on the arms of his Gothic soldiers: without them Theodoric could not make his influence felt beyond the limits of Italy or protect it from external threat, as when he gave a guarantee of protection to the Alemanni who had fled to Rhaetia after their defeat by the Frankish King Clovis or when he extended the frontier of his kingdom westwards along the shores of the Mediterranean; and it depended, secondly, on the effective exploitation of the resources of government inherited from those who had ruled before him in Italy.

According to Procopius, writing in the late 6th century, 'Of injustice towards his subjects there was hardly a trace in his government ... save only that the Goths divided among themselves the same proportion of the land of Italy which Odoacer (Odovacer) had given to his partisans'. Fighting men presumably constituted about a fifth or a quarter of Theodoric's following; and even if we accept that this was two hundred thousand strong, the number of Gothic warriors was smaller than that of the inhabitants of Rome at that time. Not surprisingly place-names of certain or probable Gothic origin or containing a Gothic personal name (which may of course originate much later) show a marked concentration in the Lombard and Venetian plains and the Alpine foothills. Finds of Gothic jewellery are more scattered. There is literary and documentary evidence for small settlements in the south in the reference to 'the thin chain of soldiers in Sicily', or the command to 'all the Goths settled in Picenum and Samnium' to attend court 'to receive our royal largesse' (the writer of the letter adding, significantly, that a warrior is 'as one dead who is not known to his lord').

If we take at its face-value the 4th- and 5th-century evidence of the gathering of lands into the hands of great *possessores*, so that the one-time small landowners became predominantly tenants, the number of men who lived by the labours of others in Italy may well have been less than that of the Goths who were to benefit from the allocation. In many instances a Goth took up residence on his lands and often an actual division took place: Theodoric later praised his first praetorian prefect Liberius for the skilful way in which he carried this out. Other Goths, perhaps even a majority, were settled in groups and received payments in cash or in horses: the *Goti*-place-names (modern Godo, Godego, etc.) may preserve the memory of such cantonments. In the course of time many more Goths became 'landed' and by no means invariably as substantial *possessores*.

'The Goth who Imitates the Roman'

When this happened, however, the Goth was in danger of abandoning his true calling. In Theodoric's view, and indeed in that of many Romans, he was there as a warrior: trained in the use of arms when young, he bore them in the king's service until physically unable to do so. Presumably there were *élite* troops who were fully professional but others were expected to turn out for training exercises as well as for war. They rode to battle and many of them fought from horseback with spear and sword which, even when dismounted, they used as a cutting weapon. Their archers, however—an important part of their army—were not horsed, and this, according to Procopius, proved a serious disadvantage. Because the Ostrogoths did not deposit grave-goods with their burials, very few of their weapons have been identified. Examples of the helmets worn by Gothic military leaders—perhaps including the *millenarii*, 'captains of thousands', who are recorded in several texts—have, however, been found in several places in Italy and elsewhere. The difficulty of finding sailors from among the Goths may explain why Theodoric had no navy until a surprisingly late date, in spite of the obvious importance of the sea-approaches to his capital, Ravenna, and to Rome.

The Goths, then, were born and brought up to fight; the native population was not. The old Roman law that forbade marriage with a barbarian was still valid, although it was sometimes got round; and, most important of all, the Goths were and remained Arians. The view attributed to Theodoric by a mid-6th-century Ravenna(?) writer that 'the Roman who imitates

f 3

p 160
(3)

the Goth is worthless, the Goth who imitates the Roman valuable' was obviously not to be taken too literally. Theodoric had a genuine regard for Roman ways; and his Gothic subjects were living, as the King (or the ministers who attributed the words to him) was never tired of telling them, in a society that was or should be characterized by *civilitas*. The Goths had to be taught to respect the law which, in so far as it concerned property, violence and obligations to the state, was the same for them as for the Romans; and to help—or force—them to do so they were subject to the jurisdiction of *comites Gothorum* in each province and in those city-territories where any of them were to be found.

This and the creation of a new office of 'count of the patrimony' (which could also be filled by Goths) to control the private domains of the King were Theodoric's only substantial modification of the administrative hierarchy that he inherited. Existing forms were retained and the higher offices filled predominantly by men whose ancestors had served the emperors in a similar capacity. Theodoric's special deference to the restricted group that now constituted the effective part of the Roman senate was partly balanced by a preference for men drawn from the provinces rather than from Rome itself: among them was the younger Cassiodorus who for nearly fifty years sought to make Goths seem like Romans, even to senators and emperors. Only slightly less important than the support of the wealthy senatorial aristocracy was that of the *curiales* (the governing class in the towns, although increasingly living in the country) and of the *possessor*-class generally. It is significant that in the 154-chapter *Edictum* of Theodoric, promulgated in the early 6th century, *servi* and their iniquities figure prominently while the *colonus* occurs by name only where he is protected from unjustly-exacted forced labour. Landowners were responsible for meeting the heavy burden of direct taxation, which continued in spite of the allocation of 'thirds', and for non-monetary levies and labour services to the state of various kinds.

It is impossible to determine the real incidence of this taxation or of the ability of the economy to support it. Many years of relative peace doubtless helped many landlords to increase their income from farms on good land. The abandonment of marginal land could mean a gain rather than a loss if population was declining: and it would be unwise to attribute much significance to the supposedly successful efforts of the senator Basilius Decius to drain part of the Pontine Marshes, which for many years past had been forming on once fertile ground. Theodoric's construction of fortified refuges for entire communities in a few key places did not imply a general movement to the hills, although

A 6th-century Ostrogothic helmet, found in a warrior's grave near the Lake of Geneva. The frame and ornamental parts are copper-gilt, the 'skull-cap' iron. (3)

this certainly took place in several areas—with consequent economic dislocation—during the wars of the imperial reconquest. It is possible to infer from evidence of the first three decades of the 6th century that Italy enjoyed an overall agricultural prosperity broken only by local, although often acute, shortage; but it is equally possible to infer that it suffered from a chronic shortage of basic foodstuffs modified only by the ability of the central government to direct available supplies to those areas where the local officials complained loudest.

A Wealth of Craftsmanship

Ravenna showed all the external signs of prosperity in the first half of the 6th century. In the eastern extension of the old city, Theodoric built or rebuilt a palace and its associated buildings: here he held court and, with his followers, ate and drank with typically Gothic gusto. Churches were built and richly endowed by private individuals. The city was a major market for both foodstuffs and the luxury products of other parts of Italy and the East. The monopolistic rights of commercial and industrial guilds (which perhaps uniquely in Ravenna survived the *débacle* of the next centuries) and royal regulation of prices may have restricted enterprise: there were clearly profits to be made, however, and the city maintained a surprising number of bankers (*argentarii*), although the *argentarius* Julian, who disposed of almost incredible sums of money for church-building in the second quarter of the century seems to have come from Constantinople. Ravenna did not stand quite alone. Theodoric commissioned new buildings and encouraged the repair and reconstruction of ancient ones, among which aqueducts could have a direct bearing on a town's well-being. Theodoric's activities at Verona were hardly on the scale that later legend suggested, but he built a palace there and repaired and perhaps even extended the walls. At Parma, on the other hand, a wall of supposedly Ostrogothic date implies a contraction of the inhabited area. What is undeniable is that in this period the transporting of timber, stone and marble and the buying and selling of corn were going on over distances and on a scale that have no parallel for several centuries thereafter; and there was evidently still a substantial class of traders in Italy among whom Jews were increasingly prominent but not predominant.

p 160–1 (3, 5) f 5, 7

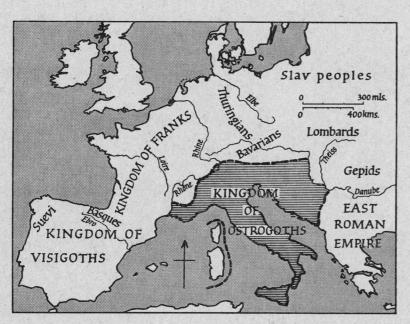

The kingdom of the Ostrogoths at the death of Theodoric (526). Theodoric ruled the whole of Italy and Sicily and the province of Dalmatia in the Balkans. Constitutionally, his position was more secure than that of the other barbarian kings; after 497 his authority was recognized at Constantinople, and his kingdom was deliberately modelled on Roman and Byzantine example. (2)

The sculptured frieze which runs round the top of Theodoric's mausoleum, underneath the massive stone roof (p. 159, pl. 1), has some interesting features. The 'pincer' motif may be debased classical ornament, or it may be native Gothic; it is found also on metalwork. This seems to be the only case of its adaptation to the hard medium of stone. (4)

p 160, 1
(4, 6)
p 162
(14)
p 161
(7)

The most important luxury imports were probably the garnets which play such a brilliant part in Ostrogothic jewellery: this, indeed, reached its highest levels of achievement in the earlier part of the 6th century, with such pieces as 'Theodoric's breast-plate' and the objects in the Cesena treasure. The contents of the Desana hoard (discovered in 1941), which seems to represent the jewel-chest of a Gothic woman, show that the newcomers patronized native craftsmen too, and such pieces as the ointment- or rouge-box could equally be the work of Goths or Italians. Germanic styles found acceptance in time among the native population: in 564 the widow of a Roman included in a quittance *fibula de bracile et de usubandilos*—an unequivocally Germanic garment. Even if we admit the intense conservatism of craftsmen trained in a distinctive tradition, it is difficult to believe that workshops in Italy continued to *recruit* on a 'nationalist' basis: and the helmets of probable Ostrogothic date which combine a type of construction developed by the Goths in Pannonia with Italianate ornament make it almost certain that they did not.

f 4
It would be equally unrealistic to suppose that no Goth ever became a stone-mason, stone-carver or even a mosaic-worker. The palaces and churches built in Italy in this period and their decoration show however few, if any, traces of non-Mediterranean influence and fit securely into the tradition of late imperial secular and Christian art. No features that are now recognizable enable us to distinguish churches built for Arians from those used by the orthodox. The books used by the Arian bishops of Ravenna, Rome, Crotone and elsewhere (and by their subordinates, who are even more shadowy figures) have largely disappeared: a notable exception is the Verona manuscript with marginalia in the Gothic language.

The Final Tragedy

Sixty years after their victorious entry into Italy, however, the Ostrogoths were on the point of almost complete destruction at the hands of imperial armies and the peace and relative prosperity of Theodoric's reign were already in the realm of legend. They had indeed always been somewhat precariously based. 'The detestable heresy of Arius' was the form of unbelief that orthodox Christians were least willing to forgive; and when the Emperor Justin issued a decree (523) against the employment in public office of pagans, Jews and heretics, it was taken by Theodoric to be an attack on himself and his people. The King reacted strongly; and the not unjustifiable suspicion that senators were entering into secret negotiations with Byzantium led to the execution of the great scholar and one-time trusted royal servant Boethius and others of his class. Yet shortly before he died (on
p 159
(2)
30th August 526) and was laid in a mausoleum just outside his capital, Theodoric enjoined the Gothic chiefs and the young grandchild who was to be their king to maintain good relations with the Roman senate and people and to retain the goodwill of the Emperor.

p 162
(8)
f 6
The Byzantine sympathies of Theodoric's daughter, Amalsuntha, who was Regent for her son, aroused deep antagonism among other Gothic leaders who finally had her murdered (535). The Emperor Justinian now had ample excuse for a 'truceless war' against the Goths. His armies invaded Dalmatia and Sicily in 536 and crossed to the mainland the next year. Naples was occupied after a siege, Rome without a fight; but the latter had subsequently to resist a siege by the new Ostrogothic King Witigis, who cut the aqueducts (an event which has been described as marking the real end of the ancient world). Subsequently the imperial armies overcame most of the Gothic contingents left to defend towns and forts on or near the Via Flaminia, at the same time suffering severe defeat further north, in campaigns that were marked by massacre and destruction on both sides. Witigis withdrew to Ravenna: here, in 540, being offered generous terms, he surrendered.

In Justinian's view the power of the Goths was at an end, even though there were garrisons still in being in the north and northwest. He had misjudged badly: the Goths were defeated but not destroyed; and the measures taken by him and his representatives alienated both his troops and many of the inhabitants of Italy. In the autumn of 541 the Gothic commander of Treviso, Baduila (Totila) was proclaimed 'King of the Goths': within two years his armies had gained control of large areas of central and southern Italy. This time there were no concessions to the landowning classes: their estates were expropriated on a large scale; the tenant *coloni*, who were mostly left undisturbed, henceforward owed their dues to the Gothic treasury; and former slaves were enlisted in the Gothic army, apparently in considerable numbers. When Totila entered Rome in 546, undermined great lengths of wall and dispersed the population, he kept with him the senators he found there; some were subsequently rescued, but the others were later put to death.

For five years the Gothic and imperial armies marched and counter-marched, lost and captured cities without either side gaining a clear-cut victory. In 550/1 Cassiodorus, a refugee in Constantinople, was still hopefully making propaganda for Gothic-Roman reconciliation; Totila, more realistically, recognized that it was a fight to the death and for the first time among barbarian kings portrayed himself in imperial insignia on his coins. Before the end of 551 an imperial army strong enough to strike a decisive blow was on its way. In the summer of 552, high up in the Apennines by the Via Flaminia, the Gothic armies were

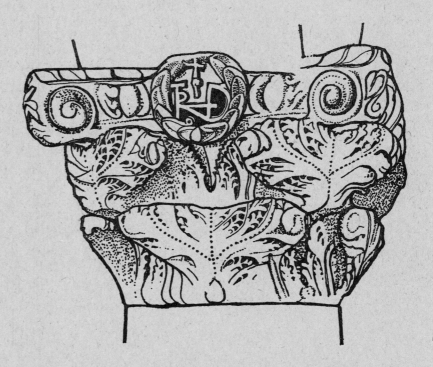

Fourteen capitals from Theodoric's palace have survived at Ravenna, most of them re-used in later buildings. Five of them, of which the best preserved is shown here, include the King's monogram in a wreath. Both this feature and the general style of the capital are strongly Byzantine. (5)

Queen Amalsuntha, who acted as regent for her son after the death of her father Theodoric. This small ivory shows her dressed in a costume closely modelled on that of Theodora in the famous S. Vitale mosaic. Her hair is gathered at the top, strings of pearls hang down on either side of her face, and she wears a heavy jewelled collar. (6)

A Second Invasion: the Lombards

The people described by Latin writers of the 1st century as *Langobardi* abandoned their north German home considerably later than the Goths and reached Italy by a less roundabout route. In the earlier 5th century the main body of them moved from the upper Elbe to the undulating plainland west of the River March (Czechoslovakia). Attila incorporated them in his 'empire'; after his death their native kings recovered their independent authority; and when the kingdom of the *Rugii* (Rugians) (on the north bank of the Danube) was finally destroyed in 487/8 by armies sent by Odovacer, the Lombards moved to the territory that they had controlled.

The presence in isolated burials and large cemeteries of characteristic types of pottery found earlier in the Elbe region is one reason for regarding these graves as 'Lombard'. Other evidence shows, however, that in the last years of the 5th century the Lombards were absorbing new influences from various sources. The discovery—first made in 1853 and confirmed in 1948—that the hill of Žuraň (from which Napoleon commanded his armies at Austerlitz) contains a limited number of unusually elaborate stonechambered burials datable to the very end of the century provides an unexpected Lombard analogy with the 'Royal Mounds' of southern Sweden. The graves of the farmer-warriors and their families, no longer cremated, were commonly in long parallel rows, the men buried with weapons, the women with brooches (usually in pairs). The shapes and polychromatic decoration of many of these derive ultimately from the late-4th-century jewellery of the Black Sea region; but while the metalworkers of the Lombards were copying and adapting current Gothic styles for some of their types, for others they found their models among the Franks, who also passed on their version of the late-Antique metalwork of the Rhineland. The neighbours whose territories the Lombards occupied may have been another source of influence. The earliest 'Lombard' wheel-pottery was surely the work of aliens whose skills the conquerors used.

Probably very soon after the death of Theodoric, the main body of the Lombards crossed the Danube. Subsequently their King Waccho (c. 510–540) established links by treaty or marriage with the Frankish kingdom of Rheims, with the Empire and with the Gepids: when in 539 the desperate Ostrogothic King sought Lombard support it was inevitably in vain. For six years after Waccho's death the Lombards acknowledged a king who was a minor, which suggests a surprising degree of political maturity.

smashed and Totila slain in a battle of epic distinction. The long-drawn-out war was not quite over. The last Ostrogothic King was killed near Vesuvius in 553; but individual garrisons held out for several years more, the last—in towns of the north-east—surrendering only in 561 or 562. A few shattered remnants sought refuge in the foothills of the Alps around Trent: a memory of one of their fortified refuges is preserved in the name (*Val di*) *Lagare* which comes, via the Lombardic, from the Gothic *Ligeris*, and the remains of another are perhaps to be identified further north at Castel Vetere near Ora; the brooches they made there are a measure of the greatness of the fall of their race.

p 162
(15)

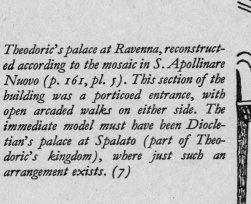

Theodoric's palace at Ravenna, reconstructed according to the mosaic in S. Apollinare Nuovo (p. 161, pl. 5). This section of the building was a porticoed entrance, with open arcaded walks on either side. The immediate model must have been Diocletian's palace at Spalato (part of Theodoric's kingdom), where just such an arrangement exists. (7)

In 546, however, a new royal dynasty was established in the person of Audoin: friendly relations between Lombards and Franks quickly ceased; and in 547/8 the Lombards were allowed to establish themselves in the ex-Ostrogothic lands as far as and even beyond the Save, in return for which they were to help the imperial armies in Italy and keep the Gepids in check. Now, in all probability, they began to adapt their existing tribal organization—based on the assembly (*gairethinx*) of, nominally, all free men (whom the king, in theory, merely represented), in practice presumably a select company of 'nobles'—to the imperial military organization of the period: by 568 a hierarchy of dukes, counts and others commanded the Lombard warrior-bands; and some of them were associated with *castella* taken over from the Byzantines. The later view that the composition of these bands (*farae*) was still determined by kin-grouping and family relationships is, however, not improbable. There is evidence that some time in the earlier 6th century *orthodox* Christian missionaries were at work among the Lombards—with very limited success: by 565 the king and his circle professed Arian Christianity (perhaps adopted from the Ostrogoths), but pagan beliefs and practices persisted for several generations more.

The New Masters of Italy

For two decades after 546 the Lombards and their eastern neighbours the Gepids—whom the imperial Court regarded as the more powerful and dangerous of the two—engaged in intermittent war alternating with truces. A promise to Audoin of imperial support was not kept; and after his death in 565 his son and successor Alboin made a 'perpetual treaty' with the recently-arrived Turco-Mongol Avars to make an end of the Gepids. In 567 these were completely destroyed by the Lombard warriors; Alboin 'made out of their dead king's head, which he carried off, a drinking goblet, called among the Lombards *scala*', and at the same time took his daughter Rosamund as his second wife.

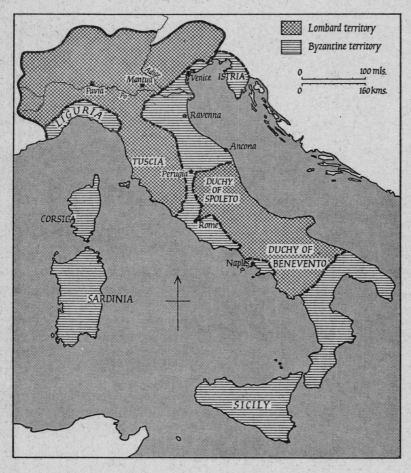

Lombard territory in 640. The division of Italy between Lombards and Byzantines was constantly fluctuating. The Lombards never conquered Rome, and Ravenna only in the mid-8th century. They were most powerful in the north (their capital was at Pavia), but Spoleto and Benevento had Lombard rulers and in 643 Liguria also fell to them. (8)

Avar-Slav pressure and the ending of imperial subsidies were perhaps the principal reasons why the Lombards now planned their final migration. In spring 568, in the words of a contemporary Burgundian writer, 'the whole Lombard army, after having set afire their own dwellings, and followed by the women and the entire population' abandoned Pannonia and crossed the Julian Alps. A few women remained behind to be annexed by the Avars, which may have given rise to the Lombard tradition that they made an agreement with the latter that if necessary they could re-occupy their lands in the future. The new invasion of Italy at first encountered only weak opposition. By September 569 the Lombards had captured all the principal cities north of the Po except Pavia. Subsequently Alboin led or sent expeditions across the Apennines, which prepared the way for the permanent annexation of much of western Emilia and of northern and central Tuscany. In ?571 two separate Lombard armies gained control of Spoleto and Benevento and their leaders subsequently established their authority—in campaigns of which almost nothing is known—over extensive territories between the central Apennines and the Adriatic and in the southern Apennines and Apulian Plain respectively. In 572 Pavia fell.

Shortly after his entry into the city that was to play a major part in the history of the Lombard and post-Lombard Italian kingdom, Alboin was murdered, in revenge for having forced his wife to drink from her dead father's skull. The eighteen-month rule of his successor Cleph was marked by the ruthless treatment of the native *possessores*. What happened on his death shows how reluctantly the Lombards, in spite of their acceptance of some of the ways of Byzantium, abandoned the traditions of a much older Germanic past: no king was chosen, and instead the dukes (traditionally thirty-five or thirty-six in number) exercised an independent authority in the territory of one or more *civitates*. The *farae* of Lombard warriors and their wives and families were mostly established in groups in easily-defended positions on the outskirts of the cities or in fortified settlements (*castella*) in the countryside; a famous passage in 'History' of the 8th-century Lombard scholar, Paul the Deacon, seems to imply that they were *f 10* maintained by requiring the greater landowners to give a 'third' of their income. A Lombard *castellum* belonging to the earliest period of settlement has been identified at Maddaloni—Monte S. Michele (near Capua), and others doubtless await discovery. Scattered archaeological finds and the evidence of place-names formed from Lombard words or names (which cannot, however, all be assumed to be of the period of settlement) suggest that many fewer of the newcomers established themselves south of the Apennines than in the Po Valley and the north-east; even in the north the Lombards were very much a minority.

In 584 the Lombard leaders re-established the kingship in the person of Authari, son of Cleph. With this Paul the Deacon associates, firstly, the establishment of a permanent patrimony for the king (which later evidence shows to have been administered in the main city-territories by a *gastald*, who also provided a check on the dukes), and, secondly, a dividing-up of what he calls the *populi*—which perhaps means that many Lombards now acquired rights (and the income from land that went with them) over peasant cultivators, free and unfree. Authari, who died in 590, only barely managed to save the Lombards from total destruction at the hands of Byzantine and Frankish armies working in concert. His widow Theudelinda, a Bavarian with Lombard ancestors, chose to succeed him, both as husband and as King, Duke Agilulf (died 615 or 616), who, in a series of campaigns that brought renewed misery to many districts of north Italy and aroused the passionate concern of Pope Gregory I (590–604), recovered much that had been lost and threatened Rome. By 605 the frontier was becoming stabilized, to leave the imperial armies and administration in control only of the Ligurian coast, the Venetian coastal strip, a solid belt of territory in central Italy including Ravenna, *f 8* Ancona and Rome, and small areas in the south and south-east. The subsequent history of the Imperial Exarchate of Italy shows a progressive adjustment of the social and administrative structure to meet the ever-present threat of invasion. A little-known and extremely interesting series of 'castles' was erected in the western Apennines and Ligurian Alps and doubtless along other

p 163
(19)
p 164
(21)
p 165
(24, 25)

frontiers. In spite of these measures, Liguria fell to Lombard armies in a single campaign in 643; and in rather more protracted fighting subsequently the Venetian frontier was pushed back to the edge of the lagoons.

Laws and Government of a Barbarian Kingdom

As a Catholic concerned for the souls of her subjects, Theudelinda maintained friendly relations with Pope Gregory and his successors: some of the gifts she received from Rome are still preserved in her favourite city of Monza. She none the less supported the north Italian clergy who were regarded by the Papacy as heterodox because they continued to defend doctrines (the so-called 'Three Chapters') that half a century earlier had been adjudged heretical by the Emperor and subsequently (and reluctantly) by the Bishop of Rome; she also found a sympathizer in the exiled Irish monk Columbanus. The foundation in 614 of a monastery at Bobbio (in the Piacenzan Apennines) with Columbanus (died 615) as Abbot seemingly had a missionary purpose: but the community's vital and enduring contribution to the Christian West was as a cultural staging-post between Ireland and the Mediterranean. When Aripert I (653–661) sought to proscribe Arianism, most Lombards who had not kept up their primitive pagan practices were still its adherents. By the end of the century, through the efforts in particular of a bishop of Pavia and of other clergy sent from Rome and partly of East Mediterranean origin, Arianism had been eliminated and the Catholic schismatics reconciled.

f 10   The extent to which the Lombards long remained a distinct ethnic group in north Italy is illustrated by Paul the Deacon's account of paintings (presumably the work of 'Romans' in the early 7th century) in Theudelinda's palace at Monza: these showed that, while normally bearded, 'they bared the neck [of hair], shaving it up to the back of the head, and had their hair parted on either side from their forehead, hanging down on their face as far as the mouth. Their garments were loose and mostly of linen, such as the Anglo-Saxons regularly wear, interwoven (*or ?bordered*) with fairly wide strips in various colours. Their boots were divided almost up to the big toe and laced cross-wise. Later on they began to use hose, over which when they rode they wore double-nap-woollen leggings—a practice they borrowed from the Romans.' Equally striking is the evidence of the cemeteries which retained their distinctive character well on into the 7th century. The grave-goods are predominantly a continuation or development of those formerly manufactured in Pannonia, together with new varieties of metalwork and glassware possibly made by the native population but specifically for the newcomers. Among a group of 7th-century graves near Chiusi (Tuscany) was one in which two egg-shells were found between the skeleton's legs, a practice followed in Pannonia earlier and one against which St Carlo Borromeo had to protest in the 16th century! The local name *Pertica (Ad Per-*

p 166   *ticas*) at Cividale and Pavia reflects the Lombard custom—record-
(26,   ed by Paul the Deacon in the late 8th century—of erecting wooden
27, 28)   posts with the figure of a bird over the tombs of the dead. Yet the

Paul the Deacon, to whose 'Historia Gentis Langobardorum' we owe nearly all our knowledge of Lombard history, was a middle-aged man when the kingdom was conquered by Charlemagne. He came from north-east Italy and was probably educated at the royal court at Benevento. In the early 780s his exceptional learning made him a prominent figure at the court of Charlemagne, but he ended his days in his beloved monastery of Monte Cassino. His 'History' covers the period from the remote origins of the Lombards on the shores of the Baltic to the death of Liutprand in 747. This drawing is the earliest known portrait of him, dating from the 11th century. (10)

Latin form of the name, the patronage of native workmen and the distinctive ribbon-animal designs found on Lombard metal-work from c. 600 and subsequently 'exported' by them to other Germanic peoples north of the Alps show that even before their conversion the Lombards were coming under the spell of 'Roman' ideas and techniques—and creating from them something new and of more than local significance.

The opposed influences in the *regnum Langobardorum* in the middle decades of the 7th century are apparent in the written code of laws, or Edict, promulgated by the Arian King Rothari (636–652) shortly after the successful Ligurian expedition. The idea of such a code is Roman although of course it was not the first of its kind in the Romano-Germanic kingdoms; and if the man or men who composed it were not Latin-speaking by birth they were obviously instructed by someone with a good knowledge of the language and of Roman 'Vulgar' law. The authority of the king and his special position before the law are clearly asserted at the beginning. The powers of the dukes are laid down, but royal officials exist who will see that they are exercised properly. The vendetta between kin was still a normal means of securing redress of grievances, although the course it might take had already been modified to take account of the attitudes of the clergy (whether Arian or Catholic) and of the right of royal officials to intervene; and the tariff of compensation due to the victims for injuries or losses suffered if feud were to be avoided occupies many clauses. The typical free Lombard was assumed to have rights over lands, flocks and slaves. But he was not a landed gentleman: he was still essentially a warrior.

This status and obligation was as important as Arianism in keeping the Lombards separate from their 'Roman' neighbours. They had, too, distinctive ways of fighting: they seem to have fought from horseback at a time when this was unusual, and favoured the use of the bow and arrow. Fighting was the normal summer occupation of many *arimanni* throughout the 7th century. The Avars and Slavs had overrun almost all the Lombard settlements outside Italy by its opening years and thereafter were a constant menace in the north-east, while the Bavarians came to be an intermittent threat further west. It has been supposed, mainly on linguistic grounds, that as a result of the devastation caused by the decades of warfare, Friuli and adjacent parts of the Venetian plain had to be substantially re-settled in the next century.

A richly decorated folding-stool (9th century) found near the Lombard capital of Pavia. Gold and silver inlays, using a combination of Roman and Germanic motifs, cover the iron frame (the leather straps are restorations). Folding-stools of this kind seem to have functioned as portable 'thrones', reserved for kings or high officials. Only two other actual examples are known (one of them associated with the Frankish King Dagobert) but pictures of them often occur in manuscript portraits. (9)

The frontier atmosphere of the duchies of Friuli and Trent, like the remoteness of Spoleto and Benevento from the main centres of royal authority (in the north), helped to keep alive a spirit of ducal independence; and few kings had not to face one or more revolts against their authority. The authority and resources of the Lombard kings was probably far greater than is commonly recognized. They increasingly used the Theodorican palace at Pavia as a settled royal residence and the city consequently emerged as a regular capital. The palace was the base for a group of lay writers of documents *(notarii)* who were whole-time functionaries of the king and came to exercise judicial functions on his behalf; and records of their decision were kept there. By the 8th century the Palace also received regular payments from various sources, including tolls levied on objects of trade; the Alpine frontier-crossings were supervized by officials who were in constant touch with the court. Rothari had claimed coinage as a royal prerogative and this was obviously effective from at least the reign of Cunicpert (688–700), when, with Pavia as the principal mint, gold coins for the first time bore the name of the Lombard king, with the figure of St Michael—who had brought Cunicpert victory in battle—on the reverse. How much of this was inherited by the Lombards directly from their predecessors is disputed: it is probable that an increasingly confident monarchy imitated and adapted Byzantine practices at various times in the 7th century and then developed them along independent lines.

The End of the 'Regnum Langobardorum'

The ending of Arianism made possible the coalescence of Lombards and Romans within the kingdom: when both Latin and German names occur in a single family the process is clearly at work; and it may be doubted whether many of the landowners who figure as founders of churches and donors of lands in the documents that survive in increasing numbers in the 8th century could claim an exclusively Lombardic ancestry. Military obligations were now laid on lands rather than on persons; and kings had to find means of creating a new class of professional warriors.

Developments such as these made possible the achievements of King Liutprand (712–744), the second member of a dynasty that was raised to the throne when Theudelinda's line finally came to an end, and probably the greatest of the Lombard kings. Until 726 he seems to have been concerned exclusively with the internal condition of his kingdom. In subsequent years, helped by the internal dissensions resulting from imperial policies, his armies steadily reduced the areas of Italy still under Byzantium; and he made the royal authority felt as never before in Spoleto and Benevento. The laws that he issued in fifteen of the annual 'national assemblies' reveal an increase in royal power and a growing opposition to violent revenge; they show a rudimentary jurisprudential thinking and the increased importance and complexity of property transactions. Royal charters and coins (gold tremisses) confirm the impression of a strong and effective monarch. Other texts point to an increasing commercial activity, particularly along the line of the Po which was the principal route of peaceful contact between the capital and other northern cities and the Byzantine territories. The Palace, finally, was a centre of Latin culture; and the effect of royal patronage can perhaps be detected in building and the associated arts. Paul the Deacon fittingly terminated his 'History' with the events of Liutprand's last years.

Liutprand's successors had not his respect for the see of Peter and this was to bring disaster on their nation: the *Liber Pontificalis* for these years reads like the chorus of a Greek tragedy. In 751 Aistulf (749–756) occupied Ravenna and the remaining Byzantine territories in Emilia and southwards along the Adriatic and then turned towards Rome. The Frankish King Pepin twice answered papal appeals for help and compelled Aistulf to surrender to the papacy much of what he had conquered. When Desiderius (756–774) sought to annex these 'Papal states' in 772, Frankish help was again sought. The Frankish armies evaded the fortifications covering the mountain-crossings of the north-west (773) and most of the towns of the kingdom quickly yielded to them. Pavia held out: when it fell in June 774, Desiderius and his remaining supporters were at the disposal of the Frankish King and the independent *regnum Langobardorum* came to an end.

The Legacy of the Ostrogoths and Lombards

Few will quarrel with the view that the earlier Ostrogothic decades witnessed a remarkable attempt at a 'Romano-Germanic synthesis' that was prematurely wrecked and therefore made a negligible contribution to the later history of the peninsula. Specifically Ostrogothic contributions to its later social and legal institutions are not detectable and the Gothic element in the Italian vocabulary and nomenclature is insignificant. The most enduring achievements of the period came from Ostrogothic patronage of architects, artists and craftsmen, although these are hardly to be despised; and we should perhaps add here, from their patronage of learning and letters. The judgment of many historians, and certainly of a majority of Italians, that the establishment of the Lombards led primarily to the barbarization of a society that began to recover only in the later 11th century is more than a little unfair—as is slowly being recognized. The society, government and culture of the kingdom in the 2nd century of its existence were all expressions of an enduring 'Romano-Germanic synthesis'.

The Lombard contribution to the Italian language was substantial. The private law of the early communal period made use of several practices introduced by the Lombards. The Palace organization created by the Lombard kings from some of the resources of central government available to their predecessors was further developed and adapted by their successors to the advantage of monarchs and subjects, until subjection to a new line of Germanic rulers brought about its dismantling. The crudity of many of the artistic monuments of the Lombard period did not exclude the creation of others that were of a very different character and quality. The artistic as well as the literary achievements of the 'Carolingian Renaissance' owed more to earlier activity in the *regnum Langobardorum* than is commonly recognized. Paul the Deacon was right in thinking that the history of his people before they experienced the wrath of the Franks deserved to be recorded for posterity; and if in the next century the independent princes of Benevento could rightly assert that they alone were still keeping alive the name of their race, they were wrong in assuming that their followers were the sole residuary legatees of the Lombard heritage.

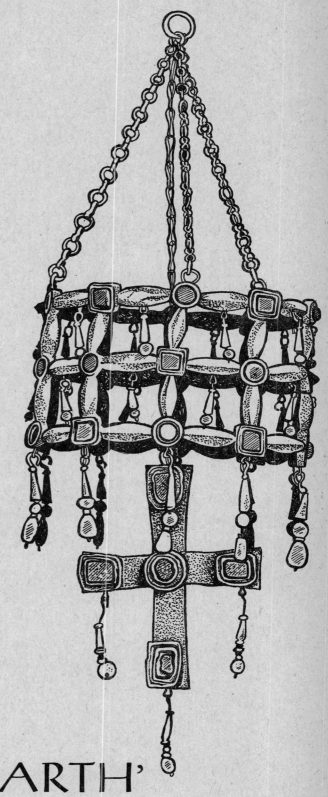

IX 'THE ENDS OF THE EARTH'

Spain under the Visigoths and Moors

WILLIAM CULICAN

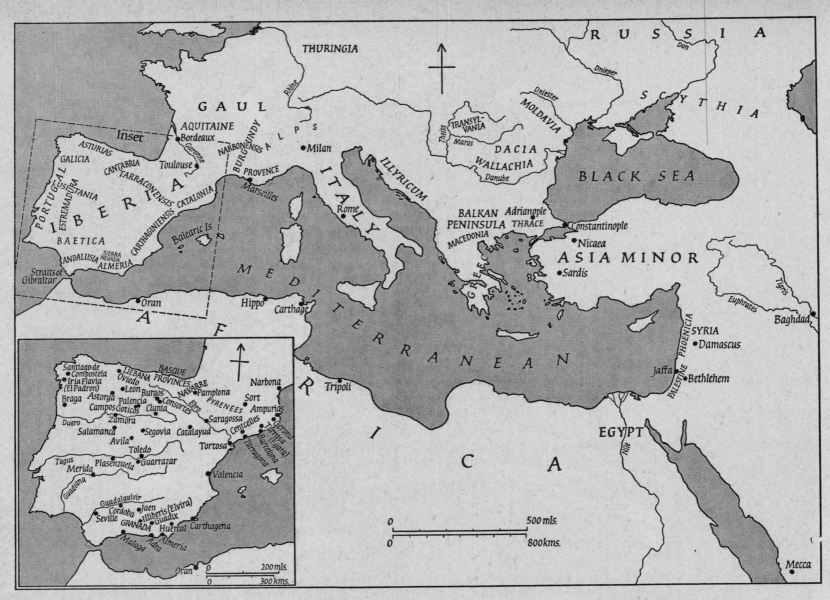

The Iberian peninsula, including the areas of Vandal, Visigothic and Arab movement

'Behold, he cometh with the clouds;

and every eye shall see him, and they which pierced him, and all the tribes of the earth shall mourn over him. Even so, Amen.' The text is the Apocalypse (1, 9), the illumination from an 11th-century Mozarabic version of Beatus' Commentary upon it, a work which can be seen as profoundly symbolic of Spain, of her history, culture and destiny.

No country in the world has displayed a more fervent and unwavering devotion to Christianity. In Roman times the early Church had already taken firm root. St James, according to legend, had preached in Galicia, and had founded the shrine of Nuestra Señora del Pilar on instructions from the Virgin herself. When in the 5th and 6th centuries Spain, like the rest of Europe, was thrown into confusion by waves of barbarian invaders, the Church did not lose its hold. In 409 came the Vandals, the Suevi and Alans, but not in such numbers as to submerge Roman civilization completely. In the 6th century it was the Visigoths—Arian Christians who transferred their allegiance to Catholicism in 589. In a series of decisive ecclesiastical councils Church and state were welded into a firm unity which was almost a theocracy.

The Visigothic kingdom was broken by the Muslim invasions of 711 which overran the whole country with the exception of the narrow coastal province of Asturias. Christianity

was tolerated, but power was entirely in the hands of the emirs, whose sophisticated capital of Cordoba has already been described in Chapter III. It was now (when, among the oppressed Christians, a cultural decline might have been expected), that Spain brought forth her most brilliant and characteristic creation—Mozarabic art, of which the Beatus manuscripts (see pls 29–31) are the most striking examples. For a time, it seems, the Apocalypse was the most revered book in Spain, its vision of the Church's sufferings and its promise of ultimate triumph no doubt offering peculiar comfort to the Spanish spirit.

The story for the next five hundred years is of one long crusade, a crusade which all Spain—and all Europe—saw as a struggle between the true and the false God. In the 9th century the tomb of St James was discovered at Compostela and soon became one of the three great pilgrimage places of Christendom, rivalling and even surpassing Rome and Jerusalem. Spanish Christianity, by the very conditions of its existence, was a militant, aggressive faith, fertile in saints and martyrs, inured to sacrifice, uncompromising, intolerant, single-minded. From the Visigothic, the Asturian and the Mozarabic churches there is a clear spiritual continuity to the world of St Teresa, St John of the Cross and El Greco. (1)

No one can say, but the belief was certainly current as early as the 7th century, possibly as early as the 5th. Later ages pictured him in the garb of a pilgrim with staff, scrip and scallop shell, the symbol of the Compostela pilgrimage (left: a Romanesque carving from the church of S. Marta de Tera, Zamora). The association of the scallop shell is obscure, but it seems to have stood for the good works and penances which accompanied the pilgrimage. At the same time St James became the rallying-cry of the crusade against Islam—Santiago 'Slayer of Moors'. (2)

The Christian communities of Roman Spain are now being revealed, more prosaically, by archaeology. Top right: detail of a sarcophagus from Gerona, showing the miracle of the loaves and fishes. Centre: fragment of a mosaic decorating the dome of a late Roman mausoleum at Centcelles (Tarragona). Religious and secular subjects are combined—Daniel, Jonah and this carefree scene of a hunt. Bottom: an Early Christian cemetery at Ampurias, near Barcelona, where a church, baptistery and many tombs and sarcophagi have been discovered. (3, 4, 5)

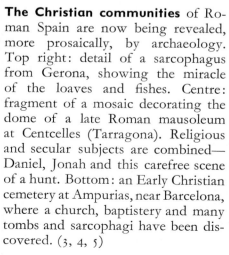

The Gothic peoples,

destined to play so dominant a part in the history of Spain, had left their homes on the coast of the Baltic in the 2nd century AD, making their way via south Russia to the Danube basin, where they came up against the frontiers of the Roman Empire. In the 4th century they were converted to (Arian) Christianity by the monk Ulfilas, who himself translated the Bible into the Gothic language. A unique fragment of this work survives, the Codex Argenteus (above), a luxury production written in silver ink on purple vellum, probably dating from the 6th century. (6)

Rome's way of dealing with the Visigothic problem was typical of her whole vascillating barbarian policy. In the Balkans they were alternately attacked, placated with tribute and employed as soldiers by the Eastern Emperor. This silver disc (a *missorium*) of Theodosius I, found in Spain, shows him flanked by his sons Honorius and Arcadius, and guarded by Germanic warriors who may well be Visigoths. Arcadius was responsible for introducing them into the Western Empire; and Honorius granted them rights in Gaul, hoping that they would act as a barrier against even more troublesome neighbours, the Vandals. (7)

The Vandals settled in Spain for less than twenty years and left few remains there. In 429 they crossed the Straits of Gibraltar and entered North Africa where they successfully founded a national state centred on Carthage. This North African mosaic, of the late-5th or early-6th centuries, shows a prosperous Vandal landowner leaving his villa. His costume and facial type are characteristically barbarian. (8)

The fortunes of the Visigoths during the 5th and 6th centuries fluctuated. Gradually they were edged out of Gaul by the Franks. In 543 Justinian's reconquest of Italy, North Africa and Spain put them once more under Byzantine rule, but towards the end of the century, under Reccared (586–621), they were able to build up a powerful and unified kingdom in Spain which was to last for the next hundred years. Its roots were still basically Roman. The *Lex Romana Wisigothorum* (right), the reformulation of the Theodosian Code made for King Euric (466–485), remained in force until the mid-7th century. (9)

Crown jewels

of the Visigothic kings came to light under a peasant's plough in 1858. It was at Guarrazar near Toledo; the treasure included nine crowns, some of them coronation dedications and one the dedication of an abbot, probably on consecration. Some years later two more were discovered but subsequently stolen and destroyed. Toledo was the capital of the Visigothic kingdom and they were probably buried at the time of the Arab invasion. Set in gold, they gleam with sapphires, pearls, agates and rock-crystals. Three had names on them—Swinthila (who reigned from 621 to 631), Recceswinth (653–672) and Sonnica, who may have been a Visigothic queen.

King Recceswinth—portrayed here with his predecessor Chindaswinth (642–653) in the Codex Vigilanus—was among the more important Visigothic rulers, and it is with him that the Guarrazar treasure seems to be mainly associated. Left: one of the 'unnamed' crowns, a network of precious stones in gold setting hanging by four chains and with a solid gold cross suspended through the centre. It is uncertain whether these crowns were ever worn; in their present form, with their attachments and crosses, they are purely votive. (10, 11)

The eagle-brooch runs like a *leitmotiv* through the art of the early Germanic peoples, appearing as far apart as Roumania and Spain. These two examples from Estremadura are possibly the finest of all. They consist basically of a circular body with head, wings and tail added. The blue and green inlays are glass, the red garnets, the white 'eyeballs' opals and the central stones quartz. (12)

Jewelled letters hang from the lower rim of Recceswinth's crown (left) making up the words RECCES-VINTHUS REX OFFERET. The crown itself is pierced gold-work, engraved to represent foliage and set with large gems—thirty pearls and thirty sapphires. A cross (below), similarly encrusted and with subsidiary pendants of its own, hangs through the centre. (13, 14)

The Visigothic nobles clearly enjoyed a life of affluence and taste, and were in close cultural touch with Byzantium. These two 7th-century bronze buckles show both the Frankish 'polychrome' style (left), with stones set geometrically, and the more Lombard type with its motif of confronted beasts. (15, 16)

A single people
but a complex interplay of cultures—
classical Roman, Byzantine, native
Visigothic, Jewish. An inscription
(below), on a slab from Tortosa, is in
three languages—Hebrew, Visigothic
Latin and (not seen) Greek. (18)

Pagan imagery lingered in vernacular religious art. This relief of the
sundisc (SOL) between angels forms
the impost of an arch in a church
near Burgos. The asymmetrical style
is probably very close to that of the
early Visigothic society in Toulouse.
(19)

Latin remained the most widely spoken language of Visigothic
Spain and was, of course, used by the Arian Church and the Law
Courts. The Ashburnham Pentateuch (above) is regarded by many
scholars as a product of Visigothic Spain—the only Visigothic
illuminated manuscript. This page shows the story of Moses: the
Israelites labouring, Moses smiting the Egyptian, the meeting
with Jethro's daughters and the Burning Bush. (17)

The churches built by the Visigoths on the eve of the Arab invasion were among the most advanced of their time in Western
Europe. San Pedro de Nave (right) was probably begun about 700,
but the ornate capitals (above, the sacrifice of Isaac and Daniel
in the Lions' Den and, below, a vine-leaf pattern) were not added
until 200 years later, when it was back in Christian hands. (20–23)

Horseshoe arches did not enter the peninsular with the Arabs, though they are one of the most characteristic features of Moorish architecture. In one of the 11th-century Beatus manuscripts (above), Babylon is shown as a Moorish house, Islamic motifs being combined with others from Visigothic ornament. (25)

'The Century of Councils', 600–700, moulded the Spanish church into a dynamic force under the leadership of the king. This page from the Codex Vigilanus, a 10th-century history of Spanish councils, shows the First Council of Toledo held in AD 400 to combat the Priscilian heresy: note the walls of Toledo, the churches of the Virgin and St Peter and the bishop with the line of priests at the bottom. (24)

'Take in eternal gift this basilica that I have dedicated, building and endowing it at my own expense and with my own heritage …' So runs King Recceswinth's dedication, dated 661, of the church of S. Juan de Baños (above and right), the finest surviving example of Visigothic architecture. The columns of the nave are looted from Roman baths, but the 'Corinthian' capitals are Visigothic work, and there are horseshoe arches in the west door, in the turret opening above, and in the sanctuary (in background, right). (26, 27)

The Arab Conquest

was not unrelieved disaster for the Spanish Christians. They were allowed to practise their religion, and in fact produced under Muslim rule the astonishing artistic flowering called the Mozarabic style (from *Musta' rib*, 'Arabized'), 9th–11th century. Separated from the main European tradition, Mozarabic illumination is a vivid combination of remote classicism, Islamic miniatures and the primitive idioms of Visigothic folk-art.

In about 776 a Spanish monk, Beatus of Liebana, wrote a Commentary on the Apocalypse, which became one of the most popular works in Spain. In the late 9th and 10th centuries it was copied in Spanish monasteries with brilliant illustrations in Mozarabic style. This corpus of 'Beatus' manuscripts (over twenty still survive) constitutes the crowning achievement of Mozarabic art. The three pictures (right) and pl. 1 of this chapter are taken from it.

Vigila the Scribe, the master of the Codex Vigilanus (see pl. 11 and 24), left this naive self-portrait on the last page. (28)

The Apocalyptic vision of St John can never have been interpreted with a bolder or more mystical imagination than in the illustrations to Beatus' Commentary. The large picture here is the Opening of the Sixth Seal (Revelations VII): 'And behold, a great multitude, which no man could number, out of every nation and of all tribes and peoples and tongues, standing before the throne and before the Lamb, arrayed in white robes and with palms in their hands; and they cry with a great voice saying, Salvation unto our God who sitteth on the throne and unto the Lamb. And all the angels were standing round about the throne and about the elders and the four living creatures; and they fell before the throne on their faces and worshipped God, saying, Amen: Blessing and glory and wisdom and thanksgiving and honour and power and might be unto our God for ever and ever.' (29)

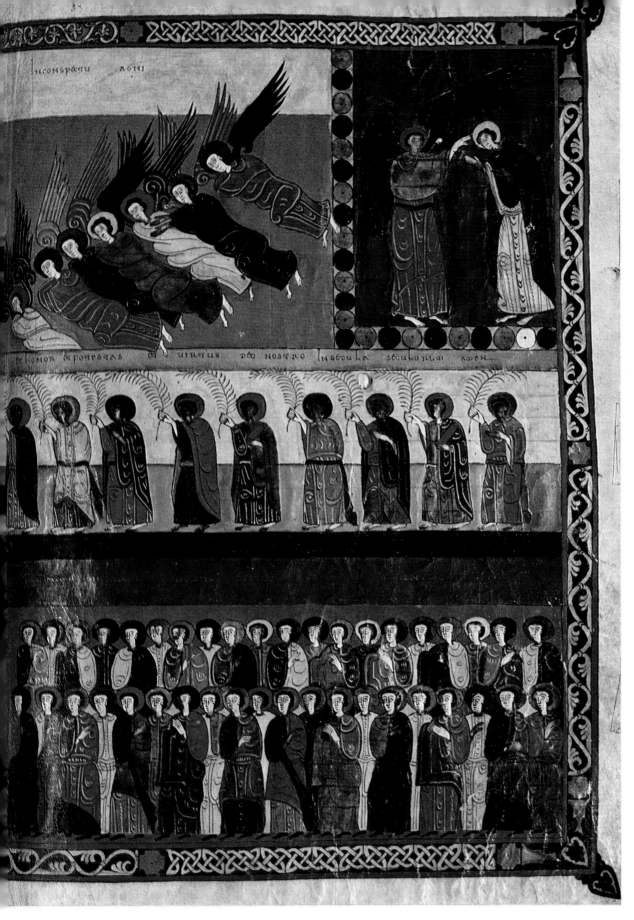

'To the angel of the church in Ephesus, write . . .' The first three chapters of the Apocalypse consist of St John's divinely revealed messages to the Christian churches of Asia. In this illustration (below) the drapery forms show the influence of European Romanesque, while the trees are more typical of Islamic art. (30)

'Daniel spake and said, I saw in my vision by night, and behold, the four winds of the heaven brake forth upon the great sea. And four great beasts came up from the sea, diverse one from another. The first was like a lion and had eagle's wings . . . a second like to a bear . . . another like a leopard which had upon the back of it four wings of a fowl; the beast had also four heads, and dominion was given to it . . . a fourth beast terrible and powerful and strong exceedingly . . . and it had ten horns . . . I beheld till thrones were placed, and one that was ancient of days did sit . . . A fiery stream issued and came forth from him'—Daniel VII. (31)

It was in combating the Adoptionist heresy that Beatus and his Commentary gained fame. This heresy used St John's Gospel to teach that Christ was only the adoptive son of God; Beatus extolled the Lamb as the symbol of Christ's sonship.

One corner of Spain

remained unconquered by the Arabs —the northern province of Asturias. Here the Visigoths held out, and by the mid-8th century had also recovered most of Galicia. Beleaguered, constantly at war and virtually cut off from the rest of Christian Europe, the little kingdom was yet able to achieve a culture of surprising originality and interest.

Outstanding among its surviving monuments, all within 25 miles of Oviedo, is the church of S. Maria de Naranco (below and right), once probably part of King Ramiro I's palace. The upper hall, reached by exterior staircases, is roofed with a round tunnel vault, the transverse ribs ending in curiously carved medallions. At each end the room opens on to loggias. (32, 33)

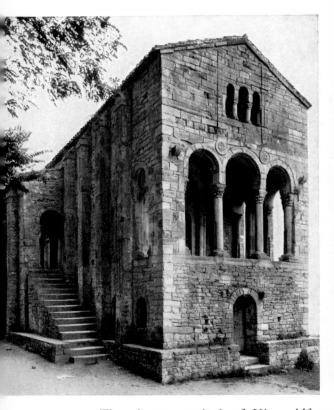

The chosen capital of King Alfonso II (791–842), Oviedo, still retains impressive reminders of the Asturian kingdom. Below: interior (restored) and exterior of S. Julian de los Prados; the wall-surfaces are covered with frescoes depicting vast buildings with pediments and fluted columns. The style can only have come from Roman wall-paintings. (34, 35)

186

Crude provincial work, unredeemed by either Asturian or Carolingian influence, was produced in the borderland ('march') between Arabs, Asturians and Franks. This altarstone, covered with embossed silver, from Gerona, shows St John the Evangelist. (36)

The Cross was finally to triumph over the Crescent in Spain, though the struggle lasted for centuries. The *Reconquista* began under King Sancho the Great of Navarre (1000–1035) who was able to hand on to his son Ferdinand a kingdom that comprised almost the whole of northern Spain. Spanish cultural isolation ended, and the new state became part of Romanesque Europe. This ivory crucifix was made for King Ferdinand in about 1063. Round the border of the cross, which is separate from the Christ figure and in a Romanesque style, is depicted the Day of Judgment—tiny naked figures who rise to salvation on the upright and are driven down into hell on the arms. (38)

By the 10th century, with Charlemagne's help, Catalonia had been largely recovered from the Moors and one of the oldest Christian sites in Spain, Tarrasa, was enriched with fine new buildings. The 6th-century baptistery (below) was restored and elaborately decorated with frescoes. (39)

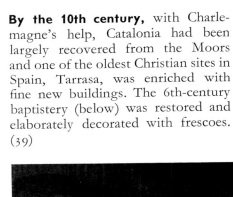

The graceful screen of S. Cristina de Lena (above), another of King Ramiro's churches, is probably made up of fragments from other buildings; the carved slabs between the central arch are typical Visigothic work. (37)

two ways of life, two cultures confronted each other as enemies in Spain during the whole of the Middle Ages. On the Christian side this gave Spanish religion its uncompromising fervour and Spanish art its peculiar intensity and violence. Moorish culture, on the other hand, doomed in the end to perish, never lost its feeling for the world of the senses, its delight in variety, its love of ornament and colour.

The Cross of the Angels (above), the masterpiece of the Asturian goldsmiths, was given to the cathedral of Oviedo in 808. The side shown here is covered with minute gold filigree and set with antique cameos (e.g. the stone at the very top) and gems.

The ivory casket (right) comes from Cordoba, first and greatest of Islamic cities in Spain. It was made in AD 970 for Ziyad ibn Aflah, Prefect of Police: its carved sides show him administering justice, hawking and (in this photograph) travelling in state on an elephant. In the intervals of the design are griffons, antelopes and eagles. (40, 41)

Spain under the Visigoths and Moors

WILLIAM CULICAN

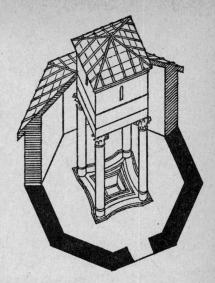

The baptistery at Tarrasa, reconstructed from remains discovered under the pavement of the church of Santa Maria. The shape of the baptismal bath is north African, but the rest of the structure is Byzantine. It dates from the 5th century AD; another baptistery was later built nearby (see p. 187, pl. 39) and a church built on the old site. (1)

NO COUNTRY IN THE WESTERN WORLD was more deeply and permanently affected by the coming of Christianity than was Spain. Tradition claims that the gospel was first preached on Iberian shores by James, son of Zebedee and close disciple of Christ. After the death of the Master, James, it is claimed, set sail from Jaffa and landed in the south of Spain, where, making his way northwards on the western network of Roman roads, he concentrated his mission in Galicia and the north-central regions. The Virgin herself miraculously visited him in the course of his work, instructing him to plant her cult in the spot where she herself would set up a pillar. Thus the city of Saragossa, where the pillar was planted, became the shrine of Our Lady of the Pillar (Nuestra Señora del Pilar) and St James returned home to meet his end in the persecutions of Herod Agrippa in AD 44. But this was not the severance of St James and Spain, for his body was miraculously transported back, some say by angels, some in a swan-drawn boat, and buried in an obscure grave near Iria Flavia (modern El Padron) in the wilds of Galicia, whose rude inhabitants he had attempted to Christianize. There he was to rest until Spain's darkest hour, when the beliefs he had implanted were in danger of extinction by the Moors.

Almost eight centuries later, at the height of the Moorish occupation, as the resistance of the remnant of the Visigothic nobility of northern Spain had taken new hope under the protection of Charlemagne, the marble sarcophagus of St James was miraculously revealed to the Bishop of Iria, Teodomir, whose own coffin has recently been found. Alfonso II (791–842), then reigning, venerated the remnants of the body and erected over the tomb the shrine which was later to grow into the great cathedral of St James (Santiago) of Compostela. Alfonso declared him patron of Spain, matamoros 'Slayer of Moors', under whose banner the Catholic armies eventually drove Islam from the land. This greatest miracle, the expulsion of the infidel from Europe, raised Compostela to Europe's greatest shrine. Through medieval times the road to Santiago was thronged with pious pilgrims from all the West. With them went artists, jugglers, fiddlers, poets and folk-singers and to build the wayside chapels and hostels came architects and sculptors, so that from the devotion to the Saint grew one of the major cultural exchanges of medieval Europe.

p 178 (2)

The Gospel in Spain

No sober historical or archaeological doubts can ever detract from the glory of Compostela; yet doubt we must. We must indeed sharply separate the evangelization of St James from the translation and discovery of his body, for the latter legendary cycle together with that of Our Lady of the Pillar is not attested until the 11th century, whereas the belief in St James' mission to Spain, whilst almost certainly without historical foundation, was widely credited in Britain and Europe in the 7th–8th centuries and there are possible references to it in the 5th. It may have arisen from some textual error in the works of Church Fathers and, unlike the translation legend, the product of a more romantic era, gained credence by its inherent possibility. The archaeological discoveries of our times have given us renewed interest in the traditions surrounding the apostolic burial places. Of Compostela all we can say is that recent excavations under the Cathedral have failed to reveal any tomb or shrine attributable to St James; but badly published excavations carried out in 1878 under the capilla mayor revealed a curious tomb shrine of the Late Roman period, surrounded by a colonnade and obviously belonging to an important person, whether pagan or Christian. From this and other considerations it seems certain that the tomb beautified by Alfonso was part of a wealthy Roman or Early Christian graveyard and that, even omitting miracles, the site was not arbitrarily chosen.

There is another tradition, believed by both John Chrysostom and St Jerome, that St Paul preached in Spain. This has certain claims to likelihood, for not only did Paul declare his intention of visiting Spain, but his awareness that the gospel was to be preached to the ends of the earth and Spain's position as finis terrae of the Roman Mediterranean make it likely that he fulfilled his intention. The extent of his work, whether a full-scale mission or a short formal visit, we do not know. Perhaps, as was his wont, he visited the Jewish communities established in the coastal cities, for the ports of the Spanish Levant had never lost touch with Old Phoenicia and the Spanish merchant Jews could not have remained unaware of the news of religious changes in their Palestinian homeland brought by the sailors from Syrian ports.

From these general considerations and traditions it seems likely that Christianity reached parts of Iberia within Apostolic times, but there seems little doubt that the first well-organized church grew up in the south, in the wealthy corn-growing province of Hispania Baetica between the Guadiana river and the Sierra Nevada. It was organized by six missionaries, Torquatus, Indalecius, Euphrasius, Cecilius, Ctesiphon and Hesichius, whose memories were honoured in the mozarabic liturgy which developed in Andalusia and Baetica in later times under the Muslims. Their names are predominantly Roman and they were most probably members of the metropolitan diaconate of Rome. Their sees were grouped in the south-west of the peninsula in Andalusia and Almeria, at Guadix, Granada, Huercal and Jaen. It is surely in consequence of the strength of this southern church that the first ecclesiastical council of Spain was called in AD 300–304 at Illiberis (Elvira) in the Granada province and that the majority of bishops attending it were from Baetica itself. In the north the church was strongest in Catalonia; Tarragona, the capital of Hispania Tarraconensis, is mentioned in the letters of St Cyprian as the earliest northern bishopric. The persecutions of Christians in the 2nd and 3rd centuries took a very heavy toll of martyrs in the Catalonian lands and catacombs similar to those of Rome were in use at Tarragona. The martyrs who perished in those centuries were commemorated in the dedications of the new basilican churches built after Constantine had officially promoted Christianity. Many outgrew mere local veneration, particularly the first martyr-bishop of Spain, Fructuoso, Bishop of Tarragona. St Fructuoso and the deacons Augurius and Eulogius, victims of the Valerian persecutions, are the earliest martyrs of whom we have full record; a 4th-century basilica once marked the scene of their death in an early Christian cemetery in Tarragona.

Besides Tarragona, strong Christian communities flourished in other Catalonian towns: at Centcelles, Gerona, Barcelona, Tarrasa (or Egara) and Ampurias graveyards, tombstones, sarcophagi, basilicas and baptisteries have been discovered testifying

p 178 (4,5) f 1

the great growth of the church in this region in the 4th and 5th centuries and providing monuments of early Christian art and architecture richer and more numerous than elsewhere in the country. By 342 Barcelona had emerged as the leading Catalonian bishopric: at the council of Sardis its bishop represented Spain: *Praetextatus ab hispaniis de Barcelona*. We may be sure that the minor characteristics of the church in the north-east differed from those of the south. Christianity had grown up in the Catalonian coastal cities among the same cosmopolitan slaves and merchants as in Rome and their seaborne traffic kept them in close cultural contact with the Christian communities of Italy, south Gaul and Africa. Thus the focus of the Spanish church moved northwards after the time of Constantine: letters of St Cyprian mention Christian communities in Astorga, Merida and Saragossa, where the second council was held in 381. Tertullian seems a little premature in his statement that in his day (about AD 200) all Spain had heard the gospel, but certainly by 330 the entire peninsula except parts of Galicia, Asturias and Cantabria had embraced Christianity, not superficially but throughout a large cross-section of society. The third council was held at Toledo in AD 400 and from this date onwards this city was frequently chosen by virtue of its centrality as the meeting place of the church.

p 183
(24)

A Fervent and Mystical Church

From its beginning, the church in Spain, whilst firm in its allegiance to Rome, identified itself with the social and national problems of the Spanish people. There is much concern in the acts of the Elvira council with interest on loans as well as with the social evils of adultery and prostitution. Already by AD 400 the church and the qualities of the Spanish character were fully wedded to produce a religious fervour full of characteristic *hispanidad*. The Spanish church produced theologians and controversialists such as Bishop Osius of Cordoba, who survived the Diocletian persecution and became adviser to Constantine in the debates against Arianism and Donatism at Nicaea and in his nineties presided at the Council of Sardis in 347. But on the whole, the spirit of arid controversy which gripped the Eastern church was absent in Spain. The Andalusian church was strongly conservative and even Osius, who in his old age favoured the admission to the church of penitent Arians, was compromised by the intransigence of Bishop Gregory of Elvira, his successor in the Cordoba see. The Spanish bent was towards devotion rather than theology: it produced in the 4th century the poet Juvencus, who rendered the Gospels in Virgilian hexameters, and Aurelius Prudentius Clemens, the true creator of Christian lyric poetry. Pope Damasus (Pope from 366 to 387), whose reign was an inspiration to Christian life, letters and music, was himself a Spaniard, poet and epigrammist. Above all, Spain was steeped in Sacred Scripture and its earliest writers drew widely on the Old Testament for inspiration and created an atmosphere of curiosity about the Bible. In AD 380, or thereabouts, the hardheaded Spanish nun Etheria set out, Bible in hand, to visit the Holy Places of Egypt, Palestine and Syria and her letters compose the first surviving piece of pilgrim literature.

With this fervour and imagination was linked the Spanish asceticism and mysticism. Anchorites were plentiful, but it seems that already by the time of the Elvira council monastic communities existed in the land following harsh disciplines. These were qualities which contributed largely to Spain's first and peculiar heresy associated with the name of Priscillian, an Asturian priest who later became Bishop of Avila. At the base of the Priscillian heresy was a certain amount of Gnosticism, either brought by the oriental mercenaries or, according to St Sulpicius, by one Marcus, an Egyptian Gnostic, whose ideas influenced the Priscillianists. A Gnostic stone found at Astorga in 1878 shows a temple façade with what seem to be representations of the sun and moon. It is inscribed *Eis Zeus Serapis Iaw*, 'Zeus, Serapis and Jahweh are one'. Similar inscriptions have been found in Egypt in a region where Asturian soldiers are known to have settled. The open hand is the Semitic symbol of adoration and greeting.

f 2

The precise theological issue for which Priscillian was condemned, first by the Saragossa council and later by the personal intervention of the Emperor Gratian, is unknown; but it is interesting to reflect on some of the incidental doctrines attributed to Priscillian or his followers and their connexion with the Spanish religious character of later times. There was a strong ascetic strain preaching fasting and continence; a doctrine of the diabolical origin of the human dilemma of spirit-locked-in-flesh; a belief of astral influences in human destiny; and above all an insistence on a highly personal and intuitive relationship between the believer and Sacred Scripture. Much of it was Gnostic and Manichaean in orientation, except that the role of personal conscience and the intuitive role of the intellect in the understanding of Scripture, even the apocryphal works, suggest a mysticism purely Spanish. Priscillian was widely followed: even those, who like St Martin of Tours saw the dangerous indiscipline of the consequences of his doctrines, regretted his condemnation.

Throughout the Early Christian period, Spain was culturally and politically an important part of the Roman Empire, exporting grain, fruit and minerals, providing recruits for the legions, skilled civil servants, tutors for the youth of the Italian aristocracy. The art of the earliest Christians, represented by scores of sarcophagi and a few mosaics, is that of Rome and the earliest churches were built on the Roman basilican plan. Here and there in the graveyards of poorer Christians at Tarragona and Ampurias burial customs of the North African Christians are followed and the baptisteries also are built on African lines, for there was constant traffic between these ports and the great African sees of Hippo and Carthage and the bulk of Spanish slaves, many of whom were Christian, were drawn from Africa. But intellectually the precise character of Spain was beginning to emerge. Shortly before the collapse of the Roman Empire, Paulus Orosius, a native of Braga (Portugal), who had visited Augustine at Hippo and Jerome at Bethlehem in AD 451, became the first Christian to write a *Universal History*. Orosius had no doubt that Spain had a destiny all its own in the Empire and opportunely pointed to the Goths, already pressing towards the Pyrenees, as about to play a providential part in the uniting of Christendom and in providing her destined opportunity. In the 'Dark Ages' which followed the fall of Roman rule in Europe, the sanctity, intellect and the loyalty of Spain both to Christianity and to the ideals of the Roman Empire saved her from an age of barbarity and preserved for her much that was constructive in Roman civilization. The physical impress of Rome in Spain is preserved until today more strongly than in any country of western Europe.

The Onslaught of the Vandals

The Roman hold on the peninsula was broken by the backwash of events in 4th-century Europe. For three quarters of a century before they entered Spain in 409, the Vandals had been moving from their settlements west of the Danube in the river valleys of the Maros and Theiss towards central and western Germany. This evacuation was in part necessitated by the pressure upon Roman Dacia of the western branch of the Eurasiatic Goths, who throughout the second half of the 4th century established their domination over all the tribes from Scythia to east Germany. These Western Goths, or Visigoths as they are most commonly known, settled in force between the River Dniester and the Alps of Transylvania, founding new settlements thickly in the territories of Moldavia and Wallachia (central and western Roumania) of which they dispossessed the Gepids, Vandals and other immigration-period tribes. Rome had experience of Visigothic power: in the third quarter of the 3rd century they had ravaged the shores of Asia Minor and Greece and the Emperor Gallus had been forced to pay tribute to them. Their conversion to Arian Christianity in the course of the 4th century possibly stabilized them a little, but the southward pressure of the Huns in the later part of that century forced the Visigoths and the Goths of Thuringia to seek new lands in Thrace and Macedonia. The road from Italy to Constantinople was thus endangered and the Emperor Valens, otherwise not ill-disposed to Visigothic loyalties, died fighting against them at Adrianople (Edirne) in 377. In January of 379 Theodosius, a Spaniard from near Segovia and a protégé of Gratian, was declared Augustus. With the aid of his Frankish generals Theodosius threw back the invaders

p 179
(6)

p 179
(7)

from Constantinople. The victory was commemorated in 396 by the erection in Constantinople of Theodosius' famous obelisk and among the sculptures on its base one records the tribute paid by the Visigothic King Athanaric.

The fate of the Western Empire was sealed when the Romans made of the homeless Visigoths, long officially *foederati* or confederates of the Empire, a pawn in the rivalries between Theodosius' two sons. Arcadius, reigning in the East, gave to Alaric and his Goths the prefecture of Illyricum, claimed by his brother Honorius, Emperor of the West. On their roundabout journey to Illyricum (Yugoslavia) Alaric's Goths took the opportunity to devastate Thrace and Greece. Arcadius was soon strong enough to rid himself of his Visigothic garrisons and left them to pursue their own ambitions by invading Italy and taking Rome.

Indirectly the Gothic invasion of Italy brought trouble to Spain. Honorius' general Stilicho was obliged to recall the Rhineland garrisons for the defence of Italy, thus throwing open the whole of Gaul to the tide of a Vandal invasion. Sweeping across the Pyrenees in 409 came the Silingian Vandals from the Rhineland, the Suevi from the Spree region and a joint group of Alans and Asdings from east Germany and Hungary. The newcomers were too few to alter the ethnic composition of Iberia, for they numbered probably less than 100,000 permanent settlers. Diverted from the Roman holdings in Hispania Tarraconensis, the invaders first settled amongst the indigenous tribes of the Palencia region. But soon they spread out: the Silings entered Baetica; the Asdings settled in southern Galicia with the Suevi to the north, whilst the Alans entered Lusitania and Hispania Carthaginiensis. These territories were indeed agreed upon in consultation with Honorius who saw the Vandals as potential allies against worse foes. Despite the partition of the land, famine and the atmosphere of suspicion and quarrelling amongst themselves, they achieved under Alan leadership a certain degree of confederate unity, enough to be able to strike at Rome in 429 when Genseric led the famine-striken Vandal warriors in the invasion of Roman Africa and the successful establishment of a Vandal kingdom stretching from Oran to Tripoli, incorporating lands which had been the granary of Rome. The impact of the Vandals on the culture of the Iberian peninsula was negligible. Spain was still Roman. Pottery and trappings from graves of the 5th century are still Roman in style. In North Africa, however, a far wealthier province, we become familiar with Vandal jewellery, seals and coinage, albeit extending over but a brief period.

p 179 (8)

Setting a thief to catch a thief, or so it sounds, Honorius agreed to the settlement of the Visigoths, after Alaric's death, in Gaul and sent them into Roman Tarraconensis to hold it as allies of Rome. Here, despite internal defections, they initially complied with Roman wishes, defeating the Silings and decimating the Alans. Athaulf, successor of Alaric as King of the Visigoths, at one point planned to destroy the West Roman Empire and put a Gothic one in its place, but he was drawn into alliance with Honorius and forced Galla Placidia, the daughter of Theodosius, taken prisoner by Alaric, to marry him. Soon he fancied himself as the restorer rather than the destroyer of the Roman heritage. In 418 the Visigoths were granted rights by Honorius to settle the lands of Aquitaine along the Garonne and for many decades Toulouse became the seat of the Visigothic kings.

The Visigoths, Watch-dogs of Rome

Before the invasion of Attila, the situation throughout the Western Empire had reached a crisis. The legions had evacuated Britain and left it open to Anglo-Saxon invasion in 441. In Spain the Suevian King Rechilas (439–446) started out from Galicia and invaded the southern Spanish territories. The Goths in France were able to take advantage of Gallo-Roman weakness to establish their local ascendancy more firmly under the Gothic King Theodoric I. Yet the Visigoths were still the watch-dogs of Rome and in 457 Theodoric II, King of Toulouse, intervened in Spain to punish the maraudings of Rechiarius of the Suevians, a Catholic convert. The military colonies left behind to keep the peace were the beginnings of Visigothic settlement in Spain. Under King Euric (466–485), by whom the Visigothic kingdom was augmented on every side and sat astride France from Bordeaux to

Gnosticism, a semi-Christian faith originating in Egypt, was brought to Spain probably by Roman legionaries and exerted some influence on the first Spanish heresy, that of Priscillian. This Gnostic stone of the 3rd or 4th century was found at Astorga. In the pediment is inscribed 'Eis Zeus Serapis' and in the open hand (a Semitic symbol of adoration) 'Yaw'— 'Zeus, Serapis and Yaweh are one'. (2)

Marseilles, the establishment of military colonies across north Spain and in the ports of the eastern coast appears as a definite prelude to civil settlement. Besides occupying Lusitania, Euric held Braga, Merida, Saragossa, Pamplona, Clunia and other cities, all it seems with the approval of Nepos, Emperor of the West in 475. Thus Euric was virtually the first Visigothic King of Spain. The beginning of his reign coincided with the Roman nadir. The fleet under Leo, Emperor of the East, and Anthemius, Emperor of the West, had failed to effect a landing in Vandal Africa and it soon appeared that Euric was not intent on taking his pact with Leo seriously. In the dispirited situation around him we can surely understand the ambitions of this energetic and gifted man, surrounded by his brilliant intellectual court and fervent Arian clergy.

The steady infiltration continued until AD 535. First went only the militaristic elements of the kingdom of Toulouse itself but later the conquests of Clovis the Frank in France and his anti-Arian sentiments accelerated the departure of civilian settlers from Visigothic-controlled lands. Even so, many of the Goths were reluctant to leave their fertile holdings in Gaul for an unknown future in Spain, so that the invaders probably did not eventually number more than a fortieth of the entire Ibero-Roman population. Of the nature of their settlement we know very little, but it appears to have been concentrated in the north-western part of the *meseta* between the middle valley of the Tagus in the south and Zamora and Pamplona in the north. From east to west the area of settlement stretched from about Salamanca to Calatayud. In these regions the Visigoths confiscated two thirds of the holdings of the Roman landowners, lands which became legally known as the *sortes gothicae* as opposed to the *tertiae Romanorum*. These official terms are preserved in the toponymy of certain parts of the peninsula by names like Sort, Consortes, Tercia and Terciar, whilst place names like Godos and Campos Goticos (Palencia) attest settlement centres probably of later times. Names like Burgos attest the presence of garrison towns.

During the first decade of the 6th century the Visigoths lost almost all their Gaulish territories except Narbonensis. During the reign of Alaric II, successor of the energetic Euric, there arose from obscurity Clovis, chief of the Sicimbri, King of the Franks, who in one of the key battles of Dark Age history, at the unknown site of Vocladum, inflicted a crushing defeat on the

Visigoths in the name of Franks, Burgundians and Catholicism. Bordeaux and Toulouse soon fell to him and the Visigoths were saved from extinction in France only by the intervention of the Ostrogothic King, Theodoric, who as Regent ruled the Visigothic destinies in Provence and Spain with remarkable liberality and success. A brilliant administrator and soldier, Theodoric set Visigothic finance and administration on its feet and by his liberality to the Spanish Catholics won the confidence of the Papacy and the Franks alike. The transition from the first Visigothic military expeditions to the period of settlement (495–535) is reflected in finds from graves. The earliest are a few circular brooches with semi-precious stones lost during the campaigns of the 5th century. Not until about AD 500 appear the first bow-fibulae in bronze, some with applied silver decoration, which imitate the Danubian or Pontic Gothic or Hunnish fibulae with but slight variations. During the reign of Theodoric (511–526) these objects and tongued buckles were particularly popular in Spain, as among the Ostrogoths, but they disappear almost entirely at the beginning of the 7th century, to be replaced by ornaments of more Byzantine character as part of the general Byzantine fashion adopted by the court of Leovigild.

Theodoric's nephew, Amalaric, for whom he was Regent, married Clotilda, Clovis' daughter. Had their marriage produced issue instead of quarrels and war, the path set by Theodoric might have been illustriously followed. A single family had ruled the Visigoths since Theodoric I in 419 until Amalaric's death in 531. The dynastic squabbles which followed and which were to mark the rest of Visigothic history led to immediate setbacks to Visigothic Spain.

A Byzantine Province

The revival of Roman power in the West under Justinian led to the first great defeat of the major Germanic kingdoms. In 543 Justinian's general Belisarius overthrew the Vandal kingdom of Gelimer in North Africa and carried in triumph to Rome not only the silver plate and golden girdles of the conquered Vandals but also a large portion of the treasure which Genseric had taken from Rome. It was reputed still to contain the sacred vessels taken from Herod's Temple in Jerusalem by Titus centuries earlier. The revival of Byzantine rule in Africa was a serious threat to the Visigoths. Rivalry between Agila and Athanagild for the Visigothic throne provided the Byzantines with an opportunity to divide and rule. For the aid which Justinian provided to Athanagild the price was the restoration to the Roman-Byzantine Empire of Baetica and much of Tarraconensis together with portions of Carthaginiensis. Malaga, Carthagena, Cordoba and Seville now became Byzantine centres and with the north-east and the Balearic islands, which had never been lost to Rome,

the Byzantine hold on eastern and southern Spain was established for a further century. The power of the Iberian Visigoths, with much of Gaul now lost and confined largely to Lusitania and central and western Tarraconensis, was temporarily greatly reduced. Athanagild was, however, a shifty ally and lost little time in regaining Baetican territory, including Seville. Nevertheless, Justinian's hold remained firm and the conversion of the Suevi to Catholicism in 560 kept the Visigoths in check. Epigraphic evidence such as the long Greek inscription of Justin II (565–578) from Plasenzuela near Merida and the inscription of the Emperor Maurice commemorating the restoration of the walls of Carthagena, as well as a number of ecclesiastical foundations of Byzantine style, attest the attempt at a Byzantine revival in the province.

Under One Crown—the Reign of Reccared

Reconquest of the peninsula by the Visigoths, beginning with the reduction of the Suevi, was largely the work of Athanagild's gifted brother Leovigild, (568–586), a personal admirer of Justinian and imitator of Byzantine customs and culture. His campaigning of 577–578 brought him dominion over Valencia, Tarragona and Saragossa, but his own son Hermenegild, married to a Frankish princess and converted to Catholicism, joined the Byzantine forces and led the rising of the south. Leovigild conquered and killed him. The year in which Hermenegild was executed also saw the end of the Suevian kingdom in Galicia and the victory of Leovigild's other son Reccared over the Frankish King Gontra of Burgundy, who had invaded Narbonensis on the pretext of assisting Hermenegild. After two victories, Leovigild established Toledo as *urbs regia* in succession to Merida and set up the Visigothic court there. He is said to have married Theodosia, daughter of the Byzantine governor of Carthagena, but his marriages are disputed and indeed any political marriage contemplated for himself or his sons bought the religious question to the fore. Leovigild's abolition of the impediments to mixed Arian-Catholic marriages in the peninsula, whilst it brought few converts to Arianism, was an important step in cementing the various groups among his people. The conversion of Crown Prince Reccared to Catholicism was more decisive. At the third Council of Toledo in 589 the majority of the Arian bishops followed King Reccared and his personal participation in the council was hailed as significant as that of Constantine at Nicaea, when the Arian heresy had been repudiated. There was indeed little opposition from the Arian clergy and Gothic aristocracy to Reccared's proclamation of the identity of the substance of the three persons of the Trinity. Pope Gregory was overjoyed and acted on behalf of Reccared in negotiating a pact with Emperor Maurice by which certain coastal possessions were left to Byzantium.

Iberia now moved swiftly towards social and religious unity and the reign of Reccared was one of the most significant of Spanish history. Church and state were now united more closely than ever in France. Arian tradition saw to it that the Church remained under royal leadership, at least until well into the 7th century when the moral authority of bishops coerced the weakened kings. Until 711 Spain was to live under a constitutional monarchy with the legislative power in the hands of the Church. It was a kind of theocracy in which the councils of Toledo acted as an intermittent congress, restoring the elective monarchy in accordance with Germanic tradition and controlling the deadly rivalries of the nobility with the weight of excommunication.

Apart from oppression of the Jews, the reign of Reccared was remarkable for its moderation and benignity and he was much occupied completing the legal codification begun by his father. The reign of his young son Liuva brought the remarkably able dynasty of Athanagild to an end. With the backing of the remnant of the Arian bishops, Witeric, an unscrupulous noble, seized the throne in Liuva's second year. Catholic dogma was, however, soon restored by the bishops at Toledo and in 612 Sisebuth was elected King. With the aid of his generals Rechila and Swinthila, he struck a final blow at the Byzantine army. The affairs of Byzantine Spain had been neglected and Heraclius could do little but sue for peace, ceding virtually all his claims in Spain.

The Visigothic reconquest of the peninsula from the Byzantines was largely due to Leovigild (568–586). In 574 he led an expedition against Cantabria and occupied its capital, Amaya. This relief from the ivory shrine of San Millan (early 11th century) shows him punishing its citizens—'Ubi Leovigildo rege Cantabros afficit (supplicio)'. (3)

Armed warriors on the march—an illustration from one of the Beatus manuscripts, showing the Babylonians riding against Jerusalem. Though painted about the turn of the 11th century, some of the details of the costume and armour go back to Visigothic traditions, the most interesting being the rows of tiny bells hanging from the saddle, harness-straps and standards. These seem to have originated in the Germanic north. At first they were exclusive to royalty or the priesthood; later they came to be worn also by the nobility and ended—ignominiously—by becoming part of the dress of the court fool. (4)

The 'Century of Councils'

When Swinthila came to the throne in 621 he was the first Visigoth to rule the entire peninsula. His ten-year reign began in a blaze of popularity, but his farewell was that of a tyrant and oppressor. Nepotism could not save him and the Fourth Council of Toledo elected the rebel Sisenand, who had been carried to the throne at Saragossa by his own and Frankish troops, as the legitimate king. The Council was presided over by Archbishop Isidore of Seville, encyclopaedist, historian, poet, philologist, wit and saint, one of the most remarkable brains of Europe, a kind of minor Dark Age combination of Doctor Johnson and Leonardo da Vinci. He came from a remarkable family: St Leander his elder brother preceded him in the Seville archbishopric and had been active in converting the Visigoths to Catholicism. Their brother, Flugentius, and sister, St Florentina, also gained pre-eminence in religious life and letters. Isidore now declared valid the 'election' of Sisenand and pronounced *anathemata* against Swinthila and his family.

The writing and learning of Spain at this period was a lamp to Dark Age Europe. Isidore's family was one of many which produced the astonishingly productive crop of saintly bishops and writers in the 6th and 7th centuries. Many of their tracts were works of apologetic, homiletic and pastoral wisdom. But along with works whose titles speak for themselves: *Formula Vitae Honestae* and Isidore's own *De Norma Vivendi*, went commentaries on those biblical books which appealed to Spanish mysticism (especially Justus' Mystical *Exposition of the Song of Songs*) and the rather rarer theological works like St Ildefonsus' *De Perpetua Virginitate Sanctae Mariae*. Others like *De Correctione Rusticorum* anticipate those quaint tracts of early Victorian England on the 'Assuagement of Drunkenness in Labourers'. In this literary atmosphere Isidore is classed as a scientist, more by his spirit of enquiry than by any scientific method, which he lacked. He was really a lexicographer and his *Etymologies*, ranging in chapters from grammar to naval engineering is a valuable source-book of life and learning in the Dark Ages, whilst his *History of the Goths*, rather an historical apologetic than history as we under-

stand it, is our main source of Visigothic annals. Like so many of the great writers of the period Isidore was Hispano-Byzantine in origin.

The 7th century has been called the 'Century of Councils'. Five and Six of Toledo, held during the reign of Sisenand's successor Chintila, were concerned with the position and protection of the monarchy and the personal sacrosanctity of the king. A splendid symbol of this theocratic rule is the collection of jewels known as the Treasure of Guarrazar, one of the major treasures of Dark Age Europe. In the course of a flood in the Huerta de Guarrazar in 1858, in a locality where there had formerly been a graveyard, a hoard of gold crowns, pectoral crosses and pendants was uncovered. Probably they were dedicated to some church near Toledo, the capital and court of the Visigothic kingdom, and were buried at the time of the Arab invasion. One crown bears in pendant letters the motto *Svinthilanus Rex Offeret* (Swinthila, 621–631) and another is dedicated by *Rex Reccesvinthus* (Recceswinth, 649–672). Other pieces belong to members of the aristocracy; a headband has the name of Abbot Theodosius worked into it and a pectoral cross once belonged to Bishop Lucetius. Sapphires, pearls, agates and rock-crystals add to the splendour of the goldwork. p 180–1 (10, 13, 14)

In spite of the sanctity accorded to the king however, the elective principle of kingship was still upheld, and in 642 Chintila's reigning son, a weakling prince, was deposed in favour of the energetic nobleman and warrior Chindaswinth, a man after the character of Leovigild. He was a legislator and man of art and letters whose aim was to end the internal rivalries of the Visigothic nobility, even by recourse to ruthless proscription, and secondly to unite the Roman and Visigothic peoples of Spain under a strong and hereditary monarchy and a single legal system. The ideal was so strongly upheld by the Church that Recceswinth, his son, had to mitigate the harsh decrees of the Eighth Council of Toledo against Froya, a powerful rebel whom he had put down. So close were the church-state relations in this council that the signatures of his Gothic lay nobility were appended to its acts. Much of Recceswinth's long and peaceful reign was directed by legislative work furthering the unification ideals of his father and promoting new facilities for the intermarriage of the two races. Under Recceswinth the old *Lex Wisigothorum* drawn up in Euric's day to regulate the personal relationships of conquerors and conquered reached its penultimate stages of development as a civil and penal code. p 180 (11) f 5 p 179 (9)

During the long reign of Recceswinth (right), the kingdom was strengthened and unified. Roman and Visigothic peoples were merged into a single nation, in the government of which the church was as powerful as the court. (5)

A Single People

It was the crowning achievement of Visigothic rule to have forged from the Romans, old Iberians, Carthaginians, Celts, Vandals and Goths a single Spanish people. They united the warrior aristocracy of the Goths with the plutocratic-bureaucratic aristocracy of the Roman world. At the end of the 6th century the ethnic and linguistic patchwork which Spain had always been in spite of Romanization was formed into a national and religious unity. Whereas the Ostrogoths invited disaster by their reluctance to renounce their Germanic characteristics, the Visigoths by abjuring Arianism integrated themselves with Spain and the Universal Church. The Visigoths, even before their entry, were the most Romanized of the Dark Age peoples and, as we gather not only from archaeological remains but also from the details of everyday life recorded by St Isidore, readily adopted in Spain

Byzantine dress and customs. They inherited from Rome not only the vision of unified empire and a universal code of law but also respect for the Latin language. If Gothic was ever widely spoken or written in Spain, certainly we have no manuscript evidence of it. Instead, Silver Latin seeded with native Celtic and intrusive Gothic and German gave birth to the Spanish language. Outside this unity stood the native elements in the Basque lands (although the cities of Braga, Astorga and Leon were fully incorporated) and to some extent the Spanish Jews.

p 182 (18)
The Jews first established themselves in Spain after their expulsion from Italy by Trajan. At this early date they found a refuge among their Semitic relatives in the old Punic cities and it is in Adra, east of Malaga, that the earliest Jewish graves are found. They fared better under the Visigoths than under the Romans but repressive measures, especially fiscal, were never removed. At one point, under Sisebuth their choice was conversion or expulsion and even under Recceswinth their position was little better. On the whole, the Toledo councils mollified the repressive measures of the kings if only for practical reasons, since the release of Christian slaves from what was often a comfortable Jewish bondage caused much misery and the presence of large numbers of *pseudoconversi*, who had accepted baptism but neglected to practice as Christians, caused nothing but embarrassment, especially as there were Christians in exactly this position. The Jewish problem was of concern to all the Christian scholars of Visigothic Spain, especially those who respected the great Rabbinic learning of Jewish scholars. They became a theological issue rather than a social problem and under the latest Visigothic kings persecution almost entirely ceased.

The strength of the Crown was further enhanced by the victories of Recceswinth's successor, a shy and reluctant noble called
f 6
Wamba, whose life and times were chronicled by St Julian. In Wamba's reign, Septimania, as so often, broke into rebellion and serious trouble broke out when the Greco-Byzantine general Paul, whom Wamba had sent to subdue the insurgents, joined the rebellion alongside the Duke of Tarragona. Wamba was forced to win back the rebel cities of Barcelona, Gerona and Narbona. The shadow which was now beginning to fall upon Spain and which was eventually to eclipse her was not cast by any rival prince or insurgent tribe. Wamba, as though he knew the coming events, fortified Toledo and introduced compulsory military service. It is recorded that his fleet fought a skirmish with the ships of the Saracens, at some unspecified time and

King Wamba (right), Recceswinth's successor, was the last great Visigothic ruler before the Arab invasions. Conscious of the immanent threat, Wamba tried to prepare for it, introducing military service and strengthening the walls of Toledo, but his realm was weakened by rebellion. Worn out and discouraged, he abdicated in 680 and spent his last years in a monastery. (6)

place. The two hundred years from Wamba to Alfonso III are covered by only one Latin chronicle written in 754, so that henceforth we see Spain largely through Arabic eyes and cannot follow in detail the defeats of the Visigothic armies.

Crescent and Cross

The Islamic invasion gave Spain a new importance in the history of Europe. Against the structure built over the centuries by Rome and Christianity now swept a force born outside the Empire's boundaries and swiftly matured. Into the speculative, philosophical and contentious world of the Christians shot the swift effective arrow of unified, undisputed and assertive dogma. The rapid Islamic conquest of North Africa and Spain did not
f 7
in fact turn the Mediterranean into a 'Muslim Lake' impairing communications between the southern Latin countries. Nor is it entirely true that the advent of Islam in the south forced the Roman Empire to function on its northern axis, for there was plenty of Byzantine activity in the Mediterranean.

Although Christianity was now on the defensive, Islamic Spain not only tolerated it but contributed largely to the art and culture of Christian Europe. In science, mathematics, medicine and astronomy, Islam had much more to teach than to learn and Muslim craftsmen brought into Europe arts of weaving, metal-founding, inlaying and engraving that had been formerly known only as imports from the Sasanian orient. Spain itself made tremendous economic advances under Muslim rule: the fertility of land was greatly increased, especially in Andalusia, by the methods of irrigation introduced from the Near East. Trade with North Africa, Egypt and Syria flourished, much of it in the control of

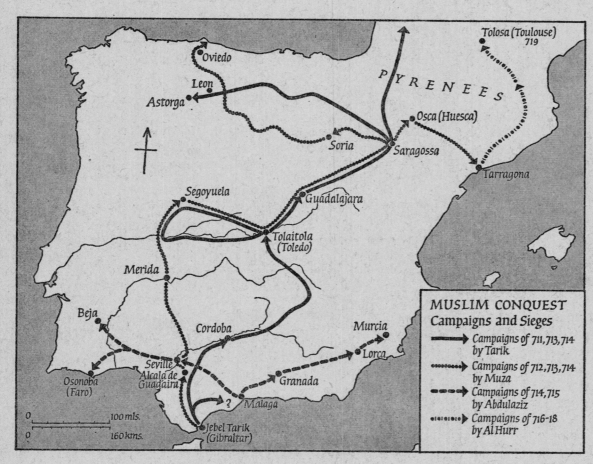

The Arab campaigns of 711 to 718, the first years of the conquest. By 720 almost the whole of Spain was under their control and they had passed over the Pyrenees and into France, leaving only the northern coastal strip, Asturias, as independent Christian territory. (7)

MUSLIM CONQUEST
Campaigns and Sieges

→ Campaigns of 711, 713, 714 by Tarik

→ Campaigns of 712, 713, 714 by Muza

→ Campaigns of 714, 715 by Abdulaziz

→ Campaigns of 716-18 by Al Hurr

Jews, now unfettered of Christian repression and taxation. Wealth and war brought new industries: Toledo produced fine weapons, Cordoba became the centre of silk weaving and leatherwork and Almeria, long dependent on export of esparto grass, became the centre of glazed-pottery making and one of the wealthiest towns in the Mediterranean. In contrast to the Germanic ideals of the landed Visigothic nobility, the Muslims were urban. The population of the new and revived cities of *al-Andalus*, more numerous than at any since Roman times, were ready consumers of the produce of the irrigated river valleys and terraced mountain slopes and of the new fruit and vegetables introduced by the conquerors.

Until the end of the 8th century the history of Arab Spain is as confused as that of the North African states themselves. The western outposts of the vast Empire were controlled from Damascus very loosely and became a profitable area for the activities of ambitious and disaffected princes whose fortunes were bound up with the rivalries between the Umayyad house of Damascus and the Abbasid house of Baghdad. One such prospecting prince was the Umayyad 'Abd ar-Rahman who p 52 succeeded in reconstructing in Cordoba the glories of the Umay- (38–40) yad court of Damascus. In 756, less than half a century after the conquest, Cordoba became a serious rival to the Orient and the anti-Abbasid warrior aristocracy of Palestine and Syria were transplanted in large numbers to Spain, where they found climatic and topographic conditions not dissimilar from those which they left.

In the first century of Muslim rule the Visigothic church continued little impaired. Even later when large numbers of Spaniards, encouraged by preferential treatment in taxation, were converted to Islam the Christian communities continued to flourish in the towns and Toledo, Seville and Merida maintained their archbishoprics. Under the comparatively isolated and unique conditions of Muslim Spain the Christian church clung to and developed the native liturgy introduced by the Visigoths with its Arian and Byzantine elements. This liturgy belonged to the Gallican branch of western liturgies, which elsewhere in the west was almost entirely supplanted by the Roman rite. Purged of Arian elements, the south Spanish Gallican liturgy had been brought into general use by the councils of Toledo under the direction of SS Leander and Isidore, as well as St Ildefonsus, and now adopted by all churches in Moorish territory. The Muslims treated those who submitted to their rule with considerable tolerance, allowing freedom of practice. Those who

Base and capital from the church of S. Pedro de Nave, Zamora. Normally the capitals of Visigothic and Mozarabic churches are of Byzantine derivation, but here they show a transition from Corinthian to the Romanesque 'cushion' style, as well as being decorated with scriptural themes—here St Philip the Apostle. (9, 10)

The roundel decoration derived from the Byzantine tree-of-paradise theme, with birds and foliage in the encircling branches, was an important influence in the art of Dark Age Europe. In Spain it is rare before Romanesque times, although it must have been well known from imported Byzantine silks. One of the few pre-Romanesque examples (9th century) is this relief from the church of Santa Maria at Quintanilla de las Viñas, near Burgos. (11)

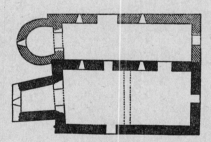

The adoption of the Mozarabic liturgy throughout the peninsula during the 7th and 8th centuries made the addition of a side-chapel necessary in many of the simpler Visigothic churches. Here at S. Miguel de Sournia the addition takes the form of a horseshoe apse—typical, like the horseshoe arch of Mozarabic architecture. (12)

By far the bulk of Visigothic decoration consisted of 'chip-carved' florets and lattice, the folk-art motifs of north Africa and Spain in Roman and pre-Roman times. This 8th-century altar-pedestal from the Mosque at Cordoba once belonged to a Visigothic church. (8)

willingly submitted were known as *Mostarabuna* or Mixt-Arabizers and their liturgy as Mozarab. Although there was nothing Arab about it, except vernacular preaching, the rite became corrupted and was suppressed after Alfonso IV captured Toledo. Mozarabic *f 12* liturgy affected architecture. Leander is known to have incorporated oriental usages and through Milan the Gallican churches were more closely in touch with Greece and Illyria than with Rome. Thus the form of the Visigothic-Mozarabic mass was more akin in many respects to that of Syria and Greece, requiring the prothesis and procession of the sacred elements before consecration. This led to the adoption of a triple-apse church-plan providing diaconal and prothetic altars flanking the main altar of celebration. Surviving churches in purely Visigothic tradition are of course few. S. Juan de Baños (Jaen) originally dedicated p 183 by Recceswinth in 661 is the outstanding example, but there are (26, 27) many later churches with the three simple barrel-vaulted apses, horseshoe arches and debased Corinthian capitals which were the hallmarks of Visigothic style, but without the carved stone panels

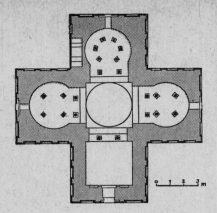

The church of S. Fructuoso, near Braga, in Portugal, was the funerary chapel of the saint, who died in 665. Its plan is a Greek cross, three arms ending in horseshoe apses with tiny arcades supporting vaults. A dome covers the crossing. S. Fructuoso's remains lay in a sarcophagus let into the exterior wall of the chancel to the left of the altar. On the outside the walls are articulated by flat niches with alternating round and triangular heads. (13)

of geometric decoration derived from Iberian and north African vernacular woodwork and peculiar to Visigothic decoration. Under Islamic influences, the development of the horseshoe arch and the elaboration of foliate decoration produced a more distinctive 'Mozarabic' architecture. In the 'Catholic lands' of Catalonia (Septimania) and Suevian Galicia, ecclesiastic architecture remained closer to Byzantine tradition, producing the baptistery of San Miguel de Tarrasa and the Byzantine cruciform church of S. Fructuoso at Braga in Portugal (665).

f 13
p 187
(39)

In the country Christian towns magistrates were appointed by the Moors to administer the Visigothic law and likewise the Jewish communities were governed by their own native legal administration parallel to that of the Qur'anic law in the Muslim cities. The lamp of Christian learning, though flickering, did not die: emirs and caliphs esteemed the wisdom and trustworthiness of Christian clergy, many of whom became more versed in Arabic than Latin, and employed them in diplomatic capacities. The initiative in fostering good relations with the Spanish Muslims was the work of Emperor Theophilus in the 9th century. Diplomatic exchanges between Cordoba and Byzantium are attested throughout the reign of 'Abd ar-Rahman II, and his son al-Hakim II petitioned Nicephorus Phocas in the 10th century for the loan of a mosaicist to execute work for the Umayyad palaces.

The impact of Cordoba in 9th–10th-century Europe was great. 'Abd ar-Rahman had founded the Cordoba mosque on the ruins

Map showing how the Muslims were slowly pushed south from the 9th to the 11th centuries. The 'Reconquista' did not end until the 15th century, with the fall of the last Arab citadel, Granada, in 1492. (14)

of a Visigothic church to be a rival of the splendour of Mecca and the sacred city of the western Muslim world. More splendid than its columns of jasper and porphyry was its claim to possess relics of Mohammed himself. Cordoba thus became the centre of pilgrimages, Qur'anic schools, art, music and poetry. There was a saying of Averroes that when a wise man died his books were sold in Cordoba and his musical instruments in Seville. To the poetess Hroswitha of Gandersheim it was the 'ornament of the world'. In its streets Christian merchants and scholars, islamized slaves and freedmen shared its culture, wealth and prosperity and from its bazaars embroidered stuffs, carved ivories, silks and metalware passed to the sacristies and homes of Europe and had a lasting influence on the minor arts of early medieval times.

The Tide Turns—Santiago 'Slayer of Moors'

No longer can we speak of 'Dark Ages'. On Spain, indeed, although there were many long shadows, full darkness never did descend. The early 9th century, which brought Charlemagne to the charge of the West Roman Empire, saw Spain amidst the splendours of a new cultural and artistic renaissance and about to begin a reintegration with western Europe. For it was with the backing of Charlemagne that the tide of Islam was turned and that there emerged from the northern remnant of the old Visigothic nobility a new leadership which was to establish a Christian Spain.

Alfonso I was the son of a Cantabrian Visigothic chieftain who married the daughter of Pelayo of Galicia, around whom the anti-Muslim resistance had concentrated. He was able to advance over much of northern Spain as far south as Segovia and Avila, whilst Charlemagne's Franks turned the Arab invasion of Septimania. His successor, Alfonso II, consolidated the neo-Gothic monarchy at Oviedo, constructing the first public buildings in which Carolingian influence is evident and which really mark the beginning of Romanesque art in Spain. Little of the Visigoths remained and the new art style was dominated by the interplay of Islamic and Carolingian styles. The southern fringes of this Asturian kingdom became exceptionally important in the cultural history of Spain. The anti-Christian feelings initially provoked in *al-Andalus* in 852 by the revolt of Eulogus in the reign of 'Abd ar Rahman II brought large-scale migrations of mozarabic clergy from Andalusia and Castile. Many were settled in succeeding years around Zamora and Leon. The convents and monasteries founded for them by the Asturian kings are some of the finest pieces of mozarabic style and it was in their scriptoria that the mozarabic tradition of manuscript illumination flourished in the 10th–11th centuries.

p 186
(32–35)

p 177 (
p 184–
(28–31)

It was under Alfonso's successor, Ramiro I, that the little northern kingdom reached its cultural peak. The tunnel-vaulted church of S. Cristina de Lena still survives almost intact. Across its east end runs a remarkable arcade of three arches—an open screen like an iconostasis. Most fascinating of all is the building (now a church) known as S. Maria de Naranco. This was originally part of the royal palace, and so provides one of the very few secular buildings of which we have direct knowledge during this period. The main hall is on the first floor, reached by an outer staircase. At each end are triple arcades opening on to loggias with stilted arches. The interior is tunnel-vaulted, with transverse arches coming down to seal-like *patera* in place of corbels.

p 187
(37)

p 186
(32, 33)

Thus with the emergence of a new Christian kingdom in Asturias and its orientation to France and Germany; with the great renaissance in art and literature; with the new Moorish and Berber populations; and above all with the new balance of western Christianity and oriental Islam, Medieval Spain was born. As often before, religion acted midwife. As a compromise with Islam Elpidius the metropolitan of Toledo (about 780) had preached 'adoptionism' which taught that Christ was a man filled with the Holy Spirit and 'adopted' by God. This was no new doctrine, but it served the interests of prudence in leaving the One-ness of Allah undivided. The Franks and Alfonso II rejected it and thereby the Christian unity of Spain was broken. But to the side of Alfonso came St James, for the revelation of his tomb in Galicia clearly showed that this last outpost of the Roman Empire, which had so long resisted orthodoxy of any kind, was the true guardian of apostolic tradition.

X PRELUDE TO EMPIRE

The Frankish kingdom from the Merovingians to Pepin

PETER LASKO

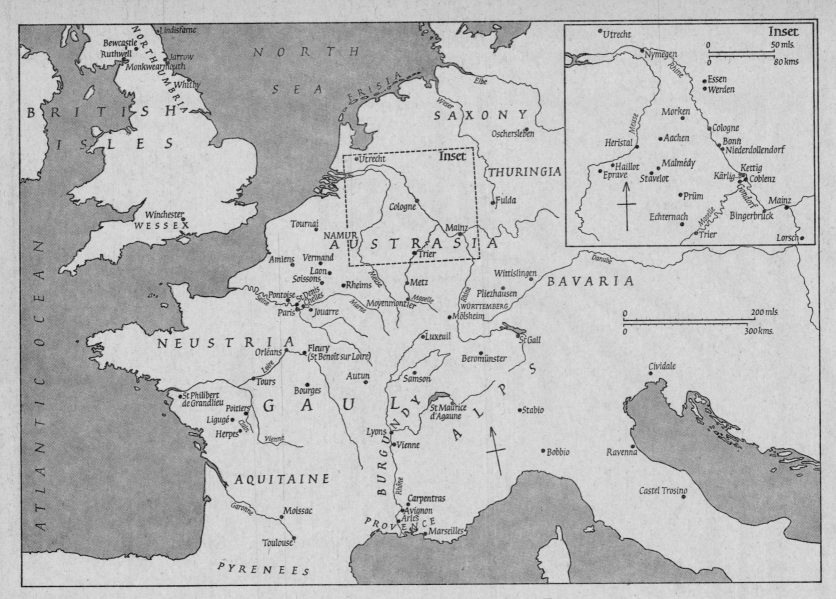

Frankish territory between the 5th and 8th centuries and important monastic centres of north-west Europe

In 486 the last Roman ruler of Gaul,

Syagrius, was defeated at Soissons. The event marked not so much the end of Roman power in Gaul (which had been disintegrating since the early years of the century under repeated attacks from the east), as the rise of the people who were destined to inherit it: the Franks.

The Franks rapidly increased their settlement west of the Rhine early in the 5th century, but there was at first nothing to show that they would eventually dominate the whole country. Other more powerful barbarian peoples (Suevi, Burgundians and above all Ostrogoths and Visigoths) surrounded them, and they were neither united nor particularly numerous. Yet, in about fifty years (464–511), under two very able leaders, Childeric and Clovis, they had succeeded in defeating or conciliating all their rivals and becoming one of the supreme powers of post-Roman Europe.

Culturally they owed nearly everything to their contact with Rome—they spoke a Latin dialect, adopted Christianity (Catholic—not, like most of the barbarians, Arian) and based their law, the *Lex Salica*, largely upon Roman example. Among the ruling classes Roman art was admired, more ancient Germanic traditions persisting among the people, though even those are probably to be traced back, more remotely, to the same source.

The line of Childeric and Clovis—the Merovingian dynasty—lasted until the middle of the 8th century, but long before that the regal authority had become a constitutional fiction. Real power lay more and more in the hands of the 'Mayors of the Palace', and it was through this office that the family of Charles Martel (later called 'Carolingian') rose to its leading position and eventually to the throne itself.

This was the beginning of a new epoch in the history of Europe and will be dealt with in a later chapter. But Merovingian culture is of significant interest in its own right, chiefly because it was a synthesis of so many separate and widely scattered influences—native Germanic, Gallo-Roman, Lombard, Byzantine, Armenian, Coptic. The tombstone or panel from a choir-screen shown here (opposite) illustrates the point. It was found at Gondorf on the Moselle and belongs to a series of Rhineland carvings of the 7th century. The man is dressed as a priest; he is bearded and portrayed full face, holding a book. In the corners of the slab are Germanic looking griffins. The two doves flanking his head have been taken to suggest that it is Christ who is represented, surrounded by creatures of Paradise—as in eastern Mediterranean ivories. The beaded border is derived from late antique art. (1)

More than forty thousand graves of the Merovingian period have been excavated by archaeologists and the amount of material recovered from them is vast. Naturally the majority belong to the lower social strata. Some, however, are richer, with spear, knife and shield in the case of men and jewellery, bronze and silver, in the case of women. The very fact of these articles being put into the graves so long after the country was officially Christian shows that ancient beliefs and customs were still widespread. A representative selection of the grave-goods other than weapons is shown here. Above: objects from northern French and Rhineland graves of the 5th and 6th centuries—a glass horn from Bingerbrück, striped coloured glass bowls from Rheims, pottery and glass beads. Left: articles from a single cemetery at Herpes (Charente)—pottery, glass, a bronze bowl and some very characteristic bronze and silver fibulae, or brooches. (2, 3)

A queen's body was recently found undisturbed beneath the crypt of the Abbey of St Denis, near Paris. She was probably Arnegunde, wife of Chlotar I, and she lay exactly as she had been buried nearly 1400 years ago, all her jewellery in place and even enough left of her rich clothes to make it possible to reconstruct her appearance in every detail (right). She was about 40 when she died, and the body had been embalmed (part of the lungs survives). The limestone coffin had been draped in a bright red woollen cloth. The queen wore, first, a fine linen shift, then a tunic of violet silk reaching to her knees, and then a long dark red silk gown with cuffs embroidered in gold thread. Over her head, with its long blonde hair, was a silken veil (also red), while on her legs and feet were linen stockings, cross-gartered, and thin leather slippers. Her jewellery included pins holding the veil, several silver belt-ends and buckles, two ear-rings, two brooches and a magnificent golden pin fastening the gown. Lying across her body, but not part of her normal dress and therefore not shown in this reconstruction, was a large belt buckle (below), probably placed there as a burial gift. (4, 5)

A female grave at Pontoise (below) yielded the normal fibulae and inlaid jewellery of a variety of designs, including birds, and S-shapes, found in the richer type of non-aristocratic burial. A silver bracelet and ear-rings complete the set. (6)

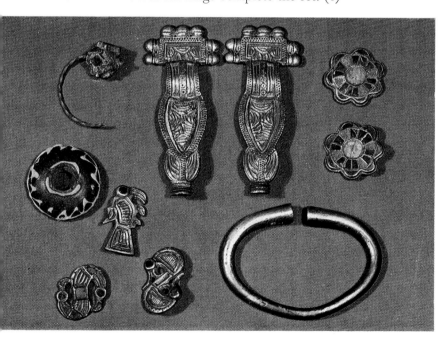

The first King of the Franks to achieve more than local eminence was Childeric. He died in 482 and was buried at Tournai. His tomb was accidentally discovered in 1653 but most of its treasures were lost when thieves robbed the Imperial Art Gallery in Paris in 1831. The most interesting relic was a gold signet-ring with a portrait of the King and the name CHILDERICI REGIS, only a cast of which survives (left). Also shown are the hilt of a sword ornamented with gold and garnets, a crystal ball, a few of the gold coins (there were a hundred gold and two hundred silver) and some of the tiny cicadas, three hundred of which were sewn over the King's cloak. They were the royal symbol of immortality. When the tomb was excavated they were mistaken for bees, and Napoleon had his coronation robe embroidered with bees, in the belief that he was perpetuating a tradition going back to the first King of France. (7)

Germanic decoration was often combined with forms derived from classical art. The chalice and paten from Gourdon (right) date from the reign of Clovis, Childeric's son and successor. Early Merovingian church plate from this period is extremely rare, and most of the surviving pieces are no older than the 8th century (e.g. pl. 44). The chalice follows the shape of a Roman decorative vase. The tendril pattern and the four 'leaves' in the corner of the paten are inlaid with turquoise; the border decoration and central cross use garnets. Although usually called a paten, the size and shape of it strongly suggest that it may be a portable altar. (8)

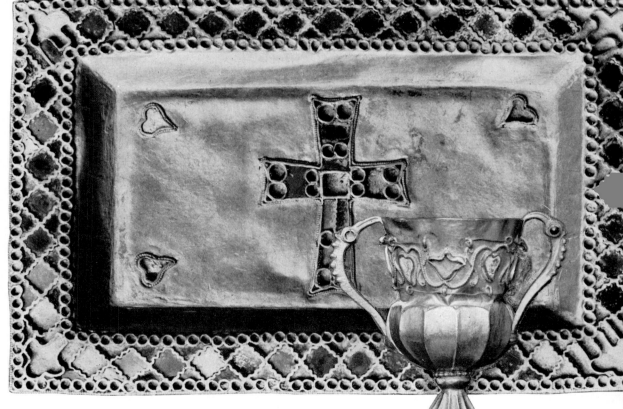

Childeric's grandson, Theodobert, (511–534) (far left) carried the Merovingian kingdom to its greatest extent, even crossing the Alps and campaigning in Italy. **Chlotar II** (584–629) (left centre) re-united the country after a generation of civil wars, but his son **Dagobert** (629–639) (left) was barely able to maintain his position. (9, 10, 11)

The Frankish warrior whose magnificent helmet *(Spangenhelm)* is shown here, was buried with his weapons and treasure at Morken in about AD 600. For him the after-life was a continuation of this world, an idea expressed on a Rhineland tombstone of some fifty years later (above) by the gesture of combing the hair. The warrior here is preyed upon by double-headed serpents—the forces of darkness—but carries a formidable *scramasaxus*, a knife-shaped sword with one edge, at his side. (12, 13)

Of Merovingian architecture hardly anything remains above ground. The baptistery of St Jean at Poitiers (right) was begun in the 5th century and much altered in the 7th. The Roman elements are clear, while the triangular niches may anticipate Lorsch (p. 274). (15)

St Radegund's reading desk (below), preserved at her convent in Poitiers, is almost certainly a gift from the East. In the centre is the Lamb, in the corners the symbols of the Evangelists. (14)

The fantastic vocabulary of forms created by Frankish manuscript illuminators in the 8th century is unique in European art. Their inspiration can only have come from the East. The three large pictures on this page, for instance, all feature a cross with the Greek letters *alpha* and *omega* hanging from the arms—a design that springs from the Eastern Mediterranean (see pl. 25). But in the first example, the Sacramentary of Gelasius (below), they are pecked at by birds of paradise; in the second, from the same MS (centre), they have turned into fish; and in the third, a MS from Laon (right), they are formed out of a continuous ribbon interlace. Bird and fish, brightly coloured, are two favourite motifs, often making up the letters themselves (e.g. the IN of 'In nomine' in the centre picture). The pillars resting on lions in the Laon MS (extreme right) recall an architectural feature of Lombard Italy deriving ultimately from antiquity. Both these manuscripts date from between 750 and 770. (17, 18, 19)

The human figure occurs only rarely in Merovingian illumination. Christ in Majesty (left) may be compared with the altar-front at Cividale on p. 166. Below right: two pages from the Gellone Sacramentary (late 8th century) showing some of its 'picture alphabet' of initials. The female figure with a cross makes the letter A, while on the second page a fish has escaped from the letter of which it formed a part and is being sternly pinned back by a hand holding a fork. (16, 20, 21)

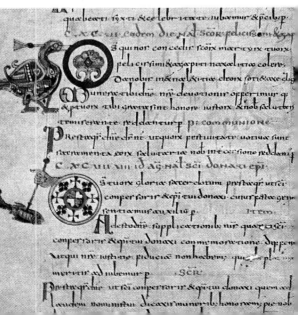

Imagery from the East

gives the key to much that is puzzling in Frankish iconography, and on this page a few selected motifs are followed through from Coptic to Merovingian art. The *alpha* and *omega* suspended on chains from a cross has already been noted in the manuscripts. It occurs also on tombstone reliefs, such as that of Bishop Boethius of Carpentras (right). The bronze cross next to it is probably original eastern Mediterranean work imported into Italy. What is especially interesting about the Boethius slab is that the artist, not understanding his model, has copied it from the wrong side, so that the Greek letters are reversed. (23, 25)

Trade contacts with Egypt are proved by a number of Coptic imports found in the West, such as this bronze bowl found near Mainz. (22)

Daniel in the Lions' Den, a popular Frankish motif, springs partly from the pottery flasks given to pilgrims at the shrine of St Menas, in Egypt (left), which bore an image, often indistinct, of St Menas between two kneeling camels. On Burgundian belt-buckles (right), the composition became more abstract, on the earlier sarcophagus of St Calentius (c. 620) at Bourges (opposite) more explicit. It could even affect a quite unrelated subject, Christ at prayer (far right), on an 8th-century bone panel from the Werden casket. (26, 27, 35, 36)

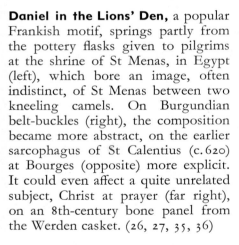

The charging horseman is another familiar Merovingian motif that can be traced back to Eastern prototypes (right). First, a Coptic textile from Egypt. Second, a plaque of bronze gilt, probably Lombard and dating from about 600, from Stabio in Switzerland. Next, two decorative bronze discs from Frankish graves, also c. 600; they probably represent the god Odin (compare the relief on the Vendel helmet, p. 221). Finally (far right), a funerary stele of c. 700 from near Oschersleben, the bearded horseman now portrayed realistically with spear, sword and round shield. (28, 29, 37, 38, 39)

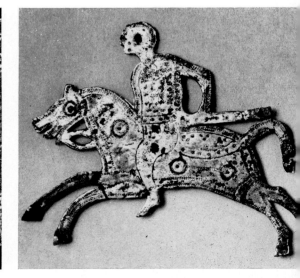

The classical pediment could have come directly from Roman examples (above left: part of a 4th-century sarcophagus at Arles), or from Coptic (above: a grave stele from Kom Buljeh). Above right is the Merovingian adaptation, a panel from the Metz choir-screen, of the middle of the 7th century. (24, 30, 31)

Interlace patterns found on the decorative edging of Coptic textiles (above left) perhaps point to Frankish buckles and strap-ends, as on this detail of an example from Amiens. (32, 33)

The transfigured Christ is probably the subject of this carving from Niederdollendorf (the reverse of pl. 13). He is shown surrounded by rays, a 'total halo'. (34)

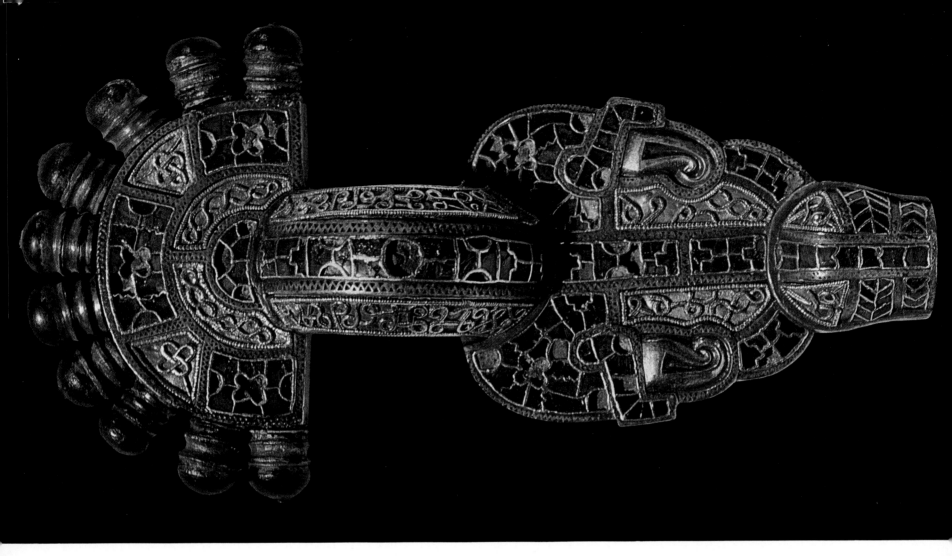

A barbaric richness still characterized the work of Merovingian jewellers of the 7th century, though in technique they owed much to Byzantium. Two of their masterpieces are illustrated here—the splendid fibula from Wittislingen (above) and the quatrefoil brooch from Mölsheim (below left). The fibula, though deposited as a burial offering, has a Christian inscription. It is of silver gilt, and set with garnets. The brooch uses an antique cameo as its centrepiece. Below: another smaller brooch showing the same cloisonné technique as the fibula. (40, 41, 42)

Four double-headed serpents, looped into a quatrefoil pattern, make up the garnet brooch shown below, also from Wittislingen. (43)

The ever-increasing popularity of relics, largely owing to the activity of Irish missionaries, ensured that much of the skilled craftsmanship of the time was devoted to shrines for their preservation. They often form miniature sarcophagi, where the remains of the saint are laid to rest. The example above (right) was found at Nymegen on the Rhine. The style combines Germanic features, such as interlace and animal-decoration, with foliage and scroll-patterns transmitted through Lombard Italy from the East. That below is from St Maurice d'Agaune, and bears an inscription on the back 'Theuderich the priest had this made in honour of St Maurice'. It is decorated with garnets, pastes and (this time) an imitation Roman cameo. (44, 45)

A unique survival

from Merovingian times, though altered in later centuries, meets us at the abbey of Notre Dame at Jouarre. The present crypt was originally two crypts belonging to two separate churches built next to each other. The vaulting and much of the fabric is later, but the west wall with its beautiful masonry (below), the capitals and several sarcophagi go back to the 7th century. (46)

Two coffins have lain in the crypt of Jouarre for 1300 years. One is that of the first Abbess, Theodochilde, who died in 662 (right). The sides are decorated with two rows of scallop shells and three bands of finely cut lettering. The second coffin (below) belongs to her brother, Agilbert. He went to England in about 650, became Bishop of Winchester and took part in the Synod of Whitby in 664. Returning to France, he was made Bishop of Paris in 668 and died soon after 685. His coffin is badly damaged, but originally showed Christ—enthroned in the centre—and twelve figures, perhaps the Apostles, their hands raised in prayer, to each side of him. (47, 48)

The head of Agilbert's coffin is carved with a Christ in Majesty (above) in a mandorla supported by the symbols of the Evangelists, of a rare form, similar to that of a 5th-century mosaic in Hosios David at Thessalonica. (49)

The Frankish kingdom from the Merovingians to Pepin

PETER LASKO

OF ALL THE PEOPLES of the continent of Europe who were absorbed into the decaying Roman Empire of the West during the migration period, only the Franks succeeded in establishing a political unity that survived the collapse and final disintegration of the Empire. No one who lived at that time and had witnessed the foundation of the powerful Ostrogothic and Visigothic kingdoms in northern Italy, southern France and Spain could have foreseen that the insignificant tribes of barbarian warriors, the Ripuarian and the Salian Franks, occupying only a comparatively small area east and west of the Rhine, were destined to lay the foundations of the culture which led to the creation of the Carolingian Empire and, through it, to western European civilization as we know it.

Settlers within Rome's Frontiers

Who were the Franks and where did they originate? The available evidence seems sufficient only to suggest that they were a political amalgamation of many small tribes which took place in the 1st and 2nd century AD in the lands between the River Weser and the Rhine. The names Franks, Alemanni, Thuringians, and so on, indicate larger groups of peoples which only superseded the older and more numerous smaller tribal units that inhabited the forests east of the Rhine at the height of imperial Roman power. Just as little is known of their material culture before they came under the influence of Roman civilization, as is known of their tribal origins.

After their early successes (mid-4th century) in breaking through the imperial frontiers into the 'Promised Land', they came to terms with the Romans and were allowed to settle within their boundaries under the obligation of hereditary military service, with the status of *foederati*. From then on, we find the so-called '*Reihengräber*' or 'Row-graves' cemeteries, a name given them because their graves are arrayed in more or less clearly defined rows, with the heads usually buried towards the west. These cemeteries are found in the frontier areas of the Empire, stretching from northern France and Belgium in the west to the Danube and the Black Sea in the south and east. The men are buried with their weapons and the women with their jewellery, as was customary among the Germanic peoples, but the mere fact that these cemeteries contain inhumations (as against the cremation practised by their forefathers) shows the extent to which they were already under the influence of Roman custom. It is in these *Reihengräber* cemeteries that we first gain a more complete picture of the material culture of the Germanic tribes, and in these finds that we must look for the beginnings of Germanic art.

The weapons, the buckles and, it seems, most of the military equipment with which the *foederati* were buried show that their taste in decoration was little more than a somewhat provincial, and at times barbarized, version of Roman motifs. The finest of these buckles and brooches mostly belong to the second half of the 4th century and are made in a technique, which is called 'chip-carving'. This technique was the result of cutting designs with broad cuts of a knife in the original wax model from which the buckles were cast by the 'lost wax' method. The designs employed—palmettes, spirals, key patterns and animal terminals—are all clearly of Roman origin, and they sometimes even include,

in the most sumptuous examples, typically Roman portrait busts. The poorer the quality of this work, the more pronounced is the degree of abstraction and the emphasis on flattened and stylized animal forms. It is difficult to say whether this abstraction is the result of the more 'native' Germanic taste of the settlers, less closely linked with the main stream of Roman culture, or whether it is merely due to less expert and less civilized workmanship practised among the lower social classes of the indigenous Gallo-Roman population and copied by the settlers. Perhaps it is just the result of the mass-production of poor quality Roman military equipment. One thing is certain, that such simply decorated objects of daily use are found only in the area forming the immediate frontier zones of the Roman Empire. Also, there is little distinction in style between the north—including even southern parts of the British Isles—and the south, right down to the lower reaches of the Danube. This might well be taken as evidence that the material is Roman, under little influence from the new settlers, because it is only the Roman element that is constant along the entire length of the imperial frontier.

The famous cemeteries at Vermand, Samson and Eprave, as well as the recently excavated cemetery at Haillot in the Namur region, provide us with material from the vital period between the late 4th and the beginning of the 6th century, which saw the change of the Salian Franks from their status of *foederati*, through the defeat of the last Roman ruler in Gaul, Syagrius, in 486, to the foundation of an independent Frankish Kingdom. After this the social pattern of the country is set for several centuries. The population consists of two separate elements—the conquering Franks and the conquered Gallo-Romans. They had different customs and for a time lived under different laws, but, as we shall see, the essence of later Merovingian culture lies in their eventual fusion.

Spear mount (4th century), from Vermand, in silver, niello and gilt. The chip-carved designs are typically Roman: at the head (right) are a cicada and two hippocamps, and lower down two serpentine animals; spirals and a rosette decorate the base and in the centre is an interlaced star. (1)

Much of the material in these cemeteries, especially the pottery and glass, is fundamentally late Roman. Certainly, the Roman glass industry of the Rhineland and the lower Rhine area, continued to flourish under the increasing control of the Franks—as did the pottery industry everywhere. But the metalwork and the weapons found there show the changes towards more truly Frankish types, and in the latest graves of the early 6th century we even find examples of cloisonné jewellery that certainly could no longer be confused with Gallo-Roman work. It is in the animal art developed in this period out of Roman prototypes that we must seek the first beginnings of Germanic art, an animal art which was defined by Salin as 'Style I'. This derives originally from the flaccid forms of late Roman dolphins and animal head terminals, but was developed by the Germanic craftsman of succeeding generations (not only among the Franks, but even more successfully among the Germanic peoples in their homelands) into an incredibly rich, varied and imaginative style. The animal forms become more and more abstracted and bisected and are spread in lavish profusion over the whole decorated surface.

Thus a synthesis was created of abstract Germanic tastes with the sophisticated techniques of metalwork, glass manufacture and goldsmith's work of the Roman Empire. At the same time, and probably of even greater importance to the development of styles in Western Europe, was the movement of peoples from the east— the Visigoths and the Ostrogoths and the invading Huns, defeated by the Romans with the help of the Franks in 451. They brought with them the tastes and techniques of the peoples beyond the eastern borders of the Roman Empire—Iranians, Parthians and Avars, and even of those who lived within the eastern provinces of the Empire itself.

The Son of Merovech

p 202
(7)

The first compelling evidence of this eastern influence can be found in the tomb of the earliest of the great Frankish rulers, Childeric, whose rich burial was accidentally discovered at Tournai in 1653. He was the son of the half-legendary Merovech, from which the name Merovingian is derived, and died in 481. Only a few fragments of this find have survived, the bulk of it having been stolen when thieves broke into the Imperial Art Gallery in Paris in 1831. Fortunately all the finds had been published soon after their discovery by the Antwerp physician Jean-Jacques Chifflet. The grave was certainly that of Childeric, because it contained a gold signet ring engraved with a full-face portrait of the King and the legend: CHILDERICI REGIS—only a cast or two of this important ring now survive. As well as this ring two swords were found in the tomb heavily ornamented with gold and cloisonné garnet inlay—they are among the earliest examples of polychrome jewellery so far found in a Frankish grave. Also in the grave were Childeric's battle axe, his spear and the head of his horse with all its harness, numerous gold buckles, gold mounts from a belt, a heavy gold bangle, a mounted crystal ball, and a purse with a hundred gold coins as well as a treasure of two hundred silver coins. No less than three hundred gold cicadas, the symbol of eternal life, their wings inlaid with garnets, were sewn on the King's brocaded cloak. No Frankish burial of comparable wealth has ever been discovered since.

Apart from the wealth of the tomb of Childeric, its archaeological importance can hardly be overestimated. It is firmly dated by the King's death, and its contents show us that the art of the court bore little, if any, relation to the mass of the material found in the *Reihengräber* cemeteries. The incipient animal art of the bronze buckles and brooches found little echo at the court, where the richer flavour of eastern art-forms played a predominant part. Indeed, in the tomb of a Germanic king near the northern borders of the Empire we find a reflection of the orientalizing tastes that can be traced in upper layers of late Roman society wherever it survived in the 5th century—in north Italy, in Rome itself and of course, more especially at the court of Constantinople. In the art which he adopted Childeric shows that he saw himself as a successor to the Roman rulers of Gaul, ready to absorb their cultural aspirations. Clearly no Germanic animal style was yet worthy of a place at court.

King Clovis

Probably much the same attitude persisted at the court, during the period of rapid Frankish expansion, under the greatest of their rulers, Childeric's son Clovis, although this would be difficult to prove. It had been Clovis who had finally put an end to Roman rule in northern Gaul by the defeat of Syagrius at Soissons in 486. In the same year Clovis, who was only twenty, having succeeded to the throne at the age of fifteen, mounted his first attack on the Thuringians—thus beginning the process of making himself ruler of all the Franks. In 496 he conquered the Alemanni and defeated the Visigoths at Tours. A few years earlier, he had married Clotilda, niece of the King of Burgundy, who had been converted to the Catholic faith, and after the defeat of the Visigoths Clovis himself was baptised an orthodox Catholic, either at Tours or at Rheims.

Clovis' conversion was of the greatest importance to the subsequent history of the Franks. By it he obtained for himself the goodwill and even the support of the Gallo-Roman population of Gaul against his powerful Germanic neighbours, the Visigoths, the Ostrogoths, and the Burgundians—all of whom subscribed to the Arian heresy, which appealed to the Germanic peoples converted to Christianity—perhaps because they found it easier to accept Christ as a man than as a divine being. The support of the orthodox majority of the Gallo-Roman population gained by Clovis' conversion was symbolized by his being granted an honorary consulship by the eastern Emperor Anastasius in 508. By his

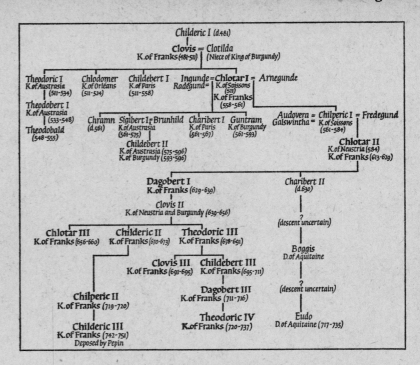

The Merovingians, or early Frankish monarchs. The first kings were succeeded by men of lesser stature. Their power was further weakened by constant division of the kingdom among the male heirs of the king, and after Dagobert I they were nothing more than puppets (see fig. 7). Rulers of the entire kingdom are shown in heavy type. (2)

conversion, the position of Clovis was also immeasurably strengthened and a firm base was created for Frankish rule in Gaul. Clovis had, by design or by the accident of his marriage to a Catholic princess, placed himself firmly on what was to be the winning side in the Arian controversy, a controversy which bedevilled the relationship of all the other Germanic rulers with the indigenous populations of the areas they attempted to control with insufficient land settlement by their own people. Clovis' strength also lay in his geographical position, which forced him to create a new centre of power in the north-west of Europe, while at the same time remaining in contact with the German homelands.

Classical Models, Barbarian Taste

What evidence we have of the period of Clovis' reign, suggests that his cultural aspirations did not differ much from those of his father. Only his acceptance of Christianity and subsequently his support of the Gallo-Roman church, adds a new dimension to the period. Of the rare pieces of early church plate to survive, the Gourdon chalice and paten are likely to date from his reign. They are ornamented with coloured inlay now partially lost, and show clearly a synthesis of Roman forms and orientalizing barbaric taste for rich and colourful decoration similar to that to be observed in Childeric's grave goods. The chalice is in the shape of a Roman decorative vase while the so-called paten, perhaps more probably a small portable altar, is decorated with the colourful stepped cell-work inlay, which was to play such a large part in Germanic polychrome jewellery of the succeeding century.

p 202
(8)

Of the architecture of the period next to nothing survives above ground, although we know of course that it must have existed. The Gallo-Roman church had been growing in strength and power long before Clovis' conversion. Already in the 2nd century the bishoprics of Lyons, Marseilles and Vienne had been founded, and in the 3rd century eight more had been added in Gaul, from Toulouse in the south to Trier in the north, while in the 4th century the bishoprics of Cologne and Mainz had been created. In the 5th century monasteries mostly as yet in the south, like Ligugé near Poitiers and St Victor at Marseilles, followed. Obviously much building activity was undertaken, and the skill of Gaulish masons is attested, admittedly later on at the end of the 7th century, by Bede's reference to masons being imported into Northumbria from Gaul, because of their superior ability in cutting stone. Perhaps something of 5th-century architectural style survives in the baptistery of St Jean at Poitiers, in spite of many

p 203
(15)

additions and alterations made in the 7th century and later. Roman brick is the main building material employed here, and the cornices, pediments and other architectural details are uncompromisingly Roman in derivation. There is of course little reason to suppose that Frankish builders, skilled no doubt only in timber and half-timbered building, could add anything to Roman traditional methods and materials. Architectural carving too, as can be seen in such rare survivals as the 5th-century capitals from 'La Daurade' at Toulouse, were entirely dependent on Roman traditions.

Frankish Power Grows

f 2 At the death of Clovis in 511, his kingdom was divided among his four sons according to Frankish custom. This had its obvious disadvantages, leading to the constant division of the kingdom. Clovis avoided the worst results of this by dividing each part of his kingdom, rather than the kingdom itself, into four parts, and each of his sons received a part of the homelands and each a part of the conquests Clovis had added to his realm. As a result none of the sons had a sufficiently unified territory to attempt sole rule, and Paris, the chief seat of the kingdom, was given into the control of all four sons. It was not the 'kingdom' but the 'royal domains'—the wealth of the King—that was divided equally among the sons. It was precisely the failure to do this at the death of Louis the Pious in 840, that finally led to the collapse of the Carolingian empire.

Under Clovis' sons, the Frankish kingdom continued to expand, and by AD 534 Burgundy came under Frankish rule, the Rhône valley and Marseilles were incorporated into the kingdom, the Bavarians were conquered, and even the Saxons east of the Rhine were beaten back and forced to pay tribute to the Frankish kings. Before the middle of the 6th century, the Frankish borders were extended as far east as the middle Danube. Frankish warriors under Clovis' grandson Theodobert even crossed the Alps to take advantage of the struggle between the Ostrogoths and the Byzantine Emperor Justinian. But with the death of Theodobert in 548 this ambitious campaign came to an end: the Merovingian kingdom had reached the point of its greatest expansion—not be substantially surpassed until the time of Charlemagne.

p 202
(9)

p 200, 1
(2, 3,
4, 6)

In spite of the adoption of the Christian faith by the court, cemetery material still abounds in the 6th and 7th century. It supplies us with a vast quantity of weapons, brooches and buckles, ornaments, pins, pottery and glass, which serve to throw considerable light on the culture of the time. The number of sites that have yielded material of this kind is quite staggering—in Württemberg alone, for example, an Alemannic area, nearly 800 different cemeteries have been recorded, some containing more than 300 individual burials. Altogether, something like 40,000 burials were estimated to have been excavated in Europe by 1961. The ornamental styles of the brooches, buckles, pins, etc. differ, of course, in the different areas of the Frankish kingdom, but it is clear that in the 6th century certain basic stylistic elements gained a wide popularity over the greater part of the area. Such elements are the 'chip-carved' techniques in the spirals, key and fret patterns, inlaid garnets and filigree ornamentation, radiate brooches, with straight foot, or with lozenge foot terminating in animal heads. Also bird forms, usually with long curving beaks, or fish-shaped ornaments, are employed as the heads of pins, or as small mounts or brooches in their own right. A large and varied vocabulary of forms is found in the vast quantity of material from the Germanic cemeteries of the period.

Treasures of a Merovingian Queen

p 208-9
(40-43)

Until recent years such material dominated the study of archaeology, and nothing seemed to survive to bridge the gap between the royal riches of Childeric's tomb of 482 and the wealth of artistic creation connected with the court of Charlemagne some 300 years later. Only occasionally, in the graves of members of the minor Frankish aristocracy, did the material give some indication of what standard of workmanship and wealth one might expect to find among the richer sections of Merovingian society. During the last fifteen years, however, two major discoveries have been made—in excavations under the cathedral of Cologne and St Denis—which substantially add to our knowledge in just this

field. The Cologne burial consisted of two graves, one of a Merovingian princess, the other of a six-year old boy of equally high standing; the St Denis burial was in all probability that of a queen. They are close together in date (Cologne probably the earlier by thirty years or so) and both were exceptionally rich in jewellery and grave-goods. Since space does not allow a full description of both, the St Denis burial will have to serve as an example to show the level achieved by Merovingian art and culture during the mid-6th century.

A large limestone coffin was found in which the remains of a female body about forty years of age at the time of death were discovered, with most of her magnificent costume still identifiable and an array of personal jewellery unprecedented among Frankish burials. Laid on a bright red blanket or cloak, the body was dressed in a fine linen shift, over which she wore a knee-length tunic of violet silk. On her legs she wore stockings with crossed leather garters. The tunic was pulled in at the hips by an open-work gilt leather girdle, fitted with silver gilt buckles and strap-ends. Over the tunic, an ankle-length dark-red silk gown completed her garments, with wide sleeves embroidered with gold thread at the cuffs. This gown was closed at the neck and at the waist by two superb circular gold brooches set with cloisonné garnet, was decorated by a magnificent large pin on the left breast, and fell open below the waist. On her head, a red satin veil was fixed by two gold pins to her long blonde hair, then fell behind to the waist. Other jewellery included a pair of ear-rings, similar to the Cologne princess' ear-rings, and silver buckles and straps fitted with strap-ends fastened her leather slippers. In addition a very large nielloed belt-buckle, with a plate and counter plate decorated with gold and garnets, had been placed just above her waist. This large buckle is certainly from a man's belt, and may have been placed in the tomb as a burial gift. Of outstanding importance is a gold ring found on her finger, inscribed with the name Arnegunde around a monogram of the word REGINE.

p 201
(5)

f 3

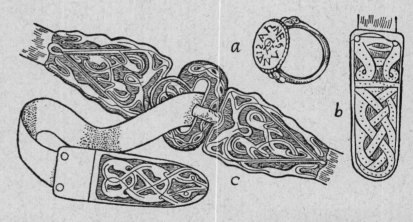

Jewellery from Arnegunde's grave included this gold ring (a) bearing the inscription ARNEGUNDIS *(genitive of Arnegunde) round a monogram of* REGINE. *The garter strap-ends (b) and buckles and strap-ends fastening the shoes (c) are decorated in an interlaced animal ornament, close to Salin's 'Style II' (see p. 239 fig. 6). (3)*

Only one Frankish Queen Arnegunde is known to history, one of the consorts of Chlotar I, King of Soissons from 511 to 558 and sole King of the Franks from 558 to 561. According to Gregory of Tours, she was the sister of Chlotar's first wife Ingunde, and Chlotar must have married her before 539, when Arnegunde's son Chilperic was born. We may assume, therefore, that she must have been born between about 520 and 525. The ring found on her finger is of course not conclusive evidence that it was she who was buried there. The ring is not a seal-ring and may have been a gift from the Queen to someone close to her. However that may be, the date of the burial is not likely to be much later than about AD 570. Among the jewellery, a pair of small silver buckles and some strap-ends are archaeologically the most important. They are decorated with a style of animal art, very close to the one classified by Salin as 'Style II'. Instead of the fragmented

f 3

animal art of Style I, in which parts of the body of creatures are broken up and re-assembled to form a pattern, in Style II, also called very aptly the 'ribbon animal' style, the bodies of the animals are elongated intertwined and interlaced in a smooth and continuous, usually symmetrically arranged, pattern. It has been said that Style II found widespread use in northern Europe only after the beginning of the 7th century, and that it had been developed in north Italy, as the result of the Lombardic invasion of Italy that took place in AD 568. At that time a new synthesis of Style I with older Mediterranean traditions of purely abstract banded interlace patterns is thought to have been created. The appearance of Style II at the Frankish court as early as the 560s, even if in a primitive stage, is therefore one of the most important aspects of the discovery of Arnegunde's tomb at St Denis.

p 239
(f 6)

These graves provide the kind of information for the 6th century which the tomb of Childeric provided for the later 5th. By contrast with Childeric's tomb it is clear that by the middle of the 6th century, the Germanic style had fully penetrated the art of the court. No longer was it necessary for the Frankish ruling families to rely on alien tastes for their personal adornment and the decoration of their material goods. Out of crude beginnings, Germanic art of the *Reihengräber* civilization had, by the middle of the 6th century, developed its aristocratic counterpart. Technically and artistically Merovingian secular art had come of age.

Mayors of the Palace

But although the material from cemeteries still remains a vital source for information as to the character of the age it is no longer our only source. The growing power of Christianity and the Church as well as the more settled and expanding nature of economic conditions in Europe led to an increase in contacts with the Mediterranean world, and to a fundamental broadening of the intellectual and cultural life of the Merovingian kingdom. This was achieved in spite of the political disintegration of Merovingian royal power. After the death of Chlotar I in 561, a series of civil wars weakened the Merovingian royal house, wars made even more bitter by the family feuds that helped to cause them. Dagobert, in a short but trenchant reign of ten years (629–639), combined the whole of the Frankish lands once more under his own rule. But even Dagobert, an unusually strong personality among the later Merovingian kings, was able to stem the flow against the Frankish royal house only for a time. The growing antagonism of the aristocracy—Dagobert complained that the nobles had robbed him of the best estates and domains in his kingdom—was too strong for the King to resist. The fact was that the kings of the early Middle Ages were able to maintain their power against their nobles only in a rapidly expanding kingdom—a condition that no longer existed after the middle of the 6th century.

p 202
(11)

The security of the supremacy of the royal house rested almost entirely on their superior wealth, for there was a need for an unremitting supply of new funds with which to pay for the loyalty of their followers. The constant division of this wealth among the sons of the king inevitably weakened the position of the rulers. Only as long as new territories were added to their royal domains by conquest, as in the time of Clovis and his immediate successors, was their position unassailable. Another difficulty, quite apart from the decline in personal ability in the quick succession of young, and on the whole dissolute, vascillating and weak kings of the Merovingian dynasty, was the growing enmity between different parts of the kingdom: the southern and western part was called Neustria—'New Lands'—and the Germanic northern and eastern part was called Austrasia—'East Lands'—names that first come into use in the late 6th century. In this struggle it was Austrasia which finally won supremacy. Not only were these 'Eastern Lands' the Frankish homelands, more fully settled by Frankish peoples and therefore the basic source of strength in the Frankish Kingdom, but also the course of history in the Mediterranean world made the final ascendancy of the area inevitable in the 8th century.

While the power of the Merovingian kings declined during the 7th century, that of the Mayors of the Palace, the leaders of

the aristocracy, increased. Chlotar II and Dagobert had been forced to surrender most of their administrative authority to the landed nobility. The country was divided into three semi-independent regions—Austrasia, Neustria and Burgundy. Each had its own laws, controlled by its own officials; the King could not appoint a nominee from outside. The great landowners in each region took it in turn to be 'Mayor of the Palace' and their loyalties were naturally local rather than national.

f 7

Charles 'the Hammer'

Predictably, the Mayors of the Palaces of Neustria, Austrasia and Burgundy were at odds, and it was Austrasia, once more under the family of Pepin, which emerged as dominant. In 687 Pepin II (of Heristal), grandson of both Arnulf of Metz and Pepin I, defeated Berthar, Mayor of the Palace of Neustria, and from that date was effective ruler of nearly all the Merovingian kingdom. He died in 714 and was succeeded (after the usual internecine struggle) by his illegitimate son Charles—known as 'Martel', 'the Hammer'.

Charles was an able ruler and a military leader of genius. His unification of the country and ability to mobilize its resources came just in time. In 719 he forced the last independent magnate, Eudo of Aquitaine, to acknowledge his suzerainty. The next year the Arabs crossed the Pyrenees.

They were held in check in the south for twelve years. Then in 732, under a new and fanatical leader, they took the field again and the tide of conquest that had begun nearly a century earlier in Arabia swept up the centre and west of France. Charles gathered an army and placed himself in a good strategic position at the confluence of the Clain and the Vienne. For seven days the two armies were encamped facing each other. Then in October 732 they joined battle—the Battle of Poitiers. Charles's long-term victory, however, was not due entirely to his own efforts. The Moors might yet have rallied had they not in their turn become split by dissension. Their later attempts on Provence and Italy were firmly repulsed. At the same time Charles again secured the eastern frontier by defeating the Saxons in 738. He re-distributed lands belonging to the Frankish church, summoned assemblies and corresponded with the Pope. At the end of his reign the foundations had been laid upon which his son and grandson, Pepin and Charlemagne, were to build the new Carolingian Empire.

All this while his official title was still 'Mayor of the Palace'. The curious constitutional fiction was preserved whereby the nominal ruler of the kingdom was always one or other of the effete *rois fainéants* of the exhausted Merovingian dynasty. It was not until the reign of Pepin (Charles Martel died in 741) that the king in fact became king in name. At first Pepin shared the government with his brother Carloman. But in 747 Carloman renounced the world and entered a monastery. In November 751, Pepin, with the approval of Pope Zacharius, deposed the last Merovingian King Childeric III and was anointed King of the Franks.

A strong Frankish Church

The rise of the Mayors of the Palace was one feature of the 7th century. The other power to increase rapidly during this time in spite of many temporary setbacks, was that of the Church, both in its secular branch under the bishops, and in its monastic branch. Although the spiritual life of the Frankish church left much to be desired, the growing control exercised over it by Frankish aristocracy augmented its political power considerably. Early in the 6th century, at the Council of Orléans, only two bishops with Germanic names attended, while no less than thirty were drawn from the ranks of the older Gallo-Roman aristocracy, but by the early 7th century, at the Council of Paris, forty-one of the bishops present were of Germanic stock and only thirty-eight were of non-Germanic origin—many of them from the Christian East. These figures indicate both the growth of the Church, and the infiltration of Frankish nobles into her ranks.

The growing power of the Church was the natural result of her tremendous expansion in wealth. Never were donations to the Church greater than in the Merovingian period. Her benefactors were many, not least among them the bishops themselves—drawn

Reliquary of St Croix, Poitiers, containing a fragment of the True Cross sent by Justin II to St Radegund. The centre panel survives but the hinged wings are known only from an 18th-century drawing; they were decorated on the outside with large carbochon gems. (4)

as they were from among the landed aristocracy. Bertram of Mans, for example, left no less than thirty-five estates to his see—and it must be remembered that all property acquired by the Church was inalienable. The Church also received other financial benefits, such as the exemption from custom dues and all sorts of taxes, while she herself was able to levy dues and tithes of many kinds. The Church always received, was never called upon to pay out, and never had to divide her property among heirs.

The monastic branch of the Church also expanded rapidly. Some 200 monasteries, mainly situated south of the Loire, were in existence in the kingdom when St Columbanus, the Irish missionary, arrived in Europe about the year 585. His arrival seems to have opened the flood gates to monastic expansion, and in no other period in history were as many monasteries founded as between the years 610 and 650—the Saint himself having died at Bobbio in north Italy in 615. By the end of the 7th century, well over 400 monasteries were in existence, and now spread over the entire kingdom as far north as the River Meuse and as far east as the upper Rhine. Some of the most famous monasteries of the Middle Ages owe their foundation to this period, including Prüm, Moyenmontier, Malmédy, Stavelot and St Gall.

Art in the Service of God

It was, of course, inevitable that expansion in wealth and power on this scale resulted in a parallel expansion of cultural output. Artistic influences from a wider background began to enrich the repertoire of Frankish art. Although pitifully little survives of early monastic art in the Merovingian kingdom, that little plainly shows these new influences at work—influences from the older centres of culture, from Italy, from Byzantium and especially from Syria and Egypt, the home of monasticism itself.

Already in the 6th century, isolated instances of such direct influences can be cited. When Chlotar I repudiated his wife Radegund, she founded the monastery of St Croix at Poitiers and became its first Abbess. In the year 569, she asked the Byzantine Emperor Justin II for a fragment of the Holy Cross, that precious relic kept at Jerusalem which had been discovered by St Helena in the 4th century in a cave near the site of Our Lord's Crucifixion. Her wish was granted and still to-day the convent of St Croix preserves a fragment of the Cross, mounted in a gold reliquary panel, decorated with cloisonné enamel and set with garnets and green pastes in rectangular cells surrounding the relic and framing the panel. In the French revolution the reliquary lost its two side wings which are known only from an 18th-century drawing. Although the documentary evidence of Radegund's acquisition of the relic is undisputed, the reliquary itself has been said to be Byzantine work of the 11th century or later. Not only is the design as difficult to parallel in the later period as in the 6th century, but it is also difficult to see how the relic could have been mounted in a later Byzantine frame while in the possession of the convent at Poitiers. St Radegund's wooden reading desk is an East Christi-

f 4

p 203 (14)

an import, while quite a number of objects of East Christian origin have been brought to light during the excavation of 6th- and 7th-century sites, especially in the Rhineland and south-western Germany. Imports from Coptic Egypt have also been found in Britain, north Italy and elsewhere in Europe.

p 206 (22)

Clearly we can assume that in a similar way, either by direct trade or by contacts through the monastic connections with the Middle East, other materials also found their way to north-western Europe. Such imports must have included textiles, decorated with abstract as well as pictorial patterns of the kind known from Egyptian burials, ivory carvings, metalwork, and pottery. Indirect evidence of such imports is plentiful. The interlace patterns found on bronze buckles and strap ends, and on the Frankish iron buckles and counter-plates inlaid with silver so popular in the 7th century, are found most frequently on the decorative roundels and strips on Coptic textiles. East Christian ivory carvings are known to have been in Europe since the early Middle Ages, some of these carvings already being copied in Carolingian times.

p 207 (32, 33)

Ideas and Images from the East

Among the stone carvings to have survived from the 7th century the tomb slab of Bishop Boethius of Carpentras, who died in 604, provides us with an interesting example of such indirect evidence. Carved on the slab is a cross, which has the *Alpha* and *Omega* suspended from its arms by small chains. This is clearly copied from a metal altar-cross, because the position of the first and the last letters of the Greek alphabet, which symbolize the Beginning and the End, are reversed on the stone carving and were obviously copied from the wrong side of a metal prototype. A number of bronze altar-crosses of the 6th century that survive from the Eastern Mediterranean show us the kind of object that the Frankish mason must have copied.

p 206 (23)

p 206 (25)

One element in the Boethius slab not mentioned so far—the upper part, carrying an inscription on a classical tabula with a pointed architectural pediment above—could not have been derived from an imported piece of metalwork, but is strictly in the monumental classical tradition. In the Boethius slab, this may well be copied from Gallo-Roman sculpture which survived into the 7th century in large quantity in France. No such source could account for the few fragments of sculpture from the church of St Peter at Metz. One of the fragments, which shows a standing saint between columns supporting a pediment, is undoubtedly derived from East Christian monastic art, probably from that of Coptic Egypt. Other Metz fragments, carved with interlace patterns, vine-scrolls and plants issuing from two-handled vases, equal-armed crosses and architectural motifs, all point to exactly the same source. Only the addition of animal heads to the ends of the strands of interlace betray the Germanic carvers. Unfortunately the date of the carvings is not certain. The church of St Peter was probably found early in the 7th century; the dates 613 or 620 have been suggested. The fragments themselves show that they were not part of the architectural structure but were most probably part of a choir screen. Certainly a date towards the middle of the 7th century, during the period of rapid monastic expansion would seem to be entirely acceptable.

p 206 (24)

p 207 (30, 31)

Among the archaeological finds, reflections of this kind of direct Mediterranean influence can also be seen. The motif of an equestrian figure, often holding a lance, found on the pierced bronze decorative discs discovered frequently in Frankish graves, is thought to have been inspired by the equestrian saints so often represented in the Christian East. The famous gold disc-brooch from Pliezhausen is probably derived from similar sources, though in this case, it may have been transmitted through north Italy. A popular type of Burgundian bronze buckle, with a rectangular plate decorated with Christian subjects such as Daniel in the Lions' Den, or pairs of birds facing a central vase, can also be shown to have been derived from well-established East Christian models. The Daniel scene especially looks very similar indeed to a very common type of pottery flask given to pilgrims at the shrine of St Menas near Alexandria, on which St Menas is represented between two camels, who kneel to the saint. The indistinct modelling of these simple flasks could easily have been

p 206, 7 (28, 29, 37-9)

f 5

p 206 (27)

p 206 (26)

Gold disc-brooch from Pliezhausen (7th century). The lancer was probably based on Mediterranean figures of mounted saints, but the protecting war demon and a barbaric vitality give it a wholly Germanic character. (5)

re-interpreted to represent the more popular and better-known subject of Daniel in the Lions' Den. In a series of Christian tombstones carved in the Rhineland in the 7th century, we find a number that show the same strong Eastern influence. Perhaps a stone from Gondorf is the most outstanding example of this trend. Not all the tomb stones show quite so much Mediterranean influence, however. That from Niederdollendorf bears a full length figure, probably intended to represent Christ with rays emanating to form a kind of mandorla—a total halo, with a fragment of interlace below. The representation on the other side, shows the deceased carrying a sword and combing his hair, to symbolize the continuation of the forces of life, while the forces of darkness are shown by two snakes, one double-headed. By his side, his grave goods are indicated by a pilgrim's flask. The mere fact that representational art was attempted at all suggests Mediterranean influence, but, both in content and style, the Germanic elements predominate here.

p 199 (1)

p 207 (34)

p 205 (13)

Craftsmanship in Gold

Much the same creative absorption and adaptation of alien influences can be seen in another category of object popular in the Merovingian kingdom in the 7th century—the large gold disc brooches, this time achieved by Frankish goldsmiths. More than forty such brooches have been found so far, varying in size from about 1½ inches to 3 inches in diameter. They are made of a bronze base, on which the pin is mounted, overlaid by a thin sheet of gold on the front, which is decorated with gold wire filigree and set with gems or glass pastes. The majority of them have been found in the Middle Rhine area, between Bonn and Coblenz.

p 208 (42)

Both in structure and design, this group of brooches differs remarkably from the traditional Germanic brooches. Although their circular form, and the use of filigree combined with symmetrically arranged gems can be found in earlier Frankish brooches, yet their total effect is very different. The quatrefoil shape employed in some of them is a new form, and the settings of gems, in a kind of gold box with a broad frame are a new form for Frankish goldsmiths. Undoubtedly, this form of setting is of Byzantine origin. Also, the fact that circular brooches of somewhat similar design and with filigree—though rarely set with simple, great settings of gems—have been found in Lombard north Italy, especially at Castel Trosino, strongly suggests that these brooches were inspired by influences from that area. Here the Byzantine traditions were firmly rooted in the area around Ravenna, which had been under the direct control of the Byzantine emperors until the later 6th century. However strong the Mediterranean influences were on these brooches, Frankish goldsmiths fully absorbed them and created an unmistakably Frankish type. In two of them, one found at Kärlich, and the other at Kettig, even Germanic animal ornament, consisting of large beaked bird heads, was successfully absorbed into the design. This ornament enables us to date these two brooches to the first half of the 7th century, others are also dated by the contexts in which they were formed to the 7th century. Perhaps the most magnificent example, found at Mölsheim, of quatrefoil shape, and set with a fine Antique cameo gem in the centre, is among the latest of the series. In its severe, precise structure we begin to see elements of the more self-conscious revival of classical forms which might suggest an early Carolingian date

p 209 (45)

p 163 (18)

f 6

p 208 (41)

for the brooch—certainly one must date it well after the year 700.

As a whole, however, these brooches show most strikingly the broadening of the cultural base in the Merovingian kingdom of the 7th century. They illustrate a period in which Frankish craftsmen were no longer restricted to their Germanic heritage, and in which they were able to absorb alien influences, especially those of the Mediterranean world, and re-interpret them creatively.

The Monastic World

In all this we have seen the first effects of the expansion of Frankish art under the influence of the growing wealth in the country as a whole, and in the Church in particular. As has been said before, secular art, or more exactly, the full evidence we gain from the Germanic burial customs, dies out early in the 8th century. But to replace it, we have the development of Christian art, under the patronage of the church, beginning about the middle of the 7th century, and growing rapidly from that time on to dominate the picture we have of art in the Frankish kingdom. We have seen the influence of the Eastern Mediterranean, and we have suggested that it was the result of the close ties that must have existed between the new monastic church in France and the older monasticism of the Eastern Mediterranean that inspired it. Such a monastic culture was to be the basis of post-classical Christian culture in western Europe. It was concerned from the first with far more than only the visual arts—its aim was the preservation of learning in the widest sense. The arts of literature, history, rhetoric, grammar, and astronomy, as well as the study of the scriptures and the writings of the Fathers of the Church were included in its orbit—a culture of far wider and deeper significance than that depending on the merely material riches of court life. This form of monastic culture saw its beginning in northwestern Europe in the period of monastic expansion in the first half of the 7th century. In the far north, in a fusion of the religious zeal of the ascetic Irish monks, with the skill of Germanic craftsmen and with the humanist learning of the classical world introduced into Britain by the Roman mission of St Augustine, a monastic culture was created during the 7th century that stands alone as the greatest single achievement in Europe before the Carolingian Renaissance. This is dealt with in another chapter of this volume.

In a more modest way, however, and at exactly the same time, the Frankish church began to take the first steps towards an understanding of culture in the same, broader sense. Perhaps the most outstanding figure in this cultural expansion—and its very beginning—was Bishop Gregory of Tours, undoubtedly the greatest historian since Roman times. He wrote his 'History of the Franks' up to the year 591 and died in 594, some three years before St Augustine landed in Britain. While in England the great *scriptoria* at Lindisfarne, Monkwearmouth and Jarrow were laying the foundations for their great works at the end of the century, and while the first magnificent high crosses were being carved at Bewcastle and at Ruthwell the Merovingian kingdom saw the earliest manuscripts to have come down to us being written and the remarkable sarcophagi at Jouarre being carved.

p 253 (35)

The Abbey of Notre-Dame of Jouarre had been founded at about AD 630 by Adon, brother of St Ouen. Of the main buildings of the abbey nothing remains, but to the north of them, in the area of the abbey's cemetery, parts of two funerary crypts survive. Nineteenth-century excavations on their site have shown that the crypts, now joined together, were originally the crypts of two churches built alongside each other; that to the north is dedicated to St Paul, the other to St Ebrigisile. The sculptured details of the latter, especially the capitals, look later than the 7th century —a date as late as the 9th century or even 10th century is likely. The marble capitals of the crypt of St Paul, however, belong to a group characteristic of the 7th century, believed to have been the work of a school of sculptors based on Aquitaine. The alterations made at this time to St Jean at Poitiers, a building mentioned earlier, included the addition of a number of very similar marble capitals, while others are known for example at Moissac, St Philibert de Grandlieu, St Denis and St Pierre de Montmartre (Paris). The vaulting of the roof of the present crypt is of course of later

p 210 (47)

date, although the disposition of the original columns makes it clear that a groined vault must have been part of the original structure. The west wall, with its very fine diaper patterns in carefully cut stone, interrupted by slim buttresses or wall arcading, may also well be part of the original late 7th-century building. Such masonry would certainly confirm the Venerable Bede's high opinion of the skill of Frankish masons.

p 210
(46)

Brother and Sister: the Coffins of Jouarre

In addition to the unique fragments of 7th-century architecture at Jouarre, the crypt contains a number of stone sarcophagi, at least two of which are of outstanding interest. The earlier of the two is the coffin of the first Abbess of Jouarre, Theodochilde, the niece of the founder who died soon after AD 662. Both sides of the sarcophagus are decorated with two rows of crisply carved seashells, with three lines of beautifully cut inscription above, between and below these rows. The steep ridge roof now on the sarcophagus, once decorated with splendid large circles of foliate scrolls of very different character, is in a poor state of preservation, which suggests that it must at some time have been separated from the tomb. Although the decoration of this coffin, especially the shells on its sides, are no doubt fundamentally of late Roman and probably Eastern origin, nothing that can account for the remarkable design of this sarcophagus as a whole has ever been put forward. But the broad, flat bands with inscription remind one somewhat of the similar inscribed broad flat frames around the figure sculpture of the Ruthwell Cross in Britain—a work of almost exactly the same time. The rather thick and simplified figure sculpture of the same cross should also be compared to a very similar treatment of the figure in relief on the second sarcophagus at Jouarre, that of Bishop Agilbert, who died probably soon after his retirement to Jouarre in 685. Agilbert, of Frankish birth and a brother of Theodochilde, is known to have gone to Britain and preached in Wessex about the year 650. He later became Bishop of the West-Saxons at Winchester, and took part in the famous Synod of Whitby in 664. Here he and Bishop Wilfred led the party that supported the Roman faction in the Anglo-Saxon Church against the Irish party in the dispute about the annual fixing of the date of Easter. Later, he returned to France and became Bishop of Paris in 668.

p 210
(47)

p 210
(48)

His sarcophagus is even more remarkable than that of his sister Theodochilde. On its long side, which decreases in height from the head-end, is a seated figure of Christ on a throne holding an unfurled scroll in his left hand. To each side of him a number of standing figures are carved, their arms raised in the early Christian pose of prayer. The damaged condition of the sculpture makes it difficult to be certain, but there seem to be six such figures on each side, probably representing the choir of the Apostles flanking the Throne. At the head of the coffin, invisible in its present position in a cramped niche of the crypt, a Christ in Majesty is known to be carved, in a mandorla supported by the four apocalyptic symbols of the Evangelists—the angel of St Matthew, the eagle of St John, the lion of St Mark and the bull of St Luke. The particular form of this composition, in which the symbols seem to be half hidden behind the mandorla, again points to East Christian models, where it appears both in Egypt in the 6th- to 7th-century wallpainting at Bawit and in the apse mosaic of the church of Hosios David at Thessalonica, a Byzantine church of the 5th century.

Merovingian Manuscripts—the Unique Synthesis

One of the earliest manuscripts to survive from the Frankish kingdom is now preserved in the Cathedral library of Cologne (No. 212). It was probably written in the south of France, perhaps at Lyons towards the middle of the 7th century—almost exactly contemporary with the earliest Northumbrian manuscripts to have come down to us. But whereas the northern manuscripts of that period are largely decorated with patterns taken directly from the Germanic goldsmith's workshops, together with some that reflect earlier Irish traditions, the Frankish manuscript draws entirely on late Roman motifs and contemporary Eastern ornament. The small bird pecking at a bunch of grapes incorporated into the initial 'D' on folio 123 B, could inhabit almost any

Gold disc-brooch from Kärlich (7th century), showing the marriage of Mediterranean and Germanic elements in Frankish craftsmanship. Along the edge are fragmented birds' heads (face and beak); it is set with garnets and glass-pastes. (6)

East Mediterranean work of decorative art, whether in stone, mosaic or painting. But it was not until the first half of the 8th century that Merovingian illumination was fully to develop its characteristic style. The colours of this style are bright and gay, its drawing lively and rapid, almost part of the written word on the page rather than a decorative addition. The illuminators made extensive use of the compass and the ruler to create their patterns. Human figures appear rarely, but animals, birds and especially fishes, often used to contruct the larger lettering itself, were spread in rich profusion over the pages. What at first sight often seems to be crude and barbaric, is in fact in its total effect handled with dash and skill and achieves a kind of sophisticated, brittle elegance. We can study this style in the 'Gothic Missal' in the Vatican library (Reg. 317) of about AD 700 probably from the monastery of Luxeuil; in the 'Chronicle of Fredegar' in the National Library of Paris (lat. 10910) of about AD 715, probably painted in eastern France; in the Sacramentary of Gelasianum, written about 750 near Paris, perhaps at Chelles, and now in the Vatican Library (Reg. Cat. 316); and in the 'Gudhinus gospels' now in the Town Library at Autun (MS 3), written at Fleury between 751 and 754. The origins of this singular style, so different from the perfection and precision of the Germanic ornament that controls much of the Anglo-Saxon style of the period, has aroused much controversy among students. Most commonly, scholars point to Coptic and Armenian manuscripts, where a very similar vocabulary of forms is to be found—although all the books that can be cited are later in date than the 8th century. Scholars who adhere to this thesis have to argue that earlier books in this style existed in the East, but have not survived. Others claim that the style was first developed in the Merovingian kingdom itself. Whatever the truth may be, the parts that make up the forms of Merovingian illumination are undoubtedly derived from the broad stream of Eastern influences to which we have constantly to refer—mixed in the manuscripts with much that is derived from the Lombard art of north Italy. In the figure style in particular, Italy may well have provided the most important sources. We need only compare the drawing of a 'Christ in Majesty' in the Fredegar manuscript in Paris, with the stone altar carved at Cividale between 737 and 744, to be convinced of this. Another element that points to Italy is to be found in a book attributed to the *scriptorium* of Laon, now in Paris (lat. 12168), dating from about AD 770. On folio Cb, the two columns that support the arch are carried on the backs of lions—an architectural form derived from classical antiquity that was so well known in Italy that it led to a revival of it in the architecture of the Romanesque period there. It should be mentioned too, that the animals on this page with interlaced legs and tails, show that Anglo-Saxon illumination was not unknown at Laon either. Merovingian illumination continued well on into the later 8th century. In the ornamental details employed in some schools, in Tours, for example, under the great British scholar Alcuin, it even lasted on into the Carolingian period of the early 9th century, in spite of the great and very different schools of illumination created by the patronage of the Emperor Charlemagne in the late 8th century.

p 204-5
(16-21)

p 204
(16)

p 166
(27)

p 205
(19)

p 281
(22)

p 282
(25)

The Relics of the Saints

The monastic workshops of the early 8th century also produced works of art other than illuminated manuscripts. The techniques learned in the development of secular goldsmith's work, and

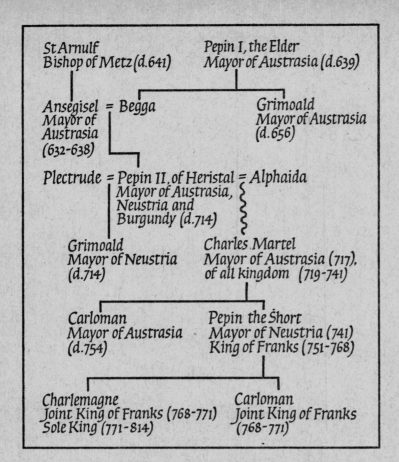

St Arnulf
Bishop of Metz (d.641)

Pepin I, the Elder
Mayor of Austrasia (d.639)

Ansegisel = Begga
Mayor of
Austrasia
(632-638)

Grimoald
Mayor of Austrasia
(d.656)

Plectrude = Pepin II, of Heristal = Alphaida
Mayor of Austrasia,
Neustria and
Burgundy (d.714)

Grimoald
Mayor of Neustria
(d.714)

Charles Martel
Mayor of Austrasia (717),
of all kingdom (719-741)

Carloman
Mayor of Austrasia
(d.754)

Pepin the Short
Mayor of Neustria (741)
King of Franks (751-768)

Charlemagne
Joint King of Franks (768-771)
Sole King (771-814)

Carloman
Joint King of Franks
(768-771)

Mayors of the Palace and ancestors of Charlemagne. Pepin I, under the Merovingian Kings Charles II and his son Dagobert I, was the first of the great Mayors of the Palace, the virtual rulers of the Frankish kingdom. With Pepin the Short's deposition of Childeric II in 751 the Merovingian dynasty came to an end and the Carolingian began. (7)

p 208
(40)
perfected in such jewellery as the Wittislingen fibula, began to be put at the service of the church. Altar vessels, covers decorated in gold, silver and jewels for the fine illuminated books, altar frontals and reliquaries were made to glorify and decorate the House of God, but practically nothing survives.

The great increase in the popularity of relics, especially among the Irish missionaries, resulted in the production of great quantities of precious reliquaries to house the sacred remains. Few though they are in number, more of these have come down to us because the reverence they commanded tended to improve their chances of survival. Probably the finest among them, is the reliquary donated by the priest Theuderich to the church of
p 209
(45)
St Maurice d'Agaune in southern Switzerland. The donation is recorded in an inscription on the back of the little shrine, which is fitted with hinged strap ends on the sides to enable it to be carried on a leather strap. Larger gem-stones and late Antique intaglio gems are attached to the surface in settings of the kind we have found on the disc brooches discussed earlier. In the centre of the front of the reliquary is mounted a glass paste cameo in classical taste, of a kind that has been shown to be of north Italian origin and of the 8th century. Although this type of reliquary is normally described as 'house-shaped' it would be more correct to see the origin of this shape in the kind of sarcophagi we have seen at Jouarre—a miniature funerary monument in which sacred relics of a saint were laid to rest. The style of the inlaid decoration would seem to be quite in keeping with 8th-century jewellery found in the Alemannic area of the Frankish kingdom in which the Abbey of St Maurice is situated, although some scholars have preferred an attribution of this reliquary to a Burgundian workshop.

Another small reliquary of very similar type was found on the
p 209
(44)
River Rhine near Nymegen and is now preserved in the Archbishop's Museum at Utrecht. It is difficult to say where in the Frankish Kingdom these reliquaries might have been made. The knowledge of both Germanic animal ornament and Byzantine ornament—the latter probably filtered into the Frankish area through north Italy—was available in most parts of the kingdom.

In the nature of their ornament these reliquaries show clearly that the craftsmen who had been responsible for the secular buckles, strap-ends and brooches were beginning to be drawn into the service of the Church. Indeed, the Church was drawing mainly on the styles available in secular Germanic art, but in a small shrine of St Mummole in the abbey church of Fleury (St Benoît-sur-Loire), decoration far closer to the East-Christian styles we have seen in the manuscripts, is employed. Linked rosettes appear below, some filled with equal-armed crosses, while on the steep roof a row of six standing figures, probably Apostles, appear under an arcade. The resemblance this decoration bears to manuscript illumination of the early 8th century shows that the other monastic arts were now beginning to turn to similar East Christian sources. The large reliquary casket, decorated with pierced and carved bone plaques preserved in the
p 207
(36)
church at Werden, near Essen, although not as closely linked with manuscript art as the Fleury reliquary, and much altered in the composition of its decorative panels, again shows the growing importance of a Christian art.

King Pepin the Short

In the early 8th century the pace of the development of a Christian culture in western Europe gathered speed and grew in significance. St Willibrord, the Anglo-Saxon missionary, had begun his work in the eastern lands of Frisia some ten years earlier. In 695 he founded the bishopric of Utrecht and two years later the monastery of Echternach was founded by Plectrude, wife of Pepin II, and Regent after his death in 714.

The 720s were the years of St Boniface's mission to the German tribes east of the Rhine. About 732 Pope Gregory III made him Archbishop of Mainz, and in the early 740s he not only founded the Abbey of Fulda, well east of the Rhine, but also began the re-organization and reform of the whole Frankish church which resulted in the acceptance of the more liberal Benedictine rule in most of the kingdoms' monasteries—a strong stimulus to cultural activity.

The coronation of Pepin, with the Pope's blessing, as legal King of the Franks marks a distinct break with the Merovingian age and a preparation for that of Charlemagne. The contrast between the Mayors of the Palace and the nominal, 'do-nothing' sovereigns had its parallel in the position of the popes *vis-à-vis* the emperor at Byzantium. As Charles Martel had always to invoke the authority of his shadow-king, so the popes continued to date their edicts by the regnal year of the Byzantine emperor, although since the iconoclastic controversy they had ceased to admit any obedience to him. In a sense the coronation of Pepin in 751 foreshadowed that of Charlemagne in 800. Both were stages towards a new orientation of western society and a new conception of Church and state.

Pepin reigned from 751 to 768. He strengthened and extended
f 7
the gains won by his father against the Moors and the Saxons, and he did much to build the new Christian church of Germany. In the winter of 753-4 Pope Stephen, threatened by the Lombards and more or less abandoned by the Emperor, came personally to Pepin, who was living in his villa on the Marne (among those sent to him was Pepin's younger son Charles, then a boy of eleven). The result of their discussion was a Frankish guarantee of the Pope's dominions in Italy, and the conferring upon Pepin of the title 'Patrician of the Romans'. It was probably at about this time also that the forged 'Donation of Constantine', the justification for the pope's temporal rule, first made its appearance. In this, as in so much else, the events of Pepin's reign provide the key to the later pattern of history.

Pepin invaded Italy in 755 and 756 and without undue hardship forced the Lombard king to acknowledge him as his overlord. He was also active at home, re-organizing the Church and adding Aquitaine finally to his kingdom. If he left other problems—Brittany, Saxony, Bavaria, Italy, the status of the papacy—for his sons to face, it is still true to say that the policy which Charlemagne so triumphantly carried out was conceived by Pepin. His achievements would certainly shine brighter were they not overshadowed by the transformation of the old kingdom of the Franks into the new 'Holy Roman Empire'.

XI FROM THE VIGOROUS NORTH

The Norsemen and their forerunners

DAVID M. WILSON

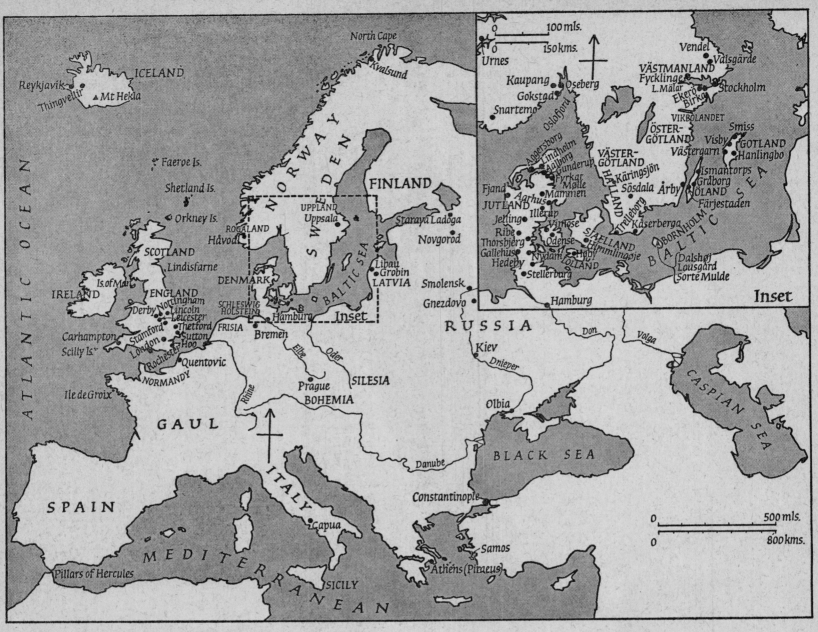

Scandinavia and areas penetrated by the Norsemen

'Out of the north

an evil shall break forth upon all the inhabitants of the land.'
When Alcuin, the great scholar of York, quoted this verse from
Jeremiah he was in no doubt that it referred to the coming of the
Norsemen. 'We and our forefathers have lived here for 350 years',
he wrote, 'and never have terrors like these appeared in Britain;
it was not thought possible that such havoc should be made.'
This view of the Norsemen may still colour our feelings towards
them, for it was also to some extent their own. Their heroes were
men of action, warriors and conquerors; the virtues they celebrated were courage and skill in war; and when a great chieftain
died it was by his weapons and armour, his sword, shield and
helmet, that he was most worthily remembered.

At the end of the 7th century such a warrior was buried at
Vendel in central Sweden. In the grave with him were placed two
of his swords with iron blades and richly decorated bronze hilts;
innumerable clasps, plates, buckles and trappings from equipment
and harness; an iron axe, arrow- and spear-heads; and—a rarity
in the northern kingdoms—the grim iron helmet shown opposite.
The ornamental parts are bronze. Over the eyes are two guards
marked with a series of triple grooves, a stylization of eyebrows.
They end in fantastic animal or bird heads. The bronze crest,
which has similar grooved markings, ends between the eyes with
the bearded head of a man. Around the edge was a row of repoussée panels, one of which remains, showing a mounted warrior

armed with a spear and round shield attacking a serpent; two
birds fly close to his head, an indication that this is Odin, the King
of the gods, with his two ravens.

The earliest migrations from Scandinavia were a curtain-raiser
for the devastating Viking raids of the 8th and 9th centuries, and
it was usually after such raids that groups of Vikings established
permanent settlements abroad. Their reputation for piracy and
destructiveness is therefore not so surprising, although their
culture itself was in many ways as sophisticated as that of the
lands they ravaged. In Dark Age Europe as a whole they stand
out for the sheer scale of their exploits. They conquered large
parts of Britain, Normandy, Sicily and Russia; they maintained
trading contacts with Byzantium, Persia and India; they discovered and colonized Iceland and Greenland and touched upon the
coasts of North America itself. And in the end, despite the fore-
bodings of Alcuin and almost every thoughtful man of the time,
they did not destroy Western civilization, but enriched it. Parts
of their legal system, their tradition of individual freedom, their
restless urge to explore the limits of the known world and (not
least) the great saga-literature of medieval Iceland which re-
creates this heroic age as no other record or relic can, have all
gone to form a living part of our tradition—that non-Roman,
non-Latin, non-Mediterranean element which still lies deep in
the consciousness of those who live in northern Europe. (1)

The bleak Scandinavian homelands, Norway, Sweden and Denmark, hap little that promised security or high civilization. Until the end of the 1st millennium there were no towns, no stone buildings, no churches, no books. Communication except by sea was hazardous and life for the bulk of the population consisted of peasant farming, together with a little trade. Only those who sought their fortune abroad were likely to grow rich.

The model (right) reconstructs a typical house of the 3rd century AD, a type which changed little with the years. The floor level would probably be slightly lower than the ground outside. The bottom of the wall was stone, the upper part wattle and daub. The roof rested on a double row of posts, and if a fire was needed the smoke escaped through a hole in it. The house was one big room, shared by men, women, children and animals. (2)

Military camps dating from the great age of Viking expansion tell of growing social cohesion and discipline. Trelleborg (above) could have housed 1200 men. It was surrounded by a circular rampart. Inside the circle were sixteen long-houses arranged in squares, and another thirteen outside. Stellerburg (below), a defended village in the south of old Denmark, reflects the necessity for the defence of even the smallest unit in those troubled times. (3, 4)

Clothes worn by warriors of the Migration period have been recovered from graves. These trousers and long-sleeved tunic are of wool, the trousers being sewn at the bottom into short stockings. Leather and fur were also used and there are traces of linen and silk. Below: a silver gilt brooch, part of the dress of a wealthy Viking, together with some late Roman coins found with it in a grave at Dalshøj, Bornholm. (5, 6, 7)

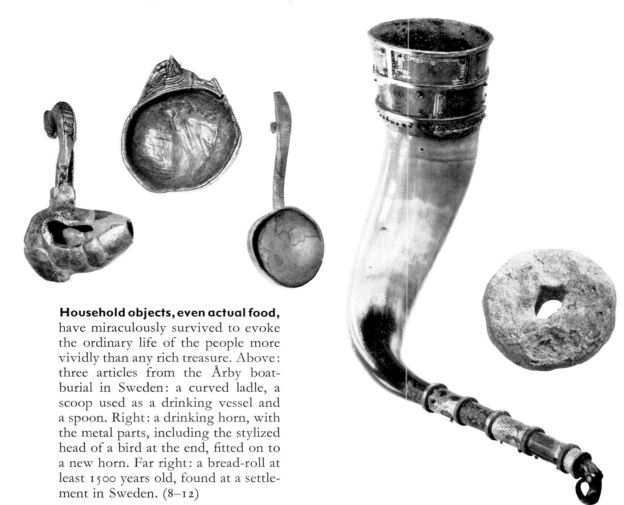

Household objects, even actual food, have miraculously survived to evoke the ordinary life of the people more vividly than any rich treasure. Above: three articles from the Årby boat-burial in Sweden: a curved ladle, a scoop used as a drinking vessel and a spoon. Right: a drinking horn, with the metal parts, including the stylized head of a bird at the end, fitted on to a new horn. Far right: a bread-roll at least 1500 years old, found at a settlement in Sweden. (8–12)

The Norse gods yielded to Christianity during the 10th century, but many of the old customs and symbols persisted under the new religion. The small amulet of Thor's Hammer (top) may be compared with the crucifix below it, the oldest known from Scandinavia. Both date from the 10th century, both are made in the same delicate repoussée and filigree style, and both probably reflect not dissimilar beliefs in supernatural protection. The Jelling stone (above right), a large roughly three-sided boulder carved with relief scenes including the crucifixion, was raised by King Harald, who (runs the Runic inscription) 'won for himself all Denmark and Norway and converted Denmark to Christianity'. (13, 14, 15)

It was the sea

that brought life, wealth and fame to the Norsemen, and their more than mundane concern for navigation and ships goes back to a very early period. Ships were often buried as offerings for the gods, to lie hermetically sealed in the heavy Danish clay for centuries. Among the most complete is that of Nydam (below; model below right), dating from the Roman Iron Age. Seventy feet long, it is made of oak and was propelled by 30 oars, 15 each side. Sails were not used until the Viking period, when they can be studied in some detail from inscribed stones, such as that from Smiss (right). A complicated array of ropes secures or furls the sail, which carries a pattern of intersecting diagonals. (16, 17, 18)

The ship of the dead, carrying the soul 'far away into the ocean' was part of ancient Scandinavian belief, and probably explains the ships carved on gravestones. Sometimes a burial would be outlined with stones in the shape of a ship (below), increasing in height towards the bow and stern. (19)

Burial inside a ship was the logical end of this mystic sea-ritual. Among the most splendid to have survived is the Oseberg ship (below), which included not only the ship itself but all its equipment, a wagon, four sledges, beds, chest, buckets and innumerable articles of daily life. (20)

On the arching prow of the Oseberg ship, one of the masterpieces of Viking art, the sculptor carved lines of interlaced animal forms ending in a serpent's head. Dating from the 9th century, the 'Oseberg style' is the creation of several different artists. The boat, which was probably the king's own ship regularly used for his voyages, was the burial place of a princess. Her body, together with that of an attendant, lay in the midst, surrounded by sacrificed horses, dogs and oxen. (23)

The art of the shipbuilders reached a level that has scarcely been surpassed. The Gokstad ship (above and below) is over 72 feet long, with a beam of 17 feet, yet its draught is only 3 feet and the planks at the bottom are less than 1 inch thick. The rudder was at the side, not the stern. In 1893 a replica of this boat crossed the Atlantic. (21, 22)

Luxuries from abroad

were among the most prized possessions of the Scandinavians, and the numbers that have survived prove the success both of their trading missions to the south and their raiding parties on the coasts of northern France and Germany. (The main trade-routes are shown on the fold-out map opposite). On these two pages it is possible to contrast the accomplished elegance of these southern imports with the much more vital and vigorous style that continued at home almost entirely uninfluenced by it.

For the northern market Roman merchants and artists produced glassware intended to appeal to local tastes, and even precise orders were carried out for Scandinavian patrons. Of the three glass cups (below) the largest, with the bull, dates from about AD 200, the other two from a century later. (25)

A Roman drinking service found at Hoby in Denmark included two very fine silver cups with relief scenes of the *Iliad*, a dish showing Venus and Cupids and this graceful bronze jug (left) with Cupid drawing his bow. The cups were engraved with the name of the owner, 'Silius'—probably the man known to have been envoy at Mainz between AD 14 and 21. The vessels could have been a diplomatic gift, or they may have been acquired by less peaceful means. (24)

The magnificent sword-hilt from ▶ Snartemo is described overleaf on p. 230. (29)

'To Apollo Grannus this gift is offered by the benefactor of the temple, Ammilius Constans'. How did a silver and copper vase of about AD 100, with this pious Latin inscription (below), find its way to a remote grave at Fycklinge in Sweden? (26)

Contact with Russia had been early established. This bronze situla from Havor, in Gotland, contained several skillets, bells, and a gold neck-ring which must have come from south Russia. In later centuries the great rivers of Russia were highways of Norse trade, and it was Viking settlers who founded the kingdoms of Novgorod and Kiev. (27)

The favourite weapon of Europe in the 1st millennium was the sword, and upon it much wealth and craftsmanship was lavished. The beautiful Snartemo sword (left), dating from about the end of the 6th century, is decorated in a sophisticated style based originally on animal forms; but by now these have become so dismembered and distorted as to be barely recognizable. The silver pommel consists of two insect-like creatures with long beaks facing each other, and the two cross-pieces are carved (in the technique called 'chip carving' in which facets at varying angles catch and reflect the light) into tendrils. Between them, the grip of the hilt is fitted with gold plates in which inextricably twisted animal shapes can just be discerned. (29)

A complete cart from the Oseberg ship was one of the most remarkable discoveries ever made in Norse archaeology. It is solidly built, with four heavy wheels and a central rib. From other evidence it appears that carts were in use in the Scandinavian lowlands, though serviceable roads must have been few. The sides of the Oseberg carriage are carved with mythological scenes, the style of the ends differing markedly from that of the long sides. The two curved cross-pieces supporting the body of the cart end in human heads, one of which is shown on the right; some scholars have seen in them portraits of old chieftains. (30, 31)

The voyage of Ohthere in the mid-9th century: he gives our earliest account of the White Sea.

To Greenland, colonized from Iceland by Eirik the Red. In 986 twenty-five ships filled with immigrants are said to have sailed for Greenland: only fourteen arrived.

Iceland: silver brooch of the 11th century. Norse emigration to Iceland took place mainly in the years before and after AD 900.

Ireland: bronze ornament found in Norway, probably seized as loot during a raid.

Middleton, Yorkshire: cross from a Viking grave, mid-10th century.

tombstone from Old St Paul's churchyard, dating from the reign of Canute.

London:

Kaupang

Birka

BALTIC SEA

Grobin

Hedeby

Lower Rhine: glass beakers and pottery; the large jug has a pattern inlaid with tin. Found at Birka.

Noirmoutier

Ile de Groix, Brittany: reconstruction of a Viking ship found in a burial mound. The 'dragon's tail' at the stern balances the head at the bow.

Rhine

Carolingian Empire: gold buckle, for joining three straps, 9th century. Found in a hoard in Norway.

Prague: Scandinavian sword of the 10th century, known as 'the sword of St Stephen'.

Kama region 9th century. Found in a [ ] Gotland.

Danub[ ]

MEDITERRANEAN

Viking trade and exploration. This map shows the main trade routes by land and sea, and the trading centres that grew up along them. Some of the imports from southern Europe and Asia are illustrated in their places of origin; all were brought to Scandinavia, where they were found in graves or the remains of trading settlements (*captions in italic*). The Vikings also left traces of their journeyings in other parts of the world, often in places they had originally visited as raiders (captions in Roman type).

Staraya Ladoga

Novgorod

Bulgar

Dnieper Gnezdovo:
Scandinavian brooch of the 10th century.

Sestovitsy, Ukraine:
horn mountings from a saddle.

ARAL SEA

Kiev

Don

Itil

*Kashmir:
statuette of
Buddha sitting on a lotus,
6th or 7th century.
Found at Helgö,
Sweden.*

: silver arm rings,

oard at Arsarve,

Olbia

C A S P I A N   S E A

B L A C K   S E A

thens:
arble lion bearing a Runic inscription,
rved there by a 'Varangian'
the service of the Byzantine Emperor.
e lion is now in Venice.

Constantinople

*Samarkand:
Arabic silver coin,
AD 903. More than 20,000
Muslim coins have
been found in Sweden.*

*Near East: censer of Persian type.
Found at Birka, Sweden.*

Baghdad

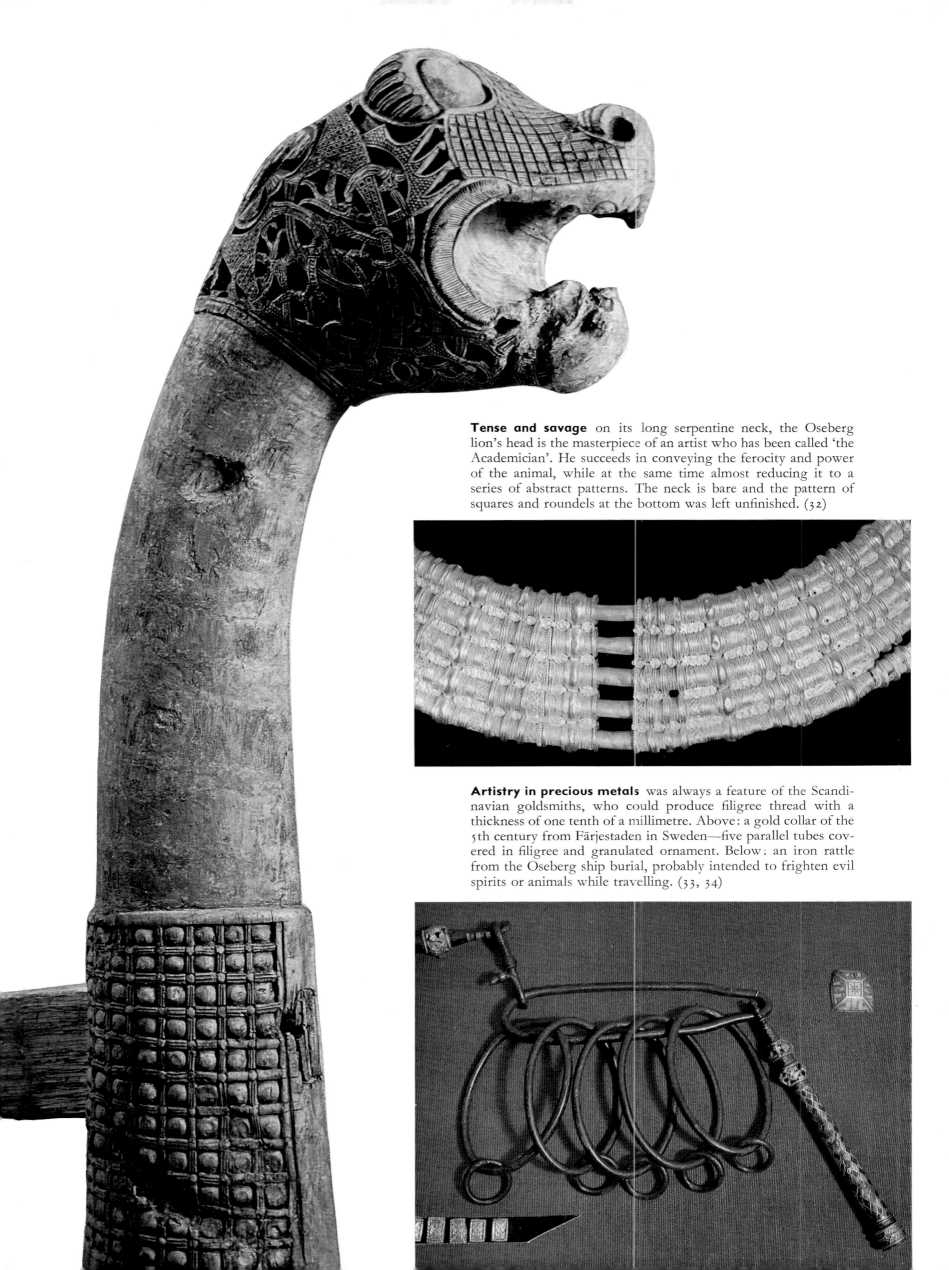

Tense and savage on its long serpentine neck, the Oseberg lion's head is the masterpiece of an artist who has been called 'the Academician'. He succeeds in conveying the ferocity and power of the animal, while at the same time almost reducing it to a series of abstract patterns. The neck is bare and the pattern of squares and roundels at the bottom was left unfinished. (32)

Artistry in precious metals was always a feature of the Scandinavian goldsmiths, who could produce filigree thread with a thickness of one tenth of a millimetre. Above: a gold collar of the 5th century from Färjestaden in Sweden—five parallel tubes covered in filigree and granulated ornament. Below: an iron rattle from the Oseberg ship burial, probably intended to frighten evil spirits or animals while travelling. (33, 34)

The first parliament

of which we have record since classical times met on the sacred ground of Thingvellir, near the west coast of Iceland (right). The custom of settling disputes and passing laws at assemblies of land-owners can be traced far back in the history of the Norsemen. In Scandinavia, however, these assemblies were under the direction of a king. In Iceland there was no king. Local meetings ('Things') took place every few months, but once a year, in June, during a special period of truce, every landowner on the island came to Thingvellir for the Great Assembly ('Althing'). It was sacrilege to violate the truce or to molest anyone on his way to or from it. Here issues of general interest were debated, private feuds ended and wrong-doers could be punished by outlawry, banishment or fines. It was a combination of parliament and high-court and in some ways resembled a body like the United Nations, since although it could pass sentence there were no means except public opinion by which its decisions could be enforced. Much of the time, too, was spent in private lobbying; every 'Thingman' set up his hut or booth where he could receive visits, canvassing for or promising support, making concessions and assessing popular feeling. This painting by the great Norse scholar W. G. Collingwood, who visited the spot with William Morris, expresses the informal atmosphere of the sessions, as well as the grandeur of their natural setting.

The Viking type of parliament survives to this day in the old Viking colony of the Isle of Man, where the laws are still promulgated every midsummer day on Tynwald Hill (below). (35, 37)

An unbroken tradition of 1000 years links the Isle of Man with the Vikings. Their first raid took place in 798; colonization followed in the 10th century. The cross of Kirk Michael (left) was set up about 950 by a craftsman called Gaut. It combines the traditional Celtic form of the Manx cross with a Norse runic inscription reading 'Mael Brigde, son of Athakan the smith, erected this cross for his own soul and that of his brother's wife. Gaut made this and all in Man'. (36)

Unique, uncompromising, unmistakable,
the art of the Norsemen is the product of a consistent evolution owing little to the Carolingian models which lay so close to it. Three of its main stages can be seen here. The gilt bronze harness-mount set with garnets (right) is the earliest, 7th century. The garnets form two eyes; but at the same time they are part of two separate animals that are almost impossible to disentangle. (39)

The Viking Age (9th–10th century) produced restless interlacing forms on a flat surface. The ceremonial axe-head (left), inlaid with gold and silver, is one of the finest examples. Finally the animal style lived again briefly in the earliest stave-churches. At Urnes (below) smooth sinuous creatures and convoluted dragons lose themselves in a coiling tracery of tendrils. (38, 40)

The Norsemen and their forerunners

DAVID M. WILSON

'IN A WORD, although there were an hundred hard-steeled iron heads on one neck, and an hundred sharp, ready, cool, never-rusting, brazen tongues in each head, and an hundred garrulous, loud, unceasing voices from each tongue, they could not recount or narrate or enumerate or tell, what all the Irish suffered in common, both men and women, laity and clergy, old and young, noble and ignoble, of hardships and of injuring and of oppression, in every house, from those valiant, wrathful, purely-pagan people.'

This hyperbolic passage from an Irish saga-writer of the 12th century summarizes the impression which the Vikings made on the western European mind. Wild statements of this sort have coloured all discussion of the great Viking adventure which brought Scandinavia for the first time into real contact with the rest of the known world. The story to be told here is of the gradual rise of an empire which, at the beginning of the 11th century, stretched from North Cape to the Isles of Scilly.

During the greater part of the 1st millennium of our era Scandinavia was both pagan and illiterate. The written history of the North depends, therefore, on such fulminations of foreign clerical pamphleteers as that quoted at the beginning of this chapter, on casual references in the general literature of European, Arab and Asian writers and on the large body of material, known as sagas, which were first written down—mainly in Iceland—in the 13th and 14th centuries, many hundred years after the events they claim to record. Such doubtful sources conspire to make it extremely difficult to sketch a consecutive history of this period in northern Europe: only a few patches of Scandinavian history can be illuminated by means of documentary sources—for the rest we rely on the abundant archaeological remains.

The first written records of Scandinavia are to be found in the works of Greek writers of the 3rd to 1st centuries BC. Strabo, Pliny, Pomponius Mela and others record that a distinguished merchant-geographer, named Pytheas, sailed in the late 4th century BC to a land called Thule, six days north of Shetland. As Iceland was, at this time, uninhabited, it seems extremely probable that the land described by Pytheas was Norway, for he discusses the people of this misty land in some detail, though at second hand. They had few cattle, but grew rye and manufactured an alcoholic drink which was probably mead. From the days of Pytheas onwards classical writers mentioned in passing various parts of Scandinavia—Pliny, Tacitus and Ptolemy each in turn describe in some detail the people who lived in Scandinavia, and particularly in Denmark, during the early centuries of our era. Tacitus, for example, mentions the Suiones, who were apparently the Sviar, or Swedes, of the powerful kingdom of central Sweden, the Finns and a number of other tribes who cannot nowadays be identified with any certainty. Ptolemy mentioned rather more tribes, particularly in Jutland and south Scandinavia including a tribe known as the Goutoi, who are almost certainly the Gautar—the Geatas of the Anglo-Saxon epic Beowulf.

The Tribesmen Look South

For the centuries when Rome dominated Europe, up to c. AD 400, archaeology supplies the most important evidence of life in Scandinavia. This period has been called, by archaeologists, the Roman Iron Age, and rightly so, for the contacts with the Roman world are the most obtrusive elements in the archaeology of southern Scandinavia. The constant wars with the Celtic and Germanic tribes, including a powerful invasion by two tribes of Danish origin, the Cimbri and the Teutoni, had caused the Romans to set up along the borders of their empire a string of fortifications and client states which, together with the strong tendency to internecine war among the Celtic and Germanic tribes to the east and north of this frontier, successfully checked any major invasion of the Roman Empire for many years. It was during this period that a considerable trade seems to have sprung up between the northern countries and the Roman lands to the south. This was not altogether a new thing for since the early Bronze Age there had been important trading connections between the Baltic lands and the Mediterranean, but now the volume of trade, if we are to judge from the archaeological remains, increased considerably.

Most of the imported objects come from grave finds and it is a fortunate coincidence that at this period, in certain parts of Scandinavia at least, the rite of inhumation gradually replaced cremation. We cannot be sure of the reason for this basic change in ritual, it may be due to contact with the religion of the peoples of Silesia and central Europe, but the new rite enables archaeologists to gain a more complete view of the material culture and of the economy of the Scandinavian people. This innovation was not universal, however, for cremation and inhumation burials occasionally occur alongside each other, while cremation was particularly favoured in Norway and on Danish Bornholm. The Roman objects found in the inhumation graves are mainly imported luxury goods—bronze vessels, glass bowls, brooches, the stamped red Samian ware (terra sigillata) and the occasional classical bronze figure.

p 226
(24–26)

Some of these objects reached Scandinavia by trade routes which were apparently controlled by the Marcomanni, who acted as middlemen between the Celts and Scandinavians and the Romans. The Marcomanni inhabited the Bohemian area of modern Czechoslovakia and merchants passed through their territory along the Elbe and the Oder to the Baltic and Scandinavia. To a lesser extent there was a trading connection from the mouth of the Rhine along the Dutch coast to the western seaboard of Scandinavia, a route demonstrated archaeologically by finds of Roman coins—particularly denarii. The Roman imports found in the Scandinavian graves are, of course, but fossils of a considerable trade; more perishable goods also came from the South —silks and other textiles, for example, and almost certainly wine, for the inhabitants of these cold northern countries had a considerable interest in alcohol as is attested by the large number of drinking vessels, in particular horns, found in their graves. Richer members of the community would presumably have been only too pleased to supplement the more barbaric drinks of mead, cider and beer with an imported Mediterranean wine.

In return the Scandinavians probably exported goods of the type for which we have documentary evidence at a later period— furs, skins, ropes of seal-skin, dairy produce and even cattle. A popular Scandinavian export in both prehistoric and historic times was Baltic amber, a substance which fetched high prices in the countries of the Western Mediterranean. Slaves were also probably sent from Scandinavia to the lands of the South.

From the Roman World—Luxury and Loot

But it is, naturally, the luxury trade which makes the most considerable impact on the modern eye. Although the perishable goods have disappeared there are, in the Scandinavian graves, such extraordinary testimonies to the far-flung trading connections of the period as the Danish grave-find of Hoby, on the island of Lolland. Chief among the objects buried in this grave are two silver beakers of remarkable quality made by a Greek craftsman—Cheirisophos—who must have been active in Rome in the 1st century AD. The grave also contained a skillet made in Capua and two bronze vessels of exceptionally high quality.

p 226
(24)

These objects are among the finest Roman products found in Scandinavia, but objects only slightly less impressive are found in graves and bogs throughout Denmark, in south and central Sweden—particularly in the rich areas of Uppland and Gotland—and, to a lesser extent, in Norway. At Fycklinge in Västmanland in central Sweden, for example, was found a most impressive bronze vessel, some 50 centimetres high. It is decorated in silver and copper and is inscribed 'to Apollo Grannus this gift is offered by the benefactor of the temple, Ammilius Constans'. Two splendid glass vessels from Himmlingøje, Sjælland (Zealand), one of which is decorated with a splendidly coloured leopard, similarly witness to the taste of Scandinavians for Roman luxury articles—whether they were simply loot or whether they came by way of trade or as diplomatic gifts.

p 226
(26)

p 226
(25)

The character of the import trade changed towards the end of the 2nd century, presumably when the Marcomannic kingdom was destroyed after their attack on the Danubian frontier of the Roman Empire in 165. From this year forward the quality of the goods imported from the Roman world declined considerably, as the axis of trade shifted from east to west. Roman objects found in Scandinavia after this date were mostly made in the Roman province of Gaul.

Throughout the 1st millennium there was a considerable contact between the East Mediterranean and Sweden by way of Russia and the rivers of eastern Europe. During the Roman Iron Age such contacts are not easily traced, but there can be little doubt that they existed. The Goths, an erstwhile Scandinavian tribe, were gradually advancing southwards out of Russia towards the Mediterranean and one may presume that a certain amount of the imported material of Mediterranean origin found in eastern Scandinavia came there by way of the Russian route to the Black Sea. More than five thousand *denarii*, spanning the whole of the Roman period, have been found on the Swedish island of Gotland. These coins can only have come to Scandinavia by way of the Gothic kingdoms established in south Russia, particularly after the consolidation of the conquest of Olbia in 236. Recent studies have demonstrated that it is difficult to differentiate between the routes, eastern and western, by which many southern imports reached Scandinavia in the Roman Iron Age; but a lively eastern contact must have existed, as is demonstrated by the 3rd-century find from Havor, Hablingbo, Gotland, excavated in 1961, which produced a bronze situla, five skillets, two bronze bells and a gold neck ring with filigree terminals which is of undoubted south Russian origin.

p 226
(27)

Swords and Ploughshares

But what of the indigenous culture of the Roman Iron Age? To judge from the material remains, as revealed in grave-finds, Roman influence was very strong. The shapes and designs of the brooches and gold pendants worn by the women and the form of the pottery which was used for both cooking and storage, were based to some extent on Roman models. Their weapons, however, and their clothes were definitely not of Roman type. The long swords and their sheaths were of a type developed among the Germanic tribes of the Roman frontier regions and, although used by auxiliary troops in the Roman forces, were of a type completely foreign to the sword used in the highly disciplined warfare of the regular Roman armies: the swords, shields and probably the spears of the Scandinavian warrior were modelled on those produced in such client states as that of the Marcomanni. Their clothes also, although our knowledge of them is imperfect due to the accidents of survival, seem to have been of Germanic form. The men wore trousers and a long-sleeved jerkin, while the women wore long trailing gowns. Woollen and linen clothes of this sort were presumably supplemented by furs in the winter, and touches of ornament were added to the dress by means of decorated leather belts like that from Vimose.

p 222
(5, 6)

Although there was obviously a considerable amount of capital tied up in trading, the economy of the Roman Iron Age was essentially agricultural. The farmers tilled their land, but we have no precise knowledge of the type of plough they used at this period; they almost certainly used the ard—a plough without mould board or wheel—although the heavier plough may have been introduced towards the middle of the 1st millennium. We have some evidence from Bornholm that emmer wheat, barley and rye were grown at different periods of the Roman Iron Age; scythes and sickles were used for harvesting and the common

saddle quern had still not been replaced by the rotary quern for grinding flour. Some of this grain was made into porridge and some was baked as bread, either in ovens or on open fires: nothing is perhaps so evocative of the life of the ordinary people as a small bread roll from the Roman Iron Age found at Vikbolandet in Östergötland, Sweden. Sheep, goats and cattle provided meat, dairy produce and clothing for the people, but only the strongest beasts were kept throughout the winter—there would be a large slaughter of all sub-standard animals in the autumn and their meat would be smoked or salted away against the hard winter months.

p 223
(12)

The Scandinavian at Home

The best evidence for houses of this period has been found in Denmark, although excavations in both Norway and Sweden have also produced house plans and outlines of villages. It is practically impossible to generalize concerning the types of settlement imposed on the landscape by the Scandinavian peoples of the Roman Iron Age—or indeed of any other period within the 1st millennium. A settlement's form depends on many factors —ecological, economic, social and political—and in an essay of this length it would be impossible to go into great detail about the differences of settlement forms and house shapes in an area which is over a thousand miles in length. The mountainous settlement of Håvodl in Rogaland, Norway, with its five mean houses cannot be compared with the rich farming community living in scattered farms on Gotland or the closely knit village communities of Jutland. It is, however, perhaps possible to make certain generalizations concerning the structure of the houses of Scandinavia in the Roman Iron Age. Generally speaking the Swedish and Norwegian houses had walls made partly of rough stone and partly of turf, they are rectangular, with roofs supported on two rows of posts, and they tended to be placed in isolation from each other although incipient villages are quite common. In Denmark and south Sweden, however, the houses were made of wood, wattle-and-daub and turf, but were of a generally similar plan to the houses found elsewhere in Scandinavia, save that the roof was occasionally carried on a single row of posts. In Denmark, and particularly in Jutland, properly integrated villages are fairly common. The variations within this classification are enormous, a house at Gunderup in north Jutland, for instance had walls of turf panelled with wood, while the walls of houses at Fjand in west Jutland were of wattle and daub. Many of these dwellings housed both men and animals; the cattle being kept at one end of the building, separated from the house proper by a partition. All the activities of life took place in one long, smoky, hall-like chamber, usually with a central fireplace: sleeping rooms were not introduced, even in the grandest houses, until the early Middle Ages.

p 222
(2)

The Sea Ways

The sea was always an important element in the life of the Scandinavian peasant; from the sea he drew food, by way of the sea came traders and invaders. His boats were therefore of some considerable importance in his life. We have evidence of a fair number of smallish boats. Larger boats have been found, for example, at Kvalsund in Norway and at Nydam in south Jutland: the Kvalsund boat had been ceremonially shattered before being placed in a bog, but the Nydam vessel survives almost whole and can be seen in the Provincial Museum for Schleswig-Holstein in Schleswig. It is a clinker-built boat, 23 metres in length, and was made of oak. Its ribs are formed of natural grown crooks, to which the planks were tied through cleats fashioned out of the solid wood. There is, practically speaking, no keel, merely a thickened plank and there is no seating for a mast. The rowlocks are thorn-shaped and longish sweeps also survive. Boats such as this were large enough to cross the North Sea—after all many an 18th-century privateer was no larger— and it was presumably in similar rowing boats that the Anglo-Saxons came to England, indeed a similar boat some 26 metres in length, was found at Sutton Hoo in Suffolk in the grave-like cenotaph of an Anglo-Saxon king who was buried about 650–660. The writings of Tacitus bear witness to the fact that there were

p 224
(17, 18)

The old faith died slowly among the Scandinavians and even in the Christian churches their attachment to pagan mythology was not suppressed. The door-jambs from Hylestad church, Sætersdal, show scenes from the story of the Volsungs. Starting bottom right: Regin forges a sword for Sigurd, who puts it to the test; he slays the dragon Fafnir, roasts and eats his heart, then murders Regin; between them is Sigurd's horse and, above, Gunnar, another character in the saga, left to die, his hands tied, in a snake pit, charming the snakes by playing the harp with his toes. (1, 2)

sailing boats in northern waters at the beginning of the 1st millennium, but there is no evidence, from the archaeological record, of sailing boats in Scandinavia before the Viking period.

Both the Kvalsund and Nydam boats were found in bogs, placed there presumably as offerings to some deity, and these are but one aspect of a fantastic phenomenon that is encountered throughout Scandinavia. The five largest and most important bog finds are those from Kvalsund, Vimose, Nydam, Thorsbjerg and Illerup; but other finds, such as that at Käringsjön, Halland in Sweden, show that the practice was widespread. The Danish bogs have produced vast quantities of weapons, clothing, idols, coins and even horses and human beings. The majority of these finds are often interpreted as booty taken from dead warriors after battle and placed in sacred bogs. Caesar's words, 'among many tribes one sees things of this kind in heaps in the holy places', are usually taken to refer to such finds. As well as plundered arms, however, there may be among them thank offerings, dedicatory offerings, etc., but, in whichever way they are interpreted, they can only be seen as a reflection of the religion or superstition of the Scandinavian peoples.

Gods of a Heroic Age

f 1, 2

Until the conversion of the Scandinavian peoples to Christianity —an object not achieved until almost the end of the 1st millennium—the people worshipped a pantheon of gods who have an origin common in Indo-European tradition. The gods have been, and were at the time, equated with their Roman counterparts—Thor, for example, is similar in many of his aspects to Jupiter. The chief evidence for Northern religion comes from Christian writings which were not exactly in favour of the strange gods: but these are the main sources on which our knowledge depends. The chief gods were Odin, Thor, Njörd and Frey. Odin was the Master of Magic and had great power and knowledge, he was also the god of war and all warriors who fell in

battle joined him in Valhalla where they lived a fully heroic life of feasting and fighting. A more popular god—although not so powerful as Odin—was Thor, whose name is associated with thunder: he was a god of immense strength which he derived from the earth (his mother was Jörd—which is to be translated as 'Earth'). His symbol—the hammer known as Mjöllnir—was very popular as an amulet in Scandinavia and as such represents his overwhelming strength: the symbol may well have been used in the consecration of the bride and in association with the burial of the dead. He was red-haired, a mighty eater and toper, and rather unsophisticated. Njörd was the god of wealth and like his son Frey was associated with fertility. There were other gods, among them Balder, Tyr, Bragi, and a number of goddesses, including Odin's wife Frigga, and Freyja, the goddess of love. The gods dwelt in Asgard where each had his own hall; here also was Valhalla. Beneath the sacred tree lived the three Norns—representing past, present and future—who span out man's destiny.

p 223
(13)

Norse mythology is permeated with the principle of evil and leads logically up to the destruction of the world—Ragnarök—in which the gods and the world are finally consumed by fire in the middle of a battle which has raged between the gods and the forces of evil, led by Loki, the instigator of all man's misfortunes and troubles. After Ragnarök a new world arises, the gods return and happiness and fertility come back to the earth—goodness finally permeates everything.

It is against this background that we must see the bog finds; for they reflect an interest and belief in the after life, while the presence of a large number of weapons would indicate the heroic nature of that life. It is interesting that the weapons were often 'killed' before they were deposited: swords were bent or mutilated, spears were broken, even whole boats were dismembered before being offered to the gods or to the heroes gathered in Valhalla. Bog finds are rarer after the Roman Iron Age, but the presence of 'killed' weapons in graves of both the Migration Period and the Viking Age would indicate that such practices survived, with the belief in the ancient gods, until the coming of Christianity in the 10th century.

'Far Away into the Ocean'

Throughout the Iron Age, Europe appears to have had some of the qualities of a maelstrom when viewed through modern eyes: the tribes of Europe were on the move, searching for richer land, for booty, for freedom from oppression and for *Lebensraum*. Although Scandinavia was on the edge of this disturbance, it was the *fons et origo* of much of its more spectacular aspects, for it was from Scandinavia that the Goths, the Burgundians, the Anglians and the Jutes originally moved to conquer large parts of the Continent and the British Isles. This restless epoch of European history is known as the Migration Period.

There are few historical sources concerning the Scandinavian people in the Migration Period, but incidental references in Frankish and Anglo-Saxon sources and in the Anglo-Saxon poem *Beowulf* introduce for the first time rather shadowy names for the members of the Scandinavian tribes. It is possible to gain a view of certain episodes in Scandinavia in the period of the great migrations, but no consecutive history is revealed, only a rather misty picture of an area racked by internecine war as the Svíar of Uppland attempted to gain control of Sweden, an impression of various wars between Norwegians and Danes, of a raid into Frisia by Swedes and of settlement in England by Danish tribes. Once again archaeology is the key to an understanding of the period.

This was a wealthy period in Scandinavia and, although the times were troubled, the people of the northern countries appear to have increased in political and economic stature. The rich graves of Vendel and Valsgärde in Sweden and the only slightly less rich grave-fields of Norway and Denmark reveal to us something of the character of the civilization of the North in this period. The burial rites became, if anything, more elaborate. Considerable mounds were erected over the dead and the bodies were often placed in a complete ship which was then covered by a mound; in certain exceptional cases the burial was surrounded by a setting of stones in the form of a ship, with taller stones at

p 221
(1)

p 224
(19, 20)

each end to represent the rising stem and stern posts of a real ship. This association of the ship with death had extremely ancient roots; in Scandinavia itself there is evidence of such an association as early as the Bronze Age: the idea of a voyage to the after life is a picturesque and natural one which would appeal especially to the mind of a seafaring nation. Something of the idea behind this type of burial can be gleaned from the description of a Scandinavian chieftain's funeral ceremony—which takes a form slightly different from that normally revealed by archaeological methods—recorded in the great Anglo-Saxon epic poem known as *Beowulf*:

> There at the haven, stood a ring-prowed ship —
> The radiant and eager ship of the lord.
> They laid down the beloved lord,
> The giver of rings, in the lap of this ship,
> The lord by the mast. They brought from afar
> Many great treasures and costly trappings.
> I never heard of a ship of this size so richly furnished
> With weapons of war, armour of battle,
> Swords and corslets. Many treasures lay
> Piled on his breast, and these were to travel
> With him far away into the ocean.

The most important group of graves of the Migration Period, other than the poorly furnished royal burial mounds at Old Uppsala (the original capital of the Kingdom of the Svíar), are the graves excavated at Vendel in the late nineteenth century by Dr Hjalmar Stolpe and those investigated at Valsgärde by Professor Sun Lindqvist and his students over the last thirty years. These aristocratic cemeteries have yielded a series of boat burials which extend from the Migration Period to the 11th century. Here were found richly ornamented swords, elaborate helmets, bridle trappings, shields mounted with highly ornamented bosses and charges, brooches, glass and more everyday objects such as tools, combs and vessels. Not only were inanimate objects laid in the graves, but the boats and their occupants were sometimes accompanied by horses—often more than one— which were placed either in the boat itself or alongside it in the trench dug to receive the ship. The burials of Vendel and Valsgärde can only be interpreted as the memorials of chieftains —possibly of royal blood—for no other class of society could have borne the capital expenditure involved. The lavish nature of these burials, particularly those of the Migration Period, give a remarkable impression not only of the wealth of their erstwhile owners but of the solidly based economy of the area.

Grave-fields of the same richness have not been found in either Norway or Denmark, but the contemporary cemetery at Lousgård on the Danish island of Bornholm and the five graves found at Snartemo in southern Norway reflect an only slightly less rich society. At Lousgård, which is a minor Vendel in that it appears to be the burial place of an aristocratic family, there is even evidence of a slave being buried with one member of the family.

Rich Burials and the Trail of War

There can be no doubt that this was a period of wealth in the Scandinavian lands, but it was also, at times, a troubled period. Both these aspects are pointedly illustrated by the rich hoards found throughout the northern countries. It is not for nothing that this is known as the Scandinavian Golden Age; one hoard, from Västergötland in Sweden, alone produced nearly a stone's weight (seven kilograms) of gold, while even richer hoards have been discovered. These hoards are particularly rich in the 5th and early 6th centuries and indicate that, although money was flowing into Scandinavia, times were very troubled, for it is only in periods of very real danger that hoards are buried and not reclaimed. Most of these hoards are composed of rings and ornaments, some of which, like the great neck-rings from Sweden, are very skilfully made and extremely beautiful. Much of the bullion is in the form of plain rings and spirals which must have formed some sort of standard of currency, but the fair number of gold coins—*solidi* from the Mediterranean empires—which have been found in Scandinavia (particularly on the Baltic islands)

indicate the source of both the metal and the wealth. It is apparent that the trade which grew up during the Roman Iron Age was continuing and that, as good-quality luxury goods became rarer in southern Europe and as the Scandinavians developed a refined and distinctive taste of their own, gold became one of the most desirable of all imports.

Professor Stenberger has demonstrated that all the evidence points to the deposition of the hoards in relatively short periods on the different Baltic islands—480–490 on Öland, 500–520 on Gotland—and that there is no evidence of a growing ritual and no evidence of less rich graves at this period. It is interesting, therefore, that this period coincides with the development of a series of forts or strongholds on the Baltic islands in Uppland and Västergötland, on the west coast of Sweden and in many parts of Norway and Finland. All the available evidence points to the fact that these forts were built during the Migration Period as temporary refuges to which the people of the district fled in case of sudden invasion by pirates or raiding parties of the kind recorded in *Beowulf*. The population on hearing of the raid would flee with its cattle to the fortresses which were set on eminences often far away from the coast and miles from the nearest arable land. The obvious wealth of the region was responsible for the raids and the hoard finds represent, in the majority of cases, the failure of the owner to return to his treasure, because either death or slavery intervened. Many of the forts—like those on Öland—are circular, but some follow the contour of the hilltop and are irregular in plan: some—like Gråborg—were used intermittently over a period of a thousand years, even being re-fortified in the Middle Ages. The result of some of these raids can be seen archaeologically: burnt farms, like those at Sorte Muld and Dalshøj on the Danish island of Bornholm, tell their own grim story of piratical depredation.

Viking Art: the Unbroken Line

But this was, as we have seen, a time of great wealth; it was also a time when the peoples of Scandinavia were becoming conscious of their own strength and of their own taste. One of the most remarkable expressions of this self-confidence is to be seen in their art, for it is during the Migration Period that there developed in Scandinavia the beginnings of an art which, in one of its aspects at least, was to continue in an unbroken tradition, until the Viking Age. There were two forms of art throughout this period, a naturalistic animal art of surprising quality and sensitivity and an abstract art of striking originality and extreme tortuousness. It is hard to evaluate the naturalistic art as so little of it survives, but where it is encountered its assured quality would indicate that this was a rich vein in the art of the North and one would wish to see more of it. Instead, we are presented with an intricate and sophisticated abstract art which is not to everyone's taste: it is an applied art, appearing almost exclusively as an embellishment on objects of utility. It occurs on brooches and swords, on pendants and helmets, it appears in metal and it appears in stone. It is a remarkable art, its elements tease the eye and often degenerate into meaninglessness. It is related to the art of the northern half of all Europe, to the art of all the Germanic peoples and was apparently impervious to influences from the formal and naturalistic art of the Mediterranean lands.

This abstract art is based on a semi-naturalistic animal ornament, whose roots can be seen in the late Roman Iron Age, when animal designs based on Romano-Celtic originals occur on objects made in Scandinavia. It appears first on objects found in the great bog finds, in a remarkable hoard from Sösdala in southern Sweden, for example, and on a beaker from Sjælland. It was also to be seen on the two great golden horns from Gallehus, Denmark, which were unfortunately melted down after having been stolen from the Royal collection in 1802. Drawings of these horns made before the robbery indicate something of their style, the applied figural scenes have few naturalistic qualities, but this is due to an abstract approach to the subject and not to bad craftsmanship.

The northern craftsmen adapted a technique from the provincial Roman repertoire which was to change these semi-naturalistic creatures into a much more abstract form. This technique was

p 221 (1)

p 229 (29)

p 231 (33)

p 222 (3)

p 222 (7)

f 3

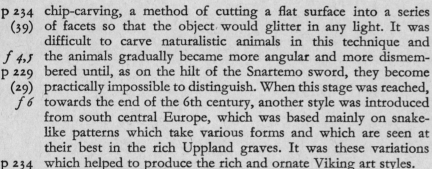

The increasing abstraction in Scandinavian art is illustrated in these examples. Above: a design on a horn found at Gallehus, c. AD 300–400; here the figures, which are isolated and easily identifiable, look back to the Romano-Celtic art of the Iron Age. Above right: the stage classified by Salin as Style I (beginning in the 5th century). The animal figures have now been broken up into separate, very stylized parts of the body, linked together without obvious coherence and interspersed with geometrical patterns. There is no continuity of line and rhythm. In its simpler form (part of a brooch from Galsted, south Jutland), the animal shapes are confined to the outer edge; in its more complex (a brooch from Vedstrup, Sjælland) they have encroached on the central space too. Lower right: Style II, which emerged in the 6th century. As on this belt-mount from Vendel, the design was entirely formed of animal shapes, now distorted beyond recognition, twisted and elongated into sophisticated snake-like patterns. (3, 4, 5, 6)

p 234
(39)

f 4,5
p 229
(29)
f 6

p 234
(38, 40)

chip-carving, a method of cutting a flat surface into a series of facets so that the object would glitter in any light. It was difficult to carve naturalistic animals in this technique and the animals gradually became more angular and more dismembered until, as on the hilt of the Snartemo sword, they become practically impossible to distinguish. When this stage was reached, towards the end of the 6th century, another style was introduced from south central Europe, which was based mainly on snake-like patterns which take various forms and which are seen at their best in the rich Uppland graves. It was these variations which helped to produce the rich and ornate Viking art styles.

During the whole of the Migration Period the economy, as in the Roman Iron Age, remained firmly based on its agricultural foundations, the religion of the people and their day-to-day life altered little and, for the vast majority of Scandinavians, this was also true of the Viking Age which was ushered in towards the end of the 8th century by a series of attacks on western Europe.

'Valiant, Wrathful, Pagan People'

The origin of the term 'Viking', despite interminable arguments by philologists and historians, has never been satisfactorily explained. The term is used here simply as a label for the Scandinavian peoples and no attempt has been made to explain it. Although there had been vague rumours of piratical action on the part of the northern barbarians for a number of years, the first real impression the Vikings made on the west was by their sack of Lindisfarne in 793. In the years that follow the pages of the chroniclers are blackened by frequent references to the activities of these pagan raiders:

'836, In this year King Egbert fought against the crews of 35 ships at Carhampton, and a great slaughter was made there, and the Danes had possession of the battle-field.'

'842, In this year there was great slaughter in London and Quentovic and in Rochester.'

'870, In this year the raiding army rode across Mercia into East Anglia and took up winter quarters at Thetford. And that winter the King Edmund fought against the Danes and the Danes had the victory and killed the King and conquered all the land.'

In Britain, as we see from these quotations, they first came to raid, but before the middle of the 9th century the raids had given way to invasions and the Vikings began to settle in districts of their own, under their own kings. The first Norwegian ruler of Ireland appeared in the 830s and during the last third of the 9th century the Vikings had settled in Yorkshire and in the area of the five Boroughs (Stamford, Nottingham, Derby, Lincoln and

Leicester)—which, with Yorkshire and the north-east of England, soon became known as the Danelaw. Normandy was not settled by the Vikings until 911, but the rest of France, together with Spain and the Low Countries were continually under Viking attack during the 9th and 10th centuries. Scotland and the Scottish Isles, the Faroes, and the Isle of Man all fell under their domination. The fortunes of the Vikings waxed and waned until in the early 11th century a Viking King, Canute, sat on the throne of England and ruled, in name at least, a vast empire which extended from the north of Norway to Cornwall. But after his reign Viking powers in most parts of the British Isles collapsed.

p 232
(35, 36)

In eastern Europe the adventures of the Swedish Vikings were of an entirely different nature. Although raids are recorded at various periods throughout the 9th and 10th century—including attacks on Constantinople itself—the main interest of these eastern Vikings lay in trade rather than in colonization. Their chief object seems to have been the control of the great Russian trade-routes along the Dnieper and the Volga, routes which opened the way to trade with Constantinople and the Near and Middle East. At various points along the Dnieper route Scandinavian warriors and merchants settled—at Staraya Ladoga, Kiev, Novgorod, Smolensk, etc., but the eastern route was controlled by the Byzantine emperor and the Khazars; merchant journeys in this direction were thus expensive owing to the taxes and dues exacted *en route*. The settlements in the north and in the west of Russia were therefore of great importance to the Vikings and the influence of the Vikings on the Slavonic peoples of these areas was of such a great political importance that they are regarded by many as founders of the Russian state.

p 227–8
(28)

The First Parliament

In the North Atlantic the Vikings colonized Iceland—a land hitherto only used as a hermitage by a few Celtic priests—and Greenland. Towards the very end of our period they visited America on a number of occasions and even wintered there, perhaps in the houses recently discovered in the north of Newfoundland by a Norwegian archaeological expedition. The most important of these Atlantic adventures was the settlement of Iceland during the period from 870 to 930. From the historical sources of the 13th century—much of which are based on earlier histories—it is possible to piece together a fairly comprehensive view of the social and political life of the island.

f 7

Iceland was not a kingdom, it was an aristocratic republic, with its own parliament meeting annually at Thingvellir not far from the modern Icelandic capital of Reykjavík. The population

p 232
(37)

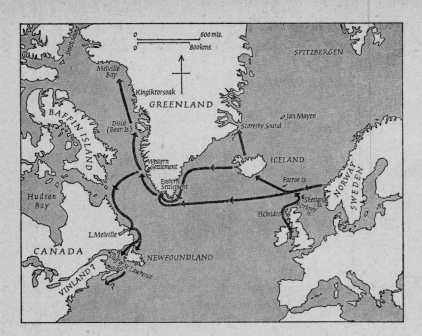

Voyages of the Norsemen in the Atlantic. Iceland was colonized by Vikings from Norway and the British Isles. In 981 Eirik the Red, banished from Iceland for manslaughter, came upon a vast new land which he named Greenland. Later Norse seamen reached North America, and called it 'Vinland' on account of the vines growing there, but the length of the communications with the West made permanent settlement impossible. (7)

was drawn from Norway and from the Norse colonies in the Celtic world and was ruled by the pagan priests *(godi)* under the formal authority of the Law-speaker, who was the president of the parliament. Laws were made and judgments were given by the parliament. The Icelandic parliament reflects a function which must have been fairly widespread in the other Viking lands—with the difference that in these other lands the king had more real power and the assembly was merely informed of his decisions. A striking survival of this Viking type of parliament is to be found to this day in the Isle of Man, where the laws are promulgated each year—on old midsummer day—on Tynwald Hill at a full assembly of all the estates of this ancient Viking kingdom.

p 232
(35)

The political history of the Viking peoples after 800 is fairly well documented. It is a complicated story of invasions and raids, of internecine war and of family feuds, which it is impossible to summarize here; but it is important to stress the fact that towards the end of the 1st millennium the Scandinavians gradually accepted Christianity and put away the old gods. During the course of the 9th century, the Vikings turned more and more to the Christian church and, although never completely accepting the new religion, became used to having a few Christians in their midst. The real turning point in the Christian mission was the conversion of Harald Bluetooth, King of Denmark, about 960–965, which followed the establishment of bishops' sees at Aarhus, Ribe and Hedeby in 948. Christianity brought literacy to Scandinavia and from this time forward the history of the north is well documented.

p 223
(13–15)

f 1, 2

But most of our information about the people of the north during the Viking period is derived from archaeology. The contents of the great ship burials at Oseberg and Gokstad provide evidence of the wealth and taste of the richer—perhaps royal—families of Norway. The treasures of Gotland provide abundant evidence of the commercial and piratical practices of the Swedish Vikings. The great camps of Denmark at Trelleborg, Fyrkat Mølle, Odense and Aggersborg witness to the disciplined military organization of the Danish armies. The foundations of the Icelandic farms, buried by the lava of Hekla in the later Middle Ages, clothe the bare bones of the political history of that island. In the colonies the story is less easy to trace archaeologically, but such antiquities as a tombstone from St Paul's in London, a Viking ship buried in Normandy, a brooch at Gnezdovo, near Smolensk, an inscription in Viking style on a lion that once stood in the Piraeus, are but a few of the remains that tell as eloquent a story of the foreign adventures of the Vikings as the contemporary chroniclers or the later saga writers.

p 224
(20)
p 225
(21–23)
p 230–1
(30–32,
34)

p 227–8
(28)

It is the archaeological remains that reveal an important and often neglected facet of Scandinavian history—the continuity of life (social, economic and political) in the North in the millennium from the beginning of the Roman Iron Age to the conversion of the 10th and 11th centuries. The life of the ordinary people changed but little, the farmers and the peasants of the Viking Age lived in the same sort of houses inhabited by their forefathers and tilled the same land in much the same way, their biggest revolution being in the change of a basic crop or in stricter taxes from their chief.

p 222
(2)

'A Civilization Sure of Itself'

Even the colonizing aspect of the Vikings was no new thing, already in the middle of the Migration Period Swedish settlers, soldiers or merchants—we know not which—had founded a fortress at Grobin, near Libau in Latvia. This venture and a number of similar excursions are only attested by the archaeological record, but this is surely but the prototype of many similar Scandinavian adventures after 800. We must even doubt the often repeated theory that a new activity of the Scandinavians in the Viking Age was trade, for this has been a constant theme of this essay at all periods. But the concentration of trade and traders into towns was an entirely new feature of Scandinavian life. Carefully placed towns, more elaborate than the trading stations we have seen in Russia, controlled the whole of the mercantile activity of the Baltic. Hedeby (near the modern town of Schleswig), Birka (in Lake Mälar a few miles from Stockholm) and Kaupang (on the west side of Oslofjord) were the chief towns founded at this period. With the exception of Kaupang, which has natural defences, they had elaborate fortifications and excellent harbours. From these great markets traders sailed to Russia, to Hamburg, Bremen, Truso and London, rounded North Cape and penetrated the Pillars of Hercules. Such a trader was Ohthere, whose account of a voyage round North Cape was recorded by King Alfred the Great. Ohthere lived in the far north of Norway and his stock-in-trade consisted of ropes made of sealskin and walrus-hide, down from the eider duck, and various furs which he probably traded through Kaupang and Hedeby, both of which are mentioned in his narrative. These towns, however, were not apparently a completely successful innovation, for none of them lasted beyond the Viking Age; Birka and Kaupang were deserted and not immediately replaced, Hedeby changed its site and a fourth town, Västergarn, south of Visby in Gotland, which has not yet been excavated, was covered by blown sand. Viking society at the end of the 1st millennium was still largely based on the individual estate and farm, villages were known, like that at Lindholm near Aalborg in Jutland, but towns were a new and altogether unproven phenomenon, not suited to the culture of the North at this period.

p 227–8
(28)

p 222
(4)

The continuity of culture which has been stressed here is nowhere better seen than in the art of the Vikings, for, as we trace its rise and growth in the indigenous art of Scandinavia, we see it taking foreign motifs and idioms into its system and modifying them to the Northern taste until, at the end of the 10th century, the art of Scandinavia is no more than a more florid development of the styles which flourished in the earlier centuries. Marc Bloch's dictum that the Vikings formed 'a civilization sure of itself' is nowhere better demonstrated than in this art which ruthlessly rejects most of the more formal influences of Carolingian and Ottonian art in favour of the barbaric and indigenous art which was its own.

The 10th and 11th centuries saw the Scandinavian countries at the peak of their international importance, never again were they to make the same impression on European life and thought. Achievements of latter-day Scandinavian heroes of the stamp of Gustavus Adolphus and Charles XII pale into insignificance by the side of the conquest of much of Britain, Normandy, Sicily and vast tracts of Russia, of the settlement of Iceland and of the establishment of colonies in Greenland. The vital civilization which the classical authors at the beginning of our millennium had only dimly perceived behind the Pythean mists had risen like a star to its zenith—an object of wonder to the civilized world of the last years of that same millennium.

XII THE COVETED ISLES

Celtic Britain and the Anglo-Saxons

CHARLES THOMAS

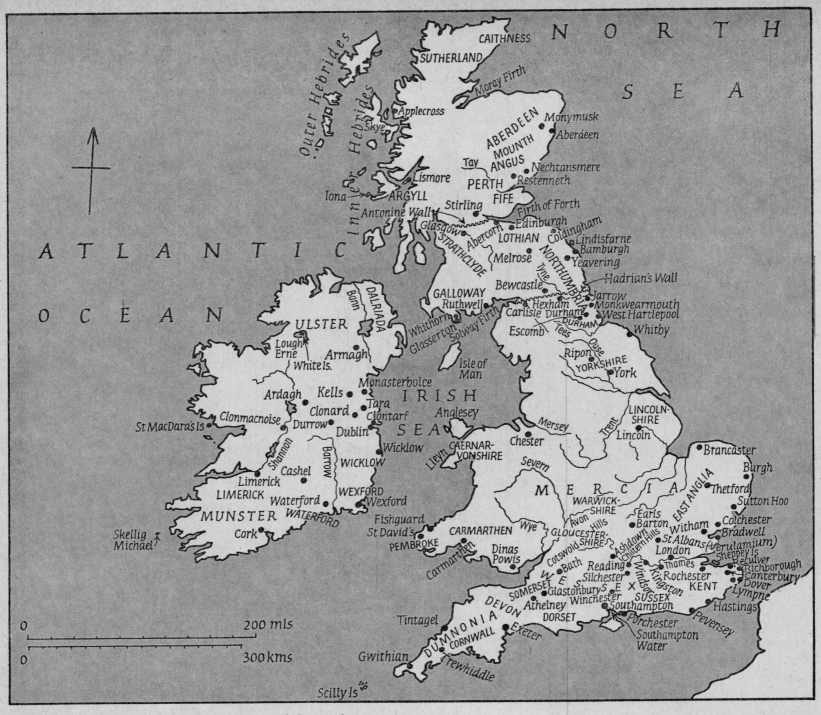

Early Christian Britain, showing important sites of the period

'Many of the Northumbrians,

as well of the nobility as private persons, laying aside their weapons, rather incline to dedicate themselves and their children to the tonsure and monastic vows than to study martial discipline. What will be the end hereof the next age will show. This is for the present the state of Britain in the 731st year of the incarnation of our Lord, in whose reign may the earth ever rejoice.'

So wrote the Venerable Bede, first and greatest of early English historians, as he neared the end of his life in the monastery of Jarrow. He died four years later. What 'the next age' did in fact show has already been glimpsed in the last chapter—the collapse of Northumbria under the savage raids of the Norsemen and the end of its Golden Age of scholarship and art.

The monk in his study (opposite) is exactly contemporary with Bede and vividly conveys the essence of his words. Although quite un-Northumbrian in style, being copied from an Italian manuscript of the 6th century (such details as the shadow of the inkwell on the floor show a certain uneasiness and lack of understanding), it does bear witness to one important element in English culture of the 8th century—its close contacts with continental Europe. It is from a Gospel book (this page shows the scribe Ezra rewriting the sacred records), made by a Northumbrian artist for Ceolfrith, Abbot of Jarrow, some time before 716. The model from which it was derived was probably acquired in Italy by Benedict Biscop (died 690), the founder of Wearmouth

and Jarrow. He went there five times to buy books and relics.

Northumbria was thus a part of Europe, though its evolution had not been typically European. It was born from the union of two separate strands of Christian culture. On the one hand was the Irish church, a vigorous monastic movement with a highly developed art, which had spread from Ireland to Scotland (Iona, founded in 563) and thence into northern—predominantly Celtic—England. On the other was the church of Rome, brought to England by Augustine, who in 597 founded the see of Canterbury in the Germanic south. When the two systems met at the Synod of Whitby in 664 it was Rome that prevailed.

On the artistic level, however, the union remained an equal and fertile one, like so many other such combinations in British history. By the 11th century, indeed, the population of Britain was, to a greater extent, perhaps, than any of the other peoples described in this book, the product of mixtures—of Celtic (the pre-Roman inhabitants, plus later Irish influence) with Germanic (Angles, Saxons, Jutes and Frisians in the 5th century and Norsemen in the 9th) overlaid with the Latin culture of southern Europe (first through the Romans, then through the Roman church and finally through the Normans, who though Norse in origin were by the time of the Conquest largely Latin in background). English history, like the English language, has a multiplicity of roots. (1)

The 'Ecclesiastical History of the English people'
of Bede describes the progress of the church in Britain from the earliest persecutions under the Romans to the great Northumbrian flowering of the 8th century, of which he was himself a part. The main emphasis is on Augustine's mission, the fate of his successors and the slow, painful conversion of the Saxon kingdoms throughout the 7th century. Bede also wrote a life of St Cuthbert, which was popular in the Middle Ages; his portrait (right) comes from a 12th-century manuscript of this work. (3)

Iona, 'an island whose monastery was ▶ for a long time the chief of almost all those of the northern Scots and all those of the Picts, and had the direction of their people' (Bede), was founded by the Irishman St Columba in 563. It was a mother house of monasticism in Scotland, and a monk from Iona, Aidan, was destined to be the founder of Lindisfarne, in Northumbria. This Celtic cross on Iona dates from the early 9th century. (6)

'Ireland is the greatest island next to Britain and lies to the west of it.' Bede gives little credit to the Irish, chiefly because they persisted in celebrating Easter on a date that he considered uncanonical. Yet it was from such barely accessible refuges as Skellig Michael (above) that the first monks had set out to evangelize Britain. (2)

'The southern Picts had long before, as is reported, forsaken the errors of idolatry and embraced the truth, by the teaching of Ninian, a most revered bishop and holy man of the British nation.' Below left: a cave at Physgyll, Wigtownshire, where a number of 6th- and 7th-century crosses have been found. Below right: a Pictish cross from the Tay valley, mid-8th century. (4, 5)

The Isle of Man is rich in early crosses, some Celtic, some Viking. The most elaborate of the former (below), a 9th-century altar frontal, shows Christ on the cross, highly stylized, with elaborate clothing that recalls examples from the East. (7)

Cornwall: there was a Celtic monastery at Tintagel (below) in the 6th century. On this rocky promontory, subsequently the site of a Norman church and a medieval castle, the monks lived in small rectangular cells built of stones and clay. Clusters of their cells can be seen on the central plateau, and on the seaward slope on the right. (8)

The Germanic settlers who came to Britain during the 5th century were pagan. The Christianity of their Celtic enemies made little impression on them, but the mission sent by Gregory I under Augustine had more success. Before the old faith died, however, it left one astonishing monument—the Sutton Hoo burial, a complete ship buried with the treasure and equipment of a Saxon king. Some of the pieces are shown here. Left: bronze plate from a helmet—a god with horned head-dress, perhaps Odin. Right: the end of a ceremonial whetstone. Below: the lid of a purse, set with garnets and coloured glass, with plaques showing the 'Daniel in the Lions' Den' motif; and two clasps.

The date of the burial was about 625. It was a cenotaph, not a grave; there was no body. (9, 10, 11)

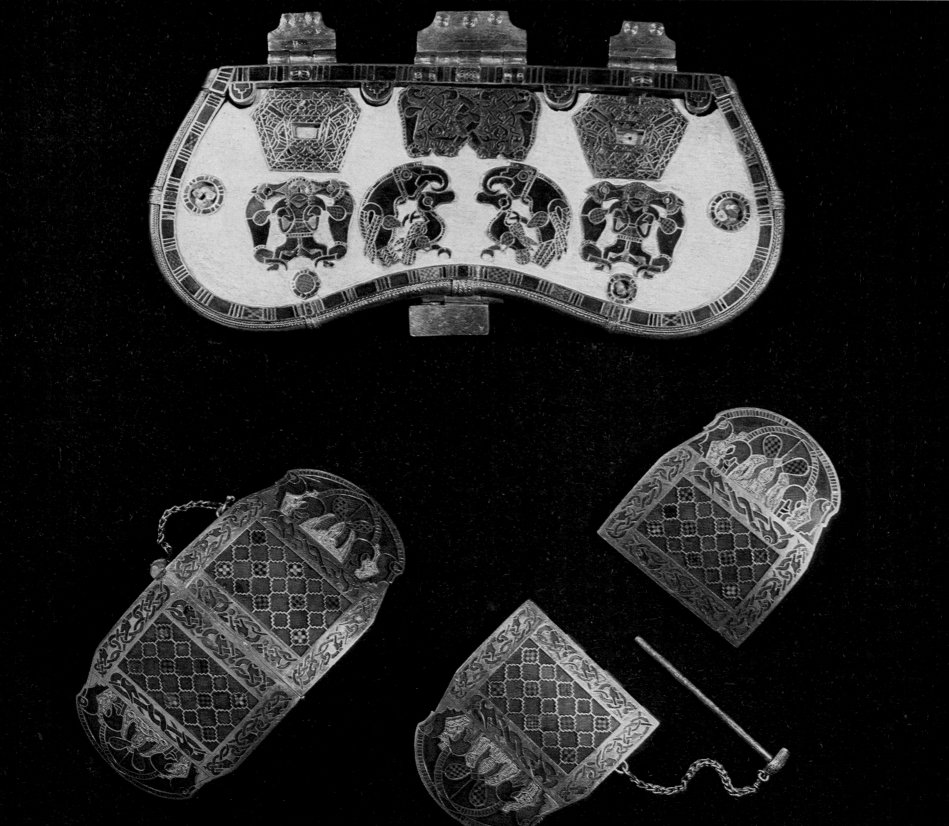

Exquisite works of jewellery were produced by the Anglo-Saxons, often showing marked affinities with their neighbours to the east and south. The Kingston Brooch (left) combines Frankish and Scandinavian motifs; it is decorated with gold filigree, cuttlefish shell, garnets and lapis lazuli. The Alfred Jewel (right) is an enamel portrait of a man holding two sceptres, very possibly King Alfred himself, for the inscription reads AELFRED MEC HEHT GEWYRCAN ('Alfred ordered me to be made'). Below, top left: a small cross containing a coin of the Byzantine Emperor Heraclius; top right: a buckle of gold filigree and garnets; centre: the Witham pins, a set of three linked pins with animal style decoration on the heads; and bottom: the Dowgate Hill Brooch, gold filigree and enamel. (12, 13, 14)

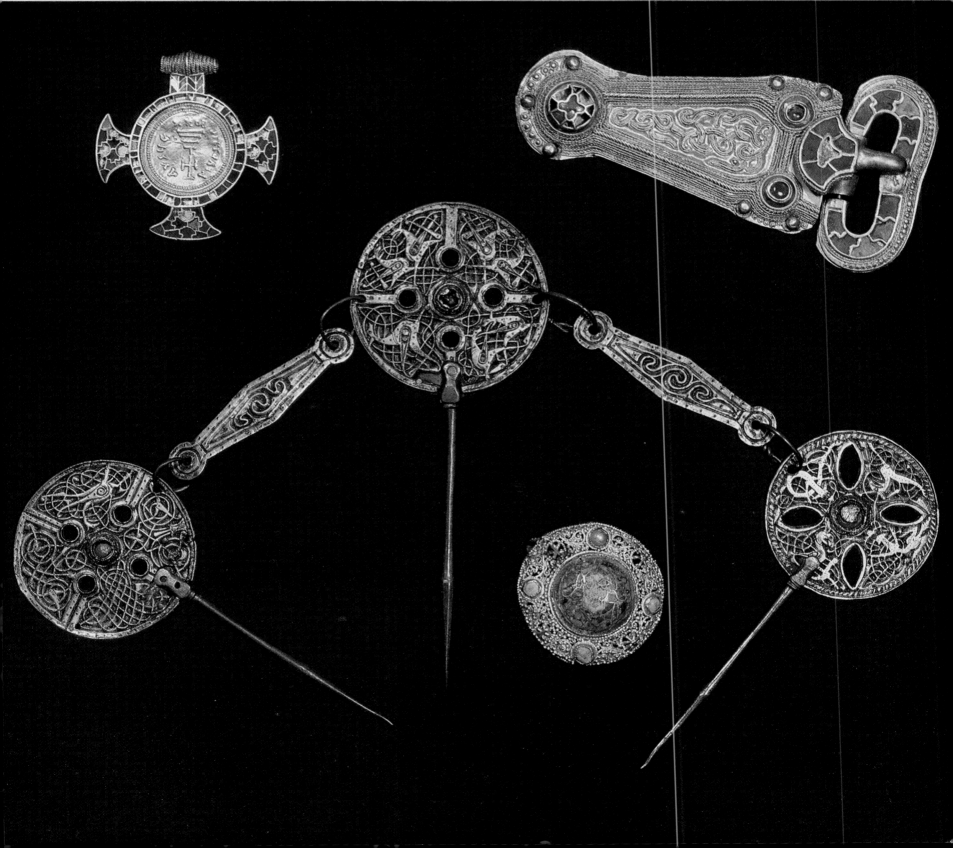

Ireland took the lead
in the conversion of Britain. Irish monks carried the Gospel to Scotland and northern England, and Irish manuscripts and metalwork formed the models for later craftsmen. Never before or since has Ireland produced works of such originality and quality.

'Scripture crosses', stone crosses of Celtic type elaborately carved with scenes in relief, are among the greatest monuments of Irish Christianity. The Cross of Muiredach, Abbot of Monasterboice (early 10th century), of which the upper part is shown here, is one of the most outstanding. The whole cross is over 17 feet high. In the centre is Christ crucified; at the top is a miniature gabled building, like a tiny stone chapel. (16)

The oldest Irish manuscript is the '*Cathach*' of St Columba, dating probably from the 6th century. The script is 'Irish majuscule' and the initials (above) are decorated with tiny scrolls like those which appear on contemporary metalwork. (15)

The heavy silver of the Ardagh Chalice (below) contrasts with its fine decoration in gold, gilt bronze, glass and enamel. Made in the early 8th century, it was hastily buried at the time of an attack and has been exceptionally well preserved. (17)

A priest, holding crosier and bell, still stands on White Island, Lough Erne, a survivor from the great age of Irish monasticism. The face is comparable in style with those of the book-cover on the right. (18)

The transformation of the figures of the Passion—Christ, two angels, Longinus with his spear and Stephaton with the sponge—into a pattern of spirals and interlacing lines is characteristic of the Irish style (right). The group is cast in bronze and probably formed part of a book-cover. The heads, in contrast to the body and clothing, are portrayed naturalistically, though over-large and with wide lentoid eyes. (19)

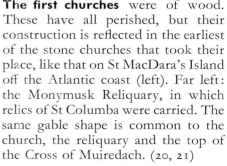

The first churches were of wood. These have all perished, but their construction is reflected in the earliest of the stone churches that took their place, like that on St MacDara's Island off the Atlantic coast (left). Far left: the Monymusk Reliquary, in which relics of St Columba were carried. The same gable shape is common to the church, the reliquary and the top of the Cross of Muiredach. (20, 21)

The pagan past

lived on in the Christian manuscripts of Ireland and Northumbria. Tendril shapes, interlacing spirals, elongated dragons and animal forms, which now crept along the borders of the Gospel-pages and Lives of the Saints, had a century before decorated the helmets and shields of pagan heroes.

The earliest example is the Book of Durrow, copied possibly on Iona in the 7th century. On the page showing St Matthew (far left) the border is filled with restless interlace, but the body, also reduced to geometrical pattern, is made up of repeated squares. The Book of Kells (left) is later, early 9th century, and was probably brought to Ireland from Iona when the Viking raids began. Here the portraits of the evangelists, though still surrounded by the unending web of interlace, have an eastern solemnity stemming from Byzantine art. (22, 23)

'Carpet pages' so called because they consist entirely of an overall pattern, are typical of the Irish and English schools, often forming frontispieces to the Gospels. This page (right) is from the masterpiece of the Northumbrian painters, the Lindisfarne Gospels, of the late 7th century. Its intricacy and detail are prodigious. In the later Middle Ages these books were thought to be the work not of men but of angels. (25)

The Lion of St Mark, designed by an artist of genius, for a Gospel book made in about 690 for the Anglo-Saxon missionary St Willibrord. (24)

The kingdom of Wessex in the south of England rose to leadership under King Alfred and during the 9th and 10th centuries, after the eclipse of the north, was the cultural centre of the country. The *scriptoria* of Winchester, its capital, produced manuscripts far closer in style to the rest of Europe than those of Ireland and Northumbria had been. This page, the Annunciation, from the Benedictional of St Aethelwold, Bishop of Winchester, compares with the richest works of Ottonian art. (26)

The urgent mission
of the church to bring Christianity to the whole of Britain made it from the beginning the most vital force in every branch of cultural life. Churchmen—revered as saints after their death—were the dominant figures of the age.

On the altar of an English church of the 9th century stood this cross, still enmeshed in the twisted tendrils of pre-Christian art. It is in many ways comparable with the 'carpet pages' of illuminated Gospels. (27)

St Columba, the founder of Iona, from a manuscript of the 9th century. (28)

St Dunstan, abbot of Glastonbury, virtually ruled England in the mid-10th century. (29)

The chair of peace, *frithstul*, at Hexham (right) is a unique Northumbrian object, Byzantine in inspiration. (30)

St Cuthbert, Bishop of Lindisfarne (above right), an austere and mystical figure, retired at the end of his life to the even more lonely island of Farne. Right: the Cross of Cuthbert, a jewel buried with him and now preserved at Durham, where his body lies. (31, 32)

'**It is the custom** of the Saxon people to erect a cross for the daily service of prayer where there is no church.' Some of these crosses were masterpieces of sculpture. Right: part of the Ruthwell Cross, showing Mary Magdalene washing Christ's feet. (35)

An archbishop of York, Wigmund (837–854), coined this large gold *solidus*, with a full-face portrait of himself. It was unprecedented in England, the only parallels being in Frankish Italy and Byzantium. Yet the coin is well designed and technically perfect. (33)

Silver plate, hidden during the 9th century when Viking attack threatened, is now being recovered. These two examples come from opposite ends of the country. Above: a chalice from Trewhiddle, Cornwall. Below: a strap-end from St Ninian's Isle, Shetland. (37, 38)

Small Saxon churches still stand, preserved by the poverty of their parishes, when greater ones have been demolished and rebuilt many times. Above: the tall north door of Bradford on Avon. Right: the tower of Restenneth, Scotland. (34, 36)

Mature Saxon architecture was distinguished by some striking features, seen here on the tower of Earls Barton church, Northants: long pilaster-strips, 'long and short work' at the corners, triangular arcading and stubby window balusters. (39)

253

The 'Seven Kingdoms'

conventionally stand for Anglo-Saxon England (though in fact there were more than seven), and the great theme of English history before the Conquest is their unification under one ruler. **Offa** (757–796) (below left), King of Mercia, was the first to call himself *rex totius Anglorum patriae*. But in the 9th century the leadership passed from Mercia (the Midlands) to Wessex, in the south. **Alfred** (871–899) (centre) turned the tide of Viking invasion and began to win back control of the territory they had conquered. **Aethelstan** (924–939)—portrayed (right) presenting Bede's 'Life of St Cuthbert' to the saint himself—and **Edgar** (959–975) (below) achieved stability and were patrons of the arts and learning. They were the last great Anglo-Saxon kings. (40–43)

Canute (1016–1035), the son of King Svein, ruled first the Dane-law and, after Aethelred's death, the whole of England. In this drawing, made at Winchester during his reign, he is depicted with his Queen Emma placing a cross on the altar of the new Abbey. (45)

The king ruled with the aid of a council, or *witenagemot*, composed of his own relatives, the leaders of the nobility and the bishops. It made laws, imposed taxes, concluded treaties and acted as supreme court of justice. In the drawing below (from Aelfric's Old Testament) it imposes the death penalty. (46)

Aethelred 'the Unready' (978–1016), Edgar's son, was unable to organize resistance to the Vikings, who began another series of attacks in 980. He was deposed by Svein, the Danish King. His nickname is a mistranslation of *unraed*, or 'lacking in counsel'. (44)

'The Forts of the Saxon Shore' in the 5th century. The modern names, from top left, are: Bradwell, Dover, Lympne, Brancaster, Burgh, Reculver, Richborough, Pevensey and Porchester. (47)

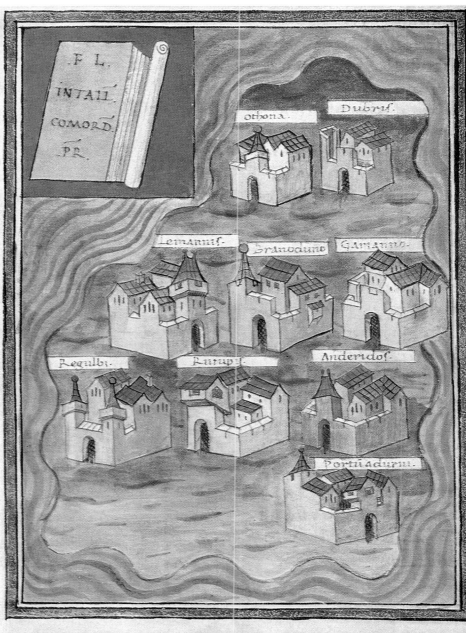

Binding together

the diverse peoples of Britain—Celtic, Saxon and Viking—ran a strong imaginitive unity, best seen in articles made for daily use or simply as decoration. The coiled serpentine forms of the Sutton Hoo gold buckle (above left)—two intertwined dragons fill the central roundel—reappear in the graceful calligraphy of the Lindisfarne Gospels (above right), Northumbrian work of some fifty years later. (48, 49)

'Chip-carving', already noted in Scandinavian art, produced some of its purest masterpieces in Celtic Ireland. This brooch (right) from Ardagh was made in the 9th century. Celtic, Saxon and Norse art share a certain *horror vacui*, yet profusion does not lead to lack of control, nor concern for technique to coldness. (50)

The five senses are the subject of this highly unusual silver brooch inlaid with niello, made in the 9th century: sight (in the middle), taste (top left), smell (top right), hearing (bottom left), and touch. The symbolism and figural style show contact with the art of continental Europe. (52)

Christianity and paganism co-exist on this whalebone casket from Northumbria (7th century). On the left Wayland the Smith, having killed the sons of Nidhad, awaits his daughter Beadohild and her servant; behind them is his brother Eigil, catching birds. On the right, the Adoration of the Magi; note the star in the sky and next to it the word MAEGI in runic. (53)

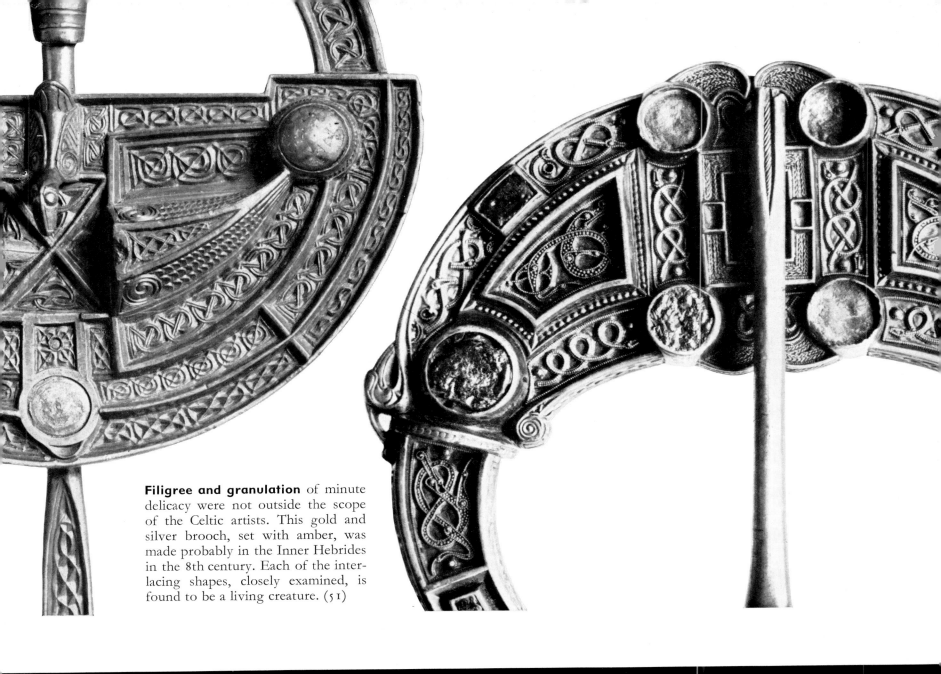

Filigree and granulation of minute delicacy were not outside the scope of the Celtic artists. This gold and silver brooch, set with amber, was made probably in the Inner Hebrides in the 8th century. Each of the interlacing shapes, closely examined, is found to be a living creature. (51)

The end of Anglo-Saxon England

came with dramatic suddenness with the Conquest by William of Normandy in 1066. The state, however, was already in decline. Danish kings had held the throne from 1013 to 1035. The political situation was chaotic, and William had at least as good a claim as Harold. It is the subsequent stability of Norman rule that makes the Battle of Hastings such a decisive turning-point, the inevitable beginning of any view of the Middle Ages in Britain.

The events of 1066 are recorded in probably the most vivid historical document ever made—the Bayeux Tapestry. It is not, in fact, tapestry at all but woollen embroidery on a linen backing,

and it dates from the last years of the 11th century. Over 230 feet long and 20 inches wide, it tells the story of Harold's oath to Duke William, of Edward the Confessor's death and Harold's accession in defiance of his promise, of Williams' invasion, the final battle and Harold's death. Three scenes from it are shown here. Above left: King Edward gives instructions to Harold (dressed in red) before he sets out for France. Above right: the death of Harold, not—as in the popular legend—by an arrow in the eye. Below: William, in the midst of the Battle, raises the vizor of his helmet to dispel a rumour that he has been killed. (54, 55, 56)

Celtic Britain and the Anglo-Saxons

CHARLES THOMAS

THE APPEARANCE OF ENGLAND, Scotland, Ireland and Wales as distinct political entities; the conversion of Britain to Christianity: the general introduction of literacy, and the predominance of English as our major native language; these are all products of the first millennium AD. They are the major legacies from an intensely formative period, and others include of course the basic pattern of our main road system, aspects of our agriculture, diet, and housing, and the location of most of our cities. Within the span of these ten centuries the British Isles, at the time of Christ no more than a conglomeration of prehistoric tribes on the occidental fringe of the Roman Empire, became part of an intricate network of European peoples. Moreover, this was a part which could never be ignored, and which on many occasions assumed an importance out of all proportion to its size and its comparatively sparse population. An acquaintance with the general course of events in Britain at this period, perhaps especially between the 4th and 8th centuries AD, is not only in itself rewarding; it is fundamental to any grasp of later developments in British history, language, art, and architecture through the Middle Ages to the present day.

Nearly all general accounts of the period tend to be unevenly biassed in favour of the Germanic-speaking invaders and their subsequent doings. The reasons for this are complex, but the main one is probably that, until the present century, almost no major historian of the period had any knowledge of, or indeed interest in, the story of the Celtic-speaking peoples of early Britain. In the nineteenth century, when a different philosophy of history held good, the Victorian moralist could find a rich quarry in the heroic behaviour and strongly-defined personalities of, say, many early kings of Northumbria and Wessex. The emotive undertones of the word 'English', and the desire to provide respectable Saxon ancestries for such national institutions as the navy, the militia, and the common law, might at one stage have led to an almost finite view of our earlier history (a view actually expressed in relation to the publication of medieval documents, regarded as absolute historical facts incapable of modification). However, under the assault of fresh scholastic techniques imported from the Continent, Anglo-Saxon texts, charters, wills, poems, and place-names were made to yield a mass of fresh information, while the physical expansion of conurbations over most of south-east England began to lay bare the rich Anglo-Saxon cemeteries lying outside what had once been Roman towns. Contemporary Celtic scholarship, largely confined to Irish material, was given powerful stimulus by the nationalistic 'Gaelic revival' in the early 1900s but it was (with French and German assistance) mainly concerned with the oldest stage of the Irish language and on what an Irishman has recently aptly called 'Irish pseudo-history', or the traditional native record of events. Yet, until the time and writings of the late H. M. Chadwick (1870–1947: main works, 1905–1940), no serious attempt was made to portray early British history in terms of both, complementary, schools of learning.

In recent decades, the superb and scholarly presentation of so much early Irish material has brought about a wider awareness of Ireland's artistic and cultural position during the Early Christian centuries. Her other role, as a centre of aggressive and vigorous expansion in the same centuries, is not so well known, and fewer still will be familiar with the parts played by the Picts, the 'northern British' (non-Germanic) kingdoms, or the Armorican settlers. These facets of early Britain therefore require stressing, as does the overlooked fact that by the half-millennium, AD 500, the area physically settled or controlled by the newcomers, be they Angles, Saxons, Jutes or Frisians, amounted to considerably less than a quarter of the British Isles.

The End of Roman Britain

The 5th century AD is still the most obscure in British history. The known background includes the withdrawal of Roman rule, the settlement of Germanic speakers in parts of east and south-east England, the survival of certain characteristics of Roman times, a variety of migrations and invasions in the north and west, and the continuance of Christianity in Ireland and Scotland, if no further afield. Even these (generally unquestioned) happenings are open to qualification. It may help to view the major events not as isolated events but as the historical counterparts of spectra in optical physics. Thus AD 410, a notional date with no archaeological counterpart, merely falls within a spectrum of declining Roman power that begins some time after the mid-4th century AD, and concludes a century or so later, allowing the term 'sub-Roman' properly to be applied to a large part of 5th-century Britain. Germanic-speaking invaders did not all arrive with Hengist and Horsa in AD 447, or any other single year, and the first Germanic settlers, in whatever capacity, were probably here before AD 400. Again, the definition and chronology of the popular movements in the Irish Sea region have to be worked out from archaeological traces and from imprecise and very much later historical sources; some of these movements cannot yet be located with confidence in any single century. The episcopal Church in the north and west associated with the saints we know as Ninian and Patrick seems more likely to have been connected with the pastoral oversight of existing Christian communities than with any attempts at wholesale conversion.

Direct literary sources for the 5th and 6th centuries are few, often oblique, invariably difficult to use, and do not constitute historical documents in the contemporary sense. Current views of the period are thus bound to be new interpretations of existing matter, rather than inferences from newly-won facts. The chance of any fresh written source can, alas, probably be ruled out. Post-war archaeology has thrown much light on purely local developments at this time, but since the inferences drawn from this work need not, by their very nature, ever have been reflected in written history, historical research tends more and more to lean on analogies cautiously drawn from the much better documented European mainland during the same centuries.

Detailed investigation of some towns at the end of the Roman period—notably Silchester, St Alban's, Winchester, and Canterbury—hints at continued urban life well into the 5th century. At Verulamium (St Alban's), large-scale rebuilding in the early 5th century must be coupled with a still-functioning aqueduct and piped water. At Canterbury, Germanic soldiers, in what role must be uncertain, appear within the city not before about 450. Silchester has yielded early 5th-century debris. A less important centre, the *vicus* at Carlisle, notable as the probable home of St Ninian and very likely a Christian town in the 5th century, was apparently occupied in the late 7th century, and may never have been deserted. Though other towns, such as Exeter, where the recorded coinage series runs out in the 380s, do appear to have been deserted at this time, the recent recognition that both silver and copper coins ceased to circulate meaningfully in Britain after about AD 430 implies that the absence of this, the major aid to dating, does not automatically indicate the end of town life.

The Native Re-assertion

There is some evidence, too, for a gradual change in the whole *character* of Britain during late and sub-Roman times. The great northern frontier of Hadrian's Wall never wholly recovered from the massive revolt of AD 367–9, a revolt in which the Celtic and other barbarians were joined by Germanic-speakers from the European mainland. The consequent necessity—consequent not only on this insurrection, but on continuous flank attacks from

Irish raiders—of arranging that local and supposedly pro-British groups should assume the status of *foederati*, that is, federates, or quasi-independent peoples charged by treaty with the defence of a particular frontier region, may ironically have hastened the very process (the dissolution of Roman Britain) that it was designed to prevent.

The recorded tribal organization of pre-Roman Britain was to some extent perpetuated during the Roman centuries, since many tribal areas, with re-adjustments, were constituted as *civitates*; regions of unequal size with local capitals, local councils, and a measure of responsibility for local administration and finance. We may suspect that the power within a *civitas* lay, by and large, in the hands of the same class that, in previous centuries, had provided the elective monarchs, the war-leaders, and the major land-holders. Downright chieftaincy, probably rendered respectable within the *civitates* by the medium of Roman titles and Roman names, flourished in border regions. Federate tribes appear to have existed, under what could be described as their own royal families, in southern Scotland, and possibly in parts of Wales. By the 5th century other groups for whose federate status no evidence exists were becoming independent kingdoms, their seats in reoccupied Iron Age hill citadels, and their reinstated monarchs provided with suitable pedigrees harking back either to Roman or to native heroes. How far, if at all, before AD 400 this process can be traced is uncertain; but Rome was either unwilling, or locally unable, to prevent the trend.

Similar British independence can be detected in spiritual matters. The official Roman religion, the state worship of deified emperors and the accepted Roman pantheon, had been the rock on which, before AD 313, Christianity had struck, in particular emperor-worship. Pagan cults in Britain had been made respectable through a convenient process (*interpretatio Romana*) which re-defined local gods or goddesses as British manifestations of official Roman deities. Yet, in the hills and thickets, un-Romanized godlings, represented by various cult-objects, may have lingered, and the mysterious healing god *Nodens*, in whose honour a large and popular temple with an attached pilgrim-centre appears in a Gloucestershire hill-fort in the 360s, seems to be wholly non-Roman and indeed a likely avatar of the Irish god *Nuada*. Nor should one overlook the distinct possibility that Christianity, as a popular rather than as an exotic religion, was on the increase in such districts as Cornwall, south Wales, the Solway Firth and the Galloway plain of south-west Scotland.

The most commonly employed archaeological index of cultural change or intrusion, whether in urban or rural settings, is that of domestic pottery. Under Roman rule, with its provision of mass-produced pottery for all classes save the extremely poor, who may have used wood and leather, and the rich, who would have preferred silver, glass, and perhaps pewter, the various native wares used to define pre-Roman cultural groupings and movements disappear, except in one or two marginal areas like Northumbria and the far south-west. But excavations today continue to reveal, in late Roman (perhaps, more often than is realized, sub-Roman) levels, the slow re-appearance of native pottery, hand-made, and not necessarily copying late Roman forms at all. It is not yet clear what this really implies. The position is further complicated by the recent recognition, on a number of western British sites of unquestionably sub- or post-Roman date (5th and 6th centuries) of wheel-made domestic pottery of Roman character. Dissemination by sea-borne trade and a source in Late Roman or Merovingian Gaul at the moment forms the most acceptable explanation.

The First Germanic Settlers

Pottery evidence has again been used to show the presence, in 4th- and 5th-century England, of groups who were neither Roman nor British. Germanic mercenaries had for years served in the Roman army, rising to high rank, and sometimes in whole tribal groups. Some students would now accept the interpretation of one account to mean that specifically Saxon and Frankish mercenaries were stationed in Britain in the late 3rd and 4th centuries, and the probability that during a subsequent period Franks, or similar, mercenaries could be found in both Ireland and Wales

relies not only on literary references but on the discovery of objects pertaining to military dress and armament of Germanic type in pre-Viking Irish contexts. In Kent, the Thames valley, and parts *f 1* of East Anglia, the presence of late 4th- or very early 5th-century settlers has also been adduced from certain finds. Whether these were *foederati*, less well-known groups like *laeti* (independent settlers with certain obligations), or merely time-expired mercenaries accepted into the general populace, cannot as yet be shown; but Myres and others would now isolate a class of pottery, called 'Romano-Saxon', Roman in ware and technique, but of shapes, and with specific ornament, which suggest that these pots were being produced in Britain to satisfy the tastes of those accustomed to similar-looking vessels in their own homelands. In a few cases, the decorative traits or shapes so closely recall the supposed prototypes that terms like 'Romano-Frisian' might just be applied.

At some stage—and the search for a single, absolute, date may be misleading if it carries the implication of a single, definite event—Germanic-speaking settlers ceased to occupy homesteads by Roman, or sub-Roman, or British, authority, and did so by right of arms. This happening is in no sense unique or special in itself; a very similar process probably occurred in south-west Wales, where Irish settlers were at the same period constructing a local kingdom. Its importance lies in the results, among which may be counted the fact this essay is being written in English, rather than Welsh or a descendant of Latin. Nor were the settlements confined to the south-east; subsequent settlement affected Wessex and Northumbria, and in parts of Lincoln and Yorkshire this may go back to the 5th century. Again, armed conflict between Britons and Anglo-Saxons may, by modern or even by Roman standards, have been on the puniest scale; but the fact that such conflict could happen at all, and the realization that, owing to some irrevocable decision in the past which first permitted the Germanic speakers to settle, they could never be dislodged, left a profound trauma on the British national consciousness.

The Anglo-Saxon Settlements

The traditional retrospective view of these events, derived from Gildas, Bede, Nennius, and the Anglo-Saxon Chronicle, and filtered through Geoffrey of Monmouth and various medieval redactors, held the field until well into the nineteenth century. It possessed the attractions of brevity, simplicity, and rationality. The legions departed, leaving a form of Roman organization behind them. Tyrants in the west seized power, and one of them, Vortigern, was obliged to invite Angles and Saxons to Britain in order to assist the British, bereft of Roman protection, in their struggles against the Picts and Scots. Having defeated these northern barbarians and tasted the measure of Britain, the Angles and Saxons sent home for further settlers, including the Jutes. Their demands for increased provisions not having been met, they now allied themselves with the Picts, and commenced to devastate Britain, paying special attention to towns, to villas, to churches, and to Christians. Temporary respite was won, somewhere in southern England, by a British victory at Mount Badon under the last of the British Romans, Ambrosius Aurelianus (in later accounts, both confused with and identified with a British warleader, Arthur). The inevitable moral aspect of the story is that the fate of the British followed wholesale corruption of state and church after the Roman withdrawal. Ecclesiastically, this was marked by the adoption of a heresy propagated by Pelagius, mainly concerned with the existence of original sin; temporarily, by the personal sins of Vortigern and subsequent British rulers (incest, adultery, murder, pride, and other offences). Despite a visit to Britain by St Germanus of Auxerre, probably in AD 429 in an attempt to check Pelagianism, when he quite incidentally directed the British in a local victory over Picts and Saxons, the course of events in the 5th and 6th centuries was, from a British angle, one of scarcely-relieved disaster representative nevertheless of Divine retribution.

While it is still just tenable that this constitutes, in rough outline, the story of the Anglo-Saxon settlement, it is an outline very largely resting on the writings of an Anglian monk in the early

8th century. The 5th-century British, or Romano-British, account is missing: Gildas' unspecific ramblings and the scattered references from late Roman historians do not begin to supply this want. Recent scholarship has concentrated, rightly, on establishing the likelihood of details within the traditional framework, rather than on forcing wholesale acceptance of the framework itself. Thus the departure of the Romans may indeed have been followed, as Bede says, by British appeals for Roman protection, the last to Aetius after AD 446. St Germanus may have visited England, and his temporary army may have been drawn from the population of St Alban's. The existence of Pelagius, and of Vortigern, is not generally doubted, though the latter, who is to be associated with central or north Wales, can only have exercised some extraordinary personal power if he really attempted to bring Germanic *foederati* to England, and his sin is as likely to have been the support of Pelagianism as any marital irregularity. That some groups of Germanic settlers were in fact federates, and became dangerous when their hosts were unable to supply the necessary corn, rings true if only because very similar things were happening, vis-à-vis the late Empire and other Germanic groups, on the Continent. The idea of a temporary British victory, associated with Ambrosius and with whatever actual person resides behind the popular Arthur, overloaded with medieval accretions, is perfectly acceptable; the location (southern England? Dorset?) and the date (within the first half of the 6th century) of the battle of Mount Badon are disputable, but the battle itself is regarded as a fact. Certain areas, even within southern England, appear to have remained British long after AD 400. Neither the Cotswolds nor the Chilterns fell to Saxons before the mid-6th century. There was a Celtic-speaking Christian enclave in Dorset until the 7th century. On the other hand—and this should be seen against the backcloth of vast Midland forests and an overall sparse population—Anglo-Saxon settlers appear to have been in Warwickshire at a surprisingly early date, and the chronology of the first landings in Wessex (Southampton Water? west Sussex?) requires re-appraisal.

Ireland's Heroic Age

The weakening of the northern and western frontiers, following the collapse of the Wall and the eventual abandonment of York and Chester, no doubt provided a fresh stimulus to barbarian invasion. A trickle of Roman finds in Ireland, reaching a peak in the later 4th and the 5th centuries, indicates a long tradition of piracy and sea-raiding, and the Picts and other peoples of the far north had really been discouraged rather than effectively debarred by the northern defences. In order to appreciate the part played by these groups in sub-Roman times, in their own lands as well as in what are now England and Wales, it is however necessary to turn to the dimly-perceived, but crucially relevant, history of Ireland at this period.

The earliest sources for Irish history, redacted by a professional literary class and confused by native origin-myths, place-name explanations, and a profound disregard both for objective fact and chronological relevance, none-the-less allow a convincing picture to be sketched. It is one of a vigorous Late Iron Age society grouped on a tribal and dynastic basis, with an economy partly pastoral and partly agricultural. This society was constrained rather than encouraged by elaborate social stratification, and by advanced concepts of tribal custom or law, internal boundaries, and the tenure of land. The inter-tribal friction which characterized a very similar stage of pre-Roman Gaul, and which in pre-Roman southern Britain could be employed by the Romans as one of the excuses for conquest, predictably applied to Ireland both during and long after the Roman period in Britain. In terms of Irish pseudo-history, the secular narratives (when not concerned with barely comprehensible mythology) revolve around warrior-kings and champions, cattle-raiding, chariot warfare, conquests, slavery, and expulsions. The material reflection can be found in the proliferation of defended homesteads, tribal hill-capitals, and frontier dykes.

In a sense, this colourful but unsettled era (which is rather more faintly detectable in the far north, among the not very dissimilar Picts) represents the Irish version of what H. M. Chad-

Square-headed bronze pin, probably 6th century, from an Anglo-Saxon cemetery at Faversham, in Kent. The pattern of Germanic settlement in England is gradually being built up from such finds. This example is unusual in using a stylized human figure as decoration. (1)

wick has called 'the Heroic Age'. The southern British counterpart was cut short by the Romans, and, sadly, has left no heroic literature behind it—though there are hints that a legend of Caractacus, who defied Rome, may have still been known in the 5th century. In Ireland, it could be argued that the Heroic Age only reached its peak in late Roman times. One effect was to bring about numerous minor invasions of the British mainland.

The reasons for this have seldom been examined, but they are likely to be social and economic. The distribution of almost any class of site or settlement in 1st-millennium Ireland suggests a population density in advance of that in contemporary Britain, and in a tribal, agricultural, society such an increasing density would be normal. The rigidity of Irish custom and the complexity of land-tenure would make it difficult for the country to absorb aggressive and younger elements on an unlimited scale. Large and sparsely-populated tracts of western Britain were not only open to them, but could be approached by well-known sea lanes, long used for piracy and slave-raiding. The earliest known settlement, from east-central Ireland to the 'pig's ear' of northern Wales, the Lleyn peninsula of Caernarvonshire, should be dated well back in the Roman period, and may at first have been locally tolerated, though by sub-Roman times it seems to have required containing by force. A far more important movement brought, according to Irish sources, most of one tribe (the Deisi) and part of another (the Ui Liathain) from southern Ireland to south-west Wales. This is best seen as a process which did actually culminate in some major event, in the late 4th century, and just possibly involved *foederatio*. It resulted in the establishment of a local Irish dynasty, a partially bilingual populace, and an Irish foothold not wholly absorbed into Wales for a good many centuries.

In the north-west, where the Irish coast is occasionally visible from the Scottish hills, settlers from at least one Ulster tribe were moving into the coastal belt of Argyll, and some of the southern islands. Again, this may have culminated in some major event, if so perhaps in the 470s. Geographical considerations led to fission into separate tribes, with coastal citadels of Iron Age type, and there need not have been many settlers in the first instance. But the Scotti or Scoti, as Bede and other writers knew them, were eventually to give not only their Gaelic language but also their name to most of northern Britain.

Southwards, the Irish settlers in Pembroke and Carmarthen spread (probably within a framework of nominal Christianity) into east Cornwall, north Devon, and parts of Somerset (certainly as far as Glastonbury), also in the later 5th century. In the 6th, further Irish—from the archaeological record, it would seem both peaceable and perhaps direct from Ireland—are to be encountered in much of west Cornwall and the Isles of Scilly.

The Tapestry of Migration

There are other migrations within Britain at this time, not necessarily connected with Ireland. Within the 5th century, either at its start (due to Roman initiative) or a little later (due to some such figure as Bede's concept of Vortigern), a large portion of the Votadini, a Late Iron Age tribe in what is now south-east Scotland, was persuaded to migrate to northern Wales; presumably as federates, presumably also to counterbalance Irish settlement in Caernarvonshire. Later historical sources explain, unconvincingly, that these Votadinians expelled the Deisi and the Ui Liathain from south Wales, but rather scanty archaeological evidence would connect them with the temporary re-occupation of some long-deserted north Welsh hillforts at this time. In the north-east, the Picts, too, were on the move. These little-known people, a mixture of a Celtic-speaking ruling class of Iron Age origins coming from the south, and a larger native Bronze Age populace, consolidated their position around the Moray Firth, and down the great pastoral belt of Aberdeen into Forfar and Fife. The Picts north of the Mounth, the belt of high land which runs east-west and into the North Sea just south of Aberdeen, spread up the coastal plain of Caithness and Sutherland, and into Orkney and Shetland; indeed, to some extent also due west, since they seem to have occupied parts of Skye.

From comparatively early in the 5th century, groups of southern British—one may locate them anywhere between Sussex and Cornwall—went overseas to the old Gallo-Roman province of Armorica, the present Brittany. By the 6th century, when this movement had gathered a certain impetus, the colonists seem mostly to have been drawn from the present Devon and Cornwall, and the Breton language results from this transfer of an insular speech. The social and linguistic links thus forged disintegrated only in the post-medieval period. It was once the fashion to explain the whole of this very extensive migration in terms of refugees from the advancing Saxons, but, chronological difficulties apart, this must now be seen as only one of a number of possible reasons. Dislike of unrest, the civil wars and famines to which Gildas and Bede allude, fear of the Irish, and the over-population in late Roman times of arable lands in Cornwall and south Devon, are all equally valid. Finally, some unsolved problems still linger. In the Isle of Man, a British population seems to have been overwhelmed, between the 5th and 7th centuries, by an Irish one, but our knowledge of this is almost wholly from linguistic sources. The post-Roman see of Britonia, in north-west Spain, complete with bishops whose names appear to be Celtic, involved Britons, Bretons, or both, but little is known about this at all; and there is an even more remote possibility, quite unexplored, that parts of eastern Scotland and Scandinavia were in contact centuries before the Norse settlers arrived.

This veritable tapestry of movement and migration—in Continental archaeology, the term 'Migration Period' is actually, and accurately, employed for it—succeeded in re-aligning for ever a Britain which, under the Romans, had not essentially changed since the 1st century BC. By some such date as AD 600, Britain, in terms of speech, ethnic content, and even partial physical appearance, would have presented a scene as strange to a Romanized Briton of the 2nd century as to an Englishman of Plantagenet times. The most obvious peculiarity would, perhaps, be the absence of urban life. In Italy, Gaul, and other parts of the late Empire, Roman towns with their walled nuclei and sprawling suburbs continued as centres of life, the majority to our own times. In Britain, there is no absolutely certain example of this. By the late 5th century, the sub-Roman British would have lacked the technology to keep a large town repaired and in working order, and outside south-eastern England, the reversion to large timber halls and re-furbished hillforts was well under way. The Irish, the Picts, and many of the Welsh, knew nothing of town life. Nor did the Anglo-Saxons. Save perhaps for Kent, where Germanic settlers were in touch with town-using kinsfolk in northern Gaul, the Anglo-Saxons tended to perpetuate a tradition of the single-family homestead, and the chieftain's communal hall with attached outworks, that stretched back in an immensely long tradition of competent timberwork to the European neolithic; that had much, too, in common (save for details of shape) with

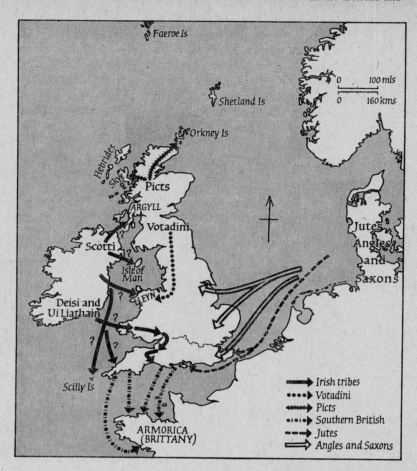

The migrations of the 6th-7th centuries determined many of the national groups of modern Britain and Brittany. Scotland, for example, acquired its name from Irish settlers, the Scotti, and Brittany from British migrants from southern England. But Angles, Saxons, and Jutes from around the Jutland peninsula (where their location is still very conjectural) were fast gaining control of areas in the east. (2)

the vernacular styles of west and north Britain. Unlike the Franks and Goths in Gaul, who, in attuning barbaric splendour to late Roman styles, inherited an administrative class to run late Roman towns for them, the Anglo-Saxons ignored urban England. Despite what Bede tells us, there is remarkably little evidence that the towns themselves were sacked; possibly those still worth sacking were also still able to fend off assault. The crumbling Roman edifices that refused to disintegrate, as a roofless timber hall would do, were *enta geweorc*, the work of giants. That extraordinary Old English poem, 'The Ruin' (perhaps about Bath), contains the poet's half-envious description of what he thought the town had formerly looked like—pinnacles, gushing fountains, paved courts and lofty gates. It is peopled nostalgically with heroic but grotesquely un-Roman concepts of mead halls and warriors' seats, gluttonous wine-feasts, and omnipresent gold and gems. Here surely, within these walls constructed beyond the skill of mere men, the gods condescended once to walk; and the eventual English resumption of town life, significantly, was in the wake of church and court, not through any spontaneous popular movement.

Christianity and the Old Gods

The end of the 6th century, archaeologically well after anything that can be called sub-Roman, historically past the point of balance of the various British migrations, forms a kind of caesura in British history. Approximately the half-way mark between the end of Roman times, and the arrival of the Norsemen, it also marks the stage at which Christianity, hitherto important but localized, begins to assume a national significance. From this general period, literacy, the concept of law, and almost all the major and minor arts, are not only firmly established but begin to exhibit progress and development comparable to their European counterparts.

Christianity may first have reached Britain (through either the Roman army or the administration, less probably through

Mediterranean traders) before the end of the 2nd century AD. It gained some foothold in the 3rd, and in 314, three bishops—of York, London, and a place which is either Lincoln or Colchester attended a council at Arles. Such slender evidence as we have hints at a British concentration on the Romanized civil province, and within that province, an urban emphasis. Survival of the faith in 5th-century southern England is attested, not only by St Germanus' visit, but by the apparent spread of Pelagianism. It now seems feasible that restricted areas in the west and the north—specifically Galloway and Carlisle, the north-west of Wales, and Cornwall—contained 5th-century Christian communities whose origins had lain within Roman Britain. In most of Ireland, Scotland, Wales, and probably widespread in the English countryside, paganism continued. In Ireland, a polytheistic religion which is amply reflected in surviving literature, archaic, conservative, and open to innumerable local variations, held the field, and the northern British and the Picts must have had religious beliefs akin to those of the other Celtic-speaking peoples. The Germanic invaders had a not dissimilar series of cults, the general character of which will be familiar to most people insofar as it survived in Norse beliefs and sagas; like all peasant communities, they also possessed an intricate web of superstitions and charms, many of which are fortunately preserved in Old English compilations of medical and herbal lore.

p 246 (9–11)

The problem of whether or not Christianity in lowland England could survive the initial centuries of pagan Anglo-Saxon settlement is still unresolved. Bede believed that it had been entirely wiped out, even though a church of the Roman period had survived in Canterbury, and was used by the Frankish Christian Queen Bertha in the 590s. Most scholars would agree with Bede on the first score, mainly because there is so little evidence that Christianity was at all widespread when the Anglo-Saxons turned on their hosts. But implicit in the same theory is the idea that Christian refugees from the horrors of heathendom took the faith to the north and west, the latter term including Ireland. This idea, in part also derived from Bede's account, must underlie the recent statement by a distinguished historian of Roman Britain that 'the so-called Celtic Church, surviving continuously in the west and north, was thoroughly Roman in creed and origin'. In matters of dogma, yes: but the disputable word here is 'continuously'.

Much of the past difficulty in approaching the related questions of 5th-century Christianity in Ireland and in north Britain has resided in the semantic undertones of the word 'missionary'. As E. A. Thompson has shown in a series of penetrating studies, it is incorrect to attribute a missionary role to the late Roman church. There is ample evidence that the arrival of a bishop at, or beyond, the northern frontiers of the Empire at this time (frontiers which of course include Hadrian's Wall and the Welsh coast) signifies, not the desire of Rome to engage in the conversion of some pagan tribe, but the response to an existing Christian community's request for spiritual leadership. Thus when Nynia, or Ninian, appears as a bishop at Whithorn in the 5th century, as Bede tells us, this is not an attempt to convert the 5th-century Gallowegians, but the establishment of an episcopal seat or even the replacement for a local bishop, and is concerned with a late Roman Christian community in that area. Such a community, whose cemetery, now located deep below the east end of the medieval Whithorn Priory, apparently intrudes into a Roman burial-ground, and possibly goes back even into the 4th century, would be in touch with others in the region; notably Carlisle, which forms the most likely background for Ninian himself. To describe Whithorn at this era as a 'Celtic monastery', and to ascribe to Ninian both the desire to convert, and the actual conversion of, the southern Picts (i.e., in Fife, Perth, and Forfar), is to follow both Bede and the author of the 8th-century poem on the Miracles of Ninian in projecting back into the 5th century concepts proper only to subsequent centuries, including Bede's own. The historical evidence for Ninian begins, after all, only with Bede, three centuries later. The archaeological evidence—

244 (3)

the nature and distribution of memorial stones—points at a regular southern Scottish diocese, between the Walls, with Christian centres corresponding roughly to the seats of sub-Roman power and the foci of population in the area.

The Apostle of Ireland

So, too, with the much more complex study of Ireland and St Patrick, it strains the evidence unwarrantably to regard the Apostle of Ireland as a super-human missionary, despatched by Rome to convert a pagan land with which he was partly familiar because he had been a slave there. It is a study admittedly confused by the unending controversy as to the identity of Patrick himself. Where and when he lived, worked, and died; whether there was more than one Patrick; as an extreme view, whether Patrick really existed at all; these are all questions which can constitute a lifetime's research in themselves. Most students would accept his *Confessio* (a stylized partial autobiography) and some limited early material either by Patrick or one of his biographers, as reflecting a real and historical person. The acceptance allows the following outline of his career. He was born of a middle-class Romano-British Christian family, probably (like Ninian) in the Carlisle area, just possibly in the *vicus* at what is now Bewcastle. As a boy, he was captured by Irish slave-raiders, and taken into slavery in the modern Ulster. He escaped, and from a southern Irish port, secured a passage to the Continent. At least a decade later, and assuming that he had undergone some form of prolonged Christian training and had been consecrated as a bishop, he returned to Ireland. There he was associated—in tradition—with other clerics, some of whom bore Latinized names. About thirty years later, he died, leaving a growing and permanent impression on his adopted land.

The official (i.e. state- and Church-supported) Irish dating is that the return to Ireland took place in 432, and Patrick's death in 461: and that the conversion of the Irish was Patrick's main intention and undertaking. The dates are derived from much later annalistic entries, and their acceptance involves explanation of other entries recording the arrival of Palladius (a bishop sent by Pope Celestine) in 431, the death of 'old Patrick' (*senex Patricius*) in 457, and even the death of Patrick in 491 or 492. Is 'old Patrick', as many think, Palladius, a colleague outshone by the other Patricius, whose real (British) name seems to have been Sucat? The later death favours an alternative chronology in which the return to Ireland is not before 461, and there is some ancillary evidence which does partly support the later dating. But, despite the lack of any direct chronological clues in Patrick's own writing, the general milieu favours—on balance—the 432–461 period.

There is nothing inherently unlikely in the *Confessio* itself, nor in many traditional details of Patrick's career. As with Ninian, problems abound unless this career is, from the outset, divorced from all concepts of a missionary expedition. Patrick's major task was surely the pastoral care of 5th-century Irish Christians, and the conversions widely and elaborately attributed to him should, in this light, be regarded as incidental. Some obscure and archaic traditions do indeed point to groups of early Christians, not necessarily around Armagh, the primatial see whose later pre-eminence seems mainly due to retrospective association with the saint. The south-east seaboard of Waterford and Wexford, and inland to central Munster, forms the focus for these traditions. The contacts between southern Ireland and south-west Wales, already discussed, and the maritime links between Ireland and some area of western Gaul, inherent in Patrick's own escape from slavery, provide the essential setting for any introduction of Christian belief into Ireland in the late 4th century. Refugee Christians from lowland England need scarcely be postulated here.

Augustine's Mission

This episcopal church, as it must have been, associated with Patrick, Ninian, and perhaps parts of western Britain besides, did not apparently survive the 6th century. The reasons for this are not primarily theological at all, and are well shown in Bede's careful transcript of Pope Gregory's instructions to St Augustine of Canterbury in 601. Augustine was in the first place to ordain twelve bishops, including one for London, within his own see; further, to ordain a bishop to serve as a second metropolitan (at York), who was himself to see to the ordination of a further twelve bishops to serve the north. These instructions are full of interest, not least in the questions they raise as to the physical

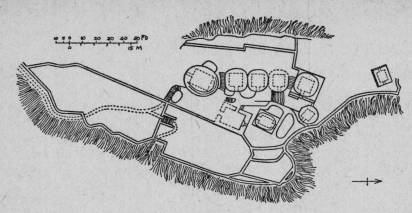

The early Celtic monastery on Skellig Michael, a 700 foot rock eight miles off the west coast of Ireland. It is almost surrounded by sheer cliffs and reached by a precipitous path from the sea consisting of 670 steps. The date of its foundation is unknown, but is recorded as existing in the early 9th century. Some of its dry-stone buildings still survive. The beehive cells (circular outside, rectangular within) cluster round a small church. (3)

state of York at this time, Augustine's own consecration as Archbishop at Arles, his dispensation to consecrate his own bishops without the necessary presence of at least two further bishops, and the specific references to contemporary British bishops who may have represented the mainland relics of the episcopal church of Roman Britain. The major point here is the geography of Gregory's instructions. These would have been both familiar and practicable in, say, Gaul, where any civil organization would be based on a surviving network of roads and cities, and where church government had long followed the hierarchic pattern of Roman civil administration. In the context of Britain, they were meaningless. The twenty-four cities, with Canterbury and York twenty-six, strangely like the traditional List of the Cities of Britain which occurs several centuries later in Nennius' writings, did not exist. The Roman view, that the countryside was merely an appendage of the town, would have been unintelligible to the English outside Kent, and Augustine in the end undertook only two ordinations, London and Rochester.

Whoever the seven or more British bishops with whom Augustine failed to reach agreement in 602 or 603 were, or others previously encountered between 597 and 601 in Wessex, and where precisely they functioned, are insoluble puzzles. We need not disbelieve in their existence, but the chances are strong that they included some from the monastic church of the west. In southern Scotland, far more so in Ireland, any attempt to extend the Patrician episcopate along the lines envisaged by Pope Gregory for Augustine's work would have equally met with failure. One cannot be sure that the Irish kingdoms even possessed permanent fixed capitals in the modern sense. The only ecclesiastical system which had a chance of winning widespread popular acceptance was one which could be assimilated to Celtic notions of land-tenure, successorship, direct personal authority, and the existence of a privileged class free to cross the dangerous tribal boundaries with impunity. The elements of just such a system were at hand. From the end of the 5th century onwards, it not only replaced the meagre sub-Roman episcopates but, having swept through almost all the Celtic-speaking areas of Britain, made important inroads on the Germanic-speaking areas, and from this base, was free to affect the European mainland as well.

The importance of the Church in Britain from about AD 500 to 800 cannot be over-emphasized. The Church was practically the sole repository of literacy and (save for a restricted field of personal ornament) the arts. The secular traditions of timber construction, re-inforced by the Anglo-Saxons, undoubtedly attained high if ephemeral standards; but the equally ancient tradition of stonework that was eventually to provide (with European assistance) the English cathedral and the English parish church, can be directly traced to ecclesiastical origins in the later 7th century. In Ireland, the only large portion of the British Isles which had not been invaded by some other group since the 1st centuries BC and AD, the Church, replacing the prolonged and ragged dynastic conflicts of earlier times, developed an inner stability

that was not shaken or eroded until the beginning of the 9th century with the advent of the Norse. Over most of England, the nascent Germanic kingdoms—insular developments from the incoming 5th-century families and clans—aligned and re-aligned themselves, the conflicts being especially elaborate in the north. Here, the surviving and powerful British states of southern Scotland, the Irish settlers in Argyll, and the Picts beyond the Forth, disputed not only with each other but with the Angles of Northumbria. In Wales, the tedious border struggles with Mercia had begun, the Welsh themselves grouping into the divisions of North and South that were to precede the eventual display of national unity. In the south-west, weakened by the emigrations to Brittany, the revived post-Roman state of Dumnonia contracted as the vigorous Saxons of Wessex pushed through Somerset to seize the rich 'red lands' of south Devon and to attain the Atlantic coast of north Cornwall. Only in Ireland does the Church of the far west, unhampered by these extraneous campaignings, attain its full development.

A New Way of Life—the Monasteries

The monastic church in Britain was derived, at some remove, from the Middle East. Communal settlements of would-be anchorites and Christian refugees can be traced as early as the 3rd century in the Egyptian deserts. A modified form of this ascetic life, associated with Pachomius, and stressing the community of life, worship and labour, attained great vogue around the East Mediterranean from the 4th century. Through the popular currency of the early 'Lives' of these desert fathers as much as through the personal contact of travellers, monasticism took root in southern Gaul by the late 4th century. Whether the immediate inspiration of such houses as Lérins (an island group off-shore from Cannes) lay in Egypt, or (more probably) in the region of Greece, Turkey, and Syria, is still disputed. There is little doubt that, by the end of the 5th century, monasticism had spread to Britain.

The chronology and geography of this implantation, a feature of insular Christianity only recently defined, remain something of a puzzle. Limited aid is afforded by the discovery that a seaborne trade (via the Straits of Gibraltar) linked a variety of Continental and Mediterranean ports with the whole of Atlantic Britain, from Argyll to Scilly. This trade, independent of the Germanic control of the Channel and the North Sea, must have originated in the Roman centuries as far as Gaul was involved, but its extension to Egypt and the Aegean is a deomnstrably later happening. Changing economic currents on the Continent and the Arab control of the Straits brought it to an end about 700, but before this time, importations of wheel-made oil or wine jars and fine table ware do afford partial indications of dates.

The south Welsh coastal plain may have seen the first establishment of monasticism, in the later 5th century. At Tintagel, in p 245 north Cornwall, a monastery probably founded by Irish Christian settlers from south Wales, the earliest Mediterranean pottery is assigned to a decade or so before 500. The later pre-eminence or Glastonbury may derive from an original monastic foundation (on the site of a Roman-period church?) at this time. Irish monasticism traditionally derived from south Wales—this is a sound tradition, inherently likely—and the emphasis on individual saints, like Finnian of Clonard (d. 549), in this context, may point to a period of widely-recognized foundation. From the middle of the 6th century, a number of major Irish centres can be traced. These include Clonmacnoise, founded about 544–7, and Iona, p 244 an Irish extension into the Dalriadic colony, founded by Columba in 563.

The western monastery succeeded, where the sub-Roman episcopate could never have done, in grafting itself on to the body politic of the post-Roman west. Self-contained and self-sufficient, the visible domain of a recognized spiritual chieftain, the monastery was yet one more manifestation of the hierarchical tribal society. Bishops indeed existed, if only to perform consecrations and ordinations, but they were wholly without territorial bishoprics. The head of a monastery, recipient of the original landgrant from some local potentate, was an abbot; like Columba on p 249 Iona, he was not necessarily a bishop at all. Successive abbots, (20) nominated and elected from the founder's kin, were (in terms of

Irish customary law) the legal heirs to the land-grant. The solitary ascetic, the man of special gifts or powers, may have been Christian, but socially he was a long-accepted facet of Irish society.

Historical sources tell us little save the occasional foundation date, the deaths of notable abbots or scribes, the more important synods, and (at a later stage) the depredations of Norse pirates. Within this sketchy framework, archaeology has done much to fill the picture. Very few monasteries have been excavated, mainly because so many of them now lie beneath later churches and burial grounds, but the basic pattern is clear. The monastery was enclosed in some kind of *enceinte* or *vallum*. A few of the very earliest seem to lie in large rectangular enclosures of the bank-and-ditch variety. This, an ultimate echo of the rectangular fortress and house plans of the Mediterranean (otherwise only known, on this scale, in Britain through Roman military engineering and town lay-out), stresses the Levantine and south Gaulish roots of monasticism. The most common *enceinte* is oval or circular, a pattern derived from the continuing Iron Age circular-fort tradition of Britain; indeed a number of monasteries were sited within deserted forts, an interesting sidelight on the times since it would appear that, deserted or not, such forts were still the property of the tribal ruler.

The Church in Ireland, by accident or design, undertook the evangelization of the north. From various west Scottish foundations, of which Iona, Lismore and Applecross are the best known, Christianity may have reached Orkney by AD 600, and at the same time was percolating into the territory of the northern Picts around the Moray Firth. The extension of the Faith to Shetland, the Faeroes, and Iceland—if no further—constitutes an extraordinary record of perilous sea-voyaging, anticipating the Norsemen by several centuries.

Scholarship, Letters and the Arts

Literacy in late Roman, and sub-Roman, times was almost certainly synonymous and coterminous with a knowledge of Latin. While the Roman (capital) letters were employed on the mainland, a curious stroke alphabet (ogam) was developed, either in south-west Wales or southern Ireland, by Irish literati in touch with what remained of Roman culture. Both alphabets were, from the 5th century, used on simple memorials to the dead. These themselves are of great interest, since they not only reveal something of the extent to which British Christian epigraphy followed Mediterranean examples, and the degree of Latinization of British personal names, but they also afford the earliest written linguistic material (save for pre-Roman coinage) for the insular Celtic languages. Precisely what written material, and in which media (wax tablets, wood, vellum, papyrus), had been used in the British church before the 5th century we shall never ascertain, but it can safely be assumed that both Ninian and Patrick possessed, in some form, the bare minima of service-books, or gospels. If Patrick's *Confessio* and certain letters be accepted as genuine, he himself must have been familiar with a rather wider range of Latin writing, and the evidence from villa mosaics alone suggests that such secular poets as Virgil had been popular in Roman Britain. The earliest British manuscript tradition, within the framework of monastic Christianity, cannot be taken back before the later 6th century, but monasticism itself must have brought fresh supplies of religious literature in its wake. In view of the sea-trade with the Mediterranean mentioned earlier, it is of interest to learn that the Church in Spain (having shed itself of the Arian heresy introduced by its own Germanic [Gothic] invaders) played some kind of part in the transmission of letters to Ireland.

Side-by-side with literacy went the arts. Here we are, unfortunately, restricted to those objects which have survived, and the potential importance of artistic development in such vanished media as wood, leather, textiles and possibly vellum, is usually forgotten. Occasional finds in bogs, and the analogy of such permafrost regions as central Siberia, where these materials have been preserved, hint at the extent of our loss. Ornamental metalwork (in gold, silver, bronze, and copper- or bronze-gilt) displays, in the 5th and 6th centuries, a variety of motifs and forms which recall, and are somehow rooted in, the so-called 'Ultimate Celtic' art which spilled over from the Iron Age into the early Roman centuries. Ireland certainly, northern Pictland and some part of Wales probably, saw the production of these Late Celtic objects, but the means by which the artistic heritage had been transmitted over the intervening centuries constitutes one of the major problems of British protohistory.

Except for the (pre-conversion) Picts, who engraved their memorial slabs with a variety of symbolic designs of Iron Age or older origin, art on stone was almost wholly Christian in context. The upright lettered memorial pillar gave way to other forms, upright or recumbent, which displayed simple crosses and other elements of early Christian iconography. Probably originating in a lost series of wooden prototypes, free-standing shaped stone crosses which were not necessarily commemorative of the dead, but could have didactic or other functions, became extremely popular; by the 8th and 9th centuries it is perfectly possible to distinguish individual schools of designs and even, occasionally, the work of individual master-craftsmen.

Conjecturally restored plan of St Wilfred's church at Hexham. The only part of the original building to survive is the crypt (shown here in outline), but there seem to have been several interesting and ambitious features, including double aisles to the nave. The small chapel standing east of the main church is paralleled at Canterbury. In both cases the two buildings were later joined together into one. (4)

The Northumbrian Golden Age

Celtic art, in the sense in which this term is generally understood, represents a fusion of these various forms; manuscripts, metalwork, sculpture. It reached, particularly in the 8th century, an extreme virtuosity, motifs and designs being freely transferable from one medium to another. Many of the earliest High Crosses in Ireland and the Irish colonies imitate, on a vast scale, ornamental metalwork or scenes from manuscripts and (imported) ivories; they possess irrelevant structural details which directly recall such things as the nails or tenon-joints of their wooden ancestors. Metalwork, at its finest using the dwindling reserves of looted Roman silver or silver-gilt (this is particularly true of Pictland), enriched with enamel or gems, could attain a pitch of craftsmanship seldom rivalled anywhere. Manuscript art, which, in addition to its devotional appeal, also attracted the finest artists of the period, blossomed into such masterworks as the Book of Kells and the Lindisfarne Gospels. It is no accident that the major art productions are all religious ones. The keenest minds, the steadiest hands, the best resources, the necessary leisure and unremitting application, were to be found in the monasteries. It is true to say that Bede's *History*, perhaps the supreme personal monument in European letters of this age, could never have been produced outside such a milieu as Jarrow.

The contact, in full post-Roman times, between the Celtic West and Saxon England, was not entirely confined to armed struggles over boundaries. An accident of history brought an area of north-east England into prominence in the 7th century. St Augustine's mission to the semi-European royal court of Kent had, as a slightly later offshoot, the despatch of the cleric Paulinus to the Anglian realm of Northumbria, where King Edwin had agreed to accept Christianity on the occasion of his betrothal to a Christian princess of Kent. Bede, a Northumbrian himself, quotes very full sources for this episode, fascinating because it includes an eye-witness account of Paulinus; 'a tall man with a

p 244 (5)
p 247–8 (16, 19)
p 256 (52)
p 252 (27)
p 250 (23, 25)
p 244 (3)
f 3
245 (6)
p 247 (12, 14)

slight stoop, with black hair, an ascetic face, and a venerable and majestic presence'. A mass conversion and baptism of the Angles took place by the river Glen, near the royal palace, about 627, but in 633, under a combined assault from pagan Mercians and Welsh, Edwin was killed and his realm ravaged. A year or so later, three northern Northumbrian princes who, for dynastic reasons, had been exiled in Scotland, returned, and eventually Oswald reconquered Northumbria for himself.

Oswald, a devout Christian, and bilingual in Old Irish and Old English, had lived among the Scots; if not actually on Iona, he must have been a familiar figure there. At his request, Aidan of Iona came to Northumbria, and, so Bede says, was given Holy Isle (Lindisfarne) as his see. The resemblance to the familiar Irish process of a land-grant to a monastic founder is no illusion, and Lindisfarne was the first of a series of monastic houses in Northumbria, from Yorkshire to the Firth of Forth, which represents no less than a direct extension of Irish monastic Christian practices into Germanic-speaking England. In retrospect, we can see that it was inevitably to be short-lived. Northumbria, now at the height of its power and influence, was in frequent contact with the European mainland and with Rome itself. If Lindisfarne, Old Melrose, Coldingham and Abercorn are physically indistinguishable from 7th-century Irish monasteries, the churches at Hexham, Ripon, Jarrow and Monkwearmouth revive an ecclesiastical strain represented by Paulinus' short-lived stone churches in Lincoln and York. Something of the splendour of Hexham, *f 4* a Mediterranean basilica implanted in the water-meads of the Tyne valley, can be felt there today. Northumbria was being absorbed into the tradition of episcopal Europe, and in 664, at the Synod of Whitby, she turned her back on Irish monasticism, *f 5* with its archaic and obsolescent tonsure, calculations of Easter, and other practices now regarded as irregular. In 710, Nectan, King of the southern Picts, and in some measure the Pictish overlord, formally brought his church and people within the Roman fold. The extent of the Picts' Christian debt to Ireland and the Irish colonies is uncertain, but it was strongest in the north, and the possibility that some southern Picts had been affected by the sub-Roman episcopate of Ninian and his successors cannot wholly be discounted. The remarkable church tower *p 253* at Restenneth, Angus, has recently (and convincingly) been *(36)* claimed as the work of Northumbrian masons shortly after 710. Between 716 and 718, the acceptance of Roman reforms took place at Iona itself, and the remaining exponents of Irish monasticism were expelled by Nectan from his Pictish demesnes. The

eventual future of the Church in Britain had been decided, even though Celtic monasticism, in an attenuated form, lingered on in parts of both Scotland and Ireland until the 11th century.

Northumbria, in what has aptly been called its Golden Age, forms an important aspect of early British history. There are grounds for believing, firstly, that a notable degree of fusion between the Anglian and British populations was accomplished, and secondly, though this is speculative, that without this century of comparative stability in the North, Christianity would have made insufficient headway amongst the other English kingdoms to withstand the first periods of pagan Norse assault. The pre-eminence of Lindisfarne itself as a source of both art and letters— *p 250* the Lindisfarne Gospels and the Codex Amiatinus are merely the *(25)* greatest surviving instances of Northumbrian book-production *p 243* during this period—needs no stressing. We should also recall that, Bede's work apart, much secular Old English poetry of great beauty is Northumbrian in origin and devolves from the same background.

The End of Peace

The British Isles, at the end of the 8th century, entered a prolonged period of unrest, generally, if not entirely, to be attributed to Norse raids and invasion. Again, as with the first Saxon settlements, a spectrum rather than any sharply-defined event, or contiguous series of events, is involved. Native annals naturally record, tersely, but with sufficient detail to allow us to appreciate what was implied, the sacking of monastery after monastery. There is no direct literary record of the Norse settlements, nor of their subsequent actions until a much later period. But for some years, it has been increasingly suspected (from archaeological finds, and from place-name work) that small groups of Scandinavians had been moving across the sea well before the 790s. Farmers and boatmen rather than pirates, their presence in the thinly-populated northern and western Isles would have led to comparatively little friction. The later phenomena of much larger settlements on the mainland, and the semi-nomadic Scandinavian army bands, reminiscent of the 5th-century Goths, blackmailing their way across country after country, have overshadowed these less well-defined groups who, coming from what was in essence a Late Iron Age agricultural background, would be unable to maintain themselves for long without recourse to this way of life. The predominantly agricultural character of the Norse colonization of Iceland bears out this view.

The course of events within both Ireland and Wales at this period is most imperfectly known; it is a period of stasis rather than progress, and though close enough to the era when most of our surviving quasi-historical sources were redacted, there is still ample room for argument in the interpretation of these sources. A most promising line of research, only newly developed, concerns the detailed settlement-history of these, and other, areas. It is probable that a great many surviving place-names can be attributed to this time; if and when these can be linked to appropriate distributions of dated settlement-types, a far clearer picture will emerge than any derived from study of those individual persons whose names, fortuitously, have been preserved in various records. 'Nothing causes more error and unfairness in man's view of history than the interest which is inspired by individual characters' wrote Lord Acton. When, as in so much of British protohistory, individual characters, and individual events of the battle, siege, and rapine type constitute practically the whole of the available written record, and when anything approaching a narrative is historically suspect because it conceals undisclosed layers of myth or pseudo-history, there is a case for a moratorium of a decade or so to allow a fresh set of inferences to be drawn from archaeological work or linguistic research.

With the 9th, 10th and 11th centuries, the 'late Saxon and Viking' period as it has been called, the essential character of post-Roman Britain disappears. The supremacy of Ireland in the West, politically, wanes. Christianity, the regular Roman form of which had been generally accepted throughout Britain by the late 8th century, has established itself beyond danger of extinction. Our knowledge of the period rests on rather different sources; among the English, the level of literacy, having spread from the Church

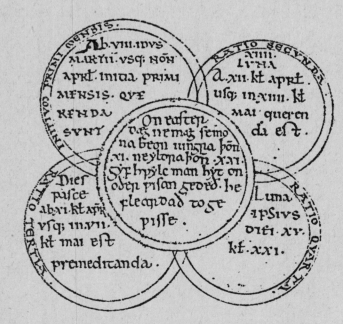

Chart for calculating Easter. When Augustine's mission succeeded in establishing Roman Catholicism as the official religion of Britain, one of the chief points on which the Celtic church had to give way was that concerning the date of Easter. The chart shown here was made by the monk Byrhtferth, a pupil of Abbo of Fleury, in an encyclopaedic manual dated 1011. (5)

to embrace the state as well, results in wills, charters, letters and biographies in addition to bare annals, and in recent decades settlement-excavation on a large scale has given us information about such late Saxon towns as Thetford, Hamwih (part of Southampton), and to a lesser extent Winchester and York; major sites such as Yeavering (a Northumbrian royal seat), Old Windsor, and many of the pottery manufactories.

The Vikings in Ireland

Within these centuries lies, omnipresent, the shadow of the Norse settlements. When considering, as some scholars have done, that the Norse contacts were sufficiently important to suggest comparison with the Roman occupation rather than with the various English settlements, it should be recalled that there is nothing particularly alien about the Norsemen at this time, as human beings. The inhabitants of Scandinavia (in particular, of Denmark and southern Norway) not only spoke a group of dialects ultimately closely related to Old English; they were the heirs of the same general material culture, the late Iron Age of north-west Europe, and their pagan religion had much in common with that of pre-Christian England.

We tend to regard Ireland as bearing the first brunt of Norse assault, probably because, having reached (in European terms) the highest level of insular culture in the modern sense, the Irish loss was in some respects the greatest. The first, isolated, coastal raids by Norwegians in search of plunder recall the less well-documented coastal piracy, by Irish seamen, of western Britain. But by the mid-9th century, such raids were penetrating deep inland. The long process of town formation, a process of which the Celts, left to themselves, appear to have been incapable, began with the fortified maritime bases like Dublin in the 830s. Wicklow, Wexford, Waterford, Cork and Limerick were in due course to arise similarly. Despite a series of struggles, in which occasionally the Irish nearly tipped the balance between defeat and victory, the position was aggravated after about 850, when a Danish fleet captured Dublin and the two rival Norse groups fought among themselves.

Recent studies have emphasized that not all Norsemen, or Vikings, were primarily after plunder, nor that the period around 800 really marks the beginning of their activities in Britain. It has now been hinted that the transmarine journeyings began after the eclipse of the (largely mercantile?) Frisian fleet after 734, and possibly a series of defeats of the generally overlooked Pictish fleet on the north-east littoral. Scattered settlement of a primarily agricultural nature in the Hebrides and the Northern Isles could have occurred, and almost certainly did, well within the 8th century. By the third quarter of the 9th century, the Norwegian jarldom of Orkney was firmly established. The Isle of Man became, probably via Ireland, a Norse kingdom at much this time. In the Norse realm of the Sudreyjar, the 'southern isles'—Man and the Hebrides—there was considerable ethnic fusion between well-to-do Norse settlers and the local Celtic-speaking inhabitants, still in a delayed Iron Age. Nowhere is this better evidenced than in the field of place-names. A curious outcome of this fusion was the appearance of groups of mixed descent—Gall-Gaedil or 'foreign Gaels' to the Irish—and their subsequent military activities, perhaps as mercenary bands, far from their homeland. They appear in Ireland in the later 9th century.

In 902, the Irish briefly re-took Dublin—an event which may be in large part responsible for the Norse settlement in north-west England, reflected not only in place-names (and dialect) but in the art of many of the later stone crosses—though Dublin was re-captured in 919. Local friction continued for a long period, despite a degree of social mingling reflected in various ways. By the mid-10th century large numbers of the Norsemen had been baptized, but (as elsewhere) the main material reflection of this fact is simply that monasteries and churchmen were, in general, left alone during the course of battle or plunder. The decisive Irish victory at Clontarf in 1014, an event which is profoundly stamped in the Irish national consciousness, led to the slow absorption of the remaining Norsemen. In terms of Irish art and culture, the robbing and obliteration of so many Irish monasteries in the 9th and 10th centuries, the removal of works

England at the end of the 9th century. A hundred years earlier the country had been divided into three main Kingdoms: Wessex, Northumbria and Mercia. In 829, under the control of Wessex, these became a unified Kingdom of England, but it was unable to survive the large-scale penetration of the Northmen which quickly followed. Alfred had finally to accept the existence of a Danelaw which stripped him of East Anglia and large parts of Northumbria and Mercia. (6)

of art (only fractionally represented in actual Scandinavian finds of this era) for their sheer bullion content, has displaced an entire chapter of our potential knowledge, particularly in the manuscript field. The shift of the Columban community (and their influence) from Iona to Kells soon after 800 may have enriched Ireland with many Northumbrian elements, notably figure representation, but it is not until the native craft revival of the 11th and 12th centuries that a few apparently direct Irish copies of Scandinavian objects appear.

The Impact on the North

In Scotland, the Angles, who had by the 640s established themselves in Edinburgh and the Forth shore, embarked on a long series of complex struggles with their northern neighbours; by no means always with success, as witness their defeat by the Picts at Nechtansmere in 685. The eventual, and perhaps inevitable, political fusion of the expanding Scots in the west and the conservative (perhaps by now divided) Pictish kingdom in the north and east took place, under Kenneth mac Alpin, in the 840s. The Norsemen, apart from their preliminary (and repeated) pillaging of such centres as Iona, turned their attention to both southern Pictland, and Strathclyde (the low-lying lands south of Glasgow) later in the 9th century. In the 10th century, the Scots occasionally entered into anti-Norse alignments with the English, though these seem to have been temporary: in 937, Athelstan defeated a mixed host which included the Scots, the Britons of Strathclyde, and the Dublin Norse. Yet the Scots, by necessity ceding the far North to the Norsemen, managed by the early 11th century to embrace not only nearly all of what had been Pictland, but also Strathclyde on the west and the Lothians on the east. The boundaries of modern Scotland took shape, though in the south-west, the modern Galloway, a settlement of Gall-Gaedil (whence the name) was laid over the successive Anglian and British occupations. With the marriage of Malcolm III ('Canmore') who ruled 1058–1093, to the formerly exiled Wessex Princess, Margaret of Hungary, the activities of their sons, notably David and Alexander, and the arrival of Norman notables and Romanesque architecture, Scotland at last entered medieval Europe.

Beyond Offa's Dyke

The detailed history of Wales during the late centuries is mainly of internal interest. The Welsh church had submitted to the Roman rule about 768; politically, the extraordinary series of frontier-works known as 'Offa's Dyke' and associated with this vigorous Mercian (Saxon) King, who ruled 756–796, marked the Welsh boundary in English eyes. The elaborate social institutions of early Wales, emphasizing ultimately the common Celtic heritage with Ireland, found some expression in the four main Welsh kingdoms, tribally sub-divided. Wales was not spared the Norse. Serious raids commenced in the 850s, and despite vigorous resistance, especially during the reign of Rhodri Mawr (who died in 878), the Norse continued to raid and on a small scale to settle. Particular attention was paid, from about 853 to 876, to Anglesey, which still bears a Norse name. A respite in the early 10th century was preceded by further struggles, and, as in Scotland, the Welsh found themselves allied with the English (of Wessex) against the Scandinavians. As the Norse embraced Christianity, they gradually ceased looting monasteries, but the last Norse raid on a Welsh religious house was as late as 1091. To the Norse, the capture of slaves seems here to have been as important as the seizure of plunder; in 989, a Welsh king was obliged to redeem many of his fighting men at a penny a head. Limited Norse settlement, particularly in the south-west, is indicated by place-names such as Fishguard, but little is physically known of this.

The outstanding figure of 10th-century Wales is the King Hywel Dda ('Howel the Good'). He succeeded, where Rhodri Mawr had failed, in uniting most of Wales under his rule, and to a large extent obliterating the archaic 'North-South' distinction. His close relations with the brilliant court of Wessex for over a quarter-century are well-known; like his hero Alfred, he visited Rome (928). His most notable monument is the code of laws redacted in his reign, a project in which (if not actually the author) he certainly played some part. Despite the existence now of these laws only in rather later transcripts, there is no doubt either as to the genuine nature of the core of the code, or its value in throwing light on the social development of early Wales.

Alfred and the Renewal of England

f 6 The Norse involvement with England came at a period when the various regional kingdoms developed from the original settlements were clearly moving toward an eventual coalescence. From time to time, but on a basis of conquest and strength rather than on broad popular acclaim, an Anglian or Saxon monarch and his realm had already, for short periods, reached some kind of supremacy. Bede, in the 8th century, lists such instances of 'over-kings' to which he gives the title *bretwalda*—it is uncertain what this concept implies. The eventual shift of power from north to south followed the decline of Northumbria in the 8th century. When the first Danish winterings, and settlement, took place in Sheppey Isle about 835, Egbert of Wessex (who died in 839) had more or less subdued and annexed the remnants of Dumnonia, the British south-west, whose precarious local independence continued only for a century or so; he conquered Mercia in 829; and he added to Wessex most of south-east England. The Danes, however, after increased plundering in the east and south-east, and even across to the west midlands, landed an 'army'—a semi-permanent land-based force—in East Anglia in 865. Their method, well-known over western Europe for the next century or so, was 'to seize a defensible position, fortify it, and ravage the surrounding country systematically until its inhabitants bought peace from them'. (Stenton). We may add that the leaders' hold at any time over their followers seems to have been proportionate to their success in obtaining, not only plunder, but food, and that (as the English found), buying-off the Danes was a process as temporary as it was often unreliable.

The Danish capture of York (866) was followed by the first important clash with Wessex, near Reading. Here a local English victory resulted (Ashdown, 870). More important from an English view was Alfred's succession, in the next year, to the Wessex throne of his brother Aethelred. Alfred represents a rare phenomenon of early British history; it is true to say, as of some of the Northumbrian kings, that he came of an exceptionally gifted family, and that he rose to the challenge of his age, but (even given the later accretions of both history and tradition) he was probably a figure who would have stood out in any milieu at any time. His capacity for leadership, particularly in reverses; his Christianity, tempered to the spirit of the times; his unusually practical and far-sighted objective in the foundation of an *English* literature; and (like Hywel Dda) his initiation of further legal codes based on the earlier compilations of Wessex, Kent and Mercia, would all allow more than a glimpse of this remarkable figure, even if we did not possess the slightly contentious biography by his friend, the Welsh Bishop Asser. p 254 (41)

The Danes, who had attempted to set up their own puppet rulers in the north and in Mercia, eventually divided their forces. The beginning of a permanent settlement based on York, to some extent reflected in archaeology as well as in place-names, dates from this period. In 874, further extensive settlement occurred in the Midlands. A treaty of 886 defined, as we might say now, the respective spheres of influence of the English and the Danes, giving us the 'Danelaw', the great slice of England in which Scandinavian, not English, custom and writ was paramount. Alfred himself, having rallied Wessex after the defeat of 878 and his own flight to Athelney (where he lost the famous 'jewel' now in the Ashmolean Museum), entered the formative period of his life which was terminated by his death in 899. The attribution to him both of the formation of some kind of permanent naval force, and the constitutional military levy ('fyrd') whose service was ended only in 1908, when the Militia became the Special Reserve, though frequently over-stated, doubtless reflects some such actual provision. p 247 (13)

The Last Great Flowering

English art achieved a period of greatness in the later 10th century, under the comparative stability of Edgar (acceded 959). While the precise dating of sculpture and certain metalwork is still difficult, the ecclesiastical reforms associated with Aethelwold and Dunstan, and an artistic involvement with the Carolingian achievements of the Continent (repeating, on a grander scale, the Northumbrian borrowings of the later 7th century), are best reflected in manuscript art; though certain sculptural achievements, individually, must be regarded as superlative. Known loosely as the Winchester School (from the illuminated charter of Edgar's New Minster, 966), this generally southern tradition continues into the 11th century, if not later. In the north, the Scandinavian contacts result in schools of cross-carving which, seen of course most fully in the Isle of Man and less clearly in the north-west and the ancient Mercia, are of visual interest rather than beauty. The eventual reflections of this, together with continuing Irish Sea traditions of stonework, are most prominent in south Wales and Cornwall, probably until well beyond 1100. p 254 (42) p 252 (29) p 251 (26)

Politically, later English history is both complex and turbulent. The submission of the Danelaw in the 950s, when England became, nominally, one kingdom, was by no means the end of Norse conflict. The Danes themselves experienced a late 10th century revival, and from the battle of Maldon (991) became again the scourge of a weakened England. The country had to submit to the Danish monarch Svein in 1013, and Svein's second son Cnut (Canute), ruler from 1016 to 1035, has left almost as deep a popular tradition as Alfred's. The tangled series of arrangements which led, following the reign of the English Edward the Confessor (1042 to 1066), to Harold's abortive attempt to assert his claim, and the victory of William of Normandy at Hastings in the same year, usher in a period which, rather illogically, is usually taken to mark the commencement of medieval Britain. Politically, the decline of English monarchy during the reign of Aethelred ('the Unready') from 978, and the resumption of Danish assaults, form a more logical horizon, and conveniently end the millennium. p 254 (45) p 258 (54–56) p 255 (44)

XIII THE GREAT KING

Charlemagne and the Carolingian achievement

PHILIP GRIERSON

Europe during the age of Charlemagne

Charlemagne—

'Carolus Magnus', 'Charles the Great'—who inherited the kingdom of the Franks in 768 and reigned until 814, was for the Middle Ages a figure of vast and legendary splendour. In the *Chansons de Gestes*, the epic tales told by minstrels in the 11th and 12th centuries, he is already larger than life:

> 'White are his locks and silver is his beard,
> His body noble, his countenance severe',

his age is 'two hundred years and more', yet he rides with the mightiest of his warriors. He is the Holy Emperor, the champion of Christendom, the father-figure of every king in Europe.

He was formally canonized in 1166 at the instance of the Emperor Frederick Barbarossa, and parts of his body were at various times removed from his tomb and placed in precious reliquaries. This bust of his head and shoulders was made about 1350 to hold parts of his skull. There is no question of its being an authentic likeness but it does powerfully express the impact that the great Frankish Emperor made upon the imagination of succeeding ages.

The legend was in fact not so very unlike the truth. We know from Einhard, who knew him in his old age, that he was an impressive man: 'Charles was large and strong, and of lofty stature, though not disproportionately tall (his height is well known to have been seven times the length of his foot); the upper part of his head was round, his eyes very large and animated, nose a little long, hair fair and face laughing and merry. Thus his appearance was always stately and dignified, whether he was standing or sitting.'

As for his achievements—history does not fall short of the *Chansons*. He was the first figure of international stature since the end of the Roman Empire, uniting most of the lands that are now France, Western Germany, Switzerland, Holland, Belgium, Austria and Italy under a government that was always firm and usually benevolent. In Spain the Moors were kept at bay; the power of the eastern Avars was broken; Saxony became part of Christendom. Above all, the concept of empire—of a political unit bigger than a single people—became again a reality in Western Europe. (1)

The best likeness of the Emperor is that on the silver deniers issued in the last year of his reign (above). The small bronze equestrian statue (right) is traditionally said to be him, though some scholars believe it to represent his grandson Charles the Bald. The horse is a 16th-century restoration, but the figure is 9th-century and agrees in some detail with Einhard's account of how Charlemagne dressed: 'He used to wear the national, that is to say, the Frank, dress; . . . hose fastened with bands covered his lower limbs and shoes his feet, and he protected his shoulders and chest by a close-fitting coat . . . Over all he flung a blue cloak'. (2,3)

Charlemagne and his second son, Pepin, whom he made King of Italy, but who died young in 810: a 10th-century copy of a 9th-century drawing. (4)

Bavaria was added to the Empire in 788 when its Duke Tassilo was brought to trial on charges of conspiring with the Avars and banished to a monastery. The chalice (right) was given by him to the abbey which he himself had founded at Kremsmunster; its date is about 780. In the ovals are Christ and the Evangelists in niello. The knotwork framing them is a Lombardic motif, a reminder that Tassilo's wife Liutperg was the daughter of Desiderius, last king of the Lombards. (6)

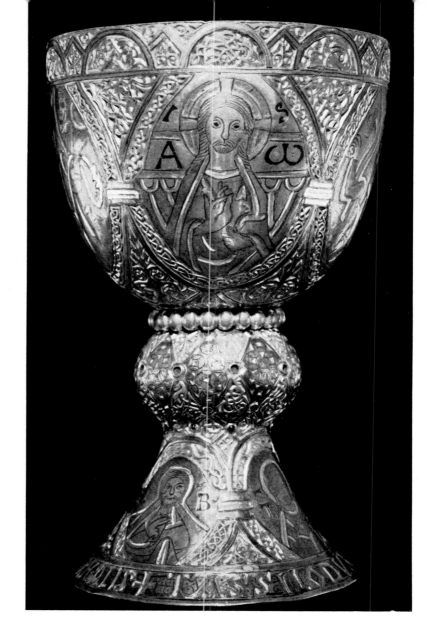

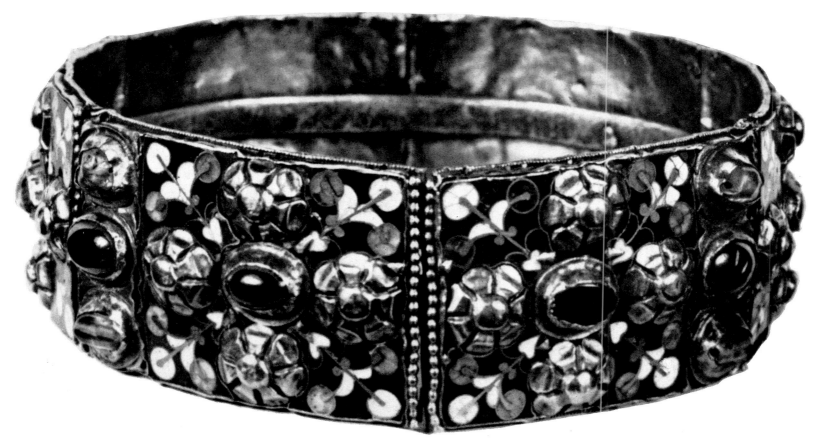

The Saxons were conquered piecemeal in eighteen savage campaigns, and as the only decisive guarantee of their submission Charlemagne forced them to become Christians. 'The Saxons', says Einhard, 'were given to the worship of devils and hostile to our religion.' Heathen practices were now ruthlessly punished by death. This copy of the baptismal vow imposed on them was made at the Abbey of Fulda in about 820. (5)

Italy fell under Frankish rule in 774 after Charlemagne had intervened in a quarrel between King Desiderius of Lombardy and Pope Adrian I. Charlemagne assumed the title of 'King of the Franks and Lombards' and it later became the custom for the emperor to be crowned three times—first at Aachen, then in Lombardy (originally at Pavia, later at Milan or at Monza) and lastly at Rome. The Lombard crown (above) is basically a work of the 10th century, though altered later; it is made of gold inlaid with jewels, but is known as the Iron Crown because round the inside is a strip of iron said to be a nail from the True Cross. (7)

273

The revival of architecture
under Charlemagne was part of a deliberate ambition to emulate the glories of ancient Rome. Early Christian basilican designs continued with few essential changes throughout the period. The church at Oberzell (left) stands on the 'monastic island' of Reichenau, and was built in the 9th century. The frescoes on the walls of the nave date from the late 10th century, but have been much restored. (8)

The classical revivalism of the 9th century is exemplified by the gatehouse to the monastery of Lorsch, Germany (below). Its immediate model was probably the gate-house of Old St Peter's at Rome; beyond that we can see the influence of the Roman triumphal arch. It stood, unattached, in the large open courtyard in front of the monastery. The fluted pilasters on the upper storey, as well as the three arches, the engaged demi-columns and Composite capitals of the ground floor are unmistakably Roman. More characteristic of its own epoch are the pattern-work masonry and row of triangular gables along the top. (10)

Massive structures at the west ends of the churches became characteristic of Carolingian architecture, and continued to be a special feature of German Romanesque. That at Corvey on the Weser (above), built between 873 and 885, has survived almost intact, though the façade and towers were heightened in the 12th century. (9)

The royal chapel at Aachen (right) was to surpass all other buildings of the age. It is a domed octagon, surrounded on the ground floor by an open ambulatory and on the upper levels by a gallery with two tiers of openings. As his model the architect, Odo of Metz, took the church of S.Vitale at Ravenna, built by Justinian some 250 years earlier and embodying for Charlemagne the imperial tradition which he was proposing to revive. The marble columns were brought from Rome and Ravenna. 'He was a constant worshipper at this church', says Einhard, 'as long as his health permitted, going morning and evening, even after nightfall, besides attending mass. He provided it with a great number of sacred vessels of gold and silver and . . . was at great pains to improve the church reading and psalmody, for he was well skilled in both, although he neither read in public nor sang, except in a low tone and with others.'

Charlemagne's throne (above) stands in the gallery at the west end facing the altar; it is of marble slabs and was used throughout the Middle Ages for imperial coronations. The bronze balustrade is part of the original fittings. The exterior of the church was later much altered but a panel of the 'Karlsschrein' (below right) showing Charlemagne dedicating it to the Virgin, preserves its appearance as built. (11, 12, 13)

'An ivory comb'

is still one of the required objects at the consecration of a Catholic bishop. The one shown here (left), one of the masterpieces of late Carolingian ivory-carving, is from Metz. Book covers are frequently of ivory-work, especially those for the Psalter (below left: King David from the Dagulf Psalter, c. 790) and the Gospels. The Gospel cover below is classical in style—Christ in a mandorla, sitting on a globe shown as a wreath of victory. Beside him are two cherubim (with six wings) and the sun and moon; in the corners the symbols of the Evangelists; round the border acanthus leaves. (14, 15, 16)

The Golden Book ('Codex Aureus') of St Emmeram (right) was made about 870, probably at Rheims or S. Denis. Each stone is held in an elaborate filigree setting. In the centre, in gold relief, sits Christ in glory; round him the four Evangelists. In the corners are four scenes from the Gospels: the woman taken in adultery, the cleansing of the Temple, the healing of the leper and the healing of the blind man. The style of these metal reliefs is close to that of the ivories.

It was the books of the Carolingian 'Renaissance' which were in the end to prove its most enduring legacy. The revival of learning was closely linked with the spread of monasticism, since the monasteries alone could provide the necessary leisure and security for study. Charlemagne encouraged the foundation of schools, libraries and *scriptoria*, and these centres of education naturally became also centres for manuscript illumination and other arts. (17)

IN PRINCIPIO—'In the beginning' —the opening words of a St John's Gospel, produced in northern France in the second half of the 9th century. The style is known as 'Franco-Saxon' since it combines the 'classicism' current in Charlemagne's Palace School (for instance the four Evangelists) with the quite different ornamental style of Anglo-Saxon art—the borders with their patterns of interlace. (18)

The pen dipped with a curiously awkward gesture into the inkwell, is symbolic of the power of the written word. In an age when every book was an act of individual devotion, there was no great gulf between the Evangelist recording the inspired message of the Gospel (in this detail St Mark from a manuscript of the Aachen Palace School) and the humble monk in his *scriptorium* retelling the same message to the greater glory of God. (19)

The Fountain of Life was an allegory of the Gospels, the fourfold spring from which the waters of Eternal Life flowed. It was often used as a frontispiece. This page from the Gospels of Saint-Médard, near Soissons, dates from the early 9th century. According to tradition it was presented to the abbey by Charlemagne's son, Louis the Pious, when he spent Easter there in 827. (20)

Fold out ▶

The 'Carolingian Renaissance'
was a complex product of many
different traditions. Against the background of Late Roman and Byzantine
art, features from other cultures—
Celtic, Germanic, Viking, Eastern—
may meet together on the same page.

The beardless Christ, from an Evan-
gelistary commissioned by Charlemagne in 781 (right), bears witness to
the Roman, or Early Christian, tradition, though the interlace pattern is
Anglo-Irish and other motifs elsewhere in the same codex can be traced
to Armenia. It was painted by a monk
called Godescalc working either at
Aachen or in one of the neighbouring
monasteries. (23)

A restless, quivering line characterizes the illuminations of the Gospel-
book made for Archbishop Ebbo of
Rheims in about 820. The drapery is
convulsed by a supernatural gale, and
the Evangelist, St Matthew, seems
scarcely able to keep pace with his
feverish inspiration. (24)

Moses delivers the Law to the
Israelites; the bearded man in the red
cloak is Aaron, the figure on the left
holding the curtain, Joshua. In this
scene from the Grandval Bible—a
product, like pl. 22, of the school of
Tours, c. 840—the late Roman influence is particularly strong. Note the
classical colonnade and the way in
which the coffered ceiling recedes in
(almost) correct perspective. (25)

The great abbeys themselves have all perished. Fragments remain of Corvey, of Lorsch, of Fulda and a few others, but hardly enough to convey their scale and importance. By good luck, however, an extremely detailed monastic plan dating from the early 9th century has been preserved, showing the entire lay-out together with the internal arrangements of each building even down to the furniture. It is now in the library of St Gall, Switzerland, and was probably sent there from one of the abbeys of the lower Rhine as a guide for the builders. How far they actually followed it is uncertain. Excavations suggest that it was probably used for the church at least.

This reconstruction shows how the St Gall plan would have looked had it been built—a 'blue-print' of the ideal monastery as the 9th century imagined it.

The church is basilican, with transepts, square tower at the crossing and an apse at both ends. At the west end (foreground) stand two separate conical towers. The entrance is by way of a small gatehouse into a curious semicircular court or *atrium*. South of the church (i.e. to the right) are the cloister and the chief monastic buildings—the dormitory on the east, refectory on the south (parallel with the church) and cellar on the west. In the background, partly hidden in the picture, are two more cloisters, one forming part of the novices' quarters, the other of the infirmary. The cemetery with its cross, the vegetable garden and circular enclosures for geese and chickens adjoin them to the south.

The farm quarters (sheep, goats, cows, pigs and horses) are on the right foreground while the south side of the whole area (on the right of the picture) is taken up by the barn, workshops, brew-house, kiln, press and kitchen. On the other side of the church is another row of substantial buildings —the abbot's house, the guests' lodgings, the school and the all-important *scriptorium* (St Gall was a leading centre of manuscript illumination).

Many of the smaller buildings are basilican in structure: that is, they have a high central space lit by a clerestory and lower rooms along one or more sides. The church and cloistral buildings would have been of stone, the rest of wood and plaster whitewashed; the roofs of lead or thatch. There was no lack of fireplaces with their chimneys, and the drainage was well worked out. (21)

The finished book is presented to a royal patron: the frontispiece of the Bible of Count Vivian, showing the monks of St Martin of Tours presenting the Bible to King Charles the Bald, Charlemagne's grandson, early in 851. He sits enthroned in the centre; the two men next to him are probably his cousins. The figure in the red cloak, to the right, without a tonsure, is Count Vivian, lay Abbot of St Martin's, while leading members of the abbey from a procession after him, those on the left carrying the Bible to be presented. The costume of the guards, as well as the architectural details of the frame, show the strong classical sympathies of the school of Tours, where the great teacher Alcuin was Abbot from 796 to 804. (22)

Engraving on rock-crystal, an expensive and difficult art, was normally confined to the court. The famous crystal of Lothar II, King of Lotharingia (855–869), is among the most exquisite examples. With its calm figures and ordered drapery, it is totally different in style from the Ebbo Gospels or the Utrecht Psalter (below). Its eight scenes tell the story of Susannah, starting at the top, going clockwise round the crystal and finishing in the middle, as follows: Susannah with the Elders in an enclosed garden, two servants hurrying to her aid; the Elders order Susannah to be brought to trial; she stands while they raise their arms in accusation; an official with a staff leads her off, but is confronted by Daniel; Daniel questions the first Elder; then the second, convicting them both of falsehood; they are stoned to death; and Susannah stands free before Daniel who sits in the judgment seat. (26)

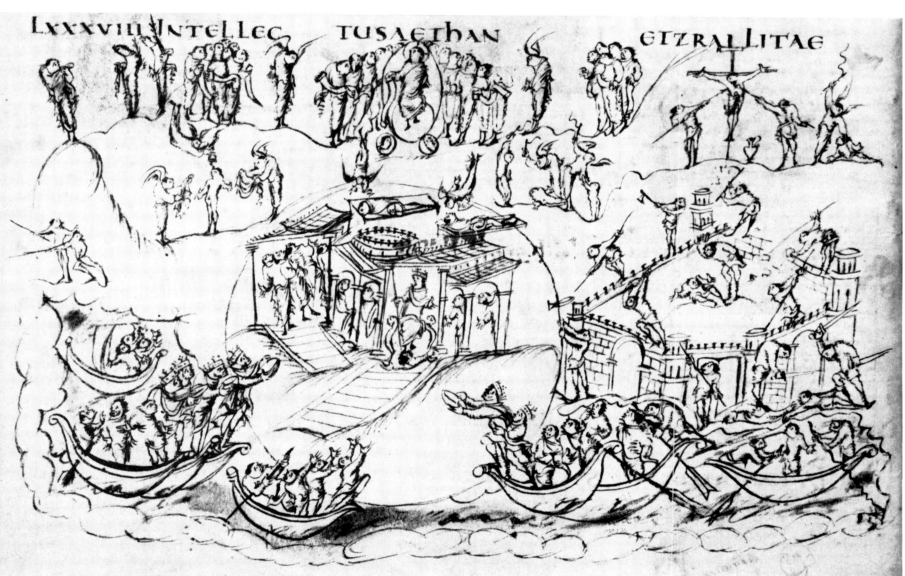

Every metaphor and figure of speech in the Psalms is translated into visual terms by the fantastic virtuosity of the master of the Utrecht Psalter (c. 820). This detail shows Psalm 89. In the middle, David in his palace: 'I have found David my servant; with holy oil have I anointed him. . . . I will set his hand also in the sea . . . Also I will make him my firstborn, higher than the kings of the earth.' The other tiny scenes all illustrate verses with the same naive literalness (right, for instance, 'Thou has brought his strongholds to ruin') and in an agitated, nervous style similar to that of the Ebbo Gospels. (27)

The art of fresco

had never died out in Italy and was revived on a large scale under Charlemagne and his successors. The general effect of a church interior decorated in this way can still be appreciated at Oberzell, pl. 8. Elsewhere isolated frescoes dating from the 9th century continue to be found, usually in a much damaged state.

The most complete cycle of Carolingian frescoes came to light only in 1947 at Müstair in Switzerland. The nave walls were once covered with five tiers of paintings, made up of no less than eighty-two identical rectangular panels. The Healing of the Dumb Man (left), like the others, is of no great artistic merit, but was doubtless the work of provincial artists imitating Roman examples. (28)

St Stephen before the High Priest (below) comes from the crypt of St Germain, Auxerre, begun in 851 by Konrad of Auxerre, a cousin of Charles the Bald. Like the Müstair frescoes, its colour-scheme is limited to a range of red and yellow ochre and bluish grey. (29)

A touch of Byzantium is recognizable in one of the few mosaics to have survived from the time of Charlemagne. The Ark of the Covenant (above) occupies the apse-ceiling of Theodulf's Oratory at Germigny-des-Prés. Theodulf was a Visigoth and a man of wide culture; it has been suggested that the choice of subject here is the result of Jewish influence. The larger angels conform exactly to the cherubim of Solomon's Temple as described in the Book of Kings. (30)

The procession of martyrs (right) was painted in the crypt of the church of St Maximin, Trier, in the late 9th century. The style is close to contemporary manuscript illumination. Norse raiders destroyed the church in 882, after which the crypt was walled in and abandoned—hence the survival of the paintings. (31)

The only son of Charlemagne

to outlive him was Louis, surnamed 'the Pious'. Stricter in morals, more scrupulous in religious exercises but weaker in force of personality than his father, he was unable to solve the many problems created by the rivalry of his sons. This portrait is from the manuscript of a poem in which the words, written right over the picture, can also be read like a crossword puzzle, so that the letters round the cross and the halo also form verses. (32)

Three years of fierce civil war, culminating in the disastrous battle of Fontenoy, followed Louis' death in 840. These scenes (right), though ostensibly illustrating a passage in the Psalms, give a good idea of war in the 9th century. But even Fontenoy settled nothing. By the Treaty of Verdun (843) the Empire that Charlemagne had created was divided between the sons of Louis the Pious. (33, 34)

Lothar, the eldest, received Lotharingia and Italy, and the title of 'Emperor'. But his territory lacked natural cohesion and after the death of his son, Lothar II, was split up between Louis and Charles. (35)

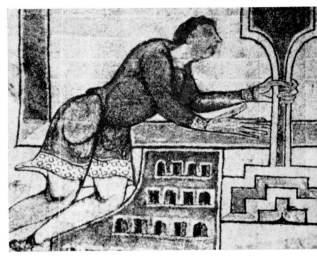

Louis the German held the kingdom of the East Franks. His long reign (843–876) gave it stability, and it was his son, Charles the Fat, who eventually reunited the whole Empire in 884. (36)

Charles the Bald was allotted the West Frankish kingdom, i.e. France. He too enjoyed a long reign (843–877), mostly spent fighting Viking raiders in the north and his own rebellious subjects in the south. (37)

287

The legitimate succession
from Charlemagne came to an end in
Germany with the abdication, or deposition, of Charles the Fat in 887. But
in the West Frankish kingdom the line
of Charles the Bald continued (with
interruptions) until nearly the end of
the 10th century.

Bishop Gauzelin, a leading churchman, later a saint, held the see of
Toul from 922–962. This was part of
the disputed province of Lotharingia,
held at the beginning of Gauzelin's
period of office by the West Franks,
then in 925 made into a dukedom
owing allegiance to the East Frankish
Kingdom. The 'Treasures of Gauzelin',
now preserved in the Cathedral
of Nancy, all date from his time. The
book-cover (left) was made for an
earlier manuscript of the Gospels. It
is an oak panel on which is fixed a
square frame and a cross of gold decorated with cloisonnée garnets, emeralds, amethysts, pearls and coral. In
the corners of the cross are engraved
silver plaques of the Evangelists and
in the centre the figure of the Virgin
('Sancta Maria'). The chalice and paten
(below) both have a base of silver
with gold applied over it, and are
encrusted with pearls and precious
stones. (38, 39)

Charlemagne and
the Carolingian achievement

PHILIP GRIERSON

The Empire of Charlemagne, showing the Frankish kingdom which he inherited and the territory gained by him during his reign, with dates of conquest. (1)

IT IS UNFASHIONABLE nowadays to write history in terms of personalities, but personalities cannot always be ignored. This is particularly true of Charlemagne. The three members of the Arnulfing family who had preceded him, Pepin of Heristal, Charles Martel, and Pepin the Short, had created a new and immensely powerful Frankish state. They had eliminated the tradition of schism between Austrasia and Neustria; they had evicted all but one of the great dukes into whose hands authority had fallen in the peripheral parts of the realm; they had given their support to Christian missions in Germany; and the last of them had intervened in Italian politics on behalf of the Pope and had displaced the last Merovingian king and assumed the royal title. It was to their policies that Charlemagne was heir and it was their policies that he carried to fruition, even if he did not always foresee the ultimate consequences of what he did.

The Man and the King

Charlemagne became King in 768, ruling for the first three years of his reign in association with his brother Carloman, and died in January 814. His biographer Einhard has left a description of his personal appearance. He was a big burly man over 6 feet in height with a large head, a thick neck, very piercing eyes, and the disconcertingly weak voice that is sometimes associated with a huge frame. He was clean shaven apart from a moustache; the long white beard traditionally associated with him is only a legend. He was immensely active, with a passion for hunting and swimming, though he was sparing in his food and sometimes suffered from insomnia. During the first half of his reign he was constantly on the move, visiting every part of his vast dominions, but in his later years he tended to stay in the vicinity of Aachen, his favourite residence. It had hot springs in which he liked to swim and there was excellent hunting in the neighbouring Ardennes. Although endlessly curious and for ever asking questions of those with whom he came into contact, Charlemagne was a doer rather than a thinker. In politics, government and war he dealt with situations as they arose without elaborating general principles or attempting to foresee the remoter consequence of his actions. Persistence rather than brilliance won him his wars and accounts for the enduring results of much of his work.

Charlemagne's predecessors had re-established the Frankish kingdom; it was his achievement to extend his authority over most of western Europe. He suppressed the semi-independent duchy of Bavaria and conquered Saxony, so that he was the first man in history to become the ruler of the whole of Germany. He annexed the Lombard kingdom, thus becoming master of the greater part of Italy, and he extended Frankish rule across the Pyrenees as far south as the Ebro. The only parts of Latin Christendom outside his kingdom were the British Isles, the semi-independent principality of Benevento in south Italy, and a group of petty Christian states in north-western Spain. Over the huge area which he ruled he established a uniform system of government, though not of law, and in it he encouraged the extension of the pattern of social relations that we term feudalism and the revival of education, learning and art that is known as the Carolingian Renaissance. Though his empire did not last —its economic system was too feebly developed and too parochial

to support such an ambitious political structure, and the Viking invasions and the civil wars of the 9th century resulted in its political collapse, so that 'Europe' had to be remade on a new basis—it was from it that all the political institutions of western Europe except those of England and the Church ultimately derived and it was in the main through its medium that the Middle Ages knew of the achievements of Roman antiquity. Even in small matters Carolingian influence still persists. It was under Charlemagne that reckoning by pounds, shillings and pence, which today survives only in England, became normal over all western Europe, and the printed forms of letters which we use today are in all essentials a product of the Carolingian Renaissance.

The First 'Germany'

Charlemagne's realm was an 'empire' in both senses in which the term is commonly used. It was an empire in that it included much territory which made no part of the *regnum Francorum* of his father's day, and it was one in the sense that in the year 800 he had conferred on him by the Pope the formal title of Emperor.

The expansion of the Frankish kingdom in Germany was no more than the completion of a policy begun by Charlemagne's predecessors. Bavaria, in the south-east, had been nominally part of the Merovingian kingdom, and both Charles Martel and Pepin had prepared the way for its annexation. Its Duke Tassilo had been compelled when a minor to take an oath of fealty to Pepin, and the organization of the Bavarian Church carried out by St Boniface had involved the wholesale intrusion of Frankish elements into the country. Tassilo made desperate efforts to preserve his independence, patronizing the great abbeys in the hope of building up a rival ecclesiastical authority to the pro-Frankish bishops, but Charlemagne was determined to make his rule a reality and end the existence of the last of the great duchies. Tassilo was compelled in 787 to promise obedience, but the next year he was brought to trial on charges of tampering with the loyalty of Charlemagne's vassals in Bavaria and intriguing with the Avars. He was condemned to death, though the penalty was reduced to one of imprisonment for life in a monastery, and Bavaria, with its great dependency of Carinthia, passed directly under Charlemagne's control.

The conquest of Saxony was the pendant to the annexation of Bavaria. Saxony was a land of small tribal units, fiercely pagan, and had never formed a part of the Frankish state. It could not be annexed by the simple process of removing its ruler, but had to be subdued in thirty years of savage fighting that lasted off and on from 772 to 803. The war was fought with great cruelty. Charlemagne regarded the conversion of the Saxons to Christianity as the only guarantee of submission, and repeated revolts were met by massacre, wholesale deportations, and the imposition of a savage penal code. When the war ended, the boundaries of the Frankish state in northern Germany had been pushed eastwards from the Rhine to the Elbe and even beyond it at one point, since the region known as Nordalbingia, corresponding to the modern Schleswig-Holstein, was included in the annexations.

Although Bavarians and Saxons continued to live according to their own legal system, Saxon law being reduced to writing for the first time, Bavaria and Saxony were treated in the fullest sense as part of the Frankish kingdom. This fact was to have the most far-reaching consequences. Charlemagne had brought about the unification of Germany, even if for the time being as part of a larger entity. In so doing he reversed a centuries-old tradition. In earlier times the closest links of Bavaria had been with the Lombard kingdom of north Italy, not with the other Germanic peoples of central Europe, while pagan Saxony had a tradition of hostility towards the Franks and but for Charlemagne's intervention would probably have been linked up with Denmark and fallen under the rule of the emerging monarchy of this country. In uniting the north and the south, therefore, Charlemagne had created the essential basis for the 'Germany' of future times. Further, merely by virtue of the huge territorial expansion which this involved, the balance of cultural forces in Europe was shifted to the east. The bishoprics and monasteries now founded in Saxony were added to those already set up by St Boniface in Franconia and others of diverse origin in Swabia and Bavaria, while the intensive settlement that followed the conquests prepared the way for the political predominance of Germany in the 10th century.

p 273
(7)
Earlier than either of these was the annexation of the kingdom of the Lombards. King Desiderius (756–774) was anxious to add the papal states to his dominions, and Pope Adrian I (772–795) appealed to Charlemagne for help. In 773 the Frankish King invaded Italy and defeated the armies of Desiderius and his son. Charlemagne had at first no intention of suppressing Lombard independence, and when he visited Rome at Easter 774, leaving his army to blockade Desiderius in Pavia, he promised Adrian an enormously enlarged territorial state which would be strong enough to protect itself against Lombard aggression in the future. Later in the year, when Desiderius surrendered and his son fled to Byzantium, Charlemagne decided to assume the title of King of the Lombards himself. A consequence of this was that the papal states as envisaged in 774 never came into existence, for the Pope, as Charlemagne saw it, would have no need to protect himself against the Franks. Like the earlier Lombard kingdom, however, that of Charlemagne never included the whole of Italy.

Venice and parts of the north east were never conquered; the papal states were independent in theory and semi-independent in practice up to 800; the south was divided between the rulers of Benevento and the Byzantine Empire. With the downfall of the Lombard kingdom in the north the rulers of Benevento took to calling themselves princes instead of dukes, and although in 788 Grimoald III agreed to recognize Frankish suzerainty, he repudiated it as soon as possible and he and his successors were in fact quite independent.

Besides unifying Germany and annexing much of Italy, Charlemagne established a vague suzerainty over many of the Slavonic peoples on his eastern frontier and in a series of expeditions in the 790s destroyed the great Avar kingdom on the middle Danube, in what is now Hungary. He likewise annexed part of north eastern Spain, the region subsequently called the Spanish March from which the county of Barcelona and the kingdom of Navarre were to develop. Only the last of these involved a fresh addition to the territory of the Frankish kingdom, and Charlemagne's Spanish adventures are best remembered as a result of the defeat of his rearguard in the Pyrenees by the Gascons in 778. One of the dead was a certain Roland, Count of the Breton March, and with Gascons transformed into Muslims the battle formed the basis of the *Chanson de Roland*, one of the great poems of European literature.

The Structure of the Realm

Charlemagne's title, from 774 onwards, was *rex Francorum et Langobardorum ac patricius Romanorum*. The first title he received by inheritance and the second by conquest; the third, which was purely honorific, had been conferred on him as a child by Pope Stephen II. Although he retained for himself supreme authority throughout his realm, he soon realized the need for some formal delegation of power. In 781 he created for his two younger sons, Louis and Pepin, the kingdoms of Aquitaine and Italy, though p 272 the men through whom their government was exercised were (4) Franks on whom he could rely and who were in reality responsible to him. He associated his eldest son Charles with him in the government in 800, and in 806 he provided in legal form for the partition of his realm after his death. It was only the accident of Charles and Pepin predeceasing their father that led to the whole Frankish state, save for a short-lived sub-kingdom in Italy for Pepin's son Bernard, passing intact to Louis the Pious. p 286
(32)
Charlemagne was therefore reconciled to the partition of the great political edifice he had put together, and he likewise never thought of disturbing the ancient practice by which his subjects lived according to their own laws. His reign indeed saw the beginning of an immense multiplication of copies of their legal codes, more particularly that of the Salian Franks. Some indeed of these codes, like the laws of the Saxons, were committed to writing for the first time at his direction, the only modifications being the condemnation of pagan practices and the bringing of some of their provisions into line with Christian ideas. He did allow himself to add new sections or chapters (*capitula*) to particular national laws, and in the course of his reign he issued great numbers of capitularies, i.e. groups of such chapters, which were mainly administrative in character and where they conflicted with customary law would normally be held to supersede it. The practice of issuing capitularies was continued by Charlemagne's successors—a formal collection of them was made during the reign of Louis the Pious—and if the Carolingian Empire had survived they would probably have developed as the laws of the realm in much the same way as statute law did in England.

Charlemagne's legislation was less important in securing the political unity of his kingdom than his use of Austrasian Franks and Frankish institutions in government. The King took his advisers from anywhere, whether inside or outside his realm— Paul the Deacon from Italy, Theodulf from Spain, Alcuin from p 285 England—the only criterion being the quality of the advice which (30) they gave. His administrators, counts and royal vassals alike, were with rare exceptions Franks, and they were installed in the newly acquired territories on the assumption that they would be loyal and could be trusted to look after Frankish interests. The genealogical table of any of the great Frankish families shows its members

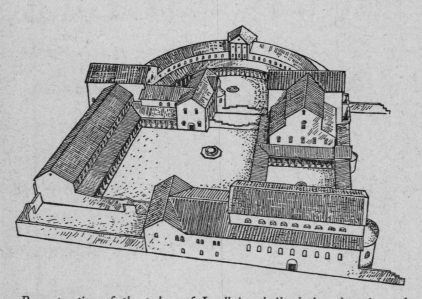

Reconstruction of the palace of Ingelheim, built during the reigns of Charlemagne and Louis the Pious. Based on classical and Byzantine models, it was grouped round a large central court. On the north side was the festival hall, leading to an attractive smaller semi-circular court. The south east corner was occupied by the Great Hall, which was linked to the church on the opposite side of a colonnaded atrium. (2)

scattered through the whole of the Empire, from Britanny to Spoleto and from Artois to Friuli, and the local dynasties which in the late 9th and 10th centuries founded their power on the ruins of the Carolingian Empire were for the most part wholly or largely Frankish in descent. When these families were used as counts in the newly-acquired provinces they naturally carried with them the procedures to which they were accustomed, so that a certain degree of institutional uniformity existed throughout the Carolingian state. This was the more easily effected since the conquered regions were all Germanic, and while the details of the laws of the various people were different their systems of courts, procedure, and evidence were not. This was true even in Italy, for however strong the influence of Roman law might be the Lombard kingdom was essentially Germanic in its structure and institutions.

The Government

The central institution of Carolingian government was the royal *palatium*. The word is better translated as 'court' than 'palace' since it was used to cover the whole personnel of the central government rather than the buildings which at any moment they occupied. The chief elements in it were the household officers, the chancellor and the chaplains. The first group of these, the constable, marshal, butler, and so forth were no longer simply performing the household services which their names imply; they were carrying out the general work of government. We hear of the royal steward being placed in command of the fleet on an expedition to Corsica. The chancery conducted the official correspondence of the king and was completely 'clerical' in personnel as well as in function. The chapel, because it was accustomed to the safe custody of ecclesiastical ornaments and relics, acted also as a record office side by side with the chancery. There was no Mayor of the Palace; the Carolingians profited by the memory of how they themselves had risen to power. Though in the later part of the reign the court tended to settle at Aachen, where Charlemagne's buildings were deliberately intended to reflect those of a Roman capital, the court was normally migratory, moving with the king from one estate to another, eating up the produce of each as it went.

Local government was not greatly changed from what it had been in early Merovingian times, before the counts had been eclipsed by the great dukes, but the power of the counts tended now to be counterbalanced by that of the great ecclesiastics and of royal vassals. The system of counts and counties was now better organized than it had been earlier and was extended into new regions; one is reminded of the way in which Napoleon extended French administrative machinery into Germany, where Hamburg was once the '*chef-lieu du département des Bouches de l'Elbe*'. The counts were now royal rather than communal officials, but they were very difficult to control. Their powers were excessive and liable to abuse, as the capitularies clearly indicate, and since the 'pay' of the counts consisted of the income of royal estates in each county set aside for their use it was extremely difficult to stop. Their power might be checked locally by that of the bishops and abbots. These were not merely the count's equals in wealth and social prestige but were often administratively independent of him, since if their property had been granted an 'immunity' the count had no jurisdiction over it and the ecclesiastical owner was answerable only to the king. The powers of the count were also diminished by the existence of royal vassals, who, though usually less wealthy, enjoyed the social prestige arising out of their personal relations with the monarch and had the privilege of bringing their own contingents directly to the royal army instead of them being merged in the forces raised by the counts.

Royal control was exercised in part by the king in person, in part through the medium of officials known as the *missi dominici* ('royal envoys'), and in part by the use of the feudal oath, more especially in the case of the royal vassals. It is indeed possible to regard the system of local government as essentially dual, exercised jointly through counts and ecclesiastics, with interlocking *missi* and interpenetrating *vassi*.

The most effective of these agents in government were the *missi*. The sending out of personal representatives of the king, somewhat resembling the itinerant justices of later medieval Eng-

p 275
(11–13)
f 7

Denier (enlarged) of Pope Leo III (795–816), minted at Rome after Charlemagne's coronation in 800. On the obverse is the name CARLUS *('Charles') set round a monogram standing for* IMPERATOR*; on the reverse is Leo's monogram encircled by the letters* SCS *('Sanctus')* PETRUS*. From 800 papal coinage bore the name of the emperor as well as that of the pope, a pattern which remained constant until the late 10th century. (3, 4)*

land, was nothing new, but the machinery was organized and regularized in a way that had not been customary before. The counties were grouped together into *missatica*, which often corresponded to archiepiscopal provinces, and the body of *missi* for each *missaticum* comprised lay and clerical elements. Two counts and one bishop was a common arrangement. They would normally receive their instructions at the May assembly, or at the beginning of summer, and would report back in the autumn. Their proceedings in each locality would begin with a sermon and exhortation, after which they would set up a court, listen to complaints against local officials, and enquire into such matters as the incidence of crime, the standard of military training, and the upkeep of roads and river banks. They could investigate the condition of the royal estates in each locality and the state of churches and monasteries, since their mixed composition and the fact that they directly represented the king gave them a jurisdiction more comprehensive than that of the counts. From the counts' point of view they were unwelcome visitors, to be satisfied and persuaded to move on as quickly as possible. They were also costly, since each member could exact on his behalf and that of his servants an allowance of 40 loaves, a pig or sheep and 2 sucking pigs, 4 hens, 20 eggs, 8 pints of wine, 2 *modii* of ale and 2 *modii* of oats for his horses.

The other elements in royal control were less effective. The personal exercise of power was necessarily reduced as the size of the realm increased; fewer men could attend the annual assembly of freemen, which was now held in May, and any particular region was less likely than before to be visited by the king on one of his journeys. Only on the highest ranks of society did the personal influence of the king still count for a good deal. As for the feudal oath, it operated in part because the counts themselves were royal *fideles* who had taken a special oath of fealty to the king, in part because there were now, in almost all parts of the Empire, royal vassals who had been endowed with estates from the royal demesne. They were privileged above ordinary freemen and specially bound to the king, and since in many cases their main title to respect was the endowment they had received from his hands they were more likely to feel loyalty towards him.

Christmas Day, 800

On Christmas Day 800 Charlemagne was crowned Emperor by Pope Leo III and acclaimed by the people in St Peter's at Rome. The reasons behind this event have been endlessly discussed by historians. During the preceding three centuries only one emperor had ever visited Rome, and no emperor had been created in Italy since 476. No emperor had ever been crowned by a pope. Up to less than half a century earlier popes had been subjects of the Byzantine emperor, dating their documents by Byzantine regnal years and announcing their election to the Byzantine exarch at Ravenna. Papal independence had come about under Stephen II (752–757) and Adrian I (772–795). Stephen II, by gift of Pepin, was the first ruler of an independent papal state, and Adrian I ceased to date documents by the regnal years of the emperor at Byzantium and minted coins in his own name. Why, in the year 800, should Leo III go out of his way to acquire a new master?

It is easier to list contributory causes than to decide which ones were decisive. Essentially it was a recognition of the shift in the balance of power in Christendom. Charlemagne was master of western Europe, head of a state much more solid in Western eyes than that of Byzantium. He had long shown himself active in the affairs of the Church, compelling the conversion of the Saxons, favouring that of the Slavs, and taking steps to counteract the spread of the Adoptionist heresy in Spain. The revival of classical and patristic studies at the Frankish court had accustomed men again to the idea of an Empire in the West. The Pope had need of a protector—Leo III had been overthrown by a conspiracy in 799 and Charlemagne was ostensibly in Rome to do justice between him and his accusers—and it could be argued that the Byzantine throne was legally vacant since it was in fact occupied by a woman, the Empress Irene. These various considerations added up to the revival of the Empire in the West. If any cause must be selected as more important than the others, it was the need of Leo III for a protector, and the one immediate consequence of the event was a change in Charlemagne's status in Rome itself, coins being henceforward struck jointly in the name of pope and emperor, not in that of a pope alone.

f 3, 4

Charlemagne and his advisers took the new title very casually. No change was made for some months in the royal style, which indeed did not become unambiguously imperial until recognition from Byzantium was forthcoming in 812, and Charles declined to wear imperial costume save when in Rome. He was subsequently heard to say that if he had known in advance the Pope's intentions he would not have gone to St Peter's, even though it was one of the major festivals of the year. His reason was probably resentment at the liberties taken by the Pope in the service, since in making the coronation precede the acclamation Leo III had virtually arrogated to himself the right of choosing the Emperor and perhaps, by altering the order of proceedings, invalidated the ceremony altogether. The pains taken by Charlemagne to secure recognition from Byzantium and his subsequent conferring of the imperial dignity on his son Louis without any reference to Rome are a sufficient indication of his attitude. In any event the acquisition of a new title by Charlemagne made no difference to the government of the Empire at the time. Its importance lay in the future.

Life and Livelihood on the Land

There is a striking contrast between the pretentious political structure of the Carolingian Empire and the backwardness of its economic organization. The population was small and the vast bulk of it was engaged in agriculture. The only centres of population were cathedral cities and abbeys; a bishop's household, a cathedral chapter, the monks of a great abbey, could draw on the resources of their estates to provide the necessary surplus of food and services, and round such institutions communities of traders and centres of industry would inevitably tend to form. Towns existing in virtue of trade alone were few in number and often impermanent. Only the stable market created by the presence of ecclesiastical or administrative institutions or the protection provided by the walls of a military stronghold could give a sufficient guarantee for the future. It is no accident that Quentovic and Duurstede, at the mouth of the Canche and on the lower Rhine respectively, two of the most important commercial centres of Charlemagne's day, failed to survive into the 10th century, since neither place was ever of the slightest ecclesiastical or administrative consequence.

p 279–80 (21)

We are much better informed about agriculture than about trade or industry in Carolingian times. The charters and registers of abbeys contain innumerable records of estates received from pious donors, and from time to time enterprising abbots would draw up surveys of their property, on the same lines as the Domesday Book but much more detailed, which were known as polyptychs (i.e. 'many leaves'). A capitulary known as the *Capitulare de villis* contains detailed directions for the management of the royal demesne, and a group of documents known as the *Brevium exempla* ('Specimens of letters') contains the actual description of a group of royal and ecclesiastical estates in the time of Louis the Pious. The *Brevium exempla* were apparently a group of reports drawn up by *missi* which were no longer required by the central government and were then handed out to some later group of envoys to serve as models on which to base their own returns.

Though small estates and holdings certainly existed, the predominant pattern was one of great estates, only small sections of which were actually cultivated. The estates of St Germain des Prés, an abbey situated in what is now Paris just south of the Seine, varied in size from 375 to 16,000 acres, most of them falling between 1500 and 5000; the royal estate of Annappes near Lille, one of those described in the *Brevium exempla*, was just over 7000 acres. Each estate included two categories of land, the *terra indominicata*, the lord's demesne, and the *terra beneficiata*, the holdings of the tenants. The *terra indominicata* had as its nucleus a small area of arable land cultivated by *coloni* and *laeti*, but the bulk of it was formed by meadow, woodlands, and waste. The *coloni* were personally free but attached to the soil, the *laeti* were personally unfree and in many cases descendants of the slave

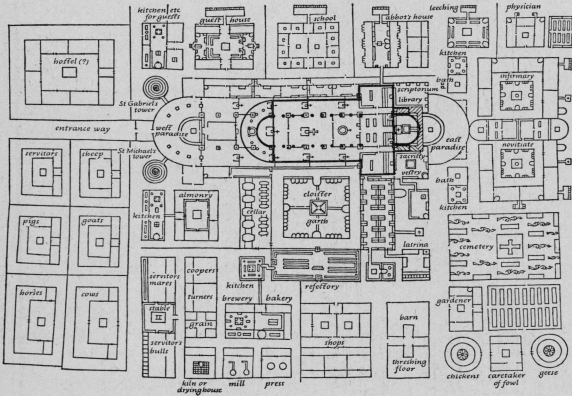

The 9th-century plan for the abbey of St Gall, which has been reconstructed on p. 279 (the view-point taken by the artist is from the bottom left-hand corner of the plan). The original manuscript contains a wealth of lettering in Latin, in very small writing, which has here been simplified and translated. Some points of interpretation still present problems (for instance the arrangement of some of the chimney-flues, and the so-called 'paradises' at each end of the church) but in essentials it presents a remarkably clear and exact picture of a wealthy Carolingian monastery. (5)

cultivators of earlier times. The *terra beneficiata*, cultivated by the *coloni* on their own behalf, consisted of arable land and the holdings were based on the concept of the *mansus*, the area necessary to support a family and varying according to the locality between about 15 and 20 acres. The main produce of the lord's demesne and tenants' holdings alike consisted of grain, vegetables, and fruit; there were varying numbers of cattle—in most places pigs were kept in large numbers, since they could live in the waste and largely fend for themselves—and wine was cultivated where soil and climate made it possible and much farther north than is the case today. Great proprietors, in organizing their estates, often grouped these together in such a way that they would complement each other's resources, even if this meant that produce would have to be conveyed from many miles away. The Annappes group of estates near Lille is associated with such an outlier near Paris which supplied the others with wine. Abbeys in Flanders are sometimes found acquiring estates in the Moselle or the Loire regions, likewise to supply them with wine, while an inland abbey might acquire an estate on the coast to supply itself with salt. The abbey of St Médard of Soissons received its salt from an estate 150 miles away.

There is ample evidence both that self-sufficiency was the ideal of the great proprietors and that they often failed to achieve it. If one were wealthy enough it would be possible to use one estate quite satisfactorily to supply the deficiencies of others, but not everyone was wealthy, and local markets played a considerable role. The replacement of the gold *tremissis* of the 7th century by the silver penny of the 8th was a sign of changing conditions, for the penny, though its purchasing power seems to us abnormally high—1d would buy 12 two-pound wheaten loaves, and 5d would buy a sheep—was well adapted to a local trade in country produce that was now beginning to grow up. The Carolingians inherited from the Merovingian age a silver penny of low weight which varied greatly in design from one locality to another and seems to have been subject to no public control at all. Pepin the Short began the process of reasserting the royal monopoly of coinage, a process which was completed by his son. Charlemagne carried out a monetary reform in c. 790 which brought into existence a silver penny of uniform design and weight, having on one face a cross and his own name and on the other the royal monogram and the name of the place where the coin was struck. A similar reform was carried out in England, and for five centuries silver pennies descended from those of Charlemagne and Offa were with rare exceptions the only coins struck in western Europe. In Charlemagne's realm their use was practically confined to Italy and to the lands west of the Rhine. Germany remained resolutely wedded to barter, despite a constant stream of legislation attempting to make the use of coin obligatory, and even in France barter no doubt persisted on a considerable scale.

Merchants and Merchandise

Mercatores and *negotiatores* are referred to from time to time in our written sources, but it is difficult to know how important they were in Carolingian economy. Two classes of them can be discerned, interregional traders dealing in staple commodities like grain, cloth and salt, and long distance merchants importing from the East such luxuries as spices and silk and exporting slaves and arms in exchange. The same terms could also cover pedlars and itinerant craftsmen—professional jewellers, tinkers and metal-workers, masons, and so on—who moved from place to place selling their skill as much as their wares. The merchants in the narrower sense of the word would conduct their business partly at such recognized centres of trade as Duurstede or Frankfurt, partly at great fairs like that of St Denis outside Paris, which we hear of as frequented by Frisians and Anglo-Saxons. They would also deal directly with great households, more especially with that of the king. Much distribution was effected by the primitive custom known to anthropologists as gift-exchange, which still survived on a large scale. Presents were then something more than the tokens exchanged at Christmas or birthdays that they are today. The letters of such men as St Boniface and Alcuin refer constantly to the carrying to and fro of gifts of all kinds, some of these being of the most

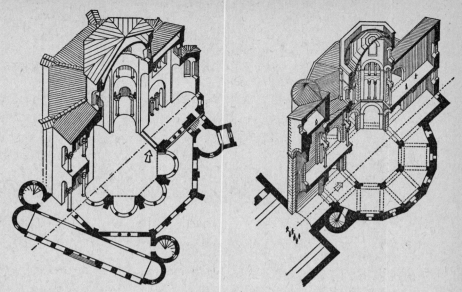

S. Vitale at Ravenna (left) compared with the royal chapel at Aachen (right). The similarity is deliberate, but the Carolingian architect (Odo of Metz) lacked the sophistication of his 6th-century model. Both plans are octagonal, with a three-storey elevation and chancel at one end. But at Ravenna each bay bulges outwards into an open niche with concave entablature, through which the ambulatory is glimpsed. At Aachen all the walls are straight and solid and the subtle interplay of space is lost. The church is nevertheless a considerable achievement for a northern builder at the turn of the 8th century. The arrows show the viewpoint of pl. 38 on p. 99 and pl. 12 on p. 275. (6, 7)

practical character. The traffic in lead, which was much prized as roofing material, seems to have been largely conducted on the basis of gift-exchange without the intervention of merchants at all.

There has been much discussion amongst scholars as to whether the Carolingian period was one of economic advance, or whether it marks a falling away from Merovingian standards. No statistics are possible, but there is good indirect evidence pointing to economic progress. Great attention was paid to the better management of royal and monastic estates: Roman writers on agriculture were much copied and studied, and abbots like Adalhard of Corbie and Hatto of Reichenau drew up elaborate regulations for the administration of monastic property. The interests of merchants were a matter of constant concern to Carolingian rulers: Charlemagne carried out a general reform of weights and measures as well as one of the coinage, and in 833 Louis the Pious granted the abbey of Corvey in Saxony the right to operate a mint on the express ground that there was no market and little trade in the vicinity and that a better supply of coin would encourage it. There is evidence of some specialization in manufacture, like that of Frisian cloth, of the opening up of new mines, and of some artistic enterprise. If the marble columns at Aachen were taken from older buildings at Ravenna, the great bronze doors were the work of craftsmen of the day. Probably agricultural and industrial production expanded during the Carolingian phase of the first half of the 9th century, and then fell off again as a consequence of the Viking invasions.

A New Flowering of the Arts

Our knowledge of the revival of letters and the arts in the Carolingian epoch is very one-sided. In architecture and sculpture there is little that has survived, and though some of it, like the interior of Charlemagne's palace chapel at Aachen, is extremely impressive, the derivative element is very strong. Charlemagne's church at Aachen was thus virtually a direct copy of S. Vitale at Ravenna, while the monastery church at St Gall would appear to have been modelled on a Roman basilica, and had apses at both ends. The cruciform church at Germigny-des-Prés, except for Aachen the best preserved Carolingian building that we have, must have followed a near eastern prototype almost exactly. Yet, even so, there is something about all these buildings that stamps them as Carolingian, and it is safe to say that an art which can be called by that name had developed by a fairly early date in the 9th century.

p 275 (11–13) f 6, 7 f 5 p 279– 80 (21)

in patria pax inuiolata in regno·
&dignitaf gloriofa regalif palatii·maxi
mo fplendore regiae poteftatif· oculif
omnium luce clariffima corufcare
atqp fplendefcere· qua fplendidiffi
mi fulgorif maximo pfufa lumine

Carolingian minuscule (meaning 'small letter'), with its bold, rounded design, was an advance in clarity and elegance. It quickly became the major book-hand of western Europe and is the basis of ordinary modern type. (8)

The fullest realization of this art came about in the sphere of painting, where the revival of Roman representational concepts tended to vie with the more primitive Germanic emphasis on stylized pattern and form. The latter style was to the fore in chapter heads and initial letters in the manuscripts, the representational element very much to the fore in the full-page illustrations and in the wall paintings which appear to have adorned the walls of most of the larger churches, though little has survived to this day.

f 2 The church at Ingelheim was thus decorated with scenes from the Old and New Testaments at the behest of Louis the Pious, and there were similar paintings in the monastery church at St Gall. These paintings must have been close in style to those

p 284 which survive, though in a rather battered condition, at Müstair
(28) in Switzerland. Byzantine and Syrian elements are present, but the style is different from anything known in the East; the art

p 285 is, in fact, already 'Carolingian'. At Germigny-des-Prés in France
(30) there was an elaborate decoration in mosaic, dating from between 799 and 818. Only a portion of it survives, showing the Ark of the Covenant between two angels, and here the work is rather more purely Byzantine in character.

The deficiencies in our knowledge of the wall paintings are happily compensated by the number of manuscripts that have survived, nearly all of them in excellent condition, for Carolingian illuminators were invariably first class technicians, and many of them were very good artists in addition. Most of the

p 282 books that contain illustrations are of a religious character: copies
(23–25) of the Gospels, books of Psalms and so on. Classical texts were
p 278 seldom illustrated. Apart from the initial letters and chapter heads
(18) of a formal character, most of the illustrations occupy whole pages and depict figures of a monumental character, such as the

p 278 Evangelists before their Gospels, David at the commencement
(19) of the Psalters, or the sovereign responsible for the execution of

p 281 the book. These portraits, especially the imperial ones, are imbued
(22) with a realism that is wholly Roman. They conform with the more straightforward, matter-of-fact character of the rest of the art, quite distinct from that which was to develop in the Byzantine world after the end of Iconoclasm. The same is true of the lovely

p 283 line drawings, as we know them in such a book as the famous
(27) Utrecht Psalter. They were to exercise a very considerable influence on future developments in the West, especially in England.

But though the realist figural trend was uppermost, hints of the old barbarian world that lay below the more cultured surface of court and monastery appear in some of the illuminations, as can be seen in a copy of the Gospels now in Paris, known as the Gospels of St Denis, where old interlacing patterns form the principal theme, and similar themes are to the fore in much of the metal work. To the 'barbarian' stream again may be attributed

p 277 the love of the ornate bejewelling which appears on most of the
(17) book covers and reliquaries of the age. The style is one which
p 288 had its birth in south Russia in Sarmatian times, and was carried
(38) west in the wake of the various barbarian invasions which characterized the centuries between the birth of Christ and the coronation of Charlemagne. But the ivories, which often form a part

p 276 of these bindings, were more sophisticated, the figures on these
(14–16) being often just as monumental in style as the portrait pages in the manuscripts.

The nature of the literature was akin to that of the illuminations. There was little of a vernacular character, and even in Latin there was little literature that one would now read for pleasure. Though Charlemagne enjoyed the German poems of his ancestors his son disapproved of either their paganism or their moral standards and had them destroyed. The positive intellectual achievements of the renaissance were small. Its theology and philosophy are appreciable only by specialists and are overshadowed by the achievements of the later Middle Ages; only John the Scot stands head and shoulders above his contemporaries, and he is virtually a discovery of modern times. Yet when all reservations are made, the Carolingian Renaissance represents a phenomenon of fundamental importance in European history, for it was due to the efforts of Carolingian scholars that the Latin past was salvaged at all.

The Revival of Learning

The basis of the renaissance was the revival of educational activity in the Empire. Secular education had never completely disappeared in Italy, and in Ireland and England, where Latin letters had come from outside and provision had consequently to be specially made for teaching the language, there were large numbers of monastic schools and a few cathedral ones. But in Gaul the old municipal schools at Bordeaux, Lyons and elsewhere had vanished in the 7th century, and nothing had grown up to take their place. The earliest of the new schools were those organized in the newly founded monasteries in Germany, where the problems of teaching Latin and extending a knowledge of the classics and patristic literature were similar to those in England. They soon spread back into Gaul, in the form of both episcopal and monastic schools, and in the reign of Charlemagne were extended both upwards and downwards, to

p 278 the Palace School on the one hand and the diocesan schools
(18, 19) on the other. The latter were in many places little more than an aspiration, but the Palace School was developed under Peter of Pisa and Alcuin into something that was both a formal school for sons of the nobility and a kind of academy in which members of the royal family and of the nobility and clergy were all called upon to participate. One result of its achievements was to endow the later Carolingians with what was an unusual phenomenon in the Middle Ages, a literate and sometimes learned aristocracy. The correspondence of Archbishop Hincmar of Rheims includes many summaries of letters to laymen dealing with unexpectedly intricate matters of religion, morality, and law, and the will of Marquis Eberhard of Friuli includes a list of books which an eminent layman might have in his library. There is in the Vatican a book which once belonged to Charlemagne's chamberlain Meginfrid.

The revival of education brought with it a revival of correct Latin for literary purposes, a reform of handwriting, and great publishing activity. The two latter were closely related to each other, since it was in the new handwriting that the copies of

f 8 books were diffused. The writing is that known as Carolingian
p 273 minuscule, a neat and regular book hand which owed much to
(5) the forms of handwriting used in the British Isles and which became widely disseminated on the continent through the activities of Irish and Anglo-Saxon missionaries and scholars. Detailed studies by a number of distinguished palaeographers of the variations of letter-forms, abbreviations and punctuation marks have now made it possible to discern the exact ways in which the blending of earlier handwritings took place and to date and place many of them with great precision. Two notable centres

p 281 were Corbie, an abbey near Amiens, important because of its
(22) great library, and St Martin of Tours, the abbey to which Alcuin
p 282 retired in his later years. Alcuin, a scholar from York, was
(25) Charlemagne's chief adviser in the middle years of the reign, and the part he played in the reform of handwriting was not the least of the services he rendered to Carolingian scholarship. When in the Italian Renaissance in the 15th century men sought to get away from the crabbed and ugly Gothic script of the later Middle Ages, they modelled their own writing on that of the classical manuscripts they were using, and since these dated in many cases from the 9th and 10th centuries it came about that Carolingian

minuscule forms the model for the printed letters we use today.

Although there are some famous exceptions, like the Vatican and Palatine Virgils and the Paris Livy, it is broadly true that the oldest manuscripts of the Latin classics date from the Carolingian Renaissance. The corollary is also valid that anything that reached the 8th century has survived for our own use today. The great gaps in Latin literature—the lost books of Livy, some of the writings of Cicero—occurred much earlier, often during the transition from papyrus to parchment. The continuity of tradition for the future was guaranteed by the multiplication of copies. In every well conducted monastery and in many cathedrals there were *scriptoria*, copying establishments with a skilled staff whose functions were essentially those of publishers. Alcuin asserted that 'to write sacred books is better than to till the soil for the vine, for the one nourishes the soul, the other only the stomach', and the prestige attached to the copying of patristic writers extended to the whole of the Latin classics as well. A large abbey like St Martin of Tours might have up to twenty copyists working at a time, and a good librarian was always on the look-out for new books to copy or better manuscripts that would provide him with variant readings which he could insert into works he already possessed. The letters of men like Alcuin and Servatus Lupus, Abbot of Ferrières, are full of references to the borrowing and lending of manuscripts, and one of the abuses of the Carolingian church, the accumulation of abbeys in the hands of a single abbot, had the unexpectedly happy result of facilitating such transactions. The exaction of pledges was simplified, and the fact that several abbeys had a common head

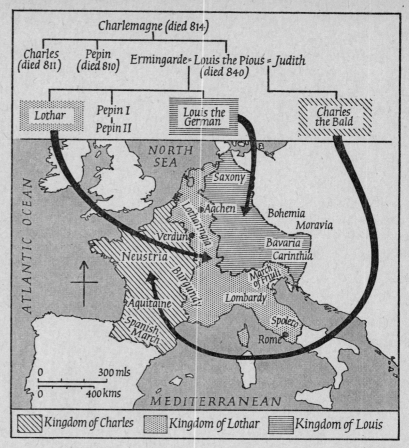

The Treaty of Verdun (843) between the sons of Louis the Pious divided Europe in a way that anticipates later national boundaries, and the Oaths of Strasbourg, which preceded it, are the first recorded prose texts of any length in the French and German languages. The East and West Frankish kingdoms enjoyed a comparatively stable history, but the middle kingdom (under the names of Lotharingia, Burgundy and Provence) was to be the subject of endless dispute. (10)

made the contents of their libraries known and accessible to the scholars of either community. Although Carolingian literary taste was not that of modern times, and some writers like Tacitus and Lucretius whom we rate very highly were so little thought of that they continued to hang by a thread, it was the universal multiplication of copies that took place in the century 750–850 that enabled scholarship to survive the disasters of the following century and hand on a legacy to the future.

The Empire Divided: Louis the Pious and his Sons

It was only by accident that Charlemagne's empire was not divided on his death. Louis had been only third in the line of succession, and had never envisaged for himself any other future than that of sub-King of Aquitaine. The deaths of his two brothers in 810 and 811 brought him to an office for which he was in many ways unfitted. He followed his father's example in raising his sons to royal rank early in his reign, and even associated his eldest son Lothar with him as Emperor, but he lacked Charlemagne's strength of personality and his ability to dominate his family, so that he could not prevent his sons becoming the tools of family ambitions and local rivalries. The intrigues of his second wife Judith and their joint endeavour to provide a suitable sub-kingdom for his youngest son Charles the Bald led ultimately to the outbreak of a civil war which lasted, with occasional interruptions and perennial shiftings of alliance, for the last twelve years of his reign. When Louis died in 840 four princes were left to dispute his inheritance: his eldest son Lothar I, who already had the imperial title and was effectively King of Italy; his third son Louis the German, already King in Bavaria; his fourth son Charles the Bald, whom he intended should succeed him in Gaul; and his grandson Pepin II, son of his second son Pepin I, who claimed the inheritance of his father in Aquitaine.

Three further years of civil war (840–843) decided the political fate of the Empire. In June 841, after much feinting and counter-marching, the forces of Lothar and Pepin met those of Louis

p 286
(32)

p 287
(35–37)
p 281
(22)

p 286
(33–34)
f 9

'. . . a harvest of spears and rivers of black steel come pouring in upon your city walls.' This vigorous illustration from the Book of Maccabees conveys as vividly as the Monk of St Gall's description the atmosphere of battle in Carolingian times, and originates in fact from the same monastery. It shows Antiochus Epiphanes' treacherous attack upon Jerusalem after a vow of peace. (9)

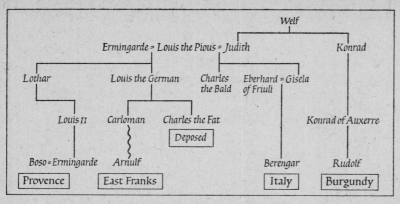

In 884 the Empire was united once more, for the last time, under Charles the Fat who, however, proved so unsuitable that in 887 he was deposed and the Empire split up into five parts, each choosing its own ruler. Four of these were connected in some way with the Carolingian family, if only by marriage. The fifth was Odo, Count of Paris, the choice of the West Franks. Italy was disputed between Berengar of Friuli and a certain Guy of Spoleto, the head of a Frankish family established south of the Alps. (11)

and Charles on the battlefield of Fontenoy near Auxerre. Lothar and Pepin were defeated, but the true losers were the Frankish nobility and the dynasty as a whole, for the death-roll on both sides was so heavy as fatally to weaken the ability of the ruling class to hold the state together. In February 842, by the oaths of Strasbourg, Louis and Charles each undertook as publicly as possible not to make a separate peace, Louis taking the oath in French so that it should be understood by the French-speaking contingents of his brother and Charles taking it in German in order to make his engagement plain to troops from the east. Lothar was forced to come to terms, and 120 commissioners were appointed to survey and value the royal demesne throughout the Empire and, Pepin's claims being disregarded, to arrange its partition between the three brothers. The outcome was the Treaty *f 10* of Verdun (August 843). The Empire was divided into three parts, the east going to Louis the German, the west to Charles the Bald, and the long central strip, from the Frisian coast to the frontier of the duchy of Benevento in southern Italy, to the eldest brother Lothar, who retained the title of Emperor but had to abandon all claims to authority over his brothers.

The Treaty of Verdun is the most famous and one of the most decisive in European history. Far sighted observers at the time regarded it as marking the end of the Carolingian state. Florus of Lyons lamented that there was no longer emperor or king, but only kinglets; no longer a kingdom, but only the fragments of one. But its decisiveness derived from subsequent accidents, not from the principles on which it was based. To posterity it seemed that France and Germany took their origins in the kingdoms of Louis and Charles, German and French respectively by race and language. In the sense that Louis and Charles were already kings in these areas and that convenience required their shares to be based on existing divisions, this may be admitted. But neither 'Germany' nor 'France' yet existed: men were conscious of being Saxons or Franks or Bavarians, or of being Neustrians or Burgundians or Provencals, not of being German or French. It was rather the long reigns of Louis the German (840–876) and Charles the Bald (840–877) that gave cohesion to the territories which they ruled, so that when subdivided in the future they always tended to come together on the same pattern. Such cohesion was denied to the portion of Lothar. It was both geographically less compact and linguistically more disunited, and it did not last long enough for loyalties to crystallize out. When Lothar I died in 855 it was divided between his three sons, and when they in turn died it was fought for between their uncles.

Louis the Pious' grandsons and great grandsons had less good fortune than his sons, and in 884, after many further partitions, the Empire of Charlemagne and Louis the Pious was re-united in the hands of a single ruler. It was his misfortune and that of his subjects that Charles the Fat, who became sole King in 884 and was crowned Emperor in the same year, was the one supremely incapable member of his house. In November 887, at

the Diet of Tribur in Franconia, he was not so much deposed as formally abandoned by his subjects, who elected kings for themselves, some of these being of Carolingian stock and others not. The East Franks chose Arnulf, a grandson of Louis the German but illegitimate; the West Franks chose Odo, a Frankish count who had earned the gratitude of his subjects by his defence of Paris against the Northmen; Italy was disputed between Berengar of Friuli and Guy of Spoleto, both of Frankish origin and the first of Carolingian descent in the female line. Burgundy chose as its King a certain Rudolf, related to the Carolingian family by marriage, but a little later Provence separated from it under Louis, son of a certain Boso who had tried to seize the throne in 879 and had married a daughter of the Emperor Louis II. Carolingian connections still counted for much, but the notion of the *regnum Francorum* as the family patrimony of the Carolingian house was formally abandoned. The title of emperor might still go on, but the history of Europe was henceforward to concern itself with the separate fragments of the Empire, not with the Carolingian state as a whole.

The Dissolution of Society

The splitting up of the Carolingian Empire was not caused by the advance of feudalism or the ravages of the Northmen, but it was these processes which explain the renewed downward plunge of western European society in the second half of the 9th century. Political fragmentation was made possible by the tradition that the Empire was analogous to a family estate subject to division between heirs; it was accentuated by the selfishness of the sons and grandsons of Louis the Pious, who never consulted any interest but their own and were quick to take advantage of any weakness or difficulty of their neighbours. It was also accentuated by the rivalries between the great Frankish noble houses, whose quarrels, now that their members held land in widely separated areas, had repercussions throughout the whole length of the Empire. Fear of attack by their own brothers, uncles or cousins made it impossible for the individual kings to control their counts or govern effectively even in the limited areas of their own kingdoms, and inability to control the counts—and the need to bribe them—led in turn to the progressive impoverishment of the kings. It was in this situation that the institution of feudalism had its role to play.

Feudalism had roots both in Germanic and Roman society, for if the property relationships involved could only be defined in terms of Roman law analogous relationships existed in both societies. For their understanding there is no need to go behind Frankish society in the Merovingian period. Any man of consequence reckoned to have in his household a large number of dependants, men whom he clothed, fed and supported and who in turn took an oath commending themselves to him and binding themselves to fight and in every way act on his behalf. These men were known as *fideles* or *vassi*, the first term implying their obligation of fealty and the second, a loan-word from Gaulish and cognate with the modern Welsh *gwas*, referring to their status, since the word was normally applied to a household servant or armed retainer. As estates owned by a landed magnate multiplied in number, it might be convenient for him to place members of his household in control of them, for such men were bound to him by a special oath of loyalty and it would be cheaper and more convenient to feed and clothe them directly from the produce of such estates than to maintain them in residence in the lord's household. The holding of land in this manner by a person who was technically termed a *vassus casatus*, a vassal endowed with a household of his own, was not so much the reward of services rendered in the past as a guarantee of services to be rendered in the future. A great landed proprietor would be able not merely to give estates to his vassals in this manner; he would attract other smaller proprietors to his service by having estates to offer in return for a promise of service and an oath of fealty. In times of social stress he might even attract not merely men but land to his service. Men would place themselves and their land at his disposal, receiving their land back as a fief in the knowledge that it was now better protected, at least against third parties, than it had been before.

Feudalism as an important feature of society had first become of consequence in the reign of Charles Martel, in part because of the development of cavalry and the convenience of placing the burden of maintaining himself fairly and squarely on the vassal's shoulders, but mainly because the widespread secularization of church property to the benefit of the ruler and the nobility had left both with a considerable surplus of land on which vassals could profitably be settled. Charlemagne, as his capitularies show, made extensive use of royal vassals in his government and granted them estates in all parts of the Empire. He also encouraged the spread of feudal bonds between other classes in society, even when it was not directly to his advantage, for in his view the multiplication of such relationships would assist in binding society together and he did not envisage the possibility of their being used to his own disadvantage. Although by the date of Charles' death feudalism had spread very widely throughout society, it had not as yet come to dominate it, and some further impulse was required before a radical transformation of society could take place. The civil wars of the last years of Louis' reign did much to further the tendency, but the true catalyst proved to be the Viking invasions.

Chaos and Anarchy—the Viking Raids

Viking raids were a new phenomenon in western Europe, where the movements of the peoples had for the most part been by land. Isolated attacks on the British Isles had begun in the last 15 years of the 8th century, and Charlemagne in 810 was driven to taking precautions against the possibility of their extension to the north coast of France. The danger which he feared made itself apparent immediately after his death, though the earliest phase of the raids was only a short one (814–819). In 837 they were resumed, and continued with occasional interruptions to the end of the century. The invaders would sail up the rivers, establish a fortified camp, and then raid over as wide an area as possible. Anything that was valuable and portable was carried off, what was not portable but was combustible was burnt, and human beings were killed and enslaved. The clumsy Frankish levies were quite unable to deal with raids of such a character; if sufficient forces were mobilized to cope with one invading group, this simply transferred itself elsewhere and set up another focus for its activities. A method that had some success involved the fortifying of the banks near the mouth of each river, so as to prevent the Vikings penetrating to the interior, and in the second half of the 9th century abbeys and towns were feverishly surrounding themselves with walls. During the Carolingian peace of the early part of the century Archbishop Ebbo of Rheims had obtained royal authority to use the stones from the city walls to construct a new cathedral. In the second half of the century his successors had hastily to rebuild the wall which he had destroyed. Charles the Bald resorted to Danegeld on a large scale, the payments being made either to induce the raiders to leave or to buy their services against other bands.

Not all of the Carolingian Empire was equally affected by the Vikings. The East Frankish kingdom got off lightly, but Hamburg was destroyed in 845 and the conversion of Scandinavia begun by St Anskar was postponed for a century and a half. In the Middle Kingdom Frisia suffered very badly, the great commercial centre of Duurstede being totally destroyed, and Lotharingia was raided from time to time; places as far inland as Liège and Aachen were plundered in 891–892. It was the West Frankish kingdom that shared with England the main destructiveness of the Vikings. Its great rivers—the Scheldt, the Somme, the Seine, the Loire, the Garonne—opened the way into the interior of the country, and in 843 a band of Vikings inaugurated a new phase in the raids by seizing and fortifying Noirmoutier at the mouth of the Loire, so that they were enabled to winter there and resume their raids in the spring.

Even when due allowance is made for the understandable exaggerations of monastic chroniclers there can be no doubt of the appalling destructiveness of the raids or the disruption of the social fabric which they caused. Towns, villages and monasteries went up in flames and their inhabitants were massacred or driven off into the woods to keep themselves alive as best they could. The raids were facilitated by the civil wars of the

middle years of the century, for some of the contestants were not above concluding temporary pacts with the invaders or at least trying to divert them from their own territories. Administration went to pieces over large areas; counts were killed and courts ceased to function, while the needs of defence diverted the attention of the kings and prevented them checking the usurpations of officials. There was widespread building of castles, since the Vikings were unskilled in siegecraft, but castles could be defended against the king as well as against the Northmen. New and larger military commands came sporadically into existence: Robert the Strong, the ancestor of the future kings of *f 12* France, is styled in the chronicles Duke of the Franks or Marquis of Neustria, since he was made head of a complex of counties intended to defend Paris. Above all, the raids resulted in the wider spread of commendation, by which free men gave themselves and their land to a lord in return for protection. A capitulary issued in 847 laid down that every free man should choose a lord for himself, and although it was never literally obeyed it marked the direction in which social relationships were evolving. The Viking invasions were the catalytic agent that transformed feudalism from an element in the social structure into its prominent and enduring feature.

These stresses came to a head in the decade 877–887. A period of short reigns and divided loyalties coincided with the worst phase of the invasions. The peace of Wedmore between Alfred and Guthrum in England in 878 diverted a major Danish army into France. Flanders and Picardy were devastated between 879 and 881. A West Frankish victory at Saucourt in 881 diverted the main attack into Lotharingia, but in 885 the invasion of northern France was renewed and continued till 892, Paris itself being subjected to a long siege in 885–886. The result was widespread anarchy which Charles the Fat was quite incompetent to check, and his deposition in 887 marked essentially the general recognition that civilization in the West would have to be saved on a local basis if it was to be saved at all.

Hope Renewed

The Europe that emerged from the wreckage of the Carolingian Empire bore little resemblance to that which had gone before. A new political unit, Christian instead of pagan and in many respects as culturally advanced as those regions which looked back to a Roman past, had come into existence east of the Rhine, and with its creation the political and cultural balance of Europe was changed decisively. Few facets of the 10th-century political scene are more striking than the predominance of the German monarchy and the virtual eclipse of that of France. If Italy was to

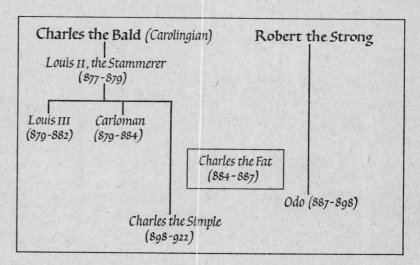

The rival kings of France. Charles the Bald had received the kingdom of the West Franks under the Treaty of Verdun (843). After his death (877) a series of short reigns followed, during which the country was divided between the two eldest sons of Louis the Stammerer. In 884 Charles the Fat re-united the whole Empire, ignoring the claims of Charles the Simple, but on his deposition (see fig. 11), the throne passed to the non-Carolingian Odo, son of Robert the Strong, ancestor of the Capetians. Odo was succeeded by Charles the Simple, but the struggle between the Carolingian and Robertian went on for nearly another century. (12)

297

some extent a political vacuum which was ultimately to be occupied by the German kings, the Carolingian period had seen a startling growth in papal power which, if for a moment in eclipse, promised steady development in the future. Everywhere society had been profoundly altered. If the advance of feudalism was a symptom of the dissolution of the state, it had provided at the same time a form of social existence which carried on in a different fashion some of its most vital functions.

It was in France, which had suffered most seriously from the Viking invasions, that the transformation of society went furthest and the advance of feudalism was most complete. The revolution of 887 revived the old kingdom of Charles the Bald, with Odo, the son of Robert the Strong, as its ruler. There was still in France, however, a Carolingian of disputed legitimacy, Charles the Simple, and in 893 a faction called him to the throne. The five years of civil war that followed continued the decline that had been almost uninterrupted since the death of Charles the Bald, when minorities and short reigns, civil war, and the fact that one sovereign was not Carolingian by descent, combined with the disruption caused by the Viking invasions to render impossible any effective assertion of royal authority. When Charles the Simple became undisputed King after Odo's death in 898 the power of the crown had virtually disappeared and effective authority had passed into the hands of the counts.

It was in fact these former representatives of royal authority who were in the best position to take advantage of the disorders of the time. They were normally great landed proprietors in their own right. They had, as counts, part of the royal demesne at their disposal, and it was no great task to assimilate it to their private estates. There existed, in almost every county, further royal estates; these in turn could be annexed when the Crown was weak and unable to assert its rights. There were also, in most counties, great abbeys which could be exploited, either by the count becoming their lay abbot or lay advocate or by simple robbery. The count, as the king's representative, was the individual who had a natural claim to the obedience of the freemen in his county; he was also, partly as a consequence of his official rank and partly by virtue of his personal eminence, the person to whom men would tend to commend themselves and their lands in times of crisis. As the office of count tended more and more to become hereditary, counties could be united by marriage and larger agglomerations of them come into existence. The principalities of medieval France often consisted not of one Carolingian county but of several. Flanders, the greatest one in the north, absorbed at its largest extent no fewer than fifteen Carolingian counties, most of these having been annexed by sheer force of arms during the anarchy of the last two decades of the 9th century.

Disputed Thrones

Against this emergence of the counts as the dominant element in French society the kings could do little or nothing. Essentially, for a hundred years, from 887 to 987, when Hugh Capet became King of France and the Carolingian dynasty came to an end, two great families were competing against each other for the crown. For most of the period, from 898 to 922 and again from 936 to 987, the throne was formally occupied by a Carolingian, but there was always in the background a representative of the Robertian house to threaten his position. The royal demesne had for the most part been dissipated and could not be recovered, and the last Carolingians sought desperately for some alternative. Again and again, taking advantage of vacancies, minorities, and disputed successions, they tried to seize either Lotharingia or one or other of the great feudal principalities, only on each occasion to be thwarted by a combination of counts who feared any reassertion of royal power. The inevitable result of the royal failure to annex a great principality was that in the end the head of a great principality would annex the crown, and it was this that Hugh Capet did in 987. But the delay of a century was almost fatal for royal power. Already Odo in 887 had become master of a royal demesne seriously weakened by a decade of short reigns and occasional civil war; a century later there was little left for Hugh Capet to inherit. Each king of the new dynasty,

however sweeping his claims, was to the other feudatories *primus inter pares* and little more.

The monarchy in Germany followed a startlingly different road. Feudalism was less strongly developed; the system of counts was less securely based; old family groupings and a sentiment of attachment to regional laws and language counted for much more. The great families that emerged were thought of as representing the older tribal units, and Bavaria, Swabia, Franconia and Saxony emerged as political entities to which there was no parallel west of the Rhine. When the Carolingian house died out in Germany the crown was therefore to pass to a much more powerful individual than in France, to a duke who was one of four instead of one of perhaps twenty, with a consequent advantage in the power of the crown. In Germany prior to 911 there had never been a non-Carolingian on the throne with a consequent weakening of loyalty; the disasters of the last decades of the 9th century had affected Germany less seriously; and the change of dynasty, when it took place, occurred more than half a century earlier than it did in France, so that less had been lost. These considerations may not fully account for the greater power of the German monarchy in 10th century Europe, but they go far towards explaining it.

France and Germany were territorially continuations of the old kingdoms of Charles the Bald and Louis the German; the Middle Kingdom, on the other hand, failed for the most part to survive. It is true that Burgundy and Italy set up their own kings in 887, and that Provence followed this example after a brief interval, but they were states of secondary importance. In the long run they were bound to succumb to one or other of their more powerful neighbours, which, since Germany was the more powerful of the two, meant in the end that, though preserving their political integrity, they were to be annexed to Germany. Lotharingia, the northern part of the Middle Kingdom, did not even become a separate state at all. Its social structure approximated to that of France, whose suffering it had shared at the hands of the Vikings, but its loyalties were strongly Carolingian. When Arnulf became King of Germany in 887/8 it became part of the German state, but when Konrad of Franconia became King in 911 it just as easily reverted to France. Henry the Fowler recovered it in 925, at a moment when a member of the Robertian house occupied the French throne, and thereafter the French never succeeded in recovering it. The Empire of Otto the Great and his successors thus came to represent two and not simply one of the kingdoms created by the Treaty of Verdun. Since Germany was stronger than France it was to it that the Middle Kingdom fell.

A New Power—the Papacy

One further great power, though in the 10th century scarcely recognizable as such, remains to be mentioned. The popes had at critical moments played a decisive role in Carolingian history. Pope Zacharias had authorized the usurpation of Pepin in 751 and Stephen II had anointed him King in 754. Half a century later, by an unexampled exercise of authority, Leo III had crowned Charlemagne Emperor. Both Charles and Louis, in crowning their own sons themselves, had shown a desire to break loose from this dependence, but again and again the popes showed their determination to retain the right of crowning the emperor till eventually it was admitted in law as well as fact. Gregory IV, albeit unwillingly, played a part in the enforced abdication of Louis the Pious in 833. Nicholas I (858–867), far from unwillingly, had intervened with success in the internal difficulties of Lothar II, forcing the King to take back his much wronged but barren wife, and had humbled Archbishop Hincmar of Rheims, the leader of the West Frankish church and the most eminent protagonist of the rights of metropolitans against popes and bishops alike. With the breakdown of imperial authority in the late 9th century, the papacy fell into the hands of the Roman nobility, whose régime in the end was best described by the term 'pornocracy' invented by Cardinal Baronius to describe it. But papal aspirations and assertions were never wholly to disappear, and when in the 11th century they were to become capable of a fuller realization than they had ever had before, it was to Carolingian precedents as much as to Petrine claims that they looked back.

XIV AFTER CHARLEMAGNE

The Empire under the Ottonians

DONALD BULLOUGH

Western Europe from the accession of Arnulf to the death of Otto III, with the chief cities and provinces

The new Empire of the West,

balancing the Byzantine Empire of the East, was by the end of the 9th century an established part of Europe's political system, though the status and authority of the Emperor outside the territories of which he was acknowledged sovereign were undefined. The office was not hereditary but its holder was generally the effective ruler of the East Frankish or Italian kingdoms and after 962 of both. The title continued to be coveted and honoured, and was destined to play a significant, if fluctuating, part in history for nearly 1000 years.

The Imperial Crown (right), now in the Treasury of Vienna, may legitimately stand as a symbol for the Saxon house, founded by Henry I in 919 and lasting (through the Salian dynasty) until 1125. The crown itself is still the centre of scholarly argument, but the most widely accepted view is that it was made (possibly

at Reichenau) for the coronation of Otto I in Rome in 961. It consists of eight plaques of gold held together by hinges secured by pearl-headed pins, so that it could easily be taken to pieces or laid flat for travelling (as was frequently necessary). Four of the plaques are filled with crudely cut gems held in gold filigree (in the manner of Carolingian reliquaries and book-covers). The other four contain panels of enamel showing God in majesty (with the inscription *Per Me Reges Regnant*—'Through me kings reign'), Solomon, David and Hezekiah with Isaiah. The upper part of the crown, an arch with a cross in front of it, dates from the time of Konrad II (1024–1039); along the two sides of the arch the words *Chuonrades Dei Gratia Romanorum Imperator Augustus* are worked in pearls. The jewelled cross has a crucifix engraved behind it. (1)

The direct Carolingian line

ended in the East Frankish kingdom when Charles the Fat, the son of Louis the German, abdicated in 887. The Empire split up into six major regions, and the magnates of each kingdom played an important part in determining the succession. The German throne was offered to Arnulf, an illegitimate son of Charles's brother. In 896 he was crowned Emperor by the Pope.

Arnulf, Louis the Child and Konrad I fill the thirty years between the abdication of Charles the Fat and the accession of the first Saxon king, Henry I. The portraits above are from seals affixed to royal charters. Arnulf (above left) died in 899 and was succeeded by his son Louis the Child (centre), then aged six. Louis lived for another twelve years, dying in 911 at the age of eighteen. Konrad (right) was an East Franconian count, a man of noble birth but not related to the Carolingian family. He was elected by the Frankish magnates and reigned until 918. All three were faced with an endless struggle to maintain their position. There were wars with the West Franks over Lotharingia, wars with the kings of Italy who laid claim to the imperial title, wars with the invading Magyars from the east, and rebellions by the powerful vassals within the kingdom itself. (2, 3, 4)

The next royal house, the Saxon dynasty, traced its descent from Liudolf, Duke of Saxony. In the genealogical tree (left), a detail from an elaborate medieval table of the Saxon, Salian and Hohenstaufen kings, he is placed at the top of the page. Under him (between his brother Bruno and sister Liutgard) is Duke Otto, *Otto dux*—Otto the Illustrious—who was offered the East Frankish throne after the death of Louis the Child but refused. Under him is Henry the Fowler, the first Saxon King, elected in 919. He is pictured with his wife Matilda. Otto I, their son, is immediately beneath them, and Otto II, *his* son, second from the right in the bottom row. In the ivory panel from an altar (right) an emperor who is thought to be Otto I is shown presenting a church to Christ, who is seated on a wreath of victory. Saints, including St Peter, stand on either side. (5, 6)

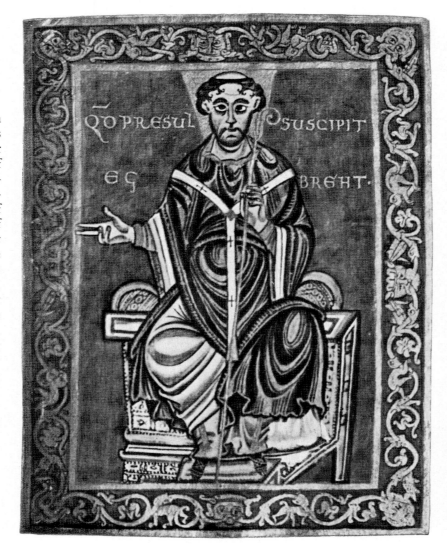

The bishops played an active part in the affairs of state and often wielded as much temporal power as a duke or count. They were also the leaders of education and patrons of the arts—names like Bernward, Bishop of Hildesheim (see pls 38–44), Willigis of Mainz, Bruno of Cologne, Notker of Liège occur wherever painting or sculpture is discussed. Two of the most outstanding of such patrons were Egbert, Bishop of Trier (right), and Gero, Bishop of Cologne (far right). Egbert, seen here on a page from a Psalter presented to him in about 983, was responsible, among much else, for the Altar of St Andrew (pl. 23) and for the famous codex illustrated in pl. 36. Gero (far right), shown receiving a book from a scribe, is remembered for the great crucifix (pl. 45) which bears his name. (9, 10)

For Otto's son, Otto II (top, in a seal impression) an imperial bride—the 16-year-old Byzantine princess Theophanu—was wooed and won. In this ivory relief (below), by a Byzantine artist, they together receive Christ's blessing. (7, 8)

The nobility, who elected the king, were still in many respects his equals and represented a constant threat to his authority. No better example of this can be found than the career of Henry, Duke of Bavaria (right), who gained for himself the nickname of 'the Wrangler'. He was a grandson of Henry I, a cousin of Otto II, and inherited the dukedom of Bavaria from his father. He rebelled twice against Otto II, was defeated, imprisoned and deprived of his duchy (976). When Otto died he led yet another revolt aimed at seizing the crown from the infant Otto III. He was in fact proclaimed king in Saxony, but his cause lost ground and he contented himself with regaining his old dukedom. He died in 995, apparently a loyal subject at last, aiding Otto against the Bohemians. The portrait comes from a manuscript painted at Regensburg in about 990. (11)

SCLAVINIA   GERMANIA   GALLIA   ROMA

The imperial family in adoration.
The ivory panel, of which this is a
detail, shows Otto II and his wife
Theophanu holding in her arms the
future Otto III. All three wear Germanic crowns. It was probably made
in Milan in about 980, when Otto II
made his state entry into that city. (12)

OTTOIMPERATOR

The boy-king, Otto III, who came to the throne when he was fourteen and died when he was twenty-one, was the visionary of the Saxon house. He tried to lay the foundations of a new Empire that was to be both Roman and Christian without ceasing entirely to be German. In the pair of pictures shown on these two pages, from a Gospel-book painted at Reichenau or at the imperial court in about 998, he is shown receiving the homage of the four chief provinces of the Empire—Sclavinia (Otto had just won a victory over the Slavs in 997), Germania, Gallia and Roma. One is reminded of the glowing words of his friend Gerbert of Rheims, later Pope Sylvester II: 'Ours, ours is the Roman Empire! Its strength rests on Italy, fertile in fruits, on Gaul and Germany, fertile in men, and on the realm of the valiant Slavs. Thou art our Caesar, our Augustus! Sprung from the noblest of Greek blood [an allusion to Otto's mother, Theophanu], you surpass the Greeks in power, you rule the Romans by hereditary right and excel both in wisdom and eloquence.'

The two pictures, in fact, are as much a diagram of a political theory as the representation of a real scene, although the four figures have recently been identified as men associated with Otto's Roman court. The Emperor is shown much larger than the other figures to symbolize his status as ruler; in his right hand he grasps the staff, in his left a globe with cross—the Christian world which is his Empire. The bishop on his right lays his hand on the cushion of Otto's throne—meaning that the Church upholds and is upheld by the throne—while the warrior on his left grips a sword in one hand and raises the other in token of allegiance. Classical as this composition is in essentials (and certainly in intention), its Germanic origin betrays itself in such details as the faces peering out of the capitals of the columns. (13, 14)

An age of saints —

of miracles, visions, legends and holy relics, but an age too of tenacious courage and faith to which mankind can still look back with admiration. The Roman Church had now become the great civilizing power of Europe. In the art produced under her patronage at this time one can recognize a new sense of majesty and purpose, almost of command. Right: a bishop (one panel of an ivory antiphonary-cover) raises his right hand in blessing; in his left he holds an open book with the opening words of Psalm 24, *Ad te, Domine, levavi animam meam* written in a curiously archaic script. The Psalm is chanted by seven priests in a half-circle and five deacons in a gallery behind. (17)

The conversion of the pagan in Eastern Europe was attended with suffering, often with death. Top: the mission and martyrdom of St Boniface, 'the Apostle of the Germans', who was killed by the Frisians in 754, refusing to defend himself. This manuscript dates from the 10th century. Bottom: St Adalbert, martyred by the Prussians in 997, intercedes with Boleslav I of Poland for the release of two slaves from a Jewish slave-trader—a scene from the bronze doors of Gniezno Cathedral (12th century), where his body was taken. (15, 16)

A dove perched on his shoulder was said to have transmitted the divine voice to St Gregory the Great when he wrote his Commentaries. In this ivory (right), which is thought to come from the same workshop (possibly Trier) as the cover opposite, he sits in a beautifully schematized study with looped curtains, an ornate writing desk, a chair like an antique capital and, in the background, a skyline of towers, gables and battlements. The lower scene shows a monastic *scriptorium* with three monks writing, one of them holding the inkwell. (19)

The Holy Lance (below) was one of the most prized relics of Christendom. A simple steel blade with a nail (from the True Cross) inserted into the middle and covered with a sheet of silver, it is in fact unlikely to be older than the 8th century. Rudolf of Burgundy acquired it from one Samson, a count in north Italy, but had to relinquish it to Henry I. Otto I carried it into battle and attributed to it his victory over the Magyars at the Lechfeld in 955. (18)

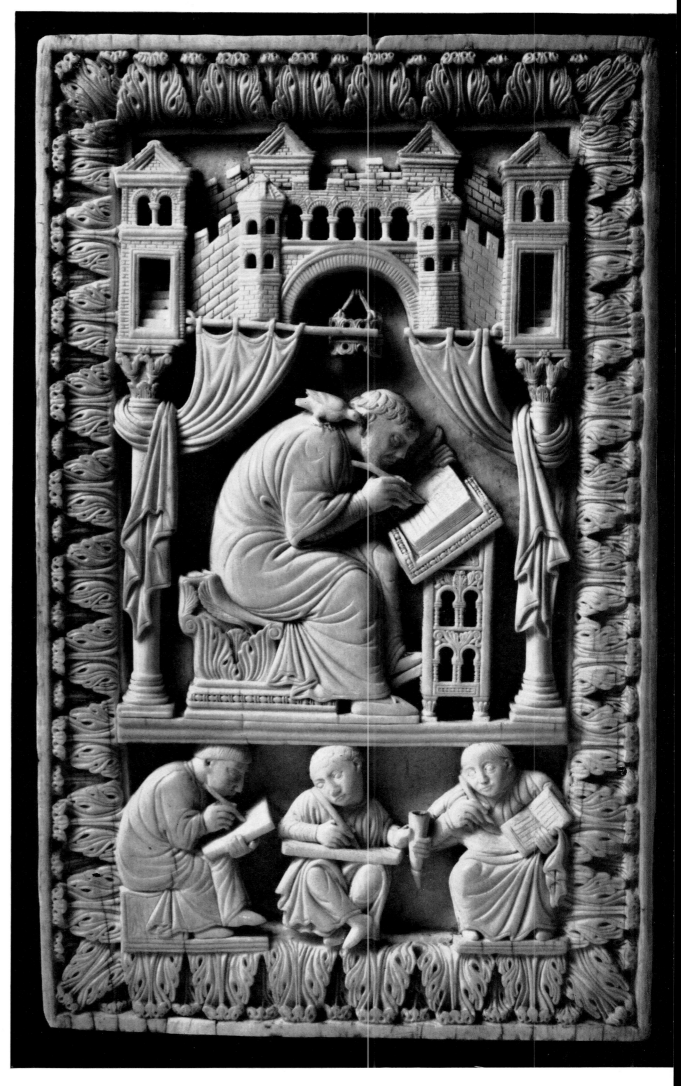

The holy image of St Foy (below) at Conques illustrates one of the most striking features of medieval religion—the devotion accorded to the relics of saints. St Foy was a young girl of twelve, martyred during the last Roman persecution in 303. In 866 some of her remains were brought to Conques and installed in the abbey. Soon tales of extraordinary miracles were circulating. One man whose eyes had been torn out was said to have regained his sight through her intercession. Pilgrims began to flock to Conques and the treasure of St Foy grew. This statue (gold plate over a wooden core) was made in about 985. As time passed a bizarre collection of valuables were fastened to it—emeralds, agates, pearls, onyx, sapphire, amethyst, crystal and even some antique Roman cameos. On her back is part of an 8th-century retable; on her chest a 13th-century triptych with quatrefoil; on her knees a gold plaque with figure of a woman; elsewhere pieces of an old Gospel cover with reliefs of Christ and the Evangelists have been fixed on wherever there was room. And in a cavity in her back, wrapped in a covering of silver, the object of all this devotion—the little saint's skull. (20)

The Golden Madonna of Essen (above) is one of the oldest (perhaps *the* oldest) free-standing figures of the Virgin in existence. Commissioned in the late 10th century by the Abbess Matilda (Otto I's granddaughter) it stands over two feet high. The wooden core was covered in gold leaf, the eyes are coloured enamel and the apple filigree. There are jewels on the halo and the book, and the footstool is covered with copper gilt. The apple is probably an allusion to the Virgin as the 'second Eve': through the first, Man fell—through the second he is redeemed. (21)

Arnulf, King of the East Franks, presented this portable altar (right) to the monastery of St Emmeran, Regensburg, in 893, three years before he was crowned Emperor in Rome. The upper part forms a canopy with four gables whose ridges are set with jewels in filigree. The gold reliefs on the sloping sides (scenes from the Gospels) belong to the same school as the Codex Aureus (see p. 277, pl. 17). A block of serpentine—mottled greenish stone—between the lower pillars served as the actual altar. It originally had a border of small enamel plaques, of which only a few remain. (22)

St Andrew's sandal is encased in this strange foot-shaped reliquary, which is also a portable altar. It was made c. 980–90 in the workshop founded by Egbert of Trier. The long sides consist of ivory panels with gold lions and symbols of the Evangelists in enamel. (23)

Christendom's growing strength

finds massive expression in the great churches of the 10th century. Saxony—pagan a century before—was now, because of the ruling dynasty, a centre of religious activity. At the same time important technical advances were made in stone-carving, vaulting and buttressing. Classical precedents, so vital to the Carolingian architects, no longer exercised such an influence. A new style, personal to its own age, began to emerge: the Romanesque.

Like all ages of transition, it was a period of bold innovation and copious variety. These five capitals—hundreds of others would make the same point—all represent a fresh look at an old problem. Right: from Hildesheim, a plain abacus surmounted by an inscribed impost-block; and Gernrode, a stylized version of Corinthian. Below: two more from Hildesheim and (far right) an unusual design from Rasdorf containing a composite picture of the symbols of the Evangelists. (24–28)

Cologne's Romanesque churches made it, until the last war, a city of unique medieval distinction. Among the earliest is St Pantaleon (left) founded soon after 966 and dedicated in 980. This view shows the characteristic high 'west-work', but the porch is a modern restoration. (29)

The nunnery of Quedlinburg (below) was founded by Henry I near his favourite home, and here in 936 he was buried. Architecturally it is notable for its groined vault and stucco capitals. The abbess of Quedlinburg was often of royal blood. (30)

In memory of his son, killed in battle in 959, the Saxon Count Gero founded another great nunnery not far from Quedlinburg—St Cyriakus at Gernrode. Left: the west end with its 'west-work' (apse added later) and tall circular towers. The nave (below) is divided into two major bays by square brick piers, and each bay subdivided by round columns, the same rhythm appearing in the gallery as two groups of six small arches. Details at this level are shown above—note the two capitals, one of which is similar to one already seen in close-up. (31, 32, 33)

A revolution
in manuscript illumination took place in Germany in the mid-10th century. Artists freed themselves from dependence on classical models and launched out boldly in search of the visionary and the dramatic. St Luke in ecstasy (left) from the Gospel Book of Otto III typifies the break with tradition. Instead of bending over a desk, the Evangelist—a giant, an Atlas—gazes straight before him and lifts a heavenly world resplendent with angels, prophets and the symbolic ox in his triumphant arms. (34)

The meaning of Holy Mass is the theme of this exhilarating yet strictly academic composition from the Uta Codex (right). The central figure, St Erhard, celebrates Mass, using the very altar of Arnulf shown in pl. 22, and dressed in the exotic robes of a high priest of the Old Covenant. (37)

St John's emblem, a huge eagle, watches over him as he writes (below left). This manuscript from Lobbes, in Lotharingia, was given by Otto I to his brother-in-law, Athelstan King of England. The Evangelists were copied by English artists, but without the *panache* of the original. (35)

The Egbert Codex (below) is a work of supreme power. 'I believe', wrote one critic, 'that almost everyone who has turned over these pages must have felt himself in the presence of a spiritual genius.' Here, in the Betrayal, Christ and Judas seem locked together with a tension unmatched till Giotto. (36)

One patron

was responsible for everything on this page except the crucifix on the far right. He was Bernward, Bishop of Hildesheim, tutor of Otto III and chaplain at the imperial court. The pair of bronze doors, of which three panels are shown (left), were made for his church of St Michael, although they were moved in about 1030 to the Cathedral. One tells the story of Genesis, the other the life of Christ. Top: the sacrifices of Cain and Abel, with the hand of God appearing in the sky. Centre: the Fall—God accuses Adam, and Adam, with a beautifully observed gesture, tries to pass the blame on to Eve, who in turn points to the Serpent. Bottom: Christ before Pilate. Satan, in the form of an ape, whispers his evil counsel in Pilate's ear. (38, 39, 40)

The small silver crucifix (above) dates from about 1007—that is, before either the door or the column—but in style it looks forward to the Middle Ages rather than back to Rome. Its feeling 'for bone structure beneath the flesh, for the sagging weight of the dead body, for the poignance of death' mark the beginning of a new realism. (41)

Bernward's visits to Rome, of which several are recorded, were obviously the key factor in the formation of his taste. His bronze doors (c. 1015) were the first of their kind to be cast in one piece in the West since the end of the Roman Empire. In the bronze column which he commissioned five years later his admiration for the classical past is even plainer. Although only 12½ feet high (being in fact simply an outsize candlestick intended to hold the Paschal candle), it is a direct imitation of the Columns of Trajan and Marcus Aurelius in Rome. Instead of the emperors' campaigns, scenes from the life of Christ wind up it in a spiral. Three details are illustrated (left). Bottom: the curing of the lame and blind. Centre: the Marriage at Cana. Top: the entry into Jerusalem. These works of Bernward's at Hildesheim, taken together, not only provide a unique ensemble of early 11th-century art, but also show how important was the personality of the patron. (42, 43, 44)

The agony of Christ's passion has left its mark on the dead figure hanging on the cross. This life-size crucifix, carved in wood and originally painted, is a work of the highest genius, overwhelming in its power, dignity and tenderness. Tradition assigns it to the period of Gero, Archbishop of Cologne between 969 and 976. He is said to have placed it 'in the middle of the church' (i.e. old Cologne Cathedral) and to have enclosed the consecrated host in the head: a small cavity does in fact exist at the base of the skull. (45)

For the coronation of an emperor this eight sided ivory situla (left) was made at Trier in about the year 1000, and was used for holding holy water at the consecration ceremony. It is encrusted with gems but is especially fascinating for the relief figures that decorate the sides. At the bottom stand armed guards in front of magnificent gates; above them miniature battlements like a town-wall. In the upper register sit a pope (centre) and an emperor, probably Sylvester II and Otto III. The other figures are two archbishops, two bishops and an abbot, all enthroned between columns draped with heavy curtains. (46)

'How can I speak of precious stones' not only useful but also wonderful to behold?' wrote Hugh of St Victor. The medieval intoxication with jewels, which modern taste is inclined to disparage, had a strong element of mysticism in it. Colours were symbolic, every stone had its ulterior meaning, and there is no doubt that in the gems with which they covered their book-covers, reliquaries and liturgical objects the men of the 10th century saw not only value but a reflection of the true splendour of Heaven. The ivory panel (above) is the centrepiece of the cover of the Golden Gospels of Echternach, made at Trier in about 990. The crucifixion too is imbued with allegory. In the corners the Sun and the Moon weep. Longinus, with the spear, represents the New Testament, opening Christ's side from which flows the redeeming blood of life. Stephaton, with the sponge, stands for the Old Covenant. The cross rests on a crouching female figure—*Terra*, the Earth. (47)

The Empire under the Ottonians

DONALD BULLOUGH

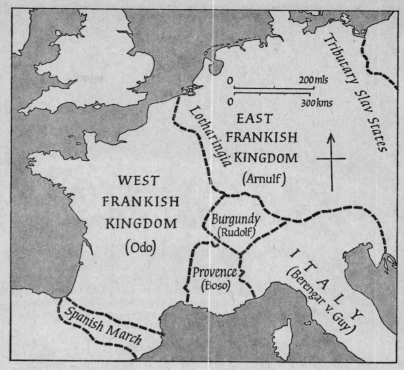

Europe at the time of Arnulf's accession, 887/8, when the Empire of Charles the Fat disintegrated. For the relationship between the various rulers see p. 296, fig. 11. The province of Lotharingia was to be a constant bone of contention between East and West Franks. (1)

p 302
(2)
f 1

BY MID-887 CHARLES THE FAT, who had temporarily re-united the territories once ruled by Charlemagne, was clearly becoming enfeebled. In the autumn he abdicated. About the same time a number of leading men from the more easterly regions of his Empire assembled at Frankfurt and proclaimed Arnulf, the illegitimate son of Charles' brother Carloman, King over the East Frankish kingdom. The impossibility of deciding whether Arnulf's 'election' followed or preceded Charles' 'abdication' exemplifies the problem of describing the break-up of the Carolingian Empire and the beginnings of separate West Frankish and East Frankish kingdoms from sources that are rarely contemporary and almost never unprejudiced.

Francia Orientalis: the Kingdom of Arnulf

p 296
(f 11)

A kingdom of *Francia orientalis*, comprising all or the greater part of the Frankish dominions east of the Rhine together with certain regions on its left bank, was created by the Treaty of Verdun in 843, when Charlemagne's Empire was divided between the three surviving sons of Louis the Pious. Granted that a German dialect was spoken in most of the territory (and there were few German-speaking districts outside it), this was a tenuous basis for political unity, although the fact and significance of a common linguistic tradition did not pass unnoticed even in the 9th century. There were marked differences in social structure and in political and cultural traditions between different regions; most conspicuously between those which had been Roman and Christian before their Germanic occupation and those in which Christian Roman civilization had been introduced by the Franks; but also between the areas occupied by different Germanic tribes. In their organization of the Church, the administration of justice and of the royal domains in their dominions the Carolingian monarchs tried to ignore and even to obliterate these differences. But while in the long run the effect of their measures was to make them largely unimportant, in the short run they often served only to emphasize them. In times of emergency or crisis the leading clergy and laity naturally came together on a regional basis and if one of their number emerged as a leader it was not difficult to identify his sphere of influence with the old 'tribal' territory.

Such men were necessarily more important as supporters of a monarch than the ordinary count, even when he came of a family long established in the area in which he exercised authority in the sovereign's name. Without their co-operation and that of the episcopacy, Arnulf could have achieved little. Throughout his reign, (887/8–899), however, it was clear that he, not they, was the arbiter of the kingdom. The determination he showed against early dissidents and a decisive defeat of the Northmen in 891 greatly enhanced his position. At least as important was the continuing magic of the Carolingian name and of its imperial aspirations. This was evident in the choice of Arnulf and in the agreement of the magnates that if he died without legitimate heir the succession should devolve on his illegitimate sons.

f 5

Yet there were obvious weaknesses. The western limits of the kingdom were far from stable, even though the clergy of Trier —who were apparently maintaining a vigorous if unoriginal intellectual tradition when most other centres of Carolingian learning were experiencing a decline—were strongly pro-Caro-

lingian; and on the long and exposed eastern frontier initiative had passed from the *Franci* to the Slavs. More than one diploma shows Arnulf making provision for the construction of a fort *(urbs)* which was obviously to provide an emergency refuge for the people of the district. In 895, following the birth of a legitimate heir, his illegitimate son Zwentibold was made king of a reconstituted Lotharingian kingdom—the last of the Frankish *divisiones regni*. The inadequacy of these measures was evident when Arnulf died leaving only a child to succeed him. Discontented Lotharingian nobles gave their allegiance to the Carolingian who now ruled the West Frankish kingdom, Charles the Simple; and in 900 the dreaded Magyars appeared for the first time on the Danube frontier—a year after their first devastating raid across the Julian Alps into north Italy. In the coming decades many more areas were to experience 'the wrath of the Magyars'.

f 1, f 5

f 1

f 2
f 5

The value to king and kingdom of the active support of able churchmen was now very apparent. Early in 900, Arnulf's legitimate son, the boy Louis, was crowned King in his palace of Forcheim—the first religious coronation in the East Frankish kingdom. Bishops and their followers were prominent in the expedition that recovered Lotharingia and in the defensive measures and battles against the Magyars; and the earliest known regulations for the maintenance of a German town wall were promulgated by the Bishop of Worms shortly before or shortly after 900. Episcopal resources and participation in the government of the kingdom were doubtless even more important after the Bavarians accepted Arnulf (of Bavaria) as their *dux* in 907: from that date the King and his court were excluded from Bavaria and its royal domains and churches were at the disposal of the Duke. Conversely, the grant to the influential Archbishop of Trier of the royal dues in his city together with the right of coining was a precedent for many similar grants in the future.

p 302
(3)

A Change of Dynasty

Louis was still a minor when he died in 911. The evidence for the steps taken to replace him and most of the evidence for the next four decades of East Frankish history come from later writers whose primary interest and guiding theme were the aims and achievements of the King and Emperor Otto. It is perhaps not surprising that there is not even rudimentary agreement among scholars as to how the evidence should be interpreted.

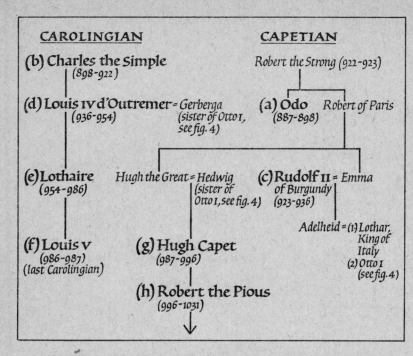

CAROLINGIAN		CAPETIAN
(b) Charles the Simple *(898-922)*		*Robert the Strong (922-923)*
(d) Louis IV d'Outremer *(936-954)*	= Gerberga *(sister of Otto I, see fig.4)*	**(a) Odo** *(887-898)* *Robert of Paris*
(e) Lothaire *(954-986)*	*Hugh the Great* = *Hedwig (sister of Otto I, see fig.4)*	**(c) Rudolf II** = *Emma of Burgundy (923-936)*
		Adelheid = (1) *Lothar, King of Italy* (2) *Otto I (see fig.4)*
(f) Louis V *(986-987)* *(last Carolingian)*	**(g) Hugh Capet** *(987-996)*	
	(h) Robert the Pious *(996-1031)* ↓	

Kings of France during the 10th century, showing the end of the Carolingian and the rise of the Capetian family. The letters a–h indicate the sequence in which the crown alternated between the two families. Note that Otto I was allied by the marriages of his sisters to both houses. (2)

p 297
(f 12)
f 2

What is certain is that the only legitimate Carolingian in 911 was the West Frankish King, Charles the Simple. The nobles of Lotharingia, as much through dynastic loyalty as discontent with the way in which they had been treated in the previous reign, promptly transferred their allegiance to him. Magnates from other parts of the kingdom assembled at Forcheim where the crown was offered first to the Saxon 'Duke' Otto who refused and

p 302
(4)

then to the East Franconian Count Konrad who accepted. What has some claim to be regarded as the first 'free' election in German history was followed by the first certain example of ecclesiastical annointment in East Francia.

Konrad I is by no means a favourite among German historians; but it has been rightly observed that even later pro-Ottonian writers regard him as a man of spirit and energy, whose enterprises were rarely blessed with success. Realizing what the loss of Lotharingia would mean, Konrad made determined efforts to

f 4

re-impose his authority there, but in vain. When Otto of Saxony died in 912, his son Henry succeeded him and subsequently used the ducal title without royal intervention. By 917 Swabia, too, had its *dux* although even in 911 it was by no means certain which of two rival families in that region would eventually emerge supreme; and in the same year Duke Arnulf re-established himself in Bavaria from which he had previously been expelled by the King with the support of bishops and abbots who objected to the Duke's secularization of church lands. Before he died

p 302
(5)

(December 918) Konrad recognized that a stronger hand than his was required by designating Henry of Saxony to succeed him.

Designation was a familiar practice of the Carolingians. But whereas in their time the chosen successor had been immediately accepted by the magnates, now there was a delay of many months, and when eventually Henry was acknowledged by an assembly at Fritzlar, in the borderlands of Franconia and Saxony where the exploitation of the land had only just begun, those taking part were predominantly from these two regions. Henry's refusal of unction may have been partly because of a fear of increasing the prestige of the already powerful Archbishop of Mainz (who expected to perform the ceremony). More important, however, was the evident implication that his authority depended on the co-operation of the leading laymen of the kingdom, especially the dukes; and his reliance on a single notary (instead of a properly-staffed writing office) shows how far he was prepared to go in not leaning on the church.

By accepting the royal dignity Henry both put a check to Saxon separatism and secured for the monarchy the benefits of

318

his predecessors' monastic foundations and acquisitions of culti-vated land. In the south, where the Bavarian Arnulf for a time claimed the royal dignity, his authority was acknowledged only after a show of force and a promise to leave the dukes a con-siderable measure of autonomy. A combination of respect for Henry and his own energies had even more important conse-

f 2

quences. Following the dispute over the kingship in West Francia (922–925) when Charles the Simple was deposed, Henry was acknowledged King in Lotharingia: the Carolingian 'Middle Kingdom' from Frisia to the Vosges watershed, with Aachen, Trier and what remained of the once rich Carolingian fisc in that area, was henceforth part of the *regnum Teutonicorum*. In 926

f 2

Henry gave new expression to his responsibilities as King when at Worms, in the presence of the Burgundian King Rudolf and the great men of his kingdom, he ordered steps to be taken to provide more fortified refuges for the inhabitants of areas exposed to attack. He extended German influence in Bohemia; and in

f 5

the late 920s his troops inflicted severe defeats on the Slavs across the Saale and middle Elbe and established permanent garrisons among them. In 933 he was victorious over a Magyar horde and a year later repelled a Danish invading-force. In his last years he was almost equally concerned with his southern neighbours. Although his own ambitions in this direction were probably never clearly formulated, the course to be followed by his successor was partly determined when he secured from King Rudolf the

p 307
(18)

'Holy Lance': for whatever may have been the original signifi-cance of this object it was now or soon afterwards regarded both as a relic and as a symbol of the right to rule over the *regnum Italiae*. Henry's last formal achievement was the desig-nation of his eldest son Otto to succeed him.

Otto I: the King and his Subjects

'After Henry, the father of his country and the greatest and best of kings, had died (2nd July 936)', Widukind tells us, 'all the people of the Franks and Saxons chose Otto for their king and

p 302-3
(5, 6)

they sent out notices of his coronation that was to take place at Aachen.' The elaborate ceremonial at the former Carolingian capital on 7th August 936 began (again according to Widukind who is our only source) with 'the dukes and the commanders of the soldiers and other military leaders raising Otto upon the throne which was erected in the portico adjoining the church of Charlemagne, and giving him their hands and promising him their fidelity and aid against all his enemies'. Otto then entered the church and was first acclaimed by the clergy and other magnates and afterwards invested with the royal insignia, each

f 8

item of which was felt to symbolize some aspect of his authority: the investiture was performed by the Archbishop of Mainz, although only after the Archbishops of Cologne and Trier had agreed not to press their alternative claims. Finally he was an-nointed and crowned; and wearing his royal garb he was led to a throne in the church which 'was so placed that he could see all and be seen by all'. The day ended with a lavish banquet in the palace (an essential part of any royal occasion) at which the four dukes acted as domestic officers.

Otto and his advisers had been at pains to emphasize that the Saxon King was entering into the full heritage of the Frankish Emperor: and they had sought to reinforce his royal authority with all the sanctions that religious and secular ceremonial could provide. The purpose of this authority, and ultimately its only justification or guarantee of lasting acceptance, was equally clear to those laity who had suffered from foreign invasion or internal disorder and to those clergy who were familiar with Augustine's *City of God* or (as the monks of Fulda and Corvey certainly were) with Einhard's portrait of Charlemagne. It was before all else to bring peace and security—a *pax* that was not merely an absence of war and destruction but was the earthly counterpart of the life of the Heavenly City in which *iustitia*, 'right order', everywhere prevailed and was nowhere perverted or disturbed.

'Justice' in a more concrete sense only incidentally engaged the attention of Otto. There is nothing to suggest that he (or his son and grandson) ever thought that he had an obligation to make this available to all the free inhabitants of the kingdom through a system of public courts. Charlemagne's innovations to this end had only slightly affected the regions east of the Rhine, where the territorial county had established itself in only a very few areas. The circumstances that had favoured the rise of the dukes had also strengthened the position of the larger (but still restricted) group that 10th-century writers refer to as *nobiles*. Their most obvious characteristic, apart from their landed wealth, was that they held courts whose proceedings and decisions were recognized (willingly or otherwise) by lesser landowners as well as by their immediate dependants. Their only rivals, or perhaps more accurately their counterparts and alternatives in some areas, were the courts of 'immune' churches—whose number grew steadily by royal grant throughout the century—and of the equally immune royal domains (fiscs), presided over by a royally-appointed advocate. So long as services were rendered, and this meant, above all, joining the royal host with a complement of troops when called upon to do so, and so long as it was recognized that even men with the ducal title were not free to act as they pleased, the powers of the *nobiles* were not likely to be challenged. Indeed, Otto and his successors apparently regarded with equanimity the abandonment to others of the money and services hitherto paid by groups of small free landowners (the so-called *Königsfrei*) to the fisc. It was evidently held that the royal authority was most secure where the king and the greatest of his subjects acknowledged their reciprocal obligation and exercised their appropriate prerogatives. It was to emphasize this, as well as to show the special intimacy reserved to the dukes, that the latter served at the coronation banquet and that they and a limited number of other magnates had previously done homage and sworn fealty and thereby become his vassals.

The implications of this 'dualist' conception of sovereignty and the limits of ducal autonomy acceptable to the monarch were soon to be revealed. In July 937 Duke Arnulf of Bavaria died and at the instigation of the Devil (according to the later chroniclers of the abbey of Tegernsee, whose lands he had secularized) his corpse was carried by hellish spirits from Regensburg to a watery grave. Two years earlier, in kingly fashion, he had publicly designated his son to succeed him. Such a succession could not be tolerated and after two expeditions Otto established his own nominee, the late Duke's brother. The Salzburg Annals record under the year 938 that 'Herold was made Archbishop by King Otto'. It is a safe inference that the new Duke had abandoned control of episcopal appointments within the duchy, and it is apparent that at the same time former royal domains and secularized ecclesiastical estates reverted to their lawful possessors. Shortly before Arnulf's death a Saxon had declined to do the service (unspecified) due from him to the 'alien' Duke Eberhard of Franconia, who thereupon sacked the community in which the offender lived. Eberhard and his following now found themselves condemned in the King's court for breaking the peace; and although the Duke was subsequently pardoned, it was only after suffering a punishment which, though seemingly trivial, was evidently regarded as very humiliating.

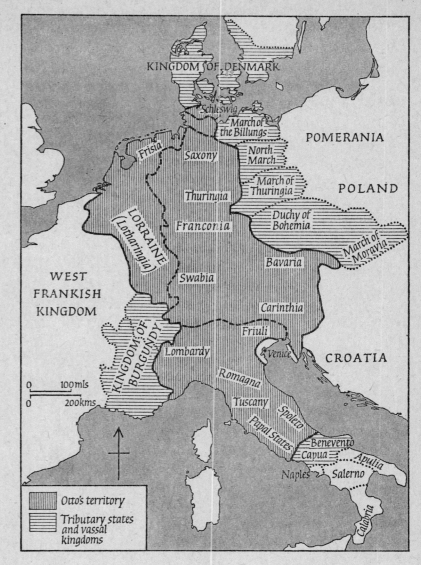

The empire of Otto I. Arnulf's kingdom (see fig. 1) expanded considerably under the early Saxon kings. Though the West Franks preserved their independence, Otto extended his rule further north and east even than Charlemagne. (3)

Discord Within—Invasion from the East

A few months later Otto had to face a challenge to his authority from magnates in all parts of the kingdom (except Bavaria) who resented the King's treatment of themselves or of others—including his brother Henry, his brother-in-law, Duke Gilbert of *f 4* Lorraine (Lotharingia), and the new Archbishop of Mainz, Frederick, who apparently objected to the treatment of church lands in his diocese and the privileged position of Fulda. In the ensuing struggle the Dukes of Franconia and Lorraine were killed (939) and the latter's widow Gerberga took refuge in *f 2, 4*

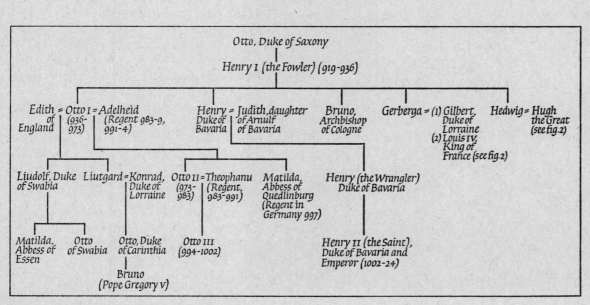

The 'Ottonian' or 'Saxon' dynasty, which ruled Germany from 936 to the middle of the 12th century, and led through a female branch to the great Hohenstaufen emperors. (4)

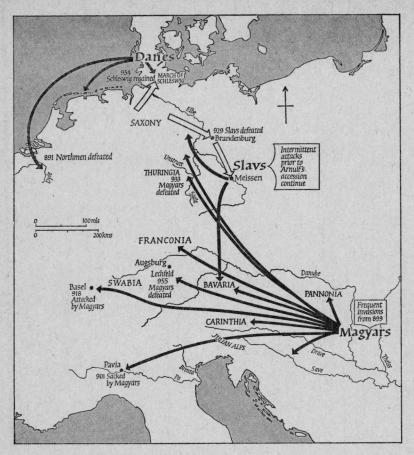

Invasions of East Frankish territory from Arnulf to Otto I. On the northern frontier lay predatory Danish forces, on the eastern marauding Slavs and, a more serious threat, the Hungarian Magyars, who began a series of almost nonstop invasions with an attack over the Italian border in 899. In the reign of Konrad they penetrated as far west as Basel and were not finally routed until 955 at the Battle of the Lechfeld. (5)

the West Frankish kingdom and subsequently married its Carolingian King, Louis d'Outremer, the son of Charles the Simple. Otto's counter-move to this was to secure the commendation to himself of a number of dissident northern French nobles. He appointed no successor to the dead Franconian duke so that any rights over lands and men previously exercised by him were in the free disposal of the King. The duchy of Lorraine was given to the ex-rebel Henry, no doubt in the hope that he would both secure the loyalty of his former co-rebels and remain loyal to his brother; but a few months later he had to be replaced by a local count.

f 4 — Otto already had one royal brother-in-law by his marriage to P 312 Edith, sister of the English King Athelstan: the two kings (35) exchanged relics and manuscripts; Otto's doings were recorded intermittently in the Anglo-Saxon Chronicle; and it was perhaps at this period that English merchants began to frequent the Rhine and German merchants to visit London. Between 942 f 2 and 944 both the French King and his Capetian rivals acknowledged his mediatory influence, which finally brought about their temporary reconciliation. The Burgundian King and the Italian Marquis Berengar both 'commended' themselves to him. This prestige abroad could not save him from rebellion at home. A more disturbing situation developed in the next few years in the two southern duchies. When the Duke of Bavaria died in 947 Otto appointed in his place the turbulent Henry; two years later f 4 he appointed his (as it proved, equally turbulent) son Liudolf to Swabia. These appointments did more credit to the King's family feelings than to his political understanding. The newcomers rapidly identified themselves with the longstanding rival aspirations southwards of their two territories: in ?949 Henry raided Aquileia, carried off the Patriarch, and perhaps dictated the choice of a successor. Liudolf was soon meditating an expedition further west. When, therefore, the widow of the Italian King Lothar, f 4 the Burgundian Adelheid, sought refuge from the usurper Berengar at the German court and then married Otto as his second wife, the German King had more than one good reason for inter-

320

(e.g. in Saxony) it was accepted that the King, as heir of the founder, was entitled simply to nominate the incumbent, whereas in the older foundations, the choice of bishop lay legally with 'clergy and people' and the royal right was merely that of declining to invest the bishop-elect. Neither direct nor indirect control of appointments, however, was of value unless there were suitable candidates to be put forward. Two factors in particular eventually ensured that there were. The first was the consequence of a movement for monastic reform that began with the monastery of Gorze (diocese of Metz), was taken up by the monastery of St Maximin, Trier in 933/4 and spread thence to innumerable other monasteries in Lorraine and beyond. Several of those who had chosen Gorze as a place in which to find a more perfect form of the religious life came from cathedral churches and believed that a strict observance of the rule of St Benedict and the right of free election of an abbot were best guaranteed by a sympathetic diocesan and an educated community. Furthermore, on grounds that were both theoretical (the unique authority divinely-bestowed in the coronation ceremonies) and practical (the need to secure their lands as far as possible against usurpation), they also identified their interests with those of the monarch. In 946 the Abbot of St Maximin, with Otto's active intervention, became Bishop of Liège, the first of many such promotions.

unbeliever. The linking of religious fervour and the subjection by force of Germany's Slav neighbours was familiar to Otto from his upbringing and was further emphasized by the promises he made at his coronation. As early as 937 he sent monks from St Maximin to establish a monastery dedicated to the warrior-saint Maurice at the frontier trading place of Magdeburg. Henry had been well-served by hard-fighting border-counts; but Otto seems to have felt that the war against the Slavs needed to be pursued with more vigour. Late in 936, he created Hermann Billung, a Saxon of distinguished birth whose family had lands, countships and churches from Lüneburg (one of Henry's foundations) to Thuringia, *princeps militiae* in the half-conquered lands between Elbe and Peene. This was effectively a revival of the earlier Carolingian notion of a 'march', the commander of which had a considerable degree of independence. The silence of the sources for nearly two decades suggests that the struggle against the Slav Redarii and Abrodites was an unrewarding one. But by the date of Hermann's death (973) there was permanent Germanic settlement in the western part of the march and the tribes beyond were subject, at least intermittently, to the payment of tribute.

f 3

In 938 Otto appointed to a *legatio* in the frontier regions further south a Count Gero who has been claimed as an *homo novus*. Between 941, when he is first referred to as *marchio*, and his death in 965, he and his family played a major part in the con-

VINEA

'Then are they truly monks when they live by the labour of their hands', said the Rule of St Benedict. Indeed, the greatest promoters of agricultural expansion were probably the monasteries, and one of the first and most active was Echternach, the home of this 10th-century Gospel book. Its illustration of the Labourers in the Vineyard, in spite of the formalized conventions, gives some idea of 10th-century methods. (6)

The formation of an educated, 'reform-minded' episcopacy was undertaken even more enthusiastically after Otto's youngest brother Bruno (the one member of his family who gave him consistently loyal support) became a dominant influence at Court. Unlike Otto, who is said to have learnt to read and write only in the 940s and never properly understood Latin, Bruno had been sent to learn letters as a child from the Bishop of Utrecht. While still a boy he had returned to his brother's court: precocious (and, one suspects, a little priggish), he was only fifteen when in 940 he made his first appearance as a *cancellarius* (i.e. writer of royal diplomas)—probably already irregularly in deacon's orders. His appointment as Arch-chaplain in 951 gave him authority over the writing-office; and two years later he was 'elected' Archbishop of Cologne, without abandoning his other responsibilities. After the suppression of the revolt of 953/4, Otto appointed no new lay duke of Lorraine but entrusted the duchy to Bruno—a combination of lay and ecclesiastical authority for which contemporaries could only coin the term *archidux* and which at quite an early date was the subject of criticism. The focus of Bruno's activity, however, continued to be the royal court. With him began the practice of using the chapel, and particularly the writing-office which was a specialized part of it, as a training-ground of promising young clerics and monks; having been imbued with the spirit of service to the monarch, they were found positions in cathedrals and abbeys where they could pass on such notions to others and help to destroy regional separatism.

f 4

All-out War against the Unbeliever

Clergy such as these were more than ordinarily familiar with the notion of the conversion of the heathen as a Christian imperative and with Augustine's dubious Christianization of the Roman doctrine of the *bellum iustum* to justify all-out war against the

quest and settlement of regions on and beyond the middle Elbe: but the range of his activities extended at times as far north as Havelberg and over much of the area between Saale and upper Elbe. Through him the Germans first encountered the Poles. To Widukind he was obviously the ideal Ottonian royal servant. His only son, who was married to a niece of Hermann and of Otto's first wife, died in battle in 959: in his memory in 961 Gero established a nunnery on newly-cleared land in the northern Harz, not far from the Ottonian family nunnery of Quedlinburg, at Gernrode (*Gern-rode*, the clearing of Gero) over which his son's widow was made abbess and where he was subsequently buried. In his own lifetime his deeds were both renowned and celebrated and his reputation survived his death: among the Slavs as a cruel and oppressive enemy, among the Germans as the strong, the swift, the noble Gere, the much-praised Markgraf Gere of the *Niebelungenlied*.

p 311
(31-33)

In 946, reference is made for the first time to a *burg-ward* in the conquered territories—the area associated with a fortress to which newly-arrived German settlers were expected to retire in an emergency and by which it was maintained. The *burg-grafen* were perhaps truly 'new men', holding office at the King's pleasure and initially without any independent sources of authority in the region; the *tributum* they collected was certainly regarded as due to the fisc. By granting market-rights and encouraging the establishment of traders and other town-dwellers around the *burgi*, and at other points where the royal court and armies were visitors, Otto seems to have been responsible for a short-lived (but interesting and important) expansion of commerce and economic lift in the eastern part of his kingdom. In 948, a year after the creation of dioceses in Denmark subject to the authority of the Archbishop of Hamburg-Bremen whose missionary-priests had at last converted the country without conquest, Otto felt able to proceed to the next stage in the 'Christianization' of northern Slavdom: with papal approval, bishoprics were established at ?Oldenburg, Havelberg and Brandenburg; and the native population was subjected to the payment of the bitterly-resented tithe. In the next decade the future ecclesiastical organization of the eastern frontier regions played an increasingly important part in Otto's plans. The aim now was the establishment of an archbishopric for the entire missionary region at Otto's beloved Magdeburg, a scheme that was unwelcome to the Archbishop of Mainz and could evidently only be carried through with the co-operation of the first bishop in Latin Christendom, the Pope. This perhaps was made to seem more urgent when the Russian princess Olga, who had only recently been baptized at Constantinople, asked Otto to send a bishop: although it was with the evident approval of the Archbishop of Mainz that the person sent was a former monk of St Alban's, at Mainz (who expressed a singular lack of enthusiasm for the undertaking).

'Rex in Italia'

Other ideas were maturing in the minds of Otto and his advisers in the same period. Unfortunately there was no Alcuin either to record or influence the notions current at Court: Luitprand, a refugee from the Italian King Berengar, who was both learned and articulate enough to have played a similar role, is silent on the decade 950–960, although it cannot be excluded that he was expressing ideas similar to those implicit in his *Historia Ottonis* and his *Legatio* for some years prior to 962. Widukind's assertion that immediately after the victory of the Lechfeld the army acclaimed Otto Emperor is an antiquarian reminiscence and cannot be regarded as a literal statement of fact: but it is hardly the less significant for that. Why the formal revival of the imperial dignity for Otto seemed in the end to be imperative is something that even the best informed of courtiers might have found as difficult to explain simply as historians do. Otto's military victories and rule over others, his services to the Christian faith, antiquarianism in clerical circles, distaste for the situation in Rome where the son of a harlot had made his son Pope, all doubtless played their part. But in the last analysis it was the logical consequence of the previous creation of close personal links between the Church and the lay power (most strikingly exemplified by the dual position of Bruno) and of the implicit belief that this was a reflection of the principle, deeply and sincerely felt, that neither was superior to the other. Of these unitary ideas, the imperial title was the most complete expression, a unique distinction bestowed by God through the intermediacy of his vicar, by which the holder's authority over all his subjects was sanctified and enhanced; even more fully than the kingship this was a living expression of the Petrine *regale sacerdotium* and the ultimate means by which Christian peace in all its fullness —spiritual and wordly—could be obtained.

In 960 Pope John XII appealed to Otto for protection against Berengar, many of whose principal subjects already regarded him as a tyrant: it was the perfect opportunity for transforming schemes and aspirations into political reality. An *ordo* for an imperial coronation was prepared (probably at St Alban's, Mainz) and a suitable crown designed and made. In the spring of 961 Otto's son by Adelheid, another Otto, was elected King at Worms and crowned at Aachen. Leaving the Archbishops of Mainz and Cologne in charge of the young King and kingdom, Otto led a magnificent host across the Brenner. The Italian capital, Pavia, was entered and bishops and magnates flocked to Otto's court, while Berengar and his family fled to the Lombard Lakes region. From this moment Otto regarded himself and was regarded by others as *Rex in Italia*.

The state of the *regnum* that Otto annexed to his own in 961, thereby linking the destinies of Italy and Germany for centuries, is not easily characterized briefly. It ceased to be independent at a time when documentary evidence exists in quantity only for a few areas; and the sole native chronicler of the period was Luitprand. Two writers whose works purport to describe conditions in northern Italy in the 950s and 960s, Rathier, Bishop (from time to time) of Verona, and Atto, Bishop of Vercelli, were passionately subjective observers, although their view that

the growing power and turbulence of the class of *milites* was creating problems for both churches and monarch is not lightly to be disregarded. Berengar II had been a failure as a king— and deserved to be: he had come to the throne by usurpation and had successively alienated a section of his courtiers, an influential section of the episcopate, an equally influential section of the magnates and the Pope; and he had failed to keep his promises to the most famous sovereign of the time. The sequence of rebellion, royal election, coronation and renewed rebellion from which only two of the last nine decades had been free had obviously not enhanced the kingly dignity. Yet the monarchy in Italy still possessed a unique asset in the permanent *palatium* at Pavia where the (lay) *iudices*, who owed allegiance only to the ruler, were trained and from which its regular sources of income were controlled.

Italy's greater wealth has sometimes been put forward as a major reason for Otto's trans-Alpine ambitions. This is questionable on several grounds. There is perhaps a tendency to exaggerate what this wealth really amounted to: in the 10th century it lay rather in Italy's material heritage from its Roman and Early Christian past, its buildings, relics and books: and to judge by his returning to Germany with Stephen of Novara in 952 and with the egregious Gunzo in ?965, Otto also thought of it as a source of scholars, however much of a disappointment they proved. Certainly, however, Venice was steadily laying the foundations of its future magnificence by trading with Greeks, Muslims and Latins, while several southern coastal towns were engaged in similar activities: and although the currently fashionable search for Byzantine influence on almost every aspect of Western life has produced little evidence that this affected Otto before 962, he can hardly have been unaware of those cities' exotic imports, if only because many of them were sold at Pavia

This graceful ink-drawing of 'The Annunciation to the Shepherds' is one of the earliest expressions of a definite Ottonian style. It appears in a 10th-century Gospel book, probably from Corvey. (7)

f 3

to pilgrims and other travellers from north of the Alps. Some of the other towns of the Po valley may already have been enjoying a modest prosperity. The known activity of the (royal) moneyers of Milan and Lucca argues a certain (local) commercial activity. Genoa was perhaps just beginning to be something more than a glorified fishing-port and Pisan ships were transporting persons and goods in the Western Mediterranean. Yet even if we can suppose that the precocious development of urban life in eastern Germany in this period was consciously planned (which seems unlikely), the subsequent handling of the *regnum Italiae* and the utilization of the resources of the Crown does not suggest that Otto and his advisers had any real understanding or appreciation of what they had acquired in 961.

The Emperor

Otto had perhaps intended that he should be crowned on Christmas Day. In fact it was on the day of the Purification of the Blessed Virgin Mary (2nd February) that he was annointed and crowned in Rome, and renewed the promise to be *protector ac defensor* of the Roman church. The future history of the German monarchy was bound up with the future of the Papacy. On 12th February the Pope issued a bull providing for the creation of an archbishopric of Magdeburg and a bishopric of Merseburg: it required five years and the confirmation of a Pope who was Otto's appointee before it was put into effect. On the following day Otto solemnly renewed the grants made to the Papacy by his royal and imperial predecessors of the former Exarchate and other territories (with the promise of more to come) and exacted from the Pope and Roman citizens an oath of loyalty. Neither part of the 'Pact' was kept. Pope John found his position intolerable and sought help from the ex-rulers of the *regnum* and from Byzantium. Otto had hitherto been unaware of, or strangely indifferent to, the likely reaction of the Court of Constantinople to his successive intervention in Russia, occupation of north and central Italy, and imperial coronation, or else he placed excessive trust in the 'Donation of Constantine'. Fortunately for him the Greek Emperor was not ready for a contest of arms in Italy; and at the end of 963 a synod presided over by Otto deposed Pope John. A similar fate subsequently befell his successor.

In an effort to solve the host of problems he had created for himself Otto spent ten of the last twelve years of his life in Italy. Three times he led expeditions to the 'deep South'—against the Arabs in the toe of Italy and against the Byzantines themselves. To judge from Luitprand, the Emperor regarded this as a duty incumbent upon him, for which those around him, however, showed little enthusiasm. Perhaps rather naively, Otto still hoped for a rapprochement with Byzantium; his illusions could hardly have survived Luitprand's report of the insulting words with which his request for an imperial bride for his son (crowned Emperor the previous year) were greeted in 968 and his own counter-insults. And the military problem remained.

The problem of the government of the *regnum* was hardly more tractable. Otto had a number of loyal supporters among the greater magnates, such as Otbert 'Marquis of Genoa' and Adelbert-Azzo 'of Canossa', the first protector of Adelheid and founder of a famous line. Consistently or otherwise with Otto's policy north of the Alps, his favours to them and others of the same class notably increased their wealth and power: Otbert was reinstated as Count of the Palace, which made him responsible for the investiture of imperial *iudices*; Adelbert received innumerable grants of land and was regularly used as a royal *missus*; and when, after a privately-organized expeditionary force had finally disposed of the Saracens of Fraxinetum, Marquis Ardoin of Turin usurped the entire valley of Susa and its revenues, the Emperor raised no objections. The alienation of royal or comital rights to bishops went far beyond anything previously practised in Germany. It is possible to justify such measures by reference to the growing menace of the lesser 'noble' landowners; and it is legitimate to stress that while the marquises and most counts continued to be men of native origin, a substantial number of bishoprics were eventually held by Germans or by men who had served an apprenticeship at the imperial court. It is also to be noted, however, that although Otto established a separate 'chan-

The coronation of a German king in the 10th century already followed a set formula, recorded in the Mainz Pontificale of c. 960, from which this drawing is taken. The ceremony normally took place in the Royal Chapel at Aachen and was attended by the archbishops of Cologne, Mainz and Trier. The king, wearing ornate chasuble and sandals, was first anointed with holy oil. He was then dressed in the ceremonial mantle and pallium (here handed to him by the archbishop on the left); and invested with the symbols of his power—the orb, the sceptre and finally the crown itself. (8)

cery' for Italian recipients, its organization and forms were entirely those of the existing writing-office: and it is difficult to avoid the conclusion that Otto had no clear or consistent policy for his Italian territories and no real understanding of their special needs and distinct traditions. This view is amply borne out by Otto's one serious attempt to be the imperial lawgiver. At Verona in 967 it was declared that because of the increasing perjury in Italian courts, the traditional process of sworn testimony should, in certain types of case (particularly but not exclusively concerned with land), be replaced by the duel (*pugna*), which contemporary Italians reasonably regarded as barbaric and generally avoided using.

Something marred nearly every apparent achievement of Otto's last years. Russia reverted to its ecclesiastical allegiance—to Constantinople—and, shortly before the appointment of the ex-missionary Bishop Adalbert as first Archbishop of Magdeburg, a separate Polish see was established at Poznan. A Byzantine bride, Theophanu, arrived for the young Otto in 972 but she was only a distant relative of the Emperor. On the other hand there were the first clear signs that the intellectual and literary achievements of some of the 'reformed' monasteries and cathedral schools were to be accompanied by creative activity in the fine arts and architecture. And nothing could detract from the impression of Otto's far-ranging prestige given by the glorious assembly of Easter 973 when Otto was residing in the family convent at Quedlinburg. For it was attended by the Dukes of Bohemia and Poland, envoys from Hungary, Bulgaria and elsewhere, and by a magnificent array of clergy and magnates from Germany and Italy.

The Second Otto: Ten Years of Strife

When Otto died on 7th May 973 his son succeeded him without immediate difficulty. There were, however, those who thought that the Emperor's cousin, the Duke of Bavaria (Henry the

p 303 (8)

p 310 (30)

p 303 (7)

f 4

p 303
(11)
Wrangler), a better choice: early in 974 the Duke rebelled, securing support from both Bohemia and Poland and from the many Bavarians who were delighted to have an opportunity of fighting the hated Saxon. The eventual suppression of the rebellion (with considerable difficulty) was followed by the establishment of a diocese of Prague, under the metropolitan authority of Mainz, and the detachment of Carinthia from Bavaria: but the two duchies were both given to relatives of the Emperor— a policy that had already been found wanting in the previous reign. Otto, indeed, seems to have been a better educated but less effective version of his father: in 978 dissensions in Lotharingia even allowed a West Frankish army to sack Aachen; and a counter-expedition that enabled his chapel to sing an Alleluia on Montmartre did not entirely restore his prestige. The one feature that distinguishes his internal policy from that of his predecessor is the more rigorous exaction of *servitia* from the wealthier churches: the stiffer demands for military contingents for his almost annual campaigns seem to have been responsible for the (unwelcome) creation of new fiefs on church lands both south and north of the Alps, with important consequences in the next century.

The restless north-eastern frontier interested Otto less than south Italy. Was it not his duty to protect Rome and the Christian religion against the infidel Arabs? And this offered the opportunity of demonstrating to the Eastern Emperor the power of the Western. It was almost as a programme that in 982 *Romanorum imperator augustus* was adopted as the normal imperial style: for Otto had summoned one of the largest armies to cross the Alps in the entire medieval period, raised in face of considerable protest from monasteries. Ill-prepared for the summer heats and fevers of Calabria, it suffered overwhelming defeat in a battle that deprived Germany of many of its finest warriors. Otto none the less began to plan a new expedition for 983/4. As a precaution
p 304
(12)
his three-year-old son by Theophanu, Otto, was sent back to Germany to be crowned King—'an unheard-of proceeding'. He was still *en route* when news reached the north of the disaster of 982. In June 983 all the conquered tribes of the Elbe–Oder area rose in revolt: they burnt and plundered the *burgen* and at Brandenburg they even disinterred the body of Bishop Dodilo whose ingenuity in exacting tithes had left bitter memories. Not for another two centuries were German authority and the Christian church re-established in the region. Shortly after Otto III's coronation at Aachen on Christmas Day 983, news reached the court of his father's death (7th December): malaria had claimed another of its royal and noble victims.

A bishop's silver crozier (c. 1000) from Hildesheim Cathedral, telling, in a delightfully compressed narrative style, the story of the Fall. The crook is in the shape of a tree which encloses the figure of Adam in adoration before God. At the foot of the tree Adam eats the forbidden fruit and— symbolic of his fall into Sin—tramples on the cardinal virtues. (11)

Two Great Women: Adelheid and Theophanu

An influential section of the clergy led by the Archbishop of Mainz foiled an attempt by the ex-Duke of Bavaria to seize the boy-king and with him the reins of government: Otto the Great's policy of identifying the interests of church and monarchy can fairly be said to have been vindicated at this time, as it was in Italy after Otto III's death. Theophanu was accepted *f 9, 10* as Regent for her son in Germany while Italy was entrusted to his grandmother. In an age of remarkable women, Adelheid was an extraordinary one: she had already outlived five *reges Italiae*, two of them her husbands; and she now showed that she could rule—and do so with the co-operation of the much-maligned Italian nobility. She had to recognize the loss of control of Rome and it was no longer possible to challenge the Eastern Empire in south Italy. But to the *regnum* and the annexed, nominally Papal, territories she gave something like a stable government for four years. The diminishing resources of the Pavian *palatium*—although its *iudices* were still important— doubtless explain the Empress' preference for the nunnery of SS Salvator and Julia, Brescia (by an ancient tradition an appurtenance of the Queen or Queen-dowager) as a residence: its dependent convents and extensive estates offered a domanial nucleus from which royal authority could be rebuilt in the future.

No satisfactory account can be given of developments in Germany in this period: a good contemporary chronicle is lacking and later writers were more interested in Otto's years of personal rule. It is clear only that royal resources were not squandered by lavish grants, whether to buy support or to reward the Regent's principal advisers. The loss of the march-regions was not admitted without a struggle and help was obtained from both Bohemia and Poland. The influence of the German court even made itself felt in northern France while Hugh Capet was consolidating his *f 2* position. The artistic activity of the period shows the first marked impact of Byzantine models. Historians have not ceased to speculate how much Otto's later notions owed to the influence of his Greek imperial mother. Others have detected a Rasputin-like evil genius in John Philagathete, a worldly Calabrian Greek cleric of the type made familiar in a more modern context by the writings of Norman Douglas, who entered the writing-office c. 980 and was subsequently the young Otto's tutor. But he had ceased to hold this position by 988/9; and his successor (until 993) was a Mainz cleric Bernward, a typical product of the Ottonian 'training-scheme', whose activities as Bishop of Hildes- *f 11* heim show him to have been a hard-headed and practical adminis- p 314– trator as well as an enlightened patron of the arts. (38–44)

In 988 John (Philagathete) was 'elected' to the bishopric of Piacenza, which the Pope was then persuaded to raise to the status of an archbishopric. The purpose behind these and similar moves was revealed when in 989, in circumstances that are entirely obscure, Theophanu ousted her mother-in-law from control of the *regnum*. For two years *missi* and *iudices* acted on her orders; and indeed she even exacted some acknowledgment of her authority from the Roman noble who had made himself *patricius* of the city. But if credit is to be given to the writer who

Otto III and his mother, the dowager Queen Theophanu, as they appear among the figures in gold relief on the cover of the Golden Gospels of Echternach (the central jewelled panel of which is illustrated on p. 316). The cover was probably made on Theophanu's orders. (9, 10)

in the earlier 11th century recorded the payments formerly made to the *camera palatii* at Pavia, the fatal step was now taken that destroyed for ever the value of the Palace to the rulers of Italy: the *ministeria* which were a major source of revenue were granted by the Empress to Archbishop John, who then disposed of them freely. When Theophanu died suddenly in June 991, Adelheid re-emerged and was accepted as Regent on both sides of the Alps. The day-to-day responsibility for Italy was entrusted to the ever-loyal Marquis Hugh of Tuscany. Adelheid herself had serious preoccupations on the north-eastern, northern and western frontiers of Germany and she was fortunate in having the loyal support of most of the leading clergy, including several who represented a 'third generation' of reformers.

Otto III, the Fourteen-Year-Old King

p 305–6
(13–14)
f 12
Probably in September 994, when he was just fourteen, Otto III's legal minority ended. He ruled for less than eight years, dying at twenty-one so that it is hardly surprising that historians do not agree on the ultimate aims of his policy. The available sources throw more light on his activities in Italy and on his relations with Germany's eastern neighbours than they do on his activity in Germany itself: it may be that this correctly represents the bias in Otto's own interests, and that it was in his reign that for the first time a grandiose conception of Empire took precedent over all other considerations. There is no doubt of his enthusiasm for the imperial idea: immediately after he came of age, Otto made preparations to go to Rome to receive the imperial crown. But an insistence on the grandiloquent, more 'fantastic' aspects of his activity without reference to their context may be as false as would be, say, an interpretation of the present-day political scene in Britain, in terms of the adulation of the monarchy. Otto's recorded actions on his first Italian expedition do not suggest the impractical visionary: he required the attendance of the Italian magnates at his courts and began the recovery of royal and ecclesiastical lands recently usurped by *nobiles* and *milites*; he confirmed the rights of the Doge of Venice—whose support he hoped for against Byzantium—to lands within the *regnum*; and a request from the ruler of Rome that he should nominate the next Pope (although not yet Emperor) is evidence either of the respect for the Ottonian line or fear of the German army in the imperial city. Otto chose his relative and chaplain Bruno of Carinthia, who took the name Gregory: and in spite of the manner of his appointment he proved no unworthy bearer of it. On 21st May 996 the new Pope bestowed the imperial crown on the sixteen-year-old Otto.

Among the visitors to Otto's court while he was in Rome were two men whose influence on him and his notions of *imperium* was decisive and undeniable. The first was the Aquitanian Gerbert, then striving to vindicate his claims to the see of Rheims; the most learned man of his time, he possessed a strong sense of 'theocracy' and was unusually qualified to re-interpret the Classical past in the context of his own day. The second was Adalbert, a Czech of noble birth, educated at Magdeburg and now for the second time a refugee from his bishopric of Prague. Whether Otto was drawn to Adalbert by his asceticism or because he already envisaged a peacefully Christianized *Slavia* is not determinable. But when Otto returned north, Adalbert was commanded to return to Bohemia or if he was still rejected, to go as a missionary to pagan lands. In fact, at the suggestion of the Duke of Poland (whose father had put the duchy under the protection

p 306
(16)
of the Pope), he chose to preach to the savage Prussians. On 23rd April 997 he was martyred. Otto heard the news while campaigning ineffectively against the Elbe Slavs. It was a time of disappointment and crisis. The Romans, with Byzantine support, had set up John Philagathete as anti-Pope. Otto gathered a large army and set out for Italy at a time of year when Alpine crossings were usually avoided. The regency in Germany was

f 4
exercised by Otto's aunt Matilda, Abbess of Quedlinburg, to whom he had given the unparalleled title of *matricia* (the feminine equivalent of *patricius*); and the two most influential figures in his immediate entourage were clearly the Arch-chancellor for Italy and Gerbert who, defeated over Rheims, had been welcomed with enthusiasm by an Emperor who acknowledged him as a

The glorification of Otto III, from the dedicatory page of a Gospel-book. The Emperor's throne is supported by Terra, the Earth. He is crowned by the hand of God, and the Living Creatures of the Evangelists hover round his head. Below, two dukes pay homage. (12)

A denarius of Otto III (983–1002). The inscriptions, beginning in the centre, read OTTO TERCIUS CI ['Caesar'] and PAPIA ['Pavia'] CIVITAS GLOR[IOSA]. Pavia was the favourite residence of Otto's grandmother Adelheid, and this laudatory epithet makes it likely that the coin was minted during her lifetime. (13, 14)

'master beloved above all others' and spoke of himself as 'most faithful of pupils': it would be difficult to have clearer indications of the direction of Otto's thoughts at this time.

While he was besieging the Roman rebels in Castel S. Angelo (April 998) Otto issued a diploma restoring to the Pavian monastery of S. Pietro property *longe tempore iniuste abstractam*': it bore (for the first time) an imperial lead *bulla* with the legend *Renovatio imperii Romanorum*. About the same date there is the first reference to Otto's Roman palace—on the Aventine, near the monastery where the martyred Adalbert had lived; in a later document there is mention of the grandiose offices (or titles) bestowed on four members of the local nobility; and the Italian Arch-chancellor now adopted the Byzantine title of *logothete*. If it was the Western Emperor's way of showing that he could match the self-styled *Imperator Romanorum* in the East in every detail, it was a modest way of doing so; if it was intended to help the Romans recall the glories of their own past, it was a symbolic rather than a

f 13, 14
practical measure. Pavia, not Rome, was the place at which Otto declared the Emperor to be once again the source of law, by a *constitutio* providing for the eventual annulment of leases from church lands (September 998). There are many signs that Otto's Roman *Renovatio* was only part of a larger plan which saw the new Empire as a means of forwarding the Christian cause where

other ways had failed. Gerbert had hinted at this in a letter written in the previous year; and on the day on which Castel S. Angelo fell, he was translated to Ravenna. The subsequent grant to Archbishop Gerbert of *comitatus* and estates in neighbouring dioceses was one of only three grants of this kind made by Otto; and whether or not we should see here some deeper political purpose, in which an alliance with Venice was also intended to play a part, Otto's ignoring of the prior rights of the Papacy is surely more significant than the apparent alienation of imperial ones.

p 316 (46) In 999 Gerbert himself became Pope, with the significant name of Sylvester II. If names meant anything, however, the new Pope was claiming a place for the *sacerdotium* in the new *imperium* which was very different from that allowed to it and its supreme earthly representative by Otto I. This mattered little only so long as the two vicars had a common approach to a jointly-assumed responsibility. For the time being both Pope and Emperor were ambitious to incorporate Slavdom in a Christian (Western) Empire; and neither showed any enthusiasm for the old policy of conquest and conversion by the sword. The veneration accorded p 306 (16) to Adalbert, whose body was at Polish Gniezno, provided a mystical link between Papal, imperial and native Slav courts which all parties were eager to exploit. Following the formal canonization of Adalbert by Papal decree—a procedure previously used only for the canonization of St Udalrich of Augsburg—Otto set out early in 1000 on a journey in which political purpose and spiritual fervour were inextricably combined. His following was unusually impressive for a peaceful expedition; and the reception of it when it reached Poland was equally impressive and indeed 'frankly beyond belief'. At the tomb of the martyr Otto proclaimed the establishment of an archbishopric of Gniezno—*ut spero legitime*, says a German chronicler cautiously. To Boleslav of Poland he gave a replica of the Holy p 307 (18) Lance, and according to one account, transferred the diadem he wore to the Duke's head. Was Otto hoping to establish an empire in which the Romano-Germanic lands were surrounded by satellite kingdoms that owed their being to the emperor? This is certainly borne out by the creation of a kingdom of Hungary the next year. But Boleslav saw the dangers.

The End of an Ideal

With so little evidence available, it is tempting to discern a powerful symbolism and detect a deep political purpose in every action of Otto's last months. In April 1000 he was at Aachen where he opened the tomb of Charlemagne and took out the cross round his neck and some of the garments in which he had been buried. (Other textiles of Byzantine manufacture were introduced into the tomb.) The autumn and winter was spent in Rome and its vicinity. A new imperial donation was made to the Pope, in which the 'Donation of Constantine' was rejected as false. But there were ominous rumblings. First Tivoli and then Rome itself rose against the 'Germans'. Finding refuge in

Castel S. Angelo, which invariably figures in the medieval history of Rome as the silent protagonist of some dramatic or strange episode, Otto upbraided the Romans for their ingratitude to one who had forsaken his own origins for love of them. Here indeed was the supreme paradox. The *patricius Romanorum*, Otto's supreme representative in the city, was an illiterate but efficient Saxon. When the hitherto-separate 'chanceries' for Germany and Italy were merged into one in 999 its head was the German Heribert who shortly afterwards was appointed Archbishop of Cologne. Unless Bishop Leo of Vercelli is regarded as an Italian rather than a Saxon, Otto's principal advisers were exclusively German; and even the greater Italian magnates were rarely at his court. The only Italian who can be supposed to have had any influence on him in his last year was the hermit Romuald. Two journeys round north and central Italy, on the first of which he visited Venice were separated by a brief sojourn in Rome: but it was clear that he could re-establish his authority there only by force. He was awaiting troops from Germany when, on 23rd January 1002, he died.

A few weeks later the Marquis of Ivrea-Vercelli was crowned King of Italy at Pavia with the support of the north Italian *milites*, some of the greater nobles and some bishops. Otto's second cousin, Henry, eventually vindicated his claim to be his rightful *f 4* successor on the throne of Germany but only by coming to terms with the magnates of two of the duchies. Otto's ideas and aspirations died with him and when 'Germany's Eastern mission' was taken up again it was through conquest, not peaceful conversion. The Empire—the Holy Roman Empire—survived long enough to be painlessly put away by Napoleon, in this as in so much else the exorcist of Europe's medieval ghosts. For centuries it was the supreme aspiration of monarchs and the inspiration of countless others. But already in the 11th century, before the fundamental premises on which the Ottonian Empire had been erected had been shattered by Gregory VII's reforming radicalism, it was much less sacral, infinitely less Roman and even less imperial than Otto had wanted it to be. We need not regret that this was so. If Otto III had lived, his reign and not that of Gregory VII might have been the one in which a challenge was thrown down to the traditions of many centuries and European policy forced to seek new foundations. There would have been little room in the new Empire for 'dualist' notions of authority and for the creation of new political organisms that enriched Europe by their individual attitudes to the cultural heritage of the past and to the political needs of the present. The lasting achievements of the Ottonians are to be sought at a humbler level—in the continued activity of the German cathedral schools and monasteries, whose achievements tend to be underrated because they represent attitudes of mind that were soon to be unfashionable and even 'reactionary'; in the masterpieces of 'Ottonian' art which were created after the death of the third Otto; and in the insistence that sovereignty is not identifiable with tyranny. Perhaps it is the nobler part.

XV THE CONCEPT
OF CHRISTENDOM

Medieval Europe takes shape

DENYS HAY

'Christ is victor, Christ is King, Christ is Emperor'

LAUDES, chanted before the King, 8th century

The Empire of Christ

was for the emergent Europe of the early Middle Ages no mere figure of speech. Its reality was expressed in various ways—not all of them consistent—but it lay nevertheless at the root of political thinking, and in the end it gave a definite and very rich meaning to the word 'Christendom'.

In the society of Western Europe there was general acceptance of a hierarchical structure. Every level of society was regarded as answerable to the one above it. But at the very top the position was never clear-cut. Not one power but two claimed to derive their authority directly from Christ—the Emperor and the Pope. Their relative precedence was the subject of endless theoretical debate and political manoeuvre intensified by political rivalry in Italy.

The Donation of Constantine, by which Constantine was supposed to have transferred supreme authority in the West to the Pope and his successors, had been fabricated in the 8th century in support of the papal case. According to the *Dictatus papae* of about 1075 the pope could make and unmake emperors (a claim supported by reference to Leo III's crowning of Charlemagne). But the emperor possessed the *de facto* power, and Otto III refused to acknowledge the pope as his superior. On the other hand, most of the kings of Europe denied the emperor's primacy but (in however vague a way) accepted that of the pope. The

struggle between emperor and pope was to continue violently until the mid-13th century and to linger on as long as the term 'Christendom' stood for a living idea. For Christendom was the unity behind the separate Christian states, a unity for which both emperor and pope, in their different spheres, were theoretically working, and which the church, as a spiritual force, did for some time actually achieve.

Thus the figure of Christ, the Saviour of the world, majestically enthroned at the centre of the cross, flanked by the symbols of the Evangelists and surrounded by the twelve Apostles, is an image that will dominate the whole of the Middle Ages, conditioning the world-view of contemporaries (in the study of nature, in history, in geography) as well as their attitude to society and public duty. The search for ultimate truth, like the search for ultimate authority, led back to a single source—the teaching of Christ.

The altar of S. Ambrogio at Milan (opposite) is one of the masterpieces of medieval craftsmanship and in some ways one of the most mysterious. It was probably made in about 835, though dates as late as the 12th century have been proposed. There is a signature on the back: VVOLVINUS MAGISTER PHABER. Who was Wolvinus? Most historians accept the name as German, 'Wulfwin', but whether he came from across the Alps or was a Lombard born in Italy cannot be known. (1)

'Behold, we give over and relinquish to our most blessed Pontiff Sylvester our palace, our city of Rome, and all the provinces, palaces and cities of Italy and the western regions, and we decree by this our godlike and pragmatic sanction that they are to be controlled by him and by his successors and we grant that they shall remain under the law of the holy Roman church.' So runs the crucial passage of the Donation of Constantine, the legal justification for the popes' claims to supremacy in western Europe. Constantine, we are told, first offered Sylvester the imperial crown itself, but the Pope refused. And so 'we placed upon his most holy head, with our own hands, a glittering phrygium of dazzling white representing the Lord's resurrection and, holding the bridle of his horse out of reverence for the blessed Peter, we performed for him the duty of a groom'. These two frescoes (above) form part of a series from the Church of the Quattro Incoronati, Rome, painted in the 13th century to popularize this legendary episode, a form of papal propaganda. (2, 3)

Charlemagne's coronation in 800 was, as we have seen, open to more than one interpretation. In the earliest representation of it, a mosaic in the Lateran (right: an 18th-century copy—the original is altered out of recognition), St Peter hands Leo the spiritual and Charlemagne the temporal power, and they seem to be equal in status. But by the 14th century (far right) Charlemagne is shown kneeling like a vassal at the Pope's feet. (4, 5)

'Christus vincit, Christus regnat', the last verse of the *laudes* or liturgical acclamation with which a new emperor was consecrated, is here inscribed on the hilt of a sword made in about 1200 for Otto IV. (6)

As ordered and hierarchic as the authority that governed it was the physical world itself. A type of map known as 'T and O' (below) shows it at its most schematic: Asia, Europe and Africa are separated by the Mediterranean, the Nile and the Don (Tanais).

Jerusalem was the centre of the earth, and is commonly shown in that position. At Madaba, Jordan, is an extraordinary mosaic map of the Holy Land made about 560. Jerusalem is fortunately among the best preserved sections (bottom). Some actual streets and buildings can be recognized, including the Church of the Holy Sepulchre, and the North Gate, the obelisk of which is the exact centre of the whole floor. (7, 8)

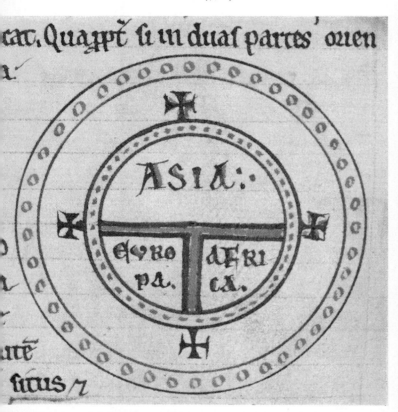

332

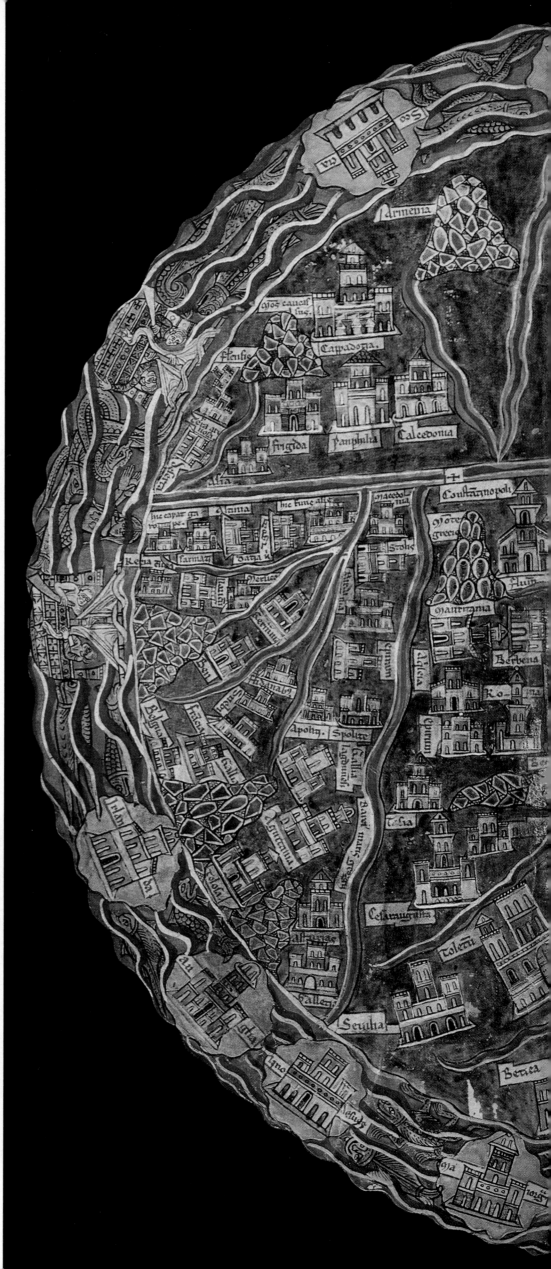

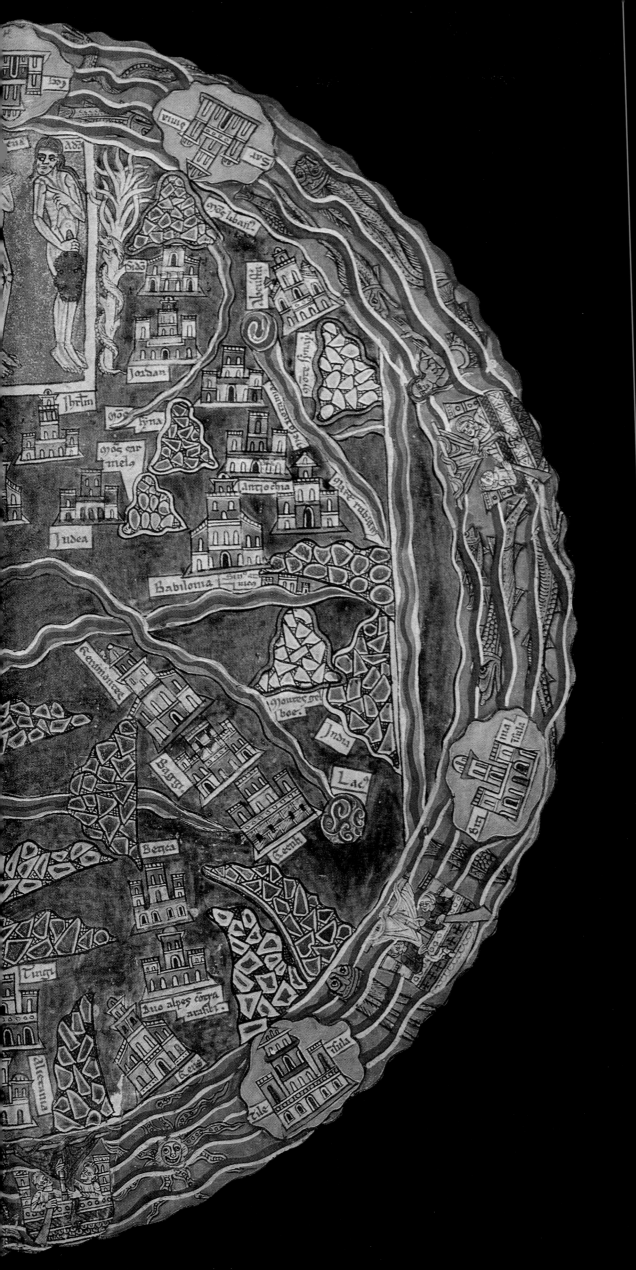

The unmoving world, as it existed in the minds of medieval scholars and philosophers, bore hardly any relation even to such geographical facts as were known. Ptolemy had discarded the idea of an all-surrounding Ocean; Roman road-maps were relatively accurate; and seamen must have used charts quite unlike any of the *mappae mundi* produced in the centres of learning. Such considerations weighed little with men who wanted a diagram or *schema* of the divine order rather than a record of scientific fact.

The map shown here is from one of the Beatus manuscripts which have already been featured in Chapter IX. These maps (about a dozen survive) differ in details according to the knowledge or imagination of the illuminator, but they all go back to a common source which was in turn probably based on the work of Isidore of Seville. The example reproduced here is from the early 13th century.

All of them show the world as a disc surrounded by Ocean (not all are circular—they may be oval or rectangular with rounded edges). East is at the top. In the sea appear the chief islands: *Archia* (Achaia, i.e. the Peloponnese), *Cecilia* (Sicily), *Sardinia*, *Bitinia insula* (Britain), *Tile insula* (Thule), *Maiorga* (Majorca), *Linodesues*, *Anglia* (England), *Irlanda* and *Scocia* (Scotland).

Towns, rivers and mountains are shown by conventional symbols. Asia Minor is top left, with *Armenia*, *Mons Caucassus*, *Calcedonia* (Chalcedon), *Cappadotia*, *Frigida* (Phrygia), etc. Bottom left is Europe, with the eastern Balkans first *(hic finis Asie)* and beyond that *Germania*, then the *flu' Danabus* marking off *Francia*, *Gallia* and *Belgua;* then *Macedonia*, leading to *Apolia*, *Spolite* and *Aquitania;* finally *Constantinopoli*, with *Tessalonica*, *Berbena* (Ravenna), *Salerna*, *Aquilaeia*, *Roma*, *Dalmatia*, *Narbona*, *Seuilia* (Seville) and *Toletum* (Toledo).

On the right is Asia: at the top the Garden of Eden, with Adam, Eve, the tree and the serpent; just beneath it *Jhrlm* (Jerusalem). The river *Jordan* flowing from *Mons Libanus*, *Mons Syna* (Mt Sinai) and *Mare Rubrum* (the Red Sea) can be identified. Across the middle of the page flows the Nile (not named) from a lake *(lacus)*. Here are *India*, *Babilonia* and other regions yet more remote and mysterious.

The narrow strip of land on the extreme right is thus described by Isidore: 'In addition to the three parts of the world, there is a fourth part beyond the ocean in the midst of the south and unknown to us on account of the heat of the sun. Within its confines the Antipodeans are fabulously said to dwell.' (9)

Pilgrimage had been a feature of the Christian life from the time of Constantine, but with the Middle Ages it became of major social importance. Jerusalem and Rome were the oldest centres. Compostela, whose origins have been described in Chapter IX, became prominent just at the end of our period. Pilgrims were of every age and class. Their motive was salvation—pilgrimage could expiate a crime or win precious remission in Purgatory. When the Last Judgment should come the pilgrims would rise with scrip, staff and scallop-emblem, to be received into Abraham's bosom, as they are in the 12th-century tympanum of Autun (right). The cross of one shows that he has been to Jerusalem; the scallop of the other stands for St James of Compostela. Left: two pilgrims on the road, a husband and wife, also of the 12th century. The journey was no light undertaking; many pilgrims set off not expecting ever to return. (10, 13)

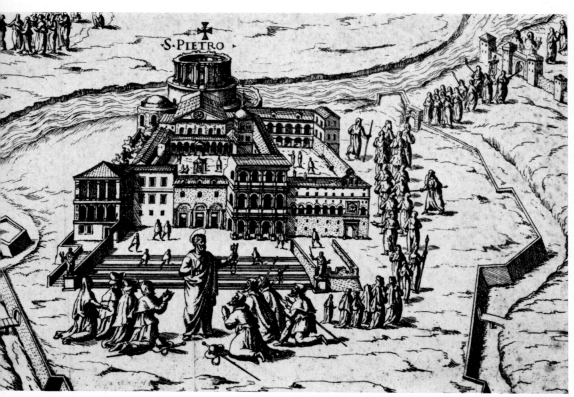

S·PIETRO

Rome has preserved its pilgrim traditions unbroken to the present day. The devout still visit the seven basilicas, ending with St Peter's. Above: a 16th-century engraving showing a stream of pilgrims coming to the feet of St Peter. In the background the old basilica is being replaced by the new. Left: a medieval misericord showing a pilgrim with emblems. Figures such as this occur everywhere in the more popular art of the Middle Ages—on choir stalls, screens and stained glass. (11, 12)

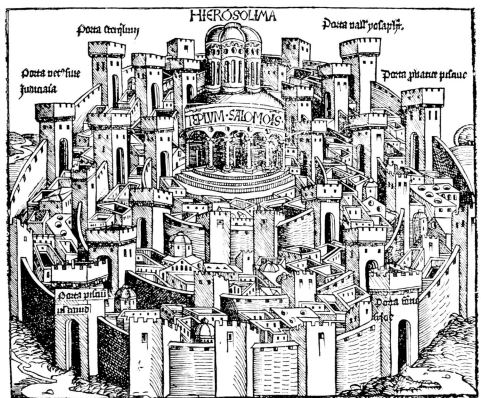

Jerusalem, the city of the Passion, was the longest and most dangerous of all the pilgrimages, especially after the Arab conquest. The plan below is a fairly accurate guide to Jerusalem in about 1150. Above is a more fanciful picture dating from the late 15th century. (14, 15)

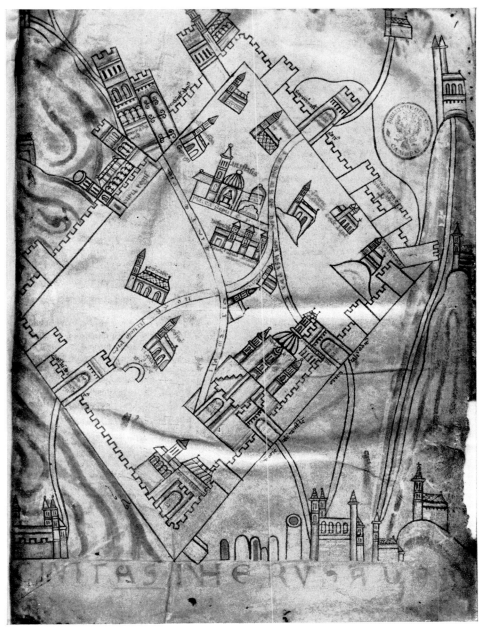

To win back Jerusalem for Christianity was the dream and the prayer of every pilgrim, but it was only with the growing solidarity of Christendom in the 11th century that the dream was capable of being realized. The First Crusade was proclaimed by Pope Urban II at the Council of Clermont in 1095. The peoples and princes of the West responded with a unity hardly to be imagined a century earlier. Armies and bands of followers crossed the

Balkans and the Byzantine Empire in 1096 and 1097 and in July 1099, after a bitter siege, they entered the Holy City. This 13th-century miniature shows the siege and capture, as well as their meaning to the medieval world. On the right soldiers bombard the city with stones from a catapult and attack the walls from a tower on wheels. Above are scenes from the Passion and, on the left, the Dormition and Assumption of the Virgin. (16)

Medieval Europe takes shape

DENYS HAY

In the 11th century members of the literate minority in Western Europe came to accept the term 'Christendom' as a description of the largest entity to which they belonged. There was nothing inevitable about this. There is no reason to suppose that primitive peoples have any need to look beyond the horizon of the tribe and tribal lands. There is every reason to assume that for the humble at any time the abstractions of the scholar remain somewhat unreal even after they are lent actuality by the politician; this we can see clearly enough in the ideological conflicts of our present world. Yet the abstractions are important for two reasons. It is the case that the politicians adopt them, consciously and unconsciously, and involve their fellows in programmes of destruction and creation which, however much they stem from elemental impulses to power, are ostensibly trying to attain spiritual or geographical frontiers. And it is also the case that occasionally such abstractions come to embed themselves so firmly in the popular mind that, having ceased merely to be terms used by writers or slogans invoked by leaders, they acquire a subterranean emotive power that lasts for centuries. Christendom was to be such a concept. As a rallying point for intellectuals, as part of the mental furniture of simple people, it survived beyond the Middle Ages, beyond the Reformation and was only relegated to the limbo of the archaic in and after the 18th century.

The Medieval World-Picture

Christendom was to have a long life. It began with a difficult birth. The word itself cannot really be firmly identified until the 11th century, a millennium after the Gospel had begun to spread. Words often follow the realities they are invented to describe, and there is no doubt that this was the case with 'Christendom'. Equally it seems clear that the idea would have found appropriate expression earlier if there had not been other grand antitheses which might have proved viable as descriptions of the polarities of the contemporary world: East and West, Civilization and Barbarism, Empire and Church—these were the main alternatives or rivals. If these notions were in the end to prove inadequate, from each of them Christendom was to derive a portion of its strength and they must briefly be considered.

East-West opposition is a fact of nature certified daily by the progress of the sun. It has indeed been argued that the very terms Europe and Asia derive from the adoption in the Greek world of the Eastern Mediterranean of Semitic words for the land of the rising sun or of light (Asia) and of the setting sun or darkness (Europe): the Aegean thus became the dividing line between two halves of the inhabited globe and the highly intelligent Greeks seem sometimes to have regarded themselves as occupying a privileged position between two vast continental extremes. In the event Europe and Asia, though capable occasionally of rousing emotion (as when Greeks and, later on, Romans used the word Asiatic as synonymous with barbaric splendour and cruel tyranny) did not prove particularly relevant for reasons which will become clear when we glance in a moment at the notions of Civilization and Empire.

The West, *Occidens*, on the other hand did continue an attenuated life. This was because the West was supposed in Greek legend to be the location of Elysium which, like the gardens of the

Christ in Majesty, beardless and seated on a throne, forms the centrepiece of the golden altar front or 'pala d'oro' in the cathedral at Aachen. It was probably made around 1000 during the reign of Otto III. (1)

Hesperides, lay in the Ocean. In this western land was bliss and, though the Romans found locations nearer at hand for Elysium and the Hesperides, the myth of a western paradise was revived in the Islands of the Blest. Such material is the stuff of dreams and it emerged from Celtic Ireland afresh, first in the Dark Age poem *Bran*, later in the *Navigatio Sancti Brendani* in which the Saint sailed to a land of promise. Such a tradition of an idyllic land in the West was to capture imagination once again in the late 15th and 16th centuries. In the meantime some of the elements of the Western Paradise had been transferred to the Eastern Eden. The authority conferred by the Bible on Asia, and by the New Testament on Asia Minor, went a long way to weaken the antithesis *Oriens-Occidens*. For the Christian peoples of the West, the East was the homeland of their religion.

Another of the influences which militated against the appropriateness of a classification *Oriens-Occidens* was the vital role exerted by the great inland sea in Greek, Roman and Dark Age politics and commerce. The Mediterranean, like other easily navigable waters at the time, was a bridge rather than a barrier and linked together not only East and West and the continents of Europe and Asia but also Africa, the third part of the world. The rivers Don and Nile, which severed the three continents, ran into the inland sea round whose borders the traffic and colonial activity of Greeks and Hellenistic peoples gravitated. For the Romans it rapidly became the heart of their Empire. At this stage it was to be elevated very nearly into an ideal, equated with the Roman world itself. *Mare nostrum*, 'our sea', the *magnum mare* or 'great sea', was possessed by the Romans, but perhaps because of the confident way in which they assumed proprietorial rights it lacked justification, lacked the polemical quality of a unifying concept: no one else claimed the sea. In any case it was a mere pond compared with the 'vast profundity obscure' of the Atlantic. Although in the Spain of the early 5th century Orosius still writes without hesitation of *magnum mare* and *mare nostrum* (I, 2), two centuries later Isidore of Seville has to add a word of explanation: *Mare magnum . . . Iste est et Mediterraneus* (*Etymologies*, XIII, xvi, 1); the Mediterranean, used absolutely and paradoxically (for the original meaning of the adjective was 'inland' not 'bounded by land'), has no connection with the world of Rome.

Implicit in these earlier categories were certain associations linking one of the partners with good qualities, the other with bad qualities. *Occidens-Europa* covered the region of the earth where civilization prevailed; *Oriens-Asia* covered the region of barbarism. In antiquity and in the Middle Ages these terms as such did not exist: 'civilization' in our sense is a product of 18th-century speculation and its definition by the French and Scottish *philosophes* also lent definition to barbarism. But in antiquity Greeks and Romans, if they had not extended the use of 'civil' to cover their own way of life, were well aware of the fundamental opposition to it of all that was barbarous. *Barbaria* (or *barbaries*)= a foreign land, all countries other than Greece and Rome, thus already had also much of the meaning of our barbarism and this was to prove a much tougher and more useful ingredient in the thought of later centuries than the simple East-West opposition with which it was necessarily associated. Asia, later on Gaul or Britain, could be described as belonging to 'Barbary'; barbarians were rough, wild, cruel and ignorant, enemies of the cultivated citizens of Greece and Rome; and, for writers of the 4th and 5th centuries, beyond the limits of *Romania*, void of *Romanitas*. Yet, while the distinction was never forgotten, it lacked clarity and it lacked urgency. Greeks regarded Romans as barbarians (a few Romans made a half-hearted attempt to reciprocate) and Byzantium in later ages and despite its growing impotence continued to apply the contemptuous epithets to Westerners, from the pope downwards. Even more compromising, the Roman world before it finally succumbed was being managed by men who on any reckoning had to be regarded as barbarians. It was also the case that the barbarians themselves were only too ready to concede the cultural superiority of their Roman masters, whose wealth they coveted, whose art and language they clumsily but perseveringly emulated. The threat to Roman notions of propriety, good manners and good scholarship, was not presented by an alternative culture, but by scattered groups of illiterate warriors infiltrating with obsequious brutality into the Promised Land they were destined to destroy.

The Earthly Empire and the Empire of God

The intellectual urge to unity, to a satisfying and simple picture of human society as an integrated organism which stemmed from Greek thought and which lay behind the generalizations we have so far considered, was able to salvage two ideas from the débâcle of the ancient world: Empire and Church. Both these terms were to have long and fruitful careers, composed in large part of their mutual interaction. And both were to share a common destiny. Each began as a programme for a single world; in the end there were to be many empires and even more churches.

Empire began as the mere power of command. It owed its subsequent importance to the possession of this power by the rulers of the Roman state. *Imperium* meant the magistrates' authority, but it also meant the whole area ruled by the Romans, combining two senses in much the same way as our word 'dominion'. With the advent of Augustus power was concentrated in one man's hands and the army thereafter so regularly gave the military title of *imperator* to the Caesar of the day that the emperor could and did become identified with the area of Roman government: 'the proud Republican term *imperium populi Romani* was transformed by the Augustans into *Imperium Romanum*'. It was into the provinces of the Empire that Christianity came, at first a religion critical of secular society and its values, but then one which came to terms. It was the Emperor Constantine who in 313 by the Edict of Milan gave Christians religious liberty, the beginning of the process by which the emperors effectively adopted Christianity.

The association of the Roman Empire and Christianity, though the events of later centuries were to strain it to breaking point, offered the inhabitants of the Roman world in the 4th and 5th

centuries a view of their ultimate purposes which might have proved longlasting. The Empire could be regarded as a Christian institution, and if Christianity had the aim of bringing all men to the peace of God, the Empire inherited ecumenical notions of civilization which also involved peace. The clergy could insert into their liturgy prayers which depend on both these concepts, like the following which still figures in the Roman Missal for Good Friday:

> Let us pray also for our most Christian emperor, so that God and our Lord will place him above all barbarous nations in order that we may live in peace hereafter.

Or like the following, which makes the Empire's role as guardian of peace part of the divine plan:

> O God who has created the Roman Empire to further the preaching of the Gospel of the eternal kingdom, give your servants our emperors heavenly weapons so that the peace of the churches may not be disturbed by the tempest of wars.

St Jerome, at the turn of the 4th and 5th centuries, also saw the earthly Empire paving the way for the Empire of God.

By this time, of course, the unity of Rome was severely impaired: in theory there were two emperors, one in the East and one in the West; in practice the Western Empire was crumbling under barbarian infiltration and attack. Yet, surprisingly enough, the existence of two separate imperial courts helped to maintain the notion of Empire. The German war leaders who established themselves in what were to become Italy, France and Spain accepted the overriding authority of the Emperors at Byzantium when they had overthrown the Emperors at Rome. They sought Roman authority and secured Roman titles in order to legitimize their *de facto* power. The autocrat in Constantinople was far away from the princelings in the West who turned to him occasionally. Even in its palmiest days the Empire had known kingdoms subject to it. Barbarian Europe saw the growth of the idea that one essential element in Empire was the transcending authority of the emperor over other, lesser princes.

> Among all the kingdoms of the earth two are reputed glorious by the rest: that of the Assyrians first and then that of the Romans . . . Other kingdoms and kings are regarded as mere appendages of these.

So Isidore of Seville, again in his *Etymologies* (IX, iii, 2–3). Such an attitude was compatible with the lofty views of their station entertained by the Eastern emperors and it accorded well enough with the situation in Western Europe, so long as there was no one ruler dominating the others. When that situation did arise, with the Carolingians, the way had been prepared for a king to be regarded as imperial precisely because he was the lord of other princes, and had brought races other than his own under his control. By then, however, elements of the imperial idea were already being associated with the Roman church and the pope of Rome.

'Christ is Victor, Christ is King, Christ is Emperor'

The coronation of Charlemagne by Leo III on Christmas Day 800 recognized the plain fact that Charles ruled over peoples other than his own: he was master of the Lombards and had a superiority in the states of the Church; his conquests had driven the frontiers of his territories east and south-west until his domains were little less extensive than those of the original Roman Empire of the West. Already the notion that a king superior over others might call himself emperor had manifested itself in Britain; *imperium* is how Bede describes the authority of an over-king; *rex Britanniae* and *Bretwalda* are related terms. Perhaps such Anglo-Saxon modes of thought were not without their influence on Carolingian ideas, through the mediation of scholars like Alcuin. In any case anointing and coronation now went together and in this, as in other ways, the ritual surrounding a Frankish monarch was similar to that associated with the Eastern emperor. With this sacred quality in kingship went responsibilities of a particular kind for the Church: here again *imperium*, empire of the Roman sort, expressed exactly the realities of Carolingian

p 330–1 (4, 5)

f 1
329 (1)
331 (6)

control over the clergy including the pope. 'Christ is victor, Christ is king, Christ is emperor' was the liturgical refrain in the 'Laudes' chanted before the King at the great feasts of the Church by the end of the 8th century in Francia, and in them Charlemagne, before he was Emperor, was treated as the highest earthly representative of divine authority. The expression 'Christian people' was sometimes used in Charlemagne's entourage as equivalent to all his subjects, and 'Christian empire' could mean the domains of the Frankish King. It cannot be doubted that the actual coronation of Charlemagne, however much it reflected the old Roman tradition of acclamation, was ultimately acceptable because of its entire appropriateness. To that extent it was not a hurried or ill-considered action; however much it may have temporarily embarrassed the new Emperor in his relations with the Eastern *Basileus*, Charlemagne firmly adopted the term.

The Empire, reborn in 800, was not to last long. It petered out in a dynasticism which showed how limited were the practical applications of universal concepts in Western Europe in the 9th century. Charlemagne died in 814. His successor Louis the Pious, who stressed even more than Charlemagne the religious element in his office, inherited an undivided realm by accident. Thereafter the Empire gradually disintegrated until the very title expired in 924. Yet if it ceased to be a practical means of government, the term 'empire' had come to stay, and that it was no longer necessarily the hereditary preserve of Frankish rulers perhaps even facilitated its survival: the title could again be applied to the possessor of power. The Carolingian tradition meant that empire was in future to be linked with German monarchs and associated with both Italy and the city of Rome, though the emergence (or re-emergence) of the term emperor in both England and Spain in the 10th century suggests that, had there not been a renewal of the German monarchy at the same time, a plurality of 'empires' might have developed. When Eadred (died 955) or Canute (died 1035) used the words 'caesar' or 'emperor' they were, however,

referring merely to their overlordship of other peoples than their own, of other kingdoms. When Otto I renewed the title it was, on the contrary, a programme which he indicated. Much of the programme had, indeed, been fulfilled. The Saxon who ruled Germany also exerted his authority in Italy and in defeating the Magyars at the Lechfeld in 955 he had exhibited a care for the Christian cause comparable to that of his distant ancestor Charlemagne. The coronation of Otto as emperor in 962 took place in Rome: the *sacrum imperium* then renewed was to last more or less unbroken until its demise, at the hands of the French *empereur* Napoleon, in 1806.

The empire of the Ottos and of the Holy Roman emperors who succeeded them was, despite its longevity, no use as a unifying concept. Empire meant the territory accepting, willingly and unwillingly, the hegemony of a German king; it was no longer coterminous with either civilization or Christianity; it was indeed a challenge to the ecumenical ambitions of the organized church. Even before Charlemagne's coronation the popes were conscious not only of their universal mission, but also of the part that Rome and Empire could be made to play in it. If an empire and an emperor might aim to represent the highest values of human society, what might be said of a Church and its leader the pope? No mere emperor of the west had as his field of activity the whole globe. *Ecclesia* was thus a viable alternative to *imperium* for those who wished to discern the boundaries of civil organization.

The Forged 'Donation of Constantine'

'Church' had, indeed, acquired much of the content of 'Empire' long before the *renovatio* of 962. In the shifting political situation of barbarian Italy the bishop of Rome was a steadier symbol of the old order than German kings, however anxious they were to acquire Roman titles, or than the distant ruler of Byzantium. The Church had been a department of state in the later Empire and when the state disintegrated the chief bishop remained in

The map of Europe, from a 15th-century manuscript of Ptolemy's 'Cosmographia', first written in the 2nd century AD. Two of the existing manuscripts state that the original maps were drawn from Ptolemy's own *specifications but none of them survive and the Renaissance translator who made the Latin version had to supply charts of the world as it was known in his own time.* (2)

possession of the City, possessed of some of the attributes of civil magistracy, and he could legitimately try to satisfy territorial as well as spiritual ambitions. Leo the Great had stressed the intention of St Peter, leader of the Apostles, to build on Roman foundations and this work of construction went on unobtrusively in the 5th and 6th centuries; it was in the late 5th century that a papal tradition began which attributed Constantine's conversion to the intervention of the pope. The activity of Justinian (it has been argued) was responsible for the evolution of a more positive papal attitude in which Gregory the Great defined the role of the earthly empire as one of service to the heavenly empire: pope and emperor were both indispensable but in practice the activities of the latter were subordinated to ends of which the former was the expositor and guardian.

p 330–1
(4, 5)

Gregory the Great died in 604. The ensuing hundred and fifty years witnessed a steady development of papal pretensions. In the middle of the 8th century circles round Pope Stephen II (752–757) produced a document which formally justified complete political authority in the west being in the hands of the Pope. The immediate circumstances of the fabrication of the Donation of Constantine are to be found in the relations of Pepin and Italy; it was produced, at any rate in large measure, to afford a precedent for Pepin's Donation of 754, in which the King of the Franks granted in perpetuity certain lands in Italy to the Pope. It was further used as a model for Charlemagne's Donation of 774 in which even greater territories were handed over to St Peter. Forgery though it was, it was nevertheless built on earlier traditions and its staggering claims did not seem (so far as one can judge) to shock 8th- and 9th-century Germans and Italians.

After a preamble in which Constantine is made to describe his miraculous conversion to Christanity at the hands of Pope Sylvester, the Emperor in thanks confers on the Pope and his successors, vicars of Christ, representatives of St Peter, holding their power from heaven, an authority even greater than that he himself possesses. The Pope is to enjoy primacy over the other patriarchs and over all churches; the Pope is to be supreme ruler over all the priests in the world. The Pope is to have the imperial palace of the Lateran as his residence and to carry all the insignia of the emperors; the clergy of Rome are entitled to wear senatorial insignia. The Emperor confers the imperial diadem on the Pope, who refuses it and so the Emperor places on the Pope's head the white *phrygium*, and has acted as his groom (holding the bridle of his horse). In order to enhance still further papal dignity the Emperor grants to the Pope and his successors not only the Lateran Palace, but also the City of Rome, as well as all provinces,

p 330–1
(2, 3)

localities and cities of Italy and the 'Western regions'. Having done all this the Donation ends with the Emperor's decision to move his Empire and his power to the 'Eastern regions', where he will build a town to be named after himself. 'Where a princely empire has been established and where is found the capital of the Christian religion it is not fitting that the earthly Emperor should exercise his power.' The Emperor curses anyone presumptious enough to alter his dispositions.

The popes of the late 8th and 9th centuries were not capable of exploiting the grander possibilities offered by the Donation in the 'Western regions': they had their time cut out to survive in Rome itself. It was, in a curious way, the emperors themselves who at first enjoyed the identification of church and empire laid down in the Donation. Charlemagne was essentially ruler of a *church*, rather than of a merely terrestrial domain. 'It was the Christian religion which gave the new Empire its basic character.... the imperial dignity reinforced Charles the Great's existing responsibility for moral and spiritual matters... The state is conceived of as the rule of wisdom in preparation for the City of God.' Charlemagne had, of course, grown up in the world that had seen the emergence of the Donation, and its ultimate relevance escaped him. Two centuries later Otto III was to arrogate to the emperor the privileges conveyed to the pope in the Donation and to denounce the document as a tissue of lies. In 1001 he issued an imperial diploma in which, while accepting Rome as the *caput mundi* and admitting that the Roman Church was the mother of all churches, he proceeded to catalogue the enormities perpetrated by the popes. Of these the chief was that they had attempted to disrupt the Empire, relying on the Donation. Otto III's own 'donation' of lands to the Pope he had appointed two years earlier was in every sense a recognition of his own supremacy: Sylvester II was to be answerable to the Emperor.

Towards the Triple Crown

In the event Otto's universalism was to be as ephemeral as Charlemagne's. The Empire of the 11th century became a German institution, though the crown and the other emblems of coronation still recalled the majestic Christian purposes of an earlier day, and the emperors continued to be attracted to Italy both for coronation and because it was, in a very real sense, a part of their directly governed lands. Not least because of the still lively sense of responsibility of emperors for the welfare of the Church, the papacy itself was reformed in the course of the 11th century and there emerged a fresh interest in the imperial element in the papal office which, though clearly laid down in the Donation of Constantine, had played little part in the public programme of the popes in the intervening period. Once again one is aware of the steady but unseen development of curial thought. Just as it had produced the Donation of Constantine so, in the pontificate of Gregory VII and his successors, the curia stated fully and unequivocally the implications of the Donation, which had been neglected by the popes and ignored or repudiated by the emperors in previous centuries. This statement is, of course, remarkable for its direct claims. But it also drew out the privileges of the pope of an incidental kind, his right (for example) to enjoy the imperial insignia, and this development is not to be underestimated in an age which attached significance of an inward kind to outward symbols. *Quod solus possit uti imperialibus insigniis*, we read in the *Dictatus papae* (c. 1075): 'the pope alone can wear the imperial insignia'. And it was from this point of time that the white *phrygium* becomes unmistakably a crown; already called a *regnum*, since the base of it was a circlet, in the mid-11th century it becomes a jewelled diadem. The imperial crown which Pope Sylvester had modestly refused in the Donation was now carried by the pope—not as a part of his regular apparel in liturgical use, but in ceremonial crown-wearings exactly parallel to those of secular kings. This was the first and the most significant step towards the threefold crown of later days, the tiara being completed in the 13th and 14th centuries.

f 3

Gregory VII's imperialism, and that of the clergy in his entourage need not be merely inferred from this. It is explicitly elaborated in the *Dictatus papae*. The pope is not only sole master of all the clergy, in a Roman Church which owed absolutely nothing

The earliest papal head-dresses were plain white caps, crowns being the sign of temporal role, but before the beginning of the 12th century the cap, or phrygium, was already decorated with one jewelled circlet. This 12th-century drawing shows Pope Paschal II and the chronicler John. (3)

to any prince. 'All princes should kiss his feet, and his alone; his name alone should be recited in churches. The name of the pope is unique. It is lawful for him to depose emperors. No council may be termed general without his mandate. From his judgment there is no appeal. The Roman Church has never erred and (as scripture shows) will never err. No one should be considered a catholic who is not of one mind with the Roman Church. The pope may release from fealty the subjects of unjust rulers.' These are some of the 27 abrupt aphorisms of the document which are expressly directed at imperial rights. Based sometimes on older sources (and probably consisting of headings for collections of supporting texts which were not in fact made), the systematic catalogue of powers made the pope a complete autocrat.

So stark a challenge to kings' *de facto* power, which many of them considered *de jure* as well, was bound to fail, just as the pope lost the real battle over appointments to bishoprics though he won a hollow victory over investiture. That story—with its culmination in *Unam Sanctam*—lies beyond the limits of this volume. We have however gone far enough to answer the question why the Church did not succeed in imposing itself as the ultimate terrestrial unit.

Even without the lofty aims of the reforming popes there was much to suggest that *ecclesia* had more reality as a unifying concept than *imperium*. The hierarchy extended into every unit and every sub-unit of the political world and had a permanency greater than that of all save the grandest lay authorities. Parishes and bishoprics remained fixed and certain; lordships fluctuated, at the mercy of the chances of war, marriage and inheritance. Even after the period of great migratory settlement came to an end and more permanent kingdoms emerged, one could identify a stranger more often by asking the question 'From what bishopric do you come? than by asking 'Who is your lord?.' Beyond that, the full enjoyment of civil rights depended on communion with the Church: excommunication deprived a man of his secular status and carried outlawry with it, as well as imperilling his spiritual resources here below and the salvation of his soul hereafter. As John Neville Figgis expressed it: 'The real state of the Middle Ages in the modern sense—if the words are not a paradox—is the Church'. Yet Church as such, like Empire, failed to establish its well-founded claim to be the largest and most logical unit of human society. It was nonetheless to colour profoundly the notion of Christendom, which in the end was to emerge as the accepted medieval description of the world. Before we consider the emergence of Christendom—a notion to which earlier universalisms, civilization, the West, Empire and Church all contributed—it is necessary briefly to review the attitude to geographical description of early medieval scholars.

The World divided by the Sons of Noah

It is necessary to stress the word *scholar*. None but the highly literate were conscious of the problem of the globe and its parts. For the vast majority even of the literate there was small need in the Dark Ages to speculate on the characteristic of any part of the earth save their immediate environment. Such speculation was based, moreover, on literary rather than scientific, let alone specifically geographical, evidence.

Ancient geography accepted a threefold division of the habitable earth. The continent of Asia was divided from Europe by the river Don, from Africa (or Libya) by the river Nile. These continents did not attract much emotion, as we have already noticed. Equally important, they did not provoke cartographical representation, so far as can be told. Mariners probably had rudimentary charts of the coasts (*periploi*), the Romans seem to have had road plans covering the Empire and, of course, precise localities were surveyed not only for road building but for town planning, irrigation and other limited practical purposes. Scientists like Aristotle had shown that the earth was a sphere; Ptolemy abandoned much popular mythology. But these views were relatively uninfluential. The broader picture of the *oecumene* or *orbis* which passed into general knowledge was diagrammatic rather than structural and the 'geographers' contented themselves with descriptions of the towns and provinces to be found in each of the continents, and continued to accept a circumambient ocean, though this had been

This 'box and V' map of the world as divided between the sons of Noah, Ham (Africa), Shem (Asia) and Japhet (Europe) comes from a 13th-century manuscript of the works of Isidore, 7th-century bishop of Seville. It reflects the curious acceptance of a schematic picture of the world. (4)

rejected by Ptolemy. It was knowledge of this kind that Dark Age scholars inherited from antiquity by way of the Fathers and which appears, for example, in Orosius and Isidore. This picture, which we may term the 'classical-popular', proved compatible with the main geographical facts of the Bible and in particular the three continents could be neatly allocated to the progeny of the three sons of Noah after the Flood. Hints of such a distribution are to be found in Josephus; in St Augustine the matter is further elaborated; and in St Jerome's commentary on Genesis, Shem is accepted as the father of the Jews, Japheth of the Gentiles, while Ham's sons are regarded as having populated Africa. p 332–3 (9)

This is the tripartite world of the Carolingian man of learning. Alcuin's commentary on Genesis, for instance, contains the following:

> *Q*. How was the world divided by the sons and grandsons of Noah? *A*. Shem is considered to have acquired Asia, Ham Africa and Japheth Europe ... *Q*. Why do we read: God shall enlarge Japheth and he shall dwell in the tents of Shem [Gen. IX, 27]? *A*. The Hebrews originated with Shem, the Gentiles with Japheth. The multitude of the faithful has been spread abroad, and Japheth's name meaning enlargement portends this.

From such material one might have expected new meaning to be poured into the continents; this did not happen. But the schematic depiction of the earth in *mappae mundi* reflects the identification of the continents with the three sons of Noah in both the 'T and O' maps and the 'box and V'. But it must be stressed that *mappae mundi* even of this elementary kind are extremely rare before the 13th century and are largely restricted before then to illustrations in texts of Isidore and the 'Beatus' maps depicting the spread of the evangelists, the *divisio apostolorum*. Neither the geographers nor their illustrators in the Dark Ages or in the Early Middle Ages make any attempt to define the frontiers of civilized or Christian society, let alone to depict as a territorial unity Empire or Church. p 332 (7) f 4 p 332–3 (9)

Yet the Christian peoples dwelling in the old Roman world and spilling out into lands beyond the old northern *limes* were gradually being drawn together. In this evolution of common characteristics, and in the more slowly developing awareness of such common characteristics, the greatest part was played, it need hardly be said, by the organized Church and to this we shall return. The Church was, however, only the formal aspect of religious emotions of a profound kind, expressing themselves in ways the purport of which men were only dimly aware. This popular religious instinct was displayed in pilgrimage and crusade, and in the apocalyptic content of this activity. At a time when the

The first church of the Holy Sepulchre in Jerusalem was erected by Constantine and destroyed by the Persians in 614. In the rebuilding, undertaken by the Crusaders, the Holy Sepulchre, the rock of Golgotha and chapels to various saints were housed under one roof. This 14th-century drawing shows the main entrance with its two large doors, the baptistery (on the left) and the open dome above the Sepulchre itself; on the right the chapel of the Franks, giving access to Golgotha. (5)

bonds of politics were weak and severely localized, when commerce was still incapable of cementing the scattered and small communities of the western world, the ambition to make physical contact with the saints and the humanity of Christ was the principal if not the only spontaneous emotion leading men to a sense of the limits of their world. For it was soon to be a paradox p 332 that the centre of their world, the navel of the earth, Jerusalem (8) itself, was to be on the edge of Christian territory.

The Journey to Jerusalem

The peculiar holiness of Jerusalem, the unique penitential value of a visit to the town where Christ had died for all men, was well established by the end of the 4th century. Shrines were built over the Holy Sepulchre and hostels provided for pilgrims. The presence of a penitent in the birth-place of Christianity was an occasion for purification and for the undertaking of vows. Of this activity the cross rapidly became a symbol. Traditionally discovered by Helena, mother of the Emperor Constantine, the cross was ceremonially displayed to devout visitors at Jerusalem and the cult of the cross spread back into even distant lands. The 7th-century stone crosses of Ireland and Northumbria replace 6th-century wooden crosses which are known to have been erected by Celtic Christians. The capture of Jerusalem by the Persians in 614 led to the cross itself being taken away; its recovery by Heraclius's efforts in 628 was commemorated in the office for the exaltation of the cross (14th September).

The journey to Jerusalem had never been easy. It became even more difficult, and of even greater merit, after the armies of Islam overran the Holy Land in 637. In the ensuing centuries, as Muslim shipping came to dominate the East Mediterranean, an element of positive combat entered into the relations of Christians and their spiritual homeland. Pope John VIII (872–882) issued a letter promising salvation to those who died fighting pagans and infidels. This was the start of the 'indulgence', the p 334, 5 heavenly reward, repeatedly offered thereafter to Christian war- (10, 12, riors. Already the pilgrim frequently divested himself of his 13) earthly possessions before embarking on the supreme journey to f 6 Jerusalem: *pauper* and *peregrinus* are linked words in many accounts of early pilgrimages. And already the attainment of Jerusalem was regarded as a culmination in any individual's earthly life. Now death while facing the Islamic enemies of Christ was to lead men to the Heavenly Jerusalem. Just as pilgrimage was p 334 undertaken to Rome, to Compostela and to other places where (11) the Apostles rested, so the sense of redemption came generally to be attached to combat with the Saracen in general. To fight in Spain was to fight for the faith just as much as it was in the East; in 1063 Alexander II formally conceded remission of sins to the

warriors in the peninsula; in 1089 Urban II directed those who intended to make a pilgrimage to Jerusalem to devote equivalent resources to the restoration of the fortress and Cathedral of Tarragona. The newly conscious sense of Christian unity felt itself to be under attack at both ends of the Mediterranean.

Urban II's principal contribution to the formation of a concrete sense of Christian identity was, of course, his preaching of the First Crusade, following on the fresh wave of Muslim attack launched by the Seljuk Turks, who had defeated the Byzantines and captured Jerusalem in 1071. His speech at the Council of Clermont (1095) has survived only in a number of versions which convey the meaning rather than the precise content. That meaning is clear. The Pope accepted the global mission of Christianity, but recognized its earthly boundaries. He recognized also the brotherhood of all Christians (including the Greek Church) and saw that this involved political as well as religious unity. The Pope outlined the occupation by the enemies of God of much of Asia, and of Africa; as for Europe, 'how small is the part of it occupied by us Christians … and even this part is attacked by Turks and Saracens'.

> Why fear death when you rejoice in the peace of sleep, the pattern of death? It is surely insanity to endanger one's soul through lust for a short space of living. Wherefore rather, my dearest brothers, if it is necessary lay down your lives for your brothers. Rid the sanctuary of God of unbelievers, expel the thieves and lead back the faithful. Let no loyalty to kinsfolk hold you back; man's loyalty lies in the first place to God. No love of your native soil should delay you, for in one sense the whole world is exile for the Christian, and in another the whole world is his country. So exile is our fatherland and our fatherland exile.

These words (they are from William of Malmesbury's account) provoked a response massive beyond the expectation of Urban, beyond the intention of the Byzantine Emperor, Alexius I, who had asked for western help in recovering his lost provinces in Asia Minor. Not only did large numbers of knights set out in great cavalcades, but the poor responded too. Was not poverty already linked with pilgrimage? Was not the Heavenly Jerusalem p 335 already confused with the real Jerusalem? (14, 15)

'The Boundaries of Christendom'

Moreover by the end of the 11th century the notion of Christendom had achieved full and self-conscious expression. The word *Christianitas*, which was to emerge in the vernaculars as *chrétienté*, *cristianità*, *cristianidad* had long existed, but in a transcendental sense, gathering together both the notion of all the faithful and also the idea of the religion itself. For this last meaning a separate word, *christianismus* was also used and it is not until the 9th century that the two expressions come to be more carefully distinguished—*christianitas* = the faithful and *christianismus* = the Christian religion. The Christian religion and its adherents were nevertheless far from being regarded territorially at this stage; *Christianitas*, Christendom as an area, is not accepted until the 11th century. That it took so long to happen demands an explanation.

The most cogent reason is surely to be found in the global aim of Christianity itself. The salvation offered by the Christian revelation was for all men. The limits of Christianity were the boundaries of the inhabited globe. In this sense it was as illogical to regard Christendom as a region on the map as it was to regard as predetermined the frontiers of civilization and barbarism. In fact the concepts of Christianity and civilization were closely associated. In the Roman world into which Christianity had come, in the end as an officially sponsored faith, the citizen who became a Christian naturally tended to treat the non-Christian as a non-Roman and it is highly significant that the word 'pagan', meaning in classical Latin a backward rustic, came to be applied to the non-Christian. Earlier Roman universalism, expressed for instance in the speech of Proculus Julius in Livy (I, 16), *Roma caput orbis terrarum sit*, thus naturally carried over into a religion which in any case had the world for its parish. It would in short be illogical to expect the catholic church to accept for itself an earthly perimeter. Yet this is what did happen.

At first the notion of limitation is found in such expressions as *Christianus orbis* or *Christianum imperium*. *Christianitas*, Christendom, with geographical overtones makes an appearance in the second half of the 9th century, as when Pope John VIII uses the expression the 'defence of Christendom' with reference to the Saracen attacks. It is however not till the mid-11th century that Christendom emerges into permanent usage. In the writings of Gregory VII we find the phrase 'the boundaries of Christendom' (*fines Christianitatis*); he describes the Roman church as 'mistress of the whole of Christendom'. From then on the word gains in frequency in both papal and non-papal sources, permeating for example the crusading propaganda which begins within a generation of Gregory VII. There can, in fact, be little doubt that crystallization of the word in its full territorial meaning in the second half of the 11th century was due, as was its evanescent use in the 9th century, to the pressure of Islam, to the consciousness of profound opposition—social, political and territorial as well as religious—between the opposed camps of Christ and Mohammed. Christian consciousness of the division may have been precipitated by the Muslim attitude itself, which divided the world into *dar-al-Islam* (the abode of peace, or of submission to God) and *dar-al-Harb* (the abode of war). If Christians through the nature of their faith accepted a universal mission, so did Muslims. And Islam had made striking advances, or so it seemed at the time. If one refers again to Malmesbury's account of Pope Urban II's speech at Clermont this can be clearly seen.

> These enemies (it should shame Christians to remember) have clearly occupied Syria, Armenia and latterly the whole of Asia Minor. Now they traverse Illyria and all the land beyond as far as the Bosphorus. They have seized control of our Lord's sepulchre (unique pledge as it is of our faith) and make our pilgrims pay for permission to enter Jerusalem ...
>
> Can anyone tolerate that we do not even share equally with them the inhabited earth? They have made Asia, which is a third of the world, their homeland ... They have also forcibly held Africa, the second portion of the world, for over two hundred years. There remains Europe, the third continent. How small a portion of it is inhabited by us Christians!

Further study of Urban's reported words would lead one to discern within the concept of Christendom the germ of the idea of Europe; and one notices the continued sense of universality—'all the world is the Christian's country'—which was in the end both to make Christendom irrelevant and to enable the notion of Europe to take its place. In this connection it is of some interest that no *mappae mundi* apparently attempted to indicate the boundaries of Christendom. On the other hand the symbol of the Cross on the coins of the crusading states gave iconographic form to the awareness of Christendom among the Christians in the Syrian frontier against Islam.

By the end of the 11th century, however, Christendom was the word which occurred to writers and speakers to describe the greatest region to which they felt they belonged. If its emergence had taken time, its roots were proportionately well established. And although by the later Middle Ages Europe was to appear as a rival, the notion of one Christian society was to linger on for centuries as an inspiration to men of good will, as a formula for politicians.

The Living Reality

As has been pointed out, the content of Christendom was formed by elements which were varied and rich. The ancient Greek and Roman sense of the brotherhood of men, and especially of the bonds of civilization, was absorbed. The notion of the West came, largely because of the domination of the East by Islam, to be identified with Christianity and Christendom. And, in different ways, both *imperium* and *ecclesia* paid their contribution to a concept which transcended both. The *imperium Christianum* of Constantine and of Charlemagne had been in many ways the first manifestation of a territorially based religion; *ecclesia* was in practice composed of precise provinces of the church under popes who were to claim and even sometimes to exercise the political leadership of Christians.

At a deeper level still the first ten centuries of the Christian era had seen western society penetrated by eschatological convictions, ill-defined but profound, linking the individual to the ultimate destinies of mankind. The notion of the pilgrim, of the pilgrim's physical poverty and spiritual wealth, had affected not only the literate and the socially important men who at second hand were familiar with literature, but simple men and women too. The merit of hardship and misery went with the reward of renewal in apocalyptic ways which coloured the popular response to the Crusade. Such sentiment turned Christendom into one of the forms in which millenarian idealism found for a time its home. Jerusalem, the centre of the earth, was thus the symbol of earthly felicity as well as the most holy place in the Holy Land. With the attainment of Jerusalem men associated strife, danger and hardship; a 'time of troubles' which would precede the coming of peace and plenty.

This is the background of 11th-century efforts which saw the Christians of the West try to replant the Cross in Jerusalem, and which witnessed the final adoption of the term Christendom. The scene in Jerusalem on 15th July 1099, when the crusaders, drenched in 'pagan' blood, loaded with the spoils of their slaughtered 'infidel' opponents, finally came, 'rejoicing and weeping for joy', to the sepulchre to adore Jesus, is the culmination of the process. They were, says the anonymous chronicler of the First Crusade, repaying their debt to Him. They were also tasting, however briefly, the rewards both spiritual and material of pilgrimage and crusade. The Earthly and the Heavenly Jerusalem were to continue for centuries to evoke and to typify the aspirations which for a time made Christendom a living reality. Christendom and its heart, Jerusalem, were thus among the most vital creations of the so-called Dark Ages, for they entered into the treasury of mythology not just of Europe but of the world.

p 336 (16)

f 5

It was customary, as a memento of one's pilgrimage, to bring back some holy water in a flask with a Christian emblem or saint stamped on it. In this example, made of lead, the figures probably represent the popular warrior saints George and Aetius. The reverse side shows Bethlehem and the Church of the Nativity. (6)

ASIA AND AFRICA

Shapur II 309..........379
Yazdgard I 399.....420
Kavadh 488..........531
570 Birth of Mohammed
610 Mohammed's vision
622 The Hijrah 661
630 Mohammed takes M
632 Mohammed dies

Ardashir II 379..383
Vahram V 420.....438
Peroz 457.....484
Mazdak preaching c. 490............529
Hormzid IV 579...590
635-641 Muslim conqu in Syria, Palestine, Persia and E

Shapur III 383 388
484 ✗ Iran defeated by Hephtalites
Khusro I 530................579
Khusro II 590............627
Yazdgard III 632....651
Musl take Carth

ARMENIA

Khosrov II 330.338
425 Beginning of Armenian script
502 Persia and Byzantium at war in Armenia
Nerses III Catholicos 641.........660

Foundation of Dvin
✗ 451 Avaraïr. Armenians defeated by Persians
645 Arab suzerainty in Georgia

387 Persia and Byzantium divide Armenia
591 Armenia divided between Persia and Byzantium
652 Arab suzera in Armenia

BYZANTIUM

Constantine the Great 306........337
Theodosius I 379.395
Anastasius I 491.........517
Justinian I 527.............565
Maurice 582.......602
Heraclius 610.......641
627 Ctesiphon captured
Justinian depo Accession of Leo

330 Constantinople becomes capital
457 466 Aspar the Alan in control of Constantinople
533 War with the Vandals
526 War with Persia
550 Spain recaptured
568 Lombards enter Italy
Phocas 602 610
626 Constantinople besieged by Persians and Avars
614 Jerusalem falls to Persians

SLAVS

HUNNIC INVASIONS 430 — 450
502 Bulgars in Illyria
557 Slavs in Thrace
600 625 Intermittent war with Byzantium

M I G R A T I O N S
512 Bulgars threaten Byzantine Empire
589 Slavs in Greece
658 Samo di
By 681 Byzant Emperor ag to pay tribute to Bulg

Bulgar attacks on Empire 527~~~566
592 Byzantine Emperor attacks Bulgarian Slavs
681 Western Bu kingdom founde

ITALY

401 Visigothic invasions
488 Ostrogoths invade Italy
553 Final defeat of Goths Italy again part of the Byzantine Empire
568 Lombard mass-migration to Italy

ROMAN EMPIRE
410 Sack of Rome by Alaric
493 Theodoric proclaimed King
526 Death of Theodoric Reign of Amalsuntha
Agilulf 590.....615
628 Death of Theudelinda
643 Liguria annexe by Lombards

St Augustine 354..............430
476 Odovacer proclaimed Emperor
Justinian invades Italy 536 540
572 Lombards control Italy
Pope Gregory I 590...604
Rothari Laws codifi 636....652

SPAIN

300 .304 1st ecclesiastical council at Elvira Conversion of the Goths to Christianity Gospels translated into Gothic by Ulfilas
400 1st Council of Toledo
Byzantine control restored 550.......... 578
Recceswinth 653...672

342 Barcelona becomes a leading bishopric
409 Vandals enter Spain
Euric 466.....485 Lex Wisigothorum
Reccared 586........621

380 Etheria's pilgrimage
457 Visigothic garrisons in Spain Consolidation of Visigothic settlements
Leovigild 568...586 Re-conquest begins
Swinthila 621...631 1st Visigothic King of all Spain

429 Vandals cross into Africa
495~~~535
589 Visigoths turn from Arianism to Roman church

FRANKS AND GERMANY

Area inhabited by native 'foederati' under Roman Empire 350~~~
486 Last Roman governor defeated
Dynastic quarrels 561~~~613
639 Rois fainéants

481 Death of Childeric and accession of Clovis
.511 Death of Clovis
Dagobert 629.639 King of all Franks
687 Pepi Mayo Austra Neustria Burgu

451 Franks and Romans defeat invading Huns
496 Clovis converted to Christianity
Chlotar I 558. 561 King of all Franks
Chlotar II 613.....629 King of all Franks

534 Burgundy annexed by Franks

NORSE

M I G R A T I O N S   A N D   S E T T L E M E N T S

BRITAIN

314 3 English Bishops at Council of Arles
Century of Germanic invasions 400~~~500
597 Augustine comes to Britain Conversion of Kent to Christianity

367-369 Celtic revolt against Romans
429 St Germanus visits Britain
601 Conversion of Kent to Christian Foundation of See of Canterbury

Patrick's mission in Ireland ?432~?461
563 Foundation of Iona
664 Syno Wh

✗ 577 Saxons victorious at Deorham
673....

800   **900**   **1000**   **1100**

CHAPTERS II and III

...mayyad caliphate at Damascus —— 750

711 Muslims enter Spain   **Harun ar-Rashid**   786 809

X 732 Poitiers (or Tours) Muslim defeat

808 ...... Aghlabid dynasty at Qairawan

872 ...... 903 **Abd ar-Rahman** caliph at Cordoba

912 961

969 Fatimid dynasty begins in Cairo

1038 Seljuks invade Persia

1058 Seljuks take Baghdad

750 Beginning of Abbasid caliphate

809-10 Muslims take Corsica and Sardinia   874 909

Samanid dynasty in Transoxiana and Khorasan

...... 999

1031 End of Umayyad caliphate in Spain

1098 Fatimids take Jerusalem

760 Rise of Isma'ili sect

762 Baghdad founded

Capital moved to Samarra 838 883

909 f. Fatimid Caliphate at Qairawan

CHAPTER IV

855 Turks stopped by **Bagrat**

806 **Ashot** becomes Prince of Armenia

902 **Gagik** allies with Turks

885 **Ashot** son of **Smbat** declared King

826 **Smbat** made General-in-Chief

...Revolt against the X 771 Bagrevand
...abs suppressed   Another revolt unsuccessful

Smbat II 890......914

799 Tiflis captured by Khazars

852 Turkish invasion

Ashot II 914......928

Ashot III 952 977

Gagik I 990 1020

1008 **Bagrat III** inherits Iberia and Georgia

1041 Byzantine invasion repulsed

1045 Ani captured by Byzantines

1065 Seljuk conquest of Armenia

X 1071 Mantzikert Turks defeat Byzantines

CHAPTERS V and VI

Leo IV 775·780

Leo V 813-820

Theophilus, last Iconoclast Emperor 829-842

Romanus I 919......944

Basil II 976 1025

Political confusion 1077

730 Beginning of Iconoclasm

787 Orthodoxy re-established by **Irene**

842 Final triumph of Orthodoxy

813 **Leo V** re-imposes Iconoclasm

Leo VI the Wise 886 912

963 First monastic foundation on Mt Athos

Arab invasions

711 Bulgarians attack Constantinople

717 Constantinople besieged by Arabs

820 Revolt of Thomas the Slav

809 Sofia captured by Krum

913 Symeon the Bulgar attacking Constantinople

972 Death of John Tzimisces

1077 Sultanate of Rum begins in Asia Minor

CHAPTER VII

Krum 802·814

Boris 825 888

716 Bulgarian independence recognized by Byzantium

X 811 Adrianopolis

Krum defeats and kills **Phocas**

863 **Cyril** and **Methodius** in Bulgaria

865 Bulgaria adopts Christianity

By 862 Varangian princes

Askold and **Ryurik** at Kiev and Novgorod

881 **Oleg** unites Novgorod and Kiev Beginning of Russia

907 **Oleg** attacks Byzantium

941 **Igor** attacks Byzantium

992 **Boleslav I.** 1025 King of Poland

996 Poland becomes Christian

971 E. Bulgaria ceded to Byzantines

963 Prince of Kiev seizes E. Bulgaria

957 **Olga** baptized at Byzantium

977 **Samuel** 1014

c. 1018 Bulgarian kingdom ends

Yaroslav the Wise 1019 ...... 1054 reigns in Kiev

Vladimir of Kiev 978 .... 1015 Christianity adopted in Russia

CHAPTER VIII

774 **Charlemagne** invades End of Lombard rule

800 **Charlemagne** Emperor

887 Disputed between **Berengar I** and **Guido**

751 **Aestulf** takes Ravenna

755 **Pepin** helps Pope against Lombards

Luitprand ...2 744

894 **Arnulf** invades

895 **Arnulf** Emperor

962 **Otto I** Emperor

967 **Otto II** co-Emperor

996 **Otto III** Emperor

999 **Pope Sylvester II**

1002 **Otto III** dies subduing revolt by Tivoli and Rome

1036 Normans begin conquest of S. Italy

772 **Desiderius** attacks papal states

995 **Pope John** banished New pope **Gregory V**

963 **Pope John** deposed New pope **Leo VIII**

CHAPTER IX

Alfonso I 739 ...... 757 rules north Spanish Kingdom

Alfonso II 791 .... 842 consolidates kingdom of Asturias

905 Foundation of kingdom of Navarre

Sancho the Great 994 .... 1035 adds Leon, Castile and Aragon to Navarre

1085 Re-capture of Toledo from Arabs

...Muslim ...quest of ...ain begins

Abd ar-Rahman I 755 ...... 788 Emir of Cordoba

Abd ar-Rahman II 822 .... 852 Emir of Cordoba

Abd ar-Rahman III 912 .... 961 Caliph at Cordoba

El Cid 1040 1099

1031 End of Cordoba caliphate

CHAPTERS X, XIII and XIV

...Rois fainéants   755 **Pepin** invades Italy

751 **Pepin the Short**

719 **Charles Martel** deposes **Childeric III** Mayor of all Kingdom

X 732 Poitiers (or Tours) **Charles** defeats Islam

738 **Charles** defeats Saxons

741 Death of **Charles**

Louis the Pious 814

Charlemagne

768 814

800 Coronation of **Charlemagne** as Emperor

812 Byzantium recognizes **Charlemagne**

Louis the German 840·876

840 **Charles the Bald** 877

X 830 Fontenoy

Lothar I 840·855

Charles the Simple 898 922

933 **Henry** repels Magyar invasion

884 Empire reunited under **Charles the Fat**

887 **Charles the Fat** deposed **Konrad** King of Germany

911·918 **Henry I**

Charlemagne 919·936

X 955 The Lechfeld Final defeat of Magyars

982 **Otto II** defeated in Calabria

Otto I Otto II Otto III 936 .... 973 · 983 ... 1002

961 **Otto** becomes King of Italy

987 Accession of **Hugh Capet**

962 **Otto** Emperor

Henry II Konrad II 1002 ... 1024 ... 1039

CHAPTER XI

787 Attacks on Britain begin

793 Sack of Lindisfarne

800 Viking kingdom in Jutland

850 Norway united by Halfdan

860 Denmark united by Gorm

870 Iceland colonized 930

860 Harald Fairhair consolidates Norway

By 862 Scandinavian princes in Novgorod and Kiev

VIKING ATTACKS ON THE CONTINENT AND BRITISH ISLES AT THEIR HEIGHT

960-965 **Harald Bluetooth** converted. Denmark becomes Christian

981 Discovery of Greenland

994 ...... 1022 Sweden becomes Christian

995-1000 Norway Christian under **Olaf Tryggvason**

1000 (or earlier) America discovered

1016 **Canute** King of England

1013 **Svein** conquers England

1028 **Canute** conquers Norway under **Olaf**

CHAPTER XII

...o Picts submit to ...oman church

768 Welsh church submits to Rome

787 Beginning of Viking raids

793 Vikings sack Lindisfarne

...nerable Bede 735

867 Northumberland conquered by Danes

X 870 Ashdown Danes defeated

Alfred the Great 871 899

886 Treaty defining Danish and English territories

X 991 Maldon Vikings defeat English

Canute King of all England 1016 ... 1035

Aethelred the Unready 978 1013

1013 **Svein** conquers England

1066 Norman conquest

Edward the Confessor 1042 ... 1066

800   **900**   **1000**   **1100**

Select Bibliography

II Beyond the Frontiers of Rome

CHRISTENSEN, A. *L'Empire des Sassanides* (Copenhagen, 1907)

GHIRSHMAN, R. *Iran: The Parthians and Sassanians* (London, 1962)

HERZFELD, E. *Archaeological History of Iran* (London, 1935) *Iran in the Ancient East* (New York, 1941)

OLMSTEAD, A. *History of the Persian Empire* (Chicago, 1948)

ORBELI, I. and TREVER, K. *Orfèvrerie Sasanide* (Leningrad, 1935)

POPE, A. U. (ed.) *A Survey of Persian Art from Prehistoric Times to the Present* 6 vols (New York, 1938; London 1958)

ROSTOVTSEV, M. *Dura and the Problem of Parthian Art*, Yale Classical Studies, Vol. 5 (New Haven, 1935)

SARRE, F. and HERZFELD, E. *Iranische Felsreliefs* (Berlin, 1910)

WILL, E. 'L'art sassanide et ses prédécesseurs' in *Syria* Vol. XXXIX (Paris, 1962)

III The Empire of the Prophet

CRESWELL, K. A. C. *A Short Account of Early Muslim Architecture* Pelican Books no. A 407 (London, 1958) *Early Muslim Architecture* 2 vols: I *Umayyads, AD 622-750;* II *Early Abbasids, Umayyads of Cordova, Aghlabids, Tulunids, and Samanids AD 751-905* (Oxford, 1932-40)

GIBB, H. A. R. *Mohammedanism* Home University of Modern Knowledge no. 197 (London, 1953)

GÓMES-MORENO, M. *El Arte Árabe Español hasta los Almohades, Arte Mozárabe* Vol. III in *Ars Hispaniae: Historia Universal del Arte Hispanico* (Madrid, 1951)

HAMILTON, R. W. *Khirbat al Mafjar: an Arabian Mansion in the Jordan Valley* (Oxford, 1959)

HERZFELD, E. and SARRE, F. *Die Ausgrabungen von Samarra* 4 vols: I *Der Wandschmuck der Bauten von Samarra und seine Ornamentik;* II *Die Keramik von Samarra;* III *Die Malereien von Samarra;* IV *Geschichte der Stadt Samarra* (Berlin, 1923-48)

LANE, A. *Early Islamic Pottery: Mesopotamia, Egypt and Persia* (London, 1947)

LEWIS, B. *The Arabs in History* Hutchinson's University Library no. 40 (London, 1950)

MARÇAIS, G. *L'Architecture Musulmane d'Occident, Tunisie, Algérie, Maroc, Espagne et Sicile* (Paris, 1954)

POPE, A. U. (ed.) *A Survey of Persian Art from Prehistoric Times to the Present* 6 vols (New York, 1938; London, 1958)

SPULER, B. *The Muslim World: a historical survey* Pt. 1 *The age of the Caliphs* in *Handbuch der Orientalistik. Geschichte der islamischen Länder* (Leiden, 1960)

IV Between West and East

ALLEN, W. E. D. *A History of the Georgian People* (London, 1932)

AMIRANASHVILI, SH. Y. *Les émaux de Georgie* (Paris, 1962)

BALTRUSAITIS, J. *Etudes sur l'art médiéval en Géorgie et en Arménie* (Paris, 1929) *Le problème de l'ogive et l'Arménie* (Paris, 1938)

DER NERSESSIAN, S. *Aght'amar. The Church of the Holy Cross* Harvard Armenian Texts and Studies, Vol. I (Cambridge, Mass., 1965) *Armenia and the Byzantine Empire* (Cambridge, Mass., 1945)

DOURNOVO, L. *Armenian Miniatures* (New York, 1961)

GROUSSET, R. *Histoire de l'Arménie* (Paris, 1947)

KARST, J. *Littérature Géorgienne chrétienne* (Paris, 1934)

LANG, D. M. *Lives and Legends of Georgian Saints* (London, 1956)

LAURENT, J. *L'Arménie entre Byzance et l'Islam, depuis la conquête arabe jusqu'en 886* (Paris, 1919)

ORMANIAN, M. *The Church of Armenia* (London, 1912)

STRZYGOWSKI, J. *Die Baukunst der Armenier und Europa* 2 vols (Vienna, 1918)

THOROSSIAN, H. *Histoire de la littérature arménienne* (Paris, 1951)

WEITZMANN, K. *Die armenische Buchmalerei des 10. und beginnenden 11. Jahrhunderts* (Bamberg, 1933)

V The Heir of Rome

BAYNES, N. H. and MOSS, H. St. L. B. (eds) *Byzantium. An Introduction to East Roman Civilization* (Oxford, 1948)

BRÉHIER, L. *Le monde byzantin. I: Vie et mort de Byzance; II: Les institutions de l'empire byzantin; III: La civilisation byzantine* (Paris, 1947-50)

BURY, J. B. *A History of the Later Roman Empire from Arcadius to Irene (395-800)* 2 vols (London, 1889) *A History of the Later Roman Empire from the Death of Theodosius I to the Death of Justinian (395-565)* 2 vols (London, 1923)

DIEHL, C. *Manuel d'art byzantin* 2 vols, 2nd ed. (Paris, 1925-6) *Byzantium: Greatness and Decline* (New Brunswick, N. J., 1957)

GOUBERT, P. *Byzance avant l'Islam* 2 vols (Paris, 1951-5)

JONES, A. H. M. *The Later Roman Empire 284-602* 3 vols (Oxford, 1964)

KRUMBACHER, K. *Geschichte der byzantinischen Literatur* 2nd ed. (Munich, 1897)

MARTIN, E. J. *History of the Iconoclastic Controversy* (London, 1930)

OSTROGORSKY, G. *History of the Byzantine State* (Oxford, 1956; 3rd ed. in German, Munich, 1964)

PARGOIRE, J. *L'église byzantine de 527 à 847,* 3rd ed. (Paris, 1923)

STEIN, E. *Histoire du Bas-Empire (284-565)* 2 vols (Paris, Brussels, Amsterdam, 1949-59)

TALBOT RICE, D. *Byzantine Art* 2nd ed. (London, 1954)

VASILIEV, A. A. *History of the Byzantine Empire* (Madison, Wisconsin, 1952)

VI The Christian Citadel

BAYNES, N. H. *The Byzantine Empire* (London, 1925; revised ed. 1943) *Byzantine Studies and Other Essays* (London, 1955)

BECK, H.-G. *Kirche und theologische Literatur im byzantinischen Reiche* (Munich, 1959)

BURY, J. B. *History of the Eastern Roman Empire from the Fall of Irene to the Accession of Basil I (802-867)* (London, 1912)

CHARANIS, P. *The Monastic Properties and the State in the Byzantine Empire* Dumbarton Oaks Papers, IV (Cambridge, Mass., 1948)

DIEHL, C. *Figures byzantines,* 2 series (Paris, 1906-8); Eng. trs. by H. Bell, *Byzantine Portraits* (New York, 1927)

DVORNIK, F. *The Photian Schism* Cambridge, 1948) *Les Slaves, Byzance et Rome au IXe siècle* (Paris, 1926)

EVERY, G. *The Byzantine Patriarchate (451-1204)* (London, 1948; 2nd ed. 1962)

FRENCH, R. M. *The Eastern Orthodox Church* (London, 1951)

HUSSEY, J. M. *Church and Learning in the Byzantine Empire 867-1185* (London, 1937) *The Byzantine World,* 2nd ed. (London, 1961)

OHNSORGE, W. *Abendland und Byzanz: Gesammelte Aufsätze zur Geschichte der byzantinisch-abendländischen Beziehungen und des Kaisertums* (Darmstadt, 1958)

RAMBAUD, A. *L'empire grec au dixième siècle: Constantin Porphyrogénète* (Paris, 1870)

RUNCIMAN, S. *The Emperor Romanus Lecapenus and his Reign. A Study of Tenth-Century Byzantium* (Cambridge, 1929) *A History of the First Bulgarian Empire* (London, 1930)

SCHLUMBERGER, G. *Un empereur byzantin au Xe siècle: Nicéphore Phocas* (Paris, 1890) *L'épopée byzantin à fin du Xe siècle;* I: *Jean Tzimisces, Basile II (969-89);* II: *Basile II (989-1025);* III: *Les Porphyrogénètes, Zoé et Théodora* (1025-57) (Paris, 1896-1905)

VII The Crucible of Peoples

BRAUN, F. *Variagi na Rusi in Beseda* Vols VI-VIII (Berlin, 1925)

DVORNIK, F. *Byzantine Political Ideas in Kievan Russia* Dumbarton Oaks Papers IX-X (Cambridge, Mass., 1956) *The Slavs in European History and Civilisation* (1963)

FASMERA *Vickingerspuren in Russland.* Preussische Akad. der Wissensch. Phil. Hist., Klasse 1931, XXIV

GRABAR, I. E., LAZAREV, V. N. and KEMENOVA, V. S. (eds) *Istoria russkogo iskusstva* (History of Russian Art) USSR Academy of Sciences, Vol I (Moscow, 1953)

KOVALEVSKIJ, A. P. *Kniga Akhmeta ibn Fadlana o go puteshestvii na Volgu v 921-922* (Kharkov, 1956)

LABANOV, A. *Recueil des pièces historiques sur la reine Anne ou Agnès, épouse de Henri Ier, roi de France, et fille de Yaroslav* (Paris, 1825)

LACKO, FATHER M. *Saints Cyril and Methodius* (Rome, 1963)

LOZINSKIJ, G. 'La Russie dans la littérature française du moyen âge' *Revue des études Slaves* Vol. IX, 1 & 2 (Paris, 1929)

MOSHIN, V. A. 'Normany v vostochnoij Evrope' *Byzantinoslavica* III (Prague, 1932) 'Khazaria pri Sviatoslave' *Seminarium Kondokovianum* Vol VI (Prague, 1933)

ROSTOVTSEV, M. 'Les origines de la Russie Kievienne' *Revue des études Slaves* (Paris, 1922)

TAUBE, M. DE *Rome et la Russie avant l'invasion des Tatars* (Paris, 1948)

THEOPHILUS *De Diversis artibus* trs. by C. R. Dodwell (London, 1961)

TIKHOMIROV, M. N. *The Towns of Ancient Rus* (Moscow, 1959)

VERNADSKIJ, G. *Kievan Russia* (New Haven, 1948) *The Mongols and Russia* (New Haven & London, 1953)

VIII Germanic Italy

ÅBERG, N. *Die Goten u. Langobarden in Italien* (Uppsala, 1923)

Archaelogisches Institut des Deutschen Reiches *Die langobardischen Fibeln aus Italien* (Berlin, 1950)

BEYERLE, F. *Die Gesetze der Langobarden* (Weimar, 1947)

BOGNETTI, G. P. 'S. Maria foris portas di Castelseprio e la storia religiosa dei Longobardi', in Bognetti et al. *Santa Maria di Castelseprio* (Milan, 1948)

Centro Italiano di Studi sull' Alto Medioevo *I Goti in Occidente* (Spoleto, 1956)
Atti del 2° Congresso internazionale di Studi sull' Alto medioevo (Spoleto, 1953)

FUCHS, S. *Kunst der Ostgotenzeit* (Berlin, 1944)

HARTMANN, L. M. *Geschichte Italiens im Mittelalter*, Vols I–II (Gotha, 1897–1903)

HODGKIN, T. *Italy and her Invaders* Vols III–VII, 2nd ed. (Oxford, 1896–99)

MOMIGLIANO, A. 'Cassiodorus and the Italian culture of his time' *Proceedings of the British Academy* XLI (London, 1955)
Secondo contributo alla storia degli studi classici (Rome, 1960)

PAUL THE DEACON *Pauli historia Langobardorum*, standard ed. by G. Waitz (Hannover, 1878); *History of the Langobards*, trs. by W. D. Foulke (New York, 1907)

PROCOPIUS trs. by H. B. Dewing, *The Loeb Classical Library* 7 vols (London & Cambridge, Mass., 1940)

SCHMIDT, L. *Geschichte der deutschen Stämme: Die Ostgermanen* 2nd ed. (Dresden, 1934)

STEIN, E. *Histoire du Bas-Empire* II (Paris, Brussels, Amsterdam, 1949)

IX 'The Ends of the Earth'

ÅBERG, N. *Die Franken und Westgoten in der Völkerwanderungszeit* (Uppsala, 1922)

GOMEZ-MORENO, M. *Iglesias mozárabes* (Madrid, 1919)

KENDRICK, T. *St James in Spain* (London, 1960)

KING, G. *Pre-Romanesque Churches of Spain*, Bryn Mawr (London, 1924)

LAMBERT, E. *Art musulman et Art chrétien dans la peninsule ibérique* (Paris-Toulouse, 1956)

MARINESCU, C., MILLÁS-VALLICROSA, J. M., and MONÉS, H. *Medieval Iberian Peninsula, Texts and Studies*, Vol. II 'Some Aspects of the Social-Economic and Cultural History of Muslim Spain, 711–1492 AD' (Leiden, 1962)

MENENDEZ PIDAL (ed.) *Historia de España* Vol. III (Madrid, 1940) containing: Camps, E., 'El arte hispano-visigodo'; Ferrandis, A. 'Las artes industriales visigodos'

NEUSS, W. *Die Apokalipse des Hl. Johannes in der Altspanischen Bibel-Illustration* (Münster, 1931)

PIJOAN, J. *Summa Artis* Vol. VIII (Barcelona, 1942)

SCHLUNK, H. 'Arte visigodo; Arte asturiano' *Ars Hispaniae* Vol. II (Madrid, 1947)

WHITEHILL, W. M., Liturgical Influences in Pre-Romanesque Apses in Spain' *Art Studies* V (Baltimore, 1927)

X Prelude to Empire

ÅBERG, N. *Die Franken und Westgoten in der Völkerwanderungszeit* (Uppsala, 1922)

BAUM, J. *La sculpture figurale en Europe à l'époque Mérovingienne* (Paris, 1937)

BURY, J. BAGNELL *The Invasion of Europe by the Barbarians, A Series of Lectures* (London, 1928)

GRABAR, A and NORDENFALK, C. *Early Medieval Painting* (New York, 1957)

GREGORY OF TOURS *The History of the Franks* (trs. by O. M. Dalton), 2 vols (London, 1927)

HUBERT, J. *L'Art pré-roman* (Paris, 1938)

JENNY, W. A. von *Die Kunst der Germanen im Frühen Mittelalter* (Berlin, 1940)

RADEMACHER, F. *Fränkische Goldscheibenfibeln aus dem Rheinischen Landesmuseum in Bonn* (München, 1940)

SALIN, B. *Die altgermanische Thierornamentik* (Stockholm, 1904)

SALIN, E. *La civilisation Mérovingienne* (ed. by A. and J. Picard & Cie., 4 vols (Paris, 1949–59)

TSCHUMI, O. *Burgunder, Alamannen und Langobarden in der Schweiz* (Bern, 1945)

VEECK, W. *Die Alamannen in Württemberg*, 2 vols (Berlin & Leipzig, 1931)

WALLACE-HADRILL, J. M. *The Long-haired Kings and other Studies in Frankish History* (London, 1962)
The Barbarian West, 400–1000 (London, 1952)

ZIMMERMAN, E. H. *Vorkarolingische Miniaturen*, 4 vols (Berlin, 1916)

Catalogue of Exhibition: *Werdendes Abendland an Rhein und Ruhr* (Essen, 1956)

XI From the Vigorous North

ARBMAN, H. *Schweden und das karolingische Reich* (Stockholm, 1937)
Birka I (Stockholm, 1940)
The Vikings (London, 1961)

BRØNDSTED, J. *The Vikings* 2nd ed. (London, 1965)

JONES, G. *The Norse Atlantic Saga* (Oxford, 1964)

KENDRICK, T. D. *A History of the Vikings* (London, 1930)

KLINDT-JENSEN, O. *Foreign Influences in Denmark's Early Iron Age* (Copenhagen, 1950)
Denmark (London, 1957)

NØRLUND, P. *Trelleborg* (Copenhagen, 1948)

SALIN, B. *Die altgermanische Thierornamentik* (Stockholm, 1904)

SAWYER, P. *The Age of the Vikings* (London, 1962)

SHETELIG, H. et. al., *Scandinavian Archaeology* (Oxford, 1937)

SHETELIG, H. and BRØGGER, A. *The Viking Ships* (Oslo, 1951)

STENBERGER, M. *Vallhagar* (Stockholm, 1951)
Sweden (London, 1962)

STRÖMBERG, M. *Untersuchungen zur jüngeren Eisenzeit in Schonen* (Lund, 1961)

XII The Coveted Isles

BLAIR, P. HUNTER *An Introduction to Anglo-Saxon England* (Cambridge, 1956)

BRØNDSTED, J. *The Vikings* 2nd ed. (London, 1965)

BROWN, G. BALDWIN *The Arts in Early England* 6 vols (London, 1903–57)

CHADWICK, N. K. *The Age of the Saints in the Early Celtic Church* (London, 1961)

DE PAOR, M. & L. *Early Christian Ireland* (London, 1958)

GOUGAUD, L. *Christianity in Celtic Lands* trs. by M. Joynt (London, 1932)

HENRY, F. *L'Art Irlandais* 3 vols (Paris, 1963–4)

RYAN, J. *Irish Monasticism. Origins and Early Development* (London, 1931)

SAWYER, P. H. *The Age of the Vikings* (London, 1962)

STENTON, F. M. *Anglo-Saxon England* 2nd ed. (London, 1947)

WAINWRIGHT, F. T. (ed.) *The Problem of the Picts* (Edinburgh, 1955)

WILSON, D. M. *The Anglo-Saxons* (London, 1960)

XIII The Great King

AMANN, E. *L'Epoque carolingienne; Histoire de l'Eglise* Vol VI, ed. by A. Fliche and V. Martin (Paris, 1937)

BECKWITH, J. *Early Medieval Art: Carolingian — Ottonian — Romanesque* (London, 1964)

BLOCH, M. *Feudal Society*, trs. by L. A. Manyon (London, 1961)

CONANT, K. J. *Carolingian and Romanesque architecture, 800–1200* Pelican History of Art (London, 1959)

DUCKETT, E. S. *Alcuin, friend of Charlemagne. His world and his work* (New York, 1951)
Carolingian portraits. A Study of the Ninth Century (Ann Arbor, 1962)

EINHARDT and THE MONK OF ST GALL *Early Lives of Charlemagne*, trs. by A. J. Grant (London, 1926)

FICHTENAU, H. *The Carolingian Empire*, trs. by P. Munz (Oxford, 1957)

FOLZ, R. *Le couronnement impérial de Charlemagne* (Paris, 1964)

GANSHOF, F. L. *Feudalism*, trs. by P. Grierson, 3rd Eng. ed. (London, 1964)

HINKS, R. *Carolingian art* (London, 1935)

KLEINCLAUSZ, A. *Charlemagne* (Paris, 1934)

LAISTNER, M. L. W. *Thought and Letters in Western Europe, AD 500–900* 2nd ed. (London, 1947)

LATOUCHE, R. *The Birth of Western Economy* (London, 1961)

LOUP DE FERRIÈRES *Correspondance*, ed. and trs. into French by L. Levillain, 2 vols (Paris, 1927–35)

MUNZ, P. *The Origin of the Carolingian Empire* (Leicester, 1960)

Son of Charlemagne. A contemporary biography of Louis the Pious, trs. by A. Cabaniss (Syracuse, N.Y., 1961)

XIV After Charlemagne

BARRACLOUGH, G. *The Origins of Modern Germany* (Oxford, 1946)

BECKWITH, J. *Early Medieval Art Carolingian–Ottonian–Romanesque* (London, 1964)

BEUMANN, H. *Widukind von Korvei* (Weimar, 1950)

BROOKE, C. N. L. *Europe in the Central Middle Ages 962–1154* (London, 1964)

CLARK, J. M. *The Abbey of St Gall* (Cambridge, 1926)

DVORNIK, F. *The Making of Central and Eastern Europe* (London, 1949)

GERBERT *The Letters of Gerbert (with his papal privileges as Sylvester II)*, trs. by H. P. Lattin (New York, 1961)

HALLINGER, K. *Gorze-Kluny* 2 vols (Rome, 1950–1)

HARTMANN, L. M. *Geschichte Italiens im Mittelalter* Vol. III (Gotha, 1911)

HAUCK, A. *Kirchengeschichte Deutschlands* Vol. III (Leipzig, 1896, reprint. 1957)

HERZOG, E. *Die Ottonische Stadt* (Berlin, 1964)

HOLTZMANN, R. *Geschichte der sächsischen Kaiserzeit* (Munich, 1941)

JOHNSON, E. N. *The Secular Activities of the German Episcopate 919–1024* Nebraska University Studies, Vols XXX–XXXI (1932)

LATOUCHE, R. *The Birth of Western Economy* Pt. IV (London, 1961)

LEEPER, A. W. A. *A History of Medieval Austria* (Oxford, 1941)

LOTTER, F. *Die Vita Brunonis des Ruotger* (Bonn, 1958)

MOR, C. G. *L'Età Feudale* 2 vols (Milan, 1952)

SCHRAMM, P. E. *Kaiser, Rom u. Renovatio* 2 vols (1st ed. Hamburg, 1929; 2nd ed. Darmstadt, 1957)

THOMPSON, J. W. *Feudal Germany* (Chicago, 1928)

TSCHAN, F. J. *Bernward of Hildesheim* 2 vols text, 1 vol. pls (Notre Dame, Indiana, 1942–52)

USLAR, R. VON *Studien zu frühgeschichtlichen Befestigungen* (Cologne, 1964)

Vescovi e Diocesi in Italia nel Medioevo, Italia Sacra V, contributions by E. Dupré Theseider, D. A. Bullough and R. Bauerreiss (Padua, 1964)

XV The Concept of Christendom

ALPHANDÉRY, P. and DUPRONT, A. *La Chrétienté et l'idée de la Croisade* 2 vols (Paris, 1954–9)

CURCIO, C. *Europa—Storia di un'idea* Vol I (Florence, 1958)

DANIEL, N. *Islam and the West* (Edinburgh, 1958)

FISCHER, J. *Oriens — Occidens — Europa* (Wiesbaden, 1957)

FOLZ, R. *L'idée d'empire en occident du Ve au XIVe siècle* (Paris, 1953)

HAY, D. *Europe: The Emergence of an Idea* (Edinburgh, 1957; new ed. New York, 1965)

KOEBNER, R. *Empire* (Cambridge, 1961)

MIRBT, C. *Quellen zur Geschichte des Papsttums und des Römischen Katholizismus* (Tübingen, 1911)

List and Sources of Illustrations

The page on which an illustration appears is shown by the first set of numerals, its plate or figure number by the second. Wherever possible the place of origin of an object is stated, together with its date and present location. The publishers acknowledge gratefully the co-operation of the many people and institutions (indicated in italic) who have supplied the pictures.

Contributing artists and photographers indicated by abbreviations are as follows: IMK Ian Mackenzie Kerr, JJOW John J. O. Webb, JDW Jon D. Wilsher, JW John Woodcock. The title page drawings are by IMK and the maps by JW.

349

IX The Ends of the Earth

X Prelude to Empire

INDEX

Index

Page numbers in *italics* indicate illustrations

357